Lectures on Complex Function Algebras

Gerald M. Leibowitz
University of Connecticut

Scott, Foresman and Company

In the editorial series of

I. M. SINGER
Massachusetts Institute of Technology

Library of Congress Catalog Card No. 75-93037
AMS 1969 Subject Classification 4655

To the memory of

Alan Robert Brodsky
Nathan Leibovitz
David S. Nathan

Preface

A complex function algebra is an algebra of continuous complex valued functions on a compact Hausdorff space S which contains the constants, separates points, and is closed under uniform convergence. One example is the algebra $C(S)$ of all continuous functions on S, and one object of interest in the subject is to find conditions on a function algebra which force it to be $C(S)$. When X is a compact set in complex n-space, there are function algebras $A(X)$ (the continuous functions on X which are analytic at each interior point), $P(X)$ (the completion of the polynomials in n variables in the maximum norm over X), and $R(X)$ (the completion of the finite valued rational functions on X). Function algebras share certain properties in common with subalgebras of $A(X)$ and it is natural to inquire to what extent one can introduce a structure with respect to which the elements of a function algebra become analytic functions. Most examples of function algebras are pieced together from subalgebras of the algebras of the types mentioned above, although the piecing can be quite bizarre.

I have attempted to write an introduction to the subject of function algebras which is structured as a text rather than a monograph or a research paper, and I have striven to proceed at a leisurely pace. I assume that the student has learned real analysis, including point set topology, linear algebra, measure theory, and complex analysis in one dimension, and that he is familiar with a few of the basic results in functional analysis. The book is not directed at experts, nor is it intended to make the reader an expert.

The general theory of Banach algebras (see the book of C. Rickart [I] cited in the bibliography) has found very little application to function algebras. What is needed about locally convex spaces and Banach algebras is presented in the first two chapters. I use Rudin's *Real and Complex Analysis*, Chapters 1–6, as a reference for measure theory, and my treatment of the elementary properties of complex measures is brief. Unfortunately, the book could not be kept self-contained without a long excursion into the theory of functions of several complex variables. I have had to be content to state some deep results from that area without proof. The interested reader will find proofs, in a more condensed style than the one adopted here, in Chapter 1 of Gunning and Rossi [C].

The book originated in a seminar which I led at Northwestern University in 1965–66 and I am indebted to the participants in that seminar for many insights. Much of the inspiration for my approach comes from courses given by John Wermer and Gabriel Stolzenberg at Harvard University and by Kenneth Hoffman at M.I.T., and any merit one may find in this presentation derives in large measure from the elegance and clarity of those courses.

I hope that a fairly comprehensive bibliography has cited nearly all the pertinent contributions to the field as of this writing. In the text itself I have usually omitted any reference to the source of particular ideas and arguments.

My thanks go to Vera Fisher for typing the manuscript and to my family for their encouragement.

G.M.L.

Contents

Chapter   One

Preliminaries

In this chapter we review some point set theory and then develop some of the functional analysis which will be used in our study of function algebras. After establishing notation, we review some facts about compactness (see §1.2) and derive a few basic results from the theory of locally convex spaces (see §1.3, §1.4, §1.5). In §1.6 we discuss three useful results about Banach spaces: the closed graph theorem, the principle of uniform boundedness, and the theorem of Banach-Dieudonné.

1.1 SPACES AND MAPS

As for notation, $\mathbf{R}$ and $\mathbf{C}$ are respectively the real and the complex fields, and $\mathbf{Z}$ is the ring of integers. $\mathbf{R}^n$ and $\mathbf{C}^n$ are real and complex n-space. T^n is the n-torus and consists of all $\lambda = (\lambda_1, \ldots, \lambda_n)$ in $\mathbf{C}^n$ with $|\lambda_1| = \cdots = |\lambda_n| = 1$. In particular, T^1 is the unit circle in the complex plane, and T^n is the n-fold Cartesian product of T^1 with itself. The empty set is denoted by $\varnothing$. If A and B are sets, then $A \backslash B$ is the complement of B relative to A. (So $A \backslash B = A \backslash (A \cap B)$.)

By a *function* we shall always mean a mapping into $\mathbf{R}$ or $\mathbf{C}$. (This will reduce the number of times we have to write " complex-valued.") The existential quantifier $\exists$ (" there exists ") and the universal quantifier $\forall$ ("for all ") will occasionally be used as abbreviations.

If F is a subset of a set S, the *characteristic function* of F (relative to S) is the function χ_F on S given by $\chi_F(s) = 1$ if $s \in F$, $\chi_F(s) = 0$ if $s \in S \backslash F$. The *inclusion map* from F to S is $i_F : F \to S$ where $i_F(x) = x$. If φ is a mapping with domain S, then the *restriction* of φ to F is the composite mapping $\varphi | F = \varphi \circ i_F$. If A is a family of mappings on S, then the restriction of A to F is the family $A |_F = \{\varphi | F : \varphi \in A\}$.

If z is a complex number, then $\bar{z}$ is the complex conjugate of z, and Re (z) is the real part of z. We carry this notation over to functions in an obvious way. A family A of functions on S is *self-adjoint* iff $\bar{f} \in A$ for every f in A. A family $\mathscr{F}$ of mappings on S *separates points* on S iff for each pair of distinct elements s_1, s_2 of S, $\exists f$ in $\mathscr{F}$ with $f(s_1) \neq f(s_2)$.

Let T be a set and $\mathscr{T}$ a collection of subsets of T. $\mathscr{T}$ is a *topology* on T iff (*i*) $T \in \mathscr{T}$, $\varnothing \in \mathscr{T}$; (ii) the intersection of any two members of $\mathscr{T}$ is a member of $\mathscr{T}$; and (iii) the union of each subfamily of $\mathscr{T}$ is a member of $\mathscr{T}$. A *topological space* is a pair $(T, \mathscr{T})$ with $\mathscr{T}$ a topology on T. (If $\mathscr{T}$ is understood, one refers to T as the space.) Given a topological space $(T, \mathscr{T})$, $U \subset T$ is *open* iff $U \in \mathscr{T}$, $F \subset T$ is *closed* iff $T \backslash F$ is open. Given $E \subset T$, int E (the *interior* of E) is the union of all open sets contained in E, $\bar{E}$ (the *closure* of E) is the intersection of all closed sets containing E, bd(E) (the *boundary* of E) is the closed set $\bar{E} \backslash \text{int} E = \bar{E} \cap \overline{(T/E)}$, and the *relative topology* of E is the family $\{E \cap U : U \in \mathscr{T}\}$ (which is a topology on E). A mapping $f : (T, \mathscr{T}) \to (T', \mathscr{T}')$ is *continuous* iff for each open set $U' \in \mathscr{T}'$, $f^{-1}(U')$ is an open set in T. f is a *homeomorphism* iff f is one-one and onto and f and f^{-1} are continuous.

1.2   COMPACTNESS

A *neighborhood* (*nbhd*) of a point p in a topological space T is a set which contains an open set which contains p. T is a *Hausdorff space* iff every pair of distinct points p, q in T has a pair of disjoint *nbhds*. A (neighborhood) *base* at a point $p \in T$ is a family $\mathscr{U}$ of *nbhds* of p such that every *nbhd* of p contains some member of $\mathscr{U}$.

Recall that a space S is *compact* iff every covering of S by open sets contains a finite subcover. (Starting in Chapter Three, we will require that a compact space be Hausdorff, but until then we demand just the covering property.) The following are some standard results on compactness. In a Hausdorff space, every compact subset is closed. Every closed subset of a compact space is also compact. A continuous mapping whose domain is compact has a compact image. A continuous one-one mapping from a compact space onto a Hausdorff space is a homeomorphism. (Thus if $(S, \mathscr{T}_1)$ is Hausdorff, $(S, \mathscr{T}_2)$ is compact, and the identity map is continuous from $(S, \mathscr{T}_2)$ to $(S, \mathscr{T}_1)$, then $\mathscr{T}_1 = \mathscr{T}_2$. That is, if a Hausdorff topology is weaker than a compact topology, then the two topologies coincide.)

Every compact Hausdorff space is normal; i.e., disjoint closed subsets have disjoint open *nbhds*. Hence all results about normal spaces apply. In particular, we have Urysohn's lemma and Tietze's extension theorem.

Theorem 1   (Urysohn's Lemma).   *Suppose that F_0, F_1 are disjoint closed subsets of a compact Hausdorff space S. Then there is a continuous function f on S such that $f(F_0) = \{0\}$, $f(F_1) = \{1\}$, and $f(S) \subset [0, 1]$. (In particular, the continuous functions separate points on S.)*

Theorem 2 (**Tietze Extension Theorem**). *Suppose that F is a closed subset of a compact Hausdorff space S and that g is a continuous function on F. Then there is a continuous function f on S such that $g = f \mid F$. (Moreover, if g maps F into a closed interval $[a, b]$ in* **R**, *then f can be taken to map S into $[a, b]$.)*

If S is a nonvoid compact space, we let $C(S)$ be the set of all continuous complex-valued functions on S. Note that Tietze's theorem asserts that if F is a nonvoid closed subset of a compact Hausdorff space S, the restriction map $f \to f \circ i_F$ carries $C(S)$ onto $C(F)$.

A topological space Y is *locally compact* iff every point of Y has a closed compact *nbhd*. In a locally compact Hausdorff space, the compact *nbhds* form a base at each point.

Suppose that Y is a locally compact Hausdorff space. Take a point ∞ not in Y, and let $Y_\infty = Y \cup \{\infty\}$. The *one-point compactification* of Y is the set Y_∞ together with the following topology $\mathcal{T}_\infty$. The open sets in $\mathcal{T}_\infty$ are the open sets of Y and the complements in Y_∞ of the compact subsets of Y. It is easy to show that Y_∞ is a compact Hausdorff space. The one-point compactification of **C** is called the *Riemann sphere*.

A continuous function f on a locally compact Hausdorff space Y *vanishes at infinity* iff f is the restriction of a continuous function g on Y_∞ for which $g(\infty) = 0$. We denote by $C_0(Y)$ the space of all such functions f. One can apply Urysohn's lemma to Y_∞ and establish separating properties of $C_0(Y)$.

The notion of weak topologies occurs frequently. Suppose that S is a set and that we are given maps $f_\alpha : S \to S_\alpha$ ($\alpha \in J$, an index set) where each S_α is a topological space. Then there is a weakest topology on S with respect to which all the maps f_α are continuous, namely, the topology $\mathcal{T}$ generated by all sets of the form $f_\alpha^{-1}(U_\alpha)$, where $\alpha \in J$ and U_α is open in S_α. $\mathcal{T}$ is called the *weak topology* defined on S by the family $\{f_\alpha\}$. For example, if X is the Cartesian product of spaces $\{X_\alpha\}$, and if $\pi_\alpha : X \to X_\alpha$ ($\alpha \in J$) is the αth coordinate projection, then the *product topology* of X is the weak topology defined by the family $\{\pi_\alpha\}$. Tychonoff's theorem asserts that $X = \prod_\alpha X_\alpha$ is compact in the product topology if each X_α is compact.

There is a basic lemma on weak topologies which goes as follows. (The proof is left as an exercise.)

Lemma 1. *Suppose that $\mathscr{F}$ is a family of continuous functions on a topological space $(Y, \mathcal{T})$, and let $\mathcal{T}_\mathscr{F}$ be the weak topology defined on Y by $\mathscr{F}$.*

   (a) *If $\mathscr{F}$ separates points on Y, then $\mathcal{T}$ and $\mathcal{T}_\mathscr{F}$ are Hausdorff topologies.*
   (b) *If $\mathscr{F}$ separates points and $(Y, \mathcal{T})$ is compact, then $\mathcal{T} = \mathcal{T}_\mathscr{F}$.*
   (c) *Suppose that $(Y, \mathcal{T})$ is a locally compact Hausdorff space, that $\mathscr{F} \subset C_0(Y)$, and that for each $y \in Y, f(y) \neq 0$ for some $f \in \mathscr{F}$. Then $\mathcal{T} = \mathcal{T}_\mathscr{F}$.*

The condition in (c) is sufficient but not necessary in order that $\mathcal{T} = \mathcal{T}_\mathscr{F}$. For example, take $Y = \mathbf{R}^1$, and let $\mathscr{F}$ contain just the identity map $x \to x$. Then $\mathscr{F}$ is not contained in C_0, but the weak topology $\mathcal{T}_\mathscr{F}$ is the usual topology of $\mathbf{R}^1$.

EXERCISE SET 1.2

1. Suppose that T is a topological space and that F is a subset of T. Show that χ_F is continuous iff F is open and closed in T. T is *connected* iff the only open-closed subsets of T are $\varnothing$ and T.

2. Show that a continuous function f on a locally compact Hausdorff space Y belongs to $C_0(Y)$ iff for every $\varepsilon > 0$, $\exists$ a compact $K \subset Y$ such that $|f| < \varepsilon$ outside of K. Prove that each $f \in C_0(Y)$ is bounded.

3. Let U be a nonempty open subset of a compact Hausdorff space S. Show that U is a locally compact Hausdorff space. What is the one-point compactification of U? What happens when U is both open and closed?

   In particular, S is the one-point compactification of $S \setminus \{p\}$ for each $p \in S$.

4. Suppose that $\sim$ is an equivalence relation on a topological space T, and let T^* be the set of $\sim$ equivalence classes. The *quotient map* Q from T to T^* is the mapping whose value at x is the equivalence class which contains x. The *quotient topology* on T^* is defined as follows: V is open in T^* iff $Q^{-1}(V)$ is open in T. The quotient map is continuous from T to T^*. If T is compact, so is every quotient space T^*.

   Given a subset E of T, the space obtained from T by *identifying E to a point* is (of course) the quotient space T^* (with the quotient topology) arising from the equivalence relation: $x \sim y$ iff $x = y$ or both $x \in E$, $y \in E$.

1.3   TOPOLOGICAL VECTOR SPACES

Let K be the real field or the complex field, and let E be a vector space over K. A topology $\mathcal{T}$ on E is *compatible* with the vector structure of E iff the maps $(f, g) \to f + g$ from $E \times E$ to E and $(\alpha, f) \to \alpha f$ from $K \times E$ to E are continuous. (Here K has the usual topology, E has the topology $\mathcal{T}$, and the products have the product topology.) A *topological vector space* (t.v.s.) over K is a vector space E over K together with a Hausdorff topology which is compatible with the vector structure.

Let E be a vector space over K. For $\lambda \in K$ and subsets A, A_1, A_2 of E, $\lambda A = \{\lambda f : f \in A\}$ and $A_1 + A_2 = \{f_1 + f_2 : f_1 \in A_1, f_2 \in A_2\}$. A subset C of A is *convex* iff C contains the line segment joining each pair of its points; i.e., $\lambda C + (1 - \lambda)C \subset C$ whenever $0 \le \lambda \le 1$. A t.v.s. E is *locally convex* iff the convex *nbhds* of 0 in E form a base; equivalently, E is locally convex iff every open set V containing 0 contains an open convex *nbhd* of 0.

The basic tool for building linear functionals on a t.v.s. is the Hahn-Banach theorem, of which the following is the real form. I assume that the result and its proof are familiar to the reader.

Theorem 3   **(Hahn-Banach).**   *Let p be a real-valued function on a real vector space E which satisfies the conditions $p(\lambda f) = \lambda p(f)$ for $\lambda \geq 0$, and $p(f + g) \leq p(f) + p(g)$ (all f, g in E). If φ is a linear functional on a linear subspace F of E such that $\varphi(f) \leq p(f)$ for all $f \in F$, then there is a linear functional ψ on E such that $\psi(f) \leq p(f)$ for all $f \in E$ and $\psi(f) = \varphi(f)$ for all $f \in F$.*

Since a complex vector space is also a real vector space, the theorem applies to complex vector spaces (but we must read "real-linear" wherever "linear" appears). If E is a t.v.s. and C is a convex *nbhd* of 0 in E, then C provides us with a function p which satisfies the hypothesis of the Hahn-Banach theorem.

Lemma 2.   *Let C be a convex nbhd of 0 in a t.v.s. E. Set $p(f) = \inf \{\lambda : \lambda > 0$ and $f \in \lambda C\}$ ($f \in E$). Then (a) $p : E \to [0, +\infty)$; (b) $p(af) = ap(f)$ if $a \geq 0$, $f \in E$; (c) $p(f + g) \leq p(f) + p(g)$ for f, g in E; (d) if $p(f) \leq 1$, then f belongs to the closure of C; (e) p is continuous at 0.*

Proof.   Since C is a *nbhd* of 0, C is absorbing. (*Cf.* Exercise 3.) Hence if $f \in E$, $\exists \lambda > 0$ with $f \in \lambda C$; so (a) is proved. If $a > 0$, then $p(af) = \inf \{\lambda > 0 : f \in a^{-1}\lambda C\} = \inf \{a\mu : \mu > 0$ and $f \in \mu C\} = ap(f)$, while $p(0) = 0$ since $0 \in \lambda C$ for every $\lambda > 0$.

Suppose that $f \in \alpha C$, $g \in \beta C$ where $\alpha > 0$, $\beta > 0$. Then since C is convex, $\frac{\alpha}{\alpha + \beta}\left(\frac{1}{\alpha}f\right) + \frac{\beta}{\alpha + \beta}\left(\frac{1}{\beta}g\right)$ belongs to C. That is, $(f + g) \in (\alpha + \beta)C$. Hence $p(f + g) \leq p(f) + p(g)$.

If $p(f) < 1$, then $f \in \lambda C$ for some $\lambda \in (0, 1)$. Then since $0 \in C$, $f = \lambda\left(\frac{1}{\lambda}f\right) + (1 - \lambda)0$ belongs to C.

If $p(f) = 1$, then for every positive integer n, $\exists \delta_n \in [0, 1/n)$ with $f \in (1 + \delta_n)C$. Hence $f \in \bar{C}$ since $(1 + \delta_n)^{-1}f \to f$.

Since C is a *nbhd* of 0, continuity of $f \to \frac{1}{\varepsilon}f$ implies that to each $\varepsilon > 0$ there corresponds a *nbhd* V of 0 in E with $\frac{1}{\varepsilon}V \subset C$. So p is continuous at 0.

We might note also that if $f \in$ int C, then $p(f) < 1$. Indeed, $f + U \subset C$ for some *nbhd* U of 0. Since U is a *nbhd* of $0 \cdot f$, $\rho f \in U$ for some $\rho > 0$. Hence $(1 + \rho)f \in f + U \subset C$. So $p(f) \leq \frac{1}{1 + \rho} < 1$.

Observe also that if p is any real-valued function on E which satisfies (b), (c), and (e), and if ψ is a real-linear functional on E such that $\psi(f) \leq p(f)$ for all $f \in E$, then ψ is continuous. (It suffices to show that ψ is continuous at 0. Given $\varepsilon > 0$, we choose a balanced *nbhd* U of 0 such that $p(f) \leq \varepsilon$ on U. (See Exercise 5.) Then if $f \in U$, $-f$ is also in U, and so $\psi(f) \leq p(f) \leq \varepsilon$ and $-\psi(f) = \psi(-f) \leq p(-f) \leq \varepsilon$, whence $|\psi(f)| \leq \varepsilon$ for all $f \in U$. So ψ is indeed continuous at 0.)

EXERCISE SET   1.3

Let E be a t.v.s. with scalar field K. Establish the following results.

1. For each $f \in E$, $\alpha \to (\alpha, f)$ is a continuous map from K to $K \times E$, and $\alpha \to \alpha f$ is continuous from K to E.

2. For each $f_0 \in E$, $f \to f + f_0$ is a homeomorphism of E onto E. If $f_0 \in E$ and U is open in E, then $f_0 + U$ is open in E. If $A \subset E$ and U is open in E, then $A + U$ is open in E. If $f_0 \in E$, then the *nbhds* of f_0 are the sets of the form $f_0 + V$ with V a *nbhd* of 0.
   A linear map $\psi : E \to K$ is continuous iff it is continuous at 0.

3. A set $U \subset E$ is *absorbing* iff $\forall f \in E$, $\exists \rho > 0$ with $\rho f \in U$. Every *nbhd* of 0 in E is absorbing.

4. If $\alpha \in K$, then $f \to \alpha f$ is a continuous linear map from E to E. Given any *nbhd* U of 0 in E, there is a *nbhd* V of 0 in E such that $\alpha V \subset U$.

5. A set $U \subset E$ is *balanced* iff $f \in U$ and $|\lambda| \le 1$ ($\lambda \in K$) imply that $\lambda f \in U$. Every *nbhd* of 0 in E contains a balanced open *nbhd* of 0. (Given a *nbhd* V of 0, find $r > 0$ and an open *nbhd* W of 0 such that $\alpha W \subset V$ whenever $|\alpha| \le r$. Let $U = \bigcup_{0 < |\alpha| \le r} \alpha W$.)

6. Given a *nbhd* V of 0 in E, there is a balanced open *nbhd* U of 0 such that $U + U \subset V$. But $\overline{U} \subset U + U$, so every *nbhd* of 0 in E contains a closed balanced *nbhd* of 0, since the closure of a balanced set is balanced. (In particular, a t.v.s. is regular: the closed *nbhds* form a base at each point.)

7. The intersection of any collection of balanced subsets of E is balanced. The whole space E is balanced, so every subset of E is contained in a smallest balanced set.
   The intersection of a finite collection of balanced absorbing sets is balanced and absorbing.

8. Let C and D be disjoint closed sets in E, and let C be compact. Then there is a *nbhd* U of 0 such that $C + U$ and $D + U$ are disjoint. (Outline: For $x \in C$, take a *nbhd* W_x of 0 such that $x + W_x$ does not meet D, and take a balanced *nbhd* V_x with $V_x + V_x \subset W_x$. Then $x + V_x$ misses $D + V_x$. Cover and intersect. Shrink again with a balanced *nbhd*.)

9. If C and D are compact sets in E, then $C + D$ is compact. If C is compact and D is closed, then $C + D$ is closed.

10. The sum of a closed subspace of E and a one-dimensional subspace of E is closed. A finite dimensional subspace of a t.v.s. is closed.

11. If C is a convex set in E, then every translate $f + C$ ($f \in E$) is convex. If C is convex, then the interior and closure of C are convex. (In fact, if

$f \in$ int C and $g \in C$, then $f + U \subset C$ for some *nbhd* U of 0, and then $\lambda f + (1 - \lambda)g + \lambda U \subset \lambda C + (1 - \lambda)C \subset C$ for each $\lambda \in (0, 1)$.)

If C is convex, so is αC for every scalar α. $C_1 + C_2$ is convex if C_1 and C_2 are convex. Every linear subspace of E is convex.

A convex subset of E is connected.

12. The intersection of any collection of convex sets is convex. Given $A \subset E$, the *convex hull* of A is the intersection of all convex subsets of E which contain A. The *closed convex hull* of A is the intersection of all closed convex subsets of E containing A.

   The closed convex hull of A is the closure of the convex hull of A. Given $f \in E$, f belongs to the convex hull of A iff there are finitely many scalars $\lambda_i \geq 0$ and finitely many $f_i \in A$ such that $\sum \lambda_i = 1$ and $\sum \lambda_i f_i = f$.

13. The convex hull of a balanced set is balanced. The interior of a balanced *nbhd* of 0 is balanced.

14. In a locally convex t.v.s. E, every *nbhd* of 0 contains a closed balanced convex *nbhd* of 0. (It suffices to show this for a convex *nbhd* U of 0. Now U contains a closed *nbhd* V, and V contains a convex *nbhd* V'. Also, V' contains a balanced *nbhd* V'' of 0. Then $W \subset U$ where W is the closed convex hull of V''.)

1.4 SEPARATION THEOREMS

The following theorem is sometimes referred to as the geometric form of the Hahn-Banach theorem.

Theorem 4. *Let E be a real t.v.s., F a linear subspace of E, C a nonempty open convex set in E, and $f_0 \in E$. Let $M = f_0 + F$, and suppose that $M \cap C = \emptyset$. Then there exists a continuous linear functional ψ on E and there is a real number α such that the hyperplane $H = \{f \in E : \psi(f) = \alpha\}$ contains M and is disjoint from C. (So if some linear variety $f_0 + F$ misses C, there is a maximal variety $f_0 + \mathrm{Ker}\,(\psi)$ through f_0 which misses C.)*

Proof. Take $f_1 \in C$, and let $D = -f_1 + C$. Then D is an open convex *nbhd* of 0. Since $M \cap C = \emptyset$, $f_1 - f_0 \notin F$. Hence each element of F', the linear span of F and $f_0 - f_1$, has a unique representation as $f = g + \lambda(f_0 - f_1)$ ($g \in F$, $\lambda \in \mathbf{R}$). If we set $\varphi(f) = \lambda$, then φ is a linear functional on F'.

Let $p(f) = \inf \{\lambda > 0 : f \in \lambda D\}$ ($f \in E$). If $g \in F$ and $\lambda > 0$, then $\lambda^{-1}g + f_0$ belongs to M and hence not to C, so $\lambda^{-1}g + (f_0 - f_1) \notin D$, whence $p(\lambda^{-1}g + (f_0 - f_1)) \geq 1$. So if $f = g + \lambda(f_0 - f_1)$ ($g \in F$, $\lambda > 0$), then $p(f) \geq \lambda = \varphi(f)$. Since $p \geq 0$, $\varphi(f) \leq p(f)$ for all $f \in F'$.

By the Hahn-Banach theorem, φ extends to a linear functional ψ on E such that $\psi \leq p$. We know that ψ is continuous since p is continuous at 0. If $f \in C$, then $f - f_1 \in D$, so $\psi(f - f_1) \leq p(f - f_1) < 1$ (since D is open) and

$\psi(f) < 1 + \psi(f_1)$. But if $f \in M$, then $f - f_0 \in F$, so $f - f_1 = (f - f_0) + (f_0 - f_1)$ belongs to F'. Thus $\psi(f - f_1) = \varphi(f - f_1) = 1$, so $\psi(f) = 1 + \psi(f_1)$. Thus the theorem is proved, with $\alpha = 1 + \psi(f_1)$. (In fact, $\psi = \alpha$ on M, $\psi < \alpha$ on C, which is slightly more than is asserted. Actually, since C is connected, if $\alpha \notin \psi(C)$, then automatically $\psi(C) < \alpha$ or $\psi(C) > \alpha$, so the strengthening of the conclusion is only apparent.)

Theorem 5.   *Let C_1, C_2 be disjoint nonempty convex subsets of a real t.v.s. E, and suppose that C_1 or C_2 is open. Then there is a closed hyperplane which separates C_1 and C_2. That is, there exists a nonzero continuous linear functional ψ on E, and there is a real number α such that $\psi \leq \alpha$ on C_2, $\psi \geq \alpha$ on C_1.*

  Proof.   We note that $C_1 + (-C_2)$ is a nonvoid open convex set in E which does not meet $M = 0 + \{0\}$. Hence there is a continuous linear functional ψ on E with $\psi(0) = 0$ and $\psi < 0$ on $C_1 + (-C_2)$. Hence $0 < \psi(f - g) = \psi(f) - \psi(g)$, $\psi(g) < \psi(f)$ for $f \in C_1$, $g \in C_2$. So $\sup_{g \in C_2} \psi(g) \leq \inf_{f \in C_1} \psi(f)$. If α is any number between the sup and the inf, then $\psi \leq \alpha$ on C_2, $\psi \geq \alpha$ on C_1.

Theorem 6.   *Let E be a real locally convex t.v.s., and let A, B be disjoint nonempty closed convex subsets of E, at least one of which is compact. Then there is a continuous linear functional ψ on E such that $\sup_B \psi < \inf_A \psi$. (A and B are strictly separated by a hyperplane.)*

  Proof.   Since A, B are disjoint sets, one of which is compact and the other closed, there is a *nbhd* V of 0 such that $A + V$ and $B + V$ are disjoint. Since E is locally convex, there is a balanced convex open *nbhd* U of 0 with $(A + U) \cap (B + U) = \emptyset$. Now $A + U$, $B + U$ are disjoint nonempty open convex sets. So there is a nonzero continuous linear functional ψ on E such that $\psi(B + U) \leq \alpha \leq \psi(A + U)$ for some α.
    If $f \in E$, then $\rho f \in U$ for some $\rho > 0$. Hence ψ cannot vanish everywhere on U since $\psi \neq 0$. Since U is balanced, $\psi(f_1) > 0$, $\psi(f_2) < 0$ where $f_1 \in U$ and $f_2 = -f_1 \in U$. If $f \in A$, then $\alpha \leq \psi(f + f_2)$, so $\psi(A) \geq \alpha - \psi(f_2)$. Similarly, $\psi(B) \leq \alpha - \psi(f_1)$. So if we choose β with $\alpha - \psi(f_1) < \beta < \alpha - \psi(f_2) = \alpha + \psi(f_1)$, the hyperplane $\{f \in E : \psi(f) = \beta\}$ separates A and B strictly.

Theorem 7 (Separation Theorem).   *Let E be a real locally convex t.v.s. Then every closed convex nonempty set $A \subset E$ is the intersection of the closed half-spaces containing A.*

  Proof.   If $f_0 \notin A$, then $\{f_0\}$ and A are disjoint nonvoid closed convex sets and $\{f_0\}$ is compact. So there exists a continuous linear functional ψ on E with $\psi(f_0) < \inf_A \psi$.
    Hence A is the intersection of those half-spaces $H(\varphi, \alpha) = \{f : \varphi(f) \geq \alpha\}$ which contain A.

Theorem 8.   *Let E be a locally convex t.v.s. If F is a closed linear subspace of E and $f_0 \in E$, then $f_0 \notin F$ iff there is a continuous linear functional φ on E such that $\varphi(f_0) = 1$ and $\varphi = 0$ on F.*

Proof.   Assume first that E is a real t.v.s. If $f_0 \notin F$, then since F is closed and convex, $\psi(f_0) < \inf_F \psi$ for some continuous linear functional ψ on E. But $\psi(F)$ is a subspace of $\mathbf{R}$. Since it is bounded below, $\psi(F) = \{0\}$. Set $\varphi = \psi(f_0)^{-1}\psi$. Then $\varphi(f_0) = 1$, $\varphi(F) = \{0\}$.

If E is a complex t.v.s. and $f_0 \notin F$, then there is a continuous real-linear map $\psi : E \to \mathbf{R}$ such that $\psi(f_0) < 0$, $\psi(F) = \{0\}$, by the same reasoning. (For E is a real t.v.s. as well as a complex t.v.s., and convexity does not depend on whether E is considered as a real space or a complex space.) If we set $\varphi(f) = \psi(f) - i\psi(if)$ ($f \in E$), then φ is a continuous linear functional on E. Since $\varphi(f_0) \neq 0$ and $\varphi(F) = \{0\}$, a scalar multiple of φ does the required job.

If E is a t.v.s., the *dual space* of E is the space E^* of all continuous linear functionals on E. If E is locally convex, then the members of E^* separate points of E from closed subspaces of E, and in particular if $f \in E$ and $f \neq 0$, then there is some φ in E^* with $\varphi(f) \neq 0$.

Let E be a vector space over K, and let $C \subset E$, $A \subset C$. Then A is an *extreme subset* of C iff the following is true. If $f \in C$, $g \in C$, and some point $\lambda f + (1 - \lambda)g$ ($0 < \lambda < 1$) of the open segment joining f to g meets A, then f and g belong to A. If C is a convex set, a nonempty convex extreme subset of C is called a *face* of C. If $f \in C \subset E$, f is an *extreme point* of C iff $\{f\}$ is an extreme subset of C. The set of all extreme points of C will be denoted by C^e. It is clear that a union or intersection of extreme subsets of C is an extreme subset of C. If A is an extreme subset of B, and if B is an extreme subset of C, then A is an extreme subset of C. If φ is any real-linear functional on E, and if $A = \{f \in C : \varphi(f) = \inf_C \varphi\}$, then A is an extreme subset of C. (Of course, A may be empty.) For if $\inf_C \varphi = \varphi(\lambda f + (1 - \lambda)g)$ where $f \in C$, $g \in C$, and $0 < \lambda < 1$, then $\inf_C \varphi = \lambda\varphi(f) + (1 - \lambda)\varphi(g) \geq \lambda \inf_C \varphi + (1 - \lambda) \inf_C \varphi = \inf_C \varphi$, so equality must hold throughout. Thus $f \in A$, $g \in A$, and A is an extreme subset of C.

Theorem 9   (Krein-Milman).   *Let A be a nonvoid compact convex subset of a locally convex t.v.s. E. Then (a) every closed face of A contains an extreme point of A; (b) A is the closed convex hull of its set of extreme points.*

Proof.   We may suppose that E is a real space.

Let F_0 be a closed face of A. Let $\mathscr{F}$ be the family of all closed faces of A which are contained in F_0. Suppose that $\{F_\alpha\}$ is a chain in $\mathscr{F}$. If $F_{\alpha_1}, \ldots, F_{\alpha_m}$ are in $\{F_\alpha\}$, then the intersection of the F_{α_i} is one of them. Hence it is nonempty. Thus $\{F_\alpha\}$ has the finite intersection property. The F_α are closed subsets of the compact space A, so $\bigcap_\alpha F_\alpha$ is nonempty. Clearly $\bigcap_\alpha F_\alpha$ is a face of A. So every chain in $\mathscr{F}$ has a lower bound in $\mathscr{F}$. By Zorn's lemma, $\mathscr{F}$ contains a minimal element. Let F be any minimal element of $\mathscr{F}$. Then F is a face of A contained in F_0. If F contained distinct elements f, g, then there would exist a linear functional $\varphi \in E^*$ with $\varphi(f) \neq \varphi(g)$. But then $F \divideontimes = \{h \in F : \varphi(h) = \inf_F \varphi\}$ is a closed nonempty extreme subset of F which is convex and does not contain both f and g. This means that $F \divideontimes$ is a member of $\mathscr{F}$ which is properly contained in F, contradicting the minimality of F. Thus $F = \{e\}$ for some $e \in F_0$, and F_0 contains an extreme point of A.

In particular, A^e is nonempty. Let C be the closed convex hull of A^e. Clearly $C \subset A$ since A is closed and convex. If there were a point $f_0 \in A \backslash C$, then by the separation theorem there would be some $\psi \in E^*$ with $\psi(f_0) < \inf_C \psi$. But the minimum set $F_0 = \{f \in A : \psi(f) = \inf_A \psi\}$ is a closed face of A; hence it contains an extreme point e of A. We have $\psi(e) = \inf_A \psi \leq \psi(f_0) < \inf_C \psi$. Since $e \in C$, this is a contradiction. So $C = A$, as asserted.

In order to prove the next theorem we need two lemmas which are of interest themselves. The proofs are left as exercises.

Lemma 3. *Let E be a vector space over K, and let $C_1, \ldots, C_n$ be convex subsets of E. Then the convex hull of $\bigcup_{i=1}^{n} C_i$ consists of all vectors of the form*

$$\sum_{i=1}^{n} \lambda_i f_i, \text{ where } \lambda_i \geq 0, f_i \in C_i \ (1 \leq i \leq n), \text{ and } \sum_{i=1}^{n} \lambda_i = 1.$$

Lemma 4. *Let E be a t.v.s. Then the convex hull of a finite union of compact convex subsets of E is also compact.*

Theorem 10. *Let E be a locally convex t.v.s. If the closed convex hull C of a compact set $A \subset E$ is compact, then every extreme point of C belongs to A.*

Proof. Suppose that $f_0 \in C^e$ but $f_0 \notin A$. Since $\{f_0\}$ and A are disjoint compact sets and E is locally convex, there is a convex *nbhd* U of 0 such that $f_0 + U$ and $A + U$ are disjoint.

Since A is compact, there is a finite set $\{f_1, \ldots, f_n\} \subset A$ with $A \subset \bigcup_{i=1}^{n} (f_i + U)$. Let C_i be the closed convex hull of $A \cap \overline{(f_i + U)}$ for each i. Since C is the closed convex hull of A, each C_i is contained in C. Hence, since C is compact by hypothesis, each C_i is a compact convex set, and $\bigcup_{i=1}^{n} C_i \subset C$. On the other hand, it is clear that $A \subset \bigcup_{i=1}^{n} C_i$. So C is the closed convex hull of the union of the C_i. By Lemma 4, C is in fact the convex hull of $\bigcup_{i=1}^{n} C_i$. Since $f_0 \in C$, f_0 has a representation as $\sum_{i=1}^{n} \lambda_i g_i$, where $g_i \in C_i$, $0 \leq \lambda_i$, and $\sum \lambda_i = 1$. Now f_0 is an extreme point of C, and each $C_i \subset C$, so it follows that $f_0 = g_j$ for some j; thus $f_0 \in C_j$.

But $\overline{f_j + U}$ is a closed convex set containing $A \cap \overline{(f_j + U)}$, so $\overline{f_j + U}$ contains C_j, the closed convex hull of the intersection. Thus we have $f_0 \in \overline{f_j + U} \subset \overline{A + U}$. Since f_0 has a *nbhd* which is disjoint from $A + U$, we have arrived at a contradiction.

Theorem 11. *Let E be a real locally convex t.v.s., and let C be a nonempty compact convex subset of E. Then* (a) *if $\varphi \in E^*$, $\varphi \,|\, C$ assumes its maximum at some extreme point of C;* (b) *$\overline{C^e}$ is the smallest closed subset of C on which every continuous linear functional $\varphi \in E^*$ assumes its maximum over C.*

Proof. (a) For each $\varphi \in E^*$, $\{f \in C : \varphi(f) = \max_C \varphi\}$ is a closed face of C, so it contains an extreme point of C (Krein-Milman). (b) It follows that $\overline{C^e}$ is a closed set on which every $\varphi \,|\, C$ assumes its maximum. On the other hand, suppose that D is a closed subset of C which does not contain every extreme point of C. Take $f_0 \in C^e$ with $f_0 \notin D$. The closed convex hull H of D is compact since $H \subset C$ and C is compact. Hence each extreme point of H belongs to D, by Theorem 10. But then $f_0 \notin H$ since otherwise f_0 would be an extreme point of H not in D. We have a point of E outside of a compact convex set. So, by the separation theorem, $\exists \varphi \in E^*$ with $\varphi(f_0) > \max_H \varphi \geq \max_D \varphi$.

Hence $\overline{C^e}$ is contained in every closed subset of C on which every continuous linear functional assumes its maximum.

This theorem will be useful in the study of boundaries for function algebras. Note that for a *complex* locally convex space E and a compact convex set C we can prove an analogue of (a): If $\psi \in E^*$, then $|\psi|$ assumes its maximum over C at some extreme point of C. (Take $f_1 \in C$ such that $|\psi(f_1)| = \max_C |\psi|$. Set $C_1 = \{f \in C : \psi(f) = \psi(f_1)\}$. Then C_1 is nonvoid, compact, and convex, so C_1 has an extreme point f_0. If $\psi = 0$ on C, then all is clear. Otherwise we can replace ψ by a scalar multiple of ψ and assume that $\psi(f_0) = 1$. Since 1 is an extreme point of the unit disk, it follows that f_0 is an extreme point of C. So $|\psi|$ attains its maximum at $f_0 \in C^e$.) But property (b) fails to hold for maximum moduli. For example, if $E = \mathbf{C}$ and C is the closed unit disk, then every linear functional $z \to \lambda z$ on E assumes its maximum modulus over C at 1 while C^e is the entire unit circle.

EXERCISE SET 1.4

1. If φ is a linear functional on a complex vector space F, and if $u = \mathrm{Re}\,(\varphi)$, then $\varphi(f) = u(f) - iu(if)\,(f \in F)$. Conversely, if u is a real-linear functional on F, then $\varphi(f) = u(f) - iu(if)$ defines a complex-linear functional on F.

2. A *seminorm* on a linear space E is a nonnegative function p on E which satisfies $p(f + g) \leq p(f) + p(g)$ and $p(\alpha f) = |\alpha| p(f)\,(\alpha \in K, f \in E, g \in E)$.

Prove that if p is a seminorm on E, and if φ is a linear functional on a subspace F of E such that $|\varphi(f)| \le p(f)$ for all $f \in F$, then there is a linear functional ψ on E which extends φ and satisfies $|\psi(f)| \le p(f)$ $(f \in E)$. (Prove this first for a real linear space E, then extend to a complex space.)

3. If φ is a linear functional on a t.v.s. E, the following are equivalent: (a) φ is continuous; (b) the null space of φ is closed in E; (c) φ is bounded on some *nbhd* of 0.

4. Let E be a t.v.s., F a linear subspace of E, and C a balanced convex *nbhd* of 0 in E. If φ is a linear functional on F such that $|\varphi| \le 1$ on $F \cap C$, show that φ extends to a linear functional ψ on E such that $|\psi| \le 1$ on C.

Hence if E is a locally convex t.v.s. and φ is a continuous linear functional on a subspace of E, then φ can be extended to a continuous linear functional on E.

5. If f and g are distinct points in a locally convex t.v.s. E, then there is a continuous linear functional ψ on E with $\psi(f) \ne \psi(g)$.

6. Let C be a subset of a vector space E. If $f_0 \in C$, show that f_0 is an extreme point of C iff whenever $f_0 = \lambda f + (1 - \lambda)g$ with f, g in C and $0 < \lambda < 1$, we must have $f_0 = f = g$. Suppose that C is a convex set and $\{f_1, \ldots, f_n\} \subset C$, $\{\lambda_1, \ldots, \lambda_n\} \subset [0, 1]$, and $\sum_{i=1}^{n} \lambda_i = 1$. Note that if $0 < \lambda_j < 1$, then

$$\sum_{i=1}^{n} \lambda_i f_i = \lambda_j f_j + (1 - \lambda_j)g \quad \text{where} \quad g = \sum_{i \ne j} \frac{\lambda_i}{1 - \lambda_j} f_i \text{ belongs to } C. \text{ Thus}$$

if f is an extreme point of a convex set C, and if f is a convex combination $\sum_{i=1}^{n} \lambda_i f_i$ (all $f_i \in C$, $0 \le \lambda_i$ and $\sum \lambda_i = 1$), then $f = f_j$ for some j.

7. In a locally convex t.v.s. E, every nonvoid compact set C has extreme points. Furthermore, C and C^e have the same closed convex hull.

8. Suppose that φ is a one-one linear map from E_1 to E_2 and that $A \subset E_1$. Show that e is an extreme point of A iff $\varphi(e)$ is an extreme point of $\varphi(A)$.

9. Suppose that S is a compact Hausdorff space. Let $A = \{f \in C(S): |f(x)| \le 1, \forall x \in S\}$. What are the extreme points of A? Is A the closed convex hull of its set of extreme points?

1.5 THE WEAK*-TOPOLOGY

Suppose that E is a locally convex t.v.s. and that E^* is the family of al continuous linear functionals on E. E^* is again a linear space, and there is a pairing of the elements of E and E^* given by $(f, \varphi) \to \varphi(f)$. By definition, $\varphi \ne 0$ iff $\varphi(f) \ne 0$ for some $f \in E$, while since E is locally convex, $f \ne 0$ iff $\varphi(f) \ne 0$ for some $\varphi \in E^*$. Each $f \in E$ determines a mapping $\varphi \to \varphi(f)$ from

E^* to the scalar field. We define the *weak*-topology* (*w*-topology*) of E^* to be the weak topology defined on E^* by the family of all these mappings as f ranges over E. With this topology, E^* is itself a locally convex space, and each $f \in E$ determines a continuous linear functional on E^*.

Conversely, if L is a linear functional on E^* which is w^*-continuous, then $\exists f \in E$ such that $L(\varphi) = \varphi(f)$ for each $\varphi \in E^*$. Indeed, since L is continuous at 0, it follows from the definition of the w^*-topology that there are $f_1, \ldots, f_n$ in E and $\varepsilon > 0$ such that if $\varphi \in E^*$ and $|\varphi(f_i)| < \varepsilon$ for $i = 1, \ldots, n$, then $|L(\varphi)| < 1$. Hence if $\varphi(f_i) = 0$ for $i = 1, \ldots, n$, then $|L(\alpha\varphi)| < 1$ for every $\alpha > 0$, and so $L(\varphi) = 0$. Therefore the kernel of L contains every φ which vanishes at $f_1, \ldots, f_n$. By Exercise 2, $L = \sum a_i f_i$ for some scalars $a_1, \ldots, a_n$.

Every normed linear space is a locally convex t.v.s. (Recall that a *norm* on E is a seminorm $f \to \|f\|$ such that $\|f\| > 0$ if $f \neq 0$. A norm determines a metric, defined by $\rho(f, g) = \|f - g\|$. Since the open balls $\{f \in E : \|f\| < r\}$ form a base at 0, E is locally convex.) A *Banach space* is a complete normed linear space (every ρ-Cauchy sequence is convergent). A linear functional L on a normed space E is continuous iff it is bounded on the unit ball of E. The operator norm of a continuous linear functional L is given by $\|L\| = \sup \{|L(f)| : \|f\| \leq 1\}$.

Suppose that E is a normed linear space and that $\Sigma^* = \{L \in E^* : \|L\| \leq 1\}$ is the unit ball in E^*. For each $f \in E$, let $C_f = \{\lambda \in K : |\lambda| \leq \|f\|\}$, and let $C = \prod_{f \in E} C_f$. By Tychonoff's theorem, C is a compact Hausdorff space in the product topology. $\xi \in C$ iff $\xi : E \to K$ and $|\xi(f)| = |\pi_f(\xi)| \leq \|f\|$ for every $f \in E$. Thus $\Sigma^* \subset C$. If $f \in E$, the restriction of the projection π_f to Σ^* is the map $L \to L(f)$, so it should be clear that the w^*-topology of E^* and the topology of C both induce the same relative topology on Σ^*. If $f, g \in E$ and $\alpha, \beta \in K$, then the map $\xi \to \xi(\alpha f + \beta g) - \alpha \xi(f) - \beta \xi(g)$ is continuous from C to K, so the set on which it vanishes is a closed subset of C. The intersection of these sets (over all f, g and all α, β) is Σ^*, and we conclude that Σ^* is a closed subset of the compact space C.

We have now proved the fundamental theorem of Alaoglu: the unit ball $\Sigma^* = \{L : \|L\| \leq 1\}$ of the dual of a normed linear space E is w^*-compact. Observe that Σ^* is also convex, and hence, by the Krein-Milman theorem, Σ^* is the w^*-closed convex hull of its set of extreme points.

EXERCISE SET 1.5

1. Suppose that E is a locally convex t.v.s. Prove that E^* is a locally convex t.v.s. with respect to the w^*-topology.

2. Suppose that $L, L_1, \ldots, L_n$ are linear functionals on a vector space E over K and that $\operatorname{Ker}(L) \supset \bigcap_{i=1}^{n} \operatorname{Ker}(L_i)$. Show that L is a linear combination of $L_1, \ldots, L_n$. (Hint: $(L_1(f), \ldots, L_n(f)) \to L(f)$ is a well-defined linear functional on a subspace of K^n.)

3. Suppose that φ is a continuous linear functional whose domain is a subspace F of a normed linear space E. Show that there is a continuous linear functional ψ on E such that ψ extends φ (i.e., $\psi \,|\, F = \varphi$) and $\|\psi\| = \|\varphi\|$.

1.6   NORMED LINEAR SPACES

In this section we review some of the basic theorems about normed linear spaces, omitting some of the proofs. (For more details consult references [F], [K].) Proofs will be given for certain important results which may be unfamiliar to the reader.

Let E, F be normed linear spaces. For a linear mapping $T : E \to F$, set $\|T\| = \sup \{\|Tf\| : f \in E, \ \|f\| \le 1\}$. T is continuous iff $\|T\| < \infty$; for this reason one refers to continuous linear maps as bounded linear transformations. The space $B(E, F)$ of all bounded linear mappings from E to F is thus a normed linear space. It is complete if F is complete. In particular, since the scalars are complete, E^* is complete.

For any normed space E, there is an embedding of E into its second dual E^{**} given by $f \to f^{**}$, where $f^{**}(L) = L(f)$ for $f \in E$, $L \in E^*$. By definition of the various norms, it is clear that $\|f^{**}\| \le \|f\|$. On the other hand, if we set $L_0(\alpha f) = \alpha\|f\|$, then L_0 is a linear functional of norm 1 on the subspace of E spanned by f, so L_0 extends to a functional $L \in E^*$ with $\|L\| = 1$. But $\|L\| = 1$ and $f^{**}(L) = L(f) = \|f\|$, so $\|f^{**}\| \ge \|f\|$. Thus $f \to f^{**}$ is an isometry.

Each T in $B(E, F)$ determines a map T^* in $B(F^*, E^*)$, where $T^*(L) = L \circ T$. If $f \in E$, $L \in F^*$, and $\|L\| \le 1$, then we have $|L(Tf)| \le \|Tf\| \le \|T\| \|f\|$, so $\|T^*\| \le \|T\|$. The same is true with T replaced by T^*, so $\|T^{**}\| \le \|T^*\| \le \|T\|$. On the other hand, T^{**} is a sort of extension of T, so $\|T\| \le \|T^{**}\|$. More precisely, $\|Tf\| = \|(Tf)^{**}\| = \|T^{**}(f^{**})\| \le \|T^{**}\| \|f\|$, so $\|T\| \le \|T^{**}\|$. We conclude that $\|T\| = \|T^*\|$.

Two fundamental theorems of functional analysis are the closed graph theorem and the principle of uniform boundedness.

Theorem 12   (Closed Graph Theorem).   *Let $T : E \to F$ be a linear mapping, where E, F are Banach spaces. Then T is continuous iff $\{(f, Tf) : f \in E\}$ is a closed subset of $E \times F$.*

Corollary 1.   *If E, F are Banach spaces and T is a one-one continuous linear mapping of E onto F, then $T^{-1} : F \to E$ is continuous.*

Corollary 2   (Open Mapping Theorem).   *If E, F are Banach spaces and T is a continuous linear mapping of E onto F, then $T(U)$ is open in F for every open set U in E.*

Theorem 13   (Uniform Boundedness Principle). *Let E be a Banach space and $\{T_\alpha : E \to F_\alpha\}$ a family of bounded linear transformations from E to normed linear spaces F_α. Suppose that for each $f \in E$, $\sup_\alpha \|T_\alpha f\| < \infty$. Then $\{\|T_\alpha\|\}$ is bounded.*

Corollary 1. *Let E be a normed linear space and $\{f_n\}$ a sequence of elements of E. Then the set of norms $\{\|f_n\|\}$ is bounded iff $\{L(f_n)\}$ is a bounded set of scalars for each $L \in E^*$.*

The next theorem gives a simple test for determining when a subspace of a dual space is w^*-closed. Although it is a special case of a stronger theorem of Krein and Šmulian, I have preferred to present Dieudonné's original argument.

Theorem 14   (Banach-Dieudonné). *Let E be a Banach space and V a subspace of E^*. Then V is w^*-closed iff $V \cap \Sigma^*$ is w^*-compact, where $\Sigma^* = \{L \in E^* : \|L\| \le 1\}$.*

Proof.   Necessity is immediate from Alaoglu's theorem. In order to prove the sufficiency we shall show that V is the annihilator of $^0V = \{f \in E : L(f) = 0 \text{ for all } L \in V\}$. What we shall actually establish is:

(1) For each $L_0 \in E^* \backslash V$, there is a sequence $\{f_n\}$ in E such that $f_n \to 0$ and $\sup_n |L(f_n) - L_0(f_n)| \ge 1$ for each $L \in V$.

To see that (1) implies that $V = (^0V)^\perp$, we argue as follows. Let (c_0) be the normed linear space of all sequences $\xi = \{\xi_n\}$ of complex numbers such that $\lim_n \xi_n = 0$, with $\|\xi\| = \sup_n |\xi_n|$. Then $(c_0) = C_0(\mathbf{Z}^+)$, where $\mathbf{Z}^+$ is the discrete space $\{1, 2, \ldots\}$. So $(c_0)^* = M(\mathbf{Z}^+)$, the space of finite complex measures on $\mathbf{Z}^+$, and this in turn is the same as ℓ^1, the space of absolutely summable sequences. Given $L \in E^*$, let $\xi(L) = \{L(f_n)\}$. Then $\xi(L) \in (c_0)$ since $f_n \to 0$ and L is continuous. The hypothesis is that $\|\xi(L) - \xi(L_0)\| \ge 1$ for all $L \in V$; so the distance from $\xi(L_0)$ to the closed subspace $\overline{\xi(V)}$ of (c_0) is at least 1. Hence there is a linear functional in $(c_0)^*$ which annihilates $\xi(V)$ but not $\xi(L_0)$. Thus there is a sequence $\{a_n\}_1^\infty$ of complex numbers such that $\sum |a_n| < \infty$, $\sum a_n L(f_n) = 0$ for all $L \in V$, but $\sum a_n L_0(f_n) \ne 0$. Since $f_n \to 0$, $\{\|f_n\|\}$ is bounded; hence $\sum \|a_n f_n\| < \infty$. Since E is complete, $f_0 = \sum a_n f_n$ exists in E, and $L_0(f_0) \ne 0$, $L(f_0) = 0$ for all $L \in V$. We have shown that if $L_0 \notin V$, then $L_0 \notin (^0V)^\perp$. So V is w^*-closed.

Suppose now that V is a linear subspace of E^* such that $V \cap \Sigma^*$ is w^*-compact and that $L_0 \notin V$. We shall construct a sequence $\{f_n\}$ in E satisfying (1). To begin with, note that for each $r > 0$, $V_r = \{L \in V : \|L - L_0\| \le r\}$ is w^*-compact. Hence each V_r is w^*-closed and therefore closed in the norm topology. Choose r so that V_r is nonvoid. If $L \in V_r$, then $\|L - L_0\| \ge \text{dist}(L_0, V_r) > 0$, while if $L \in V \backslash V_r$, then $\|L - L_0\| > r$. So $d = \text{dist}(L_0, V) > 0$.

Let us prove the following assertion.

(2) There is a nonvoid finite set $D_1 \subset E$ such that if $L \in E^*$ and $\|L - L_0\| \leq d + 1$, and if $|(L - L_0)(f)| \leq \dfrac{d}{2}\|f\|$ for all $f \in D_1$, then $L \notin V$.

Note that once (2) is proved we can replace each nonzero f in D_1 by $f/\|f\|$ and hence suppose that $\|f\| = 1$ for each nonzero f in D_1.

For each nonvoid finite set $F \subset E$, let $S(F) = \{L \in V_{d+1} : |(L - L_0)(f)| \leq \dfrac{d}{2}\|f\|, \forall f \in F\}$ and let $\overline{S(F)}$ be the w^*-closure of $S(F)$. If every $S(F)$ is nonvoid, then the intersection of any finite number of the w^*-compact sets $\overline{S(F)}$ is nonvoid (since $S(F_1) \cap \cdots \cap S(F_k) = S(F_1 \cup \cdots \cup F_k)$), so $\bigcap_F \overline{S(F)} \neq \varnothing$. But then we can find $L \in V_{d+1}$ such that each w^*-nbhd of L meets each $S(\{f\})$ ($f \in E$). Hence for each $f \in E$ and $\varepsilon > 0$, $\exists L_1 \in V$ such that $|(L_1 - L)(f)| < \varepsilon$ and $|(L_1 - L_0)(f)| \leq \dfrac{d}{2}\|f\|$. So $|(L - L_0)(f)| \leq \varepsilon + \dfrac{d}{2}\|f\|$ for all $\varepsilon > 0$, $f \in E$. Hence $\|L - L_0\| \leq d/2 < d$. Since $L \in V$, this is a contradiction. So some $S(F)$ is empty, which proves (2).

Now apply the same kind of argument recursively. We find a sequence of nonvoid finite sets $\{D_N\}$ in E such that for each $N > 1$, any L in E^* which satisfies the conditions (a) $\|L - L_0\| \leq d + N$, (b) $|(L - L_0)(f)| \leq d/2$ for all $f \in D_1$, (c) $|(L - L_0)(f)| \leq (d + k)\|f\|$ for all f in D_{k+1}, $1 \leq k < N$, does not belong to V. Again we assume that $\|f\| = 1$ for each nonzero f in D_N.

Suppose that $D_N = \{f_1{}^N, \ldots, f_{m_N}{}^N\}$. Let $\{f_n\}$ be the sequence

$$\left\{ \frac{2}{d} f_1{}^1, \ldots, \frac{2}{d} f_{m_1}{}^1, \frac{1}{d+1} f_1{}^2, \ldots, \frac{1}{d+1} f_{m_2}{}^2, \ldots \right\}.$$

Certainly $\|f_n\| \to 0$. Furthermore, given $L \in E$ such that $\sup_n |L(f_n) - L_0(f_n)| < 1$, find N such that $\|L - L_0\| \leq d + N$. Then L satisfies conditions (a), (b), (c), so $L \notin V$. That finishes the proof.

It will be of interest to us in Chapter Seven to know the conditions under which the range of a linear mapping is closed, and in particular to know that this is so iff it is true of the adjoint mapping.

Theorem 15.   *Let E, F be Banach spaces and $T : E \to F$ a bounded linear transformation. Then $T(E)$ is closed in F iff $T^*(F^*)$ is (norm) closed in E^*.*

Proof.   Suppose that $T(E)$ is closed in F. Then $T(E)$ is itself a Banach space, and $T : E \to T(E)$ is therefore an open mapping. Hence if $S = \{f \in E : \|f\| \leq 1\}$, $T(S)$ is a nbhd in $T(E)$ of 0; in particular, there is some $c > 0$ such that if $g \in T(E)$ and $\|g\| \leq c$, then $g \in T(S)$. Thus for each $g \in T(E)$, there exists some $f \in E$ such that $T(f) = g$ and $\|f\| \leq \dfrac{1}{c}\|g\|$.

Let us show that $T^*(F^*) = \{L \in E^* : L = 0 \text{ on the null space of } T\}$. This will certainly prove that $T^*(F^*)$ is closed in E^*. Since $T^*(\psi) = \psi \circ T$, it is clear that every element of $T^*(F^*)$ vanishes on $T^{-1}(0)$. Conversely, suppose that $L \in E^*$ and L vanishes on $T^{-1}(0)$. Then given f, f' with $T(f) = T(f')$, $L(f) = L(f')$. So there is a linear functional ψ_0 on $T(E)$ such that $\psi_0(T(f)) = L(f)$ for all $f \in E$. For each $g \in T(E)$, choose $f \in E$ with $T(f) = g$ and $\|f\| \leq \frac{1}{c}\|g\|$. Then $|\psi_0(g)| = |L(f)| \leq \frac{1}{c}\|g\|\|L\|$, so ψ_0 is continuous. By the Hahn-Banach theorem, ψ_0 extends to an element $\psi \in F^*$. Since $\psi \circ T = T^*(\psi) = L$, we have shown that $L \in T^*(F^*)$. So one half of the theorem is proved.

On the other hand, suppose that $T(E)$ is not closed in F. Let W be the closure of $T(E)$ in F. Note that $T^*(F^*)$ can be identified with $T^*(W^*)$ if we regard T as a mapping from E to W. (For if $\psi \in F^*$, then $T^*(\psi) = \psi \circ T = \psi_0 \circ T$ where ψ_0 is the restriction of ψ to W. Conversely, given $\psi_0 \in W^*$, ψ_0 extends to some $\psi \in F^*$, and we have $T^*(\psi) = \psi_0 \circ T$ again.) By assumption, T is not onto W. Let us prove a lemma.

Lemma 5. *Let $T \in B(E, F)$ where E, F are Banach spaces. Suppose that there exist $\varepsilon > 0$ and ρ in $[0, 1)$ such that to each $g \in F$ there corresponds some $f \in E$ with*

$(\star)$ $$\varepsilon\|f\| + \|g - T(f)\| \leq \rho\|g\|.$$

Then T is an open mapping of E onto F.

Proof. Take any $g_0 \in F$ and apply the hypothesis recursively. We see that there are $\{f_n\}$ in E such that $\varepsilon\|f_0\| + \|g_0 - T(f_0)\| \leq \rho\|g_0\|$ and $\varepsilon\|f_n\| + \|g_0 - \sum_{k=0}^{n-1} T(f_k)\| \leq \rho\|g_0 - \sum_{k=0}^{n-1} T(f_k)\|$ for all $n \geq 1$. Hence $\varepsilon\|f_n\| \leq \rho^{n+1}\|g_0\|$ and $\|g_0 - \sum_{k=0}^{n} T(f_k)\| \leq \rho^{n+1}\|g_0\|$ for all n. Since E is complete and $\sum \|f_n\| < \infty$, $f = \sum f_n$ exists in E. We have $\varepsilon\|f\| \leq \frac{\rho}{1-\rho}\|g_0\|$ and $g_0 = \lim_n \sum_{k=0}^{n} T(f_k) = T(f)$, which proves the lemma.

We now know that for each pair (ε, ρ), there is some $g_0 \in W$ such that $(\star)$ fails for all $f \in E$ (if we take $g = g_0$). So $\varepsilon\|f\| + \|g_0 - T(f)\| > \rho\|g_0\|$ for all $f \in E$. Let G be the direct sum of E and W: $G = E \times W$ with the sum norm $\|(f, g)\| = \|f\| + \|g\|$. The hypothesis implies that $(0, g_0)$ is at a distance $d \geq \rho\|g_0\|$ from the linear subspace $G_0 = \{(\varepsilon f, T(f)) : f \in E\}$. G_0 is the graph of $\frac{1}{\varepsilon} T$, so G_0 is closed in G. By a simple corollary to the Hahn-Banach theorem, there exists a linear functional L of norm 1 on G such that L vanishes on

G_0 but $L(0, g_0) = d$. If we set $\psi(g) = L(0, g)$ for $g \in W$, then we have $T^*(\psi)(f) = L(0, T(f)) = -\varepsilon L(f, 0)$ for all $f \in E$. So $\psi \in W^*$, $\|T^*\psi\| \leq \varepsilon$, and $\rho \leq \|\psi\| \leq 1$.

Take $\varepsilon_n \to 0$, $\rho_n \to 1$. Then there exist ψ_n in W^* with $\|T^*\psi_n\| \to 0$, $\|\psi_n\| \to 1$. Therefore T^* does not have a continuous inverse from E^* to W^*. T^* is one-one and linear on W^*, so the closed graph theorem implies that the range of T^* is not closed in E^*.

EXERCISE SET   1.6

1. Suppose that E is a locally convex t.v.s. and that F is a closed linear subspace of E. Let E/F be the space of cosets of E modulo F. Show that with respect to the quotient topology defined by the quotient map from E to E/F, E/F is a locally convex t.v.s.

2. Let F be a closed subspace of a normed linear space E. The quotient space E/F is a normed linear space with the following norm: $\|f + F\| =$ inf $\{\|f + g\| : g \in F\}$ (=distance from f to F). If E is a Banach space, so is E/F. The norm topology of E/F coincides with the quotient topology.

3. Let E and F be as in Exercise 2. Show that F^* is isometrically isomorphic to $E^*/F^\perp$, where $F^\perp = \{L \in E^* : L(f) = 0 \text{ for all } f \in F\}$. Furthermore, $F^\perp$ is isometrically isomorphic to $(E/F)^*$.

Chapter Two

Commutative Banach Algebras

In this chapter we develop some properties of commutative Banach algebras and give a few examples. References which contain more thorough discussions are Gelfand [B], Naimark [G], and Rickart [I].

2.1 GENERALITIES

An *algebra* over a field K is a ring A which is a vector space over K and satisfies $\alpha(fg) = (\alpha f)g = f(\alpha g)$ for all $\alpha \in K$, $f \in A$, $g \in A$. If A, B are K-algebras, a *homomorphism* (or algebra homomorphism) from A to B is a linear mapping $T: A \to B$ satisfying $T(fg) = Tf \cdot Tg$ for all f, g in A. An *ideal* in a K-algebra A is a linear subspace I of A which is a two-sided ring ideal (i.e., $fg \in I$ and $gf \in I$ for all $f \in I$, $g \in A$). If $T: A \to B$ is a homomorphism, then $T^{-1}(0) = \{f \in A : Tf = 0\}$ is an ideal of A and is called the kernel of T. Conversely, every ideal I of A is the kernel of the canonical homomorphism Q from A to the K-algebra A/I of cosets modulo I.

Let I be an ideal of A and let $u \in A$. u is a *relative identity* for I iff $(ux - x) \in I$ and $(xu - x) \in I$ for all $x \in A$, i.e., iff $Q(ux) = Q(x) = Q(xu)$ for every x. I is a *regular ideal* iff there exists a relative identity for I, or equivalently iff A/I has an identity element (which may be 0). An ideal containing a regular ideal is regular, while if A has an identity element, then every ideal of A is regular. If u is a relative identity for I, and if $u \in I$, then $I = A$.

An ideal I in A is a *maximal ideal* of A iff I is a proper ideal (i.e., $I \neq A$), but there is no proper ideal J such that $I \subset J$ and $I \neq J$. Similarly, a subalgebra B of A is a *maximal subalgebra* of A iff B is a maximal element in the partially ordered set of all proper subalgebras of A. Note that a regular maximal ideal is maximal in the family of regular ideals while a maximal regular ideal is a maximal ideal. An argument using Zorn's lemma shows that every proper regular ideal I in a K-algebra A is contained in a maximal ideal of A. If M is a regular maximal ideal of A, then A/M is a K-algebra with identity which has no nonzero proper ideals; in particular, if A/M is commutative, then A/M is a field.

If A is a K-algebra and h is a linear map from A to K, then the image of h is a subspace of K and hence is either $\{0\}$ or K. In particular, if h is a nonzero homomorphism from A into K, then $h(A) = K$, and Ker (h) is a regular maximal ideal of A.

Let A be a K-algebra with identity element 1. For each $f \in A$ and each polynomial $p(t) = \sum_{i=0}^{n} \alpha_i t^i$ with coefficients in K, we set $p(f) = \alpha_0 1 + \sum_{i=1}^{n} \alpha_i f^i$. The *spectrum* of f is the set $\sigma(f)$ of all scalars $\lambda \in K$ such that $f - \lambda 1$ has no multiplicative inverse in A. (If we must stress the algebra A, we write $\sigma_A(f)$ for $\sigma(f)$.)

In a sense, polynomials preserve spectra.

Lemma 1. *If $f \in A$ and p is a polynomial over K, then $p(\lambda) \in \sigma(p(f))$ for every λ in $\sigma(f)$.*

Proof. Suppose $\lambda \in \sigma(f)$, so that $f - \lambda 1$ is not invertible in A. By the remainder theorem for polynomials, $p(t) = (t - \lambda)q(t) + p(\lambda)$ where q is a polynomial over K. Hence $p(f) - p(\lambda) = (f - \lambda 1)q(f) = q(f)(f - \lambda 1)$. Since $f - \lambda 1$ is singular, $p(f) - p(\lambda)$ must be singular. So $p(\lambda) \in \sigma(p(f))$.

Lemma 2. *If K is algebraically closed, then $\alpha \in \sigma(p(f))$ iff $\alpha = p(\lambda)$ for some $\lambda \in \sigma(f)$.*

Proof. We need only prove the "only if" assertion. If p is a constant, the result is clear, so assume that p has degree at least 1 and that $\alpha \in \sigma(p(f))$. Set $q(t) = p(t) - \alpha$. Since K is algebraically closed, $q(t) = \beta(t - \lambda_1) \cdots (t - \lambda_n)$ where $\beta \neq 0$ and $\beta, \lambda_1, \ldots, \lambda_n$ are in K. Hence $p(f) - \alpha 1 = q(f) = \beta(f - \lambda_1 1) \cdots (f - \lambda_n 1)$ is singular in A. So some factor $f - \lambda_j 1$ is singular. That is, $q(\lambda_j) = p(\lambda_j) - \alpha$ is zero for some λ_j in the spectrum of f.

Theorem 1. *Let A, B be K-algebras with identity, and let T be an isomorphism from A onto B. Then for each f in A, $\sigma_A(f) = \sigma_B(T(f))$.*

Proof. Since T is an isomorphism, $T(1) = 1$. Also, f is invertible in A iff $T(f)$ is invertible in B. Hence if $\lambda \in K$, $T(f - \lambda 1) = T(f) - \lambda 1$ is invertible in B iff $f - \lambda 1$ is invertible in A, which proves the assertion.

EXERCISE SET 2.1

1. Show that $\sigma_K(\alpha) = \{\alpha\}$ for each $\alpha \in K$.

2. Let A be a commutative K-algebra with identity, and let $f \in A$. Show that f is invertible in A iff f belongs to no maximal ideal of A; thus $\lambda \in \sigma(f)$ iff $f - \lambda 1$ belongs to some maximal ideal of A.

3. If A is a K-algebra with identity and f is invertible in A, show that $\lambda \in \sigma(f)$ iff $\lambda \neq 0$ and $\lambda^{-1} \in \sigma(f^{-1})$.

4. Let X be a compact Hausdorff space, and let $C(X)$ be the algebra of all continuous complex-valued functions on X. (Here we define αf, $f + g$, and fg in the usual way.) Show that if $f \in C(X)$, then $\sigma(f) = f(X)$, the range of f. If X, X' are compact Hausdorff spaces and T is an algebra isomorphism from $C(X)$ onto $C(X')$, then $f \in C(X)$ and $Tf \in C(X')$ have identical ranges. For each $x \in X$, let $M_x = \{f \in C(X) : f(x) = 0\}$. Show that M_x is a maximal ideal in $C(X)$. Determine the quotient field $C(X)/M_x$.

5. Let A be a K-algebra without an identity element. Show that there is a natural extension of A to an algebra A_1 with identity. (*Hint*: Let $A_1 = A \oplus K$, and define $(f, \lambda)(f', \lambda') = (ff' + \lambda f' + \lambda' f, \lambda \lambda')$. Then A_1 is a K-algebra with identity $e = (0, 1)$. A is isomorphic to a regular maximal ideal of A_1 via the map $f \to (f, 0)$, and A_1/A is isomorphic to K. A_1 is a minimal extension of A to an algebra with identity since A and e generate A_1.)

   If $f \in A$, then f is *quasi-regular* iff $f + g = fg = gf$ for some $g \in A$. This is equivalent to $(e - f)(e - g) = e = (e - g)(e - f)$. We define the spectrum of f to be its spectrum in A_1; thus $\sigma_A(f) = \{\lambda \in K : f - \lambda e$ has no inverse in $A_1\}$. Show that $0 \in \sigma(f)$ and that if $0 \neq \lambda \in K$, then $\lambda \in \sigma(f)$ iff $\lambda^{-1}f$ is not quasi-regular. Does Theorem 1 hold if A has no identity element?

   As an example, let Y be a locally compact noncompact Hausdorff space. If $f \in C_0(Y)$, what is $\sigma(f)$?

6. Suppose that A is a commutative K-algebra and that I is an ideal in A. Then I is a K-algebra. Show that if $h_0 : I \to K$ is a nonzero homomorphism, there is exactly one homomorphism $h : A \to K$ which extends h_0.

7. Let $L^1(\mathbf{R})$ be the Banach space of all Lebesgue integrable functions on the real line. For f, g in L^1, define the *convolution* of f and g to be the function $f * g$ given by $(f * g)(x) = \int_{-\infty}^{\infty} f(x - y)g(y)\, dy$. (Prove that the integrands $(x, y) \to f(x - y)g(y)$ are measurable on $\mathbf{R}^2$, and use the Fubini theorem to show that $(f * g)(x)$ exists for almost all $x \in \mathbf{R}$ and that $f * g$ is again in L^1.) With convolution as multiplication, $L^1(\mathbf{R})$ is a commutative $\mathbf{C}$-algebra. (It has no identity element.) Show that for each real number t, the map $f \to \int_{-\infty}^{\infty} f(x)e^{-ixt}\, dx$ is a homomorphism of $L^1(\mathbf{R})$ onto the complex numbers. Show that if $\hat{f}(t) = \int_{-\infty}^{\infty} f(x)e^{-ixt}\, dx$ ($f \in L^1(\mathbf{R})$, $t \in \mathbf{R}$), then each $\hat{f}$ is a continuous function on $\mathbf{R}$. Show that $f \to \hat{f}$ is an algebra homomorphism from $L^1(\mathbf{R})$ into the space of continuous maps from $\mathbf{R}$ to $\mathbf{C}$. In fact, $f \to \hat{f}$ is an isomorphism from $L^1(\mathbf{R})$ into $C_0(\mathbf{R})$. (In particular, each $\hat{f}$ vanishes at infinity on $\mathbf{R}$. This is the famous Riemann-Lebesgue lemma. Prove it first for a smooth function f which vanishes outside an interval $[a, b]$, and then approximate an arbitrary f by such functions in the L^1-norm.) Check also that $\|f * g\|_1 \leq \|f\|_1 \|g\|_1$ and $\sup_{t \in \mathbf{R}} |\hat{f}(t)| \leq \|f\|_1$.

2.2   NORMED ALGEBRAS

A *normed algebra* over K (where $K = \mathbf{R}$ or $K = \mathbf{C}$) is a K-algebra A together with a norm on A which satisfies $\|fg\| \leq \|f\| \, \|g\|$ for all $f \in A$, $g \in A$. A *Banach algebra* (or normed ring) is a complete normed algebra.

The completion of any normed algebra is a Banach algebra. If S is a compact space, then $\|f\| = \max_{x \in S} |f(x)|$ defines a Banach algebra norm on $C(S)$. The algebra $L^1(\mathbf{R})$ of all Lebesgue integrable functions on the line is a Banach algebra (with $\|f\|_1 = \int_{-\infty}^{\infty} |f(x)| \, dx$ and convolution as multiplication).

If A is a normed algebra, and if $f_n \to f$, $g_n \to g$ in A, then $f_n g_n \to fg$; i.e., multiplication is a continuous function of both variables. If I is an ideal in A, its closure $\bar{I}$ is also an ideal. Also, $\|f^n\| \leq \|f\|^n$ for all $f \in A$ and $n = 1, 2, \ldots$.

Lemma 3.   *Let A be a Banach algebra. If $f \in A$ and $\|f\| < 1$, then there is some $g \in A$ with $f + g = fg = gf$. (I.e., f is quasi-regular.)*

Proof.   The series $\sum \|f^n\|$ converges by comparison with the geometric series $\sum \|f\|^n$. Since A is complete, $g = -\sum_{n=1}^{\infty} f^n$ exists in A. But then $f + g = -\sum_{n=2}^{\infty} f^n = fg = gf$. (Note that continuity of multiplication in A has been used. Also note that g belongs to the closed subalgebra of A generated by f.)

Lemma 4.   *Let A be a Banach algebra and let I be a proper regular ideal in A. If u is a relative identity for I, then $\|u - f\| \geq 1$ for every $f \in I$. Hence $\bar{I}$ is a proper ideal of A.*

Proof.   Assume that $\|u - f\| < 1$ for some $f \in I$. Take $g \in A$ with $u - f + g = (u - f)g$. Then $u = (ug - g) + (f - fg)$. Since u is a relative identity for I, $(ug - g) \in I$. Since $f \in I$ and I is an ideal, $(f - fg) \in I$. So $u \in I$, and I cannot be proper.

Lemma 5.   *Let M be a regular maximal ideal in a Banach algebra A. Then M is closed. In particular, if A has an identity, then every maximal ideal of A is closed in A.*

Proof. $M \subset \bar{M}$, and $\bar{M}$ is a proper ideal. So $M = \bar{M}$ by maximality.

Lemma 6.   *Let A be a Banach algebra and h a homomorphism of A into the scalars. Then h is continuous. In fact, $\|h\| \leq 1$.*

Proof.   Assume that $\|f\| < |h(f)|$ for some f in A. If $\lambda = h(f)$, then $\|\lambda^{-1}f\| < 1$, so there is some $g \in A$ with $\lambda^{-1}f + g = \lambda^{-1}fg$. Applying h to both sides, we get $1 + h(g) = h(g)$, a contradiction.

Lemma 7. *If A is a Banach algebra with identity, and if $f \in A$ and $\|1 - f\| < 1$, then f is invertible in A. If $f \in A$ and $\lambda \in \sigma(f)$, then $|\lambda| \leq \|f\|$. Thus $\sup_{\lambda \in \sigma(f)} |\lambda| \leq \|f\|$.*

Proof. If $1 - f$ has norm less than one, then $1 - f + g = (1 - f)g = g(1 - f)$ for some $g \in A$. So $1 = f(1 - g) = (1 - g)f$, and f is invertible.

If $\lambda \in K$ and $|\lambda| > \|f\|$, then $\left\| \frac{1}{\lambda} f \right\| < 1$, so $1 - \frac{1}{\lambda} f$ is invertible. Hence $f - \lambda 1 = -\lambda \left(1 - \frac{1}{\lambda} f \right)$ is invertible, so $\lambda \notin \sigma(f)$.

Theorem 2. *Let A be a complex Banach algebra, and let $f \in A$. Then* (a) $\sigma(f)$ *is a nonempty compact subset of the plane;* (b) $\|f^n\|^{1/n} \to \sup_{\lambda \in \sigma(f)} |\lambda|$ *as $n \to \infty$ (spectral radius formula).*

Proof. Since $\sigma_A(f) = \sigma_{A_1}(f)$ if A has no identity element, where A_1 is the algebra obtained by adjoining an identity to A, we assume that A has an identity. (See Exercise 5.)

If $\lambda \in \sigma(f)$, then $|\lambda| \leq \|f\|$, so $\sigma(f)$ is a bounded set in $\mathbf{C}$.

Next, $\sigma(f)$ is a closed set. For suppose $a \notin \sigma(f)$, so that $(f - a)^{-1}$ exists. If $|\lambda - a| < 1/\|(f - a)^{-1}\|$, then

$$\|1 - (f - \lambda)(f - a)^{-1}\| = \|(f - a - (f - \lambda))(f - a)^{-1}\|$$
$$= |\lambda - a| \, \|(f - a)^{-1}\| < 1$$

and $\|1 - (f - a)^{-1}(f - \lambda)\| < 1$. So $(f - \lambda)(f - a)^{-1}$ and $(f - a)^{-1}(f - \lambda)$ are invertible. It follows that $f - \lambda$ is invertible. So the complement of $\sigma(f)$ contains a neighborhood of a. The complement of $\sigma(f)$ is thus open, and $\sigma(f)$ is closed.

Now note that if f, g are invertible in A, then

$$f^{-1} - g^{-1} = f^{-1}(g - f)g^{-1} = [g^{-1} + (f^{-1} - g^{-1})](g - f)g^{-1}$$
$$= g^{-1}(g - f)g^{-1} + (f^{-1} - g^{-1})(g - f)g^{-1}.$$

So $\|f^{-1} - g^{-1}\| \leq \|g^{-1}\|^2 \|g - f\| + \|f^{-1} - g^{-1}\| \, \|g - f\| \, \|g^{-1}\|$. If $\|f - g\| < 1/\|g^{-1}\|$, then it follows that

$$\|f^{-1} - g^{-1}\| \leq \|g - f\| \, \|g^{-1}\|^2 (1 - \|g - f\| \, \|g^{-1}\|)^{-1}.$$

Hence as $f \to g$ in A, $f^{-1} \to g^{-1}$.

So if $f \in A$, the map $\lambda \to (f - \lambda)^{-1}$ is a continuous map from the complement of $\sigma(f)$ into A. If $\varphi \in A^*$ is a bounded linear functional on A, it follows that $\lambda \to \varphi((f - \lambda)^{-1}) = \Phi(\lambda)$ is analytic on the complement of $\sigma(f)$. For if $a \notin \sigma(f)$ and $\lambda \notin \sigma(f)$, then

$$\frac{\varphi((f - \lambda)^{-1}) - \varphi((f - a)^{-1})}{\lambda - a} = \varphi((f - \lambda)^{-1}(f - a)^{-1}),$$

and this approaches a limit as $\lambda \to a$. If $\sigma(f)$ were empty, then Φ would be an entire function. On the other hand, $(f - \lambda)^{-1} = \lambda^{-1}(\lambda^{-1}f - 1)^{-1} \to 0$ as

$\lambda \to \infty$, by the continuity of inversion in A. It would follow from Liouville's theorem that $\varphi((f - \lambda)^{-1}) = 0$ for every complex λ, and in particular, $\varphi(f^{-1}) = 0$. But $f^{-1} \neq 0$, so by the Hahn-Banach theorem, $\varphi(f^{-1}) \neq 0$ for some $\varphi \in A^*$, and we have a contradiction. Thus $\sigma(f)$ is nonempty, and (a) is proved.

Let $\|f\|_\sigma = \max_{\lambda \in \sigma(f)} |\lambda|$. ($\|f\|_\sigma$ is called the *spectral norm* of f.) We know that $\|f\|_\sigma \leq \|f\|$. Given $\varphi \in A^*$, we know that Φ is analytic on the complement of $\sigma(f)$ if $\Phi(\lambda) = \varphi((f - \lambda)^{-1})$. In particular, Φ is analytic on $U = \{\lambda \in \mathbf{C} : |\lambda| > \|f\|_\sigma\}$. But if $|\lambda| > \|f\|$, then $(f - \lambda)^{-1} = -\lambda^{-1}(1 - \lambda^{-1}f)^{-1} = -\lambda^{-1} \sum_{n=0}^{\infty} \lambda^{-n} f^n$, so $\Phi(\lambda) = -\lambda^{-1} \sum_{n=0}^{\infty} \varphi(f^n)/\lambda^n$ (since φ is continuous and linear). The series represents Φ on a neighborhood of ∞, so it represents Φ on U. In particular, it converges for each $\lambda \in U$. Hence for each $\lambda \in U$, there is a constant $K_\varphi(\lambda)$ such that $|\lambda^{-n} \varphi(f^n)| \leq K_\varphi(\lambda)$ for all n. Since this is true for an arbitrary $\varphi \in A^*$, it follows from the uniform boundedness principle that if $\lambda \in U$, $\{\lambda^{-n} f^n\}$ is bounded in the norm of A. Thus $\|f^n\| \leq K(\lambda)|\lambda^n|$, $\|f^n\|^{1/n} \leq K(\lambda)^{1/n}|\lambda|$, where $K(\lambda) > 0$. Take lim sup on both sides: lim sup $\|f^n\|^{1/n} \leq |\lambda|$. This is true for all λ with $|\lambda| > \|f\|_\sigma$, so lim sup $\|f^n\|^{1/n} \leq \|f\|_\sigma$.

On the other hand, if $\lambda \in \sigma(f)$, then $\lambda^n \in \sigma(f^n)$, so $|\lambda^n| \leq \|f^n\|$, $|\lambda| \leq \|f^n\|^{1/n}$. Thus $\|f\|_\sigma \leq$ lim inf $\|f^n\|^{1/n}$. This completes the proof of (b).

Note that if A is a complex Banach algebra, B a closed subalgebra of A, and $f \in B$, then the spectral norm of f as an element of B coincides with its spectral norm as an element of A, even though $\sigma_A(f)$ may be a proper subset of $\sigma_B(f)$.

If B is a complex Banach algebra with identity, and if every nonzero element of B has an inverse, then each $g \in B$ is a scalar multiple of the identity e. Indeed, $\sigma(g)$ contains some $\lambda \in \mathbf{C}$, so $g - \lambda e$ is singular and hence is zero. This is the Gelfand-Mazur theorem: A *normed complex division algebra is isomorphic to* $\mathbf{C}$. (Completeness of B was not used. See Exercise 3.)

Now if A is a complex Banach algebra and I is a closed ideal in A, then A/I is also a Banach algebra with respect to the quotient norm ($\|x + I\| = \inf_{y \in I} \|x + y\|$). Hence the following basic results hold.

Theorem 3. *Let M be a regular maximal ideal in a commutative complex Banach algebra A. Then A/M is isomorphic to* $\mathbf{C}$.

Proof. M is a closed ideal, so A/M is a field which is a Banach algebra. Hence $A/M \simeq \mathbf{C}$. (If we follow the maps through we see this: If u is a relative identity for M, then for each $f \in A$ there is some $\lambda \in \mathbf{C}$ with $f - \lambda u \in M$. The map $Q(f) \to \lambda$ is an isomorphism of A/M with $\mathbf{C}$, where $Q : A \to A/M$.)

Theorem 4. *Let A be a commutative complex Banach algebra. Then there is a one-one correspondence between the set of all regular maximal ideals of A and the set of all homomorphisms from A onto* $\mathbf{C}$.

Proof. If h is a homomorphism from A onto $\mathbf{C}$, then the kernel of h is a regular maximal ideal M. Conversely, every regular maximal ideal M in A is the kernel of the composite of $A \to A/M$ and $A/M \simeq \mathbf{C}$. Suppose that h, h' have the same kernel M. If u is a relative identity for M, then $(ux - x) \in M$ for every $x \in A$, so $h(u)h(x) = h(x)$ and $h'(u)h'(x) = h'(x)$. Thus $h(u) = h'(u) = 1$. But two linear functionals with the same kernel are scalar multiples of one another. So $h' = h$. Thus the correspondence is one-one.

Of course, this theorem is not too impressive if A has no regular maximal ideals or equivalently, when the only homomorphism from A to $\mathbf{C}$ is the zero function.

Suppose that A is a commutative complex Banach algebra with identity, and let $f \in A$. If h is a homomorphism from A onto $\mathbf{C}$, then $h(f) \in \sigma(f)$. For $h(f - h(f)1) = 0$, and so $f - h(f)1$ is not invertible. On the other hand, if $\lambda \in \sigma(f)$, then $\lambda = h(f)$ for some complex homomorphism h. Indeed, $f - \lambda 1$ is in some maximal ideal M, and M is the kernel of a homomorphism h from A onto $\mathbf{C}$. Thus $h(f - \lambda 1) = h(f) - \lambda = 0$. So in this case, $\sigma(f)$ coincides with $\{h(f): h \text{ is a homomorphism from } A \text{ onto } \mathbf{C}\}$. In the next section we shall turn things around and make each $f \in A$ into a function on the set of homomorphisms. The spectrum of f will turn out to be the range of the corresponding function $\hat{f}$.

EXERCISE SET 2.2

1. Let A be a Banach algebra. Suppose that $f_0 \in A$ and f_0 is quasi-regular. Show that if $f_0 + g_0 = f_0 g_0 = g_0 f_0$, and if $\|f - f_0\| < \dfrac{1}{1 + \|g_0\|}$, then $f + g_0 - f g_0$ is quasi-regular. Deduce that f is quasi-regular. Thus the set of quasi-regular elements in A is open. Show that if A has an identity element, then the set of invertible elements in A is an open subset of A.

2. Prove that the set of quasi-regular elements of a Banach algebra A is a group under the composition $(f, g) \to f \circ g = f + g - fg$, and show that if f^o is the quasi-inverse of f $(f \circ f^o = f^o \circ f = 0)$ then $f \to f^o$ is a continuous map from the group of quasi-regular elements onto itself.

3. Show that if A is a complex normed algebra and $f \in A$, then $\sigma_A(f)$ is nonempty. Can $\sigma_A(f)$ be an unbounded set?

4. If A is a complex Banach algebra and f is an element of A for which $\|f^n\| = \|f\|^n$ for infinitely many n, then $\|f\| = \max \{|\lambda| : \lambda \in \sigma(f)\}$. In particular, if A is any algebra of bounded functions on a set S and is complete for the norm $\|f\| = \sup_{x \in S} |f(x)|$, then the norm of each $f \in A$ is the maximum of $|\lambda|$ for λ in the spectrum of f. Is this obvious to begin with?

5. If A is a Banach algebra and A_1 is the algebra obtained by adjoining an identity to A, then A_1 becomes a Banach algebra if we set $\|(f, \lambda)\| = \|f\| + |\lambda|$. The map $f \to (f, 0)$ embeds A isometrically in A_1.

6. Find an example of an incomplete normed algebra A and a dense regular maximal ideal M in A.

7. Let a be the matrix $\begin{bmatrix} 0 & 1 \\ 0 & 0 \end{bmatrix}$, and let A be the algebra generated by a. Then A is simply the set of all scalar multiples of a. Show that A has no regular maximal ideals.

8. If A and B are complex Banach algebras, and if T is an isomorphism from A onto B, show that $\|f\|_\sigma = \|T(f)\|_\sigma$ for every $f \in A$.

9. Suppose that B is a dense subalgebra of a Banach algebra A and that h is a homomorphism from B into K, the scalar field. Show that h extends to a homomorphism from A to K iff h is continuous, and that h is continuous iff $h \in B^*$ and $\|h\| \leq 1$.

10. Let Δ be the closed unit disk in the plane, and let B be the algebra of all complex polynomials. Show that B is a normed algebra under $\|p\| = \max_{|\lambda| \leq 1} |p(\lambda)|$. Prove that if $|\alpha| > 1$, then $p \to p(\alpha)$ is a homomorphism from B onto $\mathbf{C}$ which has no extension to a homomorphism of the algebra of all uniform limits of polynomials on Δ.

2.3   THE GELFAND TRANSFORM

Throughout this section, A will be a commutative complex Banach algebra. Let $\mathscr{M}(A)$ be the set of all homomorphisms from A onto $\mathbf{C}$. Then $h \in \mathscr{M}(A)$ iff h is a nonzero multiplicative linear functional on A. The term "complex homomorphism of A" will mean "member of $\mathscr{M}(A)$" since it is convenient to exclude the zero homomorphism.

For f in A and h in $\mathscr{M}(A)$, let $\hat{f}(h) = h(f)$, and let $\hat{A} = \{\hat{f} : f \in A\}$. Then $\hat{A}$ is an algebra of functions on $\mathscr{M}(A)$, and the map $f \to \hat{f}$, which we shall call the *Gelfand map*, is a homomorphism from A to $\hat{A}$.

With the weak topology defined by the family $\hat{A}$, $\mathscr{M}(A)$ becomes a topological space which we call the *maximal ideal space* of A; its topology will be called the *Gelfand topology*.

Theorem 5.   (a) *If A has an identity element and $f \in A$, then the range of $\hat{f}$ is the spectrum of f. Hence f is invertible in A iff $\hat{f}$ never assumes the value zero. (So if $\hat{f}$ has no zeros on $\mathscr{M}(A)$, then $1/\hat{f} \in \hat{A}$.)*

(b) *If A has no identity and $f \in A$, then the spectrum of f is $\{0\} \cup (range of \hat{f})$.*

Proof. (a) $\lambda \in \sigma(f)$ iff $f - \lambda$ belongs to some maximal ideal of A, or equivalently, iff $h(f - \lambda) = 0$ for some $h \in \mathcal{M}(A)$. Since $h \neq 0$, $h(1) = 1$, so $\lambda \in \sigma(f)$ iff $\lambda = h(f) = \hat{f}(h)$ for some $h \in \mathcal{M}(A)$. In particular, f is invertible iff $0 \notin \sigma(f) =$ range of $\hat{f}$.

(b) If $\lambda \neq 0$, then the following are equivalent: (i) $\lambda \notin \sigma(f)$; (ii) $\frac{1}{\lambda} f$ is quasi-regular; (iii) $\frac{1}{\lambda} f$ is not a relative identity for any regular maximal ideal M of A; (iv) $h\left(\frac{1}{\lambda} f\right) \neq 1$ for every $h \in \mathcal{M}(A)$. So $\lambda \in \sigma(f)$ iff $\lambda = 0$ or $\lambda = \hat{f}(h)$ for some $h \in \mathcal{M}(A)$.

Theorem 6. (a) $\mathcal{M}(A)$ *is a subset of the closed unit ball of* A^*, *and the Gelfand topology is the relative topology on* $\mathcal{M}(A)$ *induced by the* w^*-*topology of* A^*.

(b) $\hat{A}$ *separates points on* $\mathcal{M}(A)$.

(c) $\mathcal{M}(A)$ *is a locally compact Hausdorff space, and every function in* $\hat{A}$ *vanishes at infinity on* $\mathcal{M}(A)$.

(d) *If* A *has an identity,* $\mathcal{M}(A)$ *is nonempty and compact.*

Proof. If $h \in \mathcal{M}(A)$, then $\|h\| \leq 1$. The w^*-topology is the weakest topology on A^* for which all the functions $L \to L(f)$ $(f \in A)$ are continuous, while the Gelfand topology is the weakest topology on $\mathcal{M}(A)$ for which the functions $h \to h(f)$ $(f \in A)$ are continuous. So (a) is obvious.

Part (b) is also clear.

Let $H = \mathcal{M}(A) \cup \{0\}$ be the set of all homomorphisms from A into **C**. Then $H \subset \Sigma^* = \{L \in A^* : \|L\| \leq 1\}$, and Σ^* is w^*-compact by the Alaoglu theorem. But if $f, g \in A$, then the functions $L \to L(fg)$ and $L \to L(f)L(g)$ are w^*-continuous, so $\{L \in A^* : L(fg) = L(f)L(g)\}$ is w^*-closed. The intersection of these sets as f, g range over A is also w^*-closed, and its intersection with Σ^* is the set H. We conclude that H is w^*-compact.

If A has an identity, then $\mathcal{M}(A) = H \cap \{L \in A^* : L(1) = 1\}$, so $\mathcal{M}(A)$ is w^*-compact. In addition, the zero ideal is contained in some maximal ideal of A, which means that there exists a complex homomorphism of A. So $\mathcal{M}(A) \neq \varnothing$.

Whether or not A has an identity, H is a compact Hausdorff space and $\mathcal{M}(A)$ is the complement in H of the zero homomorphism, say h^0. Therefore $\mathcal{M}(A)$ is a locally compact Hausdorff space with H as its one-point compactification. Since $h^0(f) = 0$ for all $f \in A$, each $\hat{f}$ extends to a continuous function on H which vanishes at h^0. Thus $\hat{A} \subset C_0(\mathcal{M}(A))$, which proves (c).

Perhaps we should add another property to the list:

(e) *If* $\mathcal{M}(A)$ *is not empty, the Gelfand map is norm decreasing.*

Here, we set $\|\hat{f}\| = \sup_{h \in \mathcal{M}(A)} |\hat{f}(h)| = \sup_{h \in \mathcal{M}(A)} |h(f)|$. Since $\|h\| \leq 1$ for each $h \in \mathcal{M}(A)$, the supremum is at most $\|f\|$. Thus $\|\hat{f}\| \leq \|f\|$, and (e) is true.

Observe that locally the Gelfand topology looks like this: Given h_0 in $\mathcal{M}(A)$, $\varepsilon > 0$, and a finite subset $E \subset A$, define $U(h_0; \varepsilon, E)$ to be $\{h \in \mathcal{M}(A) : |h(f) - h(f_0)| < \varepsilon, \forall f \in E\}$. Then the sets $U(h_0; \varepsilon, E)$ for all E and all $\varepsilon > 0$ form a base for the *nbhds* of h_0.

As an example, consider a nonvoid compact Hausdorff space S and the algebra $C(S)$ of continuous functions on S. Each $x \in S$ defines a complex homomorphism h_x of $C(S)$ where $h_x(f) = f(x)$ $(f \in C(S))$. On the other hand, every complex homomorphism of $C(S)$ is given by some $x \in S$. (Otherwise there would be a maximal ideal M in $C(S)$ which is not of the form $I_x = \{f \in C(S) : f(x) = 0\}$ for any $x \in S$. But it is not hard to show that every proper closed ideal I of $C(S)$ is contained in some I_x. For if not, then for each $x \in S$ we can choose $f_x \in I$ with $f_x(x) \neq 0$. Since $\bar{f}_x f_x \in I$, we can suppose that $f_x \geq 0$ and $f_x(x) > 0$. By continuity, $f_x > 0$ on a *nbhd* U_x of x. Finitely many of the sets U_x cover S, and the sum of the corresponding functions f_x is everywhere positive and hence invertible in $C(S)$. But this contradicts the assumption that I is a proper ideal.) Thus $S = \mathcal{M}(C(S))$, in the following sense.

Theorem 7.   *Let S be a nonvoid compact Hausdorff space. For $x \in S$, define $h_x(f) = f(x)$ $(f \in C(S))$. Then the evaluation map $x \to h_x$ is a homeomorphism from S onto the maximal ideal space of $C(S)$.*

Proof.   We have already noted that the map is onto $\mathcal{M} = \mathcal{M}(C(S))$. It is one-one since $C(S)$ separates points on S. The topology of S is the weak topology defined by $C(S)$. (Cf. Lemma 1, §1.2.) Since $\hat{f}(h_x) = f(x)$ and the topology of $\mathcal{M}$ is the weak topology defined by the functions $\hat{f}$ $(f \in A)$, the evaluation map is a homeomorphism.

As a corollary, we have an interesting result. Given compact Hausdorff spaces S_1, S_2 such that $C(S_1)$ and $C(S_2)$ are isomorphic algebras, then S_1 and S_2 must be homeomorphic. For an isomorphism of commutative Banach algebras induces a homeomorphism of their maximal ideal spaces. (Cf. Exercise 5.)

EXERCISE SET 2.3

1. Suppose that A is a commutative Banach algebra and that $\mathcal{M}(A)$ is non-empty. Show that the Gelfand map is norm preserving iff $\|f^2\| = \|f\|^2$ for every f in A. (Use the spectral radius formula; see Theorem 2, §2.2.)

2. Suppose $B \subset A$ and the linear span of B is dense in A. Show that the weak topology defined by the $\hat{f}$ with $f \in B$ is the same as the Gelfand topology of $\mathcal{M}(A)$.

3. Suppose that A is a commutative Banach algebra with no identity element and that A_1 is the algebra obtained by adjoining an identity to A. Show

that $\mathscr{M}(A_1)$ is the one-point compactification of $\mathscr{M}(A)$. (This is true even if $\mathscr{M}(A)$ is empty.)

4. Suppose that Y is a locally compact Hausdorff space which is not compact. Show that Y is the maximal ideal space of $C_0(Y)$. (Observe that the norms in $C(Y_\infty)$ and $C_0(Y)_1$ are different.)

5. Suppose that A and B are commutative Banach algebras and that T is an algebra isomorphism from A onto B. Define $T^*h = h \circ T$. Show that T^* is a homeomorphism from $\mathscr{M}(A)$ onto $\mathscr{M}(B)$.

6. Suppose that φ is a homomorphism from A into B (A, B are commutative Banach algebras). Define $\varphi^*(h) = h \circ \varphi$. Show that φ^* is a continuous map from the one-point compactification of $\mathscr{M}(B)$ into the one-point compactification of $\mathscr{M}(A)$.

7. If A is the closed subalgebra generated by an element $f \in A$, and if $\|f^n\|^{1/n} \to 0$, then $\mathscr{M}(A)$ is empty.

8. Prove a converse to Theorem 7: If S_1, S_2 are homeomorphic compact spaces, then $C(S_1)$ and $C(S_2)$ are algebraically isomorphic.

9. Let A be a commutative Banach algebra with identity. Given $f_1, \ldots, f_n$ in A, let φ be the function from $\mathscr{M}(A)$ to $\mathbf{C}^n$ defined by $\varphi(h) = (h(f_1), \ldots, h(f_n)) = (\hat{f}_1(h), \ldots, \hat{f}_n(h))$. The image of φ is the *joint spectrum* of the ordered n-tuple $(f_1, \ldots, f_n)$, and one denotes it by $\sigma(f_1, \ldots, f_n)$ (or $\sigma_A(f_1, \ldots, f_n)$ if one must emphasize the algebra). The map φ is continuous, so $\sigma(f_1, \ldots, f_n)$ is a compact set in $\mathbf{C}^n$. The origin belongs to $\sigma(f_1, \ldots, f_n)$ iff there is a maximal ideal of A which contains $\{f_1, \ldots, f_n\}$. If there is no such maximal ideal, then 1 belongs to the ideal generated by $f_1, \ldots, f_n$. By translation, we see that $\lambda = (\lambda_1, \ldots, \lambda_n) \notin \sigma(f_1, \ldots, f_n)$ iff $\sum_{i=1}^{n} (f_i - \lambda_i)g_i = 1$ for some $g_1, \ldots, g_n$ in A.

Remark. A subset S is a *set of generators* for A iff A is the smallest closed subalgebra of A which contains S and 1 (i.e., each element of A is the limit of a sequence of polynomials, in finitely many variables, of the elements of S). A is *finitely generated* iff there is a finite set of generators for A. The maximal ideal space of a finitely generated Banach algebra is the joint spectrum of a generating set. (Specifically, if $f_1, \ldots, f_n$ generate A, the map $h \to \varphi(h) = (\hat{f}_1(h), \ldots, \hat{f}_n(h))$ is a homeomorphism of $\mathscr{M}(A)$ onto $\sigma(f_1, \ldots, f_n)$.) In particular, if A is singly generated, then $\mathscr{M}(A)$ embeds as a compact set in the plane.

10. Let K be a compact set in $\mathbf{C}^n$. We define hull (K) (the *polynomial convex hull* of K) to be the set of all $\lambda \in \mathbf{C}^n$ such that $|p(\lambda)| \leq \|p\|_K = \sup_{z \in K} |p(z)|$ for every polynomial p on $\mathbf{C}^n$. K is *polynomially convex* iff $K = $ hull (K). Note that hull (K) is compact and polynomially convex.

Let $P(K)$ be the set of all functions on K which are uniformly approximable on K by polynomials in $(z_1, \ldots, z_n)$. Then $P(K)$ is a closed subalgebra of $C(K)$, where $C(K)$ is given the norm $\|f\|_K = \sup_{z \in K} |f(z)|$. Prove that to each $h \in \mathscr{M}(P(K))$ there corresponds a unique $\lambda \in$ hull (K) such that $h(p) = p(\lambda)$ for every polynomial p. Show that $h \to \lambda$ is a homeomorphism from $\mathscr{M}(P(K))$ onto hull (K).

Show that if A is a commutative Banach algebra with identity, and if $f_1, \ldots, f_n$ generate A, then $\sigma_A(f_1, \ldots, f_n)$ is a polynomially convex set in $\mathbf{C}^n$.

11. Let K be a compact nonvoid set in $\mathbf{C}^1$. Let $R(K)$ be the closure in $C(K)$ of the rational functions which are finite on K. Each $\lambda \in K$ determines a complex homomorphism of $R(K)$ by evaluation. Prove that conversely every $h \in \mathscr{M}(R(K))$ is given by evaluation at a point λ of K. (Hint: If $\lambda \notin K$, then $z - \lambda$ is invertible in $R(K)$. Here $z(\alpha) = \alpha$, $\forall \alpha \in K$.) Show that $h \to \lambda$ is a homeomorphism of $\mathscr{M}(R(K))$ onto K.

Chapter Three

C(X)

3.1 THE DUALS OF $C(X)$ AS B-SPACE AND B-ALGEBRA

Let X be a compact space. (By a compact space we shall henceforth mean a nonempty compact Hausdorff space.) $C(X)$ is the space of all continuous maps from X to $\mathbf{C}$, furnished with the pointwise operations and the sup norm. Similarly, $C_R(X)$ is the space of all continuous maps from X to $\mathbf{R}$, with the same structures. Thus $(\alpha f)(x) = \alpha f(x)$, $(f + g)(x) = f(x) + g(x)$, $(fg)(x) = f(x)g(x)$, and $\|f\| = \max_{x \in X} |f(x)|$. We note that $C(X)$ is a complex Banach algebra and that $C_R(X)$ is a real Banach algebra.

Note also that if X is a one-point space, $C(X)$ is isomorphic to $\mathbf{C}$, while if X has n elements, $C(X)$ is essentially $\mathbf{C}^n$ furnished with the componentwise operations and the norm $\|z\| = \max \{|z_1|, \ldots, |z_n|\}$. For every X, $C(X)$ contains a copy of the scalar field, namely, the subalgebra of all constant functions.

The *Borel sets* in X are the members of the σ-ring $\mathscr{B}$ generated by the closed subsets of X. A *complex Borel measure* on X is a countably additive complex valued function μ on $\mathscr{B}$ such that $\mu(\varnothing) = 0$. Each complex Borel measure μ determines a (finite) positive measure $|\mu|$ given by $|\mu|(E) = \sup \sum_{i=1}^{\infty} |\mu(E_i)|$, where the supremum is taken over all representations of E as a union of countably many disjoint Borel sets E_i; $|\mu|$ is called the *total variation* of μ. A positive Borel measure v on X is said to be *regular* iff $v(E) = \inf \{v(U): U$ open, $E \subset U\} = \sup \{v(F): F$ closed, $F \subset E\}$ for every $E \in \mathscr{B}$. A complex Borel measure μ is said to be regular iff $|\mu|$ is regular.

Complex measures μ, v are *mutually singular*, denoted by $\mu \perp v$, iff there exist disjoint Borel sets E, F such that $\mu(A) = \mu(A \cap E)$, $v(A) = v(A \cap F)$, for every $A \in \mathscr{B}$. If μ is a complex measure and v is a positive measure, then μ is *absolutely continuous* with respect to ν iff $\mu(E) = 0$ for all sets $E \in \mathscr{B}$ such that $\nu(E) = 0$. If μ is absolutely continuous with respect to ν, one writes $\mu \ll \nu$. If $\mu \geq 0$ and $\nu \geq 0$, then μ, ν are *mutually absolutely continuous* iff $\mu \ll \nu$ and $\nu \ll \mu$. Given μ, ν with $\nu \geq 0$, μ has a unique *Lebesgue decomposition* with respect to ν; $\mu = \mu_a + \mu_s$, where $\mu_a \ll \nu$ and μ_s is mutually singular with ν.

Let $M(X)$ be the space of all regular complex Borel measures on X and let $M_R(X)$ be the set of all real measures in $M(X)$. If $\mu \in M(X)$, then the norm of μ is defined to be $\|\mu\| = |\mu|(X)$. Every $f \in C(X)$ is μ-integrable for each $\mu \in M(X)$, and $f \to \int f \, d\mu$ is a bounded linear functional on $C(X)$. Theorem 1 below (the **Riesz Representation Theorem**) asserts that these are all the bounded linear forms on $C(X)$ and that the correspondence preserves norms and positivity. (Recall that $\mu \in M(X)$ is *positive* iff $\mu(E) \geq 0$ for every Borel set E, while a linear functional L is *positive* iff $L(f) \geq 0$ for every nonnegative f in $C(X)$.) For a proof of the theorem and other facts about complex measures, see Chapter 6 of Rudin [K].

Theorem 1. *For each μ in $M(X)$, $f \to \int f \, d\mu$ is a bounded linear functional L_μ on $C(X)$, and $\|L_\mu\| = \sup_{\|f\| \leq 1, \, f \in C(X)} |\int f \, d\mu| = \|\mu\|$. Conversely, every bounded linear functional on $C(X)$ has the form L_μ for some $\mu \in M(X)$. Hence $\mu \to L_\mu$ is an isometric linear mapping from $M(X)$ onto $C(X)^*$.*

Similarly, the bounded linear functionals on $C_R(X)$ are the maps $u \to \int u \, d\nu$ where $\nu \in M_R(X)$ and, moreover, $\|\nu\| = \sup_{u \in C_R(X), \|u\| \leq 1} |\int u \, d\nu|$. Thus $C_R(X)^* = M_R(X)$.

A linear functional on $C(X)$ or $C_R(X)$ is positive iff it has the form $f \to \int f \, d\mu$ where μ is a positive measure in $M(X)$.

If $\mu \in M(X)$ and F is a Borel set in X, then μ is *concentrated* on F iff $|\mu|(X \backslash F) = 0$ or, equivalently, iff $\mu(E) = 0$ for every Borel set E disjoint from F. For each measure $\mu \in M(X)$, there is a smallest closed subset on which μ is concentrated. This set is called the *closed support of* μ, and we denote it by $S(\mu)$ or supp μ. (See Exercise 1.)

A measure μ is *multiplicative* on a subalgebra A of $C(X)$ iff $\int fg \, d\mu = (\int f \, d\mu)(\int g \, d\mu)$ for all f, g in A. Since $f \to \int f \, d\mu$ is always linear, μ is multiplicative iff integration with respect to μ is an algebra homomorphism from A to $\mathbf{C}$.

Obviously the zero measure is multiplicative. The unit point masses are multiplicative on $C(X)$ (and hence on every subalgebra). That is, if for $x \in X$ we define $\delta_x(E) = 1$ if $x \in E$, and $\delta_x(E) = 0$ if $x \notin E$, then $\delta_x \in M(X)$ and $f \to \int f \, d\delta_x = f(x)$ is a complex homomorphism of $C(X)$. For subalgebras of $C(X)$ there are often many multiplicative measures, but for the entire algebra $C(X)$ there are no multiplicative measures other than those already mentioned. (Of course, this is just the fact that the maximal ideals of $C(X)$ are precisely the ideals of the form $I_x = \{f : f(x) = 0\}$ as x ranges over X, which we already know. Let's give a proof using properties of measures.)

Theorem 2. *Let $\mu \in M(X)$ be multiplicative on $C(X)$. Then either $\mu = 0$ or $\mu = \delta_x$ for some $x \in X$. (The same is true for multiplicative measures on $C_R(X)$.)*

Proof. Assume that $f \to \int f \, d\mu$ is a nonzero homomorphism of $C(X)$ into the scalars. For $F \subset X$, let χ_F be the characteristic function of F. If F is any closed subset of X, then $\mu(F) = \int \chi_F \, d\mu$ can be approximated by $\int f \, d\mu$ where $f \in C(X), f(X) \subset [0, 1]$, and $f = 1$ on F. Since $\int fg \, d\mu = (\int f \, d\mu)(\int g \, d\mu)$ for all f, g in $C(X)$, it follows that $\int \chi_{F_1} \chi_{F_2} \, d\mu = (\int \chi_{F_1} \, d\mu)(\int \chi_{F_2} \, d\mu)$, or $\mu(F_1 \cap F_2) = \mu(F_1)\mu(F_2)$ for all pairs of closed sets F_1, F_2. In particular, $\mu(F) = \mu(F)^2$, and so μ assumes only the values 0 and 1 on closed subsets of X. Since μ is regular, the range of μ on Borel sets is $\{0, 1\}$.

The closed support of μ is a nonvoid closed set S. We must have $\mu(S) = \mu(X) = 1$. Let $x \in S$. Then every open neighborhood of x has nonzero μ-measure, and this measure must thus be 1. It follows that if $y \neq x$, then $y \notin S$, for y has a neighborhood of μ-measure 0. (Take disjoint neighborhoods N_x, N_y.) Thus $S = \{x\}$ and $\mu = \delta_x$.

Since the dual of $C(X)$ is $M(X)$, it makes sense to talk about the w^*-topology of $M(X)$. This is the weakest topology on $M(X)$ which makes all the maps $\mu \to \int f \, d\mu$ (f in $C(X)$) continuous. Thus if $\{\mu_a\}$ is a net in $M(X)$, then $\mu_a \to \mu \, [w^*]$ iff $\int f \, d\mu_a \to \int f \, d\mu$ for all $f \in C(X)$. By the Alaoglu theorem, the unit ball $\Sigma = \{\mu \in M(X) : \|\mu\| \leq 1\}$ is compact in the w^*-topology.

If W is any w^*-closed linear subspace of $M(X)$, we denote by $b(W)$ the unit ball in W; i.e. $b(W) = W \cap \Sigma$. Since $b(W)$ is convex and w^*-compact, $b(W)$ is the w^*-closed convex hull of its set of extreme points, by the Krein-Milman theorem. It follows that if a w^*-continuous linear functional vanishes on this set of extreme points, it vanishes on $b(W)$ and hence on W. We shall find this observation useful when we prove the Stone-Weierstrass theorem a little later on.

EXERCISE SET   3.1

1. Let $\mu \in M(X)$. Let U be the union of all open sets in X which have $|\mu|$ measure zero. Use the regularity of μ to prove that μ is concentrated on $X \backslash U$. (Hence supp μ exists and is the complement of U.)

2. Show that a positive linear functional on $C_R(X)$ must be continuous. Show that if L is a positive linear functional on $C(X)$, then $L(u)$ is real if u is real-valued, $|L(f)| \leq L(|f|)$, and L is continuous.

3. (a) Let $\mu \in M(X)$. Prove that if $\|\mu\| = \mu(X) = 1$, then μ is positive. In fact, if $L \in C(X)^*$, then L is positive iff $L(1) = \|L\|$.

   (b) Prove the stronger result: if $L(1) = \|L\| = 1$, then for every f in $C(X)$, $L(f)$ lies in the closed convex hull of the range of f. (*Hint:* One way to do this is to prove and use Fejèr's geometric lemma: *If K is a* compact convex set in the plane, and if $w \notin K$, then there is a point $\alpha \in \mathbf{C}$ such that K is contained in the open disk with center α and radius $|w - \alpha|$.)

(c) A compact space X is *totally disconnected* iff the open-closed *nbhds* form a base at each point of X. Suppose that X is a totally disconnected compact space and that L is a linear functional on $C(X)$ or $C_R(X)$ such that $L(f)$ belongs to the range of f for every f in the domain of L. Prove that $\exists x_0 \in X$ such that $L(f) = f(x_0)$ for every f. (*Hint:* Let μ be a positive measure corresponding to L, and let $x_0 \in S(\mu)$. Show that each $x \neq x_0$ has an open-closed *nbhd* of μ-measure zero.)

Is the conclusion true if X is not assumed to be totally disconnected?

4. Let X, Y be compact spaces and let A, B be linear subspaces of $C(X)$, $C(Y)$ which contain the constants. Let T be a linear mapping from A to B. Then these two conditions are equivalent: (a) $\|T\| = 1$ and $T(1) = 1$; (b) for every f in A, the range of $T(f)$ is contained in the closed convex hull of the range of f.

5. Show that $\mathscr{P} = \{L \in C(X)^* : L(1) = \|L\| = 1\}$ is convex and w^*-compact. (That is, the set of all Borel probability measures on X ($\mu \geq 0$, $\mu(X) = 1$) is w^*-compact and convex.) Show that the extreme points of $\mathscr{P}$ are the (unit) point masses. Thus the convex combinations of point masses are w^*-dense in $\mathscr{P}$.

6. What are the extreme points of $\Sigma = \{L \in C(X)^* : \|L\| \leq 1\}$?

7. Show that if W is a w^*-closed linear subspace of $M(X)$, the set of extreme points of $b(W)$ is invariant under multiplication by any scalar of modulus 1.

8. Suppose that $\mu \in M(X)$ and that $g \in C(X)$. Define the linear functional (measure) $g\mu$ by setting $\int f \, d(g\mu) = \int fg \, d\mu$ ($f \in C(X)$). Prove that $\|g\mu\| = \int |g| \, d|\mu|$.

9. Suppose that $\mu \in M(X)$ and $g \in C(X)$. Show that if $g = 0$ a.e. $[\mu]$ then g vanishes on supp μ.

10. Let A be a closed subalgebra of $C(X)$ which separates the points of X. If the only nonzero complex measures which are multiplicative on A are the point masses, must $A = C(X)$?

11. For $A \subset C(X)$, the *annihilator* of A is $A^\perp = \{\mu \in M(X) : \int f \, d\mu = 0, \ \forall f \in A\}$. Show that $A^\perp = \{0\}$ iff A spans a dense subspace of $C(X)$. Show that $A^\perp$ is a w^*-closed subspace of $M(X)$ and that every w^*-closed subspace of $M(X)$ is an annihilator.

12. Suppose that S, T are compact spaces and that $\varphi : S \to T$ is a continuous map. Then there are maps $\varphi_* : C(T) \to C(S)$ and $\varphi^* : M(S) \to M(T)$

induced by φ, namely, $\varphi_*(f) = f \circ \varphi$ for $f \in C(T)$ and $\varphi^*(L) = L \circ \varphi_*$ for $L \in C(S)^*$.

Show that φ_* is an algebra homomorphism sending 1 to 1. Is φ^* continuous with respect to (a) the norm topologies, (b) the w^*-topologies?

If $L \in C(S)^*$ and μ is the measure corresponding to L, then the measure v corresponding to $\varphi^*(L)$ is sometimes called the *image of the measure μ under φ*. If E is a Borel set in T, what is $v(E)$? If F is a closed set in T and $i_F : F \to T$ is the inclusion map, determine $i_F^*(\sigma)$ for $\sigma \in M(F)$.

13. Suppose that L is a linear functional on a complex algebra A. Show that $L(fg) = L(f)L(g)$ for all f, g in A iff $L(f^2) = L(f)^2$ for all f in A.

3.2 THE STONE-WEIERSTRASS THEOREM

Recall that if C is a convex set in a linear space E, then C^e is the set of all extreme points of C. Combining the Hahn-Banach theorem (in the form of Theorem 8, §1.4.) with the last remark in §3.1, we obtain the following result.

Lemma 1. *Let $f \in C(X)$ and $V \subset C(X)$. Then f belongs to the closed subspace of $C(X)$ spanned by V iff $\int f \, d\mu = 0$ for every $\mu \in b(V^\perp)^e$.*

The next result is the basic step in establishing several results of a measure theoretic nature, including the Stone-Weierstrass theorem.

Lemma 2. *Let $f \in C(X)$ and $V \subset C(X)$. Suppose that (a) $V^\perp \neq \{0\}$; (b) $\mu \in b(V^\perp)^e$; (c) $\int fg \, d\mu = 0$ for every $g \in V$. Then if f is real-valued on the closed support of μ, f is constant on that support.*

Proof. Let S be the closed support of μ and suppose that $f(S) \subset \mathbf{R}$. By assumption, $\mu \in V^\perp$ and $f\mu \in V^\perp$. Hence $(af + b)\mu \in V^\perp$ for every pair of real numbers a, b. Since $f(S)$ is a compact set on the line, $(af + b)(S) \subset [1/6, 5/6]$ for some a, b with $a \neq 0$. Hence we can assume that $1 \leq 6f \leq 5$ on S, for if $af + b$ is constant on S, so is f.

Since $\mu \in b(V^\perp)^e$, $\|\mu\| = 1$. It follows that $f\mu$ and $(1 - f)\mu$ are not the zero measure, and

$$\|f\mu\| + \|(1 - f)\mu\| = \int |f| \, d|\mu| + \int |1 - f| \, d|\mu|$$

$$= \int_S |f| \, d|\mu| + \int_S |1 - f| \, d|\mu|$$

$$= \int_S f \, d|\mu| + \int_S (1 - f) \, d|\mu|$$

$$= |\mu|(S) = \|\mu\| = 1.$$

Now $\mu \in V^\perp$ and $f\mu \in V^\perp$, so $(1 - f)\mu \in V^\perp$. Hence $v_1 = f\mu/\|f\mu\|$ and $v_2 = (1 - f)\mu/\|(1 - f)\mu\|$ are in $b(V^\perp)$, while $\mu = \|f\mu\|v_1 + \|(1 - f)\mu\|v_2$ is a convex combination of v_1 and v_2. Since μ is an extreme point of $b(V^\perp)$, $\mu = v_1 = f\mu/\|f\mu\|$. This shows that $(1 - f/\|f\mu\|) = 0$ a.e. $[\mu]$, whence $f = \|f\mu\|$ a.e. $[\mu]$. Now $\{x \in X : f(x) \neq \|f\mu\|\}$ is an open set of $|\mu|$-measure 0, so it does not meet S. Thus $f = \|f\mu\|$ on S, so $f|S$ is constant.

One should observe that complex scalars are used nowhere in the proofs of the lemmas. Thus the following are true. (Note however that if V is a set of real-valued functions, what is meant by $V^\perp$ depends on whether one considers V as a subset of $C_R(X)$ or as a subset of $C(X)$.)

Lemma 1_R. *If $C(X)$ is replaced by $C_R(X)$ in Lemma 1, the corresponding result is true.*

Lemma 2_R. *Let $f \in C_R(X)$ and $V \subset C_R(X)$. Suppose that* (a) $V^\perp \neq \{0\}$, (b) $\mu \in b(V^\perp)^e$, (c) $\int fg \, d\mu = 0$ *for every $g \in V$. Then f is constant on $S(\mu)$.*

Theorem 3 (Stone-Weierstrass). *Suppose that A is a closed subalgebra of $C(X)$ (or $C_R(X)$) which separates points and is self-adjoint. Then either $A = C(X)$ $(C_R(X))$ or there is a point $x \in X$ such that A is the maximal ideal $I_x = \{f : f(x) = 0\}$.*

Proof. Note that self-adjointness is vacuously satisfied if $A \subset C_R(X)$. Since the proof in the real case is slightly simpler, we look only at the complex case.

Assume that $A \neq C(X)$. Then $A^\perp \neq \{0\}$, so each element of $b(A^\perp)^e$ has norm 1. Take $\mu \in b(A^\perp)^e$. If $f \in A$ then $\bar{f} \in A$, and so $u = \frac{1}{2}(f + \bar{f}) \in A$, $v = \frac{1}{2}i(\bar{f} - f) \in A$. By Lemma 2, u, v are constant on $S(\mu)$, so $f = u + iv$ is also constant on $S(\mu)$, for every $f \in A$. Since A separates points, $S(\mu)$ contains at most one point. But $\mu \neq 0$, so $S(\mu)$ is nonvoid; thus there is some $x \in X$ with $S(\mu) = \{x\}$. We have $\mu = a(\mu)\delta_x$ where $|a(\mu)| = \|\mu\| = 1$.

So $0 = \int f \, d\mu = a(\mu)f(x)$ for all $f \in A$, and so $f(x) = 0$; that is, $A \subset I_x$. Similarly, every $v \in b(A^\perp)^e$ has the form $v = a(v)\delta_y$ with $y \in X$, and $f(y) = 0$ for all $f \in A$. Since A separates points, the elements y must be the same for all $v \in b(A^\perp)^e$. Thus $b(A^\perp)^e = \{a\delta_x : |a| = 1\}$. By Krein-Milman, $b(A^\perp) = \{a\delta_x : |a| \leq 1\}$, and so $A^\perp$ is the set of scalar multiples of δ_x.

We have thus shown that $A \subset I_x$ and that $A^\perp \subset I_x^\perp$. By the Hahn-Banach theorem, $A = I_x$ as asserted.

EXERCISE SET 3.2

1. If B is a subalgebra of $C_R(X)$ which contains the constants and separates points, show that B is sup norm dense in $C_R(X)$.

2. If V is a subset of $C(X)$ which contains the constants, separates points, and is self-adjoint, show that the subalgebra of $C(X)$ generated by V is dense in $C(X)$.

3. Prove Weierstrass' approximation theorem: if $f \in C[a, b]$ and $\varepsilon > 0$, then there is a polynomial p for which $|f(x) - p(x)| < \varepsilon$ $(a \leq x \leq b)$.

4. Prove (a weak form of) Fejèr's theorem: if f is a continuous complex-valued function on the unit circle and $\varepsilon > 0$, then there is a trigonometric polynomial p of form $p(e^{i\theta}) = \sum_{-n}^{n} a_k e^{ik\theta}$ such that $|f(e^{i\theta}) - p(e^{i\theta})| < \varepsilon$ $(0 \le \theta \le 2\pi)$.

5. Suppose that S, T are compact spaces. Show that every continuous map $h : S \times T \to \mathbf{C}$ is uniformly approximable by finite sums of functions of the form $(s, t) \to f(s)g(t)$ with $f \in C(S)$ and $g \in C(T)$. Generalize to Cartesian products of arbitrarily many compact spaces.

6. (a) If f is a continuous function on $[0, 2\pi]$ with $f(0) = f(2\pi)$, the *Fourier coefficients* of f are the numbers $c_n = \dfrac{1}{2\pi} \displaystyle\int_0^{2\pi} e^{-inx} f(x)\, dx$ $(n \in \mathbf{Z})$.

   If f_1, f_2 are continuous periodic functions having the same sequence of Fourier coefficients, show that $f_1 = f_2$. In particular, $f = 0$ iff $\displaystyle\int_0^{2\pi} e^{inx} f(x)\, dx = 0$ for every $n \in \mathbf{Z}$.

   (b) Fourier coefficients for L^1 functions are defined in the same way. Show that if $g \in L^1(0, 2\pi)$, then $g = 0$ a.e. iff $\displaystyle\int_0^{2\pi} e^{inx} g(x) = 0$ for every integer n.

   (c) If μ is a complex Borel measure on the unit circle and if $\int z^n\, d\mu(z) = 0$ for $n = 0, \pm 1, \pm 2, \ldots$, show that μ is the zero measure.

   (d) If μ, v are complex Borel measures on $[0, 1]$ and if $\displaystyle\int_0^1 x^n\, d\mu(x) = \displaystyle\int_0^1 x^n\, dv(x)$ for $n = 0, 1, 2, \ldots$, then $\mu = v$. (A measure on $[0, 1]$ is determined by its moments.)

7. Suppose that A is a subalgebra of $C(X)$.
   (a) Show that if we define $x_1 \sim_A x_2$ iff $f(x_1) = f(x_2)$ for all $f \in A$, then $\sim_A$ is an equivalence relation on X.
   (b) A and the closure of A define the same equivalence relation. From now on assume that A is closed in $C(X)$.
   (c) For each $x \in X$, let $\tilde{x} = \{ y : x \sim_A y \}$ and let $\tilde{X}$ be the set of all equivalence classes $\tilde{x}$. The quotient map $Q : X \to \tilde{X}$ is defined by $Q(x) = \tilde{x}$ $(x \in X)$. Show that (i) for each $f \in A$ there is a function $\tilde{f}$ on $\tilde{X}$ with $f = \tilde{f} \circ Q$; (ii) $\|f\| = \max \{ |\tilde{f}(a)| : a \in \tilde{X} \}$; (iii) the map $f \to \tilde{f}$ is an algebra isomorphism of A onto its image $\tilde{A}$; (iv) $\tilde{A}$ separates points on $\tilde{X}$.
   (d) We give $\tilde{X}$ the quotient topology: $E \subset \tilde{X}$ is open iff $Q^{-1}(E)$ is open in X. Show that Q is continuous, $\tilde{X}$ is compact, and $\tilde{A}$ is a closed subalgebra of $C(\tilde{X})$. (In short, if we identify all points of X not separated by A, the resulting identification space $\tilde{X}$ is compact and A is a closed point-separating subalgebra of $C(\tilde{X})$.)

(e) Assume that A is self-adjoint and that there is a point $x_0 \in X$ such that $f(x_0) = 0$ for all $f \in A$. Show that $\tilde{A}$ is the maximal ideal of $C(\tilde{X})$ determined by $\tilde{x}_0$. Hence there is a locally compact space Y such that A is (algebraically isomorphic and isometric with) $C_0(Y)$, the space of all continuous maps $Y \to \mathbf{C}$ which vanish at infinity.

(f) Assume that A is self-adjoint and that there is no point of X at which all the functions in A vanish. Show that $\tilde{A} = C(\tilde{X})$. Thus there is a compact space S such that $A = C(S)$.

(g) Show that if the self-adjoint closed subalgebras A, A' of $C(X)$ define the same equivalence relation, then $A = A'$. (Thus a self-adjoint sub-algebra is determined by its sets of constancy.)

(h) If B is a closed subalgebra of $C_R(X)$ which is contained in no maximal ideal, then there is a compact space S such that $B = C_R(S)$.

8. Prove a Stone-Weierstrass theorem for locally compact spaces: if B is a strongly separating closed subalgebra of $C_0(Y)$, then $B = C_0(Y)$ iff B is self-adjoint. (B is strongly separating provided that B separates points and not all members of B vanish at any point of Y. *Hint:* Look at the sub-algebra of $C(Y_\infty)$ generated by B and the constants.)

9. Let I be a closed ideal in $C(X)$. Show that there is a subset K of X such that $I = \{g \in C(X) : g|K = 0\}$. (It might be a good idea to consider $b(I^\perp)^e$. Observe that you now have an alternate proof of Theorem 2, §3.1.)

3.3   SETS OF ANTISYMMETRY

Let X be a compact space and let A be a nonvoid subset of $C(X)$. A set K in X is a *set of antisymmetry* for A iff K is nonempty and every f in A which is real-valued on K is constant on K. A is *antisymmetric* provided that X is a set of antisymmetry for A.

Obviously, any one-element set is a set of antisymmetry. If K is a set of antisymmetry for A, so is its closure $\overline{K}$. For if $f \in A$ and $f|\overline{K}$ is real-valued, then f is constant on K and hence by continuity f is constant on $\overline{K}$. Further-more, if two sets of antisymmetry overlap, then their union is again a set of antisymmetry (since the constants must be the same).

Lemma 3. *Let A be a nonvoid subset of $C(X)$.*

(a) *If K_0 is a set of antisymmetry for A and if $\tilde{K}_0$ is the union of all sets of antisymmetry for A which contain K_0, then $\tilde{K}_0$ is also a set of antisymmetry for A.*

(b) *Every set of antisymmetry for A is contained in a maximal set of antisymmetry.*

(c) *Let $\mathcal{K}_A$ be the family of all maximal sets of antisymmetry for A. Then $\mathcal{K}_A$ forms a decomposition of X into pairwise disjoint closed sets.*

Proof. (a) Let $f \in A$ be real-valued on $\tilde{K}_0$. Take x_1, x_2 in $\tilde{K}_0$ and choose antisymmetric sets K_1, K_2 containing K_0 with $x_1 \in K_1$, $x_2 \in K_2$. Since $K_1 \cap K_2 \supset K_0 \neq \varnothing$, $K_1 \cup K_2$ is a set of antisymmetry for A. Since $f | K_1 \cup K_2$ is real-valued, $f | K_1 \cup K_2$ is constant; hence $f(x_1) = f(x_2)$. This shows that f is constant on $\tilde{K}_0$, as required.

(b) $\tilde{K}_0$ is clearly a maximal set of antisymmetry $\supset K_0$.

(c) Every $\{x\}$ with $x \in X$ is a set of antisymmetry, and $x \in \{\tilde{x}\}$. So X is the union of the members of $\mathcal{K}_A$. Each $K \in \mathcal{K}_A$ is closed, since $\overline{K}$ is a set of antisymmetry. And since the union of two overlapping sets of antisymmetry is again such a set, distinct maximal antisymmetric sets are disjoint. Thus $\mathcal{K}_A$ is a pairwise disjoint closed cover of X.

From Lemma 2 of §3.2, we may conclude the following strange but basic result. Combining this with the lemma above, we obtain Bishop's theorem, which asserts that A is completely determined by the family of restrictions $\{A |_K : K \in \mathcal{K}_A\}$ if A is a closed subalgebra of $C(X)$.

Theorem 4. *If A is a subalgebra of $C(X)$, then A is antisymmetric on the closed support of every extreme point of the unit ball of $A^\perp$. (Indeed this holds for any subset of $C(X)$ which is closed under multiplication.)*

Theorem 5 (Bishop). *Let A be a closed subalgebra of $C(X)$ and let $\mathcal{K}_A$ be the family of maximal sets of antisymmetry for A. If $f \in C(X)$ and $f | K \in A|_K$ for every $K \in \mathcal{K}_A$, then $f \in A$.*

Proof. Suppose that $f \notin A$. Then by Lemma 1, §3.2, $\int f\, d\mu \neq 0$ for some $\mu \in b(A^\perp)^e$. Since $S(\mu)$ is a set of antisymmetry for A, $S(\mu) \subset K$ for some $K \in \mathcal{K}_A$. By hypothesis, $f | K = g|K$ for some $g \in A$, and we have the contradiction $0 \neq \int f\, d\mu = \int_{S(\mu)} f\, d\mu = \int_K f\, d\mu = \int_K g\, d\mu = \int g\, d\mu = 0$ (since $\mu \in A^\perp$). So $f \in A$.

Corollary. *If $A|_K = C(K)$ for every $K \in \mathcal{K}_A$, then $A = C(X)$. In particular, if each point of X is a maximal set of antisymmetry for A and A is contained in no maximal ideal of $C(X)$, then $A = C(X)$. Conversely, the maximal sets of antisymmetry for $C(X)$ are the points.*

Closed supports of extreme annihilating measures are important examples of sets of antisymmetry. Similarly, supports of multiplicative measures are also antisymmetric sets, as we now prove.

Theorem 6. *Suppose that A is a subalgebra of $C(X)$ which contains the constants. If μ is a nonzero positive measure which is multiplicative on A, then $S(\mu)$ is a set of antisymmetry for A.*

Proof. Since $1 \in A$ and μ is multiplicative on A, $\mu(X)^2 = \mu(X)$, so $\mu(X) = \int 1 \, d\mu = 1$.

Now suppose that $f \in A$ and that f is real-valued on $S = \operatorname{supp} \mu$. Then $a = \int f \, d\mu = \int_{S(\mu)} f \, d\mu$ is real. We have

$$0 = \left(\int f \, d\mu - a \right)^2 = \left(\int (f - a) \, d\mu \right)^2 = \int (f - a)^2 \, d\mu = \int_S (f - a)^2 \, d\mu.$$

Hence $f - a = 0$ a.e. on S. Since f is continuous, $f = a$ on S. Thus f is constant on S, which proves the assertion.

Let us consider a basic example. Suppose that F is a continuous function on the closed unit disk which is analytic on the open disk. By the mean value property of analytic functions, $F(0) = \dfrac{1}{2\pi} \displaystyle\int_0^{2\pi} F(re^{i\theta}) \, d\theta$ if $0 < r < 1$. As $r \to 1$, $F(re^{i\theta}) \to F(e^{i\theta})$ uniformly in θ, since F is uniformly continuous. Hence the integrals converge and $F(0) = \dfrac{1}{2\pi} \displaystyle\int_0^{2\pi} F(e^{i\theta}) \, d\theta$. But if A is the set of all functions continuous for $|z| \leq 1$ and analytic for $|z| < 1$, then A is a closed subalgebra of $C(\{z : |z| \leq 1\})$ and $F \to F(0)$ is a complex homomorphism of A. What we have observed is that if $C_r = \{z : |z| = r\}$ $(0 < r \leq 1)$, then normalized arc length on C_r is a multiplicative measure μ_r on A. (If E is a subset of the closed disk, $\mu_r(E)$ is $1/2\pi$ times the Lebesgue measure of $\{\theta \in [0, 2\pi] : re^{i\theta} \in E\}$.)

Hence A is antisymmetric on each circle C_r $(0 < r \leq 1)$. In particular, if $F \in A$ and F is real-valued on the unit circle C_1, then F is constant on C_1, say $F | C_1 = \lambda \in \mathbf{R}$. But then by the maximum modulus theorem, $F - \lambda$ vanishes identically on the closed disk (since its maximum modulus on the closed disk is assumed on the boundary, where it is zero). (So C_1 is more than just a set of antisymmetry for A.)

Finally, note that the entire disk is a set of antisymmetry for A.

EXERCISE SET   3.3

1. Suppose that A, B are subsets of $C(X)$ and that $fg \in B$ whenever $f \in A$, $g \in B$. Show that for each $\mu \in b(B^{\perp})^e$, $\operatorname{supp} \mu$ is a set of antisymmetry for A. In particular, if A is a subalgebra of $C(X)$ and I is an ideal of A, then $\operatorname{supp} \mu$ is a set of antisymmetry for A for each $\mu \in b(I^{\perp})^e$.

2. Let A be a closed subalgebra of $C(X)$ and let I be a closed ideal of A. Show that **(a)** if $f \in C(X)$ and $f|K \in I|_K$ for all $K \in \mathscr{K}_A$, then $f \in I$; **(b)** if $f \in I$ and $\bar{f} \in A$, then $\bar{f} \in I$.

3. Is Lebesgue measure on $[0, 1]$ multiplicative on any closed subalgebra of $C[0, 1]$ (other than the constants, of course)?

4. Note that if Y is a locally compact space and $B \subset C_0(Y)$, then we can define the notion of set of antisymmetry for B exactly as we did for compact spaces. (Check that Y decomposes into a disjoint union of maximal sets of antisymmetry for B, each of which is closed.) Bishop's theorem is true for closed subalgebras of $C_0(Y)$.

   (The outline is as follows. Let B be a closed subalgebra of $C_0(Y)$. Let X be the one-point compactification of Y and let A be the subalgebra of $C(X)$ spanned by B and the constants. Then A consists of all functions $f + \lambda$ ($f \in B$, $\lambda \in \mathbf{C}$) and A is closed in $C(X)$. The maximal sets of anti-symmetry for A are related in a natural way to those for B—but remember the point at infinity. If $g \in C_0(Y)$ and $g|K \in B|_K$ for all $K \in \mathcal{K}_B$, then $g \in A$. Since $g(\infty) = 0$, $g \in B$.)

5. Prove that if μ is a positive measure in $M(X)$ such that $\mu(X) = 1$, and if μ is multiplicative on a subalgebra A of $C(X)$, then supp μ is a set of antisymmetry for A.

6. Let G be a compact topological group. For any $a \in G$ and any function f on G, let $f_a(x) = f(ax)$ and $f^a(x) = f(xa)$ ($x \in G$). A subset of $C(G)$ is said to be translation-invariant iff it contains all left and right translates f_a, f^a of each of its elements f.

   Show that if A is a translation-invariant subset of $C(G)$ and H is the maximal antisymmetric set for A which contains the identity element of G, then H is a closed normal subgroup of G and $\mathcal{K}_A$ is exactly the set of cosets of H.

   Hint: (1) If K is a set of antisymmetry for A, so are aK, Ka for all $a \in G$.

   (2) If $a \in G$, then $aH \in \mathcal{K}_A$ and $Ha \in \mathcal{K}_A$. Since both contain a, $aH = Ha$.

   (3) If $x \in H$ and $y \in H$, then $Hx = Hy = H$; thus $xy^{-1} \in H$.

3.4 MORE ABOUT C(X)

Bishop's theorem has as a corollary the result that if a closed subalgebra A has restrictions to each of its maximal antisymmetric sets as large as possible, then $A = C(X)$. We can also show that under certain conditions, if X breaks up into closed sets, on each of which A is all continuous functions, then $A = C(X)$. However, this is not true for subalgebras in general.

For example, let $X = [-1, 1]$ and let A be the set of all even functions in $C(X)$; $f \in A$ iff $f(-x) = f(x)$, $0 \le x \le 1$. Then $X = F_1 \cup F_2$ with $F_1 = [-1, 0]$, $F_2 = [0, 1]$. Observe that $A \ne C(X)$ but $A|_{F_1} = C(F_1)$, $A|_{F_2} = C(F_2)$. (Just extend functions by flipping their graphs.)

Even if the closed sets F_i are disjoint and $A | F_i = C(F_i)$ for $i = 1, 2$, it may be that $A \ne C(X)$. (Take $F_1 = [-2, -1]$, $F_2 = [1, 2]$, $X = F_1 \cup F_2$, and A the even functions.) However, if A separates points, then necessarily

$A = C(X)$, as we shall show below. But if $A|_{F_1} = C(F_1)$, $A|_{F_2} = C(F_2)$ and $X = F_1 \cup F_2$ but F_1, F_2 are not disjoint, then A need not be closed and hence need not be $C(X)$. (Take $F_1 = [-1, 0]$, $F_2 = [0, 1]$, and A the set of all continuous functions which are even on some neighborhood of 0. This A even separates points on $X = F_1 \cup F_2$.) So the hypotheses must fit together correctly in any possible theorem along these lines.

Lemma 4. *Let A be a subset of $C(X)$ which separates points on X. Suppose that F is a compact set in X and that $A|_F = C(F)$. If $p \in X \backslash F$, then either $f(p) = 0$ for every $f \in A$, or $f(p) \neq 0$ for some $f \in A$ which vanishes on F.*

Proof. This is the only instance I can think of where one is trying to show that a certain mapping is *not* well-defined.

Suppose that $f \in A$ and $f(F) = \{0\}$ imply that $f(p) = 0$. Then if $f, g \in A$ and $f|F = g|F$, $f(p) = g(p)$. So if we set $h(f|F) = f(p)$ for $f \in A$, then h is a well-defined homomorphism from $A|_F = C(F)$ to **C**. Either $f(p) = 0$ for all $f \in A$, or h is nonzero. In the second case, there is a point q in F with $h(\varphi) = \varphi(q)$ for all $\varphi \in C(F)$. But then $f(p) = h(f|F) = (f|F)(q) = f(q)$ for all $f \in A$. Since $p \in F$, $q \notin F$, and A separates points, the second case cannot occur.

Theorem 7. *Suppose that $X = F_1 \cup \cdots \cup F_n$ where all F_i are compact. Suppose that A is a closed subalgebra of $C(X)$ which separates the points of X, and that $A|_{F_i} = C(F_i)$ for $i = 1, \ldots, n$. Then $A = C(X)$.*

Proof. Let $K \in \mathcal{K}_A$. We shall show that K reduces to a point, and this will prove that $A = C(X)$. Note that it will suffice to prove that $K \subset F_i$ for some i. For $A|_{F_i} = C(F_i)$, so then $A|_K = C(K)$. Since $A|_K$ is antisymmetric and $C_R(K)$ separates points on K, K is a point.

Let m be the smallest integer such that $1 \leq m \leq n$ and $K \subset F_1 \cup \cdots \cup F_m$. If $m = 1$, then $K \subset F_1$, and we are done. So suppose $m > 1$. Then $K \not\subset F_1 \cup \cdots \cup F_{m-1} = F$, say. Take $p \in K \backslash F$. Then $p \notin F_i$ if $1 \leq i < m$ but $p \in F_m$. By the lemma, there exist $f_i \in A$ such that $f_i(F_i) = \{0\}$ and $f_i(p) = 1$, $i = 1, \ldots, m - 1$. (Note that $p \in F_m$ and $A|_{F_m} = C(F_m)$; so $f(p) \neq 0$ for some $f \in A$, and Lemma 4 is applicable.) Put $f = f_1 \cdots f_{m-1}$. Then $f \in A$, $f(F) = \{0\}$, and $f(p) = 1$.

We can now construct a function h in A such that $h = 0$ on F, $h \geq 0$ on K, and $h(p) = 1$. (For $A|_{F_m} = C(F_m)$, so $g|F_m = \bar{f}|F_m$ for some $g \in A$. Set $h = gf$.) Since K is a set of antisymmetry for A and $h|K$ is real-valued, $h(K) = \{h(p)\} = \{1\}$; thus $F \cap K$ is empty.

Since $K \subset F \cup F_m$, we thus have $K \subset F_m$, which means once again that K is a point. So $A = C(X)$.

Theorem 8. *Suppose that $X = F_1 \cup \cdots \cup F_n$ where the F_i are disjoint compact sets. Suppose that A is a subalgebra of $C(X)$ which separates the points of X, and that $A|_{F_i} = C(F_i)$ for $i = 1, \ldots, n$. Then $A = C(X)$.*

Proof. We may assume that $n = 2$. So let $X = F_1 \cup F_2$, $F_1 \cap F_2 = \emptyset$, and $A | F_i = C(F_i)$ for $i = 1, 2$. If $p \in F_2$, then $\exists f_p \in A$ with $f_p(p) \neq 0$, $f_p(F_1) = \{0\}$. (Once again the lemma is applicable.) We can use these f_p and a compactness argument to construct a function $g \in A$ such that $g(F_1) = \{0\}$ and $g > 0$ on F_2. (For each $p \in F_2$, find $f_p' \in A$ such that $\bar{f_p'}$ agrees with $\bar{f}_p$ on F_2. Then $g_p = f_p f_p'$ belongs to A, vanishes on F_1, and is greater than 0 on a neighborhood of p. Cover by a finite number of these neighborhoods and let g be the sum of the corresponding functions g_p.) Since $1/g$ is continuous on F_2, there is a function $g' \in A$ such that gg' is the characteristic function of F_2.

By symmetry, there exist e_1, e_2 in A with $e_1 = 1$ on F_1, $e_1 = 0$ on F_2, $e_2 = 0$ on F_1, and $e_2 = 1$ on F_2. Given any φ in $C(X)$, we choose $\varphi_i \in A$ with $\varphi_i | F_i = \varphi | F_i$ for $i = 1, 2$ and note that $\varphi = \varphi_1 e_1 + \varphi_2 e_2$; thus φ belongs to A. Hence $A = C(X)$.

Corollary 1. *Let A be a subalgebra of $C(X)$ which contains the constants and separates the points of X. If F is a nonvoid finite subset of X, then $A|_F = C(F)$.*

Proof. Let $F = \{x_1, \ldots, x_n\} = \{x_1\} \cup \cdots \cup \{x_n\}$. Then $A|_F$ is a separating subalgebra of $C(F)$ whose restriction to $\{x_i\}$ is $C(\{x_i\})$ for each i. So $A|_F = C(F)$. (There are simpler proofs of this fact, of course.)

Corollary 2. *Let A satisfy the hypothesis of Corollary 1. Suppose that μ is a nonzero complex measure on X such that μ is not a point mass but μ is multiplicative on A. Then the closed support of μ is an infinite set.*

Proof. If $S = \operatorname{supp} \mu$ is finite, then $A|_S = C(S)$. If μ_S is the restriction of μ to S ($\mu_S(E) = \mu(E)$ for Borel sets $E \subset S$), then μ_S is multiplicative on $C(S)$; thus μ_S is a point mass. So μ would be a point mass, contrary to hypothesis. Thus S is infinite.

In fact, S must be uncountable. (The simplest proof along the lines of Corollary 2 uses a fact from the theory of polynomial approximation: if X is a compact space with only a countable number of elements, then every closed subalgebra of $C(X)$ is self-adjoint; see Exercise 4. If A satisfies the hypothesis of Corollary 1 and $S = \operatorname{supp} \mu$, let B be the closure of $A|_S$ in $C(S)$. If S were countable, then B would equal $C(S)$. Since μ_S is multiplicative on $A|_S$, μ_S would be multiplicative on $C(S)$ by continuity of $u \to \int u\, d\mu_S$. Hence once again μ_S (and thus μ) would be a point mass.)

There are other theorems which assert that a closed subalgebra of $C(X)$ with suitable properties must be $C(X)$. For example, if A is a closed subalgebra which separates the points of X and contains the constant functions, and if $\operatorname{Re}(A)$ is either closed in $C_R(X)$ or a subalgebra of $C_R(X)$, then $A = C(X)$. Here $\operatorname{Re}(A)$ is the set of all $u \in C_R(X)$ such that $(u + iv) \in A$ for some $v \in C_R(X)$. (These theorems are not easily proved, and the proofs require machinery we have not yet developed.) Other characterizations assert that $A = C(X)$ if the restrictions of A to the closed sets of X have certain properties. See Glicksberg [79], Hoffman-Wermer [106], and Wermer [208].

On the other hand, one can start with a complex Banach algebra A and ask under what conditions A is isometrically isomorphic to $C(X)$ for some compact space X. If this is so, the maximal ideal space of A will be X, and this suggests a more natural question: when is the Gelfand map $f \to \hat{f}$ an isometry from A onto $C(X) = \hat{A}$? One answer is the following theorem, which is a very special case of a general representation theorem of Gelfand and Naimark.

Theorem 9. *Suppose that A is a commutative Banach algebra over $\mathbf{C}$ and that A has an identity element. If there is an involution $f \to f^*$ on A which satisfies $\|ff^*\| = \|f\|^2$ ($f \in A$), then the Gelfand map $f \to \hat{f}$ is an isometry from A onto $\hat{A}$. Furthermore, $\hat{A} = C(X)$ where $X = \mathcal{M}(A)$, and the transform of f^* is the complex conjugate of the transform of f ($f \in A$).*

Proof. First of all we recall that an involution must satisfy $(f + g)^* = f^* + g^*$, $(\alpha f)^* = \bar{\alpha}f^*$, $(fg)^* = g^*f^*$, and $(f^*)^* = f$, by definition. For a first step we note that $1^* = 1$ if 1 is the identity of A. ($1^* = 11^* = 1^{**}1^* = (11^*)^* = (1^*)^* = 1$.) Next, if $f = f^*$, then $(f^k)^* = f^k$ for all integers $k \geq 1$. So $\|f^2\| = \|ff^*\| = \|f\|^2$, and thus by induction, $\|f^{2^n}\| = \|f\|^{2^n}$ for all n. Hence if $f = f^*$, $\|f\| = \|f^{2^n}\|^{1/2^n} \to \|f\|_\sigma = \|\hat{f}\|$. Thus the Gelfand map is isometric on self-adjoint elements.

Suppose that $\alpha = a + ib$ belongs to the spectrum of f and that $f = f^*$. Then α is real. Indeed, for each real c, $\|f + ic\|^2 = \|(f + ic)(f + ic)^*\| = \|(f + ic)(f - ic)\| = \|f^2 + c^2 1\|$. Since $\alpha \in \sigma(f)$, $(\alpha + ic)^2 \in \sigma((f + ic)^2)$, so $|\alpha + ic|^2 \leq \|(f + ic)^2\| \leq \|f + ic\|^2 = \|f^2 + c^2 1\|$. Equivalently, $a^2 + (b + c)^2 = a^2 + b^2 + 2bc + c^2 \leq \|f^2 + c^2 1\|$. But $1 = 1^*$, so $\|1\| = \|11^*\| = \|1\|^2$ and thus $\|1\| = 1$. So $\|f^2 + c^2 1\| \leq \|f^2\| + c^2 \leq \|f\|^2 + c^2$ and $a^2 + b^2 + 2bc \leq \|f\|^2$. This is true for all real c, so $b = 0$ and α is real. But $\sigma(f)$ is the range of $\hat{f}$, so we conclude that if $f = f^*$, $\hat{f}$ is a real-valued function.

Now each $f \in A$ has the form $f = f_1 + if_2$, where f_1, f_2 are in A and are self-adjoint. ($f_1 = \frac{1}{2}(f + f^*)$.) So $f^* = f_1 - if_2$, and taking transforms we see that $\hat{f}$ and $\hat{f}^*$ are conjugates. Thus $\hat{f}^* = \bar{\hat{f}}$. In particular, $\hat{A}$ is a self-adjoint subalgebra of $C(\mathcal{M}(A))$. Since $\hat{A}$ separates points and contains the constants, $\hat{A}$ is dense in $C(\mathcal{M}(A))$, by the Stone-Weierstrass theorem.

It remains to show that $\|f\| = \|\hat{f}\|$ for all $f \in A$, for then $\hat{A}$ is complete, hence closed, and hence equal to $C(\mathcal{M}(A))$. But if $f \in A$, ff^* is self-adjoint, so $\|ff^*\| = \|\widehat{ff^*}\| = \|\hat{f}\hat{f}^*\| = \|\hat{f}\bar{\hat{f}}\| = \|\hat{f}\|^2$. Since $\|ff^*\| = \|f\|^2$, the Gelfand map is norm preserving.

EXERCISE SET 3.4

1. Let A be a subset of $C(X)$ which separates points on X. Suppose that F is a compact set in X and that $A|_F$ is a dense subalgebra of $C(F)$. Show that if $p \in X \backslash F$, then either $f(p) = $ for every $f \in A$, or $|f(p)| > \max_{x \in F} |f(x)|$ for some $f \in A$.

2. Let A be a closed subalgebra of $C(X)$ which separates points on X. Suppose that for each $x \in X$, there is a closed *nbhd* V_x of x such that $A|_{V_x} = C(V_x)$. Then $A = C(X)$.

3. Assume the following fact, to be proved later: if K is a compact countable set in the plane, then $P(K) = C(K)$. Show that if X is a countable compact space, then every closed subalgebra of $C(X)$ is self-adjoint.

4. Let $(S, \mathscr{S}, \mu)$ be a measure space. Let $L^\infty(S)$ be the space of all essentially bounded measurable functions on S, identifying functions which are equal a.e. $[\mu]$. Set $\|f\|_\infty =$ the essential supremum of $|f|$ on S.

   Then L^∞ is a commutative Banach algebra with identity. There is a compact space X such that L^∞ is isometrically isomorphic with $C(X)$. The topology of X is the weak topology defined by $\hat{L}^\infty$.

   Since each $f \in L^\infty$ is approximable in norm by linear combinations of characteristic functions χ_E $(E \in \mathscr{S})$, the idempotent functions $\hat{\chi}_E$ $(E \in \mathscr{S})$ define the topology of X. In particular, X has a base consisting of open-closed sets.

5. A topological space S is *completely regular* iff S is a Hausdorff space and for each pair (x, F) where F is a closed subset of S and x is a point in $S \backslash F$, there is a continuous function u on S such that $0 \le u \le 1$ on S, $u(x) = 1$, $u(F) = \{0\}$.

   Let S be completely regular. Let $BC(S)$ be the space of all bounded continuous functions on S, and for $f \in BC(S)$ let $\|f\| = \sup_{s \in S} |f(s)|$. Then $BC(S)$ is a commutative Banach algebra with identity. If βS is the maximal ideal space of $BC(S)$, then βS is a compact space and the Gelfand map is an isometric isomorphism of $BC(S)$ onto $C(\beta S)$. There is a mapping $s \to e_s$ from S into βS given by $e_s(f) = f(s)$ $(f \in BC(S))$. The topology of S coincides with the weak topology defined by $BC(S)$, so the map is a homeomorphism from S onto $e(S) \subset \beta S$. Finally, $e(S)$ is dense in βS.

   βS is called the *Stone-Čech compactification* of S.

6. If A is a ring and x, y are in A, let $x \circ y = x + y - xy$. Then $\circ$ is an associative operation on A, and if A has an identity element 1, $x \circ y = 1 - (1 - x)(1 - y)$.

7. (Raising idempotents, step 1.) Let $F = F_1 \cup \cdots \cup F_n$, where F_i are subsets of a compact space X. Let A be a subring of $C(X)$, and let $y \in X$. Suppose that y has *nbhds* $U_1, \ldots, U_n$ such that there are functions $f_1, \ldots, f_n$ in A with $f_i = 1$ on F_i and $f_i = 0$ on U_i $(1 \le i \le n)$. Then there exist $f \in A$ and a *nbhd* U of y such that $f|F = 1$ and $f|U = 0$.

8. (Raising idempotents, step 2.) Let F, K be disjoint closed subsets of a compact space X, and let A be a subring of $C(X)$. Assume that for each $x \in F$, $y \in K$, there exist *nbhds* V, W of x, y (respectively) and a function $e_{xy} \in A$ with $e_{xy} = 1$ on V, $e_{xy} = 0$ on W. Show that $\exists f \in A$ with $f|F = 1$ and $f|K = 0$.

Chapter Four

Function Algebras

4.1 SUP NORM ALGEBRAS

Let X be a compact space and $C(X)$ the algebra of all continuous complex-valued functions on X. For $f \in C(X)$, we set $\|f\| = \max_{x \in X} |f(x)|$ and call $\|f\|$ the sup norm or uniform norm of f. (Observe that $f_n \to f$ in norm iff $f_n \to f$ uniformly on X.) A norm closed subset of $C(X)$ will be referred to as uniformly closed, or merely, closed.

We shall call A a *function algebra on X* iff (a) A is a uniformly closed subalgebra of $C(X)$; (b) A separates the points of X; (c) A contains the constant functions. (Function algebras are sometimes called *uniform algebras* in the literature.) A *sup norm algebra on X* is any algebra satisfying (a) and (c). If A is a sup norm algebra on X, then A is canonically identifiable with a function algebra on the compact space obtained by identifying points of X which are identified by A. (See §3.2, Exercise 7.) By the Stone-Weierstrass theorem, a function algebra A on X is $C(X)$ iff A is self-adjoint (i.e., $f \in A$ implies $\bar{f} \in A$).

A sup norm algebra A is a commutative Banach algebra with identity. We denote by $\mathcal{M}(A)$ the maximal ideal space of A. Thus $\mathcal{M}(A)$ is compact and the elements of $\mathcal{M}(A)$ are the complex homomorphisms of A. For $f \in A$ and $h \in \mathcal{M}(A)$, we have $\hat{f}(h) = h(f)$, and the topology of $\mathcal{M}(A)$ is the weak topology defined by the transform algebra $\hat{A}$. For $x \in X$, let φ_x be the function on A given by $\varphi_x(f) = f(x)$. Then each φ_x belongs to $\mathcal{M}(A)$.

Theorem 1. *Let A be a sup norm algebra on X. Define $\varphi : X \to \mathcal{M}(A)$ by $\varphi_x(f) = f(x)$. Then φ is a continuous mapping from X onto a compact subset of $\mathcal{M}(A)$. Each $\hat{f}$ in $\hat{A}$ assumes its maximum modulus on the image of X in $\mathcal{M}(A)$, since we have the following maximum principle:*

$$\max \{|\hat{f}(h)| : h \in \mathcal{M}(A)\} = \max \{|f(x)| : x \in X\} \qquad (f \in A).$$

The Gelfand map $f \to \hat{f}$ is an algebra isomorphism and an isometry from A onto $\hat{A}$. Finally, $\hat{A}$ is a function algebra on $\mathcal{M}(A)$.

Proof. It is clear that φ maps X into $\mathcal{M}(A)$. If $x_0 \in X$, then the inverse image under φ of a basic *nbhd* $\{h \in \mathcal{M}(A) : |\hat{f}_i(h) - \hat{f}_i(\varphi_{x_0})| < \varepsilon$ for $1 \leq i \leq n\}$ of φ_{x_0} in $\mathcal{M}(A)$ is $\{x \in X : |f_i(x) - f_i(x_0)| < \varepsilon$ for $1 \leq i \leq n\}$. This set is open in X, so φ is continuous.

Now if $h \in \mathcal{M}(A)$, $\|h\| \leq 1$. (In fact, $\|h\| = 1$ since $h(1) = 1 = \|1\|$.) So $\|\hat{f}\| \leq \|f\|$. Conversely, $\|\hat{f}\| \geq \sup_{x \in X} |\hat{f}(\varphi_x)| = \sup_{x \in X} |f(x)| = \|f\|$. So $\|\hat{f}\| = \|f\|$. Since X is compact it follows that $|\hat{f}|$ assumes its maximum at some point of X. The Gelfand map is thus an isometry. Since it is clearly a homomorphism, it is an isomorphism. A normed space isometric to a complete space is complete. So $\hat{A}$ is complete and hence closed in the sup norm on $\mathcal{M}(A)$. Since $\hat{1} = 1$, $\hat{A}$ contains the constants. $\hat{A}$ separates points on $\mathcal{M}(A)$ trivially, so $\hat{A}$ is a function algebra on $\mathcal{M}(A)$.

Theorem 2. *Let A be a function algebra on X. Then the evaluation map $\varphi : x \to \varphi_x$ maps X homeomorphically onto a compact subset of $\mathcal{M}(A)$. If X is identified with its image in $\mathcal{M}(A)$, and if we set $\hat{f}(x) = \hat{f}(\varphi_x)$ for $f \in A$, $x \in X$, then $\hat{f}$ is a continuous extension of f to $\mathcal{M}(A)$.*

Proof. Since X is compact and $\mathcal{M}(A)$ is a Hausdorff space, all that we need verify is that φ is one-one if A separates points on X. But this is true by definition.

Theorem 3. *Let A, A' be sup norm algebras on compact spaces X, X'. If τ is an algebra isomorphism of A onto A', then $\tau(1) = 1$ and τ is an isometry.*

Proof. Clearly $\tau(1) = 1$. For $f \in A$, the spectrum of f in A and the spectrum of $\tau(f)$ in A' are the same. But $\|f\| = \|\hat{f}\| = \max_{h \in \mathcal{M}(A)} |\hat{f}(h)| = \max_{\lambda \in \sigma(f)} |\lambda|$ by Theorem 1 and by Theorem 5, §2.3. So $\|f\| = \|\tau(f)\|$.

In Theorem 7 we establish a converse to Theorem 3: a linear isometry of function algebras which sends 1 to 1 is multiplicative, and hence an algebra isomorphism. Also see Exercise 6.

Theorem 4. *Let A be a sup norm algebra on X. Let Σ_A be the closed unit ball of A^*, and let $T_A = \{L \in A^* : L(1) = \|L\| = 1\}$. Then Σ_A and T_A are convex and w^*-compact, and $\varphi(X) \subset \mathcal{M}(A) \subset T_A \subset \Sigma_A$.*

Every functional in T_A has an extension to a positive linear functional of norm 1 on $C(X)$. For each $L \in T_A$, there is a positive measure $m \in M(X)$ of total mass 1 such that $L(f) = \int f \, dm$ for every f in A.

Furthermore, T_A is the w^*-closed convex hull of $\varphi(X)$, and hence of $\mathcal{M}(A)$, and every extreme point of T_A belongs to $\varphi(X)$.

Proof. Note that

$$T_A = \{L \in A^* : \|L\| \le 1 \text{ and } L(1) = 1\}$$
$$= \Sigma_A \cap \{L : L(1) = 1\},$$

the intersection of Σ_A with a w^*-closed hyperplane. So since Σ_A is w^*-compact (Alaoglu), T_A is convex and w^*-compact. It is also clear that $\varphi(X) \subset \mathcal{M}(A) \subset T_A \subset \Sigma_A$.

Suppose that $L \in T_A$. By the Hahn-Banach theorem, L extends to a linear functional ψ on $C(X)$ such that $\|\psi\| = 1$. Since $\psi(1) = \|\psi\| = 1$, ψ is a positive linear functional on $C(X)$. (Suppose that $u \in C(X)$, $u \ge 0$, and $a = \min \{u(x) : x \in X\}$, $b = \max \{u(x) : x \in X\}$. Then $\psi(u) \in [a, b]$; for otherwise there is a complex number α such that $|c - \alpha| < |\psi(u) - \alpha| = |\psi(u - \alpha)|$ for all c in $[a, b]$. Hence $\|u - \alpha\| = \max \{|c - \alpha| : c \in u(X)\} \le \max \{|c - \alpha| : a \le c \le b\} < |\psi(u - \alpha)|$, so $\|\psi\| > 1$.) By the Riesz representation theorem, there is a positive measure m in $M(X)$ such that $\psi(g) = \int g \, dm$ $(g \in C(X))$. In particular, $L(f) = \psi(f) = \int f \, dm$ for $f \in A$ and $m(X) = \int 1 \, dm = L(1) = 1$.

Let K be the w^*-closed convex hull of $\varphi(X)$. Since T_A is w^*-closed and convex and contains $\varphi(X)$, $K \subset T_A$. On the other hand, if we assume that there is some L_0 in $T_A \backslash K$, we can use the separation theorem to derive a contradiction, as follows.

K is w^*-compact and convex. If $L_0 \notin K$, then L_0 and K are separated by a hyperplane; i.e., there is a w^*-continuous linear functional q on A^* such that $\text{Re} (q(L_0)) > 1$, $\text{Re} (q) \le 1$ on K. But q is given by evaluation at some point $f \in A$, so $\text{Re} (L_0(f)) > 1$, $\text{Re} (L(f)) \le 1$ for L in K. In particular,

$$\text{Re} (\varphi_x(f)) = \text{Re} (f(x)) \le 1$$

for every x in X. But there is a positive measure m_0 of total mass 1 such that $L_0(f) = \int_X f \, dm_0$, so $\text{Re} (L_0(f)) = \int_X \text{Re} (f) \, dm_0 \le 1$, and we have obtained a contradiction. Hence $K = T_A$.

Since the w^*-closed convex hull T_A of the compact set $\varphi(X)$ is compact, each extreme point of T_A belongs to $\varphi(X)$, by Theorem 10, §1.4.

Definition. Let A be a sup norm algebra on X, and let $h \in \mathcal{M}(A)$. A *representing measure* for h is a positive measure m on X such that

$$\hat{f}(h) = \int_X f \, dm \qquad \text{for all } f \text{ in } A.$$

Every complex homomorphism of A has a representing measure.

Corollary. *Let A be a sup norm algebra on X. If $f \in A$ and f is real-valued, then $\hat{f}$ is real-valued. If $f \in A$ and $f \ge 0$, then $\hat{f} \ge 0$. If $\text{Re} (f) \ge 0$, then $\text{Re} (\hat{f}) \ge 0$, while if $\text{Re} (f) > 0$, then $\text{Re} (\hat{f}) > 0$.*

Proof. All these results follow from the integral representation, $\hat{f}(h) = \int_X f\,dm$. In fact, this shows that for each f in A, the range of $\hat{f}$ is contained in the closed convex hull of the range of f.

Given a sup norm algebra A on X, let $c(A)$ be the set of all $x \in X$ such that φ_x is an extreme point of T_A. $c(A)$ is called the *Choquet boundary* of A. The closure of $c(A)$ in X is called the *Šilov boundary* of A and is denoted by $\Gamma(A)$.

Theorem 5. *Let A be a sup norm algebra on X. Then every $f \in A$ assumes its maximum modulus at some point of the Choquet boundary $c(A)$.*

In particular, if $f \in A$, $g \in A$ and the restrictions of f and g to the Šilov boundary $\Gamma(A)$ (or merely to $c(A)$) coincide, then $f = g$.

Proof. The second assertion is immediate, since equality of f and g on $\Gamma(A)$ implies that the maximum modulus of $f - g$ on X is zero.

We start with the observation that the w^*-continuous linear functionals on A^* are the maps $L \to L(f)$, with $f \in A$.

Now T_A is w^*-compact and convex, so every w^*-continuous linear functional on A^* assumes its maximum modulus at some extreme point of T_A. (See the remarks after Theorem 11, §1.4.) Hence if $f \in A$, there is some $s \in c(A)$ such that $|f(s)| = \max\{|L(f)| : L \in T_A\}$ (i.e., $|\varphi_s(f)| = \max\{|L(f)| : L \in T_A\}$). Since $\varphi_s \in \varphi(X) \subset \mathscr{M}(A) \subset T_A$, $|f(s)| = \max\{|f(x)| : x \in X\} = \max\{|\hat{f}(h)| : h \in \mathscr{M}(A)\}$.

Theorem 6. *Let A be a sup norm algebra on X, and let F be a compact subset of X. Consider the following conditions.*

(a) F contains the Šilov boundary of A.

(b) Every $f \in A$ assumes its maximum modulus at some point of F.

(c) The restriction map $f \to f|F$ from A into $C(F)$ is an isometry.

(d) Every complex homomorphism of A has a representing measure which is concentrated on F.

Then (b), (c), (d) are equivalent and (a) implies (b). If A separates points (i.e., A is a function algebra), then all four conditions are equivalent.

(Note that if A fails to separate points, $\Gamma(A)$ need not be the smallest closed subset of X on which each $f \in A$ assumes its maximum modulus. For example, if A consists of the constants, then $c(A) = \Gamma(A) = X$, but (b) holds for any one point subset of X.)

Proof. By Theorem 5, (a) implies (b). Since the norm of $f|F$ in $C(F)$ is $\max\{|f(x)| : x \in F\}$, (b) and (c) are equivalent.

If (d) holds, then each $\varphi_x \in \varphi(X)$ has a representing measure m concentrated on F. So if $f \in A$, $|f(x)| = |\int f\,dm| = |\int(f|F)\,dm| \le \|f|F\|$ ($\|m\| = 1$). Hence $\|f\| = \sup\{|f(x)| : x \in X\} \le \|f|F\|$. But $\|f|F\| \le \|f\|$ always, so $f \to f|F$ is an isometry.

Suppose that (c) holds. If f, g are in A and $f|F = g|F$, then $f = g$. Thus each $h \in \mathcal{M}(A)$ defines a complex homomorphism of $A|F$ by $f|F \to h(f)$. Since $A|F$ is isometric to A, it is a sup norm algebra on F, so this homomorphism has a representing measure $v \in M(F)$. Define m on the Borel sets of X by $m(E) = v(E \cap F)$. Then m is a positive measure, and

$$h(f) = \hat{f}(h) = \int_F (f|F)\, dv = \int_X f\, dm \qquad (f \in A),$$

so m is a representing measure for h concentrated on F. Thus (c) and (d) are equivalent.

Now suppose that A is a function algebra. Consider the real linear space $B = \{u \in C(X) : u = \mathrm{Re}\,(f)\ \text{for some}\ f \in A\}$. Then A satisfies (b) iff every $u \in B$ assumes its maximum at some point of F. (See Exercise 4.) Suppose that A satisfies (b).

Given $f \in A$, $\max_{x \in X} \mathrm{Re}\,(f(x)) = \max_{x \in F} \mathrm{Re}\,(f(x)) = \mathrm{Re}\,(f(s)) = \mathrm{Re}\,(\varphi_s(f))$, for some $s \in F$. But if $L \in T_A$, then L is represented by a positive measure m of total mass 1, so $\mathrm{Re}\,(L(f)) = \mathrm{Re}\,\left(\int_X f\, dm\right) = \int_X \mathrm{Re}\,(f)\, dm \le \mathrm{Re}\,(\varphi_s(f))$. Thus every w^*-continuous real-linear functional $L \to \mathrm{Re}\,(L(f))$ on A^* assumes its maximum over T_A on the w^*-closed set $\varphi(F)$. By Theorem 11, §1.4, the closure of the set of extreme points of T_A is the smallest w^*-closed subset of T_A on which all these functionals assume their maxima. Since $\Gamma = \Gamma(A) = \overline{c(A)}$ and φ is a homeomorphism, $\varphi(\Gamma) = \overline{\varphi(c(A))}$ is the closure of the set of extreme points of T_A; so $\varphi(\Gamma) \subset \varphi(F)$, and F contains Γ.

Theorem 7. *Let A, A' be sup norm algebras on compact spaces X, X'. If τ is a linear space isometry of A' onto A, and if $\tau(1) = 1$, then τ is an algebra isomorphism.*

Proof. Let f, g be in A'. We must show that $\tau(fg) = \tau(f)\tau(g)$. By Theorem 5, it will suffice to show that $\tau(fg)(x) = \tau(f)(x)\tau(g)(x)$ for each x in the Choquet boundary of A.

Let $\tau^* : A^* \to (A')^*$ be the adjoint of τ, given by $\tau^*(L) = L \circ \tau$. Since τ is an isometry and $\tau(1) = 1$, τ^* carries T_A onto $T_{A'}$. τ is linear and one-one, so τ^* carries the set of extreme points of T_A onto the set of extreme points of $T_{A'}$. Hence if $x \in c(A)$, then $\exists y \in c(A')$ with $\tau^*(\varphi_x) = \varphi_y$. But $\tau^*(\varphi_x)(fg) = \varphi_x(\tau(fg)) = \tau(fg)(x)$, so $\tau(fg)(x) = \varphi_y(fg) = (fg)(y) = f(y)g(y)$. Similarly, $\tau(f)(x) = \tau^*(\varphi_x)(f) = f(y)$ and $\tau(g)(x) = g(y)$. Therefore $\tau(fg)(x) - \tau(f)(x)\tau(g)(x) = f(y)g(y) - f(y)g(y) = 0$. Thus $\tau(fg) - \tau(f)\tau(g)$ does vanish on $c(A)$ and hence $\tau(fg) = \tau(f)\tau(g)$.

Theorem 8. *Let A be a sup norm algebra. Then $\mathcal{M}(\hat{A}) = \mathcal{M}(A)$.*

Proof. $\hat{A}$ is a function algebra on $\mathcal{M}(A)$, so we are to show that every complex homomorphism q of $\hat{A}$ is given by evaluation at a point of $\mathcal{M}(A)$. But $f \to q(\hat{f})$ is a complex homomorphism of A, so there is some $h \in \mathcal{M}(A)$ with $h(f) = q(\hat{f})$; that is, $q(\hat{f}) = \hat{f}(h)$ for all $\hat{f}$ in $\hat{A}$, which proves the assertion.

Let us return to Theorems 4 and 5 and note that the assumption that A is a subalgebra of $C(X)$ is used very little in the proofs.

Let B be a linear subspace of $C(X)$ or $C_R(X)$, and suppose that B contains the constant functions, but do not assume that B is uniformly closed. Let $T_B = \{L \in B^* : L(1) = \|L\| = 1\}$. Each $L \in T_B$ extends to a positive linear functional on $C(X)$ or $C_R(X)$, and thus is represented by a positive measure m of total mass 1 on X. T_B is compact and convex in the w^*-topology of B^*. There is a continuous map $x \to e_x$ from X into T_B given by $e_x(u) = u(x)$ ($x \in X$, $u \in B$), and T_B is the w^*-closed convex hull of the image of X under this map. Every extreme point of T_B has the form e_x for some $x \in X$. We define the Choquet boundary $c(B)$ and the Šilov boundary $\Gamma(B)$ exactly as we did for sup norm algebras.

For $x \in X$, let H_x be the set of all positive measures μ on X which represent e_x (i.e., the set of all Hahn-Banach extensions of e_x to $C(X)$ or $C_R(X)$). Let $F_x = \{y \in X : u(x) = u(y), \forall u \in B\} = \{y \in X : e_x = e_y\}$.

Then we have the following characterization of $c(B)$.

Theorem 9. $c(B) = \{x \in X : every \ \mu \in H_x \ is \ concentrated \ on \ F_x\}$.

Proof.   (1) Assume that $H_x \subset M(F_x)$. Suppose that $0 < t < 1$ and that $e_x = tL_1 + (1 - t)L_2$ with L_1, L_2 in T_B. There exist positive measures m_1, m_2 on X representing L_1, L_2 respectively. For $u \in B$,

$$u(x) = e_x(u) = \int u \, d(tm_1 + (1 - t)m_2).$$

So $tm_1 + (1 - t)m_2$ belongs to H_x and is thus concentrated on F_x. So m_1 and m_2 are concentrated on F_x. (If $E \subset X \backslash F_x$, then $0 = tm_1(E) + (1 - t)m_2(E)$ and $0 \le m_i(E) \le 1, 0 < t < 1$; so $m_1(E) = m_2(E) = 0$.) Thus if $u \in B$, $\int_X u \, dm_i = \int_{F_x} u \, dm_i = u(x)m_i(F_x) = u(x)$, since $u = u(x)$ on F_x and $m_i(F_x) = \|m_i\| = 1$. Thus $L_1(u) = L_2(u) = u(x)$, so $e_x = L_1 = L_2$. Hence e_x is an extreme point of T_B, so $x \in c(B)$.

(2) Assume that $x \in c(B)$. Take any $\mu \in H_x$. Let S be a Borel set in X. If $0 < \mu(S) < 1$, let $L_1(u) = \dfrac{1}{\mu(S)} \displaystyle\int_S u \, d\mu$ and $L_2(u) = \dfrac{1}{1 - \mu(S)} \displaystyle\int_{X \backslash S} u \, d\mu$ ($u \in B$). Then $L_1, L_2 \in T_B$ and $e_x = \mu(S)L_1 + (1 - \mu(S))L_2$. Since e_x is an extreme point of T_B, $e_x = L_1$. Thus

$$(\star) \qquad\qquad u(x)\mu(S) = \int_S u \, d\mu \qquad \text{for all } u \in B.$$

Note that $(\star)$ also holds if $\mu(S) = 0$ or $\mu(S) = 1$.

Suppose first that B is a subspace of $C_R(X)$. Let $u \in B$. If $u < u(x)$ on a set of positive μ-measure, then by regularity of μ, there is a compact set K with $\mu(K) > 0$ such that $u < u(x)$ on K. Hence $u \le r < u(x)$ on K for some constant r, and so $\int_K u \, d\mu \le r\mu(K) < u(x)\mu(K)$, contradicting $(\star)$. Similarly, it is not the case that $u > u(x)$ on a set of positive μ-measure. So $u = u(x)$ a.e. $[\mu]$. Hence by regularity, $\mu(X \backslash F_x) = 0$, so μ is concentrated on F_x.

Now suppose that B is a subspace of $C(X)$. We have $f(x)\mu(S) = \int_S f\, d\mu$ for all $f \in B$ and each Borel set S. Hence ($\star$) holds for each $u \in \mathrm{Re}\,(B)$, and we conclude that if $u \in \mathrm{Re}\,(B)$, then $u = u(x)$ a.e. $[\mu]$. But if $f \in B$, $f = u + iv$ where $u = \mathrm{Re}\,(f)$, $v = \mathrm{Re}\,(-if)$. So $f = f(x)$ a.e. $[\mu]$, and μ is concentrated on F_x.

Corollary. *If B separates points, then $c(B) = \{x \in X : H_x \text{ contains only the point mass } \delta_x\}$. In particular, the Choquet boundary of a function algebra A on X consists of all $x \in X$ such that the only representing measure for the homomorphism $\varphi_x \in \mathscr{M}(A)$ is the point mass at x.*

Instead of looking at the extreme points of T_B, we can consider a fixed $L \in T_B$ and look at the extreme points of the set of Hahn-Banach extensions of L. (Cf. Exercise 7.) These are thus the extreme points of the set of positive measures which represent L. For each such extreme measure, the following result holds.

Proposition. *Let $L \in T_B$, where B is a subspace of $C(X)$ or $C_R(X)$, and B contains the constants. Suppose that m is an extreme point of the set of positive measures on X which represent L. Then $\mathrm{Re}\,(B)$ is dense in $L_R^{\,1}(m)$ (the real-valued functions in $L^1(m)$).*

Proof. Suppose that $g \in L_R^{\,\infty}(m)$, $\|g\|_\infty \leq 1$, and $\int ug\, dm = 0$ for every $u \in \mathrm{Re}\,(B) = \{\mathrm{Re}\,(f) : f \in B\}$. Then $\int fg\, dm = 0$ for every f in B. Set $\mu = (1 - g)m$, $v = (1 + g)m$. Since $-1 \leq g \leq 1$ a.e., μ and v are positive measures. Since $gm \in B^\perp$, μ and v represent L, while $m = \frac{1}{2}\mu + \frac{1}{2}v$. So $m = v = \mu$, since m is an extreme point. Thus $(1 - g)m = m$, so $1 - g = 1$ a.e. and $g = 0$ in $L_R^{\,\infty}(m)$.

We conclude that the annihilator of $\mathrm{Re}\,(B)$ in $L_R^{\,\infty}(m)$ is $\{0\}$. So $\mathrm{Re}\,(B)$ is dense in $L_R^{\,1}(m)$, by the Hahn-Banach theorem and the fact that L^∞ is the dual of L^1.

Corollary. *If A is a function algebra, $h \in \mathscr{M}(A)$, and if m is an extreme point of the set of representing measures for h (for example, if h has only one representing measure m), then $\mathrm{Re}\,(A)$ is dense in $L_R^{\,1}(m)$.*

EXERCISE SET   4.1

1. Establish the analogs of Theorems 4, 5, 6 for function spaces, to the extent that they remain true.

2. Let A be a function algebra on X, and let φ be the natural embedding of X into $\mathscr{M}(A)$. Prove that the Šilov boundary of $\hat{A}$ is $\varphi(\Gamma(A))$. (Thus if we identify x with φ_x, and consider $\hat{A}$ as an extension of A to functions on $\mathscr{M}(A)$, then A and $\hat{A}$ have the same Šilov boundary.)

3. Let A be a sup norm algebra. Show that if $f \in A$, then $e^f = \sum_{n=0}^{\infty} \frac{1}{n!} f^n$ is in A and $\exp(\hat{f})$ is the Gelfand transform of e^f. Hence $e^{\int f \, dm} = \int e^f \, dm$ for every representing measure m.

4. Let A be a sup norm algebra on X, and let $S \subset X$. Show that the following conditions are equivalent: (a) every $f \in A$ assumes its maximum modulus at some point of S; (b) every u in $\mathrm{Re}(A) = \{\mathrm{Re}(f) : f \in A\}$ assumes its maximum at some point of S; (c) every $u \in \mathrm{Re}(A)$ assumes its maximum modulus at some point of S. Such a set S is called a *boundary for A*.

5. Let A be a function algebra on X and let Σ_A be the unit ball in A^*. Consider the restriction map r from $C(X)^*$ to A^*. Show that if L is an extreme point of Σ_A, then $r^{-1}(L)$ contains an extreme point of Σ, the closed unit ball of $C(X)^*$.

   Show that the extreme points of Σ are the functionals of form λh_x, where $|\lambda| = 1$ and $h_x(g) = g(x)$ $(x \in X, g \in C(X))$. So $L = \lambda \varphi_x$ for some $\lambda \in T^1$ and some $x \in X$.

   Let S be the set of $x \in X$ such that φ_x is an extreme point of Σ_A. Show that S is a boundary for A. Does $S = c(A)$?

6. (*Isometries of function algebras*) Let A be a function algebra on X. Let T be a linear isometry of A onto A. Prove that $\exists \alpha \in A$ and an algebra automorphism T_1 of A such that $1/\alpha \in A$, $|\alpha(x)| = 1$ for all $x \in X$, and $T(f) = T_1(f)\alpha$ for all $f \in A$. (Take $\alpha = T(1)$. Show that $\alpha T(fg) - T(f)T(g)$ vanishes on the set S in Exercise 5.)

7. Let $L_0 \in A^*$, A a sup norm algebra on X. A *Hahn-Banach extension of L_0* is a linear functional $L \in C(X)^*$ such that $\|L\| = \|L_0\|$ and $L(f) = L_0(f)$ for all $f \in A$. Show that the set of all Hahn-Banach extensions of L_0 is convex and w^*-compact, and hence L_0 has extreme Hahn-Banach extensions.

8. Let Y be a locally compact space and $C_0(Y)$ the Banach algebra of all continuous complex-valued functions on Y which vanish at infinity, with $\|f\| = \sup_{y \in Y} |f(y)|$. Recall that a subset E of $C_0(Y)$ is strongly separating iff E separates points on Y and $\forall y \in Y$, $\exists f \in E$ with $f(y) \neq 0$.

   Let A be a strongly separating closed subalgebra of $C_0(Y)$. Show that there exists a smallest closed subset $\Gamma(A)$ contained in Y on which every $f \in A$ assumes its maximum modulus over Y. Every complex homomorphism of A is represented by a finite positive Borel measure on Y.

9. Let A be a function algebra on X, and let F be a closed set in X which contains the Šilov boundary of A. Show that (a) $A|_F$ is a function algebra on F; (b) $\mathcal{M}(A|_F) = \mathcal{M}(A)$; (c) $\Gamma(A|_F) = \Gamma(A)$. (Note that each $\varphi \in \mathcal{M}(A|_F)$ determines a homomorphism $h \in \mathcal{M}(A)$, by $h(f) = \varphi(f|F)$. The

meaning of assertion (b) is that $\varphi \to h$ is a homeomorphism of $\mathcal{M}(A|_F)$ onto $\mathcal{M}(A)$.)

10. If A is a sup norm algebra on X and $x_0 \in X$, then x_0 is a *peak point* for A iff there is some $f \in A$ such that $|f(x_0)| = \|f\|$ while $|f(x)| < \|f\|$ for all $x \in X \setminus \{x_0\}$. Thus x_0 is a peak point for A iff there is some $f \in A$ such that $f(x_0) = 1$, $|f(x)| < 1$ for all $x \neq x_0$.

    Show that every peak point for A is in the Choquet boundary of A, and that if x_0 is a peak point for A, then the set $\{x_0\}$ is a G_δ (i.e., an intersection of countably many open sets). If X is a compact metric space, show that every point of X is a peak point for $C(X)$.

    Let Λ be an uncountable set, and let $X_\lambda = [0, 1]$ for each $\lambda \in \Lambda$. Let X be the topological product $\prod_{\lambda \in \Lambda} X_\lambda$. Then X is a compact space. For $x \in X$ and $\lambda \in \Lambda$, let $\pi_\lambda(x) = x_\lambda$ be the projection of x into X_λ. Let B be the set of all f in $C(X)$ such that there exists a countable (finite or denumerable) subset Λ_0 of Λ (Λ_0 depending on f) such that if $x, y \in X$ and $x_\lambda = y_\lambda$ for all $\lambda \in \Lambda_0$, then $f(x) = f(y)$. Then by the Stone-Weierstrass theorem, $B = C(X)$. Thus there are no peak points for $C(X)$. (Note that $[0, 1]$ can be replaced by any compact space with at least two elements.)

11. Show that a continuous homomorphism from a normed algebra into a sup norm algebra has operator norm at most 1.

12. Let A be a sup norm algebra on X, F a compact subset of X. For $f \in A$, we set $\|f\|_F = \||f| F\|$ in $C(F)$. Let $h \in \mathcal{M}(A)$. Show that the following conditions on F are equivalent.

    (a) For every f in A, $|h(f)| \leq \|f\|_F$.
    (b) There is a representing measure for h which is concentrated on F.
    (c) There is a complex measure $\mu \in M(X)$ concentrated on F such that $h(f) = \int f\, d\mu$ (all f in A).

    Any such compact set F is called a *support set* for h. Note that any closed set containing $\Gamma(A)$ is a support set for h.

    Remark. There exists a minimal support set for h, and in fact, every support set for h contains a minimal one. (By Zorn's lemma, it will suffice to show that if $\{F_\alpha\}$ is a family of support sets for h which is totally ordered under inclusion, then $F = \bigcap_\alpha F_\alpha$ is a support set for h. Note first that $\{F_\alpha\}$ has the finite intersection property, so F is a nonempty closed set. Let $f \in A$ and $E = \{x \in X : |h(f)| \leq |f(x)|\}$. Then by the same argument, $F \cap E = \bigcap_\alpha (F_\alpha \cap E)$ is nonempty. So F is a support set for h.)

    Suppose that $h \notin \varphi(X)$ and F is a minimal support set for h. Let m be a representing measure for h which is concentrated on F. For each $x \in F$, $\exists f_x \in A$ with $h(f_x) = 1$, $\varphi_x(f_x) = 0$. We see that $f_x m$ is a complex measure which represents h and is concentrated on $F\backslash\{x\}$. So by minimality of F, $\{x\}$ is not an open subset of F. Thus if $h \notin \varphi(X)$, every minimal support set for h is perfect (i.e., is a compact space with no isolated points).

As a corollary, we have the following result: *If the evaluation map φ is not onto $\mathcal{M}(A)$, then the Šilov boundary of A contains a perfect set.*

4.2 ANALYTIC FUNCTIONS ON THE UNIT DISK

In the complex plane $\mathbf{C}$, let U be the open unit disk with center at the origin. let $T = T^1$ be the unit circle, and $\Delta = \overline{U} = U \cup T$ the closed disk. The *disk algebra A* consists of all continuous functions f on Δ which are analytic on U. Denote by z the coordinate function on $\Delta : z(\alpha) = \alpha$ ($\alpha \in \Delta$). Then A is certainly a subalgebra of $C(\Delta)$ which contains z and the constants and hence separates points on Δ. A uniform limit of analytic functions is analytic, so A is a function algebra on Δ.

Note that if $f \in A$ and $\varepsilon > 0$, then the function f_ε given by $f_\varepsilon(\alpha) = f\left(\dfrac{\alpha}{1+\varepsilon}\right)$ is analytic on the disk $\{\alpha : |\alpha| < 1 + \varepsilon\}$, and hence is uniformly approximable on Δ by the partial sums of its Taylor series about the origin. But since $f \in C(\Delta)$, the restriction of f_ε to Δ converges uniformly to f as $\varepsilon \to 0$, by uniform continuity. We conclude that f is the limit in the sup norm of a sequence of polynomials. Conversely, every such uniform limit of polynomials is certainly in A. Thus the disk algebra is the uniform closure on Δ of the polynomials in z.

The disk algebra A is a singly generated Banach algebra, and hence $\mathcal{M}(A)$ can be identified with the spectrum of the generator z. In more detail, note that if $\lambda \in \Delta$, $f \to f(\lambda)$ is a complex homomorphism h_λ of A. Conversely, if $h \in \mathcal{M}(A)$ and $\lambda = h(z)$, then $|\lambda| = |h(z)| \leq \|z\| = 1$ (so $\lambda \in \Delta$), and $h(p) = \sum_{k=0}^{n} a_k \lambda^k = h_\lambda(p)$ for each polynomial $p = \sum_{k=0}^{n} a_k z^k$. Hence h and h_λ agree on a dense subset of A, so $h = h_\lambda$ (since both are continuous). A is a function algebra, and we have shown that the evaluation map $\lambda \to h_\lambda$ takes Δ onto $\mathcal{M}(A)$; thus $\Delta = \mathcal{M}(A)$ (as topological spaces).

We can use the maximum principle for analytic functions to determine the Šilov boundary $\Gamma(A)$. If $f \in A$, then $|f|$ assumes its maximum over Δ at some point of T, by the maximum modulus principle. So T contains $\Gamma(A)$. On the other hand, if $|\lambda| = 1$, then $|1 + \bar{\lambda}z|^2 = 1 + 2\,\mathrm{Re}\,(\bar{\lambda}z) + |\bar{\lambda}z|^2 \leq 2 + 2\,\mathrm{Re}\,(\bar{\lambda}z) \leq 4$, with equality holding iff $\bar{\lambda}z = 1$. Thus if $f = 1 + \bar{\lambda}z$, $f(\lambda) = 2$, but $|f(\alpha)| < 2$ if $\alpha \in \Delta\backslash\{\lambda\}$; i.e., λ is a peak point for A. Hence T is contained in the Choquet boundary $c(A)$. We conclude that $\Gamma(A) = c(A) = T$.

Therefore, each point in U has more than one representing measure. If $|\alpha| < 1$ and the closed disk of radius r about α is contained in U, then $f(\alpha) = \dfrac{1}{2\pi} \int_{0}^{2\pi} f(\alpha + re^{it})\, dt$, by the mean value property of harmonic functions.

Since T is the Šilov boundary of A, it follows that a sequence $\{f_n\}$ in A is convergent (in the sup norm over Δ) iff the restrictions $\{f_n | T\}$ converge uniformly on T. (Apply the Cauchy criterion, noting that $f_n - f_m$ and $(f_n - f_m) | T$ have the same sup norm.) Let A^1 be the image of A under the restriction map $f \to f | T$ from A to $C(T)$. By definition, A^1 is the algebra of all continuous functions on the unit circle which have continuous extensions to the closed unit disk which are analytic on the open disk. By the observations above, we note that A^1 is the uniform closure on T of the polynomials in z. Since the restriction map is an isometry, each $g \in A^1$ has exactly one extension to a function in the disk algebra A, and since it is an algebra isomorphism, $\mathscr{M}(A^1) = \mathscr{M}(A) = \Delta$ and $\Gamma(A^1) = \Gamma(A) = T$.

Let B be the closed subalgebra of $C(T)$ generated by 1, z, and $\bar{z} = 1/z$. Then B contains the constants and has a subalgebra which is self-adjoint and separates points. So $B = C(T)$, by the Stone-Weierstrass theorem. Observe that since $\bar{z} = z^{-1}$ on T, $z^k \bar{z}^m = z^{k-m}$; thus B is actually the closed linear span of the powers z^n ($n = 0, \pm 1, \pm 2, \ldots$).

Given a complex measure μ in $M(T)$ and an integer $n \in \mathbf{Z}$, we set $\hat{\mu}(n) = \int_T \bar{z}^n \, d\mu(z)$; we call $\{\hat{\mu}(n)\}$ the sequence (two-sided) of *Fourier coefficients* of the measure μ. We have immediately the uniqueness result for Fourier coefficients: if $\mu \in M(T)$ and $\hat{\mu}(n) = 0$ for all $n \in \mathbf{Z}$, then $\mu = 0$. (Equivalently, if $\hat{\mu}(n) = \hat{\nu}(n)$ for all n, then the measures μ and ν coincide.) This follows of course from the Riesz representation theorem and the observation above.

It follows that any *real* Borel measure on T which annihilates A^1 must be zero. For if μ is real and if $\int f \, d\mu = 0$ for all $f \in A^1$, then $\int z^n \, d\mu = 0$ for all $n \geq 0$ and $\int \bar{z}^n \, d\mu = 0$ also (take conjugates), whence all Fourier coefficients of μ vanish. We should note that what is going on here is that the functions of form $f + \bar{g}$ (f, g in A^1) are dense in $C(T)$. Any real annihilator of A^1 annihilates all such functions, and hence is zero.

Now T is the Šilov boundary of A and Δ is the maximal ideal space of A. So each point $\alpha \in \Delta$ has a representing measure m_α which is concentrated on T. This representing measure (remember that $m_\alpha \geq 0$) is unique. (If $\int f \, dm_\alpha = f(\alpha) = \int f \, d\sigma_\alpha$, where m_α, σ_α are positive measures concentrated on T, then the restriction of $m_\alpha - \sigma_\alpha$ to T is a real annihilator of A^1 and hence is zero. So $m_\alpha = \sigma_\alpha$.) If $|\alpha| = 1$, then the point mass δ_α is clearly the representing measure for the homomorphism $f \to f(\alpha)$. What if $|\alpha| < 1$?

Let $\alpha = re^{i\theta}$, $0 \leq r < 1$. Let m_α be the representing measure for α which is concentrated on T, and let λ_α be the restriction of m_α to T. We may think of λ_α as a measure on $[0, 2\pi]$. Since $z \in A^1$ (where $z(\lambda) = \lambda$, $\lambda \in T$) and λ_α is multiplicative on A^1, $\int z^n \, d\lambda_\alpha = (\int z \, d\lambda_\alpha)^n = \hat{z}(\alpha)^n$; i.e., $\int_0^{2\pi} e^{int} \, d\lambda_\alpha(t) = r^n e^{in\theta}$

($n = 1, 2, 3, \ldots$). Since λ_α is a real measure, $\int_0^{2\pi} e^{-int} \, d\lambda_\alpha(t) = \overline{(r^n e^{in\theta})} = r^n e^{-in\theta}$ ($n = 1, 2, 3, \ldots$). Also, $\int_0^{2\pi} d\lambda_\alpha(t) = 1$. Thus, all the Fourier coefficients of the measure λ_α are determined, and we should be able to write down λ_α explicitly.

In fact, define F_α on T by $F_\alpha(e^{it}) = \dfrac{1}{2\pi} \sum_{-\infty}^{\infty} r^{|n|} e^{int} e^{-in\theta}$ (where the term for $n = 0$ is 1, even if $r = 0$). Since $0 \le r < 1$, the series converges absolutely and uniformly on T, and hence $F_\alpha \in C(T)$. Also,

$$\int_0^{2\pi} F_\alpha(e^{it}) e^{-imt}\, dt = \sum_{n\in\mathbf{Z}} \frac{1}{2\pi} \int_0^{2\pi} r^{|n|} e^{int} e^{-imt} e^{-in\theta}\, dt = r^{|m|} e^{-im\theta},$$

since $\displaystyle\int_0^{2\pi} e^{ikt}\, dt = 0$ if $k \in \mathbf{Z}$, $k \ne 0$. (By uniform convergence, we can interchange summation and integration.)

Thus the measures $d\lambda_\alpha(t)$ and $F_\alpha(e^{it})\, dt$ have exactly the same Fourier coefficients. So they coincide. In particular, $F_0(e^{it}) = \dfrac{1}{2\pi}$ and so $d\lambda_0(t) = \dfrac{1}{2\pi}\, dt$. Thus all λ_α ($|\alpha| < 1$) are absolutely continuous with respect to λ_0. The fact that λ_0 represents the origin is a mean value property: $f(0) = \dfrac{1}{2\pi}\displaystyle\int_0^{2\pi} f(e^{it})\, dt$ for $f \in A$.

A little juggling with geometric series gives

$$2\pi F_\alpha(e^{it}) = (1 - re^{i(t-\theta)})^{-1} - 1 + (1 - re^{-i(t-\theta)})^{-1} = \frac{1 - r^2}{1 + r^2 - 2r\cos(\theta - t)}.$$

The *Poisson kernels* P_r are defined by $P_r(t) = (1 - r^2)/[1 - 2r\cos t + r^2]$ ($0 \le r < 1$, $0 \le t \le 2\pi$). So if $\alpha = re^{i\theta}$, then $d\lambda_\alpha(t) = \dfrac{1}{2\pi} P_r(\theta - t)\, dt$. The fact that λ_α represents α becomes the **Poisson Integral Formula**:

$$f(re^{i\theta}) = \frac{1}{2\pi} \int_0^{2\pi} f(e^{it}) P_r(\theta - t)\, dt \qquad (f \in A, 0 \le r < 1).$$

We have thus determined the representing measures for all $\alpha \in \Delta = \mathscr{M}(A)$ which are concentrated on $T = \Gamma(A)$. We should observe that in fact the closed support of each of these measures is the entire circle, except in the case of the point masses. (The denominator in $P_r(t)$ lies between $1 + r^2 - 2r$ and $1 + r^2 + 2r$, so $\dfrac{1-r}{1+r} \le P_r(t) \le \dfrac{1+r}{1-r}$. Thus the only open set of λ_α-measure zero is the empty set.)

If we allow representing measures with arbitrary support in Δ, the situation is very different. For example, the origin is represented by normalized arc length over each circle of radius r:

$$f(0) = \frac{1}{2\pi} \int_0^{2\pi} f(re^{it})\, dt \qquad (0 < r \le 1)$$

for $f \in A$. So there is an infinite family of representing measures for $f \to f(0)$ whose closed supports are pairwise disjoint. (For further information about the representing measures for the disk algebra, consult the article by J. Ryff in the symposium volume *Function Algebras* [A].)

We seem to have discussed each of the ideas of §4.1 for the disk algebra, except for its algebra automorphisms.

Suppose that T is an algebra isomorphism from A onto A. Set $\psi = T(z)$. Then for each polynomial $p = \sum_{n=0}^{N} a_n z^n$, $T(p) = p(T(z)) = p \circ \psi$. We know that T preserves spectra, so $\sigma_A(\psi) = \sigma_A(z)$; i.e., $\psi(\Delta) = \Delta$. Given $f \in A$, there are polynomials p_n which converge to f uniformly on $\Delta = \psi(\Delta)$, so $p_n \circ \psi \to f \circ \psi$ uniformly on Δ. Since T is continuous, $T(f) = f \circ \psi$ for all $f \in A$. Since $T(A) = A$, $z = T(f_0) = f_0 \circ \psi$ for some $f_0 \in A$. So ψ is one-one on Δ.

Now $\psi \mid U$ is a nonconstant analytic function, hence an open map from U into $\mathbf{C}$. Therefore $\psi(U)$ is an open set contained in Δ, so $\psi(U) \subset \text{int } \Delta = U$. The same is true for ψ^{-1}, so $\psi(U) = U$ and $\psi(T) = T$. Hence (see Exercise 3) there exist $\lambda \in T$, $\alpha \in U$ with $\psi = \lambda \left(\dfrac{z - \alpha}{1 - \bar{\alpha} z} \right)$.

Thus every algebra automorphism T of the disk algebra has the form $T(f)(w) = f \left(\lambda \dfrac{w - \alpha}{1 - \bar{\alpha} w} \right)$ where $|\lambda| = 1$, $|\alpha| < 1$. Conversely, each such mapping is an automorphism of A.

We can now easily determine the linear isometries from A onto A. (See Exercise 6, §4.1.) Each such isometry has the form $T_1(f) = T(f)\varphi = (f \circ \psi)\varphi$, where ψ has the form above and φ is an invertible element of A such that $|\varphi| = 1$ everywhere on Δ. Of course, such a function φ must be a constant c of modulus one, and $T_1(f) = c(f \circ \psi)$.

For later work we shall need to prove a variant of Schwarz's lemma for the disk algebra. Recall that this asserts that if $f \in A$, $f(0) = 0$, and $\|f\| \leq 1$, then $|f(\alpha)| \leq |\alpha|$ for all $\alpha \in \Delta$, and that equality holds at some α, $0 < |\alpha| < 1$, iff $f = cz$ for some $c \in \Delta$. (Given $\alpha_0 \in U$, choose r so that $|\alpha_0| < r < 1$ and apply the maximum principle to the analytic function g on U such that $f = zg$. We get $|g(\alpha_0)| \leq 1/r$, and letting $r \to 1$, $|g(\alpha_0)| \leq 1$; thus $|f(\alpha_0)| \leq |\alpha_0|$. If $|f(\alpha)| = |\alpha|$ for some α ($0 < |\alpha| < 1$), then $|g(\alpha)| = 1$, so g is constant.) If we compose with suitable Möbius transformations, we obtain the following result.

Lemma 1   (Schwarz-Pick).   *If $f \in A$ (the disk algebra) and $\|f\| \leq 1$, then*

$$\left| \frac{f(\alpha) - f(\beta)}{1 - \overline{f(\beta)}f(\alpha)} \right| \leq \left| \frac{\alpha - \beta}{1 - \bar{\beta}\alpha} \right| \qquad (|\alpha| \leq 1, |\beta| < 1).$$

Proof.   Fix $\beta \in U$. If $|f(\beta)| = 1$, then f is constant, by the maximum principle, so the assertion surely holds. (More properly, $|f(\alpha) - f(\beta)| \leq \left| \dfrac{\alpha - \beta}{1 - \bar{\beta}\alpha} \right| |1 - \overline{f(\beta)}f(\alpha)|$ in this case.) Otherwise, $|f(\beta)| < 1$, and then L and

M are Möbius transformations carrying Δ onto Δ, where $L = \dfrac{z + \beta}{1 + \bar{\beta}z}$ and

$M = \dfrac{z - f(\beta)}{1 - \overline{f(\beta)}z}$. Hence if $g = M \circ f \circ L$, then $g \in A$, $\|g\| \leq 1$, and $g(0) = 0$.

So by Schwarz's lemma, $|g(w)| \leq |w|$ for all $w \in \Delta$; that is, $\left| M\left(f\left(\dfrac{w + \beta}{1 + \bar{\beta}w} \right) \right) \right| \leq$

$|w|$, or $|M(f(\alpha))| \leq \left| \dfrac{\alpha - \beta}{1 - \bar{\beta}\alpha} \right|$ ($\alpha \in \Delta$). Hence the result is established.

Given α, β in Δ, the *pseudo-hyperbolic distance* between α and β is defined to be the number $\psi(\alpha, \beta) = \sup \{|f(\alpha)| : f \in A, \|f\| \leq 1, \text{ and } f(\beta) = 0\}$. If we let A_β be the maximal ideal of A which consists of all functions $f \in A$ which vanish at β, then $\psi(\alpha, \beta)$ is the norm of the linear functional $f \to f(\alpha)$ on the Banach space A_β. Observe that if $|\beta| < 1$ and $f \in A_\beta$, $\|f\| \leq 1$, the lemma tells us that $|f(\alpha)| \leq |(\alpha - \beta)/(1 - \bar{\beta}\alpha)|$ for every $\alpha \in \Delta$. Note that if $|\alpha| = 1$, then the right-hand side is 1, while if $|\alpha| < 1$, then it is strictly less than 1. (In the notation of the proof, L^{-1} carries U onto U, T onto T.) On the other hand, $(z - \beta)/(1 - \bar{\beta}z)$ is in A_β if $|\beta| < 1$ (it is constant if $|\beta| = 1$), and its modulus at α is precisely the right-hand side. Thus, geometrically, the lemma asserts that if $|\beta| < 1$ and $|\alpha| \leq 1$, then $\psi(\alpha, \beta) = |(\alpha - \beta)/(1 - \bar{\beta}\alpha)|$; $\psi(\alpha, \beta) < 1$ if $|\alpha| < 1$, $|\beta| < 1$; while $\psi(\alpha, \beta) = 1$ if $|\alpha| = 1$, $|\beta| < 1$. Note that if $|\alpha| < 1$ and $|\beta| < 1$, then $\psi(\alpha, \beta) = \psi(\beta, \alpha)$, since $|(\beta - \alpha)/(1 - \bar{\alpha}\beta)| = |(\alpha - \beta)/(1 - \bar{\beta}\alpha)|$. Similarly, if $|\alpha| < 1$ and $|\beta| = 1$, then $\psi(\alpha, \beta) = \psi(\beta, \alpha) = 1$, but this is not as obvious.

Let $|\alpha| < 1$, $|\beta| = 1$. Then $\psi(\beta, \alpha) = 1$ (reverse the roles of α, β above), while $\psi(\alpha, \beta) = \sup \{|f(\alpha)| : f \in A_\beta, \|f\| \leq 1\}$. We have to find $f_n \in A_\beta$ such that $\|f_n\| \leq 1$ while $|f_n(\alpha)| \to 1$. First note that if $|\alpha| < 1$, $|\beta| = 1$, and $|\gamma| < 1$, then there is a fractional linear mapping L such that $L(\alpha) = \gamma$, $L(\beta) = 1$, and $L(\Delta) = \Delta$. (Given three distinct points z_1, z_2, z_3 in $\mathbf{C} \cup \{\infty\}$ and three distinct values w_1, w_2, w_3, there is a fractional map M such that $M(z_k) = w_k$, $k = 1, 2, 3$. Hence there is a fractional map L which carries α to γ, β to 1, and $1/\bar{\alpha}$ to $1/\bar{\gamma}$. Since L takes a point on T to a point on T and sends a pair of points symmetric with respect to T into another pair of symmetric points—and a point inside to a point inside—L takes the closed disk Δ onto itself.) Hence for each $n = 1, 2, \ldots$, there is some $L_n \in A$ with $\|L_n\| = 1$, indeed L_n a Möbius transformation (cf. §4.5), such that $L_n(\beta) = 1$ and $L_n(\alpha) = -1 + 1/2n$. If $f_n = \frac{1}{2}(1 - L_n)$, then $f_n \in A_\beta$, $\|f_n\| \leq 1$, while $f_n(\alpha) = 1 - 1/4n \to 1$. So indeed $\psi(\alpha, \beta) = \psi(\beta, \alpha) = 1$.

Finally, by a suitable choice of Möbius transformation, one can show that if $|\alpha| = |\beta| = 1$ and $\alpha \neq \beta$, then $\psi(\alpha, \beta) = \psi(\beta, \alpha) = 1$.

Let α, β be points of the disk Δ. Then $\rho(\alpha, \beta) = \tanh^{-1}(\psi(\alpha, \beta))$ is often called the hyperbolic distance between α and β. ($\tanh^{-1}(y) = \log \sqrt{\dfrac{1 + y}{1 - y}}$;

$\tanh^{-1}$ carries $[0, 1]$ monotonically and continuously onto $[0, \infty]$.) We have shown that:

(a) $\psi(\alpha, \beta) = \psi(\beta, \alpha)$;

(b) $\psi(\alpha, \beta) < 1$ if $|\alpha| < 1$ and $|\beta| < 1$;
$\psi(\alpha, \beta) = 1$ if $|\alpha| = 1$, $|\beta| < 1$ or $|\alpha| < 1$, $|\beta| = 1$;
$\psi(\alpha, \beta) = 1$ if $|\alpha| = |\beta| = 1$ and $\alpha \neq \beta$.

It is also clear that

(c) $0 \leq \psi(\alpha, \beta)$, with equality iff $\alpha = \beta$.

(If $\alpha \neq \beta$, then the maximal ideals A_α, A_β are distinct; thus $f(\alpha) \neq 0$ for some $f \in A_\beta$.) In terms of hyperbolic distance, any two points in the open disk are a finite distance apart, while any point on the unit circle is an infinite distance away from all other points of the disk.

From the expression $\psi(\alpha, \beta) = |(\alpha - \beta)/(1 - \bar{\beta}\alpha)|$, which is true in all cases, we see that the Schwarz-Pick lemma asserts that each f in the closed unit ball of A contracts hyperbolic distances ($\rho(f(\alpha), f(\beta)) \leq \rho(\alpha, \beta)$). (Tracing back the proof of the lemma, we see that if equality holds for some distinct α, β in U, then f is a fractional linear map.)

In the discussion of Gleason parts for function algebras (see §4.5), we will make use of the techniques of this section to introduce a pseudo-hyperbolic metric in the maximal ideal space of any function algebra.

EXERCISE SET   4.2

1. Let B be a linear subspace of $C(X)$, where X is compact. Prove that the following conditions are equivalent.

(a) Any real measure in $M(X)$ which annihilates B is zero.
(b) If μ, ν are real measures in $M(X)$ and $\int f \, d\mu = \int f \, d\nu$ for all $f \in B$, then
$\mu = \nu$.
(c) $\text{Re}(B) = \{\text{Re}(f) : f \in B\}$ is dense in $C_R(X)$.
(d) $B + \bar{B} = \{f + \bar{g} : f \in B, g \in B\}$ is dense in $C(X)$.

Note also that if B satisfies these conditions, then B separates points on X.

2. Let $M = \dfrac{z - \alpha}{1 - \bar{\alpha}z}$, where $|\alpha| < 1$. Show that M is analytic on a *nbhd* of the closed unit disk, and hence the partial sums of the Taylor series of M converge to M uniformly on Δ. Prove that if A is a function algebra, $f \in A$, and $\|f\| \leq 1$, then $M \circ f \in A$.

3. Show that if $|\alpha_k| < 1$ $(k = 1, \ldots, n)$ and $|c| = 1$, then the function $L = c \prod_{k=1}^{n} \left(\dfrac{z - \alpha_k}{1 - \bar{\alpha}_k z}\right)$ belongs to the disk algebra A, takes U onto U, and takes T onto T.

Show that if $f \in A$ and f has a zero of order n at $\alpha \in U$, then $f = gL$ where $L = \left(\dfrac{z - \alpha}{1 - \bar{\alpha}z}\right)^n$, $g \in A$, and $g(\alpha) \neq 0$.

Now suppose that $f \in A$ and $|f| = 1$ everywhere on T. Show that $\exists c \in T$ and $\alpha_1, \ldots, \alpha_n$ in U $(n \geq 0)$ such that $f = c \displaystyle\prod_{k=1}^{n} \left(\dfrac{z - \alpha_k}{1 - \bar{\alpha}_k z}\right)$. (If $n = 0$, there are no factors, and $f = c$.)

4. Prove that the disk algebra is antisymmetric (on Δ).

5. Let f be analytic on the open unit disk U, and suppose that $f(U) \subset U$. Show that $|f'(z)| \leq \dfrac{1 - |f(z)|^2}{1 - |z|^2}$ $(z \in U)$.

4.3 THE BOUNDARY VALUE ALGEBRA

Let us continue to use the notation of §4.2. We call A^1 the *boundary value algebra*. We have seen that A^1 is the closure in $C(T)$ of the polynomials in z (really $z | T$). For many purposes it is important to have a characterization of A^1 in terms of Fourier coefficients.

Let us write dw for normalized Lebesgue measure on T. Thus $\int g \, dw = \dfrac{1}{2\pi} \displaystyle\int_0^{2\pi} g(e^{it}) \, dt$ $(g \in C(T))$. Observe that if $\lambda \in T$ and $g_\lambda(\alpha) = g(\lambda\alpha)$, then $\int g_\lambda \, dw = \int g \, dw$ (i.e., dw is translation-invariant). Given $g \in C(T)$ and $n \in \mathbf{Z}$, the nth Fourier coefficient of g is

$$\hat{g}(n) = \int \bar{z}^n g \, dw.$$

Given $g \in C(T)$ and a complex measure $\mu \in M(T)$, the *convolution* of g and μ is the function $f = g * \mu$ given by

$$f(\lambda) = \int_T g(\lambda\bar{\alpha}) \, d\mu(\alpha).$$

Clearly $g * \mu$ is continuous on T, and it follows easily from the Fubini theorem that $\hat{f}(n) = \hat{g}(n)\hat{\mu}(n)$, for every $n \in \mathbf{Z}$.

Let B consist of all continuous functions g on T such that $\hat{g}(n) = 0$ for all $n < 0$. Now $g \to \hat{g}(n)$ is a continuous linear functional on $C(T)$ $(|\hat{g}(n)| \leq \|g\|)$, so B is a closed linear subspace of $C(T)$. One computes directly that $z^k \in B$, for all $k \geq 0$ in $\mathbf{Z}$. So B contains all polynomials, and therefore B contains A^1. We shall show that $B = A^1$. By the Hahn-Banach theorem, it will suffice to show that every annihilator of A^1 is an annihilator of B.

So let ν annihilate A^1, and set $d\mu(\lambda) = d\nu(\bar{\lambda})$. (If $\tau : T \to T$ is the operation of complex conjugation, $\lambda \to \bar{\lambda}$, then $f \to \int (f \circ \tau) \, d\nu$ is a bounded linear functional on $C(T)$. Hence there is a measure $\mu \in M(T)$ such that $\int f \, d\mu = \int (f \circ \tau) \, d\nu$, for all $f \in C(T)$.) Then for each $n \geq 0$, $\hat{\mu}(n) = \int \bar{z}^n \, d\mu = \int z^n \, d\nu = 0$, since $z^n \in A^1$. On the other hand, if $g \in B$ then $\hat{g}(n) = 0$ for all $n < 0$. So the convolution $g * \mu$ has all Fourier coefficients $\hat{g}(n)\hat{\mu}(n)$ zero, and hence $g * \mu = 0$. In particular, $(g * \mu)(1) = \int g \, dv = 0$. So $v \in B^\perp$, as was to be shown.

We have proved that $f \in A^1$ iff $f \in C(T)$ and $\hat{f}(n) = 0$ for all $n < 0$.

Theorem 10   (Wermer's Maximality Theorem).   *Suppose that B^1 is a closed subalgebra of $C(T)$ which contains A^1. Then $B^1 = A^1$ or $B^1 = C(T)$.*

Proof.   If $\bar{z} \in B^1$, then B^1 contains $1, z, \bar{z}$, so $B^1 = C(T)$. If $\bar{z} \notin B^1$, then z is a noninvertible element of B^1; thus z is annihilated by some complex homomorphism h of B^1. Hence $h(z^n) = h(z)^n = 0$, for $n = 1, 2, 3, \dots$.

Let m be a representing measure for h. We have $\int z^n \, dm = h(z^n) = 0$ for all $n > 0$, and since m is real, $\int \bar{z}^n \, dm = 0$ for all $n > 0$. So $\hat{m}(n) = 0$ for all $n \neq 0$. But normalized Lebesgue measure dw also has its Fourier coefficients zero for all $n \neq 0$. Since also $\int 1 \, dw = 1 = \int 1 \, dm \, (1 \in B^1)$, $dm = dw$ by the uniqueness of Fourier coefficients. It is now clear that $B^1 \subset A^1$. Indeed, if $g \in B^1$, then $\hat{g}(-n) = \int z^n g \, dw = h(z^n g) = h(z^n)h(g) = 0$ for all $n > 0$, so $g \in A^1$. Thus $A^1 = B^1$, as asserted.

The maximality of A^1 in $C(T)$ has some interesting consequences. The theorem itself is a result in approximation theory, since it asserts that if g is continuous on the unit circle but does not extend to a function in the disk algebra, then every continuous function on T can be uniformly approximated by polynomials in z and g. Consider the set $K = \{(\alpha, g(\alpha)) : \alpha \in T\}$ (the graph of g) and the map $\psi : T \to \mathbf{C}^2$, where $\psi(\alpha) = (\alpha, g(\alpha))$. ψ is a homeomorphism from T onto K, so K is a simple closed curve in $\mathbf{C}^2$. If $F \in C(K)$, then $F \circ \psi \in C(T)$. So for each $\varepsilon > 0$, there is a polynomial P in two variables with $|P(\alpha, g(\alpha)) - F(\psi(\alpha))| < \varepsilon$ (all $\alpha \in T$); i.e., $|P(z_1, z_2) - F(z_1, z_2)| < \varepsilon$ for every pair $(z_1, z_2) \in K$. Therefore on the curve K, every continuous function is a uniform limit of polynomials in the coordinate variables. (For example, on $\{(\alpha, 1/\alpha) : |\alpha| = 1\}$, every continuous function is uniformly approximable by polynomials in two variables.)

Maximality of A^1 also shows that there are many continuous functions which are "boundary values" of analytic functions, in fact, a dense family of them. Specifically, let B consist of all $g \in C(T)$ for which there exists an analytic function G on the open unit disk such that for almost all θ in $[0, 2\pi)$, $G(z) \to g(e^{i\theta})$ as $z \to e^{i\theta}$ nontangentially. (Nontangential limits are defined more or less as follows. For $0 < \alpha < \pi/2$, let $\tilde{S}_\alpha$ be the sector $\{z \in \mathbf{C} : z \neq 0$ and $z = |z|e^{it}$ where $\pi - \alpha < t < \pi + \alpha\}$, and let $S_\alpha = \{z : |z| < 1$ and $(z - 1) \in \tilde{S}_\alpha\}$; this is sometimes called a Stolz angle at $z = 1$. Given a function G on the open unit disk and a complex number β, $G(z) \to \beta$ as $z \to 1$ nontangentially iff for every α in $(0, \pi/2)$, $G(z)$ approaches β as z approaches 1 along any path lying in S_α. G approaches λ as $z \to e^{i\theta}$ nontangentially means that $G(e^{i\theta}z) \to \lambda$ as $z \to 1$ nontangentially.) The existence of nontangential limits is a strong condition, and one might expect that B is fairly small.

However, it is clear that B is a subalgebra of $C(T)$, and that B contains the boundary value algebra A^1. We shall show that the inclusion is proper. Let $g(1) = 0$ and $g(e^{i\theta}) = (1 - e^{i\theta}) \exp\left(i \cot \dfrac{\theta}{2}\right)$ $(0 < \theta < 2\pi)$. Then $g \in C(T)$, since the exponential factor is bounded. If $G(z) = (1 - z) \exp\left(\dfrac{1 + z}{1 - z}\right)$, then G is analytic on the plane with $z = 1$ deleted, and it is clear that $G(z) \to g(e^{i\theta})$ as $z \to e^{i\theta}$ $(0 < \theta < 2\pi)$, nontangentially or not. So $g \in B$.

It turns out that $g \notin A^1$. Suppose otherwise, and let f be a function in the disk algebra which extends g. Let φ be the restriction of G to the open unit disk. Then $\varphi(z) = (1 - z)e^{M(z)}$ $(|z| < 1)$, where $M(z) = \dfrac{1 + z}{1 - z}$ $(|z| \le 1)$. M takes the unit circle onto the imaginary axis $(M(1) = \infty)$ and the open unit disk onto the open right halfplane; hence $|e^{-M(z)}| < 1$ if $|z| < 1$. Thus $\varphi(z) = \dfrac{1 - z}{e^{-M(z)}}$ is a quotient of two bounded analytic functions, neither of which vanishes at any point in U. By our assumption, $\varphi - f = \dfrac{1 - z - fe^{-M}}{e^{-M}}$ has nontangential limit 0 at all $e^{i\theta} \ne 1$. Since $|e^{-M(z)}| = 1$ if $|z| = 1$, $z \ne 1$, we will have a contradiction once we show that a bounded analytic function ψ on U cannot have nontangential limit 0 at all $e^{i\theta} \ne 1$ unless it vanishes identically. (For then it will follow that $\varphi = f$ on the open disk, which is impossible. Indeed, $\varphi(r) \to \infty$ as r increases to 1.)

Fix $\lambda \in U$. If $r > s > |\lambda|$, then by the Cauchy integral formula,

$$\psi(\lambda) = \frac{1}{2\pi i} \int_{|z| = r} \frac{\psi(z)}{z - \lambda} \, dz, \quad \text{or}$$

$$\psi(\lambda) = \frac{1}{2\pi} \int_0^{2\pi} \frac{\psi(re^{i\theta})re^{i\theta}}{re^{i\theta} - \lambda} \, d\theta.$$

If $|\psi| \le c$, then the integrands are bounded by $cr/(r - |\lambda|) \le c/(s - |\lambda|)$. Letting $r \to 1$, and using the dominated convergence theorem, we see that $\psi(\lambda) = 0$. Thus if the radial limit of ψ vanishes at all $e^{i\theta} \ne 1$ (or merely for almost all θ), then $\psi = 0$. (Actually, more is true: if there is a set $E \subset [0, 2\pi]$ of positive Lebesgue measure such that $\psi(re^{i\theta}) \to 0$ for all $\theta \in E$, then $\psi = 0$. This will follow from the Poisson-Jensen inequality for bounded analytic functions, which we shall prove in a later chapter.)

From the contradiction, we deduce that $g \in B$ but $g \notin A^1$. Since A^1 is a maximal subalgebra, B is dense in $C(T)$.

As another application of the Wermer maximality theorem, we prove the following: if F is a proper compact subset of T, then every $g \in C(F)$ can be uniformly approximated on F by polynomials. In particular, then, the restriction of the boundary value algebra to F is uniformly dense in $C(F)$.

Let B be the set of all $f \in C(T)$ whose restriction to F is in the closure of the polynomials in $C(F)$. Since $f \to f \mid F$ is a continuous homomorphism from $C(T)$ onto $C(F)$, B is a closed subalgebra of $C(T)$ and B contains A^1. But there exist functions $f \in C(T)$ with $f \mid F = 0$ but $f \notin A^1$; any such function f belongs to B, so by the maximality theorem, $B = C(T)$. (Since F is a proper closed subset of the circle, there is an open arc E disjoint from F. Take $f \in C(T)$ with $f = 0$ on $T \backslash E$ but $f \neq 0$. Since f vanishes on an arc without being identically zero, $f \notin A^1$.)

EXERCISE SET   4.3

1. Prove that if f is in the disk algebra and there is an arc on the unit circle on which f vanishes identically, then $f = 0$. (*Hint:* Rotate.)

2. Prove that the boundary value algebra A^1 is antisymmetric on T.

4.4   THE ESSENTIAL SET

Let A be a function algebra on a compact space X. Then there is a largest closed ideal of $C(X)$ which is contained in A. In fact, let $\{I_\alpha\}$ be the family of all ideals of $C(X)$ which are contained in A. ($\{0\}$ is such an ideal.) Let I be the closure of $\sum I_\alpha$, the set of all finite sums $f_1 + \cdots + f_k$ with $f_i \in I_{\alpha_i}$ for each i. Then I is the largest ideal of $C(X)$ contained in A, and I is closed.

Let $E = \{x \in X : f(x) = 0$ for every f in $I\}$. E is the zero set of the ideal I. Observe that I is exactly the set of continuous functions which vanish on E. For suppose that $g \in C(X)$ and that g vanishes on E, and let v be any extreme point of the unit ball of $I^\perp$. The support of v is a set of antisymmetry for $C(X)$ (Exercise 1, §3.3). Hence either $v = 0$ and $I = C(X)$, so $g \in I$ trivially, or supp v is a point and $v = a\delta_x$, where $|a| = 1$ and $x \in X$. Since $v \in I^\perp$, $f(x) = 0$ for all $f \in I$, so $x \in E$. Since g vanishes on E, $\int g \, dv = ag(x) = 0$. Hence g is annihilated by $b(I^\perp)^e$, so $g \in I$. (The same argument shows that every closed ideal of $C(X)$ is determined by its zero set.)

E is called the *essential set* of A. We note some obvious properties of the essential set.

(1) If $f \in C(X)$ and f vanishes on E, then $f \in A$.
(2) If $f \in C(X)$ and $f \mid E \in A \mid_E$, then $f \in A$.
(3) If S is a compact set disjoint from E, then $A \mid_S = C(S)$.
(4) If F is a closed set such that $f \mid F = 0$ implies that $f \in A$, then F contains E. (That is, E is the smallest closed set with property (1).)

(1) is just the assertion that A contains I. If $f \in C(X)$ and $f \mid E = g \mid E$ for some $g \in A$, then $f - g$ is in A, by (1), so $f = g + (f - g)$ belongs to A. Thus (2) is proved. Condition (3) follows easily from the Tietze extension theorem, since each $h \in C(S)$ has an extension to a continuous function f

on X which vanishes on E and hence belongs to A. Finally, if A contains the ideal J of all $f \in C(X)$ vanishing on F, then $J \subset I$; thus $E \subset F$, which proves (4). Observe that E is empty iff $A = C(X)$.

Theorem 11. *Let E be the essential set of a function algebra A. Then*

(a) *if K is a set of antisymmetry for A which is not a point, then $K \subset E$;*

(b) *if m is a representing measure for A which is not a point mass, then m is concentrated on E;*

(c) *if v is an extreme point of $b(A^{\perp})$, then v is concentrated on E.*

Proof. Let K be a set of antisymmetry for A, and assume that $x_0 \in K \backslash E$. Suppose that $x_1 \in K$ and that $x_1 \neq x_0$. Then $\exists\, u \in C(X)$ with $u(x_0) = 0$, $u(x_1) = 1$, $u(E) = \{1\}$, and $u(X) \subset [0, 1]$. Since u is constant on E, $u \in A$, and since u is real-valued on K, u is constant on K, a contradiction. Hence $K = \{x_0\}$.

Let $h \in \mathcal{M}(A)$, and let m be a representing measure for h. Then supp m is a set of antisymmetry for A, so either supp $m \subset E$ or m is a point mass δ_x with $x \notin E$. Similarly, if $v \in b(A^{\perp})^e$, then supp v is a set of antisymmetry for A. But supp v cannot be a point (since v annihilates 1), so supp $v \subset E$.

Corollary 1. *Let Γ be the Šilov boundary of A, and $c(A)$ the Choquet boundary of A. Then $X \backslash \Gamma \subset X \backslash c(A) \subset E$.*

Proof. Let $x_0 \in X \backslash E$. Then there is a function f in A with $f(x_0) = 1$ but $f \mid E = 0$. Hence if m is a representing measure for x_0, m cannot be concentrated on E. So m must be the point mass at x_0. Thus the only representing measure for x_0 is δ_{x_0}, so $x_0 \in c(A)$. Hence $X \backslash E \subset c(A) \subset \Gamma(A)$.

Corollary 2. *Let P be the union of all one point maximal sets of antisymmetry for A. Then E is the closure of $X \backslash P$.*

Proof. The maximal antisymmetric sets form a disjoint closed cover $\mathcal{K}_A$ of X. So if K is a maximal antisymmetric set which is not a point, then $K \cap P$ is empty. On the other hand, $K \subset E$. So $X \backslash P = \cup \{K \in \mathcal{K}_A : K \text{ is not a point}\} \subset E$. On the other hand, suppose that $f \in C(X)$ and f vanishes on $X \backslash P$. Then every v in $b(A^{\perp})^e$ annihilates f, since supp v is contained in a maximal antisymmetric set which is not a point. Hence $f \in A$. So by the minimality property of E, $E \subset \overline{X \backslash P}$. So E is the closure of $X \backslash P$.

Corollary 3. *E is the closure of $\displaystyle\bigcup_{v \in b(A^{\perp})^e}$ supp v.*

Corollary 4. *If $f \in A$ and f vanishes on E, then $\hat{f}$ vanishes on $\mathcal{M}(A) \backslash X$.*

Proof. If $h \in \mathcal{M}(A) \backslash X$ (we are identifying X with its image $\varphi(X) \subset \mathcal{M}(A)$), then h has a representing measure m which cannot be a point mass. So m is concentrated on E, which means that $\hat{f}(h) = \int_E f\, dm = 0$.

Next we observe that for each closed set F containing E, the restriction of A to F is closed in $C(F)$. That is, if $\{f_n\}$ is a sequence in A and $f_n \to g$ uniformly on F, then g has an extension to an element of A.

Theorem 12. *Let E be the essential set of a function algebra A, and let F be a compact set in X. Then (a) if $E \subset F$, then $A|_F$ is closed in $C(F)$; (b) if A contains the ideal $I_F = \{f \in C(X) : f|F = 0\}$, then $A|_F$ is closed in $C(F)$.*

Proof. (a) and (b) are equivalent, since $E \subset F$ iff $I_F \subset A$.

There is a mapping T from $A|_F$ to the quotient algebra A/I_F given by $f|F \to f + I_F$. (If $f|F = g|F$ for f, g in A, then $(f - g) \in I_F$, so $f + I_F = g + I_F$.) Now I_F is a closed ideal of A, so A/I_F is a Banach algebra under the quotient norm $\|f + I_F\| = \inf_{h \in I_F} \|f + h\|$. Hence if we prove that T is an isometry, it will follow that $A|_F$ is complete and hence closed in $C(F)$.

Lemma 2. *If $I_F \subset A$, then $f|F \to f + I_F$ is an isometry of $A|_F$ onto A/I_F.*

Proof. $\|f + h\| = \max_{x \in X} |f(x) + h(x)| \geq \max_{x \in F} |f(x) + h(x)| = \max_{x \in F} |f(x)| = \|f|F\|$ for each $f \in A$, $h \in I_F$. So T does not decrease norms. On the other hand, given $f \in A$ and $\varepsilon > 0$, $U_\varepsilon = \{x \in X : |f(x)| < \varepsilon + \|f|F\|\}$ is open in X and contains F. By Urysohn's lemma we can find $g \in C(X)$ with $g = 1$ on F, $g = 0$ on $X \backslash U_\varepsilon$, $0 \leq g \leq 1$ on X. So $h = fg - f$ belongs to I_F, while $|f + h| = |fg| < \varepsilon + \|f|F\|$ on U_ε and $f + h$ vanishes off U_ε. Thus $\|f + h\| < \varepsilon + \|f|F\|$. So $\|f + I_F\| \leq \|f|F\|$, and T does not increase norms.

We should note that the restriction of a function algebra A on X to a closed subset F need not be closed in $C(F)$. (For example, let $X = T^1$, $F = $ the closed upper semicircle, A the boundary value algebra A^1. Then $A|_F$ is dense in $C(F)$, as we showed in §4.3. But $A|_F \neq C(F)$, since any nonzero $g \in C(F)$ which vanishes at $e^{i\theta}$ for all $\theta \in [0, \pi/2]$ has no extension to an element of A.) In Chapter VII we'll take a longer look at restriction algebras.

Suppose that F is a closed set such that $I_F \subset A$. Then $A|_F$ is a function algebra on F. We now compute the maximal ideal space of $A|_F$.

Let $r_F : A \to C(F)$ be the map $f \to f|F$, and let $\varphi(q) = q \circ r_F$ for $q \in \mathscr{M}(A|_F)$. Then φ is a one-one map from $\mathscr{M}(A|_F)$ into $\mathscr{M}(A)$. If $h_0 = \varphi(q_0)$, then the inverse image under φ of $\{h \in \mathscr{M}(A) : |h(f) - h_0(f)| < \varepsilon\}$ is $\{q \in \mathscr{M}(A|_F) : |q(f|F) - q_0(f|F)| < \varepsilon\}$; so φ is continuous. If $x \in X \backslash F$, then there is a function $f \in I_F$ with $f(x) = 1$, so $\varphi(q)(f) = q(f|F) = 0$; thus $\varphi(q) \neq \varphi_x$. Hence the image of φ is a subset of $\mathscr{M}(A) \backslash (X \backslash F) = F \cup (\mathscr{M}(A) \backslash X)$. On the other hand, every $h \in F \cup (\mathscr{M}(A) \backslash X)$ has the form $\varphi(q)$ for some $q \in \mathscr{M}(A|_F)$. (If $h = \varphi_x$ with $x \in F$, let $q(f|F) = f(x)$. If $h \in \mathscr{M}(A) \backslash X$, then h has a representing measure m (on X) which cannot be a point mass, so m is concentrated on the essential set of A, and hence on F. Thus $h(f) = h(g)$ if $f|F = g|F$ (f, g in A), so $h = \varphi(q)$ for some $q \in \mathscr{M}(A|_F)$.) Since $\mathscr{M}(A|_F)$ is compact, φ is a homeomorphism from $\mathscr{M}(A|_F)$ onto $F \cup (\mathscr{M}(A) \backslash X)$. (Note that this is the union of a closed set in $\mathscr{M}(A)$ with the open set $\mathscr{M}(A) \backslash X$.)

Theorem 13. *Let A be a function algebra on X.*

(a) *If F is a closed set such that $I_F \subset A$, then $A|_F$ is a function algebra with maximal ideal space $F \cup (\mathcal{M}(A)\backslash X)$.*

(b) *If E is the essential set of A, then $\mathcal{M}(A|_E) = E \cup (\mathcal{M}(A)\backslash X)$. The topological boundary of X in $\mathcal{M}(A)$ is contained in E.*

Proof. To prove the last assertion, note that if U, V are sets in a topological space and if U is open, V is closed, and $U \cup V$ is closed, then $\mathrm{bd}(U) \subset V$. ($\mathrm{bd}(U) \subset \bar{U} \subset \overline{U \cup V} = U \cup V$, while $\mathrm{bd}(U) \cap U = \varnothing$.) Since X and $\mathcal{M}(A)\backslash X$ have the same boundary and $E \cup (\mathcal{M}(A)\backslash X)$ is compact, E contains the boundary of X.

EXERCISE SET 4.4

1. Let E be the essential set of a function algebra A on X. Show that every $\mu \in A^\perp$ is concentrated on E, and hence E is the closure of $\bigcup_{\mu \in A^\perp} \mathrm{supp}\, \mu$.

2. Let $h \in \mathcal{M}(A)$, and suppose that some representing measure for h is not a point mass. Show that every complex measure μ on $M(X)$ such that $\hat{f}(h) = \int f\, d\mu$ for all $f \in A$ must be concentrated on the essential set of A.

3. Show that if E is the essential set of A, then the essential set of $A|_E$ is E.

4. Let $\hat{E}$ be the essential set of $\hat{A}$. Show that $\hat{E} = E \cup (\mathcal{M}(A)\backslash X)$.

4.5 GLEASON PARTS

Let A be a function algebra on a compact space X. If $a \in \mathcal{M}(A)$, let $A_a = \{f \in A : \hat{f}(a) = 0\}$ be the maximal ideal of A determined by a. Given a, b in $\mathcal{M}(A)$, we set $\psi(a, b) = \sup \{|\hat{f}(a)| : f \in A_b, \|f\| \le 1\}$ and $\|a - b\| = \sup \{|\hat{f}(a) - \hat{f}(b)| : f \in A, \|f\| \le 1\}$ (the norm of $a - b$ in A^*).

A *Möbius transformation* is a fractional linear mapping $\dfrac{\alpha z + \beta}{\gamma z + \delta}$ which takes the closed unit disk Δ onto itself. The Möbius transformations have the form $\lambda \dfrac{z - \alpha}{1 - \bar{\alpha} z}$ with $|\lambda| = 1$, $|\alpha| < 1$, and hence are analytic on a neighborhood of Δ. So if L is such a map, then L is a uniform limit on Δ of a sequence of polynomials. Therefore $L \circ f \in A$ for every $f \in A$ with $\|f\| \le 1$, and the Gelfand transform of $L \circ f$ is $L \circ \hat{f}$.

Using Möbius transformations and the function ψ, we can partition $\mathcal{M}(A)$ into subsets called Gleason parts. Points in a given part turn out to be strongly related (in the sense that their representing measures fit together well), while points in different parts are strongly unrelated. For certain kinds of function algebras, the parts turn out to be sets of analyticity for the algebra, in a certain natural sense.

Lemma 3.   *Let $a, b \in \mathcal{M}(A)$. Then $\psi(a, b) < 1$ iff $\|a - b\| < 2$.*

Proof. If $f \in A$, then $f - \hat{f}(b) = g \in A_b$ and $\|g\| \le 2\|f\|$. So $|\hat{f}(a) - \hat{f}(b)| = |\hat{g}(a)| \le \psi(a, b)\|g\| \le 2\psi(a, b)\|f\|$. Hence $\|a - b\| \le 2\psi(a, b)$, and one implication is clear: if $\psi(a, b) < 1$, then $\|a - b\| < 2$.

If $\psi(a, b) = 1$, then there are f_n in A_b with $\|f_n\| \le 1$ and $|\hat{f}_n(a)| \to 1$. Replacing f_n by $e^{i\theta_n} f_n / (1 + 2^{-n})$, we can suppose that $|\hat{f}_n(a)| < 1$ and $\hat{f}_n(a) \to 1$. Now if $|\gamma| < 1$, there is a Möbius transformation L such that $L(0) = \gamma$ and $L(1) = 1$. Hence for each n there is a Möbius transformation L_n with $L_n(1) = 1$, $L_n(0) = -1 + 1/2^n$. Since $\hat{f}_k(a) \to 1$, for each n there is an integer k such that $|L_n(\hat{f}_k(a)) - 1| < 1/2^n$. Let n' be the smallest such integer, and let $g_n = L_n \circ f_{n'}$. Then $g_n \in A$, $\|g_n\| \le 1$, and $|\hat{g}_n(a) - \hat{g}_n(b)| \to 2$. So $\|a - b\| = 2$.

Lemma 4.   *Let $a, b \in \mathcal{M}(A)$. Then $\psi(a, b) < 1$ iff $f_n \in A$, $\|f_n\| \le 1$, and $\hat{f}_n(a) \to 1$ imply that $\hat{f}_n(b) \to 1$.*

Proof. Suppose that $\psi(a, b) = 1$. Then $\exists g_n \in A_b$ with $\|g_n\| \le 1$ and $|\hat{g}_n(a)| \to 1$. We may replace g_n by $e^{i\theta_n} g_n$ and have $\hat{g}_n(a) \to 1$, $\hat{g}_n(b) \to 0$. So the condition is not satisfied.

Conversely, suppose that the condition fails. Then there are f_n in A with $\|f_n\| \le 1$ such that $\hat{f}_n(a) \to 1$ but $\{\hat{f}_n(b)\}$ does not converge to 1. Passing to a subsequence, we may suppose that $\hat{f}_n(b) \to r$ and $r \ne 1$. As in Lemma 3, we may suppose that $|\alpha_n| < 1$, $|\beta_n| < 1$ for all n, where $\alpha_n = \hat{f}_n(a)$, $\beta_n = \hat{f}_n(b)$. The rest of the argument is similar to that in Lemma 3. If $|r| < 1$, choose Möbius transformations L_n with $L_n(1) = 1$, $L_n(r) = -1 + 4^{-n}$, and for each n choose n' with $|L_n(\alpha_{n'}) - 1| < 2^{-n}$, $|L_n(\beta_{n'}) + 1| < 2^{-n}$. Then $g_n = L_n \circ f_{n'}$ belongs to A, $\|g_n\| \le 1$, and $|\hat{g}_n(a) - \hat{g}_n(b)| \to 2$, so $\|a - b\| = 2$, $\psi(a, b) = 1$. If $|r| = 1$, choose a Möbius transformation L such that $L(1) = 1$, $L(r) = -1$. Then $g_n = L \circ f_n \in A$, $\|g_n\| \le 1$, and $|\hat{g}_n(a) - \hat{g}_n(b)| \to |L(1) - L(r)| = 2$, so again $\psi(a, b) = 1$.

Elements a, b of $\mathcal{M}(A)$ are said to be *equivalent* $(a \sim b)$ iff $\psi(a, b) < 1$ (or, equivalently, iff $\|a - b\| < 2$). From Lemma 4 we see that if $a \sim b$ and $b \sim c$, then $a \sim c$. So equivalence in $\mathcal{M}(A)$ is an equivalence relation, since it is clearly reflexive and symmetric. If $a \in \mathcal{M}(A)$, then the *Gleason part* of a is $P_a = \{b \in \mathcal{M}(A): a \sim b\}$.

Theorem 14.   *The Gleason parts for A form a decomposition of $\mathcal{M}(A)$ into pairwise disjoint sets, each of which is σ-compact, i.e., a union of a sequence of compact sets.*

Proof. Since $\sim$ is an equivalence relation, each $a \in \mathcal{M}(A)$ belongs to its part P_a, and distinct parts are disjoint. Since $P_a = \bigcup_n \{b : \|a - b\| \le 2 - 1/2^n\}$, P_a is σ-compact. (By the Alaoglu theorem every closed ball in A^* is w^*-compact.)

We can also see that the parts for A are open and closed in the metric topology of $\mathcal{M}(A)$ given by $\rho(a, b) = \|a - b\|$. Indeed, $P_a = \{b: \|a - b\| < 2\}$, so P_a is an open ball in $\mathcal{M}(A)$. Conversely, if $b \notin P_a$ and $\rho(b, c) < 2$, then $\rho(a, c) = 2$; so $c \notin P_a$, and the complement of P_a is also open in the metric topology.

In §4.2 we showed that every point of the unit circle is a part for the disk algebra $A(\Delta)$, while the open disk is also a part. We can use the Schwarz-Pick lemma to show that the evaluation map $\alpha \to \varphi_\alpha$ is a homeomorphism of the open disk U onto the corresponding part P, if P is given the metric topology. (It is of course a homeomorphism if P is given the Gelfand topology.) In fact, $|\alpha - \beta| = |\varphi_\alpha(z) - \varphi_\beta(z)| \le \|\varphi_\alpha - \varphi_\beta\|$, while if $f \in A(\Delta)$ and $\|f\| \le 1$, then

$$|f(\alpha) - f(\beta)| \le |1 - \overline{f(\beta)}f(\alpha)| \left|\frac{\alpha - \beta}{1 - \bar{\beta}\alpha}\right| \le 2\left|\frac{\alpha - \beta}{1 - \bar{\beta}\alpha}\right|,$$

so $\|\varphi_\alpha - \varphi_\beta\| \le 2\left|\dfrac{\alpha - \beta}{1 - \bar{\beta}\alpha}\right|$. Hence the part metric is equivalent to the usual metric on U. If $\alpha \in U$ and $|\beta| = 1$, then $\rho(\varphi_\alpha, \varphi_\beta) = 2$, so the part metric is not equivalent to the Euclidean metric on the closed disk.

If $A = C(X)$, then the Gleason parts in $\mathcal{M}(A) = X$ are one-point sets. For let x_1, x_2 be distinct points of X. Then $\exists f \in C(X)$ with $0 \le f \le 1, f(x_1) = 0$, $f(x_2) = 1$. Put $g = 2f - 1$. Then $-1 \le g \le 1$, $g(x_1) = -1$, $g(x_2) = 1$. Since $\|g\| = 1$ and $|g(x_1) - g(x_2)| = 2$, x_1 is not equivalent to x_2.

Let A be a function algebra on X. Set $B = \mathrm{Re}\,(A)$, the space of real parts of functions in A. B is a linear subspace of $C_R(X)$ and $1 \in B$. Given $a \in \mathcal{M}(A)$, define L_a on B by $L_a(u) = \mathrm{Re}\,(\hat{f}(a))$ if $u = \mathrm{Re}\,(f), f \in A$. Note that if $\mathrm{Re}\,(f) = \mathrm{Re}\,(g)$, then $\mathrm{Re}\,(f - g) = 0$; thus $\mathrm{Re}\,(\hat{f} - \hat{g}) = 0$, by the corollary to Theorem 4, §4.1. Hence L_a is well defined.

Assume that a, b are in $\mathcal{M}(A)$, and that there are sequences $\{c_n\}, \{u_n\}$ with (a) $0 < c_n < 1$, $u_n \ge 0$, $u_n \in B$; (b) $c_n \to 0$; (c) $L_a(u_n) < c_n$ and $L_b(u_n) = 1$ for all n. Then $f_n = e^{-(u_n + iv_n)}$ belongs to A for a suitable choice of v_n, and $\|f_n\| = \max(e^{-u_n}) \le 1$; while $1 \ge |\hat{f}_n(a)| = e^{-L_a(u_n)} \ge e^{-c_n} \to 1$ and $|\hat{f}_n(b)| = e^{-L_b(u_n)} = e^{-1}$. Hence a and b are not equivalent.

So if $a \sim b$, there exist no such $\{c_n, u_n\}$. Similarly, since $b \sim a$, there are no $\{d_n, w_n\}$, $w_n \ge 0$ in B, with $L_b(w_n) < d_n \to 0^+$, $L_a(w_n) = 1$. Hence there is a number c, $0 < c < 1$, such that $L_a(u) \ge c$ whenever $L_b(u) = 1$ ($u \ge 0$, $u \in B$) and $L_b(u) \ge c$ whenever $L_a(u) = 1$ ($u \ge 0$, $u \in B$). So $L_a - cL_b$ and $L_b - cL_a$ are positive linear functionals on B.

By the Hahn-Banach theorem, every positive linear functional L on B has an extension to a positive linear functional on $C_R(X)$. If $L = 0$, then this is clear. If $\|L\| > 0$, note that $-\|u\|1 \le u \le \|u\|1$ for all $u \in B$, so $-\|u\|L(1) \le L(u) \le \|u\|L(1)$; hence $\|L\| = L(1)$. Set $L_0 = L/L(1)$. Then $\|L_0\| = L_0(1) = 1$. L_0 has a norm-preserving extension to a linear functional L_1 on $C_R(X)$.

Since $\|L_1\| = L_1(1) = 1$, L_1 is positive. So $L(1)L_1$ is a positive extension of L. Hence there is a positive measure σ on X such that $L(u) = \int u \, d\sigma$ for all $u \in B$.

We apply this result to $L_a - cL_b$ and $L_b - cL_a$. There are positive measures σ, τ in $M(X)$ such that

(1) $$L_a(u) - cL_b(u) = \int u \, d\sigma$$

(2) $$L_b(u) - cL_a(u) = \int u \, d\tau, \qquad \text{for all} \quad u \in B.$$

We can now prove the following important result.

Theorem 15. *Let A be a function algebra on a compact space X. Let $a, b \in \mathcal{M}(A)$, and let $a \sim b$. Then there exist representing measures m_a, m_b for a, b which are mutually absolutely continuous and whose Radon-Nikodym derivatives $\dfrac{dm_a}{dm_b}, \dfrac{dm_b}{dm_a}$ are essentially bounded. Indeed, $\exists \, c, 0 < c < 1$, such that $cm_a \leq m_b$ and $cm_b \leq m_a$.*

Proof. If we apply (1) and (2) to $u = \text{Re}(f)$ and $v = \text{Im}(f) = \text{Re}(-if)$ for $f \in A$ and then combine, we have $\hat{f}(a) - c\hat{f}(b) = \int f \, d\sigma$, $\hat{f}(b) - c\hat{f}(a) = \int f \, d\tau$ (all $f \in A$). Hence $\hat{f}(a) = c\hat{f}(b) + \int f \, d\sigma = c^2\hat{f}(a) + c \int f \, d\tau + \int f \, d\sigma$, so $\hat{f}(a) = \dfrac{1}{1-c^2} \int f \, d(c\tau + \sigma)$. Likewise, $\hat{f}(b) = \dfrac{1}{1-c^2} \int f \, d(c\sigma + \tau)$. So we can take $m_a = \dfrac{\sigma + c\tau}{1-c^2}$, $m_b = \dfrac{\tau + c\sigma}{1-c^2}$. Since $\sigma \geq 0$, $\tau \geq 0$, and $0 < c < 1$, m_a and m_b are positive measures. So they are representing measures for a, b, respectively, while $cm_a(E) = \dfrac{c\sigma(E) + c^2\tau(E)}{1-c^2} \leq \dfrac{c\sigma(E) + \tau(E)}{1-c^2} = m_b(E)$ and $cm_b(E) \leq m_a(E)$ for each Borel set E in X. This proves the theorem. (Note that if we modify the proof, we can find m_a, m_b which are concentrated on the Šilov boundary of A in X.)

Theorem 16. *Let A be a function algebra on X, and let $a \sim b$ in $\mathcal{M}(A)$. Let λ_a be any representing measure for a. Then there is a representing measure λ_b for b with $c\lambda_a \leq \lambda_b$ $(0 < c < 1, \ c \in \mathbf{R})$. (So $\lambda_a \leq \dfrac{1}{c}\lambda_b$, $\lambda_a \ll \lambda_b$, and $d\lambda_a/d\lambda_b \in L^\infty(\lambda_b)$.)*

Proof. Choose m_a, m_b as in Theorem 15. Note that $c(\lambda_a - m_a)$ annihilates A, so $m_b + c(\lambda_a - m_a)$ represents b. Since $\lambda_b = m_b + c(\lambda_a - m_a) = (m_b - cm_a) + c\lambda_a \geq c\lambda_a \geq 0$, λ_b is a representing measure for b with the desired properties.

A converse to Theorem 15 is not hard to prove.

Theorem 17. *Let A be a function algebra on X. Suppose that $a, b \in \mathcal{M}(A)$ and that there are m_a and m_b representing a and b which are mutually absolutely continuous. Then $a \sim b$.*

Proof. By assumption, $m_a = km_b$ where $k \in L^1(m_b)$ and $k \geq 0$ a.e. Since $1 = \int 1 \, dm_a$, $\int k \, dm_b = 1$. Let $f \in A$, $\|f\| \leq 1$. Then $|\hat{f}(a) - \hat{f}(b)| = |\int f \, dm_a - \int f \, dm_b| = |\int f(k-1)dm_b| \leq \|f\|\delta$ where $\delta = \int |k-1| \, dm_b$. So it remains to show that $\delta < 2$.

But if $\delta = 2$, then $\int |k-1| \, dm_b = \int (k+1) \, dm_b$ while $|k-1| \leq k+1$. If would follow that $|k-1| = k+1$ a.e. But if $k(x_0) + 1 = |k(x_0) - 1|$, then $k(x_0) + 1 = 1 - k(x_0)$ (otherwise we have the contradiction $k(x_0) + 1 = k(x_0) - 1$), so $k(x_0) = 0$. So $|k-1| = k+1$ a.e. implies that $k = 0$ a.e., which is not the case. Hence $\delta < 2$.

Corollary. *a and b lie in the same Gleason part of $\mathcal{M}(A)$ iff there exist mutually absolutely continuous representing measures for a and b.*

We should note, however, that a given complex homomorphism of a function algebra can have a pair of mutually singular representing measures concentrated on the Šilov boundary. For example, consider the following double-disk algebra. Let Δ_1 be the unit disk with center 0, let Δ_2 be the unit disk with center 3, and let A be the algebra of continuous functions on $X = \Delta_1 \cup \Delta_2$ which are analytic on the interior of X and satisfy $f(0) = f(3)$. Then $\mathcal{M}(A)$ is X with the centers identified, and A is a function algebra on this identification space. Let C_1, C_2 be the circles bounding Δ_1, Δ_2. Let

$$m_1 = \begin{cases} \dfrac{1}{2\pi} \, d\theta & \text{on} \quad C_1 \\[2mm] 0 & \text{on} \quad C_2 \end{cases}$$

$$m_2 = \begin{cases} 0 & \text{on} \quad C_1 \\[2mm] \dfrac{1}{2\pi} \, d\theta & \text{on} \quad C_2. \end{cases}$$

Then $\int f \, dm_1 = f(0) = f(3) = \int f \, dm_2$ for all $f \in A$, while m_1 and m_2 have disjoint closed supports.

Let me say a few words about parts and analytic structure in the maximal ideal space. One of the objects of the theory of function algebras is to determine to what extent the members of a function algebra act like analytic functions of one or more complex variables, in some sense or other. The theorem below shows that any analytic structure, at least of a fairly uncomplicated kind, must be carried within individual Gleason parts of $\mathcal{M}(A)$.

Suppose that V is a domain (nonvoid open connected set) in $\mathbf{C}^n$. A map $g : V \to \mathbf{C}$ is *holomorphic* iff g is continuous on V and analytic in each variable separately. There is a local representation of holomorphic functions by means of a Cauchy integral formula (hence by means of power series) and hence estimates like those for the one variable case can be used to prove the Montel theorem on normal families: Let $\mathscr{F}$ be a uniformly bounded family of holomorphic functions on V. Then every sequence in $\mathscr{F}$ has a subsequence which converges, uniformly on compact subsets of V, to a holomorphic function. There is also a maximum principle—if g is holomorphic on V and assumes its maximum modulus, then g is constant.

Theorem 18. *Let A be a function algebra. Suppose that there is a domain V in $\mathbf{C}^n$ for some $n \geq 1$ and a mapping $\varphi : V \to \mathscr{M}(A)$ such that $\hat{f} \circ \varphi$ is holomorphic on V for every $f \in A$. Then $\varphi(V)$ is contained in some Gleason part of $\mathscr{M}(A)$.*

Proof. Take a, b in $\varphi(V)$. If a is not equivalent to b, then there are f_n in A with $\|f_n\| \leq 1$ and $\hat{f}_n(a) \to 1$, $\hat{f}_n(b) \to -1$. Take $\alpha, \beta \in V$ with $\varphi(\alpha) = a$, $\varphi(\beta) = b$. Then $\hat{f}_n \circ \varphi$ is holomorphic on V and $|\hat{f}_n \circ \varphi| \leq 1$ on V. So some subsequence $\hat{f}_{n_k} \circ \varphi$ converges to a holomorphic function g on V. But $|g| \leq 1$ on V while $|g(\alpha) - g(\beta)| = \lim_k |\hat{f}_{n_k}(a) - \hat{f}_{n_k}(b)| = 2$. So $|g(\alpha)| = 1$ and g is constant, whence we have a contradiction. Thus $a \sim b$.

In some cases, there has been success in making the parts of $\mathscr{M}(A)$ into analytic pieces, and we shall look at some of the constructions later.

One can define a "parts" relation for function spaces also. (Examine the proof of Theorem 15.) Let X be a compact space. Assume that (a) B is a linear subspace of $C_R(X)$, and (b) B contains the constants and separates the points of X. (For example, if A is a function algebra on X and $B = \mathrm{Re}\,(A)$, then B satisfies (a) and (b).)

Let $T_B = \{L \in B^* : L(1) = \|L\| = 1\}$. Corresponding to each number $d > 1$, we define a relation on T_B by: $L_1 \sim L_2(d)$ iff $1/d < L_1(u)/L_2(u) < d$ for every $u \in B$ such that $u > 0$ on X. (Since each $L \in T_B$ is a positive linear functional which is 1 at 1, $L(u) \geq \min_{x \in X} u(x)$ for all $u \in B$.) Clearly $L \sim L(d)$; $L_1 \sim L_2(d)$ iff $L_2 \sim L_1(d)$; and $L_1 \sim L_2(d)$, $L_2 \sim L_3(d')$ imply that $L_1 \sim L_3(dd')$. We shall write $L_1 \approx L_2$ iff $L_1 \sim L_2(d)$ for some $d > 1$. This is an equivalence relation on T_B. (Note that if we let $\psi(L_1, L_2) = \inf \{d > 1 : L_1 \sim L_2(d)\}$, we have $\psi(L, L) = 1$, $\psi(L_1, L_2) = \psi(L_2, L_1)$, and $\psi(L_1, L_2)\psi(L_2, L_3) \geq \psi(L_1, L_3)$. Note also that if $\psi(L_1, L_2) = 1$, then $L_1(u) = L_2(u)$ for all strictly positive $u \in B$. But if $v \in B$, then $v + t > 0$ on X for some real constant t, so $L_1(v + t) = L_1(v) + t = L_2(v + t) = L_2(v) + t$; thus $L_1 = L_2$. Hence if we set $\varphi(L_1, L_2) = \log \psi(L_1, L_2)$ for $L_1 \approx L_2$, then φ is a metric on each equivalence class. Explicitly,

$$\varphi(L_1, L_2) = \log \{\inf \{d > 1 : 1/d < L_1(u)/L_2(u) < d,\ \text{all } u > 0 \text{ in } B\}\}$$
$$= \inf \{\log d : d > 1 \text{ and } |\log L_1(u) - \log L_2(u)| < \log d$$
$$\text{for all } u > 0 \text{ in } B\}$$
$$= \inf \{c > 0 : |\log L_1(u) - \log L_2(u)| < c \text{ for all } u > 0 \text{ in } B\}.)$$

Theorem 19. *Let A be a function algebra and let B* = Re (*A*). *Each a* $\in$ $\mathcal{M}(A)$ *defines* $L_a \in T_B$ *by* $L_a(u)$ = Re ($\hat{f}(a)$) *for* u = Re (*f*), $f \in A$. *If a, b* $\in$ $\mathcal{M}(A)$, *then a* $\sim$ *b iff* $L_a \approx L_b$.

Proof. Let $a \sim b$. By the remarks preceding Theorem 15, there is a number c, $0 < c < 1$, such that $L_a - cL_b$ and $L_b - cL_a$ are positive linear functionals on *B*. So $cL_a(u) \le L_b(u)$, $cL_b(u) \le L_a(u)$ for each $u \ge 0$ in *B*. Hence $c \le L_b(u)/L_a(u) \le 1/c$ if $u \in B$ and $u > 0$ on *X*. Thus $L_a \sim L_b(d)$ for every $d > 1/c$, and $L_a \approx L_b$.

Suppose that $a \not\sim b$. Then there are $f_n \in A$ with $\| f_n \| \le 1$ such that $\hat{f}_n(a) \to 1$, $\hat{f}_n(b) \to -1$. If u_n = Re ($f_n/(1 + 2^{-n})$), $1 + u_n > 0$ on *X*. We have $L_a(u_n) \to 1$ and $L_b(u_n) \to -1$, so $L_a(1 + u_n) \to 2$ and $L_b(1 + u_n) \to 0$. Since $\dfrac{L_a(1 + u_n)}{L_b(1 + u_n)} \to \infty$, $L_a \not\approx L_b$.

Theorem 19 shows that the parts in $\mathcal{M}(A)$ are the intersections with $\mathcal{M}(A)$ of the $\approx$ parts in $T_{\text{Re}\,(A)}$. One can show that on a part in $\mathcal{M}(A)$, convergence in the metric φ defined above (with *B* = Re (*A*)) is equivalent to convergence in the metric induced by the norm in *A**. Furthermore, the equivalence classes of T_B under $\approx$ can be characterized in geometrical terms. (For proofs, see Bear [20].)

EXERCISE SET   4.5

1. Let *P* be a part in $\mathcal{M}(A)$. Suppose that $f \in A$ and $|\hat{f}(a)| = \| f \|$ for some $a \in P$. Show that $\hat{f}$ is constant on *P*.

2. Let $a, b \in \mathcal{M}(A)$. Suppose that there is a sequence $\{f_n\}$ in *A* with $\| f_n \| \le 1$ such that $|\hat{f}_n(a)| \to 1$, while $|\hat{f}_n(b)|$ does not converge to 1. Show that *a* is not equivalent to *b*.

3. Let *E* be a normed linear space and *K* the closed unit ball of *E**. Let $\psi(\alpha, \beta) = \left| \dfrac{\alpha - \beta}{1 - \bar{\beta}\alpha} \right|$ be the pseudo-hyperbolic metric on the unit disk. For $x, y \in K$, define $\rho(x, y) = \sup \{\psi(u(x), u(y)) : u \in E, |u| < 1$ on $K\}$. Show that if we set $x \sim y$ iff $\rho(x, y) < 1$, then $\sim$ is an equivalence relation on *K*. The equivalence classes are called the hyperbolic parts of *K*. Show that if *A* is a function algebra, the Gleason parts of $\mathcal{M}(A)$ are its intersections with the hyperbolic parts of Σ_A, and that on each part the metric ρ is equivalent to the norm metric.

   The notion of part can be extended to compact convex subsets of locally convex topological vector spaces, and even to slightly more general situations. (See [22] and [115].)

4. Find a commutative Banach algebra *A* and a complex homomorphism *h* of *A* such that *h* has norm less than one.

5. Let A be a function algebra, $g \in A$, and $\hat{g}(a) = 0$ for some $a \in \mathcal{M}(A)$. Suppose that g has an nth root in A for every $n = 1, 2, 3, \ldots$. Show that $\hat{g}$ vanishes on P_a.

 (We may assume that $\|g\| \leq 1$ and hence $\|g_n\| \leq 1$ for each nth root g_n of g. All $g_n \in A_a$, so $\sup_n |\hat{g}_n(b)| < 1$ for each $b \in P_a$. This implies that $\hat{g}(b) = 0$.)

 Prove that the same conclusion holds if for each n, g is a product $g = g_1 \cdots g_n$, where all $g_k \in A$ and $\|g_k\| \leq 1$ $(1 \leq k \leq n)$.

6. Let A be a function algebra on X, and let φ be the evaluation map from X into $\mathcal{M}(A)$. Prove that if x belongs to the Choquet boundary of A, then $\{\varphi_x\}$ is a one-point part in $\mathcal{M}(A)$.

7. Let A be a function algebra. Let $a, b \in \mathcal{M}(A)$. Prove that if there are representing measures m_a, m_b for a, b which are not mutually singular, then $a \sim b$.

4.6   JENSEN MEASURES

In this section we establish the existence of representing measures which satisfy an inequality analogous to a classical inequality of Jensen in analytic function theory. We begin with an elementary lemma. The proof is a standard compactness argument.

Lemma 5. *Suppose that X is a topological space, B is a compact space, and φ is a continuous mapping from $X \times B$ to $\mathbf{R}^e$ (the extended real numbers, with the usual topology). Suppose that $r \in X$ and $\varphi(r, b) > 0$ for all $b \in B$. Then there is a nbhd W of r such that $\varphi > 0$ on $W \times B$.*

Theorem 20. *Let X be a compact Hausdorff space and A a closed subalgebra of $C(X)$. Let F be a closed subset of X on which every $|f|$ $(f \in A)$ assumes its maximum over X. Then for each $x \in X$, there is a nonnegative measure $m \in M(F)$ such that $m(F) = 1$ and*

$$\log |f(x)| \leq \int_F \log |f| \, dm \quad \text{for all } f \in A.$$

 Remark. If $f(x) = 0$, then $\log |f(x)| = -\infty$ and there is nothing to prove. (Take m to be any probability measure on F.) Since $\log |f| \leq |f|$, and f is integrable with respect to every $\mu \in M(X)$, then either $\log |f| \in L^1(m)$ or $\int \log |f| \, dm = -\infty$. Part of the conclusion is that $\log |f| \in L^1(m)$ for every $f \in A$ such that $f(x) \neq 0$.

 Proof of Theorem 20.   The strategy of the proof is to produce a positive linear functional L on $C_R(F)$ which is 1 at 1 and is nonnegative at every $u \in C_R(F)$ which is greater than $\log \left(\dfrac{|f|}{|f(x)|} \right)$ on F $(f \in A, f(x) \neq 0)$. An application of the monotone convergence theorem will then complete the proof.

We assume that $f(x) \neq 0$ for some $f \in A$, and thus that $f_0(x) = 1$ for some $f_0 \in A$.

Let $C_1 = \{u \in C_R(F) : \text{there exist } f \in A \text{ and a positive rational number } r \text{ such that } |f(x)| \geq 1 \text{ and } ru > \log|f| \text{ on } F\}$, and let $C_2 = \{u \in C_R(F) : u < 0 \text{ on } F\}$. We shall show that C_1, C_2 are disjoint convex sets, one of which is open (in the norm topology of $C_R(F)$).

First of all, C_1 and C_2 are nonvoid. For example, $-1 \in C_2$ and the restriction of $\log(1 + |f_0|)$ to F belongs to C_1. If $f \in A$ and $|f(x)| \geq 1$, then $|f(y)| \geq 1$ for some $y \in F$. Hence if $r > 0$ and $ru > \log|f|$ on F, then $u(y) > 0$ for some $y \in F$. So C_1 and C_2 are disjoint. Since each $u \in C_2$ has a strictly negative minimum, it is clear that C_2 is an open convex subset of $C_R(F)$.

Now we check that C_1 is convex. In fact, C_1 is a convex cone: if $u_1, u_2 \in C_1$, then $u_1 + u_2 \in C_1$, and if $u \in C_1$ and $\xi > 0$, then $\xi u \in C_1$.

For suppose $r_j u_j > \log|f_j|$ on F $(j = 1, 2)$ where $f_j \in A$, $|f_j(x)| \geq 1$, and $r_j = m_j/n$ $(j = 1, 2)$ with m_1, m_2, n positive integers. Then $m_1 m_2 (u_1 + u_2) > \log|f_1^{nm_2} f_2^{nm_1}|$ on F. So $u_1 + u_2 \in C_1$ if $u_1, u_2 \in C_1$.

Given $u \in C_1$, choose f and r according to the definition. Then define $\varphi : (0, \infty) \times (0, \infty) \times F \to [-\infty, \infty]$ by $\varphi(s, t, y) = s\xi u(y) - t \log|f(y)|$. φ is continuous and $\varphi(r, \xi, y) > 0$ for each $y \in F$. Hence by Lemma 5, there is a set W open about (r, ξ) such that $\varphi(s, t, y) > 0$ for all $(s, t) \in W$, $y \in F$. In particular, there are positive rationals m_j/n $(j = 1, 2)$ with $(m_1/n, m_2/n) \in W$.

So $\dfrac{m_1}{m_2}(\xi u) > \log|f|$ on F, which shows that $\xi u \in C_1$.

Since C_1, C_2 are nonvoid disjoint convex sets and C_2 is open, C_1 and C_2 are weakly separated by a hyperplane. So there is a linear functional L of norm 1 on $C_R(F)$ such that $L(u) \leq \alpha$ for all $u \in C_2$, $L(u) \geq \alpha$ for all $u \in C_1$, for some real number α. Let $a = \sup\{L(u) : u \in C_2\}$, $b = \inf\{L(u) : u \in C_1\}$. Then $a \leq \alpha \leq b$.

If $a < 0$, then $2a < a$, so $2a < L(u)$ for some $u \in C_2$. But then $u/2 \in C_2$ and $L(u/2) > a$, a contradiction. So $a \geq 0$. Similarly, if $b > 0$, then $b \leq L(u) < b + 1$ for some $u \in C_1$. But then $\dfrac{b}{b+1} u \in C_1$ and $L\left(\dfrac{b}{b+1} u\right) < b$, again a contradiction. So $a = b = \alpha = 0$. Thus $\sup\{L(u) : u \in C_2\} = 0 = \inf\{L(u) : u \in C_1\}$.

If $u \in C(F)$ and $u \geq 0$ on F, then $-(u + \varepsilon) \in C_2$ for every $\varepsilon > 0$, so $-L(u) - \varepsilon L(1) \leq 0$. Hence $L(u) \geq 0$. (Let $\varepsilon \to 0^+$.) So L is a positive linear functional of norm 1. By the Riesz representation theorem, there is a positive measure m of total mass 1 in $M(F)$ such that $L(u) = \int u \, dm$ $(u \in C_R(F))$.

It remains to prove the Jensen inequality. Let $f \in A$ and set $\alpha = |f(x)|$. If $\alpha = 0$, then the inequality is obvious, so suppose that $\alpha > 0$. Put $u_n = \log\left(\dfrac{1}{n} + \dfrac{|f|}{\alpha}\right)\Big| F$. Since $\log$ is an increasing function, we have $u_n \downarrow \log\left(\dfrac{1}{\alpha}|f|\right)$

on F, and all $u_n \in C_1$. Since $L \geq 0$ on C_1, $\int u_n \, dm \geq 0$ for all n. Hence $\log\left(\dfrac{1}{\alpha}|f|\right)$ belongs to $L^1(m)$, and $\displaystyle\int_F \log\left(\frac{1}{\alpha}|f|\right) dm = \lim_n \int u_n \, dm \geq 0$, by the Lebesgue monotone convergence theorem. Since $\int 1 \, dm = 1$, this means that $\log \alpha = \log |f(x)| \leq \int \log |f| \, dm$, and the theorem is proved.

We can apply the theorem as follows. Let B be a commutative Banach algebra with identity. Take $X = \mathcal{M}(B)$, and let A be the uniform closure of $\hat{B}$ in $C(X)$. For F we take any closed set containing the Šilov boundary of $\hat{B}$ (which is the same as the Šilov boundary of A). By the theorem, for each $h \in \mathcal{M}(B)$ there is a probability measure m on F such that $\log |h(x)| \leq \int_F \log |\hat{x}| \, dm$ for all $x \in B$. (It is also true that m represents h, in the sense that $h(x) = \int \hat{x} \, dm$ $(x \in B)$. See the proof below.) The case of interest for us is that in which B is already a function algebra.

Definition. Let A be a function algebra on X and let $a \in \mathcal{M}(A)$. A *Jensen measure* for a is a positive measure m in $M(X)$ such that $\log |\hat{f}(a)| \leq \int \log |f| \, dm$ $(\forall f \in A)$. An *Arens-Singer measure* for a is a positive measure m in $M(X)$ such that $\log |\hat{f}(a)| = \int \log |f| \, dm$ for every invertible element f in A.

Theorem 21. *Let A be a function algebra and let $a \in \mathcal{M}(A)$.*

(a) *There exists a Jensen measure for a which is concentrated on the Šilov boundary $\Gamma(A)$.*

(b) *Let m be a Jensen measure for a, and let $f \in A$ and $\hat{f}(a) \neq 0$. Then $|f| > 0$ a.e. $[m]$.*

(c) *Every Jensen measure for a is an Arens-Singer measure.*

(d) *Every Arens-Singer measure for a is a representing measure for a.*

(e) *If every invertible element of A has a logarithm in A, then every representing measure for a is an Arens-Singer measure.*

Proof. (a) follows from Theorem 20, since $\Gamma(\hat{A}) = \Gamma(A)$.

(b) If $f = 0$ on a set of m-measure > 0, then $\log |f| \notin L^1(m)$, so $\int \log |f| \, dm = -\infty \geq \log |\hat{f}(a)|$. Hence $\hat{f}(a) = 0$.

(c) Let m be a Jensen measure for a. Take any invertible $f \in A$. Then
$$\int \log |f| \, dm \geq \log |\hat{f}(a)| \quad \text{and} \quad \int \log \left|\frac{1}{f}\right| \, dm \geq \log \left|\widehat{\frac{1}{f}}(a)\right| = \log |1/\hat{f}(a)|, \quad \text{or}$$
$-\int \log |f| \, dm \geq -\log |\hat{f}(a)|$. So equality holds, and m is an Arens-Singer measure.

(d) Let μ be an Arens-Singer measure for a. First of all, μ is a positive measure. Let $f = u + iv$ belong to A. Then e^f, e^{-if} are invertible elements of A. So $\log |\widehat{\exp(f)}(a)| = \log |\exp(\hat{f}(a))| = \int \log |e^f| \, d\mu$, $\log |\widehat{\exp(-if)}(a)| = \log |\exp(-i\hat{f}(a))| = \int \log |e^{-if}| \, d\mu$. That is, $\operatorname{Re}(\hat{f}(a)) = \int u \, d\mu$, $\operatorname{Im}(\hat{f}(a)) = \int v \, d\mu$. So $\hat{f}(a) = \int f \, d\mu$.

(e) Suppose that every invertible element $f \in A$ has the form $f = e^g$ with $g \in A$. If m is a representing measure for a, then $\log |\hat{f}(a)| = \log |\int f \, dm| = \log |\int e^g \, dm| = \log |e^{\int g \, dm}| = \log (e^{\mathrm{Re} \int g \, dm}) = \mathrm{Re} (\int g \, dm) = \int (\mathrm{Re} \, g) \, dm = \int \log |f| \, dm$, so m is an Arens-Singer measure.

Corollary. *Let A be a function algebra, and let $a \in \mathcal{M}(A)$. If a has a unique representing measure m concentrated on $\Gamma(A)$, then*

$$\log |\hat{f}(a)| = \log \left| \int f \, dm \right| \leq \int \log |f| \, dm$$

for every $f \in A$.

In the case of the disk algebra, each point of the open unit disk has a unique representing measure on the circle. Hence if f is in the disk algebra and $\alpha = re^{i\theta}$ ($0 \leq r < 1$), then

$(\star)$
$$\log |f(\alpha)| \leq \frac{1}{2\pi} \int_0^{2\pi} \log |f(e^{it})| \, P_r(\theta - t) \, dt$$

(where $\{P_r\}$ are the Poisson kernels). This is the classical Poisson-Jensen inequality. Note that if f is in the disk algebra and $f \neq 0$, then f cannot vanish on a set of positive Lebesgue measure on the unit circle. (For if $f = 0$ on E and $\int_E dt > 0$, then $\int_E P_r(\theta - t) \, dt > 0$, so the right side of $(\star)$ is $-\infty$. Hence $f(\alpha) = 0$ for every $\alpha \in U$. So $f = 0$ on Δ, by continuity.)

I want to mention that the hypothesis in (e), namely, that every invertible element of A is the exponential of an element of A, turns out to depend only on the topology of $\mathcal{M}(A)$ and not on the algebra A itself. This follows from a theorem of Arens [7] and Royden [150], which we shall make no attempt to prove. For any function algebra A, let A^{-1} be the group of invertible elements of A. It is easy to see that $e^A = \{e^f : f \in A\}$ is a multiplicative subgroup of A^{-1}, so one can form the quotient group A^{-1}/e^A. The Arens-Royden result is that A^{-1}/e^A is isomorphic to $\check{H}^1(\mathcal{M}(A), \mathbf{Z})$, the first Čech cohomology group of $\mathcal{M}(A)$ with integer coefficients. In particular, $e^A = A^{-1}$ (i.e., A satisfies the condition in (e)) iff this cohomology group is trivial; this is a kind of generalized simple-connectedness condition on $\mathcal{M}(A)$. In view of this result, every invertible f in A has a logarithm in A iff every nowhere vanishing continuous function on $\mathcal{M}(A)$ has a continuous logarithm.

In his thesis [135], O'Neill considers a class of function algebras in which every complex homomorphism has a unique Arens-Singer measure. He shows that for his algebras, every Gleason part which is not a point is essentially a Riemann surface, and the (Gelfand transforms of the) functions in the algebra are analytic functions on the surface. Also see [213].

EXERCISE SET 4.6

1. Let $a \in \mathcal{M}(A)$. Show that the set of Arens-Singer measures for a is convex and w^*-compact.

2. Show that the set of Jensen measures for a is convex and w^*-compact. If a is evaluation at a point $x \in X$, then $\delta_x + t(\mu - \delta_x) = t\mu + (1 - t)\delta_x$ is a Jensen measure for a if $t \geq 0$ and μ is a Jensen measure for a. (So the ray from δ_x through μ consists entirely of Jensen measures.)

4.7   THE $\dfrac{1}{4}, \dfrac{3}{4}$ CONDITION

Theorem 22. *Let A be a function algebra on X, and let $x \in X$. Then the following conditions are equivalent.*

(a) *x belongs to the Choquet boundary of A.*

(b) *For every open set U containing x, there is a function f in A such that $\|f\| \leq 1$, $|f(x)| > \frac{3}{4}$, and $|f| < \frac{1}{4}$ on $X \backslash U$.*

(c) *For every G_δ-set S containing x, $\exists f \in A$ such that $|f(x)| = \|f\|$ and $\{y \in X : |f(y)| = \|f\|\} \subset S$.*

(d) *For every open set U containing x, $\exists f \in A$ such that $|f(x)| = \|f\|$ and $\{y \in X : |f(y)| = \|f\|\} \subset U$.*

Proof. First we prove that (a) implies (b). Take $x \in c(A)$, and let $B = \text{Re}(A)$. B is a subspace of $C_R(X)$, and B contains the constants. Let us prove the following: if $g \in C(X)$, $g \geq 0$ on X, and $g(x) \geq 1$, then $\sup_{u \in B, u \leq g} u(x) \geq 1$. Otherwise $\exists \varepsilon > 0$ such that the supremum is $1 - \varepsilon$. Certainly then $g \notin B$, since $g(x) \geq 1$. Consider the subspace E of $C_R(X)$ spanned by B and g. Each element of E has form $u + \lambda g$ for unique $u \in B$, $\lambda \in \mathbf{R}$. Observe that if $u + \lambda g \geq 0$, then $u(x) + \lambda(1 - \varepsilon) \geq 0$. (If $\lambda = 0$, then this is clear. If $\lambda > 0$, then $u + \lambda g \geq 0$, so $g \geq -u/\lambda \in B$; so $1 - \varepsilon \geq -u(x)/\lambda$, and thus $u(x) + \lambda(1 - \varepsilon) \geq 0$. If $\lambda < 0$, then $(u/\lambda) + g \leq 0$, so $g \leq -u/\lambda$. Consider any $v \in B$ with $v \leq g$. Then $v \leq -u/\lambda$, so $v(x) \leq -u(x)/\lambda$. Hence the supremum over all such v is at most $-u(x)/\lambda$; i.e., $1 - \varepsilon \leq -u(x)/\lambda$, so $\lambda(1 - \varepsilon) \geq -u(x)$, $u(x) + \lambda(1 - \varepsilon) \geq 0$.) Thus the linear functional L_0 on E given by $L_0(u + \lambda g) = u(x) + \lambda(1 - \varepsilon)$ is positive. Also, $L_0(1) = 1$, so $L_0(1) = 1 = \|L_0\|$, and so L_0 is represented by a positive measure μ of total mass 1 on X. So

$$(\bigstar) \qquad u(x) + \lambda(1 - \varepsilon) = \int u \, d\mu + \lambda \int g \, d\mu \qquad (u \in B, \lambda \in \mathbf{R}).$$

In particular, $u(x) = \int u \, d\mu$ for all $u \in \text{Re}(A)$, so $f(x) = \int f \, d\mu$ for all $f \in A$. This means that μ is a representing measure for x (with respect to A). x is in the Choquet boundary, so $\mu = \delta_x$. Going back to $(\bigstar)$, we have

$$1 - \varepsilon = \int g \, d\mu = g(x), \qquad \text{contrary to hypothesis.}$$

We have proved our assertion:

If $g \geq \chi_{\{x\}}$, then sup $\{u(x) : u \in \text{Re}(A), u \leq g\} \geq 1$.

Given an open *nbhd* U of x, choose $g \in C(X)$ with $g(x) = 1$, $g(X \backslash U) = \{0\}$, and $0 \leq g \leq 1$. Take $u \in \text{Re}(A)$ with $u \leq g$ on X and $u(x) > \log 6/\log 8$. Then $e^{(\log 8)(u-1)}$ is the modulus of a function $f \in A$. Since $u - 1 \leq 0$, $\|f\| \leq 1$; $|f(x)| > \exp(\log 6 - \log 8) = \frac{3}{4}$; and since $u - 1 \leq -1$ on $X \backslash U$, $|f| \leq \exp(-\log 8) = 1/8$ on $X \backslash U$. So (b) is proved.

Now assume the $\frac{1}{4}, \frac{3}{4}$ condition (b). Let S be a G_δ containing x. We can express S as $\bigcap_{n=1}^{\infty} V_n$, where each V_n is open and $V_n \supset V_{n+1}$ for each n.

We shall construct open sets U_n and functions $g_n \in A$ with
  (i) $g_n(x) = 3(1 - 2^{-n})$;
  (ii) $\|g_n\| \leq 3(1 - 2^{-n-1})$;
  (iii) $\|g_{n+1} - g_n\| \leq 2^{-n+1}$;
  (iv) $|g_{n+1} - g_n| \leq 2^{-n-1}$ on $X \backslash U_n$;
  (v) $x \in U_n \subset V_n$.

The conditions are to hold for $n = 1, 2, \ldots$.

Suppose the construction is accomplished. By (iii), $g_1 + \sum_{n=1}^{\infty} (g_{n+1} - g_n)$ converges in the sup norm, so $\{g_n\}$ converges uniformly to a function $f \in A$. By (ii), $\|f\| \leq 3$, but by (i), $f(x) = 3$. So $|f(x)| = \|f\| = 3$. On the other hand, if $y \in X \backslash S$, then $y \notin V_n$ for some n. The V_k decrease, so $y \in X \backslash U_k$ for all $k \geq n$. But $f = g_n + \sum_{k=n}^{\infty} (g_{k+1} - g_k)$, so

$$|f(y)| \leq \|g_n\| + \sum_{k=n}^{\infty} |g_{k+1}(y) - g_k(y)| \leq 3(1 - 2^{-n-1}) + \sum_{k=n}^{\infty} 2^{-k-1}$$

$$= 3 - 2^{-n-1} < 3.$$

Thus $\{y : |f(y)| = \|f\|\} \subset S$.

It remains to construct the sequences $\{g_n\}$, $\{U_n\}$. By (b), $\exists g \in A$ with $\|g\| \leq 1$, $|g(x)| > \frac{3}{4}$, $|g| < \frac{1}{4}$ on $X \backslash V_1$. Let $g_1 = 3g/2g(x)$. Then $g_1 \in A$, $g_1(x) = 3/2$, and $\|g_1\| \leq 2 < 9/4$. So g_1 satisfies (i) and (ii) for $n = 1$.

Now suppose that $g_1, g_2, \ldots, g_k$ and $U_1, \ldots, U_{k-1}$ have been chosen to satisfy the conditions (i) through (v). Since $g_k(x) = 3(1 - 2^{-k})$, there is an open *nbhd* U of x such that $|g_k| < 3(1 - 2^{-k}) + 2^{-k-2}$ on U and hence on $U_k = U \cap V_k$. By hypothesis (b), $\exists G \in A$ with $\|G\| \leq 1$, $|G(x)| > \frac{3}{4}$, $|G| < \frac{1}{4}$ on $X \backslash U_k$. Set $h_k = 3G/2^{k+1}G(x)$ and $g_{k+1} = g_k + h_k$. We check that $g_{k+1} \in A$,

$$\|g_{k+1} - g_k\| = \|h_k\| \leq \frac{3}{2^{k+1}} \cdot \frac{4}{3} = 2^{-k+1}, \quad g_{k+1}(x) = 3(1 - 2^{-k}) + 3 \cdot 2^{-k-1} =$$

$$3(1 - 2^{-k-2}), \quad |g_{k+1} - g_k| < \frac{3}{2^{k+1}} \cdot \frac{4}{3} \cdot \frac{1}{4} = 2^{-k-1} \text{ on } X \backslash U_k, \text{ and } x \in U_k \subset V_k.$$

It remains to compute $\|g_{k+1}\|$. Now if $y \in U_k$, then

$$|g_{k+1}(y)| \le |g_k(y)| + \|h_k\|$$
$$< 3(1 - 2^{-k}) + 2^{-k-2} + 2^{-k+1}$$
$$= 3 - \frac{3/4}{2^k} = 3(1 - 2^{-k-2}),$$

while if $y \in X\backslash U_k$, then

$$|g_{k+1}(y)| \le \|g_k\| + |h_k(y)|$$
$$\le 3(1 - 2^{-k-1}) + 2^{-k-1} = 3 - 2^{-k}$$
$$< 3 - \frac{3/4}{2^k} = 3(1 - 2^{-k-2}).$$

So $\|g_{k+1}\| < 3(1 - 2^{-k-2})$. The conditions are thus satisfied by $g_1, \ldots, g_k$, g_{k+1} and $U_1, \ldots, U_{k-1}, U_k$. By induction, the construction is possible, so (c) is proved.

An open set is a G_δ, so (c) implies (d).

Assume now that (d) holds. If $X = \{x\}$, then $x \in c(A)$ trivially. Otherwise take any proper open subset U of X such that $x \in U$. By assumption, $\exists f \in A$ with $|f(x)| = \|f\|$ and $\{y : |f(y)| = \|f\|\} \subset U$. Since $f \ne 0$, we multiply by a constant, and assume that $f(x) = \|f\| = 1$ while $\{y \in X : |f(y)| = 1\} \subset U$.

Take any representing measure m for $\varphi_x \in \mathcal{M}(A)$. Then $1 = \int f \, dm$, so $1 = \int \operatorname{Re}(f) \, dm = \int 1 \, dm$, while $\operatorname{Re}(f) \le |f| \le 1$. So $1 - \operatorname{Re}(f) = 0$ a.e., $\operatorname{Im}(f) = 0$ a.e., and $f = 1$ a.e. Hence $f = 1$ on supp m. We conclude that supp $m \subset U$. Hence $m(U) = 1$ for every open *nbhd* U of x. Hence by regularity, $m(\{x\}) = 1$. This means that $m = \delta_x$, so $x \in c(A)$.

If $\{x\}$ is a G_δ, then we can take S in (c) to be $\{x\}$. If (c) holds, $\exists f \in A$ with $|f(x)| = \|f\|$, $|f(y)| < \|f\|$ for all $y \in X\backslash\{x\}$. Hence $f/f(x)$ peaks at x.

Corollary 1. *Let x belong to the Choquet boundary of A. Then x is a peak point for A iff $\{x\}$ is a G_δ.*

If $\{x\}$ is a G_δ, then x is a peak point for A, as we have just observed. Conversely, if x is a peak point, then $\exists f \in A$ with $f(x) = 1$, $|f| < 1$ on $X\backslash\{x\}$. So $\{x\} = \bigcap_{n=1}^{\infty} \{y \in X : |f(y)| > 1 - 1/n\}$.

Corollary 2. *Let $x \in X$, and suppose that $\{x\}$ is a G_δ. Then x is a peak point for A iff for every open set U containing x, $\exists f \in A$ such that $\|f\| \le 1$, $|f(x)| > \frac{3}{4}$, and $|f| < \frac{1}{4}$ on $X\backslash U$.*

Corollary 3. *Let A be a function algebra on a compact metric space. Then the Choquet boundary of A is the set of peak points for A. For each $f \in A$, there is a peak point x such that $|f(x)| = \|f\|$.*

Proof. X is metric, so every $x \in X$ is a G_δ. Indeed,

$$\{x\} = \bigcap_n \{y : \text{dist}\,(x, y) < 1/n\}.$$

So the Choquet boundary of A is the set of peak points. Since the Choquet boundary of A is a boundary, every $f \in A$ assumes its maximum modulus at a peak point.

Since a boundary for A necessarily contains every peak point for A, we see that if X is metrizable, then the Choquet boundary of A is contained in every boundary for A, and hence is a minimum boundary.

Note too that if X is compact metric and if each $\varphi_x \in \varphi(X) \subset \mathcal{M}(A)$ has only the point mass as representing measure, then every point of X is a peak point for A. In particular, the following is true.

Corollary 4. *Let A be a function algebra on a compact metric space X. If every complex homomorphism of A has a unique representing measure, then every point of X is a peak point for A. Thus the Šilov boundary and minimum boundary (the Choquet boundary) for A are X itself.*

It is sometimes useful to know that the Choquet boundary for a function algebra A "supports" (positive) representing measures for the homomorphisms in $\mathcal{M}(A)$ (and in fact, for all linear functionals in the set T_A). This is a major result in the article by Bishop and deLeeuw [37]. The proof is long and tricky, and we omit the details entirely.

Theorem 23. *Let A be a function algebra on a compact space X. Let S be any boundary for A. Let $\mathcal{S}$ be the σ-ring generated by S and the Baire sets of X. Then every L in A^* has a representation of the form*

$$L(f) = \int f \, d\mu \qquad (f \in A),$$

where μ is a complex measure on $\mathcal{S}$ such that $\mu(E) = 0$ for every $E \in \mathcal{S}$ which is disjoint from S. If $h \in \mathcal{M}(A)$, then there is a positive measure m on $\mathcal{S}$ which vanishes on the Baire sets disjoint from S and which satisfies

$$\hat{f}(h) = \int f \, dm \qquad \text{for all f in A.}$$

The measure m may not be "concentrated" on S, however, in the following sense. There is a unique regular Borel measure $\hat{m}$ on X which extends the restriction of m to the Baire sets. One can find an example where $\hat{m}(E) > 0$ for some Borel set E contained in $X \backslash S$. So the integral representation can be pathological.

EXERCISE SET   4.7

1. Consider the space $X = \Pi X_\lambda$ in §4.1, Exercise 10. Show that there are disjoint sets E_1, E_2 in X which are boundaries for $C(X)$. Hence $C(X)$ has no minimum (smallest) boundary.

2. Let Y be the real numbers with the discrete topology, and let X be the one-point compactification of X. Show that X is the Choquet boundary of $C(X)$, that the set of peak points for $C(X)$ is Y, and that Y is the minimum boundary for $C(X)$.

3. Let A be a function algebra on X. Let S be any Baire set in X which is a boundary for A. (The Baire sets are the members of the smallest σ-ring which contains the compact G_δ sets.) Prove that S contains $c(A)$. (So $c(A)$ is inside every Baire boundary. However there are examples where the intersection of the Baire boundaries for A is larger than $c(A)$. See [37, §vii].)

4. Let A be a function algebra on X, and let $x \in X$. Then x is a peak point for A iff x belongs to every boundary for A.

5. Let A be a function algebra on X, and let $x \in X$. Show that the following conditions are equivalent:
   (a) $x \in c(A)$.
   (b) For every $\varepsilon > 0$ and every open *nbhd* U of x, A contains a function f with $\|f\| \leq 1$, $|f(x)| > 1 - \varepsilon$, $|f| \leq \varepsilon$ on $X \backslash U$.
   (c) For each $y \neq x$ in X, $\exists f \in A$ with $|f(y)| < \|f\| = |f(x)|$.

6. Let A be a function algebra on a compact metric space X. Prove that the Choquet boundary of A is a G_δ. In particular, it is a Borel set.

7. Let B be a separating subspace of $C(X)$ which contains 1. Show that B and Re (B) have the same Choquet boundary.

8. Let X be a compact metric space and B a closed subspace of $C(X)$ or $C_R(X)$ which contains the constants and separates points. Then the peak points for B are dense in the Choquet boundary of B. (*Hint*: Look up the proof in Section 8 of Phelps [H].)

Chapter Five

Approximation Theory

5.1   POLYNOMIAL AND RATIONAL APPROXIMATION

Let K be a compact set in complex n-space $\mathbf{C}^n$. We define function algebras $P(K)$, $R(K)$, $A(K)$ as follows. Let $P_0(K)$ be the algebra of restrictions to K of the polynomials in the coordinate functions $z_1, \ldots, z_n$. $P(K)$ is the uniform closure of $P_0(K)$ in $C(K)$. A *rational function on K* is a quotient p/q, where p, q belong to $P_0(K)$ and q does not vanish at any point of K. The set of such functions forms a subalgebra $R_0(K)$ of $C(K)$, and $R(K)$ is the uniform closure of $R_0(K)$. The algebra $A(K)$ consists of all continuous functions on K which are holomorphic on the interior of K.

It is clear that $P(K) \subset R(K) \subset A(K) \subset C(K)$. Since $z_1, \ldots, z_n$ are in $P(K)$ and separate points, $P(K)$, $R(K)$, and $A(K)$ are function algebras on K. It is easy to show that $A(K) = C(K)$ iff the interior of K is empty. One object of this chapter is to find conditions on K which guarantee that $P(K) = C(K)$ or $R(K) = C(K)$. When $n = 1$, there is a topological characterization of those K for which $P(K) = A(K)$; we shall return to this question in the next chapter.

In §5.2 we identify the maximal ideal spaces of $P(K)$ and $R(K)$ and relate them to K. In §5.3 and §5.4 we establish a collection of results on uniform approximation by polynomials and rational functions in one variable. Section 5.5 is concerned with the Gleason parts for the algebras $R(K)$, again with $K \subset \mathbf{C}^1$. In §5.6 we outline proofs of important results about composing analytic functions with n-tuples of Banach algebra elements, and we prove Šilov's theorem relating the existence of idempotents in a function algebra A to the existence of open-closed sets in $\mathscr{M}(A)$.

5.2   POLYNOMIAL AND RATIONAL HULLS

Let K be a compact set in $\mathbf{C}^n$. The *polynomial convex hull of K* is the set hull(K) consisting of all $\lambda \in \mathbf{C}^n$ such that $|p(\lambda)| \le \sup \{|p(z)| : z \in K\}$ for every polynomial p on $\mathbf{C}^n$. Note that $\lambda \in$ hull(K) iff the homomorphism $p \to p(\lambda)$ on the normed algebra $P_0(K)$ (normed by the sup norm over K) has operator norm 1. This holds iff the homomorphism is extendable to a complex homomorphism of $P(K)$. Thus $\lambda \in$ hull(K) iff there exists a homomorphism $h \in \mathcal{M}(P(K))$ such that $h(p) = p(\lambda)$ for every polynomial p on $\mathbf{C}^n$. It is easy to see that the map $h \to \lambda = (h(z_1), \ldots, h(z_n))$ determined by this correspondence is a homeomorphism from the maximal ideal space of $P(K)$ onto hull(K), which we observe is the joint spectrum of $(z_1, \ldots, z_n)$ in the algebra $P(K)$. K is said to be *polynomially convex* iff $K =$ hull(K).

Conversely, let A be any finitely generated function algebra with generators $f_1, \ldots, f_n$. Let $K = \sigma_A(f_1, \ldots, f_n)$. Then we see that A is isomorphic to $P(K)$ (with f_i mapping to z_i for each i), and K is polynomially convex. (Let $\lambda \in$ hull(K). If $w = (h(f_1), \ldots, h(f_n))$ belongs to K, then $p(w) = q(w)$ for any polynomials p, q on $\mathbf{C}^n$ such that $p(f_1, \ldots, f_n) = q(f_1, \ldots, f_n)$; so $p - q$ vanishes on K and hence at λ. So $p(f_1, \ldots, f_n) \to p(\lambda)$ is a well-defined continuous homomorphism on a dense subalgebra of A. Thus $\exists h \in \mathcal{M}(A)$ with $\lambda_i = h(f_i)$ $(1 \le i \le n)$, so $\lambda \in K$.)

A compact set K is polynomially convex iff the evaluation map from K into $\mathcal{M}(P(K))$ is onto. In particular, if $P(K) = C(K)$, then K is polynomially convex.

Polynomial convexity is not a topological property. Observe that the unit circle T in $\mathbf{C}^1$ is not polynomially convex, since hull(T) = Δ, the closed unit disk. On the other hand, we know that if $K = \{(\lambda, \lambda^{-1}) : \lambda \in T\}$, then $P(K) = C(K)$; thus K is a polynomially convex simple closed curve in $\mathbf{C}^2$. (Note that K is in fact a " plane curve," since K sits in $\{z \in \mathbf{C}^2 : z_1 = \bar{z}_2\}$, a real two-dimensional subspace of $\mathbf{R}^4$.)

By the separation theorem (cf. §1.4), a compact set K in $\mathbf{C}^n$ is convex iff for each $\lambda \notin K$, there is a real-linear functional ψ on $\mathbf{C}^n$ with $\psi(\lambda) > \max_K \psi$. This may suggest why the phrase " polynomially convex" is used.

Since hull(K) = $\mathcal{M}(P(K))$, every $f \in P(K)$ has a natural continuous extension $\hat{f}$ to hull(K), where $\hat{f}$ is the Gelfand transform of f. (More specifically, if $\lambda \in$ hull(K), and p_n are polynomials converging uniformly to f on K, then $\hat{f}(\lambda) = \lim_n p_n(\lambda)$.) The extension still satisfies $|\hat{f}(\lambda)| \le \max_K |f|$ for every $\lambda \in$ hull(K).

Theorem 1.   *Let K be a compact set in $\mathbf{C}^n$. Then:*

(a) *the Šilov boundary of $P(K)$ is contained in the topological boundary of* hull(K) *in $\mathbf{C}^n$;*

(b) $\mathbf{C}^n \backslash$ hull(K) *is connected.*

Proof. (a) Let $f \in P(K)$. Then f is a uniform limit of polynomials $\{p_n\}$ on K, so $\|f\| = \lim \|p_n\|$ and $\|\hat{f}\|_{\mathrm{bd(hu}(K))} = \lim \|p_n\|_{\mathrm{bd(hu}(K))}$. Thus it suffices to prove that every $p \in P_0(K)$ assumes its maximum modulus over K at a point of bd(hull K). But by the definition of the hull and by the maximum modulus principle for polynomials, $\max_K |p| = \max_{\mathrm{hu}(K)} |p| = \max_{\mathrm{bd(hu}(K))} |p|$, so (a) is proved.

(b) hull(K) is compact and hence lies inside a ball in $\mathbf{C}^n$. So $\mathbf{C}^n \backslash \mathrm{hull}(K)$ has one unbounded component. We show that it has no bounded components. If U is a bounded component of $\mathbf{C}^n \backslash \mathrm{hull}(K)$, then every polynomial p assumes its maximum modulus over U on $\mathrm{bd}(U) \subset \mathrm{hull}(K)$; so $U \subset \mathrm{hull}(K)$ by the definition of the hull; thus there is no such U.

Theorem 2. *If K is a compact set in $\mathbf{C}^1$, then the Šilov boundary of $P(K)$ is* bd(hull(K)).

Proof. $\Gamma(P(K)) \subset \mathrm{bd(hull}(K))$, by Theorem 1(a). Assume $\alpha \in \mathrm{bd(hull}(K))$, but $\alpha \notin \Gamma$. Then there is a closed disk D with center say $\beta \in \mathbf{C} \backslash \mathrm{hull}(K)$, such that $\alpha \in D$ but $D \cap \Gamma = \varnothing$. (If $r = \mathrm{dist}\,(\alpha, \Gamma)$, take $\beta \in \mathbf{C} \backslash \mathrm{hull}(K)$ with $|\alpha - \beta| < r/3$, and let D be the closed disk of radius $r/3$ about β.) Then $z - \beta \in P(K)$ and has no zeros on the maximal ideal space hull(K), so $z - \beta$ is invertible in $P(K)$. But

$$|(z - \beta)^{-1}(\alpha)| = |(\alpha - \beta)^{-1}| > \max_{\Gamma(P(K))} |(z - \beta)^{-1}| = \max_K |(z - \beta)^{-1}|,$$

so $\alpha \notin \mathrm{hull}(K)$.

For sets in the plane, the polynomial hull is obtained by filling in the holes.

Theorem 3. *Let K be a compact set in $\mathbf{C}^1$. Then* hull(K) *is the union of K with the bounded components of* $\mathbf{C} \backslash K$.

Proof. $K \subset \mathrm{hull}(K)$ always, and each bounded complementary component $U \subset \mathrm{hull}(K)$ by the maximum modulus theorem. (See the argument for Theorem 1(b) above.) Let Ω be the unbounded component of $\mathbf{C} \backslash K$ and let $\alpha \in \Omega$. Suppose that $\alpha \in \mathrm{hull}(K)$. Choose $\beta \in \Omega \backslash \mathrm{hull}(K)$. Since Ω is connected and meets hull(K) and its complement, Ω meets $\mathrm{bd(hull}(K)) = \Gamma(P(K))$, so Ω meets K. This is a contradiction, so $\Omega \cap \mathrm{hull}(K)$ is empty.

Theorem 4. *A compact set K in $\mathbf{C}^1$ is polynomially convex iff its complement is connected.*

Again let K be a compact set in $\mathbf{C}^n$. The *rational convex hull of K* is the set R-$hull(K)$ consisting of all $\lambda \in \mathbf{C}^n$ such that $|g(\lambda)| \leq \max_K |g|$ for all rational functions g which are finite on K. Observe that $K \subset R$-hull$(K) \subset \mathrm{hull}(K)$. K is *rationally convex* iff $K = R$-hull(K).

Theorem 5. (a) $\lambda \in R\text{-hull}(K)$ *iff* $p(\lambda) \in p(K)$ *for every polynomial p on* $\mathbf{C}^n$. (b) $R\text{-hull}(K)$ *is the maximal ideal space of* $R(K)$.

Proof. (a) If there is a polynomial p such that $p(\lambda) \notin p(K)$, then $p - p(\lambda)$ is a polynomial with no zeros on K, so the rational function $(p - p(\lambda))^{-1}$ is finite on K. Since this function has value ∞ at λ, $\lambda \notin R\text{-hull}(K)$. Conversely, if $\lambda \notin R\text{-hull}(K)$, then there are polynomials p, q such that $|q| > 0$ on K and $|p(\lambda)/q(\lambda)| > \max_K |p/q|$. We multiply by a constant and suppose that $p(\lambda)/q(\lambda) = 1$. Then $r = p - q$ is a polynomial, and $r(\lambda) = 0 \notin r(K)$.

(b) If $\lambda \in R\text{-hull}(K)$, then $g \to g(\lambda)$ is a continuous homomorphism from $R_0(K)$ onto $\mathbf{C}$, so it extends to a complex homomorphism h_λ of $R(K)$.

Conversely, let $h \in \mathcal{M}(R(K))$. Then the restriction of h to $P(K)$ is a complex homomorphism, so there is a point $\lambda \in \text{hull}(K)$ such that $h(p) = p(\lambda)$ for every polynomial p. Given g in $R_0(K)$, $g = p/q$ where p, q are polynomials and q vanishes nowhere on K. Since q is an invertible element of $R(K)$, $q(\lambda) \neq 0$. Thus $p = qg$, so $p(\lambda) = q(\lambda)h(g)$ and $h(g) = p(\lambda)/q(\lambda)$. Note that condition (a) has the following equivalent form: if a polynomial vanishes at λ, it vanishes somewhere on K. So we see that $\lambda \in R\text{-hull}(K)$, and h agrees with h_λ on a dense subalgebra. Hence $h = h_\lambda$.

Corollary 1. *Every compact set in* $\mathbf{C}^1$ *is rationally convex.*

Corollary 2. *Every f in* $R_0(K)$ *extends to be holomorphic on a nbhd of R-hull(K).*

Proof. $f = p/q$ on K, where p and q are polynomials and q vanishes nowhere on K. By (a), q vanishes nowhere on $R\text{-hull}(K)$, so f extends to a rational function on $R\text{-hull}(K)$. (If $f = p_1/q_1$ also on K, then $qp_1 - q_1p$ vanishes identically on $R\text{-hull}(K)$, so the extension is independent of how we represent f on K.)

Let's sketch the proof of an interesting result about rational hulls of sets in $\mathbf{C}^n$ $(n > 1)$ which is far from true in $\mathbf{C}^1$. (A rigorous proof would require too long a detour to be worth giving.)

Theorem 6. *Let U be a nonempty bounded open set in* $\mathbf{C}^n$, *where* $n > 1$. *Then* $U \subset R\text{-hull}(\text{bd}(U))$. *(If a polynomial vanishes at a point in U, it vanishes somewhere on the boundary of U.)*

Proof. By translating coordinates, we can suppose that $0 \in U$ and $p(0) = 0$, where p is a polynomial on $\mathbf{C}^n$. Let $V = \{z \in \mathbf{C}^n : p(z) = 0\}$. We must show that V meets $\text{bd}(U)$. If not, then $W = V \cap U = V \cap \bar{U}$ is a compact set containing 0, and W is open in V.

For each $t \geq 0$, let C_t be the set of points $(\lambda, t, t, \ldots, t) \in \mathbf{C}^n$, where λ is arbitrary in $\mathbf{C}$. (Each C_t is a complex plane sitting in $\mathbf{C}^n$.) By assumption, $0 \in C_0 \cap W$. Since $|(\lambda, t, \ldots, t)|^2 = |\lambda|^2 + (n-1)t^2$, the distance from 0 to C_t is $t\sqrt{n-1}$ and this $\to \infty$ as $t \to \infty$. W is bounded and the distances increase monotonically with t, so $\{t : \mathrm{dist}\,(0, C_t) \leq \max_{z \in W} |z|\}$ is a closed interval $[0, T]$. If C_{t_n} meets W for a sequence $\{t_n\}$ in $[0, T]$ and if $t_n \to t$, then C_t meets W. So $\{t : C_t \text{ meets } W\}$ is closed in $[0, T]$ and hence has a largest element t_0.

Let $f_t(\lambda) = p(\lambda, t, t, \ldots, t)$. Each f_t is a polynomial on $\mathbf{C}$ whose coefficients are polynomials in t. Either f_{t_0} is identically zero, or f_{t_0} has only finitely many zeros. If $f_{t_0} = 0$, then p vanishes identically on C_{t_0}. Now C_{t_0} meets W and hence meets U. Since U is bounded, C_{t_0} meets the complement of U. Hence since C_{t_0} is connected, C_{t_0} meets $\mathrm{bd}(U)$. But then if $f_{t_0} = 0$, p would vanish at a point of $\mathrm{bd}(U)$, which we are assuming is not true.

Let $w_1, \ldots, w_m$ be those zeros of f_{t_0} for which $(w_1, t_0, \ldots, t_0), \ldots, (w_m, t_0, \ldots, t_0)$ belong to W. (Repeat multiple roots according to their multiplicities.) The coefficients of λ in $f_t(\lambda)$ are continuous functions of t, and the roots of a polynomial are continuous functions of its coefficients. (This follows from Rouché's theorem.) Hence $\exists \varepsilon > 0$ such that if $|t - t_0| < \varepsilon$, f_t has m roots $w_1(t), \ldots, w_m(t)$ which come arbitrarily close to $w_1, \ldots, w_m$. Since W is a nbhd of the points $(w_j, t_0, \ldots, t_0)$ in V, there is a $t > t_0$ for which all the $(w_j(t), t, \ldots, t)$ belong to W. Hence C_t meets W, and we have a contradiction.

It is clear that $P(K)$ is finitely generated, with generators $z_1, \ldots, z_n$. It is less obvious that $R(K)$ is finitely generated, but this also turns out to be true.

Theorem 7. *Let X be a compact set in $\mathbf{C}^n$. Then there is a function $f \in R(X)$ such that $z_1, \ldots, z_n, f$ generate $R(X)$.*

Proof. Let Q_1 be the family of all rational functions of form $1/p$, where p is a polynomial vanishing nowhere on X. Then $z_1, \ldots, z_n$ and Q_1 generate $R(X)$. Let P_1 be the family of all polynomials p on $\mathbf{C}^n$ such that p vanishes nowhere on X and all the coefficients in p have rational real and imaginary parts. P_1 is countable. Enumerate its members as $p_1, p_2, \ldots$. Since X is compact, the family $Q = \{1/p : p \in P_1\}$ is dense in Q_1. So $R(X)$ is generated by the countable set $Q \cup \{z_1, \ldots, z_n\}$.

Choose positive numbers a_i such that $a_1 = 1$ and

$$\|p_k\| a_k^{-1} \sum_{i=k+1}^{\infty} a_i \left\| \frac{1}{p_i} \right\| < 1 \qquad \text{for } k = 1, 2, \ldots,$$

where the norm is the sup norm over X. (For example, take $a_1 = 1$ and

$$a_{k+1} = \frac{1}{2^{k+2}} \left\| \frac{1}{p_{k+1}} \right\|^{-1} \min\left(\frac{a_1}{\|p_1\|}, \ldots, \frac{a_k}{\|p_k\|} \right) \qquad \text{for } k = 1, 2, \ldots.)$$

Set $f = \sum_{i=1}^{\infty} \dfrac{a_i}{p_i}$. Since $\sum_{i=2}^{\infty} a_i \left\| \dfrac{1}{p_i} \right\| < \infty$, $f \in R(X)$. We prove that $z_1, \ldots, z_n, f$ generate $R(X)$.

It suffices to prove that each p_i^{-1} belongs to the closed subalgebra A generated by f and the polynomials. Since $\|p_1 f - 1\| = \left\| \sum_{i=2}^{\infty} \dfrac{a_i p_1}{p_i} \right\| < 1$, $p_1 f$ is invertible in A. (See Chapter Two.) But then $p_1^{-1} = f(p_1 f)^{-1}$ belongs to A. Assume now that $1/p_1, \ldots, 1/p_k$ belong to A. Then

$$\left\| \frac{p_{k+1}}{a_{k+1}} \left(f - \sum_{i=1}^{k} \frac{a_i}{p_i} \right) - 1 \right\| = \left\| \frac{p_{k+1}}{a_{k+1}} \sum_{i=k+2}^{\infty} \frac{a_i}{p_i} \right\| < 1,$$

so $p_{k+1} a_{k+1}^{-1} \left(f - \sum_{i=1}^{k} a_i p_i^{-1} \right)$ is an invertible element of A. Thus $1/p_{k+1}$ belongs to A. By induction, every p_i^{-1} is in A, so the theorem is proved.

EXERCISE SET 5.2

1. Suppose that K is a compact set in $\mathbf{C}^n$ and every point of K has real coordinates. Then K is polynomially convex.

2. Every compact set in $\mathbf{C}^n$ is homeomorphic to a polynomially convex set in $\mathbf{C}^{2n}$.

3. The torus $T^n = \{(z_1, \ldots, z_n) \in \mathbf{C}^n : |z_1| = \cdots = |z_n| = 1\}$ has a connected complement in $\mathbf{C}^n$ if $n > 1$, but T^n is not polynomially convex. So Theorem 4 is a one-dimensional theorem only.

4. Let $K_1 = \{\lambda \in \mathbf{C} : 1 \leq |\lambda| \leq 2\}$. The Šilov boundary of $P(K_1)$ is a proper subset of $\mathrm{bd}(K_1)$, so K_1 and $\mathrm{hull}(K_1)$ have distinct boundaries.

5. Let K be the bicylinder $\{(\lambda_1, \lambda_2) \in \mathbf{C}^2 : |\lambda_1| \leq 1, |\lambda_2| \leq 1\}$. K is polynomially convex. The Šilov boundary of $P(K)$ is T^2. (Each $(\lambda_1, \lambda_2) \in T^2$ is a peak point for $(1 + \bar{\lambda}_1 z_1)(1 + \bar{\lambda}_2 z_2)$.) The topological boundary of K is the union of two intersecting solid tori, hence is three-dimensional, while $\Gamma(P(K))$ is a two-dimensional object.

6. Let $K = \{(\lambda, \lambda^{-1}) : |\lambda| = 1\} \cup \{(\lambda, \lambda^{-1}) : |\lambda| = 2\}$. Show that $\mathrm{hull}(K) = \{(\lambda, \lambda^{-1}) : 1 \leq |\lambda| \leq 2\}$. In this case the hull of the union of two "circles" is an "annulus."

7. If a polynomial p vanishes identically on K, then p vanishes identically on $\mathrm{hull}(K)$.

8. Let A be a sup norm algebra on a compact space X, and let $f \in A$. Show that $\mathrm{bd}(\sigma_A(f)) \subset f(X)$.

9. Let K be a compact set in the plane. Show that the Šilov boundary of $R(K)$ is $\mathrm{bd}(K)$ and the Šilov boundary of $A(K)$ is $\mathrm{bd}(K)$.

10. Let A be the function algebra on the closed unit disk Δ generated by z and $|z|$. Show that $\mathcal{M}(A)$ is a solid cone (or rather, a frustrum of such a cone).

5.3 UNIFORM APPROXIMATION IN THE PLANE

Theorem 8. *Let X be a compact set in the plane whose complement $\mathbf{C}\backslash X$ is connected. Then $P(X) = R(X)$.*

Proof. A rational function f has a partial fraction decomposition,
$$f(z) = \sum_{v=0}^{N} \sum_{j=1}^{m_v} \frac{c_{jv}}{(z - z_v)^j} + p(z), \text{ where } p \text{ is a polynomial. So it suffices to show}$$
that for every $\alpha \notin X$, $(z - \alpha)^{-1} \in P(X)$.

Let $\mu \in M(X)$ annihilate $P(X)$. We must show that $\int_X (z - \alpha)^{-1} \, d\mu(z) = 0$ for all $\alpha \in \mathbf{C}\backslash X$. Note that if $F(\alpha) = \int_X (z - \alpha)^{-1} \, d\mu(z)$ ($\alpha \in \mathbf{C}\backslash X$), then F is analytic on the complement of X. Let $R > \max_{z \in X} |z|$. Then if $|\alpha| > R$, $z \to (z - \alpha)^{-1}$ is analytic on the disk of radius R about 0, so $(z - \alpha)^{-1} = \sum_{n=0}^{\infty} c_n z^n$, the series converging uniformly on X. Hence if $|\alpha| > R$, then $F(\alpha) = \sum c_n \int_X z^n \, d\mu(z) = 0$, since $\mu \in P(X)^{\perp}$. Since $\mathbf{C}\backslash X$ is a domain and F vanishes on a nonvoid open subset of $\mathbf{C}\backslash X$, $F = 0$; i.e., μ annihilates $(z - \alpha)^{-1}$ for every $\alpha \notin X$.

Conversely, if $P(X) = R(X)$, then $\mathbf{C}\backslash X$ is connected. For if $P(X) = R(X)$, then their maximal ideal spaces are the same. So hull$(X) = R$-hull$(X) = X$ (remember that $X \subset \mathbf{C}^1$) and $\mathbf{C}\backslash X$ is connected. Since $R(X) \subset A(X)$, note also that if $\mathbf{C}\backslash X$ is not connected, then $P(X) \neq A(X)$. Mergelyan's theorem, which we shall prove later, asserts that the converse is also true: if $\mathbf{C}\backslash X$ is connected, then $P(X) = A(X)$. The proof is much more difficult than the easy proof of Theorem 8.

The next result is a basic one concerning singular integrals. Its proof goes back at least as far as the work of A. Denjoy in the 1930's.

Lemma 1. *Let σ be a positive measure in $M(X)$. Then for almost all α in the plane, $(z - \alpha)^{-1} \in L^1(\sigma)$. Furthermore, if $F(z) = \int_X \frac{d\sigma(\zeta)}{|\zeta - z|}$, then F is integrable* (*with respect to Lebesgue measure in the plane) over every compact set.*

Proof. A few measure theoretic words may be in order. We write $dx\,dy$ for the restriction of two-dimensional Lebesgue measure to the Borel sets in $\mathbf{C} = \mathbf{R}^2$. The "almost everywhere" statement above is a.e.$[dx\,dy]$. Define $F(z)$ to be $+\infty$ for each z such that $|\zeta - z|^{-1} \notin L^1(\sigma)$.

The proof uses the Fubini theorem. Note that $|\zeta - z|^{-1}$ is a Borel measurable nonnegative function on $X \times \mathbf{C}$. Let E be a square containing X. Let R be the diameter of E, and for each $\zeta \in X$, let D_ζ be the closed disk with center ζ and radius R. Then if $\zeta \in X$,
$$\iint_E \frac{dx\,dy}{|\zeta - z|} \le \iint_{D_\zeta} \frac{dx\,dy}{|\zeta - z|} = \iint_{D_\zeta \backslash \{\zeta\}} \frac{dx\,dy}{|\zeta - z|} = \int_0^{2\pi} \int_{(0,R]} \frac{r\,dr\,d\theta}{r} = 2\pi R.$$

(Here we use the fact that $\{\zeta\}$ has $dx\, dy$ measure 0, and change to polar co-ordinates: $z = \zeta + re^{i\theta}$ ($0 < r \le R$), on $D_\zeta \backslash \{\zeta\}$.) Thus

$$\iint_E F(z)\, dx\, dy = \iint_E \left(\int_X \frac{d\sigma(\zeta)}{|\zeta - z|} \right) dx\, dy$$

$$= \int_X \left(\iint_E \frac{dx\, dy}{|\zeta - z|} \right) d\sigma(\zeta) \le 2\pi R \, \|\sigma\| < \infty.$$

So by Fubini-Tonneli-Hobson, $F(z)$ is finite a.e. on E and $F \in L^1(dx\, dy)$ over E. So F is integrable over every compact set.

As a consequence of the lemma, if $\mu \in M(X)$, then $\int_X \frac{d|\mu|(\zeta)}{|\zeta - z|} < \infty$ for almost all $z \in \mathbf{C}$. So for almost all z, $\int_X \frac{d\mu(\zeta)}{\zeta - z}$ exists. For example, if $\{\zeta_n\}$ is a countable dense subset of X and $\{c_n\}$ is a sequence of complex numbers such that $\sum |c_n| < \infty$, then $\sum \frac{c_n}{\zeta_n - z}$ converges absolutely for almost all $z \in \mathbf{C}$.

Lemma 2. *Let X be a compact set in the plane. Let $\mu \in M(X)$. If $\int_X \frac{d\mu(\zeta)}{\zeta - z} = 0$ for almost all z, then $\mu = 0$.*

The lemma will follow easily once we establish the following proposition. In terms of Schwartz distributions, it says that in $\mathbf{R}^2$, $-\frac{\partial}{\partial \bar{z}} \left(\frac{1}{z} \right)$ is the Dirac delta distribution. (This result goes back to D. Pompeiu (1912).)

Theorem 9. *Let f be a continuously differentiable function on $\mathbf{R}^2$ which vanishes outside a compact set. Set $f_{\bar{z}} = \frac{1}{2} \left(\frac{\partial f}{\partial x} + i \frac{\partial f}{\partial y} \right)$. Then for every $\alpha = a + ib$ in $\mathbf{C}$,*

$$(\star) \qquad\qquad f(a, b) = -\frac{1}{\pi} \iint_{\mathbf{R}^2} \frac{f_{\bar{z}}(x, y)}{x + iy - \alpha}\, dx\, dy.$$

Proof. Let $\alpha = a + ib$ be any complex number. Since $f_{\bar{z}}$ is bounded and continuous and vanishes outside a compact set E, $\iint_E \frac{|f_{\bar{z}}|}{|z - \alpha|}\, dx\, dy < \infty$, as we saw in the proof of Lemma 1. Hence the right side of $(\star)$ exists. Let $\varepsilon > 0$ and $D_\varepsilon = \{ z \in \mathbf{C} : |z - \alpha| \ge \varepsilon \}$. Then as $\varepsilon \to 0$,

$$\delta(\varepsilon) = -\frac{1}{\pi} \iint_{D_\varepsilon} (z - \alpha)^{-1} f_{\bar{z}}\, dx\, dy$$

approaches the right side of (★) (by the dominated convergence theorem, since $\chi_{D_\varepsilon}|z-\alpha|^{-1}|f_{\bar z}| \leq |z-\alpha|^{-1}M\chi_E \in L^1$ for some M, and by the fact that $\{\alpha\}$ has $dx\,dy$ measure 0). Change to polar coordinates and use the chain rule: if $F(r,\theta) = f(a + r\cos\theta, b + r\sin\theta)$ $(\varepsilon \leq r < \infty, 0 \leq \theta \leq 2\pi)$, then

$$[F_r \quad F_\theta] = [f_x \quad f_y]\begin{bmatrix} \cos\theta & -r\sin\theta \\ \sin\theta & r\cos\theta \end{bmatrix},$$

so

$$[f_x \quad f_y] = [F_r \quad F_\theta]\begin{bmatrix} \cos\theta & -r\sin\theta \\ \sin\theta & r\cos\theta \end{bmatrix}^{-1}$$

$$= \frac{1}{r}[F_r \quad F_\theta]\begin{bmatrix} r\cos\theta & r\sin\theta \\ -\sin\theta & \cos\theta \end{bmatrix}.$$

Hence $f_{\bar z} = \frac{1}{2}f_x + \frac{i}{2}f_y = \frac{e^{i\theta}}{2}\left(F_r + \frac{i}{r}F_\theta\right)$ where $F_r = \dfrac{\partial F}{\partial r}$, $F_\theta = \dfrac{\partial F}{\partial \theta}$. So $-\delta(\varepsilon) = \dfrac{1}{2\pi}\displaystyle\int_\varepsilon^\infty \int_0^{2\pi}\left(F_r + \frac{i}{r}F_\theta\right) d\theta\, dr$. Since F is periodic in θ, $\displaystyle\int_0^{2\pi}F_\theta\, d\theta = 0$. Thus

$$-\delta(\varepsilon) = \frac{1}{2\pi}\int_\varepsilon^\infty \int_0^{2\pi} F_r\, d\theta\, dr$$

$$= \frac{1}{2\pi}\int_0^{2\pi}\int_\varepsilon^R \frac{\partial F}{\partial r}(r,\theta)\, dr\, d\theta$$

where R is chosen so that f vanishes for $|z - \alpha| \geq R$. So

$$\delta(\varepsilon) = \frac{1}{2\pi}\int_0^{2\pi} F(\varepsilon,\theta)\, d\theta$$

$$= \frac{1}{2\pi}\int_0^{2\pi} f(a + \varepsilon\cos\theta, b + \varepsilon\sin\theta)\, d\theta.$$

As $\varepsilon \to 0$, the integrands approach $f(a,b)$, uniformly in θ, so $\delta(\varepsilon) \to f(a,b)$ as $\varepsilon \to 0$, and (★) is established.

Now we prove Lemma 2. Lef f be a continuously differentiable function which vanishes outside a compact set E containing X. Then

$$\int_X f(\lambda)\, d\mu(\lambda) = \int_X \left(\iint_E -\frac{1}{\pi}(z-\lambda)^{-1}f_{\bar z}\, dx\, dy\right) d\mu(\lambda)$$

$$= \iint_E -\frac{f_{\bar z}}{\pi}\left(\int_X \frac{d\mu(\lambda)}{z-\lambda}\right) dx\, dy = 0.$$

(We can use the Fubini theorem, since the integrand is Borel measurable and $f_{\bar z}$ is bounded. Cf. Lemma 1.) Thus μ annihilates every such f. Since the functions of this kind are dense in $C(X)$, μ is the zero measure.

Theorem 10.   *Let X be a compact set in the plane. Then if every point of X is a peak point for $R(X)$, $R(X) = C(X)$.*

Proof.   Suppose that $R(X) \neq C(X)$. Then $R(X)^\perp$ contains a nonzero complex measure μ. For each $\alpha \in \mathbf{C}\backslash X$, $\int_X (z - \alpha)^{-1} d\mu(z) = 0$. But $\mu \neq 0$, so by Lemma 2, $\exists z_0 \in X$ such that $\int |z - z_0|^{-1} d|\mu|(z) < \infty$ and

$$\int (z - z_0)^{-1} d\mu(z) \neq 0.$$

We can multiply μ by a constant, and suppose that $\displaystyle\int_X \frac{d\mu(z)}{z - z_0} = 1$.

If $f \in R_0(X)$, then $\dfrac{f(z) - f(z_0)}{z - z_0}$ is in $R_0(X)$, so it is annihilated by μ.

Hence $\displaystyle\int_X \frac{f(z)}{z - z_0} d\mu(z) = f(z_0)$. So $(z - z_0)^{-1} d\mu(z)$ is a complex measure on X which represents evaluation at z_0 on $R_0(X)$.

Take $g \in R(X)$ and f_n in $R_0(X)$ with $f_n \to g$ uniformly on X. The sup norms of the f_n are uniformly bounded and $|z - z_0|^{-1} \in L^1(|\mu|)$, so by the dominated convergence theorem,

$$\int (z - z_0)^{-1} f_n(z)\, d\mu(z) \to \int (z - z_0)^{-1} g(z) d\mu(z).$$

Thus $(z - z_0)^{-1} d\mu(z)$ represents evaluation at z_0 on $R(X)$. (Thus we have shown that if $\mu \in R(X)^\perp$, then there is a function a such that $\dfrac{a(z_0)\, d\mu(z)}{z - z_0}$ "pseudo-represents" evaluation at z_0 for each $z_0 \in X$ such that $\int (z - z_0)^{-1} d\mu(z)$ converges absolutely to a nonzero number.)

Note that since $|z - z_0|^{-1} \in L^1(|\mu|)$, $|\mu|(\{z_0\}) = 0$.

Now we use the hypothesis that every $x \in X$ is a peak point for $R(X)$. There is a function $g \in R(X)$ such that $g(z_0) = 1$ but $|g| < 1$ on $X\backslash\{z_0\}$. For each positive integer n, $\displaystyle\int_X \frac{g^n(z)}{z - z_0} d\mu(z) = g(z_0)^n = 1$. But $g^n \to \chi_{\{z_0\}}$ boundedly on X, so $g^n \to 0$ boundedly a.e. $[|\mu|]$ on X. Hence $\displaystyle\int_X \frac{g^n(z)}{z - z_0} d\mu(z) \to 0$ (again by dominated convergence), and this is a contradiction. So $R(X)^\perp = \{0\}$ and $R(X) = C(X)$.

Theorem 11.   *Let X be a compact set in the plane.*

(a) *If the interior of X is empty, then for every nonzero annihilator μ of $R(X)$, the closed support of μ has positive planar measure.*

(b) *If X has a nonempty interior, then there is a nonzero annihilator of $R(X)$ whose closed support has planar measure zero.*

Proof.   (a) Suppose that int $X = \varnothing$. Take $\mu \in R(X)^\perp$. Let E be the closed support of μ, and let $F(\alpha) = \displaystyle\int_E (z - \alpha)^{-1} d\mu(z)$. Then F is analytic on the complement of E, and F vanishes on $\mathbf{C}\backslash X$. Since int $X = \varnothing$, $X\backslash E \subset X =$

bd($\mathbf{C}\backslash X$), so by continuity F vanishes on $X\backslash E$. Thus F vanishes on $\mathbf{C}\backslash E$. If E has planar measure zero, then $\int_X (z - \alpha)^{-1} d\mu(z) = 0$ for almost all α; thus $\mu = 0$ by Lemma 2.

(b) Take z_0 in the interior of X, and choose $r > 0$ so that every point of the closed disk with center z_0 and radius r is in the interior of X. By the mean value property of analytic functions,

$$f(z_0) = \int_X f \, d\delta_{z_0} = \frac{1}{2\pi} \int_0^{2\pi} f(z_0 + re^{it}) \, dt$$

for every f in $R(X)$. So $\delta_{z_0} - \frac{1}{2\pi} d\theta$ is a nonzero annihilator of $R(X)$ whose closed support has planar measure 0.

There are no known geometric conditions on X which are necessary and sufficient for $R(X)$ and $C(X)$ to coincide. One obvious necessary condition is that the interior of X be empty. However, this condition is not sufficient, as is shown by Mergelyan's "Swiss cheese" algebras, which we now describe.

Let Δ be the closed unit disk. Construct a sequence of open disks $\{D_n\}$ in Δ with radii $\{r_n\}$ such that:

(1) $D_i \cap D_j = \varnothing$ if $i \neq j$;
(2) $\sum r_n < \infty$;
(3) $X = \Delta\backslash\bigcup_{n=1}^{\infty} D_n$ has an empty interior.

(We construct examples of such disks below, and in the examples we have further that $\bar{D}_i \cap \bar{D}_j = \varnothing$ if $i \neq j$.)

Let γ_n be the positively oriented boundary of D_n and γ the positively oriented unit circle. Define a complex measure μ as follows:

$$\int_X f \, d\mu = \int_\gamma f(z) \, dz - \sum_{n=1}^{\infty} \int_{\gamma_n} f(z) \, dz \qquad (f \in C(X)).$$

By (2), $\mu \in M(X)$. It is clear that $\mu \neq 0$, and it is easy to see that μ annihilates $R(X)$. So $R(X) \neq C(X)$. (Let f be a rational function on X. If no pole of f lies in D_j, then $\int_{\gamma_j} f(z) \, dz = 0$, by Cauchy's theorem. f has only a finite number of poles, so $\sum_n \int_{\gamma_n} f(z) \, dz$ is a finite sum. Finally, by the residue theorem, if $b_1, \ldots, b_s$ are the distinct poles of f inside Δ, then $\int_\gamma f(z) \, dz = 2\pi i \sum_1^s \mathrm{Res}\,(f; b_i) = \sum_n \int_{\gamma_n} f(z) \, dz$; thus $\int f \, d\mu = 0$.)

Since X has an empty interior, this is our first example of a finitely generated function algebra (which is proper) whose Šilov boundary and maximal ideal space coincide. (Note that the annihilator μ is concentrated on a set of planar measure zero. Compare with Theorem 11.)

Here is a way to construct Swiss cheeses in the closed unit disk Δ. For $a \in \mathbf{C}$ and $r > 0$, let $D(a, r)$ be the open disk of radius r about a. Take any

$a_1 \in$ int Δ. Choose r_1 so that $0 < r_1 < \min\left(\frac{1}{2}, \text{dist}\,(a_1, \text{bd}(\Delta))\right)$, and let $D_1 = D(a_1, r_1)$, $X_1 = \Delta \backslash D_1$. Then X_1 is compact and connected, and X_1 has a nonvoid interior. Define d_1 on X_1 by $d_1(x) = \text{dist}\,(x, \text{bd}(X_1))$. Then d_1 has a strictly positive maximum at some point $a_2 \in X_1$. Choose $r_2 > 0$ so that

$$r_2 < \min\left(\frac{1}{2^2}, d_1(a_2)\right), \quad \text{and let}\quad D_2 = D(a_2, r_2), \quad X_2 = \Delta \backslash (D_1 \cup D_2).$$

The pattern is now clear. We obtain disks $D_n = D(a_n, r_n)$ and compact sets $X_n = \Delta \backslash (D_1 \cup \cdots \cup D_n)$ such that the $\bar{D}_n$ are pairwise disjoint and

$$r_{n+1} < \min\left(\frac{1}{2^{n+1}}, d_n(a_{n+1})\right) \text{ for all } n, \text{ where } d_n(x) = \text{dist}\,(x, \text{bd}(X_n))\ (x \in X_n)$$

and a_{n+1} is chosen so as to maximize d_n.

Let $X = \bigcap_n X_n = \Delta \backslash \bigcup_{n=1}^{\infty} D_n$. We have to check that X has an empty interior. If not, then there is a closed disk $\bar{D} = \bar{D}(z_0, r)$ contained in the interior of X. Since $\bar{D}$ is interior to each X_n, $r \leq \text{dist}\,(z_0, \text{bd}(X_n)) \leq d_n(a_{n+1})$ for all n. But then for all distinct n and m, $|a_n - a_m| \geq r$. (Fix n and let $1 \leq j < n + 1$. Then $\text{bd}(D_j) \subset \text{bd}(X_n)$. The line segment from a_j to a_{n+1} meets $\text{bd}(D_j)$ in a point b_{jn}, so $d_n(a_{n+1}) = \text{dist}\,(a_{n+1}, \text{bd}(X_n)) \leq |a_{n+1} - a_j|$.) This is clearly a contradiction, since some subsequence of $\{a_n\}$ must converge in Δ.

Lemma 3. *Let K be a compact set in the plane, and let U be an open set containing K. Then there exist oriented line segments $\gamma_1, \ldots, \gamma_n$ lying in $U \backslash K$ such that for every function f analytic in U, the Cauchy formula $f(z) =$*

$$\sum_{j=1}^{n} \frac{1}{2\pi i} \int_{\gamma_j} \frac{f(\xi)}{\xi - z}\, d\xi \text{ holds for every } z \in K.$$

   Proof. See p. 255, [K] for the details. One lays down a grid of lines parallel to the x- and y-axes with the distance between consecutive lines equal to one-third the distance from K to $\text{bd}(U)$. (If U is the whole plane there is no problem.) Take all the closed squares which meet K, delete common boundaries of abutting squares, and retain the remaining closed segments. These are $\gamma_1, \ldots, \gamma_n$. For a point of K inside one of the squares, the formula follows from the usual Cauchy formula, the integrals over all but one of the squares vanishing by Cauchy's theorem. A continuity argument shows that it holds for every z in K.

Theorem 12   (Runge's Theorem). *Let K be a compact set in the plane whose complement is connected. Then every function f which is analytic on an open nhbd of K is uniformly approximable by polynomials on K.*

   Proof. The Cauchy formula in the lemma shows that f is uniformly approximable on K by linear combinations of the functions $z \to (\xi - z)^{-1}$ with $\xi \in \gamma_1 \cup \cdots \cup \gamma_n$. (Consider the Riemann sums for the integrals.) Since $R(K) = P(K)$, $f\,|\,K \in P(K)$, as asserted.

The disk algebra coincides with the uniform closure of the polynomials on the closed unit disk. In particular, every rational function on the disk is a uniform limit of polynomials. Let us now show that, conversely, every polynomial on the disk can be uniformly approximated by rational functions of a simple type.

Theorem 13. *The Möbius transformations span a dense linear subspace of the disk algebra $P(\Delta)$, where Δ is the closed unit disk.*

Proof. We have to show that if μ is a Borel measure on Δ which annihilates all functions M_α of form $M_\alpha(z) = \dfrac{z - \bar{\alpha}}{1 - \alpha z}$ ($|\alpha| < 1$), then μ annihilates all polynomials. Since $\int M_\alpha(z)\, d\mu(z) = 0$, $\int \dfrac{z}{1 - \alpha z}\, d\mu(z) = \bar{\alpha} \int \dfrac{1}{1 - \alpha z}\, d\mu(z)$ for all α in the open unit disk U. So $f(\alpha) = \bar{\alpha} g(\alpha)$ ($\alpha \in U$), where

$$f(\alpha) = \int z(1 - \alpha z)^{-1}\, d\mu(z) \qquad \text{and} \qquad g(\alpha) = \int (1 - \alpha z)^{-1}\, d\mu(z).$$

Since f and g are analytic on U and $\bar{z}$ is nowhere analytic, we conclude that g and f vanish identically on U.

So if $|\beta| > 1$, $g\left(\dfrac{1}{\beta}\right) = \beta \int (\beta - z)^{-1}\, d\mu(z) = 0$.

Let p be a polynomial. By the Cauchy integral formula,

$$p(z) = \frac{1}{2\pi i} \int_{|\beta| = 2} p(\beta)(\beta - z)^{-1}\, d\beta \qquad (z \in \Delta).$$

So

$$2\pi i \int p(z)\, d\mu(z) = \int_\Delta \left(\int_{|\beta| = 2} p(\beta)(\beta - z)^{-1}\, d\beta \right) d\mu(z)$$

$$= \int_{|\beta| = 2} p(\beta) \left(\int_\Delta (\beta - z)^{-1}\, d\mu(z) \right) d\beta = 0.$$

(Use of the Fubini theorem is justified, since $(z, \beta) \to p(\beta)(\beta - z)^{-1}$ is continuous on $\Delta \times \{\beta : |\beta| = 2\}$ and $d\mu(z)$, $d\beta$ are finite Borel measures.) So μ does annihilate all polynomials; hence μ annihilates $P(\Delta)$.

Here is a theorem which was mentioned implicitly in Chapter III.

Theorem 14. *Let X be a compact set in the plane which has countably many elements. Then $P(X) = C(X)$.*

Proof. Note first that the complement of X is connected. For take z_1, z_2 in $\mathbb{C} \backslash X$. Since X is countable and $[0, 2\pi)$ is uncountable, there is a direction such that the ray L emanating from z_1 in that direction is disjoint from X. There are uncountably many points on L, and the line segments

$[z_0; z_2)$ with $z_0 \in L$ are disjoint, so one of them, say $[z_0^*; z_2)$, misses X. So z_1 can be joined to z_2 in $\mathbf{C} \backslash X$ by the broken line $[z_1; z_0^*] \cup [z_0^*; z_2]$.

The planar measure of X is zero, so $R(X) = C(X)$. (See Exercise 1.) And $P(X) = R(X)$, by Theorem 8. So $P(X) = C(X)$.

Corollary. *Let X be a compact space with countably many elements. Then every closed subalgebra of $C(X)$ is self-adjoint, and $C(X)$ is the only function algebra on X.*

Proof. Take a closed subalgebra A in $C(X)$, and let $f \in A$. Then $f(X)$ is a compact plane set with at most denumerably many elements, and so is $\{0\} \cup f(X)$. By the theorem there are polynomials p_n converging uniformly to $\bar{z}$ on $\{0\} \cup f(X)$. Let $q_n = p_n - p_n(0)$. The q_n are polynomials without constant term which converge uniformly to $\bar{z}$ on $f(X)$. Since A is a closed subalgebra, $\bar{f} = \lim (q_n \circ f)$ belongs to A, so A is self-adjoint. If A is a function algebra, then self-adjointness implies that $A = C(X)$.

EXERCISE SET 5.3

1. Let X be a compact set in $\mathbf{C}$ whose planar measure is zero. Show that $R(X) = C(X)$. (This is a theorem of Hartogs and Rosenthal.)

2. For K a compact set in $\mathbf{C}^n$, let $H(K)$ be the set of all functions on K which are uniformly approximable by functions which are holomorphic in a *nbhd* of K. (The *nbhds* vary: $f \in H(K)$ iff $\forall \varepsilon > 0$, $\exists U$ open with $K \subset U$ and F holomorphic on U such that $|f - F| < \varepsilon$ on K.)
   Show that if $n = 1$, then $H(K) = R(K)$.

3. Let F be analytic on a simply connected plane domain Ω. Then F is uniformly approximable by polynomials on every compact subset of Ω. There is a sequence of polynomials $\{p_n\}$ such that for every compact set K contained in Ω, $p_n \to F$ uniformly on K.

4. Let X be a compact set in $\mathbf{C}$. Show that the following conditions are equivalent. Observe that if X satisfies these conditions, then the interior of X is necessarily empty.
   (a) $R(X) = C(X)$.
   (b) X is the Choquet boundary of $R(X)$.
   (c) Each $x \in X$ is a peak point for $R(X)$.
   (d) If E is the set of peak points for $R(X)$, then $X \backslash E$ has planar measure zero.
   (e) Every complex homomorphism of $R(X)$ has a unique representing measure.

5. Suppose that for each i, D_i is an open disk of radius r_i and that $\sum_{i=1}^{\infty} r_i < 1$. Let Δ be the closed unit disk and $X = \Delta \backslash \bigcup_{i=1}^{\infty} D_i$. Then $R(X) \neq C(X)$.

(For each n, let $X_n = \Delta \backslash \bigcup_{i=1}^{n} D_i$. Then $X = \bigcap_n X_n$, the intersection of a decreasing sequence of compact sets. For each n, let $\mu_n \in M(\Delta)$ be the measure which is dz on the positively oriented boundary of X_n and is zero elsewhere. If r is a rational function with poles off X, then by the finite intersection property, $\int r \, d\mu_n = 0$ for all sufficiently large n. Since $\|\mu_n\| \leq 4\pi$ for all n, $\{\mu_n\}$ has a w^*-cluster point $\mu \in M(\Delta)$. Again by the f.i.p., μ is concentrated on X, and μ clearly annihilates $R(X)$. We have $\int \bar{z} \, d\mu = \lim \int \bar{z} \, d\mu_{n_k} = \lim A_k$ for a suitable subsequence $\{n_k\}$, where A_k is the Lebesgue measure of X_{n_k}. Hence $\int \bar{z} \, d\mu > 0$ and so $\mu \neq 0$. Thus $R(X) \neq C(X)$.)

6. Suppose that X is a compact set in the plane and that the interior of X is empty. Show that for every compact set $F \subset X$ of planar measure 0, $R(X)|_F$ is dense in $C(F)$.

7. Prove that our Swiss cheese set X is connected and has empty interior. (Can you think of a physical interpretation of this result?)

8. Let S be a closed subset of Δ which has empty interior. Show that the Swiss cheese X can be chosen so that all $\bar{D}_n$ are disjoint from S; so X contains S and still satisfies the relevant conditions. For example, we can take a Cantor-like set E on $[-1, 1]$ and let S be the set of vertical chords passing through E.

9. Suppose that X is a compact set in the plane and that σ is any positive measure in $M(X)$. Show that $\int_X |\log|\xi - z|| \, d\sigma(\xi)$ is Lebesgue integrable over every compact set and hence is finite a.e. $[dx \, dy]$.

10. (Laplacian in polar coordinates). Let f be a C^2 function on $\mathbf{R}^2$, i.e., f has continuous second order partial derivatives. Set $f_{\bar{z}} = \frac{1}{2}\left(\frac{\partial f}{\partial x} + i \frac{\partial f}{\partial y}\right)$, $f_z = \frac{1}{2}\left(\frac{\partial f}{\partial x} - i \frac{\partial f}{\partial y}\right)$, $\Delta f = \frac{\partial^2 f}{\partial x^2} + \frac{\partial^2 f}{\partial y^2}$. Show that $f_{z\bar{z}} = f_{\bar{z}z} = 4 \, \Delta f$.

If (a, b) is fixed and $f(x, y) = F(r, \theta)$ ($x = a + r \cos \theta$, $y = b + r \sin \theta$), compute that $f_z = e^{-i\theta}\left(F_r - \frac{i}{r}F_\theta\right)$, $f_{\bar{z}} = e^{i\theta}\left(F_r + \frac{i}{r}F_\theta\right)$, $\Delta f = \frac{1}{r}\frac{\partial}{\partial r}\left(r\frac{\partial F}{\partial r}\right) + \frac{1}{r^2}\frac{\partial^2 F}{\partial \theta^2}$ away from (a, b).

11. Suppose that f is a C^2 function on $\mathbf{R}^2$ and that f vanishes outside a compact set. Show that $f(\alpha) = -\frac{1}{2\pi}\iint_{\mathbf{R}^2} \Delta f(z) \log \frac{1}{|z - \alpha|} \, dx \, dy$ ($z = x + iy$) for every α in $\mathbf{R}^2$.

12. Suppose that X is a compact set in the plane, that $\mu \in M(X)$, and that $\int_X \log \frac{1}{|z - \xi|} \, d\mu(\xi) = 0$ a.e. on the plane. Show that $\mu = 0$.

13. Let X, Y be compact spaces and f a continuous map from Y onto X. Let $\mathscr{F}$ be the family of all compact sets $F \subset Y$ such that $f(F) = X$, and order $\mathscr{F}$ by inclusion. Then $\mathscr{F}$ has a minimal element.

14. If T is a topological space, then x is an *isolated point* of T iff $\{x\}$ is open in T. A Hausdorff space P is *perfect* iff P is compact (hence nonvoid) and has no isolated points. A compact space Q is *scattered* iff Q contains no perfect subsets.
  (a) Show that no uncountable compact subset of the plane is scattered.
  (b) Show that if Q is a scattered compact space and if the compact space X is the continuous image of Q, then X is scattered.
  (c) Prove that if Q is scattered, then $C(Q)$ is the only function algebra on Q.

15. Fill in the details of this proof of Theorem 8: Since $\mathbf{C} \backslash X$ is connected, $X = \text{hull}(X)$. So if $\alpha \notin X$, $z - \alpha$ is invertible in $P(X)$. Hence $P(X) = R(X)$.

5.4 WALSH'S THEOREM

We are now going to prove the theorem of J. Walsh† which states: if X is a compact set in the plane and X is the boundary of the unbounded component of $\mathbf{C} \backslash X$, then $\text{Re}\,(P(X))$ is dense in $C_R(X)$. (Walsh phrases the theorem in terms of uniform approximation of real-valued harmonic functions by real trigonometric polynomials.) The result is not transparent, and we shall need some preliminary results similar to those in §5.3. (Cf. in particular Exercises 9, 10, 11, 12, §5.3.)

Lemma 4. *Let z_0, z, y be complex numbers such that $0 < \varepsilon < |z - z_0|$ and* $|z - y| < \varepsilon/2$. *Let* $w = z_0 + \dfrac{|z - z_0|}{|y - z_0|}(y - z_0)$ *be the point on the ray from z_0 through y such that $|w - z_0| = |z - z_0|$. Then each point of the segment from w to y lies in the open disk $D(z; \varepsilon)$, as does each point $h(t) = z_0 + (z - z_0)e^{it\theta}$* $(0 \le t \le 1)$, *where* $\theta = \arg\left(\dfrac{w - z_0}{z - z_0}\right)$; *that is, the shorter arc from z to w at distance $|z - z_0|$ from z_0 lies in $D(z; \varepsilon)$.*

  Proof.   Since $0 < \varepsilon < |z - z_0| \le |z - y| + |y - z_0| < \varepsilon/2 + |y - z_0|$, $|y - z_0| > 0$. Hence w exists, and $|w - z_0| = |z - z_0|$. Since $w - y = (y - z_0)$ $\left(\dfrac{|z - z_0|}{|y - z_0|} - 1\right)$, $|w - y| = \big||z - z_0| - |y - z_0|\big| \le |z - y|$; thus $|w - z| \le 2|z - y| < \varepsilon$.   Similarly, $|w + t(y - w) - z| = |y - z + (1 - t)(w - y)| \le 2|z - y| < \varepsilon$ if $0 \le t \le 1$. So $[w; y] \subset D(z; \varepsilon)$.

---

† Über die Entwicklung einer harmonischen Funktion nach harmonischen Polynomen, *Journal für die reine und angewandte Mathematik*, 159 (1928).

Now $h(t) - z = (z - z_0)(e^{it\theta} - 1)$, so $|h(t) - z| = |z - z_0| \, |e^{it\theta} - 1|$. In particular, $|w - z| = |z - z_0| \, |e^{i\theta} - 1|$, so $|e^{i\theta} - 1| = \dfrac{|w - z|}{|z - z_0|} < 1$. Hence $|\theta| \leq \pi/3$, so for $0 \leq t \leq 1$, $|e^{it\theta} - 1| \leq |e^{i\theta} - 1|$. Thus $|h(t) - z| \leq |w - z| < \varepsilon$, so the arc lies in $D(z; \varepsilon)$.

Lemma 5. *Let Ω be a domain in the plane, and let z_0 be a boundary point of Ω. Then there is a sequence $\{x_n\}$ in Ω such that*

(a) $x_n \to z_0$;

(b) $|x_1 - z_0| > |x_2 - z_0| = |x_3 - z_0| > |x_4 - z_0| = |x_5 - z_0| > \cdots$;

(c) *for each odd n, the segment $[x_n; x_{n+1}] \subset [z_0; x_n] \cap \Omega$.*

Proof. Given $x \in \Omega$, let E_x be the set of all points y in Ω which can be chained to x in the following manner: $y \in E_x$ iff there is a closed interval $[a, b]$, a continuous map $g : [a, b] \to \Omega$, and a partition $a = t_0 < t_1 < \cdots < t_n = b$ of $[a, b]$ such that for each i, either g takes $[t_{i-1}, t_i]$ one-one onto the segment $[g(t_{i-1}); g(t_i)]$ and this segment lies on the ray from z_0 through $g(t_i)$, or $|g(t) - z_0| = |g(t_i) - z_0|$ for all t in $[t_{i-1}, t_i]$. E_x contains x, and it follows from Lemma 4 that E_x is open and closed in Ω. Since Ω is connected, $E_x = \Omega$.

Given any $\delta > 0$, since z_0 belongs to $\overline{\Omega}\backslash\Omega$, there are $\{y_n\}$ in Ω such that $y_n \to z_0$ and $|y_{n+1} - z_0| < |y_n - z_0| \leq \delta$ for all n. Since y_n is chained to y_{n+1} in finitely many steps (for each separate n), the construction of $\{x_n\}$ in $\Omega \cap \overline{D}(z_0; \delta)$ is now clear.

Given Ω, $\{x_n\}$, z_0 as in Lemma 5, let S be the union of the open segments $(x_n; x_{n+1})$ for n odd, and let $a_i = |x_{2i+2} - z_0|$, $b_i = |x_{2i+1} - z_0|$ ($b_0 > a_0 = b_1 > a_1 = b_2 > \cdots$). Set $V = \bigcup_{i=0}^{\infty} (a_i, b_i)$. There is a piecewise linear homeomorphism h from V onto S, and we can use h to carry Lebesgue-Borel measure on V over to S. So there is a nonnegative Borel measure σ on S such that for every f in $L^1(\sigma)$, $f \circ h$ is in $L^1(V)$ and $\int_S f \, d\sigma = \int_V f(h(t)) \, dt = \int_0^{b_0} f(h(t)) \, dt$.

If Ω is an unbounded domain, then for any $\delta > 0$ we can find such a set $S = S(\delta)$ with the additional property that $\sigma(S) = |x_1 - z_0| = \delta$. Indeed, Ω meets the punctured disk $D(z_0; \delta)\backslash\{z_0\}$ and its exterior, so Ω must meet the circle C of radius δ about z_0. We take y_1 with $|y_1 - z_0| = \delta$ and choose our initial point x_0 suitably on C. Note that if $0 < r_1 < r_2 \leq \delta$, then $\sigma(\{z \in S : r_1 < |z - z_0| < r_2\}) = r_2 - r_1$.

The purpose of introducing the measure σ, which is concentrated on segments, is to enable us to compute explicitly some integrals below and get suitable estimates which will justify some applications of the Fubini theorem.

Lemma 6. *Let Y be a compact set in the plane, and let the complement of Y be a connected set $\Omega = \mathbf{C}\backslash Y$. Define f on $\mathbf{C} \times \mathbf{C}$ as follows: $f(z, w) = \log 1/|z - w|$ if $z \neq w$, $f(z, z) = 0$. Let $\alpha \in M(Y)$ be a real measure, and set*

$u(z) = \int_Y f(z, \xi) \, d\alpha(\xi)$ *if the integral converges absolutely, while* $u(z) = 0$ *if it does not. Then u is a Borel measurable function, and the integral converges absolutely for almost all z in* **C**.

Suppose that $u(z) = 0$ *for all z in* Ω. *Then* $u(z) = 0$ *for all z in* $\overline{\Omega}$.

Proof. Take a point z_0 in bd(Ω) such that $\int_Y |f(z_0, \xi)| \, d|\alpha|(\xi) < \infty$. We must show that $u(z_0) = \int f(z_0, \xi) \, d\alpha(\xi)$ vanishes.

Fix ρ with $0 < \rho < \frac{1}{2}$. Consider any δ with $0 < \delta < \rho$. Take $S \subset \Omega$, a union of open segments, and a positive measure σ on S such that $\sigma(\{z \in S : r_1 < |z - z_0| < r_2\}) = r_2 - r_1$ for all $0 < r_1 < r_2 \le \delta$. Note that $\sigma(S) = \delta$.

Suppose that $\xi \in Y$ and $|\xi - z_0| \le \rho$. We compute

$$\frac{1}{\delta} \int_S f(z, \xi) \, d\sigma(z) = \frac{1}{\delta} \int_S \log \frac{1}{|z - \xi|} \, d\sigma(z)$$

$$\le \frac{1}{\delta} \int_S \log \left(\frac{1}{\left| |z - z_0| - |\xi - z_0| \right|} \right) d\sigma(z)$$

$$\le \frac{1}{\delta} \int_0^\delta \log \frac{1}{|r - r_0|} \, dr$$

$$= \log \frac{1}{r_0} + \frac{1}{\delta} \int_0^\delta \log \frac{1}{|1 - r/r_0|} \, dr$$

$$= \log \frac{1}{r_0} + \frac{r_0}{\delta} \int_0^{\delta/r_0} \log \frac{1}{|1 - t|} \, dt$$

if $\xi \ne z_0$, where $r_0 = |\xi - z_0|$. (If $\xi = z_0$, then the upper estimate is

$$\frac{1}{\delta} \int_0^\delta \log \frac{1}{r} \, dr = 1 - \log \delta,$$

since $r \log r \to 0$ as $r \to 0^+$.) So if $\xi \in Y$ and $0 < |\xi - z_0| \le \rho$, then $\frac{1}{\delta} \int_S f(z, \xi) \, d\sigma(z) \le f(z_0, \xi) + C$, where $C = \sup_{T > 0} \frac{1}{T} \int_0^T \log \frac{1}{|1 - t|} \, dt$. (One computes that $C < \infty$, and in fact C is the solution of the transcendental equation $T = 1 + e^{-T}$, so $1 < C < 2$.)

Since $\xi \to |f(z_0, \xi)|$ is in $L^1(|\alpha|)$ by hypothesis, and $f(z_0, \xi) = \log \frac{1}{|z_0 - \xi|}$ for $\xi \ne z_0$, it follows from the regularity of α that $\alpha(\{z_0\}) = 0$. Let $E(\rho) = \{\xi \in Y : 0 < |\xi - z_0| < \rho\}$, $F(\rho) = \{\xi \in Y : |\xi - z_0| \ge \rho\}$. Since $f \ge 0$ on $S \times E(\rho)$ and f is continuous on $\overline{D}(z_0; \rho) \times F(\rho)$ (which contains $S \times F(\rho)$), the Fubini theorem is applicable:

$$\int_S \int_Y |f(z, \xi)| \, d|\alpha|(\xi) \, d\sigma(z) = \int_Y \int_S |f(z, \xi)| \, d\sigma(z) \, d|\alpha|(\xi) < \infty.$$

Equality is therefore true with $|f|$ replaced by f and $|\alpha|$ replaced by α. So we have $\int_S u(z)\, d\sigma(z) = \int_Y g(\xi)\, d\alpha(\xi)$, where $g(\xi) = \int_S f(z, \xi)\, d\sigma(z)$ if the integral converges absolutely and $g(\xi) = 0$ otherwise. But u vanishes identically on Ω, so $\int u\, d\sigma = 0$.

Thus $\int g\, d\alpha = 0$, and since $\alpha(\{z_0\}) = 0$ this means that

$(\star)$
$$\left| \int_{F(\rho)} \frac{1}{\delta} g\, d\alpha \right| = \left| \int_{E(\rho)} \frac{1}{\delta} g\, d\alpha \right| \le \frac{1}{\delta} \int_{E(\rho)} |g|\, d|\alpha|$$

$$\le \int_{E(\rho)} [f(z_0, \xi) + C]\, d|\alpha|(\xi).$$

Note that g depends on δ, since S and σ do. Since f is uniformly continuous on $\bar{D}(z_0; \rho) \times F(\rho)$, $\frac{1}{\delta} g_\delta(\xi)$ converges to $f(z_0, \xi)$ uniformly on $F(\rho)$ as $\delta \to 0^+$. So if we let $\delta \to 0$ in $(\star)$, we have

$(\star\star)$
$$\left| \int_{F(\rho)} f(z_0, \xi)\, d\alpha(\xi) \right| \le \int_{E(\rho)} [f(z_0, \xi) + C]\, d|\alpha|(\xi).$$

As ρ decreases to 0, the sets $E(\rho)$ decrease to the empty set, so the right hand side of $(\star\star)$ approaches 0. ($f(z_0, \xi) \ge 0$, since $|z_0 - \xi| \le \frac{1}{2}$ on $E(\rho)$. So the dominated convergence theorem will apply.) By countable additivity of α, the left hand side of $(\star\star)$ approaches $\left| \int_Y f(z_0, \xi)\, d\alpha(\xi) \right|$, so $u(z_0) = \int f(z_0, \xi)\, d\alpha(\xi) = 0$, as was to be shown.

We are now in a position to prove Walsh's theorem, and we can establish slightly more at the same time. Recall that a function G is *harmonic* on an open set $U \subset \mathbf{C}$ iff G is C^2 on U and $\Delta G = 0$ on U, where ΔG is the Laplacian of G.

Theorem 15. *Let Y be a compact plane set whose complement Ω is connected. Let X be the boundary of Y. Define $B = \{g \in C_R(X) : g$ is the uniform limit on X of real parts of polynomials in $z\}$, and let H be the set of functions $g \in C_R(X)$ for which there is a continuous function G on Y such that $G = g$ on X and G is harmonic on int Y.*

Then (a) B is a closed subspace of H containing the constants, and H is a closed subspace of $C_R(X)$; (b) each $g \in H$ has a unique harmonic extension $G \in C(Y)$; (c) for $a \in Y$, let $U_a(g) = G(a)$ $(g \in H)$; then $\|U_a\| = U_a(1) = 1$, and the set M_a of positive measures λ_a on X such that $U_a(g) = \int g\, d\lambda_a$ for all $g \in H$ is nonvoid; (d) let $a \in$ int Y and $\lambda_a \in M_a$; then $\int_X \left| \log \dfrac{1}{|z_0 - \xi|} \right| d\lambda_a(\xi)$ exists for every $z_0 \in X$, and

$$\int_X \log \frac{1}{|z_0 - \xi|}\, d\lambda_a(\xi) = \log \frac{1}{|z_0 - a|}\ ;$$

(e) $B = H = C_R(X)$. (*In particular, the Dirichlet problem for Y is solvable:
every real-valued continuous function on bd(Y) has a continuous extension to
Y which is harmonic on the interior of Y.*)

Proof. (a) The real part of an analytic function is harmonic, and a uniform limit of harmonic functions is harmonic. Also, by the maximum
principle for harmonic functions, if a sequence Re (p_n) of real parts of polynomials is uniformly convergent on X, then it is uniformly convergent on Y.
Thus H is closed in $C_R(X)$ and B is a closed subspace of H.

(b) If G_1, G_2 are continuous on Y and harmonic on int Y, then $G_1 - G_2$ is
harmonic on int Y; so $\|G_1 - G_2\|_Y = \|G_1 - G_2\|_{\mathrm{bd}(Y)}$. Hence if $G_1|X = g =
G_2|X$, then $G_1 = G_2$.

(c) Let $U_a(g) = G(a)$ $(g \in H)$. Since $\|G\|_Y = \|g\|_X$, $|U_a(g)| \leq \|g\|$. So
$\|U_a\| \leq 1$. On the other hand, $U_a(1) = 1$, so $\|U_a\| = U_a(1) = 1$. By the Hahn-
Banach and Riesz representation theorems, $M_a = \{\lambda_a \geq 0$ in $M(X) : U_a(g) =
\int g\, d\lambda_a, \forall g \in H\}$ is nonvoid.

(d) Fix a in the interior of Y. Let $f(z, w) = \log \dfrac{1}{|z - w|}$ if $z \neq w$, and

$f(z, z) = 0$. Let $f_z(\xi) = \log \dfrac{1}{|z - \xi|}$, $z \in \Omega$, $\xi \in Y$. Then f_z is continuous on Y

and harmonic on the interior of Y. So $U_a(f_z) = \log \dfrac{1}{|z - a|} = \int_X f_z(\xi)\, d\lambda_a(\xi) =$

$\int_X \log \dfrac{1}{|z - w|}\, d\lambda_a(w)$.

Since Y is bounded, we can choose $R > 1$ such that the disk $D(0; R)$
contains Y. Let $z_0 \in X = \mathrm{bd}(\Omega)$. Take $\{z_n\}$ in $\Omega \cap D(0; 2R)$ converging to z_0,

and let $s = \log(3R)$. Then $\log \left(\dfrac{1}{|z_n - \xi|}\right) + s > 0$ and $\log \left(\dfrac{1}{|z_0 - \xi|}\right) + s > 0$

for every $\xi \in X$. Thus $0 \leq \int_X \liminf_n (f_{z_n} + s)\, d\lambda_a \leq \liminf_n \int_X (f_{z_n} + s)\, d\lambda_a$,
by Fatou's lemma. But

$$\liminf_n (f_{z_n}(\xi) + s) = \begin{cases} \log \dfrac{1}{|z_0 - \xi|} + s & (\xi \neq z_0) \\ +\infty & (\xi = z_0) \end{cases}$$

and $\int_X (f_{z_n} + s)\, d\lambda_a = \log \dfrac{1}{|z_n - a|} + s$ for each n. So

$$0 \leq \int \left(\log \dfrac{1}{|z_0 - \xi|} + s\right) d\lambda_a \leq \log \dfrac{1}{|z_0 - a|} + s.$$

We conclude that $\log \dfrac{1}{|z_0 - \xi|} + s$ is λ_a-integrable, and since constants are

λ_a-integrable, $\log \dfrac{1}{|z_0 - \xi|}$ is in $L^1(\lambda_a)$.

Set $\lambda(E) = \lambda_a(E \cap X)$ for Borel sets E in Y, and let δ_a be the point mass at a. Then

$$\int_Y f(z, \xi) \, d\lambda(\xi) = \int_Y \log \frac{1}{|z - \xi|} \, d\lambda(\xi) = \log \frac{1}{|z - a|} = f(z, a)$$

$$= \int_Y f(z, \xi) \, d\delta_a(\xi)$$

for all $z \in \Omega$, so $\mu = \delta_a - \lambda$ annihilates $w \to f(z, w)$ for every $z \in \Omega$. We have just shown that $w \to f(z_0, w)$ is μ-integrable for every $z_0 \in \mathrm{bd}(\Omega)$, so by Lemma 6, $\int f(z_0, w) \, d\mu = 0$ and $\mu(\{z_0\}) = 0$ for every z_0 in $\mathrm{bd}(\Omega) = X$. Hence $\int_X \log \frac{1}{|z_0 - \xi|} \, d\lambda_a(\xi) = f(z_0, a) = \log \frac{1}{|z_0 - a|}$.

(e) Let α be a real measure in $M(X)$ which annihilates B. If p is a polynomial, then $\int p \, d\alpha = \int (\mathrm{Re}\, p) \, d\alpha + i \int (\mathrm{Im}\, p) \, d\alpha = 0$, since $\mathrm{Re}\,(p)$ and $\mathrm{Im}\,(p) = \mathrm{Re}\,(-ip)$ are in B. Now $\log(1 - w) = -\sum_1^\infty \frac{w^n}{n}$, the series converging uniformly on each closed subdisk of the unit disk. We have $Y \subset D(0; R)$, so $\int_X \log\left(1 - \frac{\xi}{z}\right) d\alpha(\xi) = -\sum_1^\infty \frac{1}{nz^n} \int_X \xi^n \, d\alpha(\xi) = 0$ if $|z| > R + 1$.

(Note that $\left|\left(1 - \frac{\xi}{z}\right) - 1\right| < 1$, so $\xi \to \log\left(1 - \frac{\xi}{z}\right)$ is continuous.) So $\int_X \mathrm{Re}\left(\log\left(1 - \frac{\xi}{z}\right)\right) d\alpha(\xi) = \int_X \log\left|1 - \frac{\xi}{z}\right| d\alpha(\xi) = 0$. Since α annihilates the constants,

$$\int_X \log \frac{1}{|z - \xi|} \, d\alpha(\xi) = 0 \qquad (|z| > R + 1).$$

Let $f(z, w) = \log \frac{1}{|z - w|}$ $(z \neq w)$, $f(z, z) = 0$, and let

$$u(z) = \int_X \log \frac{1}{|z - \xi|} \, d\alpha(\xi)$$

if the integral converges absolutely, and $u(z) = 0$ otherwise. u is continuous on Ω and is harmonic there, since we can compute partial derivatives under the integral sign. Since u vanishes for $|z| > R + 1$, $u = 0$ on Ω.

So $u(z) = 0$ for all $z \in X$, by Lemma 6.

Take $a \in \mathrm{int}\, Y$, and use the notation of (d). f is a Borel measurable function on $X \times X$ and $0 \le f(z, \xi) + s$ $(z \in X, \xi \in X)$. So by the Fubini-Tonelli theorem,

$$\int_X \int_X [f(z, \xi) + s] \, d|\alpha|(z) \, d\lambda_a(\xi) = \int_X \int_X [f(z, \xi) + s] \, d\lambda_a(\xi) \, d|\alpha|(z)$$

$$= \int_X [f(z, a) + s] \, d|\alpha|(z)$$

by (d), and this is finite since $a \in \text{int } Y$ and so $z \to f(z, a) + s$ is continuous on X. Therefore $f + s$ is integrable on $X \times X$, and so f is $|\alpha| \times \lambda_a$ integrable.

Let $F = \{\xi \in X : z \to f(z, \xi) \notin L^1(|\alpha|)\}$. Then F is λ_a-measurable, and $\lambda_a(F) = 0$. Since $f(z, \xi) = f(\xi, z)$, $\xi \to f(z, \xi)$ is in $L^1(|\alpha|)$ for all $z \notin F$. We thus have

$$0 = \int_X u(z) \, d\lambda_a(z)$$

$$= \int_{X \backslash F} u(z) \, d\lambda_a(z)$$

$$= \int_{X \backslash F} \left(\int_X f(z, \xi) \, d\alpha(\xi) \right) d\lambda_a(z)$$

$$= \int_X \left(\int_{X \backslash F} f(z, \xi) \, d\lambda_a(z) \right) d\alpha(\xi)$$

$$= \int_X \int_X f(z, \xi) \, d\lambda_a(z) \, d\alpha(\xi)$$

$$= \int_X \int_X f(\xi, z) \, d\lambda_a(z) \, d\alpha(\xi)$$

$$= \int_X \log \frac{1}{|\xi - a|} \, d\alpha(\xi),$$

by (d) and the Fubini theorem. So $u(a) = 0$.

Hence $u(z) = 0$ for all $z \in \mathbf{C}$.

So $\alpha = 0$, by Exercise 12, §5.3. This proves that $B^\perp = \{0\}$, so $B = C_R(X)$.

Corollary 1 (Walsh's Theorem). *Let X be a compact set in the plane which is the boundary of its unbounded complementary component. Then $\text{Re}(P(X))$ is dense in $C_R(X)$.*

Corollary 2. *If X satisfies the condition in Corollary 1, then $R(X) = C(X)$. (For every complex homomorphism of $R(X)$ has a unique representing measure.)*

Theorem 16 (Lavrentiev's Theorem). *Let X be a compact set in the plane. Suppose that the complement of X is connected and that X has empty interior. Then $P(X) = C(X)$.*

Proof. X satisfies the hypotheses of Corollary 1, so $R(X) = C(X)$. But $\mathbf{C} \backslash X$ is connected, so $P(X) = R(X)$. Thus the theorem is proved. (Note that Lavrentiev's theorem includes Theorem 14 as a special case.)

EXERCISE SET 5.4

1. Let J be a Jordan arc lying in the plane (i.e., J is the homeomorphic image of a closed interval $[a, b]$). Prove that $P(J) = C(J)$.

2. Let A be a singly generated function algebra on the closed interval $[0, 1]$. Prove that $A = C[0, 1]$.

3. Prove that the harmonic measures λ_a in Theorem 15 are unique. What is the relation between (d) and the Jensen measures for $P(X)$?

4. Suppose that A is a function algebra on a compact space X, and that A contains a function f such that the range of Re (f) is not connected. Prove that A contains a nonconstant (idempotent) function e such that $e^2 = e$, and hence $\mathscr{M}(A)$ is not connected. (Since Re $(f)(X)$ is not connected, $f(X)$ splits into two chunks. Use Runge's theorem to find polynomials p_n which converge uniformly on $f(X)$ to the characteristic function of one chunk.)

5. Let A be a singly generated function algebra on a compact space X. Show that unless $A = C(X)$, $\Gamma(A)$ is a proper subset of $\mathscr{M}(A)$.

5.5 GLEASON PARTS FOR $R(X)$

Let X be a compact set in the plane. In [215], Wilken observed that a modification of Bishop's arguments concerning $R(X)$ (cf. Theorem 10) yields the interesting fact that a Gleason part in $X = \mathscr{M}(R(X))$ is either a one-point set, in which case the point is a peak point, or the part has positive planar measure. We will prove this using an argument of A. Browder and get a slightly stronger conclusion.

Here is some notation. Given $\mu \in M(X)$, define $\tilde{\mu}(z) = \int_X \dfrac{d|\mu|(\xi)}{|\xi - z|}$ for $z \in \mathbb{C}$, and let $\hat{\mu}(z) = \int_X \dfrac{d\mu(\xi)}{\xi - z}$ if $\tilde{\mu}(z) < \infty$. We know that $\hat{\mu}$ is defined a.e. $[dx\, dy]$, and it is clear that $|\hat{\mu}(z)| \le \tilde{\mu}(z)$. Let $dm(z) = dx\, dy$ be planar Lebesgue measure.

Lemma 7. *Let* $\mu \in M(X)$, $x \in \mathbb{C}$, $\Delta_n = \{\xi : |\xi - x| \le 1/n\}$. *Then*

$$\frac{1}{m(\Delta_n)} \int_{\Delta_n} |z - x| \tilde{\mu}(z)\, dm(z) \to |\mu|(\{x\}) \text{ as } n \to \infty.$$

Proof. Set $F_n(\xi) = \dfrac{1}{m(\Delta_n)} \int_{\Delta_n} |(z - x)(z - \xi)^{-1}|\, dm(z)$. Observe that $F_n(x) = 1$, and if $\xi \ne x$, then $|F_n(\xi)| \le \dfrac{1}{nm(\Delta_n)} \int_{\Delta_n} |z - \xi|^{-1}\, dm(z) \le \dfrac{1}{n}\left(|\xi - x| - \dfrac{1}{n}\right)^{-1}$ as soon as $n > |\xi - x|^{-1}$. Hence $F_n(\xi) \to 0$ as $n \to \infty$, if $\xi \ne x$. So $F_n \to \chi_{\{x\}}$ pointwise.

Observe that if E is any measurable set in the plane with $0 < m(E) < \infty$, and if D is the closed disk with center the origin and $m(D) = m(E)$, then $\int_E \frac{dm(w)}{|w|} \leq \int_D \frac{dm(w)}{|w|}$. (It suffices to prove that $\int_{E\setminus D} \frac{dm(w)}{|w|} \leq \int_{D\setminus E} \frac{dm(w)}{|w|}$, since $\int_{E\cap D} = \int_{D\cap E}$. But if $w \in E\setminus D$, then $|w| \geq$ radius of $D = \sqrt{m(E)/\pi}$, while if $w \in D$, then $|w| \leq \sqrt{m(E)/\pi}$. Thus

$$\int_{E\setminus D} \frac{dm(w)}{|w|} \leq \sqrt{\frac{\pi}{m(E)}}\, m(E\setminus D) = \sqrt{\frac{\pi}{m(E)}}\, m(D\setminus E) \leq \int_{D\setminus E} \frac{dm(w)}{|w|}.$$

This proves the observation.)

If $\xi \neq x$, then we have $\int_{\Delta_n} \frac{dm(z)}{|z - \xi|} = \int_{\Delta_n'} \frac{dm(w)}{|w|}$, where Δ_n' is the disk of radius $1/n$ centered at $x - \xi \neq 0$, and $\int_{\Delta_n} \frac{dm(z)}{|z - x|} = \int_{\Delta_n''} \frac{dm(w)}{|w|}$, where Δ_n'' is the disk of radius $1/n$ centered at the origin. By our observation,

$$\int_{\Delta_n} |z - \xi|^{-1}\, dm(z) \leq \int_{\Delta_n} |z - x|^{-1}\, dm(z).$$

Thus

$$F_n(\xi) = \frac{1}{m(\Delta_n)} \int_{\Delta_n} |z - x|\,|z - \xi|^{-1}\, dm(z)$$

$$\leq \frac{1}{nm(\Delta_n)} \int_{\Delta_n} |z - \xi|^{-1}\, dm(z)$$

$$\leq \frac{1}{nm(\Delta_n)} \int_{\Delta_n} |z - x|^{-1}\, dm(z)$$

$$= 2.$$

(Change to polar coordinates and compute.) Hence by the dominated convergence theorem, $\int_X F_n(\xi)\, d|\mu|(\xi) \to |\mu|(\{x\})$.

On the other hand, $\int F_n\, d|\mu| = \frac{1}{m(\Delta_n)} \int_{\Delta_n} |z - x|\tilde{\mu}(z)\, dm(z)$, by the Fubini theorem. So the lemma is proved.

Lemma 8. *Let $\mu \in M(X)$, $x \in X$, and suppose that μ represents evaluation at x on $R(X)$. (μ is a complex measure.) Let $\varepsilon > 0$ and $\delta = \varepsilon/(1 + \|\mu\| + \varepsilon)$. If $z \in \mathbb{C}$ and $|z - x|\tilde{\mu}(z) < \delta$, then $z \in X$ and $\|\varphi_z - \varphi_x\| < \varepsilon$.*

Proof. Since $\int f\, d\mu = f(x) = \varphi_x(f)$ for all $f \in R(X)$, $\hat{\mu}(z) = \int \frac{d\mu(\xi)}{\xi - z} = \frac{1}{x - z}$ if $z \notin X$. Hence $|x - z|\tilde{\mu}(z) \geq |x - z|\,|\hat{\mu}(z)| = 1 > \delta$.

Assume now that $|z - x| \tilde{\mu}(z) < \delta$. We know that $z \in X$. Since $\tilde{\mu}(z) < \infty$, $\hat{\mu}(z)$ exists. Set $c = \int_X \frac{\xi - x}{\xi - z} d\mu(\xi)$. c exists (since $|\xi - x| \le \text{diam}(X) < \infty$) and equals $\tilde{\alpha}(z)$, where $d\alpha(\xi) = (\xi - x) d\mu(\xi)$. But $\xi - x$ belongs to $R(X)$ and vanishes at x, while μ represents evaluation at x. So α is an annihilator of $R(X)$. By an observation in the proof of Theorem 10, $\frac{1}{c} \frac{d\alpha(\xi)}{\xi - z} = \frac{1}{\tilde{\alpha}(z)} \frac{d\alpha(\xi)}{\xi - z}$ is a complex measure which represents φ_z (evaluation at z) on $R(X)$. ($c = 1 + (z - x)\hat{\mu}(z)$, so $|c| \ge 1 - \delta > 0$.) Let ν be this measure.

Now $|\varphi_z(f) - \varphi_x(f)| = |\int f \, d(\nu - \mu)| \le \|f\| \, \|\mu - \nu\|$ for all $f \in R(X)$; thus $\|\varphi_z - \varphi_x\| \le \|\mu - \nu\|$. So it remains to compute $\|\mu - \nu\|$. Since $d(\nu - \mu)(\xi) = \left[\frac{1}{c} \frac{\xi - x}{\xi - z} - 1 \right] d\mu(\xi)$, we first simplify the term in brackets.

$$\frac{1}{c} \frac{\xi - x}{\xi - z} - 1 = \frac{1}{c(\xi - z)} (\xi - x - c(\xi - z))$$

$$= \frac{1}{c(\xi - z)} (\xi - x - (1 + (z - x)\hat{\mu}(z))(\xi - z))$$

$$= \frac{1}{c(\xi - z)} (z - x - (z - x)\hat{\mu}(z)(\xi - z))$$

$$= \frac{1}{c} \frac{z - x}{\xi - z} (1 - \hat{\mu}(z)(\xi - z)).$$

Hence

$$\|\nu - \mu\| = \int \frac{1}{|c|} \left| \frac{z - x}{\xi - z} \right| |1 - \hat{\mu}(z)(\xi - z)| \, d|\mu|(\xi)$$

$$= \frac{|z - x|}{|c|} \int \left| \frac{1}{\xi - z} - \hat{\mu}(z) \right| \, d|\mu|(\xi)$$

$$\le \frac{|z - x|}{|c|} (\tilde{\mu}(z) + |\hat{\mu}(z)| \, \|\mu\|)$$

$$\le |c|^{-1} |z - x| \tilde{\mu}(z)(1 + \|\mu\|)$$

$$< |c|^{-1} \delta(1 + \|\mu\|).$$

So $\|\nu - \mu\| < \dfrac{\delta}{1 - \delta} (1 + \|\mu\|) = \varepsilon$. Thus $\|\varphi_z - \varphi_x\| < \varepsilon$.

Fix $x \in X$ and let $\varepsilon > 0$. Set $P_\varepsilon = \{z \in X : \|\varphi_z - \varphi_x\| < \varepsilon\}$. (If $\varepsilon = 2$, then P_ε is precisely the Gleason part containing x. If $\varepsilon > 2$, then $P_\varepsilon = X$.)

Theorem 17. *If x does not belong to the Choquet boundary of R(X), then*

$$\frac{m(P_\varepsilon \cap \Delta_n)}{m(\Delta_n)} \to 1 \ as \ n \to \infty, \ where \ \Delta_n = \{z \in \mathbf{C} : |z - x| \le 1/n\}. \ In \ particular,$$

P_ε *has positive measure.*

Proof. The crucial step is to construct the right pseudo-representing measure μ. Since x is not in the Choquet boundary, there is a representing measure ν for x with $\nu \ne \delta_x$. So $0 \le \nu(\{x\}) < 1$. Let $t = (1 - \nu(\{x\}))^{-1}$, and set $\mu = (1 - t)\delta_x + t\nu$. Then the real measure μ represents φ_x on $R(X)$, and $\mu(\{x\}) = 0$. So of course $|\mu|(\{x\}) = 0$ also.

By Lemma 7, $\dfrac{1}{m(\Delta_n)} \displaystyle\int_{\Delta_n} |z - x|\, \tilde{\mu}(z)\, dm(z) \to 0$ as $n \to \infty$. By Lemma 8, $P_\varepsilon \cap \Delta_n$ contains $E_n = \{z \in \Delta_n : |z - x|\tilde{\mu}(x) < \delta\}$, where $\delta = \varepsilon(1 + \|\mu\| + \varepsilon)^{-1}$. Hence

$$\frac{m(P_\varepsilon \cap \Delta_n)}{m(\Delta_n)} \ge \frac{m(E_n)}{m(\Delta_n)} = 1 - \frac{m(\Delta_n\backslash E_n)}{m(\Delta_n)}.$$

But if $z \in \Delta_n\backslash E_n$, then $-\dfrac{|z - x|\tilde{\mu}(z)}{\delta} \le -1$; thus

$$-\frac{1}{\delta} \int_{\Delta_n\backslash E_n} |z - x|\tilde{\mu}(z)\, dm(z) \le -m(\Delta_n\backslash E_n).$$

Hence

$$1 \ge \frac{m(P_\varepsilon \cap \Delta_n)}{m(\Delta_n)} \ge 1 - \frac{1}{\delta m(\Delta_n)} \int_{\Delta_n\backslash E_n} |z - x|\, \tilde{\mu}(z)\, dm(z)$$

$$\ge 1 - \frac{1}{\delta} \frac{1}{m(\Delta_n)} \int_{\Delta_n} |z - x|\, \tilde{\mu}(z)\, dm(z).$$

So the conclusion is clear.

Corollary (Wilken's Theorem). *If P is a Gleason part for R(X), then either P has positive planar measure, or P = {x} where x is a peak point for R(X).*

Proof. Since X is compact metric, the Choquet boundary for $R(X)$ is the same as the set of peak points. Hence either $x \in X$ is a peak point (and then the part containing x is $\{x\}$) or the part containing x has positive measure.

Thus $R(X) = C(X)$ iff every Gleason part for $R(X)$ is a point. Also, $R(X) = C(X)$ iff every Gleason part for $R(X)$ has planar measure zero. If $x \in X$, then x is a peak point for $R(X)$ iff $\{x\}$ is a one-point part. Moreover, there can be only countably many parts lying in the complement of the set of peak points.

We have not determined the parts for $R(X)$, but we have learned something about them.

EXERCISE SET   5.5

1. Let X be a compact set in the plane and let $x \in X$. Show that x belongs to the Choquet boundary of $R(X)$ iff evaluation at x is an isolated point in $\mathcal{M}(R(X))$ with respect to the metric topology.

5.6   APPLICATION OF ANALYTIC FUNCTIONS

Let A be a function algebra on a compact space X, and let $f \in A$. Suppose that F is an analytic function on an open set U containing the spectrum of f. By Lemma 3, we can find $\xi_1, \ldots, \xi_m$ in $U \backslash \sigma(f)$ and scalars $a_1, \ldots, a_m$ such that $|F(z) - \sum_1^m a_i(z - \xi_i)^{-1}| < \varepsilon$ for every $z \in \sigma(f)$. In particular, $|F(f(x)) - \sum_1^m a_i(f(x) - \xi_i)^{-1}| < \varepsilon$ for all $x \in X$, since $\sigma(f)$ contains the range of f. But the ξ_i belong to the complement of $\sigma(f)$, so each $f - \xi_i$ is an invertible element of A. Thus we have shown that there is a function $g \in A$ with $\|F \circ f - g\| < \varepsilon$. So $F \circ f$ is uniformly approximable by A, and thus $F \circ f$ belongs to A.

One can modify the proof to get a result for an arbitrary commutative Banach algebra A with identity: if $f \in A$ and F is analytic on a *nbhd* of $\sigma_A(f)$, then $F \circ \hat{f}$ belongs to $\hat{A}$. (Since $\hat{A}$ needn't be uniformly closed, this does not follow from the result just established.) Take the representation $F(z) = \frac{1}{2\pi i} \sum_{j=1}^n \int_{\gamma_j} F(\xi)(\xi - z)^{-1}\, d\xi$ ($z \in \sigma(f)$, all γ_j lying in the complement of $\sigma(f)$), and note that the Riemann sums for the vector valued integral

$$\frac{1}{2\pi i} \sum_{j=1}^n \int_{\gamma_j} F(\xi)(\xi - f)^{-1}\, d\xi$$

converge to an element $g \in A$ in norm. Since the norm in A dominates that in $\hat{A}$, $\hat{g} = F \circ \hat{f}$.

The same kind of theorem is true if we take, instead of a single element f and its spectrum $\sigma_A(f)$, any ordered n-tuple of elements $f_1, \ldots, f_n$ and the joint spectrum $\sigma_A(f_1, \ldots, f_n)$; but now the proofs depend crucially on some highly nontrivial theorems about holomorphic functions of several complex variables. We shall state these without proof as we need them; the reader is referred to Chapter 1 of [C] for proofs.

The crucial lemma reduces the problem to a similar one for finitely generated algebras. The joint spectrum is then polynomially convex, and one can invoke suitable approximation arguments (which are generalizations of Runge's theorem to $\mathbf{C}^n$, $n > 1$) and complete the proofs.

Lemma 9. *Let A be a commutative Banach algebra with identity, and let $f_1, \ldots, f_n$ belong to A. Suppose that U is an open set in $\mathbf{C}^n$ which contains*

$\sigma_A(f_1, \ldots, f_n) = \{(h(f_1), \ldots, h(f_n)) : h \in \mathcal{M}(A)\}$. *Then there is a finite set $E \subset A$, possibly empty, such that if B is the closed subalgebra of A generated by $1, f_1, \ldots, f_n$, and E, then $\sigma_B(f_1, \ldots, f_n) \subset U$.*

Proof. Note that if B is any subalgebra of A which contains $1, f_1, \ldots, f_n$, then $\sigma_A(f_1, \ldots, f_n) \subset \sigma_B(f_1, \ldots, f_n)$. (The larger the algebra, the smaller the joint spectrum.) Let A_0 be the closed subalgebra generated by $1, f_1, \ldots, f_n$, and let σ_0 be the joint spectrum of $f_1, \ldots, f_n$ in the algebra A_0.

If $\sigma_0 \subset U$, we take E to be empty, and the conclusion follows. Otherwise, $\sigma_0 \backslash U$ is a nonempty compact set in $\mathbf{C}^n$. Since $\sigma_A(f_1, \ldots, f_n) \subset U$, $\sigma_0 \backslash U$ is disjoint from $\sigma_A(f_1, \ldots, f_n)$. So if $w \in \sigma_0 \backslash U$, there exist $g_1{}^w, \ldots, g_n{}^w$ in A such that $\sum_{i=1}^{n} g_i{}^w(f_i - w_i 1) = 1$. Let $A_1(w)$ be the closed subalgebra of A generated by $1, f_1, \ldots, f_n, g_1{}^w, \ldots, g_n{}^w$, and let $\sigma_1(w)$ be the joint spectrum of $f_1, \ldots, f_n$ in $A_1(w)$. Since $A_0 \subset A_1(w) \subset A$, $\sigma_A \subset \sigma_1(w) \subset \sigma_0$. By construction, $f_1 - w_1 1, \ldots, f_n - w_n 1$ lie in no proper ideal of $A_1(w)$, so $w \notin \sigma_1(w)$. Since $\sigma_1(w)$ is a closed set, w has a *nbhd* N_w disjoint from $\sigma_1(w)$.

The *nbhds* $\{N_w : w \in \sigma_0 \backslash U\}$ cover the compact set $\sigma_0 \backslash U$, so there is a finite subcover $N_{w_1}, \ldots, N_{w_k}$. Let $E = \{g_i{}^{w_j} : 1 \leq i \leq n, 1 \leq j \leq k\}$, and let B be the closed subalgebra generated by $1, f_1, \ldots, f_n$ and E.

Since $A_0 \subset B$, $\sigma_B(f_1, \ldots, f_n) = \sigma_B \subset \sigma_0$. Suppose $z \notin U$. Then if $z \notin \sigma_0$, certainly $z \notin \sigma_B$. If $z \in \sigma_0 \backslash U$, then $z \in N_{w_j}$ for some j; thus $z \notin \sigma_1(w_j)$. But $A_1(w_j) \subset B$, so $\sigma_B \subset \sigma_j(w_j)$; hence $z \notin \sigma_B$. Thus $z \notin U$ implies that $z \notin \sigma_B$, or $\sigma_B \subset U$. The lemma is proved.

Now in order to utilize the lemma we state the **Oka-Weil Approximation Theorem:** *If K is a polynomially convex compact subset of $\mathbf{C}^n$, then $P(K) = H(K)$*; i.e., every function holomorphic on a *nbhd* of K is uniformly approximable by polynomials in $(z_1, \ldots, z_n)$ on K.

We can now prove the function algebra version of the theorem on application of holomorphic functions.

Theorem 18   **(Arens-Calderôn).**   *Let A be a function algebra on a compact space X, and let $f_1, \ldots, f_n$ belong to A. If F is a function holomorphic on a nbhd of $\sigma_A(f_1, \ldots, f_n)$ in $\mathbf{C}^n$, then $F(f_1, \ldots, f_n) \in A$.*

Proof. Let F be holomorphic on an open set U containing $\sigma_A = \sigma_A(f_1, \ldots, f_n)$. Use the notation of the proof of the lemma. If $E = \varnothing$, then $\sigma_0 \subset U$. Since $f_1, \ldots, f_n$ generate A_0, σ_0 is polynomially convex. By Oka's theorem, there are polynomials p_k converging to F uniformly on σ_0. If $x \in X$, then $(f_1(x), \ldots, f_n(x)) \in \sigma_A \subset \sigma_0$; thus $p_k(f_1, \ldots, f_n) \to F(f_1, \ldots, f_n)$ uniformly on X. Since A is a function algebra, $F(f_1, \ldots, f_n) \in A$.

If $E = \{h_1, \ldots, h_m\}$ where $m \geq 1$, then B is generated by $\{1, f_1, \ldots, f_n, h_1, \ldots, h_m\}$, and $\sigma_B(f_1, \ldots, f_n) \subset U$. But

$$\sigma_B(f_1, \ldots, f_n, h_1, \ldots, h_m) \subset \sigma_B(f_1, \ldots, f_n) \times \mathbf{C}^m \subset U \times \mathbf{C}^m.$$

Set $F^*(z_1, \ldots, z_{n+m}) = F(z_1, \ldots, z_n)$. Then F^* is holomorphic on $U \times \mathbb{C}^m$. By the first paragraph, $F^*(f_1, \ldots, f_n, h_1, \ldots, h_m)$ belongs to B (generators!), so $F(f_1, \ldots, f_n) \in B \subset A$, and the theorem is proved.

If A is an arbitrary commutative Banach algebra with identity, a proof along the lines above will fail, because $\hat{A}$ needn't be uniformly closed, and there is no reason for $F(\hat{f}_1, \ldots, \hat{f}_n)$ to wind up in $\hat{A}$. But the result is nonetheless true.

Theorem 19   (**Arens, Calderôn, Šilov, Waelbroeck**).   *Let A be a commutative Banach algebra with identity, and let $f_1, \ldots, f_n$ belong to A. Let F be holomorphic on a nbhd U of $\sigma_A(f_1, \ldots, f_n)$. Then $\exists g \in A$ with*

$$\hat{g}(a) = F(\hat{f}_1(a), \ldots, \hat{f}_n(a)) \quad \text{for all } a \in \mathcal{M}(A).$$

Proof.   The idea is to keep raising the dimension enough so that we can replace F by a function holomorphic on a suitable polydisk and then use the Cauchy integral formula.

First use the lemma to find a finite set $E \subset A$ such that $\sigma_B(f_1, \ldots, f_n) \subset U$, where B is the closed subalgebra of A generated by $1, f_1, \ldots, f_n, E$. If we can find $g \in B$ which works for $F^*(\hat{f}_1, \ldots, \hat{f}_n, \hat{E})$ on $\mathcal{M}(B)$, then by projecting and restricting we have it for F. Thus we can (and do) assume that $1, f_1, \ldots, f_n$ generate A.

In this case $\sigma = \sigma_A(f_1, \ldots, f_n)$ is compact and polynomially convex, but now Oka's theorem won't succeed. But a lemma used to prove Oka's theorem will help: *if K is a compact set in $\mathbb{C}^n$, then* hull(K) *is the intersection of all open polynomial polyhedra containing K.* (Let $c > 0$ and let $p_1, \ldots, p_r$ be polynomials on $\mathbb{C}^n$, where $r \geq 0$. Then $P(p_1, \ldots, p_r; c) = \{z \in \mathbb{C}^n : |z_i| < c$ for $1 \leq i \leq n$ and $|p_j(z)| < c$ for $1 \leq j \leq r\}$. If $r = 0$, then P is just a product of disks of radius c.) Since $\sigma \subset U$, a compactness argument (replace open polyhedra by closed polyhedra) shows that there exists an open polynomial polyhedron $P = P(p_1, \ldots, p_r; c)$ such that $\sigma \subset P \subset U$. We can replace U by P. So now F is holomorphic, with domain an open polynomial polyhedron P containing σ.

Define $\mu : P \to \mathbb{C}^{n+r}$ by $\mu(z_1, \ldots, z_n) = (z_1, \ldots, z_n, p_1(z_1, \ldots, z_n), \ldots, p_r(z_1, \ldots, z_n))$, and let $M = \mu(P)$. M is a closed submanifold of the polydisk $D = \{w \in \mathbb{C}^{n+r} : |w_i| < c, 1 \leq i \leq n + r\}$, so by a theorem in several complex variables, every holomorphic function on P lifts through M; i.e., there is a holomorphic function h on D such that $F = h \circ \mu$.

This is a substantial improvement, since h is holomorphic on a polydisk containing $\Sigma = \{(\hat{f}_1(a), \ldots, \hat{f}_n(a), p_1(\hat{f}_1(a), \ldots, \hat{f}_n(a)), \ldots, p_r(\hat{f}_1(a), \ldots, \hat{f}_n(a))) : a \in \mathcal{M}(A)\} \subset \mathbb{C}^{n+r}$. Σ is just the joint spectrum of $(f_1, \ldots, f_n, p_1(f_1, \ldots, f_n), \ldots, p_r(f_1, \ldots, f_n))$. If we prove the theorem for h, then we have it for F, since $F = h \circ \mu$ and $\Sigma = \mu(\sigma(f_1, \ldots, f_n))$.

Thus we may suppose that F is holomorphic on $D = \{z \in \mathbb{C}^n : |z_i| < R, 1 \leq i \leq n\}$, $R > 0$, where $\sigma(f_1, \ldots, f_n) \subset D$. Since $\sigma \subset D$,

$$\|\hat{f}_i\| = \sup_{a \in \mathcal{M}(A)} |\hat{f}_i(a)| < R - \varepsilon < R$$

for a suitable $\varepsilon > 0$, $i = 1, \ldots, n$. Since $\|\hat{f}\| = \sup_{\lambda \in \sigma(f)} |\lambda|$, we see that if λ_i is on the circle C in $\mathbf{C}^1$ with center 0 and radius $R - \varepsilon$, then $\lambda_i 1 - f_i$ is invertible in A. Set

$$g = \left(\frac{1}{2\pi i}\right)^n \int_{C \times \cdots \times C} F(\lambda_1, \ldots, \lambda_n)(\lambda_1 1 - f_1)^{-1} \cdots (\lambda_n 1 - f_n)^{-1} \, d\lambda_1 \cdots d\lambda_n.$$

(Note that the integrand is continuous, since inversion is a continuous function in a Banach algebra. The Riemann sums converge, in the norm of A, to an element $g \in A$, since A is a Banach algebra.) Any $m \in \mathcal{M}(A)$ is a continuous algebra homomorphism and in particular must commute with the definite integral. Hence

$$\hat{g}(m) = m(g) = \left(\frac{1}{2\pi i}\right)^n \int_{C \times \cdots \times C} \frac{F(\lambda_1, \ldots, \lambda_n)}{(\lambda_1 - \hat{f}_1(m)) \cdots (\lambda_n - \hat{f}_n(m))} \, d\lambda_1 \cdots d\lambda_n$$

$$= F(\hat{f}_1(m), \ldots, \hat{f}_n(m)),$$

by the Cauchy integral formula.

Theorem 20 (Šilov's Theorem on Idempotents). *Let A be a commutative Banach algebra with identity. Suppose that $\mathcal{M}(A)$ is the union of two disjoint closed sets K_0 and K_1. Then for some $f \in A$, $\hat{f} = 0$ on K_0 and $\hat{f} = 1$ on K_1.*

Proof. The first step is to produce a finite number of elements $\hat{f}_1, \ldots, \hat{f}_n$ in $\hat{A}$ such that under the map $a \to (\hat{f}_1(a), \ldots, \hat{f}_n(a))$ the sets K_0 and K_1 have disjoint images. Suppose that this has been done. Since the map is continuous, the images of K_0, K_1 are disjoint compact sets in complex n-space, so they have disjoint open *nbhds* U_0, U_1. If $F = \begin{cases} 0 \text{ on } U_0 \\ 1 \text{ on } U_1 \end{cases}$, then F is holomorphic on $U_0 \cup U_1$, a *nbhd* of $\sigma(f_1, \ldots, f_n)$; thus, by the theorem above, $F(\hat{f}_1, \ldots, \hat{f}_n)$ belongs to $\hat{A}$. This means that $\exists f \in A$ with $\hat{f} = 0$ on K_0, $\hat{f} = 1$ on K_1, and completes the proof, except for the details.

Given $p \in K_0$, $q \in K_1$, find f_{pq} in A with $\hat{f}_{pq}(p) = 0$, $\hat{f}_{pq}(q) = 1$. This is possible since $\hat{A}$ separates points and contains the constants. By continuity, p and q have open *nbhds* V_p^q, W_p^q (respectively) such that $\text{Re}(\hat{f}_{pq}) \leq \frac{1}{4}$ on V_p^q and $\text{Re}(\hat{f}_{pq}) \geq \frac{3}{4}$ on W_p^q. Cover K_1 by finitely many *nbhds* $W_p^{q_1}, \ldots, W_p^{q_k}$ ($k = k(p)$), and let $V_p = V_p^{q_1} \cap \cdots \cap V_p^{q_k}$. V_p is a *nbhd* of p, so by compactness, K_0 is covered by finitely many *nbhds* $V_{p_1}, \ldots, V_{p_m}$. Take the corresponding f_{p_i, q_j} for $f_1, \ldots, f_n$.

Corollary 1. *If A is a function algebra on X and X is connected, then $\mathcal{M}(A)$ is connected.*

Proof. If $\mathcal{M}(A)$ splits, then A contains an element f such that $\hat{f}$ takes $\mathcal{M}(A)$ onto $\{0, 1\}$. Since $f^2 = f$, $f(X) = \{0, 1\}$ also. Thus X splits.

Corollary 2. *A function algebra A has a connected maximal ideal space iff A has the following "connected range property": for each $f \in A$, $\text{Re}(f)$ has a connected range.*

Proof. By Exercise 4, §5.4, A has the *CRP* iff A contains no nonconstant idempotent functions. By Šilov's theorem, this is equivalent to $\mathcal{M}(A)$ being connected.

Corollary 3. *If K is a connected compact subset of $\mathbf{C}^n$, then the polynomial convex hull of K is connected.*

Corollary 4. *Let X be a compact totally disconnected space. Then there is no function algebra, other than $C(X)$, which has maximal ideal space X.*

Proof. Suppose that A is a function algebra on X, and that the evaluation map $X \to \mathcal{M}(A)$ is onto. Then by Šilov's theorem, A contains the characteristic function χ_F of every open-closed subset $F \subset X$. But by the Stone-Weierstrass theorem, the linear span of the functions χ_F (F open-closed in X) is dense in $C(X)$, so $A = C(X)$.

Theorem 21. *Let A be a function algebra, and let $a \in \mathcal{M}(A)$. Then a is an isolated point of $\mathcal{M}(A)$ iff $a \in \Gamma(A)$ and a is an isolated point of $\Gamma(A)$.*

Proof. If a is an isolated point of $\mathcal{M}(A)$, then A contains a function f whose Gelfand transform is $\chi_{\{a\}}$, by Šilov's theorem. Hence $a \in \Gamma(A)$ and $\{a\}$ is open-closed in $\Gamma(A)$.

Conversely, suppose that a is an isolated point in $\Gamma = \Gamma(A)$. Then there is an open set U in $\mathcal{M}(A)$ with $U \cap \Gamma = \{a\}$. By definition of the Šilov boundary, $\exists f \in A$ with $f(a) = 1$ and $|f| < 1$ on $\Gamma \backslash U = \Gamma \backslash \{a\}$. Since f^n converges to $\chi_{\{a\}}$ uniformly on Γ, $\exists g \in A$ with $g(a) = 1$ and $g(x) = 0$ for all $x \in \Gamma \backslash \{a\}$.

Since $g^2 = g$ on Γ, $g^2 = g$ in A. Hence $\hat{g}^2 = \hat{g}$. So if $p \in \mathcal{M}(A)$, then either $\hat{g}(p) = 1$ or $\hat{g}(p) = 0$. But it is now obvious that $\hat{g}(p) = 1$ only if $p = a$. Indeed, p has a representing measure m concentrated on Γ; if $\hat{g}(p) = 1$, then $1 = \int g\, dm = m(\{a\})$, so $m = \delta_a$. Thus $\{a\} = \{p \in \mathcal{M}(A) : \hat{g}(p) \neq 0\}$ is open in $\mathcal{M}(A)$.

EXERCISE SET 5.6

1. Let A be a function algebra on X. Let F, G be open-closed subsets of $\mathcal{M}(A)$ for which $F \cap X = G \cap X$. Then $F = G$. In particular, every non-void open-closed subset of $\mathcal{M}(A)$ meets X.

2. Show that the maximal ideal space of an antisymmetric function algebra is connected.

3. Let A be a function algebra whose maximal ideal space is not connected, Prove that there are closed ideals I, J of A such that $A = I + J$, $I \neq 0$, $J \neq 0$, but $I \cap J = 0$.

Chapter Six

Abstract Function Theory

Many results in this chapter are generalizations of classical theorems concerning functions on the unit circle which are boundary values of analytic functions. The original results are due mainly to F. Riesz, M. Riesz, G. Szegö, R. Nevanlinna, and A. Beurling. An excellent account of the development of the main ideas, together with a careful discussion of the inter-relationship of the major theorems (and proofs of additional results), can be found in the article by Srinivasan and Wang in [A].

6.1   UNIQUE REPRESENTING MEASURES

In the abstract theory some sort of uniqueness of representing measures is always assumed, so in this section we discuss some classes of function algebras in which representing measures are unique. First consider a single complex homomorphism. Throughout this chapter, X designates an arbitrary compact space, unless otherwise specified.

Theorem 1.   *Let A be a function algebra on X, and let P be a Gleason part in $\mathcal{M}(A)$. Suppose that some $a \in P$ has a unique representing measure on X. Then every member of P has a unique representing measure.*

Proof.   Let $b \in P$, and let λ_b, λ_b' be representing measures for b. Since $a \sim b$, it follows from Theorem 16, §4.5 that there are representing measures m_a, m_a' for a such that $\lambda_b \le \frac{1}{c} m_a$, $\lambda_b' \le \frac{1}{c'} m_a'$ (c, c' positive constants). By hypothesis, a has a unique representing measure m, so $m_a = m_a' = m$. Thus $\lambda_b = gm$, $\lambda_b' = g'm$ where g, g' are in $L_R^\infty(m)$.

Recall that Re (A) is dense in $L_R^1(m)$, since m is an extreme point in the set of representing measures for a. (Cf. the Proposition in §4.1.) Since $\int f \, d\lambda_b = \int f \, d\lambda_b' = \hat{f}(b)$ for all $f \in A$, $\int f(g - g') \, dm = 0$, therefore $\int \mathrm{Re}\,(f)(g - g') \, dm = 0$ also. Hence $g = g'$ a.e. $[m]$; thus $\lambda_b = \lambda_b'$.

If B is a set of functions, let $\bar{B} = \{\bar{f} : f \in B\}$ and $\mathrm{Re}\,(B) = \{\mathrm{Re}\,(f) : f \in B\}$. If B is a complex linear space, so is $\bar{B}$, and $\mathrm{Re}\,(B)$ is a real linear space. Note, too, that in this case $\mathrm{Re}\,(B) + i\,\mathrm{Re}\,(B) = B + \bar{B}$, since $\mathrm{Re}\,(f) + i\,\mathrm{Re}\,(g) = \frac{1}{2}(f + \bar{f}) + \dfrac{i}{2}(g + \bar{g}) = \frac{1}{2}(f + ig) + \frac{1}{2}(\overline{f - ig})$ and $f + \bar{g} = \mathrm{Re}\,(f + g) + i\,\mathrm{Re}\,(ig - if)$.

Now let A be a function algebra on a compact space X. A is a *Dirichlet algebra* iff $\mathrm{Re}\,(A)$ is uniformly dense in $C_R(X)$. Observe that $\mathrm{Re}\,(A)^\perp$ is the same as the set of all real Borel measures in $A^\perp$. Hence A is a Dirichlet algebra iff the only real measure which annihilates A is the zero measure. It follows immediately that each $a \in \mathcal{M}(A)$ has a unique representing measure if A is a Dirichlet algebra, since the difference of two such measures annihilates A. In particular, each $x \in X$ is represented on A only by δ_x, so the Choquet boundary of A is all of X, and so $\Gamma(A) = X$ also. (Also see Exercise 1, §4.2.)

In §4.2 we noted that the boundary algebra A^1 (the restriction of the disk algebra to the unit circle) is a Dirichlet algebra. Walsh's theorem shows that, more generally, if X is a compact plane set which coincides with the boundary of its unbounded complementary component, then $P(X)$ is a Dirichlet algebra. Our theorems on $R(X)$ (see §5.3) imply that if $X \subset \mathbf{C}$, then $R(X) = C(X)$ iff $R(X)$ is a Dirichlet algebra.

Recall that A^1 is the uniform closure of the polynomials in $e^{i\theta}$ on T^1. Let A^{11} be the closure on T^2 of the polynomials $p = \sum\limits_{n=0}^{N} \sum\limits_{m=0}^{N} a_{nm} e^{in\theta} e^{imt}$. Then A^{11} is a function algebra on T^2 but is not a Dirichlet algebra, for the real measure $(e^{i\theta}e^{-it} + e^{-i\theta}e^{it}) \, d\theta \, dt$ annihilates A^{11}.

Let us call a set $S \subset \mathbf{Z}^2 = \mathbf{Z} \times \mathbf{Z}$ a *half-plane* iff (a) S is a semigroup (i.e., S is closed under addition), (b) $S \cup (-S) = \mathbf{Z}^2$, (c) $S \cap (-S) = \{(0, 0)\}$. (For example, if α is a positive irrational, then $S_\alpha = \{(n, m) : n + m\alpha \geq 0\}$ is a half-plane.) Let Λ_S be the closure on T^2 of the polynomials $p = \sum\limits_{(n,\,m)\,\in\,S} a_{nm} e^{in\theta} e^{imt}$. ($\Lambda_S$ consists of all $g \in C(T^2)$ such that $\hat{g}(n, m) = \dfrac{1}{4\pi^2} \int_0^{2\pi} \int_0^{2\pi} g(e^{i\theta}, e^{it}) e^{-in\theta} e^{-imt} \, d\theta \, dt$ vanishes for all $(n, m) \notin S$.) Then Λ_S is a Dirichlet algebra on the torus T^2, and it is easy to see that Λ_S is antisymmetric on T^2. (Actually Λ_S is a Dirichlet algebra iff (a) and (b) are satisfied.)

The boundary value algebra A^1 has an interesting structural property which turns out essentially to characterize it among Dirichlet algebras on the circle. (For a deep extension of the ideas below to arbitrary compact groups— abelian or not—see [146].) Let T be the unit circle. For $f \in C(T)$, $\alpha \in T$, let $f_\alpha(z) = f(\alpha z)$ $(z \in T)$. f_α is called the translate of f through α. Note that if $f \in A^1$, then $f_\alpha \in A^1$ for every $\alpha \in T$, so A^1 is translation-invariant.

Let A be a function algebra on the circle such that A contains the translates of each of its members. Let H be the maximal set of antisymmetry for A which contains 1. Then H is a closed subgroup of T, and the maximal antisymmetric sets for A are the cosets of H. (See Exercise 6, §3.3.) Therefore $H = T$ or there is some $n \geq 1$ such that H is the group of nth roots of unity. But if $H \neq T$, then H is finite, so $A \mid_H = C(H)$. Since H is a set of antisymmetry for A, it follows that if $H \neq T$, then $H = \{1\}$.

If $H = \{1\}$, then every maximal antisymmetric set for A is a point; thus $A = C(T)$, by Bishop's theorem. Otherwise $H = T$, and then A is antisymmetric.

Recall that the convolution of f, g in $C(T)$ is defined by $(f * g)(z) = \int f(zw^{-1})g(w)\, dw$, where $dw = \dfrac{1}{2\pi}\, d\theta$ for $w = e^{i\theta}$. Observe that $f * g \in C(T)$ also, and that if $f \in A$ and $g \in C(T)$, then $f * g \in A$. (Indeed, if $\mu \in A^{\perp}$, then $\int (f * g)\, d\mu = \iint f(zw^{-1})g(w)\, dw\, d\mu(z) = \iint f(zw^{-1})g(w)\, d\mu(z)\, dw = \iint f_{w^{-1}}(z)g(w)\, d\mu(z)\, dw = 0$, so $f * g \in A$.) In particular, if $f \in A$, then $f * z^n \in A$ for all $n \in \mathbf{Z}$. But $(f * z^n)(e^{i\theta}) = \hat{f}(n)e^{in\theta}$, so $\hat{f}(n)z^n \in A$ for all $n \in \mathbf{Z}$, $f \in A$. ($\hat{f}(n)$ is the nth Fourier coefficient of f.)

Since A does not reduce to the constants, $\hat{f}(n) \neq 0$ for some $f \in A$ and some $n \neq 0$. So if A is a translation-invariant function algebra on the circle, A contains z^n for some nonzero integer n.

Theorem 2. *Let A be a translation-invariant Dirichlet algebra on the unit circle, and let A^1 be the boundary value algebra. Then either $A = C(T)$, $A = A^1$, or $A = \{\bar{f} : f \in A^1\}$.*

Proof. Assume that $A \neq C(T)$. Since A is a Dirichlet algebra, $f_n + \bar{f}_n \to z + \bar{z}$ uniformly on T for some sequence $\{f_n\}$ in A. Therefore, $\hat{f}_n(1) + \hat{\bar{f}}_n(1) \to \hat{z}(1) + \hat{\bar{z}}(1) = 1$. So either $\hat{f}(1) \neq 0$ or $\hat{\bar{f}}(1) \neq 0$ for some $f \in A$. By the remarks above, we conclude that either $z \in A$ or $\bar{z} = z^{-1} \in A$. In the first case $z^n \in A$ for all $n \geq 0$ (in the second, $z^n \in \bar{A}$ for all $n \geq 0$), so $A = A^1$ ($\bar{A} = A^1$), by Wermer's maximality theorem.

If A is an algebra of functions and $1 \in A$, we let A^{-1} be the group of invertible elements of A and $\log |A^{-1}| = \{\log |f| : f \in A^{-1}\}$. A *logmodular algebra* on a compact space X is a function algebra on X such that $\log |A^{-1}|$ is dense in $C_R(X)$ in the sup norm.

Every Dirichlet algebra is logmodular, since $e^A \subset A^{-1}$ and $\mathrm{Re}(f) = \log |e^f|$. We shall see examples below of logmodular algebras which are not Dirichlet algebras.

Theorem 3. *Let A be a logmodular algebra on X. Then every $a \in \mathcal{M}(A)$ has a unique representing measure on X, and X is the Šilov boundary of A.*

Proof. Let $a \in \mathcal{M}(A)$, and let μ, ν be representing measures for a. We have to show that $\int u\, d\mu = \int u\, d\nu$ for every u in $C_R(X)$. Let's give the basic argument here and then comment on the details below.

For each $f \in A^{-1}$, $\int f \, d\mu = \hat{f}(a)$, $\int f^{-1} \, dv = \hat{f}(a)^{-1}$ $(f^{-1} = 1/f)$, and so $(\int |f| \, d\mu)(\int |f^{-1}| \, dv) \geq 1$. Given $u \in C_R(X)$, there are $f_n \in A^{-1}$ with $\log |f_n| \to u$ uniformly on X. Hence $|f_n| \to e^u$ and $|f_n^{-1}| \to e^{-u}$ uniformly. So $(\int e^u \, d\mu)(\int e^{-u} \, dv) \geq 1$.

Fix $u \in C_R(X)$ and let $\rho(t) = (\int e^{tu} \, d\mu)(\int e^{-tu} \, dv)$. Then $\rho(t) \geq 1$ for all real t, and $\rho(0) = 1$. So ρ has a minimum at $t = 0$. Hence $\rho'(0) = 0$. But $\rho'(t) = (\int ue^{tu} \, d\mu)(\int e^{-tu} \, dv) - (\int e^{tu} \, d\mu)(\int ue^{-tu} \, dv)$, so $\rho'(0) = \int u \, d\mu - \int u \, dv = 0$, which shows that $\mu = v$ and proves the first conclusion of the theorem. It also shows that X is the Choquet boundary of A, so $X = \Gamma(A)$.

Remark. If $g_n \to g$ uniformly on X and if $h : \mathbf{C} \to \mathbf{C}$ is continuous, then $h \circ g_n \to h \circ g$ uniformly since $\{\|g_n\|\}$ is bounded and h is uniformly continuous on compact sets. In particular, $|f_n| \to e^u$ uniformly if $\log |f_n| \to u$ uniformly.

Let $\psi(s) = \int e^{su} \, d\mu$, where $u \in C_R(X)$, $\mu \in M(X)$. For fixed s, the series $\sum_0^\infty \dfrac{s^n}{n!} u^n$ converges uniformly to e^{su}, and μ is a continuous linear functional. Thus $\psi(s) = \sum_0^\infty c_n s^n / n!$ for each complex s, where $c_n = \int u^n \, d\mu$. This shows that ψ is an entire function, and the series can be differentiated term by term. Thus $\psi'(s) = \int ue^{su} \, d\mu$, and the formula for ρ' follows immediately.

Now that we know that representing measures for points in $\mathcal{M}(A)$ are unique when A is logmodular, we are in a position to prove the powerful lemma of F. Forelli. First we prove two elementary measure-theoretic lemmas.

Lemma 1. *Let m be a probability measure in $M(X)$. Let K be a compact set with $m(K) = 0$. Then for every $\varepsilon > 0$, there is a function $u \in C_R(X)$ with $u > 0$ on X, $u > 1$ on K, and $\int u \, dm < \varepsilon$.*

Proof. There is an open set U containing K with $m(U) < \varepsilon/3$. Choose a Urysohn function v with $v = 1$ on K, $v = 0$ on $X \setminus U$, $0 \leq v \leq 1$, and let $u = v + \varepsilon/3$. Then $u \geq \varepsilon/3$ on X, $u = 1 + \varepsilon/3$ on K, and

$$\int u \, dm = \frac{\varepsilon}{3} + \int_U v \, dm \leq \frac{2\varepsilon}{3}.$$

Lemma 2. *Let v be a positive measure in $M(X)$, and let v be concentrated on a Borel set E. Then there is a σ-compact set $S \subset E$ on which v is concentrated.*

Proof. Since v is regular, there are compact $E_n \subset E$ with $v(E_n) > v(E) - \dfrac{1}{n}$. Set $K_n = E_1 \cup \cdots \cup E_n$. Then $v(K_n) \geq v(E_n) > v(E) - \dfrac{1}{n}$ for each n, K_n is compact, and $K_n \subset K_{n+1}$. Hence if $S = \bigcup_n K_n$, then $v(S) = \lim_n v(K_n) = v(E)$. So v is concentrated on the σ-compact set S.

Lemma 3   (Forelli's Lemma).   *Let A be a logmodular algebra on X and m a representing measure for $a \in \mathcal{M}(A)$. Let S be an F_σ-set in X with $m(S) = 0$. Then there is a sequence $\{f_n\}$ in A such that (1) $\|f_n\| \le 1$ for all n, (2) $f_n \to 0$ pointwise on S, (3) $f_n \to 1$ a.e. [m].*

Proof.   We can suppose that $S = \bigcup\limits_{n=1}^{\infty} K_n$ where the K_n are compact sets and $K_n \subset K_{n+1}$ $(n \ge 1)$. Choose $\rho_n \in C_R(X)$ with $\rho_n > 0$ on X, $\rho_n > 1$ on K_n, and $\int \rho_n\, dm < 1/n^2$ (Lemma 1). Set $u_n = -n\rho_n$. Then $u_n < 0$, $u_n < -n$ on K_n, and $\int u_n\, dm > -1/n$. By hypothesis, we can find $f_n \in A^{-1}$ such that (a) $\log |f_n| < 0$ on X, (b) $\log |f_n| < -n$ on K_n, (c) $\int \log |f_n| > -2/n$. Since f_n is invertible, $\hat{f}_n(a) \ne 0$, so we can multiply f_n by a constant of modulus 1 and also assume that (d) $0 < \hat{f}_n(a) = \int f_n\, dm$.

Since m is the unique representing measure for a, m is an Arens-Singer measure. So we can rewrite (a)-(d) as (e) $\|f_n\| < 1$, (f) $|f_n| < e^{-n}$ on K_n, (g) $\log |\int f_n\, dm| = \int \log |f_n|\, dm > -2/n$, or $\int f_n\, dm > e^{-2/n}$.

By (f), $f_n \to 0$ pointwise on S, and by (e), (1) holds. From (e) and (g) it follows that $\int f_n\, dm \to 1$. But $\int |1 - f_n|^2\, dm = \int (1 - 2 \operatorname{Re}(f_n) + |f_n|^2)\, dm \le 2(1 - \int \operatorname{Re}(f_n)\, dm)$. Hence $f_n \to 1$ in $L^2(m)$. But then some subsequence $\{f_{n_i}\}$ converges to 1 a.e. $[m]$ and the f_{n_i} satisfy conditions (1), (2), (3).

Now consider a logmodular algebra A, a complex homomorphism $a \in \mathcal{M}(A)$, and the representing measure m for a on $\Gamma(A)$. For any measure $\mu \in M(X)$, let μ_a, μ_s be the absolutely continuous and singular parts of μ with respect to m, so that $\mu = \mu_a + \mu_s$, $\mu_a \ll m$, $\mu_s \perp m$. Let $A_a = \{f \in A : \hat{f}(a) = 0\}$ be the maximal ideal determined by a.

Theorem 4   (Generalized F. and M. Riesz Theorem).

(a) *If μ annihilates A, then μ_a and μ_s annihilate A.*

(b) *If μ annihilates A_a, then μ_s annihilates A and μ_a annihilates A_a.*

Proof.   By Lemma 2, μ_s is concentrated on an F_σ-set S with $m(S) = 0$. By Forelli's lemma, there exist $f_n \in A$ satisfying (1), (2), (3).

Let $f \in A$. Then $ff_n \to f$ a.e. $[m]$, $ff_n \to 0$ on S, and $\|ff_n\| \le \|f\|$ for all n. Hence by the dominated convergence theorem, $\int ff_n\, d\mu_a \to \int f\, d\mu_a$ and $\int ff_n\, d\mu_s \to 0$.

(a) Suppose that $\mu \in A^\perp$. Then $\int ff_n\, d\mu = 0$ for all n, so $0 = \lim_n \int ff_n\, d\mu_a + \lim_n \int ff_n\, d\mu_s = \int f\, d\mu_a$. Hence $\mu_a \in A^\perp$, as was to be shown. (Since $\mu_s = \mu - \mu_a$, $\mu_s \in A^\perp$ also.)

(b) Suppose instead that $\mu \in A_a^\perp$ and set $c = \int 1\, d\mu$, so that $\nu = \mu - cm$ annihilates A. By part (a), the singular part of ν also annihilates A, so $\nu_s = \mu_s \in A^\perp$. Since μ_a is the difference of two annihilators of A_a, $\mu_a \in A_a^\perp$, so (b) is proved.

Corollary 1.   *Let A be a logmodular algebra on X, and let $x \in X$. Then for each $\mu \in A^\perp$, $\mu(\{x\}) = 0$. (Hence $\mu(C) = 0$ for every countable set C in X.)*

Proof. We take $a =$ evaluation at x, $m = \delta_x$, and decompose μ as $c\delta_x + \mu_s$, where c is a scalar and $\mu_s(\{x\}) = 0$. By the theorem, $c\delta_x \in A^\perp$, and in particular, $c = \int 1\, d(c\delta_x) = 0$. So $\mu = \mu_s$, and we're done.

Corollary 2   (Classical F. and M. Riesz Theorem).   *Let μ be a complex Borel measure on the unit circle such that $\int z^n\, d\mu(z) = 0$ for $n = 1, 2, \ldots$. Then μ is absolutely continuous with respect to Lebesgue one-dimensional measure on the circle.*

Proof.   Let A be the boundary value algebra A^1, and let m be the measure $\dfrac{1}{2\pi}\, d\theta$ on the circle T. A is a Dirichlet algebra and m is multiplicative on A, since $\int f\, dm = \hat{f}(0)$ for $f \in A$, where $\hat{f}$ is the analytic extension of f. By assumption, $\int z^n\, d\mu(z) = 0$ ($n \geq 1$), so μ annihilates the maximal ideal $A_0 = \{f \in A : \hat{f}(0) = 0\}$. Hence the singular part μ_s annihilates A. Thus $\int z^n\, d\mu_s(z) = 0$ for all $n \geq 0$. But then $\bar{z}\, d\mu_s$ annihilates A_0 and is singular with respect to m, so $\bar{z}\, d\mu_s$ annihilates A; i.e., $\int z^n\, d\mu_s(z) = 0$ for all $n \geq -1$, so one more Fourier-Stieltjes coefficient of μ_s is zero. By induction on n, $\bar{z}^n\, d\mu_s(z)$ is in $A^\perp$ for every $n \geq 0$, so $\int z^k\, d\mu_s(z) = 0$ for every $k \in \mathbf{Z}$. Hence $\mu_s = 0$, so μ is indeed absolutely continuous with respect to m.

Observe that logmodularity of A is used in Theorem 4 and Corollary 1 only to invoke the Forelli lemma. Observe also that we can express Corollary 2 in a somewhat different form. By the Radon-Nikodym theorem, $\mu = h\, dm$ where $h \in L^1(m)$. Since $\mu \in A_0{}^\perp$, $\displaystyle\int_0^{2\pi} h(e^{i\theta})e^{-in\theta}\, d\theta = 0$ for $n = -1, -2, -3, \ldots$; that is, the negative-order Fourier coefficients of h all vanish. So if $\mu \perp A_0$, $d\mu = h\, dm$ where $h \in L^1(m)$ and h is "analytic," in the sense that $\hat{h}(n) = 0$ for all $n < 0$. Moreover, if we modify the argument at the beginning of §4.3 we can show that h is the L^1 limit of a sequence of polynomials. (An annihilator in $(L^1)^*$ of the polynomials is a function $\varphi \in L^\infty$ with

$$\int \varphi(z)z^n\, dm(z) = 0 \quad \text{for all } n \geq 0.$$

Set $\psi(z) = \varphi(\bar{z})$ and consider the convolution $\psi * h$. By Fubini's theorem, all its Fourier coefficients vanish. But $\psi \in L^\infty$, $h \in L^1$, so $\psi * h$ is continuous. Hence $\psi * h = 0$, and in particular $(\psi * h)(1) = 0$; i.e,. φ annihilates h. By the Hahn-Banach theorem, h is approximable by polynomials in L^1.)

Suppose now that X is a compact set in the plane and X is the boundary of the unbounded component of $\mathbf{C} \backslash X$. By Walsh's theorem, $P(X)$ is a Dirichlet algebra, so the generalized Riesz theorem is applicable. Combining the Riesz theorem with Lemma 2, §5.3, we can prove the following theorem about annihilators of $P(X)$.

Theorem 5.   *Let Y be a compact set in the plane with connected complement and let $X = \mathrm{bd}\,(Y)$. Suppose that $\mu \in P(X)^\perp$ and μ is mutually singular with every representing measure for $P(X)$. Then $\mu = 0$.*

Proof. It will be enough to show that $\int (z - z_0)^{-1} d\mu(z) = 0$ for every z_0 such that $\int |z - z_0|^{-1} d|\mu|(z)$ is finite. Since $\mathbf{C}\backslash Y$ is connected, $R(Y) = P(Y)$, so this is clear for $z_0 \in \mathbf{C}\backslash Y$.

Suppose now that $z_0 \in Y$ and $|z - z_0|^{-1} \in L^1(|\mu|)$. We know that $Y = \text{hull}(X) = \mathcal{M}(P(X))$, so z_0 has a representing measure σ on X with respect to $P(X)$. If g is any function in $P(X)$ such that $\hat{g}(z_0) = \int g \, d\sigma = 0$, there are polynomials q_n converging uniformly to g on X. Subtracting off $\int q_n \, d\sigma$, we have polynomials p_n such that (i) $p_n(z_0) = 0$ for all n, (ii) $\|p_n - g\|_X \to 0$. Because of (i), $p_n(z)/(z - z_0)$ is a polynomial for each n, so $\int \dfrac{g(z)}{z - z_0} \, d\mu(z) =$

$\lim_n \int \dfrac{p_n(z)}{z - z_0} \, d\mu(z) = 0$.

We have now shown that the finite Borel measure $(z - z_0)^{-1} d\mu(z)$ annihilates every $g \in P(X)$ with $\hat{g}(z_0) = 0$. But by assumption, μ is singular with respect to σ, so $(z - z_0)^{-1} d\mu(z)$ is also singular. Hence by the generalized Riesz theorem, $(z - z_0)^{-1} d\mu(z)$ annihilates 1. But this is precisely what we had to show, so we conclude that $\mu = 0$.

The proof of the Wermer maximality theorem in §4.3 used two facts crucially: (i) A^1 is a Dirichlet algebra on the circle, and (ii) if a complex homomorphism of a larger algebra annihilates z, then it must be determined by the multiplicative measure (relative to A^1) which annihilates z. The same approach has been used successfully to prove the maximality of certain other Dirichlet algebras. (For example, see [103].) The next theorem is an essential step in the argument.

Theorem 6. *Let A, B be function algebras on X, with $A \subset B$. Suppose that every complex homomorphism of A has a unique representing measure (which holds, for example, if A is logmodular or Dirichlet on X).*

Suppose that $h_0 \in \mathcal{M}(A)$ and h_0 has an extension to a complex homomorphism h of B. Then

(★) $h(f) = \int f \, dm \qquad (f \in B)$

where m is the representing measure for h_0. (In particular, h_0 has at most one extension $h \in \mathcal{M}(B)$, and the representing measure for h_0 (relative to A) is a representing measure for h (relative to B).) Hence $\mathcal{M}(B)$ is homeomorphic to a closed subset of $\mathcal{M}(A)$, via the restriction mapping.

Proof. Suppose $h_0 \in \mathcal{M}(A)$ extends to $h \in \mathcal{M}(B)$. Let m_0 be the representing measure for h_0, and let m be any representing measure for h. Since $A \subset B$, $\int f \, dm = h(f) = h_0(f) = \int f \, dm_0$ for all $f \in A$, so m is also a representing measure for h_0. Thus $m = m_0$ (by uniqueness of multiplicative measures on A) and (★) holds.

For algebras in general one can obtain an analogous result if one makes the assumption that every representing measure for h_0 is multiplicative on B.

Theorem 7. *Suppose that A and B are function algebras on X with $A \subset B$. Let $a \in \mathcal{M}(A)$. Suppose that every representing measure for a is multiplicative on B. Then a has a unique extension $\tilde{a} \in \mathcal{M}(B)$. Moreover, the set of representing measures for a (relative to A) is the same as the set of representing measures for $\tilde{a}$ (relative to B).*

Proof. Since a has a representing measure, a has at least one extension to a complex homomorphism of B, by hypothesis. Suppose that a_1, a_2 in $\mathcal{M}(B)$ restrict to a and take representing measures λ_1, λ_2 for a_1, a_2. Then $\frac{1}{2}(\lambda_1 + \lambda_2)$ is a representing measure for a (the set of representing measures for a is convex), so $\frac{1}{2}(\lambda_1 + \lambda_2)$ is multiplicative on B; i.e., $\frac{1}{2}(a_1 + a_2) \in \mathcal{M}(B)$. But this is impossible if $a_1 \neq a_2$; for then $\hat{g}(a_1) = 1$, $\hat{g}(a_2) = 0$ for some $g \in B$, and $\int g^2 \, d\left(\frac{\lambda_1 + \lambda_2}{2}\right) = \frac{1}{2}$ while $\left[\int g \, d\left(\frac{\lambda_1 + \lambda_2}{2}\right)\right]^2 = \frac{1}{4}$. Hence a has exactly one extension $\tilde{a}$. Because of the uniqueness of $\tilde{a}$, it is clear that a and $\tilde{a}$ have the same set of representing measures.

Corollary. *If $A \subset B \subset C(X)$ are function algebras, and if every multiplicative measure for A is multiplicative on B, then the restriction map from $\mathcal{M}(B)$ to $\mathcal{M}(A)$ is a homeomorphism of $\mathcal{M}(B)$ onto $\mathcal{M}(A)$.*

EXERCISE SET   6.1

1. Let A be a Dirichlet algebra on X. Show that each $x \in X$ is a one-point part in $\mathcal{M}(A)$.

2. Let A be a logmodular algebra on a compact metric space X. Prove that every $x \in X$ is a peak point for A.

3. Let A be a logmodular algebra on X, and let $a \in \mathcal{M}(A)$. Show that if m is the representing measure for a on X, then $\log |\hat{f}(a)| \leq \int \log |f| \, dm$ for all $f \in A$, and equality holds for all $f \in A^{-1}$.

4. Let A be a function algebra on X. Suppose that the linear span of $\log |A^{-1}|$ is dense in $C_R(X)$. Prove that every $a \in \mathcal{M}(A)$ has exactly one Arens-Singer measure.

5. Let A be a function algebra on X. Suppose that every $a \in \mathcal{M}(A)$ has a unique representing measure. Prove that if λ_1, λ_2 are representing measures for points in $\mathcal{M}(A)$, then either λ_1 and λ_2 are mutually absolutely continuous, or λ_1 and λ_2 are mutually singular.

6. Let G be an additive abelian group. We give G the discrete topology. Let $\ell^1(G)$ be the space of all functions ψ on G such that $\|\psi\|_1 = \sum_{x \in G} |\psi(x)|$ is finite. Then with the pointwise linear operations and convolution as multiplication: $(\psi_1 * \psi_2)(x) = \Sigma_y \, \psi_1(x - y)\psi_2(y)$, $\ell^1(G)$ is a commutative

Banach algebra with identity. The complex homomorphisms of $\ell^1(G)$ can be identified as follows. (See [B], [F], [G], or [J] in the bibliography.) A *character* of G is a (continuous) map $\alpha : G \to T^1$ such that $\alpha(x + y) = \alpha(x)\alpha(y)$ for all x, y in G. Each character of G defines a complex homomorphism of $\ell^1(G)$ by the formula $\psi \to \tilde{\psi}(\alpha) = \sum_{x \in G} \psi(x)\alpha(x)$, and these turn out to be all the complex homomorphisms of $\ell^1(G)$.

Let Γ be the set of all characters of G. Γ is a group under pointwise multiplication (the *character group* of G), and if we carry the Gelfand topology of $\mathscr{M}(\ell^1(G))$ over to Γ, then Γ becomes a compact space and the group operations $(\alpha, \beta) \to \alpha\beta$, $\alpha \to \alpha^{-1} = \bar{\alpha}$ are continuous. Thus Γ is a compact abelian topological group. For $x \in G$, $\alpha \in \Gamma$, set $\varphi_x(\alpha) = \alpha(x)$. Then the topology of Γ is the weak topology defined by $\{\varphi_x : x \in G\}$ (i.e., it is the topology of pointwise convergence on G).

An ordering of G gives rise to the concept of generalized analytic functions on Γ. We want the sum of two nonnegative elements to be nonnegative, so we work with semigroups. (S is a semigroup in G iff $x + y \in S$ for all $x \in S$, $y \in S$.) Assume that (a) S is a semigroup in G, and (b) $S \cup (-S) = G$. Let $\ell^1(S)$ be the set of all $\psi \in \ell^1(G)$ such that ψ vanishes outside S, and let Λ_S be the closed linear span of the monomials φ_x with $x \in S$. Prove that (i) Λ_S is a Dirichlet algebra on Γ; (ii) $\ell^1(S)$ is a closed subalgebra of $\ell^1(G)$; (iii) the closed linear span of $\{\varphi_x : x \in G\}$ is dense in $C(\Gamma)$, and $\varphi_x = 1$ iff $x = 0 \in G$; (iv) Λ_S is the uniform closure of the transforms $\tilde{\psi}$, $\psi \in \ell^1(S)$.

Because of (iv), Λ_S and $\ell^1(S)$ have the same maximal ideal space. Prove that the complex homomorphisms of $\ell^1(S)$ can be identified with the semicharacters of S. (ζ is a *semicharacter* of S iff $|\zeta(x)| \leq 1$ for all $x \in S$, $\zeta(0) = 1$, and $\zeta(x + y) = \zeta(x)\zeta(y)$ for $x \in S$, $y \in S$.) The Gelfand map on $\ell^1(S)$ is simply $\psi \to \tilde{\psi}$, where $\tilde{\psi}(\zeta) = \sum_{x \in S} \psi(x)\zeta(x)$, $\psi \in \ell^1(S)$. (Thus the maximal ideal space of Λ_S is the "disk" of semicharacters of S, and the Šilov boundary is the character group Γ.)

Some remarks are in order. First, suppose that G is the additive group $\mathbf{Z}$ and that $S = \{n \in \mathbf{Z} : n \geq 0\}$. Then $\Gamma = T^1$, with $\varphi_n(e^{i\theta}) = e^{in\theta}(n \in \mathbf{Z}, e^{i\theta} \in \Gamma)$. Each semicharacter ζ is uniquely determined by the complex number $z = \zeta(1)$, and the compact space of semicharacters is just the closed unit disk. The transform algebra $\{\tilde{\psi} : \psi \in \ell^1(S)\}$ on Γ is the set of absolutely convergent Taylor series $\left\{ \sum_{n=0}^{\infty} a_n e^{in\theta} : \Sigma |a_n| < \infty \right\}$, and Λ_S is the disk algebra.

Secondly, Λ_S can always be characterized in terms of Fourier coefficients. To see this we need to know that Γ carries an analogue of normalized Lebesgue measure on the circle T^1. This is indeed the case (see the references mentioned above): there is a positive Borel measure μ on Γ such that $\mu(\Gamma) = 1$ and $\int f(\alpha\beta) \, d\mu(\alpha) = \int f(\alpha) \, d\mu(\alpha)$ for all $\beta \in \Gamma$ and $f \in C(\Gamma)$. (μ is called the *Haar measure* of Γ.) An argument using convolutions of measures (cf. §4.3) will show that $f \in C(\Gamma)$ belongs to Λ_S iff $\int \overline{\alpha(x)} f(\alpha) \, d\mu(\alpha) = 0$ for all $x \notin S$. (To prove this, you will have to show that distinct φ_x, φ_y are orthogonal in $L^2(\mu)$ and that a continuous function all of whose Fourier coefficients vanish is identically zero.)

For further discussion of these and related ideas consult Arens and Singer [10], Hoffman [93], [94], [97], and Hoffman and Singer [103].

6.2 H^p SPACES

Let m be a probability measure (i.e., a positive measure of total mass 1 with domain some σ-algebra of sets), and let A be a subalgebra of $L^\infty(m)$ which contains the constant functions. Assume that m is multiplicative on A; then:

(i) $\int fg \, dm = (\int f \, dm)(\int g \, dm)$ for all f, g in A.

Given m and A, we define function spaces $H^p(m)$ as follows. If $1 \leq p < \infty$, then H^p is the closure of A in $L^p(m)$, while $H^\infty(m) = H^2(m) \cap L^\infty(m)$. For $f \in L^1(m)$, we set $\hat{f}(0) = \int f \, dm$ and let $H_0^p = \{f \in H^p : \hat{f}(0) = 0\}$ ($1 \leq p \leq \infty$), $A_0 = \{f \in A : \hat{f}(0) = 0\}$.

Note that if $f_n \to f$ in $L^p(m)$ ($1 \leq p < \infty$), then $\hat{f}_n(0) \to \hat{f}(0)$, by Hölder's inequality. Hence if $f \in H_0^p$, p finite, and if we set $g_n = f_n - \hat{f}_n(0)$ where the f_n are in A and converge to f in L^p norm, then $g_n \in A_0$ and $\|g_n - f\|_p \to 0$. So we have:

(1) For $1 \leq p < \infty$, H_0^p is the L^p closure of A_0.

Some additional facts are not hard to establish:

(2) The L^2 closure of H_0^∞ is H_0^2.
(3) H^∞ is a norm closed subalgebra of L^∞.
(4) $\int fg \, dm = (\int f \, dm)(\int g \, dm)$ for all f, g in H^2.
(5) If $f \in H^\infty$, then $e^f \in H^\infty$ and $\int e^f \, dm = e^{\int f \, dm}$, while $\int f^n \, dm = (\int f \, dm)^n$ for all integers $n \geq 1$.
(6) A_0 is an ideal in A. H_0^∞ is an ideal in H^∞.

To see (3), note that H^∞ is the intersection of two linear spaces, hence is a subspace of L^∞. Given f_0, g_0 in H^∞ and $\varepsilon > 0$, choose f, g in A with $\|f - f_0\|_2 < \varepsilon/2\|g_0\|_\infty$ and $\|g - g_0\|_2 < \varepsilon/2\|f\|_\infty$. Then $\|fg - f_0 g_0\|_2 < \varepsilon$. So $fg \in H^2 \cap L^\infty = H^\infty$. Hence H^∞ is an algebra. To see that it is norm closed, let f belong to the closure of H^∞ in L^∞. Given $\varepsilon > 0$, choose f_1 in H^∞ with $\|f - f_1\|_\infty < \varepsilon/2$, and choose f_2 in A with $\|f_1 - f_2\|_2 < \varepsilon/2$. Then since $\|g\|_2 \leq \|g\|_\infty$ for all $g \in L^\infty(m)$, $\|f - f_2\|_2 < \varepsilon$. So $f \in H^2 \cap L^\infty = H^\infty$. Hence H^∞ is norm closed.

Given f, g in H^2, choose f_n, g_n in A with $f_n \to f$ and $g_n \to g$ in L^2. Then the inner products $(f_n, \bar{g}_n) = \int f_n g_n \, dm$ converge to $(f, \bar{g}) = \int fg \, dm$. But m is multiplicative on A, so $\int f_n g_n \, dm = (\int f_n \, dm)(\int g_n \, dm) \to (\int f \, dm)(\int g \, dm)$. So (4) is proved.

Property (5) follows since H^∞ is a Banach algebra with 1 and $f \to \int f \, dm$ is a multiplicative linear functional on H^∞. Its kernel is the maximal ideal H_0^∞.

Lemma 4.   *Let* $u \in \mathrm{Re}\,(H^\infty)$, *and let* $\alpha(u) = \inf_{f \in H_0^\infty} \int |1 - f|^2 e^u \, dm$. *Then* $\alpha(u) = e^{\int u \, dm}$.

Proof.   First suppose that $u = \mathrm{Re}\,(g)$ where $g \in H_0^\infty$. Then by (3) and (5), $1 - e^{-g/2}$ also belongs to H_0^∞, so $\alpha(u) \le \int |1 - (1 - e^{-g/2})|^2 e^u \, dm = \int |e^{-g}| e^u \, dm = \int 1 \, dm = 1$. On the other hand, if $f \in H_0^\infty$, then $(1 - f)^2 e^g = e^g + f_1$ where $f_1 \in H_0^\infty$. Thus $\int (1 - f)^2 e^g \, dm = \int e^g \, dm = e^{\int g \, dm} = 1$, so $1 = |\int (1 - f)^2 e^g \, dm| \le \int |1 - f|^2 e^u \, dm$ for all $f \in H_0^\infty$. Thus $\alpha(u) \ge 1$, and the lemma is proved for $u \in \mathrm{Re}\,(H_0^\infty)$.

If $g \in H^\infty$, then $g - a \in H_0^\infty$, where $a = \int g \, dm$. So if $u \in \mathrm{Re}\,(H^\infty)$, then $u - b \in \mathrm{Re}\,(H_0^\infty)$, where $b = \int u \, dm$. Hence

$$\inf_{f \in H_0^\infty} \int |1 - f|^2 e^u \, dm = e^b \inf_{f \in H_0^\infty} \int |1 - f|^2 e^{u-b} \, dm = e^b = e^{\int u \, dm},$$

which proves the lemma.

If we make an additional assumption we will be able to prove that $\alpha(u) = e^{\int u \, dm}$ for every $u \in \mathrm{Re}\,(L^\infty) = L_R^\infty$ and obtain some interesting results along the way.

Consider the following uniqueness hypothesis for m:

(ii) If h is an a.e. nonnegative function in $L^1(m)$ such that $\int f h \, dm = \int f \, dm$ for all $f \in A$, then $h = 1$ a.e. $[m]$. (That is, the only measure ≥ 0 which is absolutely continuous with respect to m and represents $f \to \hat{f}(0)$ on A is m.)

Lemma 5.   *Assume that m satisfies* (i) *and* (ii). *Let w be a nonnegative function in* $L^1(m)$. *Let P be the orthogonal projection of* 1 *into the closure of A_0 in the Hilbert space* $L^2(w \, dm)$. *Then*
(a) $|1 - P|^2 w$ *is constant a.e.* $[m]$,
(b) *the constant equals* $\alpha = \inf \{\int |1 - f|^2 w \, dm : f \in A_0\}$,
(c) $\alpha = \inf \{\int |1 - f|^2 w \, dm : f \in H_0^\infty\}$.

Proof.   Note that (c) asserts that $\mathrm{dist}\,(1, A_0) = \mathrm{dist}\,(1, H_0^\infty)$ in $L^2(w \, dm)$; it does not assert that A_0 and H_0^∞ have the same closures in $L^2(w \, dm)$. Let us use the notation E^- for the closure of a set E in $L^2(w \, dm)$.

Since P is the projection of 1 into A_0^-, $P \in A_0^-$ and $1 - P \perp A_0$ in $L^2(w \, dm)$. There are $f_n \in A_0$ with $f_n \to P$ in $L^2(w \, dm)$. Therefore $f(1 - f_n) \to f(1 - P)$ for all $f \in A_0$, since

$$\int |f(1 - f_n) - f(1 - P)|^2 w \, dm \le \|f\|_\infty^2 \int |f_n - P|^2 w \, dm.$$

But all $f(1 - f_n) \in A_0$ if $f \in A_0$, so we conclude that if $f \in A_0$, then $f(1 - P) \in A_0^-$. Hence $1 - P \perp f(1 - P)$, or $\int |1 - P|^2 f w \, dm = 0$, for all $f \in A_0$.

By hypothesis (ii), there is a constant $\beta \geq 0$ such that $|1 - P|^2 w = \beta$ a.e. $[m]$. Since P is the projection of 1 into A_0^-, $\beta = \int |1 - P|^2 w \, dm = \text{dist}^2(1, A_0^-) = \alpha$, where α is defined in (b).

The rest of the proof depends crucially on the fact that $(1 - P)w \in L^2(m)$. (Since $w \in L^1(m)$, $\alpha w \in L^1(m)$, which means that $|1 - P|^2 w^2 \in L^1(m)$.) For $1 - P \perp A_0$ in $L^2(w \, dm)$, so $(1 - P)w \perp A_0$ in $L^2(m)$. Hence $(1 - P)w$ is orthogonal in $L^2(m)$ to H_0^∞, since the $L^2(m)$-closure of A_0 is $H_0^2 \supset H_0^\infty$. So we see finally that $1 - P$ is orthogonal to $(H_0^\infty)^-$ in $L^2(w \, dm)$.

But this means that the decomposition $1 = P + (1 - P)$ is the decomposition associated with $L^2(w \, dm) = (H_0^\infty)^- \oplus (H_0^\infty)^\perp$. So P is the projection of 1 into $(H_0^\infty)^-$ in $L^2(w \, dm)$, and thus $\alpha = \text{dist}^2(1, A_0^-) = \text{dist}^2(1, (H_0^\infty)^-)$; i.e., $\alpha = \inf \{\int |1 - f|^2 w \, dm : f \in H_0^\infty\}$ also.

Lemma 6. *Assume that m satisfies* (i) *and* (ii), *and let* $w = e^u$ *where* $u \in L_R^\infty$. *Then* $P \in H_0^\infty$, $\int (1 - P)^2 \, dm = 1$, *and* $|1 - P|^2 e^u = \alpha(u)$ *a.e.* $[m]$, *where* $\alpha(u)$ *is defined as in Lemma* 4.

Proof. Note that $a \leq u \leq b$ a.e., so $0 < e^a \leq e^u \leq e^b$ a.e. $[m]$. Thus the closure of a subset of L^∞ in $L^2(e^u \, dm)$ is the same as its closure in $L^2(1 \, dm)$. In particular, $A_0^- = H_0^2$. Since $P \in A_0^-$, $P \in H_0^2$. But $|1 - P|^2 e^u = \alpha$ a.e., by Lemma 5, so $|1 - P|^2 \leq \alpha e^{-a}$ a.e. Hence $P \in H_0^\infty$. Finally, $\int (1 - P)^2 \, dm = [\int (1 - P) \, dm]^2 = 1$ since $\int P \, dm = 0$.

Lemma 7. *Suppose that L is a positive linear functional on L_R^∞ such that* $L(u) = \int u \, dm$ *whenever* $u \in \text{Re}\,(H^\infty)$. *Then if m satisfies* (i) *and* (ii), $L(u) = \int u \, dm$ *for all* $u \in L_R^\infty$.

Proof. If E is a measurable set and u is the characteristic function of E, then $e^u = 1 + \sum_{n=1}^\infty \frac{u^n}{n!} = 1 + (e - 1)u$ and $e^{-u} = 1 + \left(\frac{1}{e} - 1\right)u$. Now use Lemma 6 to find $F \in H^\infty$ with $\int F \, dm = 1$ and $|F|e^u = \alpha$, a nonnegative constant. ($F = (1 - P)^2$.) Of course $\alpha > 0$ since $F \neq 0$. Note that

(a) $$\frac{1}{\alpha} = \int \frac{1}{\alpha} F \, dm = \text{Re}\,\left(\int \frac{1}{\alpha} F \, dm\right) = L\left(\text{Re}\left(\frac{1}{\alpha} F\right)\right),$$

by the hypothesis on L.

Since $L \geq 0$ it follows from (a) that $\frac{1}{\alpha} \leq L\left(\left|\frac{1}{\alpha} F\right|\right) = L(e^{-u}) = 1 + \left(\frac{1}{e} - 1\right)L(u)$ (since $L(1) = \int 1 \, dm = 1$). Hence $\frac{e - 1}{e} L(u) \leq \frac{\alpha - 1}{\alpha}$. On the other hand,

$$\alpha = \inf_{f \in A_0} \int |1 - f|^2 e^u \, dm \leq \int e^u \, dm = 1 + (e - 1) \int u \, dm,$$

so $\dfrac{\alpha - 1}{\alpha} \le \dfrac{e-1}{\alpha} \int u\, dm$. We conclude that

(b) $$L(u) \le \frac{e}{\alpha} \int u\, dm, \qquad u = \chi_E.$$

So (b) holds for u if u is a finite linear combination $\sum a_i \chi_{E_i}$ with $a_i \ge 0$. By monotone increasing approximation, using the fact that $L \ge 0$, we see that $L(u) \le \dfrac{e}{\alpha} \int u\, dm$ for every nonnegative $u \in L^\infty$. Hence for an arbitrary $u \in L_R^\infty$, $|L(u)| \le L(|u|) \le \dfrac{e}{\alpha} \int |u|\, dm = \dfrac{e}{\alpha} \|u\|_1$. Thus L is continuous on L_R^∞ with respect to the L^1 norm, so L extends to a unique $\Lambda \in (L_R^1)^*$.

The dual of L_R^1 is L_R^∞, so $\exists v \in L_R^\infty$ such that

(c) $$\Lambda(u) = \int vu\, dm \qquad (u \in L_R^1).$$

But $L \ge 0$ so $v \ge 0$ a.e. If we apply (c) to each $u \in \mathrm{Re}\,(A)$, we see that $\int f\, dm = L(\mathrm{Re}\,(f)) + iL(\mathrm{Im}\,(f)) = \int vf\, dm$ for all $f \in A$. Hence by hypothesis (ii), $v = 1$ a.e. But then $\Lambda(u) = \int u\, dm \ (u \in L_R^1)$, and in particular, $L(u) = \Lambda(u) = \int u\, dm$ for all $u \in L_R^\infty$, as asserted.

The conclusion of Lemma 7 can be rephrased as follows: if m satisfies (i) and (ii), then the linear functional $f \to \int f\, dm$ on H^∞ has a unique norm-preserving extension to a linear functional on L^∞. Thus it will not be too surprising to find out that H^∞ turns out to be logmodular on the maximal ideal space of L^∞; we will prove this fact below.

Lemma 8. *Suppose that m satisfies* (i) *and* (ii). *Let* $u \in L_R^\infty$, *and let* $\alpha(u) = \inf_{f \in H_0^\infty} \int |1 - f|^2 e^u\, dm$. *Then* $\alpha(u) = e^{\int u\, dm}$.

Proof. The linear functional $h \to \int h\, dm$ on $\mathrm{Re}\,(H^\infty)$ has a unique Hahn-Banach extension to L_R^∞, i.e., a unique positive linear extension. Hence for every $u \in L_R^\infty$, $\sup \{\int h\, dm : h \in \mathrm{Re}\,(H^\infty), h \le u\} = \int u\, dm = \inf \{\int h\, dm : h \in \mathrm{Re}\,(H^\infty), h \ge u\}$ (the inequalities are supposed to hold a.e. $[m]$), for otherwise one could find an extension other than the obvious one. (To see this, look carefully at the proof of the Hahn-Banach theorem.) Exponentiating on both sides, we have

$$\sup \{e^{\int h\, dm} : h \in \mathrm{Re}\,(H^\infty), h \le u\} = \sup \{\alpha(h) : h \in \mathrm{Re}\,(H^\infty), h \le u\}$$
$$= e^{\int u\, dm}$$
$$= \inf \{\alpha(h) : h \in \mathrm{Re}\,(H^\infty), h \ge u\}.$$

But the functional α is monotone, so $\alpha(u)$ lies between the sup and the inf, and we must have $\alpha(u) = e^{\int u\, dm}$.

Suppose that m satisfies (i) and (ii). Then the following is true.

Theorem 8. *Given u in $L_R^\infty = \mathrm{Re}\,(L^\infty)$, $\exists F \in H^\infty$ such that $1/F \in H^\infty$ and $u = \log |F|$.*

Proof. Use Lemma 6 to find F, G in H^∞ such that $\int F\,dm = 1 = \int G\,dm$ and $|F|e^u = \alpha(u)$, $|G|e^{-u} = \alpha(-u)$. By Lemma 7, $\alpha(u)\alpha(-u) = 1$, so $|FG| = 1$ a.e., while $\int FG\,dm = (\int F\,dm)(\int G\,dm) = 1$. Since $\|m\| = 1$, it follows that $FG = 1$ a.e. $[m]$. Hence $e^u = |G|/\alpha(-u) = |\alpha(u)G|$ where $\alpha(u)G \in H^\infty$ and $\dfrac{1}{\alpha(u)G} \in H^\infty$, which proves the theorem.

Although we are dealing with an arbitrary probability measure m and a subalgebra of $L^\infty(m)$ for which (i) and (ii) hold, there is a function algebra interpretation of Theorem 8. First of all, $L^\infty(m)$ is a commutative Banach *-algebra in which $\|ff^*\| = \|f\|^2$. So by the commutative form of the Gelfand-Naimark theorem (cf. §3.4), the Gelfand map $f \to \tilde{f}$ carries L^∞ onto $C(Z)$, where $Z = Z(m)$ is the maximal ideal space of L^∞. The map $f \to \tilde{f} = Tf$ is an isometry and preserves complex conjugates, and the space Z is totally disconnected. The map T carries H^∞ onto a closed subalgebra $\tilde{H}^\infty$ of $C(Z)$, $|Tf| = T(|f|)$, and $T(\log g) = \log (Tg)$ if $g > 0$ (a.e.), $g \in L^\infty$. Hence Theorem 8 asserts that every real-valued continuous function $\tilde{u} \in C_R(Z)$ has the form $\tilde{u} = \log |\tilde{F}|$ where $\tilde{F}$ is an invertible element of the sup norm algebra $\tilde{H}^\infty$. This certainly shows that $\tilde{H}^\infty$ separates points on Z, and we conclude the following.

Theorem 9. *If m satisfies* (i) *and* (ii), *then $\tilde{H}^\infty(m)$ is a logmodular algebra on the maximal ideal space Z of $L^\infty(m)$. In particular, Z is the Šilov boundary of $H^\infty(m)$.*

Since L^∞ is carried isometrically by T onto $C(Z)$, every bounded linear functional on L^∞ is given by a (regular Borel) measure on the compact space Z. In particular, m corresponds to a measure $\tilde{m}$ on Z, and we have $\int f\,dm = \int_Z \tilde{f}\,d\tilde{m}$ for all $f \in L^\infty$. Condition (4) says that the map $\tilde{f} \to \int \tilde{f}\,d\tilde{m}$ is a complex homomorphism of $\tilde{H}^\infty$. (So far, all this is true whether or not (ii) is satisfied.) When $\tilde{H}^\infty$ is logmodular (e.g., when (ii) is satisfied), $\tilde{m}$ is the unique representing measure for this homomorphism, so $\tilde{m}$ is a Jensen measure for $\tilde{H}^\infty$. That is, $\log |\int \tilde{f}\,d\tilde{m}| \le \int \log |\tilde{f}|\,d\tilde{m}$ $(\tilde{f} \in \tilde{H}^\infty)$. We pull this inequality back via T and conclude the following.

Theorem 10. *Let m satisfy* (i) *and* (ii). *Then*

(iii) $$\log \left| \int f\,dm \right| \le \int \log |f|\,dm$$

for all $f \in H^\infty(m)$, and in particular for every f in A.

Actually, the Jensen inequality is satisfied on every $H^p(m)$, $1 \le p \le \infty$.

Theorem 11. *Suppose that m is multiplicative on A, and that Jensen's inequality* (iii) *is true for every* $f \in A$. *Then* (iii) *is true for every* $f \in H^1(m)$.

Proof. Take $f \in H^1$ and choose $\{f_n\}$ in A converging to f in $L^1(m)$. Then $\hat{f}_n(0) \to \hat{f}(0)$, so by adding constants we can suppose that $\hat{f}_n(0) = \hat{f}(0)$ for all n. By assumption, then, $|\hat{f}(0)| \leq \int \log |f_n|\, dm$ for every n.

Observe that if $\varepsilon > 0$, then $|\log(|a| + \varepsilon) - \log(|b| + \varepsilon)| \leq \dfrac{1}{\varepsilon} |a - b|$ for

all a and b. $\left(\log \dfrac{|a| + \varepsilon}{|b| + \varepsilon} \leq \dfrac{|a| + \varepsilon}{|b| + \varepsilon} - 1 = \dfrac{|a| - |b|}{|b| + \varepsilon} \leq \dfrac{1}{\varepsilon} |a - b|.\right)$ Now for each

$\varepsilon > 0$, $\log(|f| + \varepsilon)$ and $\log(|f_n| + \varepsilon)$ are in $L^1(m)$. (They are certainly measurable, and $\log \varepsilon \leq \log(|f| + \varepsilon) \leq |f| + \varepsilon$, so $0 \leq \log(|f| + \varepsilon) - \log \varepsilon \leq |f| + \varepsilon - \log \varepsilon$. Since m is a finite measure and $f \in L^1$, the right side is integrable. Hence $\log(|f| + \varepsilon) - \log \varepsilon$ is in $L^1(m)$. Hence so is $\log(|f| + \varepsilon)$.) By the inequality above, $\log(|f_n| + \varepsilon) \to \log(|f| + \varepsilon)$ in $L^1(m)$. So $\int \log(|f_n| + \varepsilon)\, dm \to \int \log(|f| + \varepsilon)\, dm$. Hence $\int \log(|f| + \varepsilon)\, dm \geq |\hat{f}(0)|$.

Now let ε decrease to 0. By the monotone convergence theorem, $\int \log |f|\, dm \geq |\hat{f}(0)|$.

As a consequence, if m satisfies (i) and (ii), and if $f \in H^1(m)$ and $\int f\, dm \neq 0$, then $\log |f| \in L^1(m)$.

The next result is a special case of an inequality for convex functions due to Jensen.

Lemma 9 (Arithmetic-Geometric Mean Inequality). *Let w be a nonnegative function in* $L^1(m)$, *where m is a positive measure of total mass* 1. *Then:*

(7)
$$\int \log w\, dm \leq \log \left(\int w\, dm\right).$$

Equality holds in (7) *iff w is constant a.e.* [m].

Proof. If $\log w \notin L^1$, then $\int \log w\, dm = -\infty$, so there is nothing to prove. So suppose that $\log w \in L^1$. For every constant $c > 0$, $\log c + \log w = \log(cw) \leq cw - 1$ ($\log t \leq t - 1$ for every $t \geq 0$). Hence $\log c + \int \log w\, dm \leq c \int w\, dm - 1$, since $\int 1\, dm = 1$. Choose $c = \exp(-\int \log w\, dm)$. The left side vanishes and (7) follows upon simplifying the expression on the right.

If $\int \log w\, dm = \log(\int w\, dm)$, then with c chosen as above, $\log(cw) = cw - 1$ a.e. [m]. Hence $cw = 1$ a.e. and $w = 1/c$ a.e. [m].

(We can now add an inequality to Jensen's inequality in Theorem 10: $\log |\int f\, dm| \leq \int \log |f|\, dm \leq \log(\int |f|\, dm), f \in H^1$.)

Consider a nonnegative integrable function w on the unit circle, and let L_w^2 be the set of all measurable f on the circle such that

$$\|f\|_w^2 = \frac{1}{2\pi} \int_0^{2\pi} |f(e^{it})|^2 w(e^{it})\, dt < \infty.$$

It is easy to see that the functions z^n, $n = 0, \pm 1, \pm 2, \ldots$ span L_w^2. We now ask: when is the closed linear span of the z^n with $n \geq 0$ equal to L_w^2? (This can be phrased in pseudoprobabilistic language as, "When can the past be predicted, knowing the future?") By shifting over one power at a time (since $|z| = 1$), we see that this is so iff 1 belongs to the closed subspace spanned by $\{z^n\}_{n=1}^{\infty}$, so the question becomes: when is $\inf \int_0^{2\pi} |1 - p|^2 w \, dt/2\pi = 0$?, where the inf is taken over all polynomials p such that $p(0) = 0$. The next theorem, due to G. Szegö, answers the question in terms of w (1 is in the span iff $\log w \notin L^1$) and gives an explicit measurement of the prediction error.

Theorem 12   (**Szegö's Theorem**).   *Consider the assertion*

(iv) $$\inf_{f \in A_0} \int |1 - f|^2 w \, dm = \exp \left(\int \log w \, dm \right)$$

for every $w \geq 0$ in $L^1(m)$. Then if m satisfies conditions (i) *and* (ii), (iv) *is also satisfied.*

Proof. If we look at Lemma 8, we see that we have proved (iv) in the case where $w = e^u$, $u \in L_R^{\infty}$; i.e., when w is bounded above and bounded away from zero a.e. The proof for an arbitrary nonnegative $w \in L^1(m)$ can be accomplished in a sequence of steps by approximating w carefully. Note that part of the conclusion is that the inf is 0 iff $\log w$ is not in $L^1(m)$.

Assume first that w is bounded away from zero, say $w \geq r > 0$ a.e. Set $w_n = \min(w, n)$. Then $w_n \in L^1$, $r \leq w_n \leq n$, $r \leq w_n \leq w$, $w_n \uparrow w$. Hence $w_n = e^{u_n}$ where $u_n = \log w_n \in L_R^{\infty}$, and $u_n \uparrow \log w$. By the monotone convergence theorem, $\int (w - w_n) \, dm \to 0$ and $\int u_n \, dm \to \int \log w \, dm$. So $\alpha_n = e^{\int u_n \, dm} \to \alpha = e^{\int \log w \, dm}$.

By what is known, $\alpha_n = \inf_{f \in A_0} \int |1 - f|^2 w_n \, dm$ for all n. Let P_n be the projection of 1 into the closure of A_0 in $L^2(w_n \, dm)$. Then $|1 - P_n|^2 w_n = \alpha_n$ a.e. $[m]$ and $P_n \in H_0^{\infty}$ (by Lemmas 5 and 6). We have

(8) $$\int |1 - P_n|^2 w \, dm = \int |1 - P_n|^2 w_n \, dm + \int |1 - P_n|^2 (w - w_n) \, dm,$$

whence

(9) $$\int |1 - P_n|^2 w \, dm = \alpha_n + \int |1 - P_n|^2 (w - w_n) \, dm.$$

Now $|1 - P_n|^2 w_n = \alpha_n$, so $|1 - P_n|^2 \leq \dfrac{\alpha_n}{r}$ a.e. From (9) we have

$$\int |1 - P_n|^2 w \, dm \leq \alpha_n \left(1 + \frac{1}{r} \int (w - w_n) \, dm \right) \leq \alpha \left(1 + \frac{1}{r} \int (w - w_n) \, dm \right).$$

So $\inf_n \int |1 - P_n|^2 w \, dm \leq \alpha$ (since $\int (w - w_n) \, dm \downarrow 0$). Since all P_n are in H_0^{∞}, $\inf_{f \in H_0^{\infty}} \int |1 - f|^2 w \, dm \leq \alpha$.

Conversely, if $f \in A_0$ and $n \geq 1$, then $\int |1 - f|^2 w \, dm \geq \int |1 - f|^2 w_n \, dm \geq$ $\inf_{g \in A_0} \int |1 - g|^2 w_n \, dm = \alpha_n$. This holds for all n, so $\int |1 - f|^2 w \, dm \geq \alpha = \lim \alpha_n$. Thus $\inf_{f \in A_0} \int |1 - f|^2 w \, dm \geq \alpha$ and Szegö's theorem is proved when w is bounded away from zero.

Now take an arbitrary $w \geq 0$ in $L^1(m)$. Set $g_n = \max(w, 1/n)$. Then $g_n \geq 1/n > 0$ and $g_n \downarrow w$, while all $g_n \in L^1(m)$. So $\log g_n \downarrow \log w$, and $e^{\int \log g_n \, dm} \to e^{\int \log w \, dm}$ by monotone convergence. Since each g_n is bounded away from zero, $e^{\int \log g_n \, dm} = \inf_{f \in A_0} \int |1 - f|^2 g_n \, dm \geq \inf_{f \in A_0} \int |1 - f|^2 w \, dm$ for all n, so in the limit $e^{\int \log w \, dm} \geq \inf_{f \in A_0} \int |1 - f|^2 w \, dm$. This proves part of the Szegö theorem, and we can use it to finish off the proof.

Take $g \in A_0$ and apply the last result to $|1 - g|^2 \in L^1$. We have

$$e^{\int \log |1 - g|^2 \, dm} \geq \inf_{f \in A_0} \int |1 - f|^2 |1 - g|^2 \, dm.$$

But if $f \in A_0$, then $(1 - f)(1 - g) = 1 - k$ where $k \in A_0$; thus

$$\int |1 - f|^2 |1 - g|^2 \, dm = \int (1 - k)(1 - \bar{k}) \, dm = 1 + \int |k|^2 \, dm \geq 1.$$

So if $g \in A_0$, then $e^{\int \log |1 - g|^2 \, dm} \geq 1$.

Given $w \geq 0$ in $L^1(m)$ and $g \in A_0$, it follows that

$$e^{\int \log w \, dm} \leq e^{\int \log w \, dm} e^{\int \log |1 - g|^2 \, dm} = e^{\int \log (|1 - g|^2 w) \, dm} \leq \int |1 - g|^2 w \, dm.$$

(The arithmetic-geometric mean inequality was used at the last step.) This is true for all $g \in A_0$, so $e^{\int \log w \, dm} \leq \inf_{g \in A_0} \int |1 - g|^2 w \, dm \leq e^{\int \log w \, dm}$, and the theorem is proved.

It may be of interest to note that the Szegö theorem as we have stated it in (iv) is in fact equivalent to the uniqueness hypothesis (ii).

Theorem 13.   *Let m be a probability measure and A a subalgebra of $L^\infty(m)$ on which m is multiplicative. Let $A_0 = \{f \in A : \int f \, dm = 0\}$. Then if the Szegö theorem (iv) holds, m satisfies (ii).*

Proof.   We are given $w \geq 0$, $w \in L^1(m)$, satisfying $\int wf \, dm = \int f \, dm$ for every $f \in A$. In particular, $\int w \, dm = 1$ and $\int wf \, dm = 0$ for every $f \in A_0$. Thus if $f \in A_0$, $\int |1 - f|^2 w \, dm = \int (1 - f - \bar{f} + |f|^2) w \, dm = 1 + \int |f|^2 w \, dm \geq 1 = \int w \, dm$. By Szegö's theorem, $e^{\int \log w \, dm} = \inf_{f \in A_0} \int |1 - f|^2 w \, dm \geq \int w \, dm$. But the reverse inequality is also true, and we conclude from Lemma 9 that w is constant a.e. $[m]$. Since $\int w \, dm = 1$, the constant is 1, so (ii) is satisfied.

Before we continue with the general measure theory and Hilbert space arguments, let us look at an obvious instance where the hypotheses (i) and (ii) are satisfied. Suppose that A is a function algebra on X, and that some $a \in \mathcal{M}(A)$ has a unique representing measure m. Then A is identifiable with a subalgebra of $L^\infty(m)$, and (i) and (ii) hold. (In fact, for each b in the Gleason part P_a, (i) and (ii) hold with m replaced by the unique representing measure

m_b for b.) We define the spaces $H^p(m)$ as above, and thus have the following results.

(10) $H^\infty(m)$ is a logmodular algebra on $Z = \mathcal{M}(L^\infty(m))$; in fact,

$$\log |(H^\infty)^{-1}| = \mathrm{Re}\,(L^\infty) = L_R^\infty.$$

(11) $\log |\int f\,dm| \leq \int \log |f|\,dm$ $(\forall f \in H^1(m))$, and in particular, if $\int f\,dm \neq 0$, then $\log |f| \in L^1(m)$ and $|f| > 0$ a.e. $[m]$.

(12) For each $h \geq 0$ in $L^1(m)$, $\inf \{\int |1 - f|^2 h\,dm : f \in A, \int f\,dm = 0\} = \exp(\int \log h\,dm)$, and the same is true with A replaced by $H^\infty(m)$ (Szegö's theorem).

But we can prove somewhat more under our present hypothesis. Let μ be any positive measure in $M(X)$, and let P be the projection of 1 into the closure of $A_a = \{f \in A : \hat{f}(a) = 0\}$ in $L^2(\mu)$. Let us follow the proof of Lemma 5.

Set $\alpha = \int |1 - P|^2\,d\mu = \mathrm{dist}^2(1, A_a)$ in $L^2(\mu)$. If $\alpha > 0$, then $\frac{1}{\alpha}|1 - P|^2\mu$ is a probability measure which annihilates A_a, so it is a representing measure for a. By the uniqueness hypothesis, $|1 - P|^2\mu = \alpha m$. The last equality is also true when $\alpha = 0$, since then 1 belongs to the closure of A_a, so $P = 1$.

Let the Lebesgue decomposition of μ with respect to m be $\mu = \mu_a + \mu_s$ where $\mu_a \ll m$ and $\mu_s \perp m$. Then $|1 - P|^2\mu = |1 - P|^2\mu_a + |1 - P|^2\mu_s = \alpha m$. By uniqueness of the Lebesgue decomposition, $|1 - P|^2\mu_a = \alpha m, |1 - P|^2\mu_s = 0$. So

(13) $$\alpha = \int \alpha\,dm = \int |1 - P|^2\,d\mu = \int |1 - P|^2\,d\mu_a.$$

Since $P = 1$ a.e. $[\mu_s]$, $\int f(1 - \bar{P})\,d\mu_a = \int f(1 - \bar{P})\,d\mu = 0$ for all $f \in A_a$, so $1 - P$ is orthogonal to A_a in $L^2(\mu_a)$. But P belongs to the $L^2(\mu_a)$ closure of A_a (since there are $f_n \in A_a$ with $\|f_n - P\|_{L^2(\mu_a)} \leq \|f_n - P\|_{L^2(\mu)} \to 0$), so it follows that P is the projection of 1 into the closure of A_a in $L^2(\mu_a)$. Hence, by (13), $\mathrm{dist}^2(1, A_a)$ in $L^2(\mu)$ equals $\mathrm{dist}^2(1, A_a)$ in $L^2(\mu_a)$.

Theorem 14 (Generalized Kolmogorov-Szegö-Krein Theorem). *Let A be a function algebra on X, and suppose that some $a \in \mathcal{M}(A)$ has a unique representing measure m. Let μ be any positive measure in $M(X)$, and let the Lebesgue decomposition of μ with respect to m be $\mu = wm + \mu_s$ ($w \geq 0$, $w \in L^1(m)$, $\mu_s \perp m$). Then*

$$\inf_{f \in A_a} \int |1 - f|^2\,d\mu = \inf_{f \in A_a} \int |1 - f|^2 w\,dm = \exp\left(\int \log w\,dm\right),$$

where A_a is the maximal ideal determined by a.

This is as far as the extension can go, at least for function algebras. For Lumer [116] has proved that if A is a function algebra on X, if $a \in \mathcal{M}(A)$, and if the generalized *K-S-K* theorem is true for every representing measure *m* for *a* and every nonnegative $\mu \in M(X)$, then *a* has a unique representing measure. (However, one should note that there are function algebras *A* and representing measures *m* satisfying the Szegö theorem, or equivalently, hypothesis (ii), such that *m* is *not* the only representing measure for the homomorphism $f \to \int f\, dm$ ($f \in A$). For example, let *m* be normalized Lebesgue measure on the unit circle, and let *A* be the subalgebra of the boundary value algebra consisting of all *f* such that $f(1) = \int f\, dm = \hat{f}(0)$. Then *m* satisfies (i) and (ii), but *m* and the unit mass at 1 both represent the same complex homomorphism of *A*.)

Because of Jensen's inequality (iii) for $f \in H^1(m)$, where *m* satisfies (i) and (ii), we see easily that if $f \in H^1(m)$ and $\int f\, dm \neq 0$, then $\log |f|$ is integrable. For the H^1 space associated with the complex homomorphism of the disk algebra defined by evaluation at the origin, a stronger conclusion can be drawn. The strengthened result does not hold in the general context of (i) and (ii).

Theorem 15.   *Let m be normalized Lebesgue measure on the unit circle, and let $H^1 = H^1(m)$ be the closure of the boundary value algebra in $L^1(m)$. Suppose that $f \in H^1$ and $f \neq 0$. Then $\log |f|$ is integrable with respect to m.*

Proof.   For each integer *n* let $\hat{f}(n) = \int f \bar{z}^n\, dm$. Since $f \in H^1$, *f* is an L^1 limit of polynomials in *z*, so $\hat{f}(n) = 0$ for all $n < 0$. If $f \neq 0$, then some Fourier coefficient of *f* is not zero, so there is a smallest integer *k* such that $\hat{f}(k) \neq 0$. This means that fz^{-k} has all negative order Fourier coefficients 0, so $fz^{-k} \in H^1$. Thus Jensen's inequality is applicable:

$$-\infty < \log |\hat{f}(k)| = \log \left| \int fz^{-k}\, dm \right| \leq \int \log |fz^{-k}|\, dm = \int \log |f|\, dm.$$

Hence $\log |f| \in L^1(m)$. (In particular, $f^{-1}(0)$ has measure zero.)

The projection technique used to prove Lemma 5 and Theorem 14 also yields an interesting result about representing measures.

Theorem 16.   *Let A be a subalgebra of $L^\infty(m)$ which contains the constants, where m is a probability measure which is multiplicative on A. Let μ be a complex measure such that $\int f\, d\mu = \int f\, dm$ for all $f \in A$. Then there exists a positive measure σ which is absolutely continuous with respect to $|\mu|$ such that $\int f\, d\sigma = \int f\, dm$ ($f \in A$).*

Proof.   Let $A_0 = \{f \in A : \int f\, dm = 0\}$. Then μ annihilates A_0, and $\int 1\, d\mu = 1$. If $f \in A_0$, then $\int |1 - f|^2\, d|\mu| \geq |\int (1 - f)^2\, d\mu| = |(\int (1 - f)\, d\mu)^2| = 1$. So $\alpha = \inf_{f \in A_0} \int |1 - f|^2\, d|\mu| \geq 1$ (in particular, $\alpha \neq 0$). So if *P* is the projection of 1 into the closure of A_0 in $L^2(|\mu|)$, then $1 - P$ is orthogonal to A_0 and $\int |1 - P|^2\, d|\mu| = \alpha$. Thus $\sigma = \frac{1}{\alpha} |1 - P|^2 |\mu|$ is a positive measure of mass 1, and since $f(1 - P)$ belongs to the $L^2(|\mu|)$-closure of A_0 for each

$f \in A_0$, $\int f|1 - P|^2 \, d|\mu| = \int f \, d\sigma = 0$ for all $f \in A_0$. Hence $\sigma \geq 0$, $\sigma \ll |\mu|$, and $\int f \, d\sigma = \int f \, dm$ for each $f \in A$.

Using Theorem 16, we can prove a variation of Theorem 5 on completely singular annihilators.

Proposition 1. *Let X be a compact set in the plane. Suppose that $\mu \in R(X)^{\perp}$ and μ is mutually singular with every representing measure for $R(X)$. Then $\mu = 0$.*

Proof. Suppose that $\mu \in R(X)^{\perp}$ but $\mu \neq 0$. Then, by Lemma 2, §5.3, there is some $x \in X$ such that $\int |z - x|^{-1} \, d|\mu|(z) < \infty$ but $\int (z - x)^{-1} \, d\mu(z) = c \neq 0$. As we observed in the proof of Theorem 10, §5.3, $dv(z) = \dfrac{1}{c} \dfrac{d\mu(z)}{z - x}$ is a complex measure on X which represents evaluation at x on $R(X)$. By Theorem 16, there exists a positive measure $\sigma \in M(X)$ which represents x and which is absolutely continuous with respect to $|v|$. So certainly μ and σ are not mutually singular.

EXERCISE SET 6.2

1. Prove that $H^p \subset H^1$ for $1 \leq p \leq \infty$.

2. Show that the product of two H^2 functions belongs to H^1. Show that if $f \in A$ and $g \in H^p$, then $fg \in H^p$ ($1 \leq p \leq \infty$).

6.3 INVARIANT SUBSPACES AND FACTORIZATION THEOREMS

In his 1949 paper [25], Arne Beurling solved the following problem: determine the closed subspaces of ℓ^2 (the space of square summable sequences $\{\xi_n\}_0^{\infty}$) which are invariant under the shift operator $T : \ell^2 \to \ell^2$ which sends $\{\xi_0, \xi_1, \xi_2, \ldots\}$ to $\{0, \xi_0, \xi_1, \xi_2, \ldots\}$. Each $\xi \in \ell^2$ determines a function f in L^2 of the circle, namely the function with Fourier series $f(e^{i\theta}) \sim \sum_{n=0}^{\infty} \xi_n e^{in\theta}$. When ξ corresponds to f, $T\xi$ corresponds to $e^{i\theta}f(e^{i\theta})$. So the invariant subspaces of T are in one-one correspondence with the subspaces of H^2 of the circle which are invariant under the operation of multiplication by the coordinate function z. Beurling showed that the nonzero closed invariant subspaces of H^2 were exactly the subspaces of the form $qH^2 = \{qf : f \in H^2\}$, where $q \in H^2$ and $|q| = 1$ almost everywhere. Furthermore, the representation was essentially unique: if $qH^2 = q_0 H^2$, then $q = \lambda q_0$ where λ is a constant of modulus 1.

The Beurling result has since been generalized in several directions. The general structure of nonunitary isometries on Hilbert spaces has been studied.

Operators whose lattice of invariant subspaces is the same as that of the shift operator have been discovered, and various other Hilbert space generalizations have been explored. Another direction of generalization will be of interest to us. Note that $S \subset H^2$ is invariant under multiplication by z iff S is invariant under multiplication by all polynomials. One can ask to what extent Beurling's invariant subspace theorem remains true when normalized Lebesgue measure on the circle is replaced by an arbitrary probability measure m, and the polynomials and their L^2 closure H^2 on the circle are replaced by an algebra A on which m is multiplicative and its L^2 closure $H^2(m)$. We shall give some answers in this section.

We begin with a collection of lemmas.

Lemma 10. *Let m be a probability measure. Suppose that g is a real-valued function in $L^2(m)$ such that $\int \log |1 - tg| \, dm \geq 0$ for every real number t in some interval $(-\delta, \delta)$. Then $g = 0$ a.e. $[m]$.*

Proof. Apply the hypothesis to t and $-t$ and add the results. We obtain $\int \log |1 - t^2 g^2| \, dm \geq 0$ $(0 \leq t < \delta)$. Let E_t be the set where $g^2 < 1/t^2$, and let F_t be its complement. Then

$$0 \leq \int_{E_t} \log (1 - t^2 g^2) \, dm + \int_{F_t} \log (t^2 g^2 - 1) \, dm.$$

Now $\log (1 - u) \leq -u$ if $u < 1$, and $\log (u - 1) \leq u$ if $u \geq 1$, so

$$0 \leq -t^2 \int_{E_t} g^2 \, dm + t^2 \int_{F_t} g^2 \, dm$$

or

$$0 \leq - \int_{E_s} g^2 \, dm + \int_{F_s} g^2 \, dm \qquad (0 < t < \delta).$$

Since $g^2 \in L_R^1(m)$ and $m(E_t) \to 1$ as $t \to 0^+$, we have $0 \leq -\int g^2 \, dm$ and therefore $g = 0$ a.e.

Lemma 11. *Let m be a probability measure and h a nonnegative function in $L^1(m)$. Then $\exp (\int \log h \, dm) = \inf \{\int e^u h \, dm : u \in L_R^1(m), \int u \, dm = 0\} = \inf \{\int e^u h \, dm : u \in L_R^\infty(m), \int u \, dm = 0\}$.*

Proof. First suppose that $\log h$ is integrable. Then if $u \in L_R^1(m)$ and $\int u \, dm = 0$, $\int e^u h \, dm \geq \exp (\int \log (e^u h) \, dm) = \exp (\int u \, dm + \int \log h \, dm) = \exp (\int \log h \, dm)$ by the arithmetic-geometric mean inequality. So $\exp (\int \log h \, dm) \leq \inf \{\int e^u h \, dm : u \in L_R^1, \int u \, dm = 0\}$. But if $g = -\log h + \int \log h \, dm$, then $g \in L_R^1$ and $\int g \, dm = 0$, while $\int e^g h \, dm = e^{\int \log h \, dm} \int dm = \exp (\int \log h \, dm)$. So equality is obtained.

If $\log h \notin L^1(m)$, then $\int \log h \, dm = -\infty$, so $\exp (\int \log h \, dm) = 0$. So again $\exp (\int \log h \, dm) \leq \inf \{\int e^u h \, dm : u \in L_R^1, \int u \, dm = 0\}$. For each $\varepsilon > 0$, $\log (h + \varepsilon)$ is integrable. We apply the case above to it and then let ε decrease to 0. Again the inf equals $\exp (\int \log h \, dm)$.

The infima corresponding to L_R^∞ and to L_R^1 can be shown to be equal by monotonicity arguments. (See Hoffman [97], page 289.)

Theorem 17. *Let m be a probability measure. Suppose that A is a subalgebra of $L^\infty(m)$ which contains the constants and that (i) m is multiplicative on A; (ii) if $\int fh\,dm = \int f\,dm$ for all $f \in A$, where h is nonnegative and in $L^1(m)$, then $h = 1$ a.e. [m]. Then the following hold.*
  (1) *If $g \in L^2(m)$ and $\int fg\,dm = 0$ for all $f \in A$, then $\int \log|1 - g|\,dm \geq 0$.*
  (2) *$A + \bar{A}$ is dense in $L^2(m)$.*
  (3) *$L^2(m) = H^2(m) \oplus \overline{H_0^2(m)}$.*
  (4) *If $f \in H^2(m)$ and f is real-valued, then f is constant a.e. [m].*

Proof. (1) Assume that $\int fg\,dm = 0$, $\forall f \in A$. Then if $f \in H^\infty$, $\int fg\,dm = 0$ also. Thus $\int f\,dm = \int (1 - g)f\,dm$, so $\log|\int f\,dm| \leq \log\int |1 - g|\,|f|\,dm$ for all $f \in H^\infty$. But m satisfies Jensen's inequality on H^∞, so

$$\int \log|f|\,dm = \log\left|\int f\,dm\right| \leq \log\int |1 - g|\,|f|\,dm$$

for every invertible element $f \in H^\infty$. But we know that $L_R^\infty = \log|(H^\infty)^{-1}|$. Hence $\int u\,dm \leq \log\int |1 - g|e^u\,dm$ for every $u \in L_R^\infty$; in particular,

$$\inf\left\{\int |1 - g|e^u\,dm : u \in L_R^\infty, \int u\,dm = 0\right\} \geq 1.$$

So (1) follows from Lemma 11.
  (2) We must show that if $g \in L^2(m)$ is orthogonal to A and $\bar{A}$, then $g = 0$ a.e. [m], or equivalently, if g and $\bar{g}$ are orthogonal to A in L^2, then $g = 0$.
  So suppose that $g \in L_R^2(m)$ and $\int fg\,dm = 0$ for all $f \in A$. Then by (1), $\int \log|1 - tg|\,dm \geq 0$ for all real t. So $g = 0$ a.e. by Lemma 10.
  (3) Note that H^2 and $\overline{H_0^2}$ are closed subspaces of L^2. They are orthogonal since $\int f\bar{g}\,dm = \int fg\,dm = (\int f\,dm)(\int g\,dm) = 0$ if $f \in H^2$, $g \in H_0^2$. Finally, their direct sum is all of L^2, since by (2), any element of L^2 which is orthogonal to H^2 and $\overline{H_0^2}$ must be 0.
  (4) Suppose $f \in H^2$ and $f = \bar{f}$ a.e. [m]. Let $\lambda = \int f\,dm = \hat{f}(0)$. Then λ is a real constant and $f - \lambda \in H_0^2$. So $f - \lambda$ belongs to $H^2 \cap \overline{H_0^2} = \{0\}$. Hence $f = \lambda$ a.e. [m].

Corollary. $H^\infty = \{g \in L^\infty : \int fg\,dm = 0$ for all $f \in A_0\}$.

Proof. If $f \in A_0$ and $g \in H^\infty$, then $0 = (\int f\,dm)(\int g\,dm) = \int fg\,dm$. Conversely, if $g \in L^\infty$ and $\int fg\,dm = 0$ for all $f \in A_0$, then $\bar{g}$ is orthogonal to A_0 in L^2 and hence $\bar{g}$ is orthogonal to H_0^2. Since H^2 is the orthogonal complement of $\overline{H_0^2}$, $g \in H^2$. So $g \in H^\infty = L^\infty \cap H^2$.

Next we have a factorization theorem for nonnegative functions.

Theorem 18. *Suppose that the hypotheses of Theorem* 17 *are satisfied.*
Let w *be a nonnegative function in* $L^1(m)$. *Then* $\log w \in L^1(m)$ *iff* $w = |g|^2$
a.e. for some $g \in H^2(m)$ *such that* $\hat{g}(0) \neq 0$.

Proof. If $w = |g|^2$ a.e., then $\log w = 2 \log |g|$. But $g \in H^2$ and $\hat{g}(0) \neq 0$,
so $\log |g|$ is integrable. (Indeed, since $H^2 \subset H^1$, $\int \log |g| \, dm \geq \log |\int g \, dm| >$
$-\infty$ by Jensen's inequality.) So $\log w$ is integrable.

On the other hand, if $\log w \in L^1(m)$, then $\alpha = \exp(\int \log w \, dm) =$
$\inf_{f \in A_0} \int |1 - f|^2 w \, dm > 0$, by Szegö's theorem. So if P is the projection of
1 into the closure of A_0 in $L^2(w \, dm)$, then $|1 - P|^2 w = \alpha > 0$ a.e. $[m]$ and
$w = |g|^2$ where $g = \sqrt{\alpha}(1 - P)^{-1}$. Since $w \in L^1(m)$, $g \in L^2(m)$. Also, $\hat{g}(0) =$
$\int \sqrt{\alpha}(1 - P)^{-1} \, dm = \alpha^{-1/2} \int (1 - \bar{P}) w \, dm$. Since $1 - P$ is orthogonal to P in
$L^2(w \, dm)$, $\hat{g}(0) = \alpha^{-1/2} \int (1 - \bar{P})(1 - P) w \, dm = \alpha^{-1/2} \int |1 - P|^2 w \, dm > 0$ (indeed, $\hat{g}(0) = \sqrt{\alpha}$). Finally we observe that $g \in H^2(m)$ since g is orthogonal to
$\overline{A_0}$ and hence to $\overline{H_0}^2$. (For if $f \in A_0$, then $\int g f \, dm = \sqrt{\alpha} \int (1 - P)^{-1} f \, dm =$
$\alpha^{-1/2} \int (1 - \bar{P}) f w \, dm = 0$ since $1 - P$ is orthogonal to A_0 in $L^2(w \, dm)$.)

Now we prove extensions of Beurling's invariant subspace theorems.
We assume that the hypotheses of Theorem 17 are satisfied. A subspace S of
$L^2(m)$ will be called *invariant* iff $AS \subset S$, i.e., $fg \in S$ for all $f \in A$, $g \in S$.
Equivalently, S is invariant iff $A_0 S \subset S$. S is *simply invariant* iff the closure
of $A_0 S$ in $L^2(m)$ is a proper subspace of S. (S is *doubly invariant* iff S is the
closure of $A_0 S$.)

Theorem 19. *Under the hypotheses of Theorem* 17, *if* S *is a simply invariant
closed subspace of* $L^2(m)$, *then* $S = qH^2$ *where* $q \in L^\infty$ *and* $|q| = 1$ *a.e. The
function* q *is uniquely determined by* S *up to multiplication by constants of
modulus* 1.

Proof. By hypothesis, the closure of $A_0 S$ in L^2 is a proper subspace of S,
so there is a nonzero function $g \in S$ orthogonal to $A_0 S$. Since $g \neq 0$ we may
assume that $\|g\|_2 = 1$. For each $f \in A$, $f - \hat{f}(0)$ is in A_0, so g is orthogonal to
$g(f - \hat{f}(0))$. This means that $\int |g|^2 f \, dm = \hat{f}(0) \int |g|^2 \, dm = \hat{f}(0) = \int f \, dm$ for all
$f \in A$. Hence by the uniqueness assumption (ii), $|g| = 1$ a.e.

Since S is an invariant subspace, $gA \subset S$. So $gH^2 \subset S$, since $g \in L^\infty$. The
inclusion is an equality. Note that gH^2 is a closed subspace of S: if $\{f_n\} \subset H^2$
and $gf_n \to f$ in L^2, then $f_n \to \bar{g} f \in H^2$, so $f \in gH^2$. Thus $gH^2 = S$ provided that
any $h \in S$ which is orthogonal to gH^2 is 0. But $\int h \bar{g} \bar{f} \, dm = 0$ for all $f \in A$,
so $h\bar{g}$ is orthogonal to A in L^2. But g is orthogonal to $A_0 S$, so $h\bar{g}$ is also
orthogonal to $\overline{A_0}$. Since $A + \overline{A_0}$ is dense in L^2, $h\bar{g} = 0$ a.e. So $h = h\bar{g}g = 0$
a.e. Thus $S = gH^2$.

If $qH^2 = q_1 H^2$ where q and q_1 are of modulus 1 a.e., then $\bar{q} q_1 H^2 = H^2 =$
$q\bar{q}_1 H^2$. Hence $q\bar{q}_1$ and its complex conjugate lie in H^2. So $q\bar{q}_1$ is constant
a.e. (Apply (4) of Theorem 17 to Re $(q\bar{q}_1)$, Im $(q\bar{q}_1)$.) Therefore $q = \lambda q_1$ where
λ is constant. So uniqueness is proved.

Theorem 20. *Suppose that conditions* (i), (ii) *are satisfied. Let S be an invariant closed subspace of $H^2(m)$ such that $\int f \, dm \neq 0$ for some $f \in S$; i.e., 1 is not orthogonal to S. Then $S = qH^2$ where $q \in H^\infty$ and $|q| = 1$ a.e.*

Proof. By assumption, $A_0 S \subset S$. Since m is multiplicative on H^2, $\int fg \, dm = 0$ for all $f \in A_0$, $g \in S$. Hence $\int h \, dm = 0$ for all h in the L^2 closure of $A_0 S$. Since 1 is not orthogonal to S, the closure of $A_0 S$ is proper in S. So S is simply invariant. Thus $S = qH^2$ for some $q \in L^\infty$ with $|q| = 1$ a.e. But $1 \in H^2$, so $q \in S \subset H^2$. Hence $q \in H^\infty$.

In the classical case of the boundary value algebra, every nonzero closed invariant subspace of H^2 is of the form qH^2 for some $q \in H^\infty$ with $|q| = 1$ a.e. (For example, $H_0^2 = zH^2$.) But in general the representation fails to hold without the hypothesis that 1 is not orthogonal to S.

Each member $g \in H^2(m)$ generates an invariant subspace, namely, $Ag = \{fg : f \in A\}$. Let S be the L^2 closure of Ag. When does $S = H^2$? Note that since S is invariant and A is dense in H^2, $S = H^2$ iff $1 \in S$.

Theorem 21. *Given a measure m and an algebra A satisfying* (i), (ii), *let $g \in H^2(m)$. Then Ag is dense in $H^2(m)$ iff $\int \log |g| \, dm = \log |\int g \, dm| > -\infty$.*

Proof. Note that since m is multiplicative on H^2, $\int g \, dm \neq 0$ if Ag is dense in H^2. So we can replace g by a constant multiple and assume that $\int g \, dm = 1$. We now must show that Ag is dense in H^2 iff $\int \log |g| \, dm = 0$.

If Ag is dense, there exist f_n in A with $f_n g \to 1$ in $L^2(m)$. So $\int f_n \, dm = \int f_n g \, dm \to 1$. Thus we may suppose that $\int f_n \, dm = 1$ for all n (replace f_n by $f_n / \hat{f}_n(0)$). We have $\int |1 - f_n g|^2 \, dm = 1 - 2 \operatorname{Re}(\int f_n g) \, dm + \int |f_n|^2 |g|^2 \, dm \to 0$. So $\int |1 - g_n|^2 |g|^2 \, dm \to 1$, where $g_n = 1 - f_n$ belongs to A_0. Conversely, if there exist g_n in A_0 with $\int |1 - g_n|^2 |g|^2 \, dm \to 1$, then Ag is dense in H^2. But if $f \in A_0$, then $1 = |\int (1 - f)g \, dm|^2 \leq \int |1 - f|^2 |g|^2 \, dm$. So density of Ag is equivalent to $\inf_{f \in A_0} \int |1 - f|^2 |g|^2 \, dm = 1$.

But by Szegö's theorem, the infimum equals $\exp(\int \log |g|^2 \, dm) = \exp(2 \int \log |g| \, dm)$. So Ag is dense iff $\int \log |g| \, dm = 0$, as asserted.

An *inner function* is a function $q \in H^\infty(m)$ with $|q| = 1$ a.e. An *outer function* in $H^2(m)$ is a function g such that $\int \log |g| \, dm = \log |\int g \, dm| > -\infty$. Theorems 20 and 21 tell us how inner and outer functions are related to invariant subspaces in $H^2(m)$. The next theorem gives a factorization of an arbitrary H^2 function (not in H_0^2) into inner and outer factors.

Theorem 22. *Assume* (i) *and* (ii). *Let $f \in H^2(m)$ and $\int f \, dm \neq 0$. Then there are q, g with q inner and g outer such that $f = qg$. The factorization is unique up to multiplication by constants of modulus 1.*

Proof. Let S be the closure of Af in $L^2(m)$. Then S is a closed invariant subspace of H^2 and 1 is not orthogonal to S. So $S = qH^2$ where q is an inner function. Thus $f = qg$ for some $g \in H^2$. Now $Af = q(Ag)$ while the closure of

Af is $S = qH^2$. So Ag must be dense in H^2 and therefore g is an outer function. (Given $h \in H^2$, there are f_n in A with $qf_ng \rightarrow qh$ in L^2. Since $|q| = 1$, $f_ng \rightarrow h$. So Ag is dense in H^2.)

On the other hand, if f has the factorization qg with q inner and g outer, then qH^2 is the closure of Af. So q is unique, since the inner function in Theorem 20 is unique.

Corollary (Szegö's Factorization Theorem).   *Let w be a nonnegative function in $L^1(m)$. Then the following are equivalent*: (a) $\log w \in L^1(m)$; (b) $w = |f|^2$ *where $f \in H^2$ and $\int f\, dm \neq 0$*; (c) $w = |g|^2$ *for some outer function $g \in H^2$.*

This follows at once from Theorems 18 and 22. But note, too, that the function constructed in the proof of Theorem 18 (given w and $\log w$ in $L^1(m)$) is already an outer function. For $\log |\hat{g}(0)| = \log \sqrt{\alpha} = \log(\exp(\frac{1}{2}\int \log w\, dm)) = \frac{1}{2}\int \log w\, dm = \frac{1}{2}\int \log |g|^2\, dm = \int \log |g|\, dm > -\infty$.

Theorem 23.   *Let A be a function algebra on a compact space X. Let $a \in \mathcal{M}(A)$ and suppose that a has a unique representing measure m on X. Let σ be the representing measure for a point of the Gleason part of $\mathcal{M}(A)$ which contains a. Set $A_\sigma = \{f \in A : \int f\, d\sigma = 0\}$ and $w = d\sigma/dm$. Let μ be a positive measure in $M(X)$, and let the Lebesgue decomposition of μ with respect to m be $\mu = hm + \mu_s$ ($h \in L^1(m)$, $\mu_s \perp m$). Then*

$$\inf_{f \in A_\sigma} \int |1 - f|^2\, d\mu = \exp\left(\int \log w\, dm\right) \cdot \exp\left(\int \log h\, d\sigma\right).$$

Remark.   Perhaps we should observe that Theorem 23 is more of a genuine generalization of Szegö's original theorem of the 1920's than our previous "abstract Szegö theorem." For the classical result goes as follows.

Corollary.   *Let $\alpha = re^{i\theta}$ lie in the open unit disk. Let m be normalized Lebesgue measure on the circle, P_r the Poisson kernel, and A the disk algebra. Then for each $h \in L^1(m)$, $h \geq 0$, we have*

$$\inf_{f \in A, f(\alpha) = 0} \int |1 - f|^2 h\, dm = (1 - r^2) \exp\left(\frac{1}{2\pi}\int_0^{2\pi} \log h(t)P_r(\theta - t)\, dt\right).$$

The Lebesgue decomposition here is taken with respect to m, the representing measure on $T^1 = \Gamma(A)$ for the origin, while the L^2 distance is computed with respect to the maximal ideal determined by an arbitrary α in the open disk.

To prove the corollary, note first that the boundary value algebra is a Dirichlet algebra, so Theorem 23 applies. The open disk is a single part, and the representing measure σ for α is given by $d\sigma(t) = P_r(\theta - t)\, dm(t)$. So the infimum equals

$$\exp\left(\int \log P_r(\theta - t)\, dm(t)\right) \cdot \exp\left(\int \log h(t)P_r(\theta - t)\, dm(t)\right),$$

where we have written $h(t)$ for $h(e^{it})$. Thus we must verify that $\frac{1}{2\pi} \int_0^{2\pi} \log P_r(\theta - t)\, dt = \log(1 - r^2)$ if $0 < r < 1$. Since $P_r(\theta - t) = \frac{1 - r^2}{1 - 2r\cos(\theta - t) + r^2}$, this is equivalent to

(1) $$\int_0^{2\pi} \log(1 - 2r\cos t + r^2)\, dt = 0.$$

But if $f(z) = 1 - rz$, then f is an invertible element of the disk algebra. So $\int_T \log|f(z)|\, dm(z) = \log\left|\int_T f(z)\, dm(z)\right| = \log 1 = 0$, since m is an Arens-Singer measure, and this proves (1). So the corollary is established.

Now for the proof of the theorem:

By hypothesis, the complex homomorphisms of A determined by σ and m belong to the same part P in $\mathscr{M}(A)$, and each point in P has a unique representing measure. Hence $\sigma = wm$, where $w \geq 0$ and w and $1/w$ are in $L^\infty(m)$.

Given a positive measure $\mu \in M(X)$ with Lebesgue decomposition $\mu = hm + \mu_s$, $h \in L^1(m)$, the Lebesgue decomposition of μ with respect to σ is $\mu = \frac{h}{w}\sigma + \mu_s$. Hence by the Kolmogorov-Szegö-Krein theorem,

$$\inf_{f \in A_\sigma} \int |1 - f|^2\, d\mu = \inf_{f \in A_\sigma} \int |1 - f|^2 \frac{h}{w}\, d\sigma = \exp\left(\int \log\frac{h}{w}\, d\sigma\right).$$

So in order to prove the theorem, it remains to show that

(2) $$\exp\left(\int \log\frac{1}{w}\, d\sigma\right) = \exp\left(\int \log w\, dm\right).$$

Let $A_m = \{f \in A : \int f\, dm = 0\}$, and let P be the orthogonal projection of 1 into the closure of A_m in $L^2\left(\frac{1}{w}\, dm\right)$. Since $w \in L^\infty$, $f \to \int f\, dm$ is a continuous linear functional on $L^2\left(\frac{1}{w}\, dm\right)$; thus $\int P\, dm = 0$. If we look at the proofs of Theorem 18 and the Corollary to Theorem 22, we see that $|1 - P|^2 \frac{1}{w} = \beta$ a.e. $[m]$, where $\beta = \exp\left(\int \log\frac{1}{w}\, dm\right)$, and $g = (1 - P)^{-1}$ is an outer function in $H^2(m)$ such that $|g|^2 = \frac{1}{\beta w}$ a.e. Since the closures of Ag in $L^2(m)$ and $L^2(\sigma)$ are the same, g is also an outer function in $H^2(\sigma)$.

Hence $\int \log|g|\, d\sigma = \log\left|\int g\, d\sigma\right| = \log\left|\int gw\, dm\right|$. But $gw = \frac{1 - \bar{P}}{\beta}$ a.e., so $\int \log|g|\, d\sigma = \log\left|\frac{1}{\beta}\int(1 - \bar{P})\, dm\right| = \log 1/\beta$. Since $1/w = \beta|g|^2$, we have $\int \log\frac{1}{w}\, d\sigma = \log\beta + 2\int \log|g|\, d\sigma = \log 1/\beta = \int \log w\, dm$. So (2) is proved.

EXERCISE SET 6.3

1. Show that the function q in Theorem 20 is a constant multiple of the projection of 1 into S.

2. Prove that every nonzero closed subspace of H^2 of the circle which is invariant under multiplication by z has the form qH^2 where q is an inner function.

3. Show that if q is an inner function in $H^\infty(m)$, then qH^2 is a closed invariant subspace of H^2.

4. Show that under the hypothesis of Theorem 23, $\inf_{f \in A_\sigma} \int |1 - f|^2 \, dm = \inf_{f \in A_m} \int |1 - f|^2 \, d\sigma$.

5. Assume that the hypotheses (i) and (ii) are satisfied. For $S \subset L^2(m)$, let $[S]$ be the closed linear span of S in $L^2(m)$. Prove that if $f \in L^2(m)$ and $f \notin [fA_0]$, then $f = qg$ where g is an outer function in $H^2(m)$, $q \in [fA]$, and $|q| = 1$ a.e.; g is unique up to multiplication by constants of modulus 1. Show next that if $f \in L^1(m)$ and $|f|^{1/2} \notin [|f|^{1/2}A_0]$, then $f = qg^2$ where $|q| = 1$ a.e. and g is an outer function in $H^2(m)$. Show that if g is an outer function in H^2, then Ag^2 is dense in H^1. Prove that $|f|^{1/2} \in [|f|^{1/2}A_0]$ iff f belongs to the closure of $A_0 f$ in $L^1(m)$; so if $f \notin [A_0 f]_1$, f factors as qg^2 with g^2 "outer" in $H^1(m)$.

6.4   ANALYTIC DISKS

Let A be a function algebra on a compact space X. Let $a \in \mathcal{M}(A)$, and suppose that a has a unique representing measure m. Then each point b in the Gleason part P containing a also has a unique representing measure m_b (Theorem 1). The measures m, m_b are mutually absolutely continuous, with dm/dm_b and dm_b/dm essentially bounded (Theorem 15, §4.5). The L^p closures of A are thus the same: $H^p(m) = H^p(m_b)$, $1 \le p < \infty$, and of course $H^\infty(m) = H^\infty(m_b)$. Note, however, that the inner products in $H^2(m)$ and $H^2(m_b)$ are in general different and that orthogonality has different meanings in the two spaces.

Now suppose that P contains a point b distinct from a. We fix b and let $\sigma = m_b$ be the representing measure for b. Since a, b are distinct homomorphisms, there is some f_0 in A with $\int f_0 \, dm = 0$, $\int f_0 \, d\sigma \ne 0$. Note that $H_0^2(m) = \{f \in H^2 : \int f \, dm = 0\}$ is a closed subspace of $H^2(m) = H^2(\sigma)$ which is invariant under multiplication by A, since m is multiplicative on H^2. Since $f_0 \in H_0^2(m)$ and $\int f_0 \, d\sigma \ne 0$, 1 is not orthogonal to $H_0^2(m)$ in $L^2(\sigma)$. So we apply Beurling's invariant subspace theorem and deduce that $H_0^2(m) = ZH^2(\sigma) = ZH^2(m)$, where $Z \in H^\infty$ is an inner function, i.e., $|Z| = 1$ a.e.

For any representing measure λ which represents a point of P, $\hat{Z}(\lambda) = \int Z \, d\lambda$ exists. We are going to prove that $\hat{Z}$ is a one-one mapping of P onto the open unit disk, and furthermore that for each $f \in A$, there is a function F analytic on the disk such that $\hat{f}(\lambda) = F(\hat{Z}(\lambda))$ for all λ in P (or rather, representing points of P). Thus P has the structure of an "analytic disk" relative to A, with a as center of the disk, since $\hat{Z}(m) = 0$.

First we show that $\hat{Z}$ maps P into the open disk. Given $\lambda \in P$, $|\hat{Z}(\lambda)| = |\int Z \, d\lambda| \le \int |Z| \, d\lambda = 1$ since λ is a probability measure and $|Z| = 1$ a.e. $[\lambda]$. If equality holds, then Z is a constant of modulus 1 a.e. But $H_0^2(m) = ZH^2 \ne H^2$, so this is impossible. Hence

(1) $$|\hat{Z}(\lambda)| < 1 \qquad \text{for all } \lambda \in P.$$

Again, since $H_0^2(m) = ZH^2$ and $|Z| = 1$ a.e., $Z \in H_0^\infty(m)$. Therefore $Z^n \in H_0^\infty(m)$ for $n = 1, 2, \ldots$. So

(2) $$\int Z^n \, dm = 0 \qquad \text{for } n = 1, 2, \ldots.$$

If $f \in H^2$ and $\lambda \in P$, we use the notation $\hat{f}(\lambda) = \int f \, d\lambda$. Also, we write $\|f\|$ for the norm of f in $L^2(m)$. The function Z defines a linear operator $T : H^2 \to H^2$ as follows. Given $f \in H^2$, $f - \hat{f}(m)$ belongs to $H_0^2 = ZH^2$. Hence $Tf = \bar{Z}(f - \hat{f}(m))$ belongs to H^2. T is clearly linear. We have

(3) $$Z \cdot Tf = f - \hat{f}(m) \qquad \text{for all } f \in H^2.$$

To compute the operator norm of T, note that $f - \hat{f}(m)$ and the constants are orthogonal in $L^2(m)$; so $\|f - \hat{f}(m)\|^2 + \|\hat{f}(m)\|^2 = \|f\|^2$. But $\|Tf\|^2 = \int |\bar{Z}(f - \hat{f}(m))|^2 \, dm = \int |f - \hat{f}(m)|^2 \, dm = \|f - \hat{f}(m)\|^2$, so $\|Tf\| \le \|f\|$. Hence T has operator norm at most 1.

Given $f \in H^2$, set $a_n = \int \bar{Z}^n f \, dm$ $(n = 0, 1, 2, \ldots)$. We claim that

(4) $$a_n = \int T^n f \, dm \qquad (n = 0, 1, 2, \ldots).$$

The assertion is certainly true when $n = 0$. Assume it is true for $n \ge 0$, for every $f \in H^2$. Then $a_{n+1} = \int \bar{Z}^{n+1} f \, dm = \int \bar{Z}^n \bar{Z} f \, dm$ while $\bar{Z} f = \bar{Z}(f - \hat{f}(m)) + \hat{f}(m)\bar{Z} = Tf + \hat{f}(m)\bar{Z}$. Hence $a_{n+1} = \int \bar{Z}^n (Tf) \, dm + \hat{f}(m) \int \bar{Z}^{n+1} \, dm$. By (2) and the induction hypothesis, $a_{n+1} = \int T^n(Tf) \, dm = \int T^{n+1} f \, dm$. So the induction step is proved, and (4) is true. It follows easily that $T^n f = a_n + Z \cdot T^{n+1} f$ for all n. For $T^n f - Z \cdot T^{n+1} f = T^n f - (T^n f - \int T^n f \, dm)$ by (3), and by (4) this is just a_n. Applying the relation recursively, starting with $n = 0$, we obtain a Taylor formula

(5) $$f = a_0 + a_1 Z + a_2 Z^2 + \cdots + a_{N-1} Z^{N-1} + Z^N \cdot T^N f.$$

Take λ in the Gleason part P. We wish to integrate (5) with respect to λ and write $\widehat{Z^n}(\lambda) = \int Z^n \, d\lambda = \hat{Z}(\lambda)^n$ for each n. This is justified as follows. For any f, g in $H^2(m) = H^2(\lambda)$, there exist f_n, g_n in A with $f_n \to f$ and $g_n \to g$ in $L^2(m)$. Since λ and m are boundedly absolutely continuous, convergence also holds in $L^2(\lambda)$. Hence the dot products $\int f_n g_n \, d\lambda$ converge to $\int fg \, d\lambda$. But λ is multiplicative on A. So $\int fg \, d\lambda = (\int f \, d\lambda)(\int g \, d\lambda)$. Since $Z \in H^\infty$, $Z^n \in H^2$ for every n, so in fact $\int Z^n \, d\lambda = (\int Z \, d\lambda)^n = \hat{Z}(\lambda)^n$.

The integrated remainder is $\int Z^N \cdot T^N f \, d\lambda = \hat{Z}(\lambda)^N \int T^N f \, d\lambda$. Now $f \to \int f \, d\lambda$ is a bounded linear functional on H^2 and $\|T^N\| \leq 1$. So there is a constant K such that $\left| \int Z^N \cdot T^N f \, d\lambda \right| \leq K|\hat{Z}(\lambda)|^N \|f\|$. By (1), the remainder approaches 0 as $N \to \infty$.

We may therefore conclude that

$$(6) \qquad \hat{f}(\lambda) = \sum_{n=0}^{\infty} a_n \hat{Z}(\lambda)^n$$

for all $f \in H^2(m)$, $\lambda \in P$, where $a_n = \int \bar{Z}^n f \, dm$. For a given $f \in H^2$, $|a_n| \leq \int |f| \, dm$ for all n, so $\{a_n\}$ is a bounded sequence. So the series $\sum_{n=0}^{\infty} a_n z^n$ converges on the open unit disk to an analytic function $z \to F(z)$, and we have $\hat{f}(\lambda) = F(\hat{Z}(\lambda))$.

It is now clear that $\lambda \to \int Z \, d\lambda = \hat{Z}(\lambda)$ is one-one. For if $\hat{Z}(\lambda_1) = \hat{Z}(\lambda_2)$, then $\hat{f}(\lambda_1) = F(\hat{Z}(\lambda_1)) = F(\hat{Z}(\lambda_2)) = \hat{f}(\lambda_2)$ for all $f \in A$. Since $\hat{A}$ separates points, $\lambda_1 = \lambda_2$.

The next task is to prove that $\hat{Z}$ maps P onto the entire disk.

Recall that $Tf = \bar{Z}(f - \hat{f}(m))$ and $a_n(f) = \int T^n f \, dm$, $f \in H^2$. It is clear that $T(H^{\infty}) \subset H^{\infty}$. Now given f, g in A and any $N \geq 0$,

$$f = \sum_{n=0}^{N} a_n(f)Z^n + Z^{N+1}f_{N+1},$$

$$g = \sum_{n=0}^{N} a_n(g)Z^n + Z^{N+1}g_{N+1},$$

where f_{N+1}, g_{N+1} lie in H^{∞}. (See (5).) So

$$fg = \sum_{n=0}^{N} \left(\sum_{j=0}^{n} a_j(f)a_{n-j}(g) \right) Z^n + Z^{N+1}R_N,$$

where $R_N \in H^{\infty}$. Hence if $0 \leq k \leq N$, then

$$a_k(fg) = \int \bar{Z}^k fg \, dm = \sum_{n=0}^{N} \left(\sum_{j=0}^{n} a_j(f)a_{n-j}(g) \right) \int \bar{Z}^k Z^n \, dm + \int Z^{N+1-k} R_N \, dm.$$

Now $Z^{N+1-k}R_N \in H_0^{\infty}$, so the last integral is 0. It follows from (2) and the fact that $|Z| = 1$ a.e. that $\int \bar{Z}^k Z^n \, dm = \delta_{nk}$, so we have

$$(7) \qquad a_k(fg) = \sum_{j=0}^{k} a_j(f)a_{n-j}(g) \qquad (\forall f, g \text{ in } A)$$

for every $k \leq N$. Since N is arbitrary, (7) holds for all $k \geq 0$. Hence if we set $\tilde{f}(z) = \sum_{k=0}^{\infty} a_k(f)z^k$ ($f \in H^2$, $|z| < 1$), then $f \to \tilde{f}$ is an algebra homomorphism of A into the algebra of analytic functions on the unit disk. For any $f \in H^2$, $\tilde{f}$ is the analytic function F such that $\hat{f}(\lambda) = F(\hat{Z}(\lambda))$, $\lambda \in P$.

Each z in the open unit disk U defines a complex homomorphism $\lambda_z \in \mathcal{M}(A)$ by $\lambda_z(f) = \sum_{k=0}^{\infty} a_k(f) z^k = \tilde{f}(z)$. (Note that $\lambda_z(1) = 1$ because of (2).) We can show that $\lambda_z \in P$ ($\forall z \in U$) and $\hat{Z}(\lambda_z) = z$. (Here we identify λ_z with its representing measure.)

First of all, if $f \in A$, $\|f\|_\infty \le 1$, and $\hat{f}(m) = 0$ (the ∞ norm here is the sup norm in A), then $|\tilde{f}(z)| = |\lambda_z(f)| \le \|f\|_\infty \le 1$ for all $z \in U$ (since λ_z is a complex homomorphism of the Banach algebra A) and $\tilde{f}(0) = \lambda_0(f) = a_0(f) = \hat{f}(m) = 0$. So by Schwarz's lemma, $|\lambda_z(f)| = |\tilde{f}(z)| \le |z|$ ($\forall z \in U$). Hence $\psi(\lambda_z, m) = \sup \{|\lambda_z(f)| : f \in A, \hat{f}(m) = 0\} \le |z| < 1$, where ψ is the pseudohyperbolic metric on $\mathcal{M}(A)$. Hence $\lambda_z \in P$ for each $z \in U$.

Given $g \in H^2$, $|a_k(g)| = \left|\int \bar{Z}^k g \, dm\right| \le \int |g| \, dm \le \left(\int |g|^2 \, dm\right)^{1/2} = \|g\|$. So $|\tilde{g}(z)| = \left|\sum a_k(g) z^k\right| \le \|g\|/(1 - |z|)$ for each $z \in U$. Choose f_n in A converging to g in L^2 norm. Then $\tilde{f}_n \to \tilde{g}$ pointwise by the estimate just established (convergence is uniform on compact subsets of the disk), so $\tilde{g}(z) = \lim_n \tilde{f}_n(z) = \lim_n \int f_n \, d\lambda_z = \int g \, d\lambda_z = \hat{g}(\lambda_z)$ (since the representing measure λ_z is in the same part as m). In particular, $\hat{Z}(\lambda_z) = \tilde{Z}(z) = z$ ($\forall z \in U$). So $\hat{Z}$ maps P one-one onto U, and the inverse map to $\lambda \to \hat{Z}(\lambda) = \int Z \, d\lambda$ is the map $z \to \lambda_z$.

Let us summarize our results.

Theorem 24. *Let A be a function algebra on a compact space X. Let $a \in \mathcal{M}(A)$ and suppose that a has a unique representing measure m on X. Suppose also that the part P of $\mathcal{M}(A)$ which contains a, contains a point distinct from a.*

Then there is an inner function $Z \in H^\infty(m)$ such that $\lambda \to \hat{Z}(\lambda) = \int Z \, d\lambda$ is a one-one map of the part P onto the open disk U. The inverse map τ is a one-one continuous mapping of the disk onto P, and for every f in A, the composite function $\hat{f} \circ \tau$ is analytic on U.

Proof. We have proved all the assertions but one. To see that τ is continuous (recall that P has the Gelfand topology), note that for fixed $f \in A$, $z \to \tau(z)(f) = \lambda_z(f) = \tilde{f}(z)$ is analytic on U and hence is continuous.

Wermer [205] gives an example of a Dirichlet algebra A and a non-one point part P in $\mathcal{M}(A)$ which is not homeomorphic to the disk. In particular, the coordinatizing map $\tau : U \to P$ does not have a continuous inverse. Wermer also shows that if A is a Dirichlet algebra and if a "disk part" P in $\mathcal{M}(A)$ is given the *metric* topology, then the map $\tau : U \to P$ is a homeomorphism. (A basic lemma shows that if $m_1 = w_1 m$, $m_2 = w_2 m$ are representing measures for points a_1, a_2 in P, then $\|m_1 - m_2\| \le e^2 \|a_1 - a_2\|$.)

Corollary. *Let A be a logmodular algebra (for example, a Dirichlet algebra). If P is a part in $\mathcal{M}(A)$, then either P is a point or there exists a one-one continuous map τ of the open unit disk onto P such that $\hat{f} \circ \tau$ is analytic on U for each $f \in A$. In particular, P is connected.*

The result of Wermer cited above shows that if the maximal ideal space $\mathcal{M}$ of a Dirichlet algebra is given the metric topology, then the connected components of $\mathcal{M}$ coincide with the parts, and each is either a point or homeomorphic to the open disk.

Recall that we have shown in §5.5 that if X is a compact set in $\mathbf{C}^1$ and $A = R(X)$, which is Dirichlet only if $R(X) = C(X)$, then the one-point parts coincide with the Choquet boundary.

Suppose now that A is any Dirichlet algebra. Each part in $\mathcal{M}(A)$ is either an analytic disk or a point. Since $X = c(A)$, each point of X is a one-point part in $\mathcal{M}(A)$. Can there be one-point parts off the Choquet boundary? It turns out that the answer is *yes*. We will give a class of examples below. The algebras will be algebras of "generalized analytic functions," which were introduced in Exercise 6, §6.1.

Let G be an additive subgroup of the reals, and let G_+ be the set of non-negative elements of G. We consider G as a discrete topological group. Let $\Gamma = \hat{G}$ be the character group of G (the set of homomorphisms $\alpha : G \to T^1$, with the topology of pointwise convergence), and let Δ be the set of semi-characters of G_+ (the homomorphisms ζ of G_+ into the multiplicative semigroup $\{z : |z| \leq 1\}$ for which $\zeta(0) = 1$). We can consider Γ to be a closed subset of Δ; $\zeta \in \Delta$ extends to a character of G iff $\zeta(G_+) \subset T^1$. The "disk" Δ turns out to be the maximal ideal space of a Dirichlet algebra $A(G)$ on Γ. We will describe $A(G)$ below.

The "origin" in Δ is the semicharacter ρ_0 defined by

$$\rho_0(x) = \begin{cases} 1 & \text{if } x = 0 \\ 0 & \text{if } x > 0, x \in G. \end{cases}$$

Since the ordering in G is archimedean, we see the following:

(8) If $\zeta \in \Delta$ vanishes somewhere on G_+, then $\zeta = \rho_0$.

For let $\zeta(x_0) = 0$. Given $x > 0$ in G, $nx \geq x_0$ for some positive integer n; so $nx - x_0 \in G_+$. Hence $\zeta(nx) = \zeta(nx - x_0)\zeta(x_0) = 0$. So $\zeta(x)^n = 0$, $\zeta(x) = 0$. Thus $\zeta = \rho_0$.

Suppose $\zeta \in \Delta \backslash \{\rho_0\}$. By (8), ζ has no zeros on G_+. Let $\rho = |\zeta|$, $\alpha = \zeta/|\zeta|$. Then $\rho \in \Delta$, $\rho \geq 0$, $\alpha \in \Gamma$, and $\zeta = \rho\alpha$. Hence every $\zeta \neq \rho_0$ has a unique polar decomposition: $\zeta = \rho\alpha$ where ρ is a nonnegative semicharacter and α is a character. On the other hand, $\rho_0 = \rho_0\alpha$ for every α in Γ.

The nonnegative semicharacters have a simple form.

(9) If $\rho \geq 0$, $\rho \in \Delta$, and $\rho \neq \rho_0$, then $\exists r \in (0, 1]$ with $\rho(x) = r^x$ for all $x \in G_+$. Conversely, if $0 < r \leq 1$, then the formula $\rho(x) = r^x$ $(x \in G_+)$ defines a nonnegative element of $\Delta \backslash \{\rho_0\}$.

In order to prove (9) we must make a few observations. Take $0 < \rho \leq 1$ in Δ. If $x \geq y \geq 0$ in G, then $x - y \geq 0$, so $\rho(x) = \rho(x - y)\rho(y) \leq \rho(y)$. Thus ρ is decreasing.

Fix $x_0 > 0$ in G. Let $x \in G$, $x > 0$. Consider positive integers n, m such that $n/m < x/x_0$. Then $nx_0 < mx$ in G_+, so $\rho(nx_0) = \rho(x_0)^n \geq \rho(x)^m = \rho(mx)$. Hence $\rho(x_0)^{n/m} \geq \rho(x)$. Let n/m approach x/x_0. We conclude that $\rho(x_0)^{x/x_0} \geq \rho(x)$. Approximating from above by rationals, we have the reverse inequality. So $\rho(x) = \rho(x_0)^{x/x_0} = r^x$ where $r = \rho(x_0)^{1/x_0}$. Since $0 < x_0$ and $0 < \rho(x_0) \leq 1$, $0 < r \leq 1$. Equality holds at $x = 0$ also, so (9) is established.

If we make the convention that $0^0 = 1$, then the representation in (9) holds even for $\rho = \rho_0$. Hence to each $\zeta \in \Delta$ there corresponds a pair $(r, \alpha) \in [0, 1] \times \Gamma$ such that $\zeta(x) = r^x \alpha(x)$ for all $x \geq 0$ in G.

Consider the Banach space $\ell^1(G)$ of all functions $\psi : G \to \mathbf{C}$ for which $\|\psi\|_1 = \sum_{x \in G} |\psi(x)|$ is finite. If we set $(\psi_1 * \psi_2)(x) = \sum_{y \in G} \psi_1(x - y)\psi_2(y)$, then $\ell^1(G)$ becomes a commutative Banach algebra with identity, with convolution as multiplication. Let $B = \{\psi \in \ell^1(G) : \psi = 0 \text{ outside } G_+\}$. Then $B = \ell^1(G_+)$ is a closed subalgebra of $\ell^1(G)$ containing the identity element $e = \chi_{\{0\}}$. Each $x \in G$ defines a translation operator on $\ell^1(G)$ given by $\psi^x(y) = \psi(y - x)$ $(\psi \in \ell^1(G), y \in G)$. If $x \in G_+$ and $\psi \in B$, then $\psi^x \in B$. By the Fubini theorem, $\psi_1{}^x * \psi_2 = \psi_1 * \psi_2{}^x$. Note that for each $x \in G$, e^x is the characteristic function of $\{x\}$.

Lemma 12. *There is a one-one correspondence* $\zeta \leftrightarrow h_\zeta$ *between* Δ *and* $\mathcal{M}(B)$, *given by* $h_\zeta(\psi) = \tilde{\psi}(\zeta) = \sum_{x \in G_+} \psi(x)\zeta(x)$ $(\forall \psi \in B)$. *The map* $\zeta \to h_\zeta$ *is a homeomorphism.*

Proof. Given $\zeta \in \Delta$, one verifies directly that h_ζ is a complex homomorphism of B. Given $h \in \mathcal{M}(B)$, $h(e) = 1$ since e is the identity element of B. We have $e^x * e^y = e * (e^y)^x = e * e^{x+y} (x, y \in G_+)$, so $h(e^x)h(e^y) = h(e^{x+y})$. Hence if we set $\zeta(x) = h(e^x)$ for $x \in G_+$, then $\zeta(0) = 1$, $\zeta(x + y) = \zeta(x)\zeta(y)$. Furthermore, since $\|h\| = 1$, $|\zeta(x)| = |h(e^x)| \leq \|e^x\|_1 = 1$, so $\zeta \in \Delta$. Any $\psi \in B$ is the sum of a norm convergent series $\psi = \sum_{x \in G_+} \psi(x)\chi_{\{x\}} = \sum_{x \in G_+} \psi(x)e^x$, so $h(\psi) = \sum_{x \in G_+} \psi(x)h(e^x) = \tilde{\psi}(\zeta)$. Hence $h = h_\zeta$, as asserted.

Since the functions $\{e^x : x \in G_+\}$ generate B as a Banach algebra, it is clear that the Gelfand topology of $\mathcal{M}(B)$ coincides with the (pointwise convergence) topology of Δ. So $\zeta \to h_\zeta$ is a homeomorphism.

This proves the lemma. Simple modifications of the argument show that the complex homomorphisms of $\ell^1(G)$ are the maps $\psi \to \tilde{\psi}(\alpha)$ $(\alpha \in \Gamma)$ and that Γ is homeomorphic to $\mathcal{M}(\ell^1(G))$.

Let $\tilde{B}$ be the transform algebra $\{\tilde{\psi} : \psi \in B\}$, viewed as functions on Δ. We know that the continuous complex homomorphisms of $\tilde{B} \subset C(\Delta)$ are the evaluations at the points of Δ. Next observe that the restriction map from $\tilde{B}$ to $\tilde{B}|_\Gamma$ is an isometry.

Lemma 13. Γ *is the Šilov boundary of* $\tilde{B}$.

Proof. By the spectral radius formula,

$$\|\tilde{\psi}\| = \max_{\zeta \in \Delta} |\tilde{\psi}(\zeta)| = \lim_{n \to \infty} \|\psi^{(n)}\|_1^{1/n},$$

where $\psi^{(n)}$ is the n-fold convolution of ψ with itself. Since $B \subset \ell^1(G)$ and Γ is the maximal ideal space of $\ell^1(G)$, $\lim_{n \to \infty} \|\psi^{(n)}\|_1^{1/n} = \max_{\alpha \in \Gamma} |\tilde{\psi}(\alpha)|$ also. So Γ is a closed boundary for $\tilde{B}$. Hence if S is the Šilov boundary of $\tilde{B}$, S is contained in Γ.

Given $\alpha \in \Gamma$, we see that the pointwise product $\psi\alpha$ of α with any $\psi \in B$ is again in B and that $\widetilde{\psi\alpha}(\zeta) = \tilde{\psi}(\zeta\alpha)$ for all $\zeta \in \Delta$. Hence $S\alpha$ is a closed boundary for $\tilde{B}$. So $S \subset S\alpha$ and (by the same token) $S \subset S\alpha^{-1}$. So $S = S\alpha$. Choose any $\alpha_0 \in S$. Then $S = S\alpha_0^{-1}\alpha$, so $\alpha = \alpha_0(\alpha_0^{-1}\alpha)$ belongs to S for any $\alpha \in \Gamma$. So $S = \Gamma$.

For $x \in G$ and $\alpha \in \Gamma$, let $\varphi_x(\alpha) = \alpha(x) = \langle x, \alpha \rangle$. Let $\mathbf{A}(G)$ be the closed subspace of $C(\Gamma)$ spanned by the φ_x for $x \in G_+$. Since G_+ is a semigroup containing $0 \in G$, $\mathbf{A}(G)$ is a closed subalgebra of $C(\Gamma)$ which contains the constants. The closed linear span of $\{\varphi_x : x \in G\}$ is dense in $C(\Gamma)$, by the Stone-Weierstrass theorem, so $\mathbf{A}(G)$ is a Dirichlet algebra on Γ. Observe that if $x \geq 0$, φ_x is the restriction to Γ of $\widetilde{e^x}$, so $\mathbf{A}(G)$ is the uniform closure of the restriction of $\tilde{B}$ to its Šilov boundary. Thus the Šilov boundary of $\mathbf{A}(G)$ is Γ and the maximal ideal space of $\mathbf{A}(G)$ is Δ. The specific action of Δ on $\mathbf{A}(G)$ is as follows. If $f = \tilde{\psi} | \Gamma$ where $\psi \in B$, then $\hat{f}(\zeta) = \tilde{\psi}(\zeta) = \sum_{x \in G_+} \psi(x)\zeta(x)$. If $\zeta = \rho\alpha$ where $\rho(x) = r^x$ $(0 \leq r \leq 1)$, then $\hat{f}(\zeta) = \sum_{x \in G_+} \psi(x)r^x\alpha(x)$. In particular, if f is a finite sum $\sum_{i=1}^{n} c_i \varphi_{x_i}$ (so that $f(\beta) = \sum_{i=1}^{n} c_i \beta(x_i)$, $\beta \in \Gamma$), then $\hat{f}(\zeta) = \sum_{i=1}^{n} c_i r^{x_i}\alpha(x_i)$; these finite sums $\sum c_i \varphi_{x_i}$ are dense in $\mathbf{A}(G)$. Note that if $f = \tilde{\psi} | \Gamma$, then $\hat{f}(\rho_0) = \psi(0)$.

Since $\mathbf{A}(G)$ is a Dirichlet algebra, each $\zeta \in \Delta$ determines a unique probability measure $m_\zeta \in M(\Gamma)$ which represents the homomorphism $f \to \hat{f}(\zeta)$. A probability measure $m_0 \in M(\Gamma)$ equals m_ζ iff $\int \varphi_x \, dm_0 = \zeta(x)$ for all $x \in G_+$. We can determine the representing measures m_ζ explicitly.

Because of the polar decomposition $\zeta = \rho\alpha$ $(\rho \geq 0$ in Δ, $\alpha \in \Gamma)$, it will be enough to find the measures m_ρ. Indeed, a calculation shows that $\int f(\alpha\beta) \, dm_\rho(\beta) = \hat{f}(\rho\alpha)$ for f a finite sum $\sum c_i \varphi_{x_i}$ $(x_i \in G_+)$, so $m_{\rho\alpha}$ is the measure corresponding to the positive linear functional $f \to \int f(\alpha\beta) \, dm_\rho(\beta)$ on $C(\Gamma)$.

The origin ρ_0 is represented by the Haar measure $d\alpha$ of Γ, since

$$\int \langle x, \alpha \rangle \, d\alpha = \begin{cases} 1 & \text{if } x = 0 \\ 0 & \text{if } x \neq 0, \, x \in G. \end{cases}$$

Before we describe the measures m_ρ $(\rho \neq \rho_0)$, we need a little lemma.

Lemma 14. *Let* $c(t) = \dfrac{1}{\pi}(1 + t^2)^{-1}$, $-\infty < t < \infty$. *Then*

$$\hat{c}(\lambda) = \int_{-\infty}^{\infty} e^{i\lambda t}c(t) \, dt = e^{-|\lambda|} \qquad (\lambda \in \mathbf{R}).$$

Proof. This is a standard exercise in contour integration. Since c is an even function, $\hat{c}(\lambda) = \int_{-\infty}^{\infty} \cos(\lambda t)c(t) \, dt = \hat{c}(-\lambda)$, so we may assume that

$\lambda \geq 0$. Given $R > 1$, we integrate $\dfrac{1}{\pi} \dfrac{e^{i\lambda z}}{1 + z^2}$ over the contour composed of $[-R, R]$ and the semicircle $z = Re^{i\theta}$, $0 \leq \theta \leq \pi$. The integral equals $e^{-\lambda}$, by the residue theorem. As $R \to \infty$, the integral over the semicircle approaches 0, so $\hat{c}(\lambda) = \lim_{R \to \infty} \int_{-R}^{R} e^{i\lambda t} c(t)\, dt = e^{-\lambda}$.

Now given $\rho \geq 0$ in Δ with $\rho \neq \rho_0$, we choose $r \in (0, 1]$ such that $\rho(x) = r^x$ for all $x \in G_+$. Let r^{it} be the character of G given by $r^{it}(x) = r^{itx} = \exp(itx \log r)$. Since $\log r \leq 0$, $\hat{c}(x \log r) = e^{x \log r} = r^x$ for each $x \in G_+$. Taking linear combinations and limits, we have a formula for m_ρ:

$$\int_\Gamma f\, dm_\rho = \int_{-\infty}^{\infty} f(r^{it}) c(t)\, dt \qquad (f \in C(\Gamma)).$$

Suppose now that $0 < r < 1$. If E is any Borel set in Γ, then $m_\rho(E) = \int_{-\infty}^{\infty} \chi_E(r^{it}) c(t)\, dt$. So the measure m_ρ is concentrated on the subgroup $\Lambda = \{r^{it} : -\infty < t < \infty\}$ of Γ. For an arbitrary real number s, let $\alpha_s(x) = e^{-isx}$ $(x \in G)$. Then $\alpha_s \in \Gamma$. For a given $r \in (0, 1)$, the numbers $t \log r$ fill up $\mathbf{R}$ as t ranges over $\mathbf{R}$. Hence $\Lambda = \{\alpha_s : s \in \mathbf{R}\}$, which is independent of r.

So we have the following situation. Let $\zeta = \rho\alpha$. If $\rho = \rho_0$, then m_ζ is the Haar measure of Γ. If $\rho \neq \rho_0$ and ρ is not identically 1, then m_ζ is concentrated on the coset $\alpha\Lambda$ of the one-parameter subgroup $\{\alpha_s : s \in \mathbf{R}\}$ of Γ. If $\rho = 1$, then $m_\zeta = m_\alpha$ is the point mass at α.

The measures m_ρ, $0 < \rho < 1$, are mutually absolutely continuous. In fact, if $s = -\log r > 0$, then $\int f\, dm_\rho = \int_{-\infty}^{\infty} f(\alpha_{st}) c(t)\, dt = \int_{-\infty}^{\infty} \dfrac{1}{\pi} \dfrac{s}{s^2 + t^2} f(\alpha_t)\, dt$ for every bounded Borel function f on Γ. So for any Borel set E in Γ,

$$m_\rho(E) = \int_{\{t \in \mathbf{R}^1 : \alpha_t \in E\}} \dfrac{1}{\pi} \dfrac{s}{s^2 + t^2}\, dt.$$

Hence $m_\rho(E) = 0$ iff $\{t \in \mathbf{R}^1 : \alpha_t \in E\}$ has Lebesgue one-dimensional measure 0. Since the m_ρ are mutually continuous, the homomorphisms $\{\rho\alpha : 0 < \rho < 1\}$ for fixed $\alpha \in \Gamma$ all lie in one Gleason part of $\mathcal{M}(A(G))$. Similarly, if $\zeta = \rho\alpha_\sigma$ $(0 < \rho < 1, \ \sigma$ real$)$, then $\int f\, dm_\zeta = \dfrac{1}{\pi} \int_{-\infty}^{\infty} \dfrac{s}{s^2 + t^2} f(\alpha_{\sigma+t})\, dt = \dfrac{1}{\pi} \int_{-\infty}^{\infty} \dfrac{s}{s^2 + (t - \sigma)^2} f(\alpha_t)\, dt$ where $s = -\log \rho$. So $\rho\alpha_\sigma$ is in the same part as ρ. Hence $Q = \{\rho\alpha : 0 < \rho < 1, \alpha \in \Lambda\}$ is contained in a single Gleason part of Δ, and similarly αQ is contained in one part, for each $\alpha \in \Gamma$.

Lemma 15. *If* $F \in C(\Gamma)$, *then* $M(F) = \lim_{T \to +\infty} \dfrac{1}{2T} \int_{-T}^{T} F(\alpha_t)\, dt$ *exists and equals* $\int_\Gamma F(\alpha)\, d\alpha$.

Proof. For each $F \in C(\Gamma)$ for which the limit exists, let $M(F)$ be the indicated limit. If $x \in G$ and $x \neq 0$, then $\dfrac{1}{2T} \displaystyle\int_{-T}^{T} \varphi_x(\alpha_t)\, dt = \dfrac{1}{2T} \displaystyle\int_{-T}^{T} e^{-ixt}\, dt = \dfrac{\sin xT}{xT}$, so $M(\varphi_x) = 0 = \displaystyle\int \langle x, \alpha \rangle\, d\alpha = \displaystyle\int_{\Gamma} \varphi_x(\alpha)\, d\alpha$. Clearly $M(\varphi_0) = M(1) = 1 = \displaystyle\int_{\Gamma} 1\, d\alpha$. M is linear, so $M(F)$ exists for every trigonometric polynomial $F = \displaystyle\sum_{i=1}^{n} c_i \varphi_{x_i}$ and coincides with the Haar integral on the dense subspace of $C(\Gamma)$ consisting of the trigonometric polynomials.

Now let $F \in C(\Gamma)$ be arbitrary. Choose trigonometric polynomials F_n converging uniformly to F on Γ. Then $M(F_n - F_m) = M(F_n) - M(F_m)$ exists for all n, m, and $|M(F_n - F_m)| \leq \|F_n - F_m\| \to 0$. So $M(F_n)$ converges to some complex number λ. We assert that $M(F)$ exists and equals λ. Since $\lambda = \lim_n M(F_n) = \lim_n \displaystyle\int_{\Gamma} F_n(\alpha)\, d\alpha = \displaystyle\int_{\Gamma} F(\alpha)\, d\alpha$, this will establish the lemma.

The argument is a standard uniform convergence argument for interchanging limit operations. Let $\varepsilon > 0$. Choose N such that $\|F_N - F\| < \varepsilon/3$. Since $|M(F_N) - M(F_m)| \leq \|F_N - F_m\|$ for all m, we have $|M(F_N) - \lambda| \leq \|F_N - F\|$ (let $m \to \infty$), so $|M(F_N) - \lambda| < \varepsilon/3$ also. Choose T_0 such that $\left| M(F_N) - \dfrac{1}{2T} \displaystyle\int_{-T}^{T} F_N(\alpha_t)\, dt \right| < \varepsilon/3$ for all $T \geq T_0$. Since $\left| \dfrac{1}{2T} \displaystyle\int_{-T}^{T} F(\alpha_t)\, dt - \dfrac{1}{2T} \displaystyle\int_{-T}^{T} F_N(\alpha_t)\, dt \right| \leq \|F - F_N\| < \varepsilon/3$, it follows from the triangle inequality that $\left| \dfrac{1}{2T} \displaystyle\int_{-T}^{T} F(\alpha_t)\, dt - \lambda \right| < \varepsilon$ for all $T \geq T_0$. So $\lim_{T \to +\infty} \dfrac{1}{2T} \displaystyle\int_{-\infty}^{\infty} F(\alpha_t)\, dt$ exists and equals λ.

Lemma 16. Λ *is a dense subgroup of* Γ.

Proof. For the proof we will need a fundamental result of harmonic analysis, the Pontrjagin duality theorem. (See §1.7 of [J].) This asserts that if G is a locally compact abelian group and Γ is the group of all continuous characters of G, given the topology of uniform convergence on compact subsets of G, then the character group of Γ is G (i.e., each continuous character of Γ is a point evaluation, and the topology of G is that of uniform convergence on compact sets in Γ). Actually, we will need only some special cases of the duality theorem.

Let H be the closure of Λ. If $H \neq \Gamma$, then Γ/H (with the quotient topology determined by the canonical map $\kappa : \Gamma \to \Gamma/H$) is a nontrivial compact abelian group. So by the duality theorem, there exists a continuous character σ of Γ/H which is not identically 1. But then $\sigma \circ \kappa$ is a continuous character φ of Γ such that $\varphi = 1$ on H but $\varphi \not\equiv 1$. By duality, $\exists x \in G$ such that $\varphi(\alpha) = \alpha(x)$ for all $\alpha \in \Gamma$. In particular, $e^{-ixt} = \varphi(\alpha_t) = 1$ for all real t, so $x = 0$. But then φ is identically 1, and we have arrived at a contradiction.

Lemma 17. *If G is not isomorphic to $\mathbf{Z}$, then Λ has Haar measure zero. Hence the measures $m_{\rho\alpha}$ for $0 < \rho < 1$ in Δ are singular with respect to Haar measure m.*

Proof. Since G is not isomorphic to $\mathbf{Z}$, G has no smallest positive element. Hence if a positive integer N is given, there exist arbitrarily large numbers $R > 2N$ such that $\pi/R \in G$. Fix any such R, and let f be a continuous function on $[-R, R]$ such that $0 \leq f \leq 1$, $f = 1$ on $[-N, N]$ and $f = 0$ outside $[-2N, 2N]$. Extend f by periodicity to a continuous function on the line. Since f is periodic with period $2R$, we have

$$(10) \quad \lim_{T \to +\infty} \frac{1}{2T} \int_{-T}^{T} f(t)\, dt = \frac{1}{2R} \int_{-R}^{R} f(t)\, dt = \frac{1}{2R} \int_{-2N}^{2N} f(t)\, dt \leq \frac{2N}{R}.$$

The trigonometric polynomials are dense in $C(T^1)$, so $f(t)$ is uniformly approximable on the line by functions of form $\sum_{k=-n}^{n} c_k e^{-ikt\pi/R} = \sum_{k=-n}^{n} c_k e^{-ix_k t}$, where $x_k = k\pi/R$ belongs to G. Each such function determines a continuous function φ on Γ, given by $\varphi = \sum c_k \varphi_{x_k}$ (i.e., $\varphi(\alpha) = \sum c_k \alpha(x_k)$, $\forall \alpha \in \Gamma$), and the corresponding functions φ are uniformly convergent on Λ. Since Λ is dense in Γ, the φ's converge uniformly on Γ (by the Cauchy criterion), so there exists some $F \in C(\Gamma)$ such that $F(\alpha_t) = f(t)$ for all real t. From (10) and Lemma 15, it follows that $\int F(\alpha)\, d\alpha \leq 2N/R$.

Now let $\Lambda_N = \{\alpha_t : |t| \leq N\}$. We have shown that for each $R > 2N$ such that $\pi/R \in G$, there is a continuous function F on Γ with $F \geq \chi_{\Lambda_N}$ and $\int F(\alpha)\, d\alpha \leq 2N/R$. Since R can be chosen arbitrarily large, $m(\Lambda_N) = 0$. (For any Borel set $E \subset \Gamma$, $m(E) = \inf \{\int F(\alpha)\, d\alpha : F \in C(\Gamma), \chi_E \leq F\}$.) But $\Lambda = \bigcup_{N=1}^{\infty} \Lambda_N$, so $m(\Lambda) = 0$ also. By translation-invariance of m, each coset $\alpha\Lambda$ also has Haar measure 0. The measures m_ζ ($\zeta = \rho\alpha, 0 < \rho < 1$) are concentrated on $\alpha\Lambda$, so they are all mutually singular with respect to m.

Here is the theorem we have been seeking.

Theorem 25. *Let G be an additive subgroup of the reals which is not isomorphic to the integers. Let Γ be the character group of G and Δ the space of semi-characters of $G_+ = \{x \in G : x \geq 0\}$. Then Δ is the maximal ideal space of the algebra $\mathbf{A}(G)$ of generalized analytic functions determined by G_+, and $\mathbf{A}(G)$ is a Dirichlet algebra on Γ. The homomorphism ρ_0 of $\mathbf{A}(G)$ given by $\hat{f}(\rho_0) = \int_\Gamma f(\alpha)\, d\alpha$ constitutes a one-point part in $\mathcal{M}(\mathbf{A}(G))$ which does not belong to the Šilov boundary Γ (unless G is the trivial subgroup $\{0\}$).*

Proof. All assertions except the last have been established. But ρ_0 has representing measure m, the Haar measure of Γ. If $\zeta \neq \rho_0$, then $\zeta = \rho\alpha$ where $\alpha \in \Gamma$, $\rho \in \Delta$, and $0 < \rho \leq 1$. If $\rho(x) = 1$ for some $x \in G_+$, then ρ is identically 1. In that case, $\zeta = \alpha$ belongs to Γ and hence the representing measure $m_\zeta = \delta_\alpha$. If $0 < \rho < 1$, then m_ζ is concentrated on $\alpha\Lambda$, a set of Haar measure zero. Thus for each $\zeta \neq \rho_0$ in $\mathcal{M}(\mathbf{A}(G)) = \Delta$, m_ζ and the representing measure for ρ_0 are mutually singular. So ζ and ρ_0 belong to distinct Gleason parts.

If we start with the boundary value algebra A and let m be normalized Lebesgue measure (arc length) on the unit circle, the logmodular algebra $H^\infty = H^\infty(A; m)$ turns out to be isomorphic to the algebra of bounded analytic functions on the unit disk. (H^∞ is logmodular since A is a Dirichlet algebra and m is multiplicative on A. See Theorem 9, §6.2. Each point $re^{i\theta}$ in the open disk U determines a Poisson measure $P_r(\theta - t)\, dm(t)$ which is absolutely continuous with respect to m; these measures remain multiplicative on H^∞, so U is contained in $\mathcal{M}(H^\infty)$. See [E] for a detailed account of the properties of H^∞.) The parts in $\mathcal{M}(H^\infty)$ and the coordinatizing maps $\tau : U \to P$ (P a part in $\mathcal{M}(H^\infty)$) have been determined by Hoffman [98] and turn out to be very natural objects, even though $\mathcal{M}(H^\infty)$ is quite bizarre. The coordinatizing maps can be described as follows. Given $\zeta \in U$, let $\tau_\zeta(z) = \dfrac{z + \zeta}{1 + \bar{\zeta}z}$ ($|z| < 1$); we regard τ_ζ as a map from U into $\mathcal{M}(H^\infty)$. The disk is dense in $\mathcal{M}(H^\infty)$ (this is the affirmative solution of the "corona problem"; see Carleson [46]), and as points $\zeta \in U$ converge to a point $a \in \mathcal{M}(H^\infty)$, the maps τ_ζ converge pointwise to a map τ_a from U into $\mathcal{M}(H^\infty)$. It turns out that $\tau_a(U) = P_a$, the Gleason part through a; τ_a is analytic, i.e., $\hat{f} \circ \tau_a$ is analytic on U for each $f \in H^\infty$; and τ_a is either constant or one-one. An algebraic condition on a which is necessary and sufficient in order that $P_a \neq \{a\}$ (and hence be an analytic disk) is that some f in the maximal ideal A_a is not the product of two members of A_a, or roughly, $P_a = \{a\}$ iff $A_a^2 = A_a$. Finally, there is an analytic condition: $P_a \neq \{a\}$ iff a lies in the closure of an interpolating sequence $\{\zeta_n\} \subset U$, i.e., a sequence of points in U such that $\inf_n \prod_{k \neq n} \psi(\zeta_k, \zeta_n) > 0$ (where ψ is the pseudohyperbolic metric on U).

One may ask whether weaker hypotheses than uniqueness of representing measures (uniqueness of Arens-Singer measures, for example) still imply that a Gleason part or some nontrivial subset of a part must carry some sort of analytic structure, though perhaps not a disk structure. Affirmative results along these lines have been obtained by Ahern and Sarason [2] and Wermer [210], among others.

6.5 DECOMPOSITION OF MEASURES

In this section we derive a formula for the annihilators of logmodular algebras. In §6.6 we shall apply the formula to prove Mergelyan's theorem on polynomial approximation.

Theorem 26.   *Let A be a logmodular algebra on a compact space X, and let m be a representing measure for a complex homomorphism of A. Then for each $h \in H^\infty(m)$ there exists a sequence $\{h_n\}$ in A such that $\|h_n\| \leq \|h\|_\infty$ for all n and $h_n \to h$ a.e. $[m]$.*

Proof.   We may assume that $\|h\|_\infty \leq 1$. Since h belongs to $H^2(m)$, there is a sequence in A which converges to h in L^2 norm. Some subsequence $\{f_n\}$ converges to h a.e. $[m]$ and in $L^2(m)$.

Let $E_n = \{x \in X : |f_n(x)| \geq 1\}$. We shall prove that

$$(1) \qquad \int_{E_n} \log |f_n| \, dm \to 0 \qquad \text{as} \quad n \to \infty.$$

Fix $\varepsilon > 0$ and let $F_n = \{x \in X : |f_n(x)| \geq 1 + \varepsilon\}$. On F_n, $\log |f_n| \leq |f_n| = |(f_n - h) + h|$, so $\int_{F_n} \log |f_n| \, dm \leq \int_{F_n} |f_n - h| \, dm + \int_{F_n} |h| \, dm$. By the Schwarz inequality, $\int_{F_n} |f_n - h| \, dm \leq \|f_n - h\|_2$, so $0 \leq \int_{F_n} \log |f_n| \, dm \leq \|f_n - h\|_2 + m(F_n)$. Since ε is fixed and $|f_n| \to |h| \leq 1$ a.e. $[m]$, $m(F_n) \to 0$. So there exists $n_0(\varepsilon)$ such that $0 \leq \int_{F_n} \log |f_n| \, dm \leq \varepsilon$ for all $n \geq n_0(\varepsilon)$. But on $E_n \backslash F_n$, $\log |f_n| < \log (1 + \varepsilon)$. So for $n \geq n_0(\varepsilon)$, $0 \leq \int_{E_n} \log |f_n| \, dm \leq \varepsilon + \log (1 + \varepsilon)$. This proves (1).

Set $w_n = \log (\max (1, |f_n|))$. Then

$$w_n(x) = \begin{cases} \log |f_n(x)|, & x \in E_n \\ 0, & x \notin E_n. \end{cases}$$

So $w_n \in C_R(X)$ and $w_n \geq 0$ on X. Since A is logmodular, there exists $g_n \in A^{-1}$ such that

$$(2) \qquad -\frac{1}{2n} < \log |g_n| + w_n + \frac{1}{2n} < \frac{1}{2n}$$

on X. Multiplying g_n by a constant of modulus 1 does not affect the truth of (2), so we may assume that $\int g_n \, dm > 0$ for all n. Since m is an Arens-Singer measure,

$$-\frac{1}{n} - \int w_n \, dm \leq \int \log |g_n| \, dm = \log \left(\int g_n \, dm \right) \leq -\int w_n \, dm$$

for all n, or $-\frac{1}{n} - \int_{E_n} \log |f_n| \, dm \leq \log \left(\int g_n \, dm \right) \leq -\int_{E_n} \log |f_n| \, dm$. Since the extreme terms in the inequality approach 0 as $n \to \infty$ (by (1)), $\int g_n \, dm \to 1$.

Now $\log |g_n| \leq -w_n$ on X, so $|g_n| \leq 1$ everywhere on X and $|g_n| \leq |f_n|^{-1}$ on E_n. By the definition of E_n, $\|f_n g_n\| \leq 1$. Since $|g_n| \leq 1$ and $\int g_n \, dm \to 1$, it follows exactly as in the proof of the Forelli lemma that $g_n \to 1$ in $L^2(m)$. So some subsequence g_{n_i} converges to 1 a.e. $[m]$. Set $h_i = g_{n_i} f_{n_i}$. Then $h_i \in A$, $\|h_i\| \leq 1$, and $h_i \to h$ a.e. $[m]$.

Corollary.   *Under the hypothesis above,* $H_0^1(m) = \{f \in L^1(m) : \int fg\, dm = 0$ *for all* $g \in A\}$.

Proof.   If $f \in H_0^1(m)$ and $g \in A$, then $\int fg\, dm = (\int f\, dm)(\int g\, dm) = 0$. (Since m is multiplicative on A, it is easy to show that m is multiplicative on $H^1 \cdot A$.) Conversely, let $f \in L^1(m)$ and $\int fg\, dm = 0$ for all $g \in A$. In particular, $\int f\, dm = 0$. To show that f belongs to $H_0^1(m)$ it will suffice, by the Hahn-Banach theorem, to show that any continuous linear functional on $L^1(m)$ which annihilates $H^1(m)$ also annihilates f. So let $\varphi \in L^\infty(m)$ satisfy the conditions $\|\varphi\|_\infty \leq 1$, $\int g\varphi\, dm = 0$ for all $g \in H^1(m)$. Now $L^\infty(m) \subset L^2(m)$, and the conditions say that φ is orthogonal to $\bar{A}$ in $L^2(m)$. But $L^2 = H^2 \oplus \overline{H_0^2}$, so it follows that $\varphi \in H^2 \cap L^\infty = H^\infty$.

By the theorem, there exist h_n in A such that $\|h_n\| \leq 1$ for all n and $h_n \to \varphi$ a.e. $[m]$. By the dominated convergence theorem, $\int fh_n\, dm \to \int f\varphi\, dm$. But $\int fh_n\, dm = 0$ for all n by assumption, so $\int f\varphi\, dm = 0$. Hence $f \in H^1$.

The corollary can be phrased as follows. Any annihilator $\mu \in A^\perp$ which is absolutely continuous with respect to m has the form $\mu = km$ where $k \in H_0^1(m)$, and conversely each such measure is an annihilator of A.

Theorem 27.   *Let A be a logmodular algebra on X, and let $\mu \in A^\perp$. Then there is a sequence of representing measures $\{m_i\}$ for points of $\mathscr{M}(A)$ and there are functions $k_i \in H_0^1(m_i)$ such that $\mu = \sum\limits_{i=1}^{\infty} k_i m_i + \sigma$ where $\sigma \in A^\perp$ and σ is singular with respect to every multiplicative measure on A.*

Proof.   Given a point a in $\mathscr{M}(A)$, let m_a be its representing measure. If m is any positive measure in $M(X)$ and $\lambda \in M(X)$, let us denote by λ_m, λ'_m the absolutely continuous and singular parts of λ with respect to m. Note that if m and $\sigma \geq 0$ are mutually absolutely continuous, then $\lambda_m = \lambda_\sigma$ and $\lambda'_m = \lambda'_\sigma$. In particular, $\lambda_m = \lambda_\sigma$ if $m = m_a$, $\sigma = m_b$, and a, b lie in the same Gleason part.

Given $\mu \in A^\perp$, let $\mathscr{P}$ be the set of all parts P such that $\mu_m \neq 0$ for some $m = m_a$ with $a \in P$. We shall prove that if $P_1, \ldots, P_n$ are distinct members of $\mathscr{P}$, and if $m_i \in P_i$, $1 \leq i \leq n$, then $\sum\limits_{i=1}^{n} \|\mu_{m_i}\| \leq \|\mu\|$. So the number of distinct parts $P \in \mathscr{P}$ is at most denumerable, and if we choose one m in each distinct P, then $\sum\limits_{m} \mu_m$ is norm convergent in the Banach space $M(X)$. Since $\mu \in A^\perp$, every $\mu_m \in A^\perp$ by the F. and M. Riesz theorem, so $\sum\limits_{m} \mu_m$ is also in $A^\perp$. We note that $\mu_m = k_m m$ where $k_m \in H_0^1(m)$, by the Corollary to Theorem 26. We then set $\sigma = \mu - \sum\limits_{m} \mu_m$ and have to verify that σ is completely singular.

If complex homomorphisms a, b have representing measures which are not mutually singular, then $a \sim b$. For let $m = m_a$, $\lambda = m_b$, and let $\lambda = \lambda_0 + \lambda_s$ where $\lambda_0 \ll m$, $\lambda_s \perp m$. Set $c = \int d\lambda_0$; $c > 0$ by assumption. But for any

$g \in A$, $(g - \hat{g}(b))\lambda$ annihilates A; so $(g - \hat{g}(b))\lambda_0 \in A^\perp$ also, by the Riesz theorem. In particular, 1 is annihilated by $(g - \hat{g}(b))\lambda_0$, so $\int g \, d\lambda_0 = c\hat{g}(b)$. By uniqueness of representing measures, we conclude that $\lambda = \dfrac{1}{c}\lambda_0 \ll m$. By symmetry, $m \ll \lambda$. So m_a, m_b are mutually absolutely continuous.

Given $m_i \in P_i \, (1 \le i \le n)$, set $v = \mu - \sum\limits_{i=1}^{n} \mu_{m_i}$. Then since $v = \mu'_{m_j} - \sum\limits_{i \ne j} \mu_{m_i}$, v is singular with respect to each m_j. Hence v is singular with respect to $\sum\limits_{j=1}^{n} \mu_{m_j}$. But it is a basic fact about the total variation norm that if $\lambda_1 \perp \lambda_2$, then $\|\lambda_1 + \lambda_2\| = \|\lambda_1\| + \|\lambda_2\|$. So $\|\mu\| = \left\| v + \sum\limits_{j=1}^{n} \mu_{m_j} \right\| = \|v\| + \left\| \sum\limits_{j=1}^{n} \mu_{m_j} \right\| = \|v\| + \sum\limits_{j=1}^{n} \|\mu_{m_j}\|$. Thus the inequality is proved.

Since $\sigma = \mu - \sum\limits_{m} \mu_m$ and $A^\perp$ is norm closed, $\sigma \in A^\perp$. Given any representing measure m_0, we have $\sigma_{m_0} = 0$. Indeed, if m_0 represents a point not in any $P \in \mathscr{P}$, then $\mu_{m_0} = 0$ while all μ_m are absolutely continuous with respect to the corresponding m and hence singular with respect to m_0; so $\sigma_{m_0} = \mu_{m_0} - \sum\limits_{m}(\mu_m)_{m_0} = 0$. If m_0 represents a point $a \in P$ for some $P \in \mathscr{P}$, choose $m \in P$ such that μ_m occurs in the sum defining σ; then $\sigma_{m_0} = \sigma_m = \mu_m - \mu_m = 0$. So σ is singular with respect to every multiplicative measure on A.

We are going to apply the Corollary to Theorem 26 to obtain a theorem about bounded analytic functions on parts in $\mathscr{M}(A)$, but first we need the classical result for functions on the unit disk.

Theorem 28. *Let f be an analytic function on the open unit disk, and suppose that $|f(z)| \le 1$ for all z with $|z| < 1$. Then there is a sequence of polynomials $\{p_n\}$ such that $p_n(z) \to f(z)$ for every z $(|z| < 1)$, and $|p_n(z)| \le 1$ for all n and for all z with $|z| < 1$. (A bounded analytic function on the open disk is a pointwise limit of a sequence of polynomials with the same bound.)*

The theorem will follow at once if we establish:

Lemma 18. *Let $f(z) = \sum\limits_{n=0}^{\infty} a_n z^n$ be analytic for $|z| < 1$. For any integer $n \ge 0$, set $s_n(z) = \sum\limits_{k=0}^{n} a_k z^k$, $t_n(z) = \dfrac{1}{n+1} \sum\limits_{k=0}^{n} s_k(z)$. Then $|f(z)| \le 1$ for all z in the open unit disk iff $|t_n(z)| \le 1$ for all n and for all z on the unit circle.*

For $s_n \to f$ pointwise, so by a fact about Cesaro means from advanced calculus, $t_n \to f$ pointwise. If all t_n are bounded by 1 on $|z| = 1$, then they are bounded by 1 on $|z| \le 1$ by the maximum modulus theorem.

Proof of Lemma 18.   If $|t_n| \leq 1$ for all n, then $f = \lim_n t_n$ is also bounded by 1 on the disk. So one implication is trivial. Now assume that $|f(z)| \leq 1$, $|z| < 1$. Then for each real θ the function f_θ given by $f_\theta(z) = f(e^{i\theta}z)$ is also analytic and bounded by 1, while its Cesaro means τ_n^θ satisfy $\tau_n^\theta(1) = t_n(e^{i\theta})$. It will therefore suffice to show that $|t_n(1)| \leq 1$ for all $n \geq 0$.

Recall that if $\sum_{n=0}^{\infty} \alpha_n z_0^n$ and $\sum_{n=0}^{\infty} \beta_n z_0^n$ are absolutely convergent, and if $\gamma_n = \sum_{k=0}^{n} \alpha_k \beta_{n-k}$, then $\sum_{n=0}^{\infty} \gamma_n z_0^n$ converges absolutely and has the sum $(\sum \alpha_n z_0^n)(\sum \beta_n z_0^n)$. Hence $\left(\sum_{n=0}^{\infty} z^n\right)\left(\sum_{n=0}^{\infty} a_n z^n\right) = \sum_{n=0}^{\infty} \left(\sum_{k=0}^{n} a_{n-k}\right)z^n = \sum_{n=0}^{\infty} s_n(1)z^n$ and $\left(\sum_{n=0}^{\infty} z^n\right)^2 \left(\sum_{n=0}^{\infty} a_n z^n\right) = \sum_{n=0}^{\infty} (n+1)t_n(1)z^n$ if $|z| < 1$.

Therefore $(n+1)t_n(1)$ is the nth Taylor coefficient for $f(z)/(1-z)^2$. So if $0 < r < 1$, then $(n+1)t_n(1) = \dfrac{1}{2\pi i} \int_{|z|=r} \dfrac{f(z)}{(1-z)^2 z^{n+1}} \, dz$, by the Cauchy integral formula. If we add to the integrand any function h which is analytic on the unit disk, the value of the integral remains unchanged, since $\int_{|z|=r} h(z) \, dz = 0$ by Cauchy's theorem. Put $h(z) = (-2 + z^{n+1})f(z)/(1-z)^2$. Then the formula reduces to $(n+1)t_n(1) = \dfrac{1}{2\pi i} \int_{|z|=r} \dfrac{f(z)(1 - z^{n+1})^2}{(1-z)^2 z^{n+1}} \, dz = \dfrac{1}{2\pi i} \int_{|z|=r} \dfrac{f(z)}{z^{n+1}}(1 + z + z^2 + \cdots + z^n)^2 \, dz$.

Estimate the integrals, with $z = re^{i\theta}$. Since $|f| \leq 1$ on the open disk,
$$(n+1)|t_n(1)| \leq \frac{1}{2\pi} \int_0^{2\pi} \frac{1}{r^{n+1}} |1 + z + \cdots + z^n|^2 r \, d\theta. \text{ But}$$

$$\left| \sum_{k=0}^{n} z^k \right|^2 = \sum_{k=0}^{n} \sum_{j=0}^{n} r^{k+j} e^{(k-j)i\theta}$$

and $\int_0^{2\pi} e^{im\theta} \, d\theta = 0$ if m is a nonzero integer, so $(n+1)|t_n(1)| \leq \dfrac{1}{2\pi} \int_0^{2\pi} \dfrac{1}{r^n} \sum_{k=0}^{n} r^{2k} \, d\theta = \left(\sum_{k=0}^{n} r^{2k}\right)/r^n$, where $0 < r < 1$ and r is arbitrary. Letting $r \to 1$, we have $(n+1)|t_n(1)| \leq n + 1$, or $|t_n(1)| \leq 1$, which is what remained to be proved.

Theorem 29.   *Let A be a logmodular algebra. Suppose that $a \in \mathcal{M}(A)$ and that the part P which contains a contains a point distinct from a. Let Z be the inner function in $H^2(m)$ and $\tau : U \to P$ the coordinatizing map determined in Theorem 24, where m is the representing measure for a. Suppose that φ is a bounded analytic function on P, in the following sense: $\varphi \circ \tau$ is analytic on U and $|\varphi| \leq c < \infty$ on P. Then there is a sequence $\{g_n\}$ in A with $\|g_n\| \leq c$ such that $\hat{g}_n(\lambda) \to \varphi(\lambda)$ for all $\lambda \in P$.*

Proof. We assume without loss of generality that $c = 1$. There is an analytic function f on the open unit disk U such that $\varphi(\lambda) = f(\hat{Z}(\lambda))$ for all $\lambda \in P$. (Once again we are using the same notation for points in a part and their representing measures.) Since $|f| \leq 1$ on U, there exist polynomials p_n converging pointwise to f on U such that $|p_n| \leq 1$ on U for all n. Since $Z \in H^\infty(m)$ and $H^\infty(m)$ is an algebra, $\{p_n(Z)\}$ is a sequence in the unit ball of $H^\infty(m)$. Regard $H^\infty(m)$ as a subspace of $L^\infty(m) = L^1(m)^*$. The unit ball of $L^\infty(m)$ is w^*-compact, so $\{p_n(Z)\}$ has a w^*-accumulation point $g \in L^\infty(m)$ such that $\|g\|_\infty \leq 1$. But it is clear from the Corollary to Theorem 17 that $H^\infty(m)$ is w^*-closed in $L^\infty(m)$, so $g \in H^\infty(m)$.

Given $\lambda \in P$, $\lambda = wm$ where $w \in L^1(m)$, indeed $w \in L^\infty(m)$. By w^*-convergence, $\widehat{p_n(Z)}(\lambda) = \int p_n(Z)w \, dm$ has $\int gw \, dm = \hat{g}(\lambda)$ as an accumulation point. At the same time, since λ is multiplicative on $H^\infty(m)$, $\widehat{p_n(Z)}(\lambda) = p_n(\hat{Z}(\lambda)) \to f(\hat{Z}(\lambda)) = \varphi(\lambda)$. So $\varphi(\lambda) = \hat{g}(\lambda)$.

By Theorem 26, there is a sequence $\{g_n\}$ in the unit ball of A which converges a.e. to g. By bounded convergence, we have $\hat{g}_n(\lambda) = \int g_n w \, dm \to \int gw \, dm = \hat{g}(\lambda) = \varphi(\lambda)$. So the proof is finished. (Perhaps the fact that $\varphi(\lambda) = \hat{g}(\lambda)$ for all $\lambda \in P$, where $g \in H^\infty(m)$, is more interesting than the final conclusion.)

6.6 MERGELYAN'S THEOREM

Let us return now to the questions of polynomial and rational approximation, some of which were discussed in Chapter V. Suppose that X is a compact set in the plane and that $\mathbf{C}\backslash X$ is connected. Let S be the boundary of X. We know that X is polynomially convex, so X is the maximal ideal space of the function algebra $P(X)$; we also know that S is the Šilov boundary of $P(X)$, so that the restriction map from $P(X)$ onto $P(S)$ is an isometric algebra isomorphism. By Walsh's theorem, $P(S)$ is a Dirichlet algebra, with maximal ideal space $X = \text{hull}(S)$.

The Gleason parts of $\mathscr{M}(P(S))$ are the one-point sets $\{x\}$ with $x \in \text{bd}(X)$ and the components of the interior of X. That each $x \in S$ forms a part is clear, since δ_x is the unique representing measure for x (on S). Since each $\hat{f} \in P(X)$ is analytic on each component Ω of int X ($f \in P(S)$), Ω is contained in a single part of $\mathscr{M}(P(S))$, by Theorem 18, §4.5. But the parts for a Dirichlet algebra are connected, by Theorem 24, §6.4, so it follows that Ω is a part. We can say more. There is a one-one map τ of the unit disk U onto Ω such that $\hat{f} \circ \tau$ is analytic on U for each $f \in P(S)$. In particular, we can take $f(z) = z$. So τ is a one-one analytic map of U onto Ω. Hence $\tau^{-1} : \Omega \to U$ is a one-one analytic mapping. So the map $\hat{Z} = \tau^{-1}$ associated with a component Ω of int X (and a fixed representing measure) is a conformal mapping of Ω onto the open unit disk. (In particular, Ω is simply connected.)

Each point $z \in X$ determines a complex homomorphism h_z of $P(S)$, and h_z has a unique representing measure λ_z concentrated on S. A bounded function φ defined on a component Ω of int X is analytic iff $\varphi \circ \tau$ is analytic on U, where $\tau^{-1} : \Omega \to U$ is the conformal map described above. Hence if φ is bounded and analytic on Ω, it follows from Theorem 29 that there is a sequence $\{g_n\}$ in $P(X)$ such that $\|g_n\| \leq \sup_\Omega |\varphi|$ and $g_n \to \varphi$ pointwise on Ω. Moreover, from the proof of Theorem 29 we know that if we fix a point $z_0 \in \Omega$, then there is some $\Phi \in H^\infty(\lambda_{z_0})$ such that $|\Phi| \leq \sup_\Omega |\varphi|$ a.e. and $\varphi(z) = \int_S \Phi \, d\lambda_z$

for all $z \in \Omega$. (If $K_z = d\lambda_z/d\lambda_{z_0}$, then $\varphi(z) = \int_S \Phi K_z \, d\lambda_{z_0}$, $\forall z \in \Omega$.) So we have a type of Poisson integral representation of bounded analytic functions on Ω in terms of H^∞ functions on S.

Theorem 28 is true for bounded analytic functions on Ω: if φ is analytic on Ω and $\sup_{z \in \Omega} |\varphi(z)| = c < \infty$, then there are polynomials p_n such that $|p_n| \leq c$ on X and $p_n \to \varphi$ pointwise on Ω. (Take $g_n \in P(X)$ with $\|g_n\| \leq c$ and $g_n \to \varphi$ on Ω. Approximate g_n uniformly by a polynomial q_n so that $\|g_n - q_n\| < 1/n$. Then $\|q_n\| < c + \dfrac{1}{n}$ and $q_n \to \varphi$ on Ω. Set $p_n = \dfrac{c}{c + \dfrac{1}{n}} q_n$. Then the poly-

nomials p_n have the asserted properties.)

Theorem 30 (Mergelyan's Theorem). *Let X be a compact set in the plane such that $\mathbf{C} \backslash X$ is connected. Then $P(X) = A(X)$.*

Proof. Recall that $F \in A(X)$ iff $F \in C(X)$ and F is analytic on int X. Let $S = \text{bd}(X)$. Then each $F \in A(X)$ assumes its maximum modulus on S, so $A = A(X)|_S$ is a function algebra which contains the Dirichlet algebra $P(S)$. Thus A is a Dirichlet algebra.

Each $f \in A$ has a unique extension $F \in A(X)$, so each $z \in X$ determines a complex homomorphism $f \to F(z)$ of A. Let μ_z be the representing measure for this homomorphism. Then $\int f \, d\mu_z = \int f \, d\lambda_z$ for every $f \in P(S)$, so since $P(S)$ is a Dirichlet algebra, $\mu_z = \lambda_z$. Thus λ_z is multiplicative on A. Let $H^1(\lambda_z)$ be the closure of $P(S)$ in $L^1(\lambda_z)$, and let $H^1(\mu_z)$ be the closure of A in $L^1(\lambda_z)$.

In order to prove that $A = P(S)$ we need only show that each $\mu \in P(S)^\perp$ annihilates A. But by Theorems 27 and 5, $\mu = \sum_{n=1}^\infty k_n \lambda_{z_n}$ where $\{z_n\}$ is a sequence in X and $k_n \in H_0^1(\lambda_{z_n})$. But $H_0^1(\lambda_{z_n}) \subset H_0^1(\mu_{z_n})$, so $\int f \, d\mu = \sum_n \int f k_n \, d\lambda_{z_n} = \sum_n (\int f \, d\lambda_{z_n})(\int k_n \, d\lambda_{z_n}) = 0$ for all $f \in A$. Hence $A = P(S)$.

So for each $F \in A(X)$, there are polynomials p_n converging uniformly on S to $f = F|S$. By the maximum principle, the p_n converge uniformly on X to a function $F_0 \in P(X)$. Since $F - F_0$ vanishes on S and belongs to $A(X)$, $F - F_0 = 0$. So $A(X) \subset P(X) \subset A(X)$, and the theorem is proved.

We have shown along the way that $P(S)$ is maximal in the class of function algebras A such that $\Gamma(A) \subset S$ and $\mathcal{M}(A) \supset X$.

Recall that we had proved in §5.3 that if $\mathbf{C}\backslash X$ is connected, then $P(X) = R(X)$. Mergelyan's theorem says that if $\mathbf{C}\backslash X$ is connected, then $R(X) = A(X)$. Mergelyan [123] extended the last result to the case where $\mathbf{C}\backslash X$ has finitely many components, or even infinitely many components, provided that their diameters stay bounded away from zero. Mergelyan's proof is constructive and extremely complicated, but we shall give a proof (due principally to Garnett) which follows the measure-theoretic approach of §5.3 and uses the special case already established in Theorem 30.

The argument leans strongly on the observation that rational approximability is essentially a local question.

Theorem 31. *Let $f \in C(X)$ where X is a compact set in $\mathbf{C}$. Assume that each point x in X has a closed nbhd V_x in X such that $f | V_x$ is in $R(V_x)$. Then $f \in R(X)$.*

In order to prove the theorem we derive two lemmas. The first characterizes the measures which annihilate $R(X)$ (we shall have to prove that every $\mu \in R(X)^{\perp}$ also annihilates f). The second provides a means for constructing annihilators of $R(V_x)$, given an annihilator of $R(X)$. Finally, we construct a way to recover a given annihilating measure $\mu \in R(X)$ from the subannihilators it induces.

Lemma 19. *Let X be a compact set in the plane, and let $\mu \in M(X)$. Define*
$$\tilde{\mu}(z) = \int_X \frac{d|\mu|(\xi)}{|\xi - z|} \text{ and let } \hat{\mu}(z) = \int_X \frac{d\mu(\xi)}{\xi - z} \text{ for each } z \in \mathbf{C} \text{ for which } \tilde{\mu}(z) < \infty.$$
Then $\mu \in R(X)^{\perp}$ iff $\hat{\mu}(z) = 0$ for all $z \in \mathbf{C}\backslash X$.

Proof. If $\mu \in R(X)^{\perp}$ and $z \in \mathbf{C}\backslash X$, then $\xi \to |\xi - z|^{-1}$ is continuous on X and $\xi \to (\xi - z)^{-1}$ is in $R(X)$; hence $\tilde{\mu}(z) < \infty$ and $\hat{\mu}(z) = 0$.

Conversely, suppose that $\hat{\mu}(z) = 0$ for all $z \in \mathbf{C}\backslash X$. Given $z_0 \in \mathbf{C}\backslash X$, let
$$f(\xi) = (\xi - z_0)^{-1}. \text{ Then } \frac{f(\xi + 1/n) - f(\xi)}{1/n} = n\left[\left(\xi + \frac{1}{n} - z_0\right)^{-1} - (\xi - z_0)^{-1}\right]$$
converges to $f'(\xi) = -(\xi - z_0)^{-2}$ uniformly on X. So since $z_0 - \frac{1}{n} \in \mathbf{C}\backslash X$ for all sufficiently large n, $\int d\mu(\xi)/(\xi - z_0)^2 = 0$. By induction, $\int d\mu(\xi)/(\xi - z_0)^n = 0$ for all $n \geq 1$. Any rational function f on X is the sum of a polynomial p and a linear combination of functions of form $\xi \to (\xi - z_0)^{-n}$, so $\int f \, d\mu = \int p \, d\mu$. But $\int p \, d\mu = 0$, as can be shown using the reasoning employed in the proof of Theorem 13, §5.3. (Choose R greater than $\max_{\xi \in X} |\xi|$. Then
$$2\pi i p(\xi) = \int_{|z|=R} \frac{p(z)}{z - \xi} \, dz \ (\xi \in X), \text{ so } 2\pi i \int p \, d\mu = \int_X \left(\int_{|z|=R} \frac{p(z)}{z - \xi} \, dz\right) d\mu(\xi) =$$
$$\int_{|z|=R} p(z)\hat{\mu}(-z) \, dz = 0.) \text{ So } \mu \in R(X)^{\perp}.$$

Lemma 20.   *Let $\mu \in M(X)$. Let φ be a C^1 function on $\mathbf{R}^2$ which vanishes outside a compact set E. Set $\sigma = -\dfrac{1}{\pi}\,\varphi_{\bar{z}}\,\hat{\mu}m_2$, where m_2 is two-dimensional Lebesgue measure. Then $\varphi\hat{\mu} = \widehat{\varphi\mu} + \hat{\sigma}$.*

Proof.   Consider any $\alpha \in \mathbf{C}$ such that $\tilde{\sigma}(\alpha) < \infty$. Then $\hat{\sigma}(\alpha) = -\dfrac{1}{\pi}\displaystyle\int_X\int_X (z - \alpha)^{-1}\varphi_{\bar{z}}(z)(\xi - z)^{-1}\,d\mu(\xi)\,dm_2(z)$. Invert the order of integration, write $(z - \alpha)^{-1}(\xi - z)^{-1}$ as $(\xi - \alpha)^{-1}[(\xi - z)^{-1} + (z - \alpha)^{-1}]$, and apply Theorem 9, §5.3. We obtain $\hat{\sigma}(\alpha) = -\dfrac{1}{\pi}\displaystyle\int_X \frac{1}{\xi - \alpha}(\varphi(\xi) - \varphi(\alpha))\,d\mu(\xi) =$

$\varphi(\alpha)\displaystyle\int_X \frac{1}{\xi - \alpha}\,d\mu(\xi) - \int_X \frac{\varphi(\xi)}{\xi - \alpha}\,d\mu(\xi) = \varphi(\alpha)\hat{\mu}(\alpha) - \widehat{\varphi\mu}(\alpha)$.

Corollary.   *If $\mu \perp R(X)$, then $\varphi\mu + \sigma \perp R(X \cap E)$.*

Proof of Theorem 31.   Given $x \in X$, there is an open set U_x about x in $\mathbf{C}$ such that f is uniformly approximable by rational functions on $X \cap \overline{U}_x$. Let S_x be a closed rectangular box centered at x and contained in U_x. By compactness of X, finitely many S_{x_i} cover X, and f is in $R(X \cap S_{x_i})$ for each i.

Let $\mu \in R(X)^{\perp}$. We prove that $\displaystyle\int_X f\,d\mu = 0$. For each i, let ψ_i be a C^1 function such that $\psi_i = 1$ on S_{x_i} and $\psi_i = 0$ outside U_{x_i}. Set $\varphi_1 = \psi_1$, $\varphi_2 = (1 - \psi_1)\psi_2, \ldots, \varphi_n = (1 - \psi_1)(1 - \psi_2)\cdots(1 - \psi_{n-1})\psi_n$. Then each φ_i is C^1 on $\mathbf{R}^2$, $\varphi_i = 0$ outside U_{x_i}, and $\displaystyle\sum_{i=1}^{n}\varphi_i = 1 - \prod_{i=1}^{n}(1 - \psi_i)$. Hence $\displaystyle\sum\varphi_i = 1$ on $S_{x_1} \cup \cdots \cup S_{x_n}$, which is a *nbhd* of X. So $\displaystyle\sum\frac{\partial\varphi_i}{\partial\bar{z}} = \frac{\partial}{\partial\bar{z}}\left(\sum\varphi_i\right) = 0$ on X. (The set $\{\varphi_i\}$ is called a C^1 partition of unity, subordinate to the cover $\{U_{x_i}\}$.)

Set $\sigma_i = -\dfrac{1}{\pi}\dfrac{\partial\varphi_i}{\partial\bar{z}}\,\hat{\mu}m_2$ on X, and let $\nu_i = \varphi_i\mu + \sigma_i$. By the Corollary, ν_i is orthogonal to $R(X \cap S_{x_i})$. Note that ν_i is concentrated on $X \cap S_{x_i}$. But f is in $R(X \cap S_{x_i})$, so we have $\displaystyle\int_X f\,d\nu_i = 0$ for each i. But $\displaystyle\sum_{i=1}^{n}\nu_i = \left(\sum_{i=1}^{n}\varphi_i\right)\mu - \dfrac{1}{\pi}\left(\sum_{i=1}^{n}\dfrac{\partial\varphi_i}{\partial\bar{z}}\right)\hat{\mu}m_2 = \mu$, so $\displaystyle\int_X f\,d\mu = 0$. Hence f is annihilated by every $\mu \in R(X)^{\perp}$, whence $f \in R(X)$.

Theorem 32 (Mergelyan).   *Let X be a compact set in the plane. Let $\{G_n\}$ be the set of components of $\mathbf{C}\backslash X$. Assume that $\inf_n \{\operatorname{diam}(G_n)\} > 0$. Then $R(X) = A(X)$.*

Proof. Let $0 < \delta < \inf_n \{\text{diam}\,(G_n)\}$. For each $x \in X$, let $\Delta_x = \{z \in \mathbf{C} : |z - x| \le \delta/2\}$, $\Delta'_x = \mathbf{C} \backslash \Delta_x$, $K_x = \Delta_x \cap X$. Then K_x is a compact *nbhd* of x in X, and $\mathbf{C} \backslash K_x = \Delta'_x \cup (\mathbf{C} \backslash X) = \Delta'_x \cup (\bigcup_n G_n)$. Since $\text{diam}\,(\Delta_x) < \text{diam}\,(G_n)$ for each n, Δ'_x meets each G_n. So $\mathbf{C} \backslash K_x$ is connected. Hence by Theorem 30, $A(K_x) = R(K_x)$. But if $f \in A(X)$, then $f \,|\, K_x \in A(K_x)$ for all $x \in X$; thus $f \in R(X)$ by Theorem 31.

Chapter Seven

Restriction Algebras

7.1 PEAK SETS

Let X be a compact space and A a subspace of $C(X)$. A set $F \subset X$ is a *peak set* for A iff F is nonvoid and there is a function $g \in A$ such that $g = 1$ on F and $|g| < 1$ on $X \backslash F$; any such g is a *peaking function* for F. Peak sets are compact, and if $x \in X$, x is a peak point for A iff $\{x\}$ is a peak set for A. Note that a peak set must meet every boundary for A, and that X itself is a peak set for A, if A contains the constants.

Given $f \in A$, let $M_f = \{x \in X : |f(x)| = \|f\|\}$ be the set on which f assumes its maximum modulus. If F is a peak set with peaking function g, then certainly $F = M_g$. However, sets of the form M_f need not be peak sets. (For example, let A be the disk algebra on the unit disk X, and let F be the unit circle. Then $F = M_z$ but F is not a peak set for A.) If A contains the constants, then M_f can be broken up into peak sets. For if F is nonempty, where $F = \{x \in X : f(x) = \|f\|\}$ ($f \in A$), then F is a peak set, with peaking function $g = \frac{1}{2}(1 + \|f\|^{-1}f)$ (unless $f = 0$, in which case we take $g = 1$). Replace f by αf ($|\alpha| = 1$) to produce other peak slices.

Theorem 1. *Let A be a closed subspace of $C(X)$. (a) Let F be a nonempty set which is the intersection of countably many peak sets for A. Then F is a peak set for A. (b) Suppose that F is a nonempty set which is an intersection of peak sets for A. Then for every open set U containing F, there is a peak set S such that $F \subset S \subset U$. Hence if K is any closed set disjoint from F, there is a function $f \in A$ such that $\|f\| = 1, f = 1$ on F, and $|f| < 1$ on K.*

Proof. If $F = F_1 \cap \cdots \cap F_n$ where each F_i is a peak set for A and if g_i is a corresponding peak function, then $\dfrac{1}{n}(g_1 + \cdots + g_n)$ peaks exactly on F.

If $F = \bigcap_{n=1}^{\infty} F_n$ and for each n, $g_n \in A$, $g_n = 1$ on F_n and $|g_n| < 1$ on $X \backslash F_n$, then $g = \sum 2^{-n} g_n$ belongs to A and peaks exactly on F. So (a) is proved.

Suppose that $F = \bigcap_{\alpha} F_{\alpha}$ where each F_{α} is a peak set for A, and let U be an open *nbhd* of F. The F_{α} are closed sets and X is covered by U and the complements $X \backslash F_{\alpha}$, so there are finitely many $\alpha_1, \ldots, \alpha_m$ with $F \subset S = F_{\alpha_1} \cap \cdots \cap F_{\alpha_m} \subset U$. S is a peak set, so (b) is proved.

We now turn to an examination of the properties of peak sets for function algebras, in particular the properties of restriction algebras $A|_F$ where F is a peak set for A. In fact, the technical condition which is usually relevant is that F be (nonvoid and) an *intersection* of peak sets for A.

Lemma 1 (Bishop's Lemma). *Let A be a function algebra on X and let $f \in A$. Suppose that F is nonempty in X and that F is the intersection of peak sets for A. Set $\|f\|_F = \max_F |f|$ and take any $x_0 \in F$ with $|f(x_0)| = \|f\|_F$.*

Set $E = \{x \in F : f(x) = f(x_0)\}$. Then there is a peak set S for A such that $S \cap F = E$. In particular, if F is a peak set, so is E.

Proof. If $f(x_0) = 0$, then there is nothing to prove. So suppose that $f(x_0) \neq 0$ and set $g = \frac{1}{2}\left(1 + \frac{f}{f(x_0)}\right)$. Then g is in A, $\|g\|_F = g(x_0) = 1$, and $E = \{x \in F : g(x) = 1\} = \{x \in F : |g(x)| = 1\}$. So E is a peak set for $A|_F$, and we are to show that $E = S \cap F$ where S is a peak set for A.

Consider the open sets $U_n = \{x \in X : |g(x)| < 1 + 1/2^n\}$. Each of them contains F, so there exist $g_n \in A$ with $g_n = 1$ on F, $\|g_n\| = 1$, and $|g_n| < 1$ on $X \backslash U_n$. Since $X \backslash U_n$ is compact, $|g_n|$ is bounded away from 1 on $X \backslash U_n$; so there are positive integers p_n such that $\max_{X \backslash U_n} |g g_n^{p_n}| < 2^{-n}$. Set $h = \sum_1^{\infty} g g_n^{p_n}/2^n$. Since $\|g_n^{p_n}\| = 1$, the series converges uniformly, and $h \in A$. Note that $h|F = g|F$ since every $g_n = 1$ on F.

Let's check that the weights have been chosen in such a way that $\|h\| = 1$. (So we have extended $g \mid F$ to an element of A without increase of sup norm.) Certainly $\|h\| \geq 1$ since $h(x_0) = 1$. If $x \in \bigcap U_n$, then $|g(x)| \leq 1$, so $|h(x)| \leq \sum \|g_n^{p_n}\| 2^{-n} = 1$. If x belongs to no U_k, then $|h(x)| \leq \sum |g(x) g_n(x)^{p_n}| 2^{-n} < \sum 1/2^{2n} < 1$. Otherwise, for some n, x belongs to $U_1, \ldots, U_{n-1}$ but not to U_n. In this case,

$$|h(x)| \leq \sum_1^{n-1} 2^{-k} |g(x)| |g_k(x)|^{p_k} + \sum_n^{\infty} 2^{-k} |g(x)| |g_k(x)|^{p_k}$$

$$< (1 + 2^{-n+1}) \sum_1^{n-1} 2^{-k} + \sum_n^{\infty} 2^{-2k}$$

$$= (1 + 2^{-n+1})(1 - 2^{-n+1}) + \left(\frac{4}{3}\right) 2^{-2n} = 1 - \left(\frac{2}{3}\right) 2^{-2n+2} < 1.$$

So $\|h\| = 1$.

Let $S = \{x \in X : h(x) = 1\}$. Then S is a peak set for A, and since $h = g$ on F, $S \cap F = \{x \in F : g(x) = 1\} = E$. So the lemma is proved.

Here is an application of Bishop's lemma.

Proposition 1. *Let A be a function algebra. Assume that A has a minimal boundary, say S. Then every point of S is a peak point for A, so S is in fact a minimum boundary for A.*

Proof. Let $x_0 \in S$. Then $S \backslash \{x_0\}$ is a proper subset of S, so $S \backslash \{x_0\}$ is not a boundary for A. Hence there is a function $f \in A$ such that $|f|$ does not assume its maximum on $S \backslash \{x_0\}$. But S is a boundary for A, so $|f(x_0)| = \|f\|$, $|f(x)| < \|f\|$ for all $x \in S \backslash \{x_0\}$. Now $f(x_0) = \alpha |f(x_0)|$ where α is a complex number of modulus 1. So if $g = \bar{\alpha} f$, then $g \in A$, $g(x_0) = \|g\|$, $|g(x)| < \|g\|$ for all $x \in S \backslash \{x_0\}$. But in fact, g assumes its maximum modulus only at x_0.

For suppose that $x_1 \neq x_0$ and $|g(x_1)| = \|g\|$. Set $g_1 = \dfrac{g}{g(x_1)}$ and let $F = \{x \in X : g_1(x) = 1 = \|g_1\|\}$. Note that $g_1 \in A$ and $x_1 \in F$. Since A separates points, $h(x_1) = 1$, $h(x_0) = 0$ for some $h \in A$. Take $x_2 \in F$ such that $|h(x_2)| = \|h\|_F$, and let $E = \{x \in F : h(x) = h(x_2)\}$. Note that F is a peak set for A and that the rest of the hypotheses in Bishop's lemma are satisfied. So E is a peak set. A peak set meets every boundary, so $E \cap S$ is nonvoid. But $E \subset F$ and F is disjoint ftom $S \backslash \{x_0\}$, so $E \cap S = \{x_0\}$. But $x_0 \in E$ would imply that $h(x_0) = h(x_2)$, or $0 = \|h\|_F$, which contradicts the fact that $h(x_1) = 1$ and $x_1 \in F$. So we have a contradiction.

Hence $g(x_0) = \|g\|$, $|g(x)| < \|g\|$ for all $x \in X \backslash \{x_0\}$. So x_0 is a peak point for A.

We can also use Bishop's lemma to prove that every maximal set of antisymmetry is an intersection of peak sets (Theorem 2 below). Combining this result with Theorem 3, we see that the restriction of a function algebra to a maximal antisymmetric set is again a function algebra (i.e., the restriction algebra is uniformly closed). It then becomes obvious that certain problems for function algebras in general can be reduced to problems for antisymmetric function algebras, which can be very helpful.

Theorem 2. *Let K be a maximal antisymmetric set for a function algebra A. Then K is an intersection of peak sets for A.*

Proof. Let F be the intersection of all peak sets for A which contain K. (X is such a peak set.) Then $K \subset F$. We prove that F is a set of antisymmetry for A, and hence $K = F$.

Suppose that $f \in A$ and that f is real-valued on F. Then f is real-valued on K, so there is a real number c such that $f = c$ on K. There is a polynomial p such that $p(c) = 1$ but $0 \leq p(t) < 1$ if $t \in f(F) \backslash \{c\}$. Set $g = p \circ f$. Then

$g \in A$, $g = 1$ on K, and if $x \in F$, $g(x) = 1$ iff $f(x) = c$, while $\|g\|_F = 1$. Thus by Bishop's lemma, if $E = \{x \in F : g(x) = 1\}$, then there is a peak set S such that $S \cap F = E$. So S is a peak set containing K (since $K \subset E \subset S$), from which we conclude that $F \subset S$ and hence that $E = S \cap F = F$. So $f = c$ on F. Thus F is a set of antisymmetry, so $K = F$.

Corollary. *Let K be a maximal antisymmetric set for A, and let U be an open nbhd of K. Then there is a peak set F for A such that $K \subset F \subset U$.*

Let A be a closed subalgebra of $C(X)$. For any closed set F in X, we define the *kernel* of F to be the set $kF = \{f \in A : f \mid F = 0\}$. kF is a closed ideal of A, and hence A/kF is a Banach algebra under the quotient norm $\|f + kF\| = \inf_{g \in kF} \|f + g\|$. There is an algebra isomorphism T of $A\mid_F$ onto A/kF given by $T(f \mid F) = f + kF$. (T is well defined and one-one by the definition of kF.) We give $A\mid_F$ the sup norm: $\|f\|_F = \|f \mid F\|$ in $C(F)$ and ask, when is $A\mid_F$ closed in $C(F)$?

Theorem 3. *Let A be a closed subalgebra of $C(X)$. Let F be a compact subset of X. Then*

(a) $\|f \mid F\| \le \|f + kF\|$ *for all $f \in A$;*

(b) $A\mid_F$ *is closed in $C(F)$ iff $\exists c_F > 0$ such that $c_F \|f + kF\| \le \|f \mid F\|$ for all $f \in A$;*

(c) *if F is an intersection of peak sets for A, then the map $f \mid F \to f + kF$ is an isometry from $A \mid F$ onto A/kF, and $A\mid_F$ is closed in $C(F)$. (In particular, this is true if F is a peak set for A.)*

Proof. (a) If $g \in kF$, then $\|f + g\| \ge \|f + g\|_F = \|f\|_F$, so $\inf_{g \in kF} \|f + g\| \ge \|f \mid F\|$.

(b) If there is a positive number c such that $c\|f + kF\| \le \|f \mid F\| \le \|f + kF\|$ ($f \in A$), then T and T^{-1} are continuous ($T(f \mid F) = f + kF$). Since A/kF is a Banach space, $A\mid_F$ is complete and hence closed in the sup norm.

Conversely, suppose that $A\mid_F$ is closed in $C(F)$. By (a), T^{-1} is a one-one continuous linear map from one Banach space onto another. By the closed graph theorem, $T = (T^{-1})^{-1}$ is also continuous. So $\|f + kF\| \le \|T\| \|f\|_F$ ($f \in A$), and we may take $c = \|T\|^{-1}$.

(c) This is a modification of the proof we gave to show that A restricted to its essential set is closed. Let F be an intersection of peak sets. We want to show that $\|f + kF\| \le \|f\|_F$ for every $f \in A$, and it will suffice to show that $\|f + kF\| \le \|f\|_F + \varepsilon$ for every $\varepsilon > 0$. So the problem is this: given $\varepsilon > 0$, find a function f_0 in A which coincides with f on F and which gets no larger than $\|f\|_F + \varepsilon$ anywhere on X. Since F is an intersection of peak sets, it turns out that f_0 can be found.

Given $\varepsilon > 0$, let $U = \{x \in X : |f(x)| < \|f\|_F + \varepsilon\}$. By Theorem 1, there is a peak set S with $F \subset S \subset U$. Take $g \in A$ with $g = 1$ on F, $|g| < 1$ off U, and $\|g\| = 1$. Since $X \setminus U$ is compact, $\|g\|_{X \setminus U} = \delta < 1$ and hence $g^n \to 0$

uniformly on $X \backslash U$. Choose n so that $\|f\| \delta^n < \|f\|_F + \varepsilon$. Then if $x \in U$, $|f(x)g(x)^n| \le |f(x)| < \|f\|_F + \varepsilon$, while if $x \in X \backslash U$, $|f(x)g(x)^n| \le \|f\| \delta^n < \|f\|_F + \varepsilon$. But $f_0 = fg^n$ belongs to $f + kF$, since $g = 1$ on F. So $\|f + kF\| = \inf\{\|h\| : h \in f + kF\} \le \|f_0\| < \|f\|_F + \varepsilon$, which proves the inequality.

Theorem 4. *Let F be an intersection of peak sets for a closed subalgebra A of $C(X)$, and assume that F is not empty. Then A interpolates $A|_F$ with preservation of norm. That is, for each $\varphi \in A|_F$, $\exists g \in A$ with $g|_F = \varphi$ and $\|g\| = \|\varphi\|$.*

Proof. If $\varphi = 0$, then there is no problem, so we assume that $\|\varphi\| = \max_F |\varphi| = 1$. Since $A|_F$ is isometric with A/kF, we can find $f \in A$ such that $f|F = \varphi$ and $\|f\| < \|\varphi\| + \frac{1}{2} = \frac{3}{2}$.

Since $f|F = \varphi$, $|f| \le 1$ on F. Note that there is a peak set S such that $F \subset S \subset \{x \in X : |f(x)| \le 1\}$. (Set $V_n = \left\{x \in X : |f(x)| < 1 + \dfrac{1}{n}\right\}$. Each V_n is open and $F \subset V_n$, so there is a peak set S_n with $F \subset S_n \subset V_n$. Take $S = \bigcap_n S_n$.)

Let $h \in A$ be a peaking function for S. Unfortunately, $\{x \in X : |f(x)| \le 1\}$ is not open, so we have no uniform control over the modulus of h on its complement, as we did in Theorem 3. We can get around the difficulty in the following way.

Set $K_n = \left\{x : 1 + \dfrac{1}{2^{n+1}} \le |f(x)| \le 1 + \dfrac{1}{2^n}\right\}$. The K_n are compact sets disjoint from S, so there are positive integers p_n with $|h^{p_n}| < 4^{-n}$ on K_n. Set $g = \sum_{n=1}^{\infty} 2^{-n} f h^{p_n}$. Then g is a norm-preserving extension of φ.

Since the series converges uniformly on X, $g \in A$. On F, $f = \varphi$ and $h = 1$, so $g|_F = \varphi$. If $x \in X$ and $|f(x)| \le 1$, then $|g(x)| \le \sum_1^{\infty} 2^{-n} \|h\|^{p_n} = 1$, while if $|f(x)| > 1$, then $x \in K_m$ for some m, and we have

$$|g(x)| = \left| 2^{-m} f(x) h(x)^{p_m} + \sum_{n \ne m} 2^{-n} f(x) h(x)^{p_n} \right|$$

$$\le \left(1 + \frac{1}{2^m}\right)\left(2^{-m} 4^{-m} + \sum_{n \ne m} 2^{-n}\right) < 1.$$

So $\|g\| = \|\varphi\| = 1$ and the norm is preserved.

Suppose that F is a peak set for A. We can then take $h = 1$ on F, $|h| < 1$ on $X \backslash F$. If we replace g by gh, we can strengthen the conclusion of Theorem 4 as follows.

Theorem 5. *Let F be a peak set for A, a closed subalgebra of $C(X)$. Then every nonzero φ in $A|_F$ has an extension $f \in A$ such that $|f(x)| < \|\varphi\|$ for all x in $X \backslash F$. (Peak sets allow "peak interpolation.")*

Next we show that peak points for A remain peak points for $\hat{A}$. The corresponding result for peak sets is false. (For example, X is always a peak set for A, but X is not a peak set for $\hat{A}$ unless $\mathcal{M}(A) = X$.)

Theorem 6. *Let A be a function algebra on X, and suppose that $x_0 \in X$ is a peak point for A. Then x_0 is a peak point for $\hat{A}$.*

Proof. Choose $f \in A$ with $f(x_0) = 1$ and $|f| < 1$ on $X \backslash \{x_0\}$. Suppose that $a \in \mathcal{M}(A)$ and that a does not coincide with evaluation at x_0. Let μ be a representing measure for a on X. If $\int |f|\, d\mu = 1$, then since $1 - |f| \geq 0$ on X, $1 - |f| = 0$ a.e. with respect to μ. But this would imply that $\mu(\{x_0\}) = 1$ and therefore that $a = x_0$, contrary to our assumption. Hence $|\hat{f}(a)| = \left| \int f\, d\mu \right| \leq \int |f|\, d\mu < 1$. Since a is arbitrary, $\hat{f}$ peaks exactly at x_0.

EXERCISE SET   7.1

1. Show that x belongs to the Choquet boundary of a function algebra A iff $\{x\}$ is an intersection of peak sets for A.

2. Let A be a function algebra and f a real-valued function in A. Prove that every set of constancy for f is a peak set for A.

3. Let A be a subalgebra of $C(X)$ with $1 \in A$. Let $F \subset X$ be a compact set. Suppose that $\forall x \in X \backslash F$, $\exists f_x \in A$ with $f_x = 1$ on F, $|f_x(x)| < 1$, and $\|f_x\| = 1$. Show that F is an intersection of peak sets for A.

4. Let I be a closed ideal in a function algebra A, and let $K \in \mathcal{K}_A$. Show that $I|_K$ is closed in $C(K)$ and is in fact isometric with $I/I \cap kK$. (The same is true if I is replaced by any closed subspace B of $C(X)$ which is an A-module.)

5. Let A be a function algebra and $K \in \mathcal{K}_A$ a maximal antisymmetric set for A. Show that if K does not reduce to a point, then K contains a perfect set.

6. Let A be a function algebra on X, and let F be a compact G_δ in X. Show that if F is an intersection of peak sets for A, then F is itself a peak set. In particular, if X is metrizable, every (nonvoid) intersection of peak sets is a peak set.

7. Show that there are closed ideals in the disk algebra which are not representable as kernels of closed sets. (For a complete discussion of the ideal theory of the disk algebra, consult [E].)

8. Let A be a function algebra on X, and let $x \in X$. Let S_x be the intersection of all peak sets for A which contain x. Let T_x consist of all $y \in X$ such that $f(y) = f(x)$ for all $f \in A$ such that $x \in M_f$. (a) Prove that $S_x = T_x$. (b) Prove that S_x is a set of antisymmetry for A.

9. Let A be a function algebra with Choquet boundary $c(A)$, and let F be an intersection of peak sets for A. Prove that $F \cap c(A) = c(A|_F)$.

7.2   *A*-CONVEX HULLS

Let A be a function algebra on X. If U is a nonvoid subset of X, we denote by A_U the uniform closure of $A|_U$ in $C(\overline{U})$. The *A-hull of U* is the set $\widetilde{U} = \{a \in \mathcal{M}(A) : |\hat{f}(a)| \leq \sup_U |f|, \ \forall f \in A\}$. U is *A-convex* iff $U = \widetilde{U}$.

Note that U and $\overline{U}$ have the same *A*-hull and that $\widetilde{U}$ is compact.

Theorem 7. $\widetilde{U}$ *is the maximal ideal space of* A_U.

Proof. Since $A_U = A_{\overline{U}}$ by definition, we may assume that U is a compact set $F \subset X$.

Let h be a complex homomorphism of A_F. Then $f \to h(f|F)$ is a complex homomorphism of A (note that $1 \to 1$). So $\exists a \in \mathcal{M}(A)$ with $h(f|F) = \hat{f}(a)$ (all $f \in A$). Since $\|h\| = 1$, $|\hat{f}(a)| \leq \|f|F\|$, $\forall f \in A$. So $a \in \widetilde{F}$.

Conversely, let $a \in \widetilde{F}$. The mapping $f|F \to \hat{f}(a)$ is well defined, since $f|_F = g|_F$ implies that $(f - g)|_F = 0$, so $(f - g)\hat{}(a) = 0$. It is a continuous homomorphism from $A|_F$ to $\mathbf{C}$, since $|\hat{f}(a)| \leq \|f\|_F$. Hence it extends to a complex homomorphism $h : A_F \to \mathbf{C}$.

So we have a map $h \to a$ from $\mathcal{M}(A_F)$ onto $\widetilde{F}$, where $h(f|F) = \hat{f}(a)$. It is now an easy matter to verify that this map is a homeomorphism, so the proof is finished.

I leave the proof of the next theorem to the reader.

Theorem 8.   *Let F be a compact set in X. Then* $a \in \widetilde{F}$ *iff there is a representing measure for a which is concentrated on F.*

Let us recall that if μ is an extreme point of $b(A^\perp)$ (the unit ball in the annihilator of A) or if μ is a representing measure for some $a \in \mathcal{M}(A)$, then $S = \text{supp } \mu$ is a set of antisymmetry for A. (Cf. §3.3.) So certainly S is a set of antisymmetry for $A|_S$. But more is true.

Theorem 9.   *Let* $\mu \in b(A^\perp)^e$ *or let* μ *be a representing measure for some* $a \in \mathcal{M}(A)$. *Let F be a closed set in X which contains* $S = \text{supp } \mu$. *Then S is a set of antisymmetry for* A_F.

Proof. If $\int f \, d\mu = \hat{f}(a)$ for all $f \in A$, then $a \in \widetilde{F} = \mathcal{M}(A_F)$, and by uniform convergence on S, μ (restricted to F) represents a on $A_F = \overline{A|_F}$. Similarly, if μ is an extreme point of $b(A^\perp)$ and μ is concentrated on F, then μ (restricted to F) is an extreme point of $b(A_F{}^\perp)$. So by the results cited above, $S = \text{supp } \mu = \text{supp } (\mu|_F)$ is a set of antisymmetry for A_F.

It should not be assumed that a set of antisymmetry for $A|_F$ is always a set of antisymmetry for A_F. (I am grateful to R. P. Boas and D. Chalice for pointing out the following interesting example.)

Consider the disk algebra A on the closed unit disk Δ. Let I_0 be the segment $\{x + iy : |x| \leq \frac{1}{2}, y = 0\}$, and let $I_n = \left\{x + iy : |x| \leq \frac{1}{2}, y = \dfrac{1}{n+1}\right\}$ $(n = 1, 2, 3, \ldots)$. Let F be the union of I_0 and the I_n $(n \geq 1)$. F is a compact subset of Δ. Since the interior of F is empty and F does not separate the plane, it follows from Lavrentiev's theorem that $A_F = C(F)$. Nevertheless, F is a set of antisymmetry for A! For suppose that $f \in A$ and $f \mid F$ is real-valued. If $f \mid I_0$ is constant, then f is constant, by the identity principle for analytic functions. Otherwise, $f'(x_0) \neq 0$ for some $x_0 \in (-\frac{1}{2}, \frac{1}{2})$. But then there is an open disk V centered at x_0 such that $f \mid V$ is a homeomorphism from V onto the open set $f(V)$. The image under f of the segment $V \cap I_0$ is a connected set on the line, so it is an interval with $f(x_0)$ not an endpoint. But then (for all n sufficiently large) $f\left(x_0 + \dfrac{i}{n+1}\right) \notin f(V \cap I_0)$, so $\left\{f\left(x_0 + \dfrac{i}{n+1}\right)\right\}$ cannot converge to $f(x_0)$. This contradicts the continuity of f, so the assumption that $f \mid I_0$ is nonconstant is false.

As a corollary to Theorem 9 we have the following.

Theorem 10. *Let μ be as in Theorem 9. Then the A-hull of supp μ is connected.*

Proof. A_S is an antisymmetric function algebra, $S = \text{supp } \mu$. Hence $\tilde{S} = \mathcal{M}(A_S)$ is connected, by Šilov's theorem on idempotents. (See Exercise 2, §5.6.)

Corollary. *If m is a nonzero positive measure on the closed unit disk Δ, and if $\int fg \, dm = (\int f \, dm)(\int g \, dm)$ for all f, g in the disk algebra, then hull (supp m) is connected.*

We now consider the restriction of an algebra to a subset which is an intersection of peak sets.

Theorem 11. *Let F be a nonempty set in $\mathcal{M}(A)$ which is an intersection of peak sets for $\hat{A}$. Then*
  (a) $F = A\text{-hull } (F \cap X) = \hat{A}\text{-hull } (F)$;
  (b) $F = \mathcal{M}(A_{F \cap X}) = \mathcal{M}(\hat{A}_F)$;
  (c) $\Gamma(\hat{A}_F) \subset F \cap \Gamma(A)$.

Proof. (a) and (b) are equivalent statements.

Take $p \in \mathcal{M}(A) \backslash F$. There is an open set U in $\mathcal{M}(A)$ with $F \subset U$, $p \notin U$ (by normality of a compact space). Since F is an intersection of peak sets, $\hat{g} = 1$ on F, $|\hat{g}| < 1$ off U, for some $g \in A$. So if $f = 1 - g$, then $f \in A$, $\hat{f} \otimes 0$ on F, and $\hat{f}(p) \neq 0$. Hence $p \notin \tilde{F}$. Since $F \subset \tilde{F}$ always, $F = \tilde{F} = \hat{A}\text{-hull } (F)$.

$F \cap X \subset F$, so $A\text{-hull } (F \cap X) = \hat{A}\text{-hull } (F \cap X) \subset \tilde{F} = F$. On the other hand, take any $a \in F$. Let μ be a representing measure for a. Then μ is concentrated on $F \cap X$. (If $\mu(X \backslash F) > 0$, then $\mu(E) > 0$ for some compact set

$E \subset X \backslash F$. Take $g \in A$ with $\|g\| = 1$, $\hat{g} = 1$ on F, $|\hat{g}| < 1$ on E. Then $1 = \hat{g}(a) = \int_X g \, d\mu \leq |\int_{X \backslash E} g \, d\mu| + |\int_E g \, d\mu| < \mu(X \backslash E) + \mu(E) = 1$, a contradiction.) So a belongs to the A-hull of $F \cap X$. So (a), (b) are proved.

If we apply (a) to the function algebra $A|_\Gamma$ ($\Gamma = \Gamma(A)$), which has the same $\hat{A}$ and $\mathcal{M}(A)$ (or merely modify the proof to note that if μ is a representing measure for a which is concentrated on Γ, then supp $\mu \subset F \cap \Gamma$), we see that every $a \in \mathcal{M}(\hat{A}_F) = F$ has a representing measure concentrated on $F \cap \Gamma$. So $F \cap \Gamma$ is a boundary for $\hat{A}_F$, and it must therefore contain the Šilov boundary of $\hat{A}_F$. (Note too that $F = A$-hull $(F \cap \Gamma(A))$.)

Corollary 1. *If F is a nonempty set in $\mathcal{M}(A)$ which is an intersection of peak sets for $\hat{A}$, then F meets $\Gamma(A)$. Hence $F \cap X$ and $F \cap \Gamma(A)$ are nonvoid.*

Corollary 2. *If F is a nonempty intersection of peak sets for $\hat{A}$, and if $F \cap X$ is a point $\{x\}$, then $F = \{x\}$.*

Proof. If $f \in A$, then $\hat{f} - f(x)$ assumes its maximum modulus over F on $F \cap X = \{x\}$; i.e., $\hat{f}|F$ is constant. Since $\hat{A}$ separates points, $F = \{x\}$.

We end this section with a result which is in the spirit of §3.4. The technique is similar to one used in algebra in the construction of idempotents. For more theorems of a similar nature, see [129] and §7.5.

Proposition 2. *Let A be a function algebra on X, and let $F_1, \ldots, F_n$ be compact sets with $X = F_1 \cup \cdots \cup F_n$. Suppose that for each k, $1 \leq k \leq n$, every complex homomorphism of $A|_{F_k}$ is given by evaluation at a point of F_k. Then $X = \mathcal{M}(A)$.*

Proof. Let M be a maximal ideal of A. For each k, $M|_{F_k}$ is an ideal in $A|_{F_k}$. If $M|_{F_k} = A|_{F_k}$ for $k = 1, \ldots, n$, then there are $f_1, \ldots, f_n$ in M such that $f_i = 1$ on F_i. Let $h_1 = f_1$, $h_2 = f_1 + f_2 - f_1 f_2 = h_1 + f_2 - h_1 f_2$, and define $h_{j+1} = f_{j+1} + h_j - h_j f_{j+1}$ for $j = 1, \ldots, n-1$. Since M is an ideal, all $h_i \in M$, and we note that $h_1 = 1$ on F_1, $h_2 = 1$ on $F_1 \cup F_2, \ldots$, $h_n = 1$ on $F_1 \cup \cdots \cup F_n = X$. That is, $1 \in M$, contradicting the assumption that M is a proper ideal in A.

Hence $M|_{F_k}$ is a proper ideal in $A|_{F_k}$ for some k. By hypothesis, it follows that $\exists x \in F_k$ such that $M|_{F_k} \subset \{f|_{F_k} : f \in A$ and $f(x) = 0\}$; i.e., $M \subset \{f \in A : f(x) = 0\}$. Since M is a maximal ideal it follows that M is the kernel of the homomorphism $f \to f(x)$.

EXERCISE SET 7.2

1. Let A be a function algebra on X, with $X = \mathcal{M}(A)$. Let $f \in C(X)$, and let B be the closed subalgebra generated by A and f. We are concerned with determining $\mathcal{M}(B)$ in terms of $\mathcal{M}(A)$. (See [214].) For $m \in \mathcal{M}(B)$, let

$r(m)$ be the restriction of m to A, and let $s(m) = (r(m), m(f)) \in X \times \mathbf{C}$. Note that s is a homeomorphism from $\mathcal{M}(B)$ into $X \times \mathbf{C}$, and that $s(X)$ is the graph of f.

For each complex λ, let F_λ be the A-hull of $f^{-1}(\lambda)$. Set $H = \bigcup_{\lambda \in \mathbf{C}} F_\lambda \times \{\lambda\} = \{(a, \lambda) : \lambda \in f(X), a \in F_\lambda\}$. Prove that H embeds in $\mathcal{M}(B)$ in the following sense: $s(\mathcal{M}(B)) \supset H \supset s(X)$.

Prove that $\sigma_B(f)$ is the union of $f(X)$ with those of its bounded complementary components which meet $\sigma_B(f)$. Show that if $f(X)$ has empty interior and connected complement, then $\sigma_B(f) = f(X)$ and $s(\mathcal{M}(B)) = H$. Thus in this case we can determine $\mathcal{M}(B)$ explicitly in terms of f and $\mathcal{M}(A)$.

Show that either $f^{-1}(\lambda)$ is A-convex for every λ, or $\mathcal{M}(B)$ is properly larger than $\mathcal{M}(A)$.

2. Let A be a function algebra. Show that if S is a peak set for $\hat{A}$, every non-void open-closed subset of S is a peak set for $\hat{A}$.

7.3   PROPERTIES OF THE ANTISYMMETRIC DECOMPOSITION

In this section, A is a function algebra on a compact space X, and $\hat{A}$ is the transform algebra on the maximal ideal space $\mathcal{M}(A)$. The family of maximal antisymmetric sets for A is $\mathcal{K} = \mathcal{K}_A$, and $\hat{\mathcal{K}} = \mathcal{K}_{\hat{A}}$ is the family of maximal antisymmetric sets for $\hat{A}$. If $K \in \mathcal{K}$, then K is an intersection of peak sets for A, so $A|_K = A_K$ is a function algebra. Its maximal ideal space is $\tilde{K}$, the A-hull of K in $\mathcal{M}(A)$.

The maximal ideal space and Šilov boundary of A can be recovered piecemeal from those of the A_K, as one would suspect from Bishop's theorem.

Theorem 12. *$\mathcal{M}(A)$ is the disjoint union $\bigcup_{K \in \mathcal{K}} \tilde{K}$.*

Proof. Let K_1, K_2 be distinct members of $\mathcal{K}$. Then K_1 is an intersection of peak sets and K_2 is a closed set disjoint from K_1, so there is a function g in A with $\|g\| = 1$, $g = 1$ on K_1, $|g| < 1$ on K_2. Since $1 - g \in A$ and vanishes on K_1, $1 - \hat{g}$ vanishes identically on $\tilde{K}_1$. On the other hand, on $\tilde{K}_2$, $|\hat{g}| \le \|g\|_{K_2} < 1$. So $\tilde{K}_1$ and $\tilde{K}_2$ are disjoint.

It remains to be shown that every $a \in \mathcal{M}(A)$ lies in $\tilde{K}$ for some $K \in \mathcal{K}$. Take a representing measure m for a. Then A is antisymmetric on the closed support of m, so m is concentrated on some $K \in \mathcal{K}$. Hence $a \in \tilde{K}$, since $|\hat{f}(a)| = |\int f \, dm| = |\int_K f \, dm| \le \|f\|_K$ for each $f \in A$.

Theorem 13. *$\Gamma(A)$ is the closure of $\bigcup_{K \in \mathcal{K}} \Gamma(A_K)$.*

Proof. (i) Take x in the Choquet boundary of A. x belongs to some $K \in \mathcal{K}$. Let U be any *nbhd* of x in X. Then, since $\{x\}$ is an intersection of peak sets, $\exists f \in A$ with $\|f\| = 1$, $|f(x_0)| = 1$, and $|f| < 1$ on $X \backslash U$. In particular, $|f| < 1$ on $K \backslash U$. Thus x belongs to $\Gamma(A_K)$. So $c(A) \subset \bigcup_{K \in \mathcal{K}} \Gamma(A_K)$. Since $\Gamma(A)$ is the closure of $c(A)$, $\Gamma(A)$ is contained in $\overline{\bigcup \Gamma(A_K)}$.

(ii) Conversely, let $K \in \mathcal{K}$ and $x_0 \in \Gamma(A_K)$. Let U be an open set about x_0 in X. Then $\exists g \in A$ with $\|g\|_K = 1$, $|g(x)| < 1$ on $K \backslash U$. Take $x_1 \in K$ such that $|g(x_1)| = 1$, and let $E = \{x \in K : g(x) = g(x_1)\}$. By Bishop's lemma, E is an intersection of peak sets for A. But $E \subset U$, so there is a peak set S with $E \subset S \subset U$. So $\exists f \in A$ with $\|f\| = 1$, $f = 1$ on E and $|f| < 1$ on $X \backslash U$. We have therefore shown that $x_0 \in \Gamma(A)$. Thus $\bigcup_{K \in \mathcal{K}} \Gamma(A_K) \subset \Gamma(A)$ and the theorem follows.

Note that $\Gamma(A)$ need not coincide with $\bigcup_{K \in \mathcal{K}} \Gamma(A_K)$, since this union may not even be closed in X. For example, let $X = \Delta \times [0, 1]$, Δ the closed unit disk. Let $D_0 = \Delta \times \{0\}$, $C_0 = T^1 \times \{0\}$. Let A be the set of all $f \in C(X)$ such that $z \to f(z, 0)$ is analytic on the open unit disk (the functions which are in the disk algebra on the slice D_0). If $0 < t_0 \le 1$, then each point (z, t_0) (with $z \in \Delta$) is a maximal set of antisymmetry for A. For if $(z_1, t_1) \ne (z, t_0)$ there is a function $u \in C_R(X)$ with $u(D_0 \cup \{(z_1, t_1)\}) = 0$, $u(z, t_0) = 1$, and of course u belongs to A. The disk D_0 is also a maximal set of antisymmetry for A, since $A|_{D_0}$ is the disk algebra. Hence $\bigcup_{K \in \mathcal{K}_A} \Gamma(A_K) = C_0 \cup \{(z, t) \in X : t > 0\}$, which is not closed and cannot be the Šilov boundary of A. It is, however, the Choquet boundary of A. (It is easy to construct explicit peaking functions for each point of $C_0 \cup \{(z, t) : t > 0\}$.)

Note that for this function algebra A, $\bigcup_{K \in \mathcal{K}} \Gamma(A_K)$ is dense in X. We know that the maximal ideal spaces $\tilde{K} = \mathcal{M}(A_K) = K$, so we conclude that $X = \Gamma(A) = \mathcal{M}(A)$ for the "bottom slice" algebra. It is also of interest to note that A is finitely generated—in fact, $t, z, t\bar{z}$ is a set of generators for A. (Let C be the subalgebra of $C_0(X \backslash D_0)$ generated by $t, tz, t\bar{z}$. C is a self-adjoint subalgebra of $C_0(X \backslash D_0)$, and C separates points and contains a function (namely t) which vanishes at no point of $X \backslash D_0$. So by the Stone-Weierstrass theorem, C is dense in $C_0(X \backslash D_0)$. Given $f \in A$, let $g(z, t) = f(z, t) - f(z, 0)$. Then if $\varepsilon > 0$ is given, there is a polynomial p (without constant term) such that $|g(z, t) - p(t, tz, t\bar{z})| < \varepsilon/2$ on $X \backslash D_0$ and hence on X. Since f is in the disk algebra on the bottom slice, there is a polynomial $q = \sum_0^N a_n z^n$ such that $|f(z, 0) - q(z)| < \varepsilon/2$ on Δ. So $|f(z, t) - (q(z) + p(t, tz, t\bar{z}))| < \varepsilon$ for all $(z, t) \in X$. Thus $\{1, t, z, tz, t\bar{z}\}$ generates a dense subalgebra of A.)

Remark. For a function algebra A, if $K \in \mathcal{K}_A$, A_K is an antisymmetric function algebra. So its maximal ideal space $\tilde{K}$ is connected. (This follows from Šilov's theorem on idempotents, since an antisymmetric algebra contains no nonconstant idempotent.) Thus the decomposition in Theorem 12 represents $\mathscr{M}(A)$ as a disjoint union of compact connected sets. If A is a proper subalgebra (of $C(X)$), then at least one of those sets is not a point.

If we cut a maximal antisymmetric set for $\hat{A}$ down to X, we get a maximal antisymmetric set for A, and all $K \in \mathscr{K}_A$ are obtained in this way.

Theorem 14. *The members of $\mathscr{K}$ are the sets $K' \cap X$ with $K' \in \hat{\mathscr{K}}$.*

Proof. Let $K' \in \mathscr{K}_{\hat{A}}$. If $f \in A$ is real-valued on $K' \cap X$, then f is real-valued on $\Gamma(\hat{A}_{K'})$, by Theorem 11. Hence $\hat{f} \mid K'$ is real-valued, e.g., because it is obtained by integrating f with respect to a positive measure on $\Gamma(\hat{A}_{K'})$. Since K' is a set of antisymmetry, $\hat{f}$ is constant on K', hence on $K' \cap X$. So $K' \cap X$ is a set of antisymmetry for A.

Take F closed in X with $K' \cap X \subsetneqq F$. Then K' is a proper subset of $K' \cup F$, so $K' \cup F$ is not a set of antisymmetry for $\hat{A}$. Some $\hat{f} \in \hat{A}$ is real-valued on $K' \cup F$, constant on K', but not constant on $K' \cup F$. Since $K' \cap F$ is not empty (it contains $K' \cap X$), f is not constant on F. Hence we have shown that $K' \cap X$ is a maximal set of antisymmetry for A.

On the other hand, if $K \in \mathscr{K}$, then K is a set of antisymmetry for $\hat{A}$, so K is contained in some $K' \in \hat{\mathscr{K}}$. By maximality, $K = K' \cap X$. So $\mathscr{K} = \{K' \cap X : K' \in \hat{\mathscr{K}}\}$.

Conversely, if we start with a maximal antisymmetric set $K \in \mathscr{K}_A$, then the set $K' \in \mathscr{K}_{\hat{A}}$ which cuts down to K is just the A-hull of K.

Theorem 15. *Let $K \in \mathscr{K}_A$, and let $K' \in \mathscr{K}_{\hat{A}}$ be such that $K = K' \cap X$. Then $K' = A\text{-hull}(K) = \tilde{K}$. Thus the decomposition of $\mathscr{M}(A)$ in Theorem 12 is the antisymmetric decomposition defined in $\mathscr{M}(A)$ by the function algebra $\hat{A}$.*

Proof. K' is an intersection of peak sets for $\hat{A}$. So

$$K' = A\text{-hull}(K' \cap X) = A\text{-hull}(K).$$

Let $a \in \mathscr{M}(A)$, and let P be the Gleason part of $\mathscr{M}(A)$ containing a. Let K' be the maximal antisymmetric set for $\hat{A}$ containing a. If U is any open set containing K', then there is a function $\hat{f} \in \hat{A}$ with $\hat{f} = 1$ on K', $|\hat{f}| < 1$ on $\mathscr{M}(A)\backslash U$, and $\|\hat{f}\| = 1$. Since $\hat{f}(a) = 1 = \|\hat{f}\|$, $\hat{f}(b) = 1$ for every $b \in P$. (See Lemma 4, §4.5.) It follows that $P \subset U$. Since K' is the intersection of all open sets $U \supset K'$, we conclude that $P \subset K'$. (Note that the argument works just as well for any decomposition of $\mathscr{M}(A)$ into a disjoint union of intersections of peak sets.)

Theorem 16. *If P is a part in $\mathscr{M}(A)$, there is a maximal antisymmetric set $K \in \mathscr{K}_A$ such that $P \subset \tilde{K}$.*

This follows from Theorem 15 and the discussion above. So every maximal antisymmetric set $\tilde{K}$ (for $\hat{A}$) is a union of parts.

EXERCISE SET   7.3

1. Consider the bottom slice (or "tomato can") algebra A on $X = \Delta \times [0, 1]$. Determine the Gleason parts for A. Show that each point $(z, 0)$ ($|z| < 1$) in the "inside" of the bottom slice has representing measures which have disjoint closed supports, and hence has a representing measure (concentrated on $X =$ the Šilov boundary of A) with a disconnected closed support.

Note, too, that D_0 is a peak set for $A = \hat{A}$ but $\Gamma(A_{D_0})$ is a proper subset of $D_0 \cap \Gamma(A) = D_0$. (Here $D_0 = \Delta \times \{0\}$.)

2. Show that if A is a function algebra, then $c(A) = \bigcup_{K \in \mathcal{K}} c(A_K)$.

7.4   ANTISYMMETRY AND UNIFORM APPROXIMATION

Let us start with some definitions. A sup norm algebra A on a space X is antisymmetric iff X is a set of antisymmetry for A; i.e., $f \in A$ and f real-valued imply that f is constant. (Equivalently, if $f \in A$ and $\bar{f} \in A$, then f is constant.) A is said to be *pervasive* iff $A|_F$ is dense in $C(F)$ for every proper compact subset F of X. A is said to be *analytic* iff the only element of A which vanishes on a nonvoid open set in X is 0. (This is clearly a generalization of the identity principle for analytic functions.) A is an *essential* algebra on X iff X is the essential set for A; i.e., A contains no nonzero ideal of $C(X)$.

We shall prove a number of interrelationships among these properties. One should also note that some of the conditions are satisfied by A on X iff they are satisfied by $\hat{A}$ on $\mathcal{M}(A)$. For example, A is antisymmetric on X iff $\hat{A}$ is antisymmetric (and thus this is so iff A is antisymmetric on its Šilov boundary). This follows from results in §7.3, but it is easy to prove directly. Similarly, since the essential sets for A and $\hat{A}$ satisfy $\hat{E} = (\mathcal{M}(A)\backslash X) \cup E$, A is an essential algebra iff $\hat{A}$ is essential. We have proved (see §4.3) that the boundary value algebra is pervasive; i.e., the disk algebra is pervasive on its Šilov boundary, but it is clear that the disk algebra is far from pervasive on the disk. So the property of being pervasive is dependent on which representing space X (X compact, $\Gamma(A) \subset X \subset \mathcal{M}(A)$) one is using for A. The facts for analyticity are more elusive. (But see the Corollary to Theorem 27 below.)

We will call a measure $\mu \in M(X)$ *global* iff supp $\mu = X$; i.e., $|\mu|(U) > 0$ for every nonvoid open set U in X.

Theorem 17.   *Let A be a sup norm algebra on X. Then A is pervasive iff every nonzero annihilator of A is global.*

Proof.   Assume that A is pervasive. Take $\mu \in A^{\perp}$ and let F be the closed support of μ. If $F \neq X$, then $A|_F$ is dense in $C(F)$. But $\mu|_F$ is clearly an annihilator of $A|_F$, so $\mu|_F$ annihilates $C(F)$. Therefore $\mu|_F$ is the zero measure, so $\|\mu\| = |\mu|(F) + |\mu|(X\backslash F) = 0$. Hence if $\mu \in A^\perp$ is not global, $\mu = 0$.

Conversely, assume that every nonzero μ in $A^\perp$ is global. Take any proper compact set $F \subset X$. If $\nu \in M(F)$ annihilates $A|_F$, then ν extends to a measure $\mu \in M(X)$ which annihilates A ($\mu(E) = \nu(E \cap F)$) for all Borel sets E in X). Since μ is concentrated on F, a proper closed subset of X, $\mu = 0$ by hypothesis. So $(A|_F)^\perp = \{0\}$, and $A|_F$ is therefore dense in $C(F)$. So A is pervasive.

Theorem 18. *Let A be a pervasive function algebra on X. Let $a \in \mathscr{M}(A)\backslash X$, and let λ_a be a representing measure for a. Then λ_a is global.*

Proof. Let S be the closed support of λ_a. If $S \neq X$, then $A_S = C(S)$ by assumption. So $\mathscr{M}(A_S) = \tilde{S} = S$. But λ_a is a representing measure for a which is concentrated on S, so $a \in \tilde{S}$. Since $S \subset X$ and $a \notin X$, this is a contradiction. Therefore $S = X$.

Lemma 2. *Let A be a function algebra on X, with Šilov boundary Γ. Then $A|_\Gamma \neq C(\Gamma)$ unless $A = C(X)$.*

Proof. We have essentially proved this already. Suppose that $A|_\Gamma = C(\Gamma)$. If $x \in X\backslash\Gamma$, then $\exists f \in A$ with $|f(x)| > \sup_\Gamma |f|$, by Lemma 4, §3.4. This is absurd, so $X = \Gamma$, $A = C(X)$.

Theorem 19. *If A is pervasive on X, then $X = \Gamma(A)$.*

Proof. $A|_\Gamma$ is closed in $C(\Gamma)$. If Γ were proper, then $A|_\Gamma$ would be dense in $C(\Gamma)$ and so $A|_\Gamma$ would be $C(\Gamma)$, which contradicts the lemma.

Theorem 20. *Let A be a pervasive function algebra on X and $A \neq C(X)$. Then A is analytic on X.*

Proof. Let $f \in A$ vanish on a nonvoid open set $V \subset X$. Since $A \neq C(X)$, there is a nonzero $\mu \in A^\perp$. Now $f\mu \in A^\perp$ also, and $f\mu$ is not global. Since A is pervasive, $f\mu = 0$. Hence $\|f\mu\| = \int |f|\,d|\mu| = 0$, so $f = 0$ a.e. $[|\mu|]$. But μ is global, so $f = 0$ everywhere on X. Hence A is analytic.

Theorem 21. *An analytic sup norm algebra is an integral domain.*

Proof. Let A be analytic and f, g nonzero elements of A. Take $x_0 \in X$ with $f(x_0) \neq 0$. There is a set U open about x_0 such that $|f| > 0$ on U, by continuity of f. Since A is analytic and $g \neq 0$, there is a point $x \in U$ at which g does not vanish. Since $(fg)(x) \neq 0$, $fg \neq 0$. So A is an integral domain.

Theorem 22. *Let A be a sup norm algebra on X. Suppose that A is an integral domain. Then A is antisymmetric.*

Proof. Set $B = \{f \in A : \bar{f} \in A\}$, the "symmetric part" of A. B is a self-adjoint sup norm algebra, so by the Stone-Weierstrass theorem there is a compact space Y such that $B = C(Y)$. But B is an integral domain, so Y is a point. Thus B contains only the constants, and A is antisymmetric.

Theorem 23.   *An antisymmetric sup norm algebra is essential.*

Proof.   This is true because every nonzero closed ideal in $C(X)$ contains nonconstant real-valued functions.

So for proper subalgebras of $C(X)$ we have A pervasive $\Rightarrow A$ analytic $\Rightarrow A$ is an integral domain $\Rightarrow A$ is antisymmetric $\Rightarrow A$ is essential. We shall see below that these conditions are equivalent if A is a maximal algebra on X, but there are examples to show that in general none of the implications can be reversed.

Note that a pervasive algebra A has this property: if λ is a representing measure for a point in $\mathcal{M}(A)$, then either λ is global or λ is a point mass. (If S is the closed support of λ, then λ is multiplicative on $A|_S$, hence, by continuity, on A_S. If $S \neq X$, $A_S = C(S)$, so λ is a point mass.) The converse is undoubtedly true: any algebra with this property is pervasive; but I don't see how to prove it.

If we change the condition slightly, we get a class of algebras somewhat intermediate to those studied above. Let us say that a function algebra A *has global measures* iff every $a \in \mathcal{M}(A) \backslash X$ has a representing measure which is global. (Every pervasive algebra has global measures.) We call A a *maximum modulus algebra* provided these conditions are satisfied: (i) $X \neq \mathcal{M}(A)$; (ii) if $f \in A$ and $\hat{f}$ assumes its maximum modulus at a point of $\mathcal{M}(A) \backslash X$, then f is constant.

Theorem 24.   *Let A be a function algebra on a compact space X. Then* (a) *if A has global measures and $X \neq \mathcal{M}(A)$, A is a maximum modulus algebra;* (b) *if A is a maximum modulus algebra, A is antisymmetric.*

Proof.   (a) Take $f \in A$ such that $|\hat{f}(a)| = \|f\|$ for some $a \in \mathcal{M}(A) \backslash X$. We may assume that $\hat{f}(a) = 1 = \|f\|$. If A has global measures, then a has a representing measure μ whose closed support is X. But $1 = \int f \, d\mu = \int \mathrm{Re}\,(f)\, d\mu$, so $1 - \mathrm{Re}\,(f) \geq 0$ and $\int (1 - \mathrm{Re}\,(f))\, d\mu = 0$. Hence, since $1 - \mathrm{Re}\,(f)$ is continuous, $1 - \mathrm{Re}\,(f) = 0$ on supp $\mu = X$. Thus $f = 1$.

(b) Suppose that A is a maximum modulus algebra. There is a point $a \in \mathcal{M}(A) \backslash X$. Take a representing measure μ for a. Then μ is concentrated on a maximal antisymmetric set $K \in \mathcal{K}_A$, and we need only show that $K = X$. If not, there is a function $f \in A$ with $\|f\| = 1$, $f = 1$ on K, but f not constant, since K is an intersection of peak sets. But then $1 = \int_K f \, d\mu = \int f \, d\mu = \hat{f}(a) = \|f\|$, and $\hat{f}$ assumes its maximum modulus at a point not in X, contrary to hypothesis. Hence $K = X$ and A is antisymmetric.

A function algebra can have global measures and yet not be an integral domain (hence not analytic or pervasive). For example, consider the double-disk algebra on its Šilov boundary: take $\Gamma_0 = \{(z, 0) : |z| = 1\}$, $\Gamma_1 = \{(z, 1) : |z| = 1\}$, two disjoint copies of the unit circle, and let $X = \Gamma_0 \cup \Gamma_1$. Let A consist of all $f \in C(X)$ such that there are functions f_0, f_1 in the disk algebra with $f_0(z) = f(z, 0)$, $f_1(z) = f(z, 1)$ if $|z| = 1$, and $f_0(0) = f_1(0)$. Then if Δ_0, Δ_1 are the corresponding copies of the closed unit disk, $\mathcal{M}(A) = \Delta_0 \cup \Delta_1$ with the centers identified. A is certainly not an integral domain, but every point of $\mathcal{M}(A) \backslash X$ has a global representing measure.

We know that the origin has two badly singular representing measures, so the measure which is $\dfrac{1}{4\pi} dt$ on Γ_0 and $\dfrac{1}{4\pi} dt$ on Γ_1 represents the origin (i.e., the "center"). If $z_0 = re^{i\theta}$, $0 < r < 1$, let μ be $\dfrac{1}{2\pi}\left(P_r(\theta - t) - \dfrac{1 - r}{1 + r}\right) dt$ on Γ_0 and $\dfrac{1}{2\pi}\dfrac{1 - r}{1 + r} dt$ on Γ_1, where $\{P_r\}$ are the Poisson kernels. Then μ is a (positive) global representing measure for $(z_0, 0)$. Similarly, we obtain a global measure for $(z_0, 1)$. Thus we have a computational proof that A is an algebra with global measures. (Also cf. Exercise 6.)

A function algebra A is a *maximal subalgebra* of $C(X)$ iff $A \neq C(X)$ and A is contained properly in no proper closed subalgebra of $C(X)$.

Theorem 25. *For a maximal subalgebra A of $C(X)$, the following are equivalent: (a) A is pervasive; (b) A is analytic; (c) A is an integral domain; (d) A is antisymmetric; (e) A is essential.*

Proof. We need only verify that (e) implies (a) when A is maximal. The proof is identical to the one we gave for the boundary value algebra. Given a proper closed set F in X, F nonvoid, let $B = \{g \in C(X) : g|_F \in A_F\}$. B is a closed subalgebra of $C(X)$ containing A. Since A does not contain the ideal of all $g \in C(X)$ which vanish on F, $B \neq A$. By maximality, $B = C(X)$, so $A_F = C(F)$, which shows that A is pervasive.

If we restrict a maximal algebra A to its essential set E, we obtain an essential maximal subalgebra of $C(E)$. In particular, $A|_E$ is antisymmetric, so E is a set of antisymmetry for A. There is another way to look at this result which may be of interest.

Theorem 26. *Let A be a maximal subalgebra of $C(X)$. Then there is exactly one maximal antisymmetric set for A in X which is not a point, and this set is the essential set for A.*

Proof. Since $A \neq C(X)$, at least one such set is not a point, by Bishop's theorem. Assume that there are distinct maximal antisymmetric sets K_1, K_2 such that $A|_{K_i} \neq C(K_i)$ for $i = 1, 2$. We derive a contradiction.

Since $A \mid K_1 \neq C(K_1)$, some nonzero Borel measure μ concentrated on K_1 annihilates A. Let I be the ideal $\{g \in C(X) : g = 0 \text{ on } K_1\}$, and let B be the closure of $A + I$. Then B is a closed subalgebra of $C(X)$ containing A. $B \neq C(X)$ since $0 \neq \mu \in B^{\perp}$, but $B \neq A$ since $B|_{K_2} = I|_{K_2} = C(K_2)$. This contradicts maximality of A.

So there is exactly one $K \in \mathscr{K}$ such that $A|_K \neq C(K)$, i.e., such that K is not a point. Since the essential set E is the closure of the union of the non-point maximal antisymmetric sets, $E = K$.

Corollary. *If A is a maximal subalgebra of $C(X)$, there is exactly one maximal set of antisymmetry for $\hat{A}$ in $\mathscr{M}(A)$ which is not a point.*

Now let's establish an invariance property of analyticity for function algebras.

Theorem 27. *Let A be a function algebra, and let S be a closed boundary for A. Suppose that $f \in A$ and that f vanishes on a relatively open subset U of S. Then $\hat{f}$ vanishes on the complement of A-hull $(S \backslash U)$ in the maximal ideal space of A.*

Proof. Let $a \in \mathscr{M}(A)$, $g \in A$. Then since $f = 0$ on U and S is a boundary for A, $|\hat{f}(a)| |\hat{g}(a)| \leq \|f\|_{S \backslash U} \|g\|_{S \backslash U}$. The same is true with g replaced by g^n, so if $\hat{f}(a) \neq 0$ we have $|\hat{g}(a)|^n \leq c(\|g\|_{S \backslash U})^n$ for every positive integer n, where $c = \|f\|_{S \backslash U} |\hat{f}(a)|^{-1}$. Take nth roots and let $n \to \infty$. We obtain $|\hat{g}(a)| \leq \|g\|_{S \backslash U}$. So if $\hat{f}(a) \neq 0$, $a \in A$-hull $(S \backslash U)$.

Corollary. *Suppose that A is a function algebra, and that A is analytic on its maximal ideal space; i.e., $\hat{A}$ is an analytic algebra. Then A is analytic on its Šilov boundary.*

For if $f \in A$ and f vanishes on a nonvoid open subset U of $\Gamma(A)$, then by Theorem 27, $\hat{f}$ vanishes on the open set $\mathscr{M}(A) \backslash A$-hull $(\Gamma \backslash U)$. By hypothesis, either $\hat{f} = 0$ or A-hull $(\Gamma \backslash U) = \mathscr{M}(A)$. But the second alternative means that $\Gamma \backslash U$ is a closed boundary for A, which is impossible. So $\hat{f} = 0$ and hence $f \mid \Gamma = 0$. (We have proved slightly more than is asserted in the Corollary: for any function algebra A, if $f \in A$ vanishes on a nonvoid relatively open subset of $\Gamma(A)$, then $\hat{f}$ vanishes on a nonvoid open subset of $\mathscr{M}(A)$.)

Here is an example which shows that the Šilov boundary cannot be replaced by an arbitrary closed boundary in the last corollary. Let A be the disk algebra, and let $S = T^1 \cup \{0\}$. S is a boundary for A and z vanishes on $\{0\}$, a nonvoid open subset of S. So A is not analytic on S. Nevertheless A is analytic on $\Delta = \mathscr{M}(A)$ (naturally).

Let's return to the notation of Theorem 27. We showed that if $f = 0$ on U, then $\hat{f}(a) = 0$ for all $a \notin \widetilde{S \backslash U}$. But in fact, given $a \notin \widetilde{S \backslash U}$, $\exists \lambda$, $0 < \lambda \leq 1$, such that $|\hat{f}(a)| \leq (\sup_U |f|)^{\lambda} (\sup_{S \setminus U} |f|)^{1-\lambda}$ for every $f \in A$. (This is an abstract form of the Hadamard three circles theorem of complex analysis.) To prove this, take a Jensen measure μ for a which is concentrated on the closed boundary S. Then $\int f \, d\mu = \hat{f}(a)$ and $\log |\hat{f}(a)| \leq \int_S \log |f| \, d\mu \, (f \in A)$. So if $M_1 = \sup_U |f|$, $M_2 = \sup_{S \setminus U} |f|$, then

$$\log |\hat{f}(a)| \leq \int_U \log |f| \, d\mu + \int_{S \setminus U} \log |f| \, d\mu$$

$$\leq \lambda \log M_1 + (1 - \lambda) \log M_2,$$

where $\lambda = \mu(U)$. If $\lambda = 0$, then μ is concentrated on $S \setminus U$, and then a belongs to A-hull $(S \setminus U)$, contrary to hypothesis. Hence $0 < \lambda \leq 1$ and $|\hat{f}(a)| \leq M_1{}^{\lambda} M_2{}^{1-\lambda}$.

EXERCISE SET 7.4

1. Can a pervasive sup norm algebra fail to separate points?

2. If $C(X)$ is an integral domain, show that X is a point.

3. Let X be the union of two closed disks (in the plane) which are externally tangent, e.g., $\bar{D}(0; 1) \cup \bar{D}(2; 1)$. Let A be the algebra $A(X)$ of continuous functions on X which are analytic on the interior of X. Show that A is antisymmetric but not an integral domain (hence not analytic, not pervasive).

4. Let $X = \Delta \times [0, 1]$, Δ the closed unit disk. Let A be the set of functions $f \in C(X)$ such that $z \to f(z, t)$ is in the disk algebra on every slice $(0 \leq t \leq 1)$. Show that A is an essential algebra which is not antisymmetric.

5. Suppose that A is a maximal subalgebra of $C(X)$. Prove that $X = \Gamma(A)$.

6. Let A be the double-disk algebra on $X = \Gamma_0 \cup \Gamma_1$. Show that $\mathscr{M}(A) \setminus X$ is a Gleason part in $\mathscr{M}(A)$. Let a be the "center" in $\mathscr{M}(A)$ and $b \neq a$, $b \in \mathscr{M}(A) \setminus X$. Note that a has a representing measure μ whose closed support is all of X. Use the results of Chapter IV to prove that b also has a global representing measure.

7. Let A be a function algebra on X. Prove that if A is analytic on X, then A is analytic on $\Gamma(A)$.

8. Let γ be a Jordan curve in the plane, and let Ω be the "interior" of γ. Let A_γ be the set of functions continuous on $\bar{\Omega} = \Omega \cup \gamma$ and analytic on Ω. Suppose that $f \in A_\gamma$ and f vanishes on an open arc α of γ. Prove that $f = 0$.

7.5 SEPARATION PROPERTIES

Let X be a compact space. Since X is normal, $C(X)$ has the following property: given disjoint compact sets F_0, F_1 in X, $\exists f \in C(X)$ with $f(F_0) = \{0\}$, $f(F_1) = \{1\}$. In this section we are concerned with function algebras which have this property or similar separating properties on X. (Note that by Urysohn's lemma the function $f \in C(X)$ can be chosen to have range in [0, 1]. For more general algebras this will no longer be possible.)

Let A be a family of functions on X. We say that A is *regular* iff for each x_0 in X and for each compact set F not containing x_0, $\exists f \in A$ with $f(x_0) = 0$, $f(F) = \{1\}$. A is *normal* iff for each pair of disjoint compact sets F_0, F_1 in X, $\exists f \in A$ with $f(F_0) = \{0\}$, $f(F_1) = \{1\}$. A is *approximately normal* iff for each $\varepsilon > 0$ and for each pair of disjoint compact sets F_0, F_1 in X, $\exists f \in A$ with $|f| < \varepsilon$ on F_0 and $|1 - f| < \varepsilon$ on F_1.

Examples of normal, or even regular, function algebras (other than $C(X)$, of course) are difficult to construct, and for several years it was conjectured that none existed. An example of a regular function algebra which is not normal can be given as follows. Let H^∞ be the subalgebra of L^∞ of the unit circle consisting of all functions whose negative order Fourier coefficients all vanish. (H^∞ can be identified via a Poisson integral representation with the algebra of bounded analytic functions on the open unit disk.) Then $L^\infty = C(Z)$ where Z is the maximal ideal space of L^∞, and H^∞ is a function algebra on Z. Above each point α on the unit circle lies a fiber $\mathcal{M}_\alpha = \{h \in \mathcal{M}(H^\infty) : h(z) = \alpha\}$ in the maximal ideal space of H^∞. Each $\mathcal{M}_\alpha$ is a peak set for $\hat{H}^\infty$, so $A_\alpha = \hat{H}^\infty \mid \mathcal{M}_\alpha$ is a function algebra on $\mathcal{M}_\alpha$. It turns out that the restriction of A_α to $Z \cap \mathcal{M}_\alpha$ is a regular function algebra isomorphic to A_α. For details see the last chapter in [E].

In [120] one can find an example of a compact plane set X, a sort of infinitely superimposed family of Swiss cheeses, such that $R(X)$ is a normal function algebra but $R(X) \neq C(X)$.

We will not discuss these examples in any detail but will merely collect some general properties of regular function algebras.

Approximately normal algebras are easier to find. In particular, we shall see that Dirichlet algebras are approximately normal, as are the algebras $R(X)$ when X is a compact planar set whose interior is empty. (Since $R(X) = C(X)$ iff $R(X)$ is a Dirichlet algebra, this will provide us with an abundance of non-Dirichlet approximately normal function algebras.)

We begin by noting that bounded approximate normality is possible only for $C(X)$.

Theorem 28. *Let A be a closed subspace of $C(X)$. Suppose that there is a constant M such that for every $\varepsilon > 0$ and every pair F_0, F_1 of disjoint closed sets in X, A contains a function f such that $\|f\| \leq M$, $|f| < \varepsilon$ on F_0, and $|1 - f| < \varepsilon$ on F_1. Then $A = C(X)$.*

Proof. We have to show that if $\mu \in A^\perp$, then $\mu = 0$. Let $\varepsilon > 0$ and let F be any compact set in X. Choose V open in X with $F \subset V$ and $|\mu|(V \backslash F) < \varepsilon$. By hypothesis, $\exists f \in A$ with $\|f\| \leq M$, $|f| < \varepsilon$ on $X \backslash V$, $|1 - f| < \varepsilon$ on F.

Since $f \in A$ and $\mu \in A^\perp$, $\int f \, d\mu = 0$. So

$$\left| \int_F f \, d\mu \right| = \left| \int_{X \backslash F} f \, d\mu \right| \leq \varepsilon |\mu|(X \backslash V) + M |\mu|(V \backslash F) \leq \varepsilon(M + \|\mu\|).$$

Thus, since $\mu(F) = \int_F f \, d\mu + \int_F (1 - f) \, d\mu$, $|\mu(F)| \leq \varepsilon(M + 2\|\mu\|)$. Since ε is arbitrary, $\mu(F) = 0$. Since F is arbitrary, $\mu = 0$. So $A^\perp = \{0\}$ and $A = C(X)$.

It is clear that if A is approximately normal on X and S is a closed subset of X, then A_S is approximately normal on S.

Lemma 3. *Let A be an approximately normal function algebra on X. Then X is the Šilov boundary of A.*

Proof. This is clear. For if F is any proper closed subset of X and $x_0 \in X \backslash F$, then $\exists f \in A$ with $|f(x)| < \frac{1}{4}$ for each $x \in F$ and $|1 - f(x_0)| < \frac{1}{4}$. Hence $|f(x_0)| > \frac{3}{4} > \|f\|_F$, so F is not a boundary for A.

The next theorem summarizes some of the important properties of approximately normal algebras.

Theorem 29. *Let A be a function algebra on X. Then the following statements are equivalent.*

(a) *A is approximately normal.*

(b) *For each compact set F in X and each open-closed subset G of F, $\chi_G \in A_F$.*

(c) *Every representing measure for A has a connected closed support.*

(d) *If E, F are disjoint closed sets in X, then A-hull $(E \cup F) = A$-hull $(E) \cup A$-hull (F) and the A-hulls of E and F are disjoint.*

Proof. (a) $\Rightarrow$ (b) Let F be compact in X and G open-closed in F. Then G and $F \backslash G$ are disjoint closed sets in X, so for each $n > 0$ in $\mathbf{Z}$, $\exists f_n \in A$ with $|f_n| < 1/n$ on $F \backslash G$, $|1 - f_n| < 1/n$ on G. It is clear that $f_n \to \chi_G$ uniformly on F, so $\chi_G \in A_F$.

(b) $\Rightarrow$ (c) Let μ be a representing measure for A on X. Suppose that $\operatorname{supp} \mu$ is the union of disjoint closed sets E, F. Then by hypothesis, $\chi_E \in A_{E \cup F}$. But A-hull $(\operatorname{supp} \mu) = A$-hull $(E \cup F) = \mathscr{M}(A_{E \cup F})$ is connected, by Theorem 10, §7.2, so χ_E must be constant. Thus E or F is empty, and $\operatorname{supp} \mu$ is connected.

(c) $\Rightarrow$ (d) Take disjoint closed sets E, F in X. Now $\widetilde{E \cup F}$ consists of all $h \in \mathscr{M}(A)$ which have a representing measure concentrated on $E \cup F$. By hypothesis, each such measure has a connected support and must thus be concentrated either on E or on F. So $\widetilde{E \cup F} = \tilde{E} \cup \tilde{F}$.

On the other hand, if $\tilde{E}$ and $\tilde{F}$ meet, then some $h \in \mathscr{M}(A)$ has representing measures μ concentrated on E and ν concentrated on F. But then $\frac{1}{2}(\mu + \nu)$ would be a representing measure for h with disconnected closed support, contrary to hypothesis. So $\tilde{E}$ and $\tilde{F}$ are disjoint.

(d) $\Rightarrow$ (a)   Let E, F be disjoint closed sets in X. By assumption, $\widetilde{E \cup F}$ is the disjoint union of $\tilde{E}$ and $\tilde{F}$. But $\tilde{E} \cup \tilde{F} = \mathscr{M}(A_{E \cup F})$, so Šilov's theorem implies that the characteristic function of E is uniformly approximable on $E \cup F$ by members of A. But this means precisely that A is approximately normal.

Corollary 1.   *Let A be an approximately normal function algebra on X. Then X is connected iff $\mathscr{M}(A)$ is connected.*

Proof.   If X is connected, then $\mathscr{M}(A)$ is connected, by Šilov's theorem. If G is an open-closed set in X, then $\chi_G \in A$ if A is approximately normal, so $\hat{\chi}_G \in C(\mathscr{M}(A))$. Hence if $\mathscr{M}(A)$ is connected, $\hat{\chi}_G$ is constant, so χ_G is constant. Hence if $\mathscr{M}(A)$ is connected, X is connected.

For approximately normal algebras one can strengthen Theorem 29 as follows.

Corollary 2.   *Let A be an approximately normal function algebra on X. Let μ be an extreme point of $b(A^\perp)$. Then supp μ is connected.*

Proof.   Let $S = $ supp μ. We know that $\tilde{S} = \mathscr{M}(A_S)$ is connected. But A_S is approximately normal, so S is connected.

Corollary 3.   *Let A be an approximately normal function algebra on X, and let $\{C_\alpha\}$ be the family of components of X. Then if $f \in C(X)$ and $f \,|C_\alpha \in A|_{C_\alpha}$ for all α, it follows that $f \in A$.*

Proof.   The proof is the same as the proof of Bishop's theorem in §3.3. There each $\mu \in b(A^\perp)^e$ was concentrated on a maximal set of antisymmetry. Now since supp μ is connected, μ is concentrated on some C_α. So if f satisfies the hypothesis of the corollary, every $\mu \in b(A^\perp)^e$ annihilates f, and thus $\in A$.

Corollary 4.   *If X is a compact totally disconnected space, then $C(X)$ is the only approximately normal function algebra on X.*

If A is approximately normal, and if $\{C_\alpha\}$ is the family of components of X, $\{C_\alpha\}$ acts much like the family of maximal antisymmetric sets $\mathscr{K}_A$ (cf. Corollary 3). Observe that since X is compact, each C_α is an intersection of open-closed sets (cf. the Corollary to Lemma 5). Each nonvoid open-closed set $G \subset X$ is a peak set for A (since χ_G belongs to A), so each C_α is an intersection of peak sets. In particular, $A\,|_{C_\alpha}$ is uniformly closed. Nonetheless, the components of X need not be sets of antisymmetry for A (A approximately normal). For an example, see [177].

Theorem 30. *Every Dirichlet algebra is approximately normal.*

For let E, F be disjoint closed sets in X. If A is a Dirichlet algebra on X, then $B = A_{E \cup F}$ is a Dirichlet algebra on $E \cup F$. We must show that $\chi_F \in B$, so we need only prove the following lemma.

Lemma 4. *If A is a Dirichlet algebra on X and F is an open-closed set in X, then $\chi_F \in A$.*

Proof. $\chi_F \in C_R(X)$. So $\exists f \in A$ with $\|\chi_F - \operatorname{Re}(f)\| < \frac{1}{3}$. Hence $f(F)$ and $f(X \backslash F)$ can be enclosed in disjoint rectangular regions R_1, R_0. By Runge's theorem, there are polynomials p_n converging uniformly to 1 on R_1 and to 0 on R_0. Hence $\chi_F = \lim p_n \circ f$ belongs to A.

Corollary. *Let A be a Dirichlet algebra on X. Then every representing measure for A has connected closed support, and so does every $\mu \in b(A^\perp)^e$. Furthermore, if X is totally disconnected, then $A = C(X)$.*

Theorem 31. *If X is a compact set in the plane, then $R(X)$ is approximately normal iff int X is empty.*

Proof. Note first that if $R(X)$ is approximately normal, then $X = \Gamma(R(X)) = \operatorname{bd}(X)$, so int $X = \varnothing$.

Conversely, suppose that int $X = \varnothing$. Let F be closed in X.

Let us show first that $R(X)_F = R(F)$. Every rational function with poles off X has a restriction to F which lies in $R(F)$, so $R(X)_F \subset R(F)$. On the other hand, z and the functions $\dfrac{1}{z - \alpha}$ with $\alpha \in \mathbf{C} \backslash F$ generate $R(F)$; so for the reverse inclusion it will suffice to show that if $\alpha \notin F$, then $(z - \alpha)^{-1}$ can be uniformly approximated by $R(X)$ on F. This is clear for α outside of X, so consider $\alpha \in X \backslash F$. The interior of X is empty, so there are α_n in $\mathbf{C} \backslash X$ converging to α. So $z - \alpha_n \to z - \alpha$ uniformly on F. Since inversion is continuous in a Banach algebra, $(z - \alpha_n)^{-1} \to (z - \alpha)^{-1}$ in $R(F)$. Hence $(z - \alpha)^{-1} \in R(X)_F$, and we have proved the assertion.

In particular, the $R(X)$-hull of F, considered as a subset of $X = \mathscr{M}(R(X))$, equals F; i.e., $F = \mathscr{M}(R(X)_F)$. Now take any open-closed set $G \subset F$. By Šilov's theorem, $\chi_G \in R(X)_F$, so we conclude that $R(X)$ is approximately normal. (We can avoid the use of Šilov's theorem here as follows. G and $F \backslash G$ are disjoint closed sets, so they have disjoint open *nbhds* U, V. But then the function which is 1 on U and 0 on V is analytic on a *nbhd* of F, so by Exercise 2, §5.3 (or an explicit integral formula—find one), its restriction to F is in $R(F) = R(X)_F$. This means that $\chi_G \in R(X)_F$, as we asserted above.)

The Swiss cheese algebras $R(X)$ are thus examples of non-Dirichlet approximately normal function algebras. Observe too that if int $X = \varnothing$, and if $K \subset X$ is a maximal antisymmetric set for $R(X)$, then $R(K) = R(X)_K$ is an antisymmetric approximately normal algebra. So if $R(X) \neq C(X)$, at least one $R(K)$ is a proper antisymmetric approximately normal algebra. At the other extreme, Steen [177] has constructed an approximately normal $R(X)$ which contains a nonconstant real-valued function (with X connected—if X is not connected, there's no problem).

We know that Dirichlet algebras are approximately normal. But a log-modular algebra need not be approximately normal. For example, H^∞ is a logmodular algebra whose Šilov boundary Z is totally disconnected, yet $H^\infty \neq L^\infty = C(Z)$, so H^∞ is not approximately normal on Z.

We mentioned above that a component of a compact space is an inter-section of open-closed sets. Let us show this. First we prove a topological lemma.

Lemma 5. *Let $\{F_v\}$ be a family of open-closed sets in a compact space X, and let $F = \bigcap\limits_v F_v$. If there exist disjoint closed sets A, B in X such that $F = A \cup B$, then there exist disjoint open-closed sets V, W with $A \subset V$ and $B \subset W$.*

Proof. X is normal, so A, B have disjoint open *nbhds* C, D. Set $M = X \backslash D$, $N = X \backslash C$. Then M, N are closed sets whose union is X, and $A \cap N = \varnothing = B \cap M$, while $A \subset C \subset M$, $B \subset D \subset N$.

Since $M \cap N \cap F$ is empty, by compactness there are indices $v_1, \ldots, v_n$ such that $M \cap N \cap F_0 = \varnothing$ where $F_0 = \bigcap\limits_{j=1}^{n} F_{v_j}$. F_0 is open-closed in X. Set $V = M \cap F_0$, $W = N \cap F_0$. Then V, W are disjoint closed sets in X and $A \subset V$, $B \subset W$. It remains to show that V, W are open. But bd$(M) \cap F_0 = M \cap (\overline{X \backslash M}) \cap F_0 \subset M \cap N \cap F_0 = \varnothing$, so $V = $ int $M \cap F_0$ is open. Similarly, W is open.

Corollary. *Let C be a connected nonempty subset of a compact space X, and let D be the component of X which contains C. Then D is the intersection of all open-closed sets in X which contain C.*

Proof. Let F be the intersection of all open-closed sets containing C. If U is open-closed and $C \subset U$, then $U \cap D$ and $(X \backslash U) \cap D$ are disjoint closed sets whose union is the connected set D, so one of them is empty. But $U \cap D$ contains $C \neq \varnothing$, so $(X \backslash U) \cap D$ must be empty. Hence $D \subset U$. Taking the intersection of all such U, we see that $D \subset F$.

D is a maximal connected set containing C, so if F is shown to be connected, we'll know that $F = D$. So assume that F is the union of disjoint closed sets A, B. By the lemma, there are disjoint open-closed sets V, W in X with $A \subset V$ and $B \subset W$. Since $D \subset F \subset V \cup W$, $V \cap D$ and $W \cap D$ form a disjoint closed cover of D, so one of them is empty. Say $W \cap D = \varnothing$. Then

$D \subset V$. So V is an open-closed set containing C, and thus $F \subset V$. But then $B = B \cap F \subset W \cap F \subset W \cap V = \varnothing$, so B is empty. Hence F is connected, as was to be shown.

We can use the corollary to see another application of Šilov's theorem on idempotents.

Lemma 6. *Let A be a function algebra on X. Then every component of $\mathscr{M}(A)$ contains a component of X.*

Proof. Let D be a component of $\mathscr{M}(A)$. Then D is an intersection of open-closed sets in $\mathscr{M}(A)$. By Šilov's theorem, the characteristic function of each such set belongs to $\hat{A}$, so D is an intersection of peak sets for $\hat{A}$. Hence $D \cap X$ is not empty. Take $x_0 \in D \cap X$, and let C be the component of X containing x_0. Since C is a connected set in $\mathscr{M}(A)$ containing x_0, $C \subset D$.

Now let us establish some facts about regular and normal function algebras. Further results can be found in [E] and [F].

Theorem 32. *Let A be a function algebra. Suppose that $\hat{A}$ is regular on $\mathscr{M}(A)$. Then $\hat{A}$ is normal. (An algebra regular on its maximal ideal space is normal.)*

Proof. We may as well replace A by $\hat{A}$ and assume that A is regular on $X = \mathscr{M}(A)$. Let F, S be disjoint closed sets in X, and let $I = kF$, $J = kS$ be their kernels. Note that if $x \in X$, then either $f(x) \neq 0$ for some $f \in I$, or $g(x) \neq 0$ for some $x \in J$. (For if $x \in F$, then $x \notin S$, so $\exists g \in A$ with $g(x) \neq 0$, $g \mid S = 0$; while if $x \notin F$, $\exists f \in A$ with $f(x) \neq 0$, $f \mid F = 0$.) So $I \cup J$ is contained in no maximal ideal of A. Hence the ideal generated by $I \cup J$ is A; i.e., $A = I + J$. So $\exists f \in I$ such that $(1 - f) \in J$. That is, $f \in A$, $f = 0$ on F, $f = 1$ on S. So A is normal.

Theorem 33. *Suppose that A is a normal function algebra on X. Then $X = \mathscr{M}(A)$ (so $A = \hat{A}$).*

Proof. Let $h \in \mathscr{M}(A)$. Take a minimal support set S for h, and let μ be a representing measure for h concentrated on S. Note that if $f \in A$ and f vanishes on a nonvoid relatively open subset V of S, then $h(f) = 0$. For if not, then $\nu = \dfrac{1}{h(f)} f\mu$ is a complex measure which represents h and is supported on $S \backslash V$, contradicting minimality of S. But then normality of A implies that S is a point $x_0 \in X$, and hence $h = x_0$ and $\mathscr{M}(A) = X$. (For if S contains distinct points x, y, then since S is a compact space, x and y have disjoint closed *nbhds* in the space X. So there are relatively open subsets V_0, V_1 of S with $x \in V_0$, $y \in V_1$, and $\overline{V}_0 \cap \overline{V}_1 = \varnothing$. By normality, $\exists f \in A$ with $f = 0$ on $\overline{V}_0$, $1 - f = 0$ on $\overline{V}_1$. It follows that $h(f) = h(1 - f) = 0$. This contradiction implies that S is a singleton set.)

Theorem 34.   *Let A be a regular function algebra on X. Let $x_0 \in X$ and let m be a Jensen measure for x_0. Then m is the point mass at x_0.*

Proof.   Let $x \neq x_0$, $x \in X$, and take a closed *nbhd S* of x with $x_0 \notin S$. Then $\exists f \in A$ with $f(x_0) = 1$, $f(S) = \{0\}$. Since $0 = \log|f(x_0)| \leq \int \log|f| \, dm$, $\log|f|$ is integrable with respect to m, yet $\log|f| = -\infty$ on S. So $m(S) = 0$. Hence supp $m = \{x_0\}$, so $m = \delta_{x_0}$.

Note that if X is a compact set in the plane, and if $R(X)$ is a proper normal function algebra on X (as in McKissick's example, cf. [120]), then some point in X is not a Choquet boundary point for $R(X)$. (Otherwise $R(X) = C(X)$; see §5.3.) Thus there are homomorphisms of $R(X)$ which have Jensen measures not supported on the Choquet boundary. Each homomorphism has a unique Jensen measure, but not all representing measures are unique.

Using Jensen measures, we can extend Proposition 2 at the end of §7.2 to countable decompositions.

Lemma 7.   *Let A be a function algebra on X, and let μ be a Jensen measure for $a \in \mathcal{M}(A)$. Then if F is a closed set in X such that $\mu(F) > 0$ and $A|_F$ is closed in $C(F)$, then $a \in \mathcal{M}(A|_F)$.*

Proof.   The mapping $f|F \to \hat{f}(a)$ on $A|_F$ is well defined. For if f, g are in A and $f|F = g|F$, then $\log|\hat{f}(a) - \hat{g}(a)| \leq \int_X \log|f - g| \, d\mu = -\infty$, so $\hat{f}(a) = \hat{g}(a)$. Hence a determines a complex homomorphism of the function algebra $A|_F$.

Theorem 35.   *Let A be a function algebra on X. Suppose that $X = \bigcup\limits_{i=1}^{\infty} F_i$, where F_i is closed in X and $A|_{F_i}$ is closed in $C(F_i)$ for each i. Then $\mathcal{M}(A) = \bigcup\limits_{i=1}^{\infty} \mathcal{M}(A|_{F_i})$.*

Proof.   Take $a \in \mathcal{M}(A)$. Let μ be a Jensen measure for a. (One exists.) Then $\mu(F_i) > 0$ for some i, so $a \in \mathcal{M}(A|_{F_i})$. Hence $\mathcal{M}(A) \subset \bigcup\limits_{i=1}^{\infty} \mathcal{M}(A|_{F_i})$. Conversely, for each i, $\mathcal{M}(A|_{F_i}) = A$-hull $(F_i) \subset \mathcal{M}(A)$, so equality is proved.

The results of §3.4 on restriction algebras also extend to countable decompositions of X.

Theorem 36.   *Let A be a function algebra on X. Let E be the essential set of A. Then $X \backslash E = P \cap Q$ where $P = \{x \in X : x$ has a closed nbhd F such that $A|_F = C(F)\}$ and Q is the Choquet boundary of A.*

Proof. One inclusion is easy to prove. Take $x \in X \backslash E$. Since x has a closed *nbhd* disjoint from E, $x \in P$. (See (3) in §4.4.) Let U be an open set containing x. Then $\exists u \in C(X)$ such that $0 \le u \le 1$, $u(x) = 1$, and $u = 0$ outside $U \cap (X \backslash E)$. Hence $u \in A$ and $x \in \{y \in X : |u(y)| = \|u\|\} \subset U$. So $x \in Q$. (Alternately, we can quote Corollary 1, §4.4.)

Conversely, take $x \in P \cap Q$. Choose an open set V with $x \in V$ and $A|_{\overline{V}} = C(\overline{V})$. Find $f \in A$ such that $f(x) = 1$, $\|f\| = 1$, and $|f| < 1$ on $X \backslash V$. Since $X \backslash V$ is compact, there is a positive integer k such that $|f^k| < \frac{1}{2}$ on $X \backslash V$. Let $f_0 = f^k$. Then $f_0 \in A$, $f_0(x) = 1 = \|f_0\|$, and $|f_0| < \frac{1}{2}$ on $X \backslash V$. Choose an open set U about x such that $|1 - f_0| < \frac{1}{4}$ on U. Then $U \subset V$, and the compact sets $f_0(\overline{U})$, $f_0(X \backslash V)$ lie in disjoint disks in the plane. So by Runge's theorem there are polynomials p_n ($n \ge 1$) such that $p_n(f)$ converges uniformly to 1 on $\overline{U}$ and $p_n(f)$ converges uniformly to 0 on $X \backslash V$. Since $A|_{\overline{V}} = C(\overline{V})$, $\exists g \in A$ with $g = 0$ on $\overline{V} \backslash U$ and $g(x_0) = 1$. Set $g_n = p_n(f)g$. Then $\{g_n\}$ converges uniformly on X, and $g_0 = \lim g_n$ satisfies these conditions: $g_0 = 0$ on $X \backslash U$, $g_0(x_0) = 1$, $g_0 \in A$.

Set $W = \{y \in X : |1 - g_0(y)| < \frac{1}{4}\}$; W is an open *nbhd* of x and $W \subset U \subset V$. Let h be any function in $C(X)$ which is zero on $X \backslash W$. Since $A|_{\overline{V}} = C(\overline{V})$, $\exists h_0 \in A$ such that $h_0(y) = h(y)/g_0(y)$ ($y \in W$), $h_0(y) = 0$ ($y \in V \backslash W$). Then $h = h_0 g_0 \in A$. So A contains every continuous function which is zero on $X \backslash W$. Hence $E \subset X \backslash W$, so x has a *nbhd* disjoint from E.

Remark. If A is approximately normal on X, then $X \backslash E = P$. (So if $x \in P$, then x belongs to $c(A) = Q$. For let $x \in P$. Choose V open about x such that $A|_{\overline{V}} = C(\overline{V})$. Take an open set U such that $x \in U \subset \overline{U} \subset V$. Since A is approximately normal, there are f_n ($n \ge 1$) in A with $f_n \to 1$ uniformly on $\overline{U}$, $f_n \to 0$ uniformly on $X \backslash V$. We can now argue as above that if $h \in C(X)$ and $h = 0$ on $X \backslash U$, then $h \in A$. Hence $E \subset X \backslash U$, so $x \notin E$. Thus $P \subset X \backslash E$.) For algebras in general, $X \backslash E$ does not always coincide with the set P defined in the theorem. (See Exercise 8.) Mullins [129] has shown that if $X = \mathscr{M}(A)$ and X is metrizable (so Q is the set of peak points for A), then $E = X \backslash P$. His proof uses the local maximum modulus theorem of §7.7. The argument given in the proof of Theorem 36 is a modification of Mullins' argument.

Theorem 37. *Let A be a function algebra on X. Suppose that $X = \bigcup_{i=1}^{\infty} F_i$, where F_i is closed in X and $A|_{F_i} = C(F_i)$ for each i. Then $A = C(X)$.*

Proof. First we observe that A is approximately normal. For if F is any compact set in X, it follows from Theorem 35 that A_F has maximal ideal space F. (Set $E_i = F \cap F_i$. Then $F = \bigcup_{i=1}^{\infty} E_i$ and $A_F|_{E_i} = C(E_i)$ for each i. So $\mathscr{M}(A_F) = \bigcup \mathscr{M}(C(E_i)) = \bigcup E_i = F$.) This clearly implies that A is approximately normal. (For example, see Exercise 5.)

So the essential set E for A is given by $E = X \backslash P$, where $P = \{x \in X : x$ has a *nbhd* V such that $A|_V = C(\overline{V})\}$. Suppose that E is nonvoid. Then E is a compact space and $E = \bigcup_{i=1}^{\infty} (E \cap F_i)$, so by the Baire category theorem some $E \cap F_j$ has a nonempty interior in E. Hence $E \cap F_j$ contains a closed set V which is a *nbhd*, relative to E, of some point of E. But $A|_{F_j} = C(F_j)$, so $A|_V = C(V)$. This means that $V \subset P$, which is disjoint from E. Since $V \subset E$ and V is nonvoid, this is a contradiction. So E is empty, and hence $A = C(X)$. (The careful reader will observe that we have used the fact that $A|_E = A_E$ is approximately normal and has essential set E.)

EXERCISE SET   7.5

1. Let A be an approximately normal function algebra and $K \in \mathcal{K}_A$ a maximal set of antisymmetry for A. Prove that K is connected.

2. Let A be a proper pervasive subalgebra of $C(X)$. Prove that A is approximately normal iff X is connected.

3. Let A be a function algebra on X, and let E be the essential set of A. Show that A is approximately normal iff A_E is approximately normal.
   Show that a maximal subalgebra of $C(X)$ is approximately normal iff its essential set is connected.

4. Prove that each of the following is equivalent to the others if A is a function algebra on X.
   (i) A is approximately normal.
   (ii) For every compact set $F \subset X$, the map $U \to U \cap F$ is one-one from the family of open-closed sets in $\mathcal{M}(A_F)$ onto the family of open-closed sets in F.
   (iii) For each compact set $F \subset X$, the map $C \to C'$ is one-one from the family of components of F to the family of components of $\mathcal{M}(A_F)$. Here C' is the component of $\tilde{F}$ which contains C.
      If (i) holds, then in (ii) the inverse map is $U \cap F \to A$-hull $(U \cap F)$, and in (iii) the map $C \to C'$ is given by $C' = A$-hull (C).

5. If X is a compact set in the plane and int X is empty, prove that either $R(X) = C(X)$ or some maximal antisymmetric set K for $R(X)$ has positive Lebesgue measure.

6. Prove that a singly generated function algebra A on X cannot be normal unless $A = C(X)$. (McKissick's example has two generators.)

7. Let A be the subalgebra of $C(\Delta)$ consisting of all functions f whose restriction to $X = \{0\} \cup T$ belongs to the restriction of the disk algebra to $\{0\} \cup T$. Show that the essential set of A is X but 0 has a closed *nbhd* on which A is all continuous functions.

7.6 RESTRICTIONS OF MEASURES

Let X be a compact space. Given μ in $M(X)$ and a Borel set F in X, we define the measure μ_F by setting $\mu_F(E) = \mu(E \cap F)$ for Borel sets E in X; i.e., $\mu_F = \chi_F \mu$. Note that $\mu_F = 0$ iff $|\mu|(F) = 0$ (equivalently, iff $\mu(E) = 0$ for every Borel set E contained in F).

Suppose that F is a peak set for a function algebra A on X. If $f \in A$ is a peaking function for F, then $f^n \to \chi_F$ boundedly as $n \to \infty$. Hence by the dominated convergence theorem, $f^n \mu$ converges to μ_F in the w^*-topology, for every μ in $M(X)$. Since A is an algebra, $f^n \mu$ annihilates A if $\mu \in A^\perp$, so we conclude that for every μ in $A^\perp$, μ_F also belongs to $A^\perp$. This is so when F is a peak set for A. If F is an intersection of peak sets, then we have the same conclusion by the regularity of $\mu \in A^\perp$. (Given $g \in A$ and $\varepsilon > 0$, choose an open set U with $F \subset U$ and $\|g\| \, |\mu|(U \backslash F) < \varepsilon$. There is a peak set S with $F \subset S \subset U$, so $\left| \int g \, d\mu_F \right| = \left| \int g \, d(\mu_S - \mu_F) \right| < \varepsilon$ if $\mu \in A^\perp$. Hence $\mu_F \in A^\perp$.)

The converse is also true: if F is a compact subset of X, and if $\mu_F \in A^\perp$ for every μ in $A^\perp$, then F is an intersection of peak sets for A. The strategy of the proof is as follows. Let B_0 be the set of all functions in A which are constant on F. B_0 is a sup norm algebra on X, so B_0 is isomorphic to a sup norm algebra B on the space X^* obtained from X by identifying F to a point p. X^* is compact, and we have to show that p is an intersection of peak sets for B. The first step is to prove that B separates points and hence is a function algebra on X^*. The second is then to show that p belongs to the Choquet boundary of B. If this is not the case, then there is a real measure σ on X^* which represents p with respect to B such that $\sigma(\{p\}) = 0$. (See the proof of Theorem 17, §5.5.) So $\nu = \delta_p - \sigma$ is a nonzero annihilator of B with $\nu(\{p\}) = 1$. But because of the hypothesis on F, one can show that for every $\nu \in B^\perp$, $\nu(\{p\}) = 0$, so this is a contradiction. Thus p does belong to the Choquet boundary of B, and the assertion follows.

The details of the two major steps in the argument above are complicated and tricky. The proofs use facts about restrictions of measures to which we turn now.

Our first task is to obtain a dual formulation of Theorem 3, §7.1. So let A be a closed subspace of $C(X)$, and let F be a compact subset of X. We can embed $M(F)$ in $M(X)$ in a natural way: to each $\nu_0 \in M(F)$ there corresponds $\nu \in M(X)$ such that $\nu(E) = \nu_0(E \cap F)$ (E Borel in X). There will be no harm in identifying ν_0 with $\nu = \nu_F$, and we make the identification.

Let $r: A \to A|_F$ be the restriction map $f \to f|F$. Then r^* maps $(A|_F)^* = A_F^* = M(F)/A_F^\perp$ into $A^* = M(X)/A^\perp$, where $r^*(L) = L \circ r$ (L in A_F^*). r^* is continuous and linear. A bounded linear map has a closed range iff its adjoint has a closed range, so $A|_F$ is closed in $C(F)$ iff the range of r^* is closed in A^*. (See Theorem 15, §1.6.)

Note that $A_F^\perp = \{\nu \in M(F): \int \varphi \, d\nu = 0, \ \forall \varphi \in A|_F\} = M(F) \cap A^\perp$, so $r^*: M(F)/M(F) \cap A^\perp \to M(X)/A^\perp$. The action of r^* is given explicitly as follows: $r^*(v + A_F{}^\perp) = v + A^\perp$, $v \in M(F)$. (Indeed, $r^*(L)(f) = L(f \mid F)$, $L \in (A \mid_F)^*, f \in A$. So if L is determined by $v \in M(F), L(f \mid F) = \int_F (f \mid F)\, dv = \int_X f\, dv$, so $r^*(L)$ is also determined by $v \in M(X)$.) Clearly if $v \in M(F)$, then $\|r^*(v + A_F{}^\perp)\| = \|v + A^\perp\| = \text{dist }(v, A^\perp) \le \text{dist }(v, A_F{}^\perp)$ (since $A_F{}^\perp \subset A^\perp) = \|v + A_F{}^\perp\|$, so r^* is norm-decreasing. Since $v \in A^\perp$ implies that $v \in M(F) \cap A^\perp$ ($v \in M(F)$), r^* is one-one. Hence by the closed graph theorem, the range of r^* is closed (or equivalently, complete) iff r^* has a continuous inverse. The condition for this is that $(r^*)^{-1}$ is bounded, i.e., $\exists c > 0$ such that $\|v + A_F{}^\perp\| \le c\,\|v + A^\perp\|$ for every $v \in M(F)$. (If such a c exists, necessarily $c \ge 1$.)

Theorem 38.   *Let A be a closed subspace of $C(X)$, and let F be a compact set in X. Then* (a) $A \mid_F$ *is closed in $C(F)$ iff there is a number $c \ge 1$ such that* (i) $\|v + A_F{}^\perp\| \le c\,\|v + A^\perp\|$ *for all $v \in M(F)$ (equivalently, dist $(v, M(F) \cap A^\perp)$ $\le c$ dist $(v, A^\perp)$);* (b) *when* (i) *holds, $A \mid_F$ and A/kF are topologically isomorphic, and c dominates the norm of the isomorphism;* (c) (i) *holds with $c = 1$ iff $A \mid_F$ and A/kF are linearly isometric (via the natural map).*

Proof.   We have proved part (a) already. Suppose that (i) holds. Then $r : A \to A \mid_F$ has a closed range, and the kernel of r is $kF = \{f \in A : f \mid F = 0\}$; hence the induced map $T : A/kF \to A \mid_F$ is a continuous linear isomorphism. (Again we use the closed graph theorem.) The adjoint map $T^* : A_F{}^* \to (A/kF)^*$, i.e., from $M(F)/A_F{}^\perp$ to $(kF)^\perp \subset A^*$, is also a continuous linear isomorphism. One computes that $T^*(v + A_F{}^\perp)(f) = \int (f \mid F)\, dv = r^*(v)(f)$, $v \in M(F)$, so T^* and r^* can be identified.

Condition (i) is the assertion that the operator norm of $(r^*)^{-1}$ is at most c, and we already know that $\|r^*\| \le 1$. Hence $\|T^{-1}\| = \|(T^{-1})^*\| = \|(T^*)^{-1}\| \le c$ and $\|T\| \le 1$. Clearly $c = 1$ iff $\|T^{-1}\| \le 1$, i.e., iff T^{-1} is an isometry.

Corollary.   *Suppose that A is a closed subspace of $C(X)$, F is a compact set in X, and $\mu_F \in A^\perp$ for every $\mu \in A^\perp$. Then $A \mid_F$ is closed in $C(F)$, and $A \mid_F$ and A/kF are isometric.*

Proof.   We have $(A \mid_F)^\perp = M(F) \cap A^\perp = \{\mu_F : \mu \in A^\perp\}$, since $\mu \in A^\perp$ implies $\mu_F \in A^\perp$. So if $v \in M(F)$, $\|v + (A \mid_F)^\perp\| = \inf \{\|v - \mu_F\| : \mu \in A^\perp\} = \inf \{\|(v - \mu)_F\| : \mu \in A^\perp\} \le \inf \{\|v - \mu\| : \mu \in A^\perp\} = \|v + A^\perp\|$. Hence (i) holds with $c = 1$.

We can use Theorem 37 to show that $A \mid_F = C(F)$ iff annihilators of A are balanced toward the complement of F.

Theorem 39.   *Let A be a closed subspace of $C(X)$, and let F be a compact set in X. Then $A \mid_F = C(F)$ iff for some $c \ge 1$, $\|\mu_F\| \le c\,\|\mu_{X \setminus F}\|$ for all $\mu \in A^\perp$. When this is so, c dominates the norm of the isomorphism from $C(F)$ onto A/kF.*

Proof. If $A|_F = C(F)$, then $A|_F$ is closed in $C(F)$ and $A_F^\perp = 0$, so $\exists c \geq 1$ such that $\|v\| \leq c\|v + A^\perp\|$ for every $v \in M(F)$. In particular, if $\mu \in A^\perp$, then $\|\mu_F\| \leq c\|\mu_F + A^\perp\| \leq c\|\mu - \mu_F\| = c\|\mu_{X\setminus F}\|$.

On the other hand, suppose the condition is satisfied. We see at once that $(A|_F)^\perp = 0$, so $A|_F$ is dense in $C(F)$. (Take v in $(A|_F)^\perp = M(F) \cap A^\perp$. Then $\|v\| \leq c\|v_{X\setminus F}\| = 0$.) Therefore everything will follow if we show that $\|v\| \leq c\|v + A^\perp\|$ for every v in $M(F)$. Since the norm of the sum of two mutually singular measures is the sum of their norms, and since $c \geq 1$, then

$$\|v - \mu\| = \|(v - \mu_F) - \mu_{X\setminus F}\| = \|v - \mu_F\| + \|\mu_{X\setminus F}\| \geq \frac{1}{c}\|v - \mu_F\| + \|\mu_{X\setminus F}\|$$

$$\geq \frac{1}{c}\|v\| + \|\mu_{X\setminus F}\| - \frac{1}{c}\|\mu_F\| \geq \frac{1}{c}\|v\| \quad (v \in M(F), \mu \in A^\perp).$$

Hence $\|v\| \leq c\inf_{\mu \in A^\perp}\|v - \mu\| = c\|v + A^\perp\|$, which completes the proof.

Corollary 1 (Generalized Rudin-Carleson Theorem). *Suppose that $\mu_F = 0$ for all $\mu \in A^\perp$. Then $A|_F = C(F)$, and every $\varphi \in C(F)$ has extensions f_ε in A with $\|f_\varepsilon\| \leq (1 + \varepsilon)\|\varphi\|$. (The second assertion is merely that A/kF and $C(F)$ are isometric, via $f + kF \to f|F$.)*

Actually, as noted above (but not proved), if $\mu_F = 0$ for all $\mu \in A^\perp$, then certainly $\mu_F \in A^\perp$ for all $\mu \in A^\perp$, which means that F is an intersection of peak sets for A. Hence by Theorem 4, §7.1, every $\varphi \in C(F)$ has an extension $f \in A$ with $\|f\| = \|\varphi\|$.

Corollary 2 (Rudin-Carleson Theorem). *Let F be a closed set of measure zero on the unit circle. Then every $\varphi \in C(F)$ extends to a function in the disk algebra.*

Proof. Let X be the circle and let A be the boundary value algebra on X. If $\mu \in A^\perp$, then μ is absolutely continuous with respect to Lebesgue measure on X, by the F. and M. Riesz theorem. Hence $\mu_F = 0$ for all $\mu \in A^\perp$, so $A|_F = C(F)$.

For example, we can take F to be a nowhere dense perfect set of measure zero on the circle, i.e., a Cantor set of measure zero. Then every $\varphi \in C(F)$ has an extension which is continuous on the closed disk and analytic on the open disk. Now every compact metric space is the continuous image of the Cantor set, so we conclude that given any compact set E in the plane, there is a function f in the disk algebra which maps the unit circle onto a set containing E. (Lots of space-filling curves are boundary values of uniformly continuous analytic functions on the unit disk.)

We return now to the general discussion.

Lemma 8. *Let A be a closed subspace of $C(X)$, F a compact set in X, and $kF = \{f \in A : f | F = 0\}$. Then $A^\perp + M(F)$ is a w*-dense linear subspace of $kF)^\perp$.)*

Proof. If $\mu \in A^\perp$ then $\mu \in (kF)^\perp$, and if μ is concentrated on F then $\mu \in (kF)^\perp$, so $A^\perp + M(F)$ is a subspace of $(kF)^\perp$. To show that it is w^*-dense we must show that every w^*-continuous linear functional $\mu \to \int f \, d\mu$ which annihilates $A^\perp + M(F)$ annihilates $(kF)^\perp$. So take $f \in C(X)$ such that $A^\perp + M(F)$ annihilates f. Then $A^\perp$ annihilates f, so $f \in A$ by the Hahn-Banach theorem, and every δ_x with $x \in F$ annihilates f, so $f \in kF$. Hence $(kF)^\perp$ annihilates f.

Lemma 9. *Given the hypothesis of Lemma 8, suppose that $A|_F$ is closed in $C(F)$. Then $A^\perp + M(F) = (kF)^\perp$.*

Proof. Since $A^\perp + M(F)$ is dense in $(kF)^\perp$, it suffices to prove that it is w^*-closed. By the Banach-Dieudonné theorem, it will be enough to show that the unit ball of $A^\perp + M(F)$ is w^*-closed.

Take a generalized sequence $\{\mu_a + v_a\}$ with $\mu_a \in A^\perp$, $v_a \in M(F)$, such that all $\|\mu_a + v_a\| \le 1$ and $\mu_a + v_a$ converges w^* to some $\mu \in M(X)$. The unit ball Σ of $M(X)$ is w^*-closed, so $\mu \in \Sigma$.

By Theorem 38, there is some $c \ge 1$ such that dist $(v, A_F^\perp) \le c$ dist $(v, A^\perp)$ for all $v \in M(F)$. Hence for each a there is some $\lambda_a \in A_F^\perp$ such that $\|v_a - \lambda_a\| \le 2c$ dist $(v_a, A^\perp) \le 2c \|v_a + \mu_a\| \le 2c$. Notice that $\lambda_a \in A_F^\perp \subset M(F) \cap A^\perp$. By the Alaoglu theorem, $\{v_a - \lambda_a\}$ has a w^*-cluster point v, and since $M(F)$ is w^*-closed in $M(X)$, it follows that $v \in M(F)$. But $\{\mu_a + \lambda_a\}$ clusters at $\mu - v$ (since $\mu_a + \lambda_a = (\mu_a + v_a) - (v_a - \lambda_a)$) and $A^\perp$ is w^*-closed, so $\mu - v$ is in $A^\perp$. So $\mu = (\mu - v) + v$ lies in $\Sigma \cap (A^\perp + M(F))$. Thus the unit ball of $A^\perp + M(F)$ is w^*-closed.

Lemma 10. *Let T be an isometric linear mapping from a normed linear space X into a normed linear space Y. Then the adjoint $T^* : Y^* \to X^*$ carries Y^* onto X^*.*

Proof. Let $\psi \in X^*$. Since T is linear, $T(X)$ is a subspace of Y. The map $T(x) \to \psi(x)$ is a well-defined linear functional on that subspace (since T is one-one), and it is continuous since $|\psi(x)| \le \|\psi\| \|x\| = \|\psi\| \|T(x)\|$. So by the Hahn-Banach theorem it extends to a continuous linear functional φ on X. But $\varphi(T(x)) = \psi(x)$ for all $x \in X$, which means that $\varphi \circ T = T^*(\varphi) = \psi$.

We can now prove the theorem mentioned at the beginning of this section and strengthen our Rudin-Carleson theorems.

Theorem 40. *Let A be a function algebra on X, and let F be a compact subset of X. Then F is an intersection of peak sets for A iff $\mu_F \in A^\perp$ for every μ in $A^\perp$.*

Proof. If F is an intersection of peak sets, then the condition is satisfied, as we have already observed. Conversely, suppose that $\mu_F \in A^\perp$ for every $\mu \in A^\perp$. By the corollary to Theorem 38, $A|_F = A_F$ is closed in $C(F)$, so

$(kF)^{\perp} = A^{\perp} + M(F)$ by Lemma 9. Note too that if $\mu \in A^{\perp}$, then $\mu_{X\backslash F} = \mu - \mu_F$ is also in $A^{\perp}$.

Let $B_0 = \{f \in A : f \,|\, F \text{ is constant}\} = kF + \mathbf{C}1$. Let X^* be the space obtained from X by identifying F to a point p, and let B be the subalgebra of $C(X^*)$ corresponding to B_0. It is clear that B is a sup norm algebra on X^*. In fact, B is a function algebra on X^*, since the following two conditions hold: (a) given $x \in X\backslash F$, $f(x) \neq 0$ for some $f \in kF$; (b) given distinct x, y in $X\backslash F$, $f(x) \neq f(y)$ for some $f \in kF$. So B separates points. (If $f(x) = 0$ for all $f \in kF$, then $\delta_x \in (kF)^{\perp} = A^{\perp} + M(F)$, so $\delta_x = \mu + \nu$ for some $\mu \in A^{\perp}$, $\nu \in M(F)$. Hence $\delta_x = \mu_{X\backslash F} + (\mu_F + \nu_F)$. Since $x \in X\backslash F$, $\mu_F + \nu_F = 0$, $\delta_x = \mu_{X\backslash F}$. But then $\delta_x \in A^{\perp}$, which is a contradiction since $1 \in A$. So (a) is proved. Similarly, if (b) fails then $\delta_x - \delta_y \in (kF)^{\perp}$, hence $\delta_x - \delta_y \in A^{\perp}$ by the same argument, and this contradicts the hypothesis that A separates points on X.)

In order to show that F is an intersection of peak sets for A, we must prove that $\{p\}$ is an intersection of peak sets for B, i.e., that p belongs to the Choquet boundary $c(B)$. It will suffice to prove that if $\tau \in B^{\perp}$, then $\tau(\{p\}) = 0$. (See the remarks at the beginning of this section.)

Let $Q : X \to X^*$ be the identification map, $Q_* : C(X^*) \to C(X)$ the map which sends g to $g \circ Q$ (the range of Q_* is the set of functions in $C(X)$ which are constant on F), and $Q^* : M(X) \to M(X^*)$ the adjoint of Q_*. Explicitly, $Q^*(\sigma) = \tau$ iff $\int (g \circ Q)\, d\sigma = \int g\, d\tau$ for all $g \in C(X^*)$. Now Q_* is clearly an isometry, so Q^* is onto $M(X^*)$, by Lemma 10. So each $\tau \in M(X^*)$ is the image of some $\sigma \in M(X)$ under Q^*.

Take $\tau \in B^{\perp}$. Set $J = \{h \in B : h(p) = 0\}$. Then $\tau \in J^{\perp}$ and $\int 1\, d\tau = 0$. Choose $\sigma \in Q^{*-1}(\tau)$. Since $Q_*(J) = kF$, $\int f\, d\sigma = \int (g \circ Q)\, d\sigma = \int g\, d\tau = 0$ for all $f \in kF$ ($g \in J$). So $\sigma \in (kF)^{\perp} = A^{\perp} + M(F)$, say $\sigma = \mu + \nu$ where $\mu \in A^{\perp}$, $\nu \in M(F)$. Then $\tau = Q^*(\mu_{X\backslash F}) + Q^*(\mu_F + \nu_F)$. Since $\mu_F + \nu_F$ is concentrated on F, $Q^*(\mu_F + \nu_F)$ is a scalar multiple $\alpha\delta_p$ of the point mass at p. As observed above, $\mu_{X\backslash F} \in A^{\perp}$, so $\int 1\, dQ^*(\mu_{X\backslash F}) = \int 1\, d\mu_{X\backslash F} = 0$. Hence $0 = \int 1\, d\tau = \int \alpha\, d\delta_p = \alpha$. So $\tau = Q^*(\mu_{X\backslash F})$, which means precisely that $\tau(\{p\}) = 0$. Hence the theorem is proved.

Corollary 1. *If F is a compact set in X such that $\mu_F = 0$ for every $\mu \in A^{\perp}$ (A a function algebra on X), then F is an intersection of peak sets for A, $A\,|_F = C(F)$, and every $g \in C(F)$ has an extension $f \in A$ with $\|f\| = \|g\|$.*

Corollary 2. *Let F be a closed set of measure zero on the unit circle. Then F is a peak set for the boundary value algebra A^1, and $A^1\,|_F = C(F)$. Every $g \in C(F)$ has an extension $f \in A^1$ with $\|f\| = \|g\|$. Furthermore, there is a function f_1 in the disk algebra such that $\{z : |z| \leq 1 \text{ and } f_1(z) = 0\} = F$.*

All the assertions follow from Theorem 40 and the Rudin-Carleson theorem (and the F. and M. Riesz theorem) except the last, which follows from the next lemma.

Lemma 11. *Let A be a function algebra and $F \subset X$ a compact set such that (a) F is a peak set for A, (b) $A|_F = C(F)$. Then $\exists f \in A$ such that F is exactly the zero-set of $\hat{f}$ on $\mathscr{M}(A)$. (Peak-interpolation sets are zero-sets in $\mathscr{M}(A)$.)*

Proof. F is a peak set, so there exists $f \in A$ such that $f = 1$ on F, $|f| < 1$ on $X \backslash F$. We shall show that if $a \in \mathscr{M}(A) \backslash X$, then $|\hat{f}(a)| < 1$ also.

Take a representing measure m for a (concentrated on X). Then $m(X \backslash F) > 0$, since m is not concentrated on F. (Indeed, if supp $m \subset F$, then $a \in \hat{F} = \mathscr{M}(A_F) = \mathscr{M}(C(F)) = F$, which is absurd.) So

$$|\hat{f}(a)| \le \int_F |f|\, dm + \int_{X \backslash F} |f|\, dm = m(F) + \int_{X \backslash F} |f|\, dm$$

$$< m(F) + m(X \backslash F) = 1.$$

Let $f_0 = 1 - f$. Then $\hat{f}_0 = 0$ exactly on F.

Theorem 41. *For a logmodular algebra A on X and a compact set F in X, the following conditions are equivalent: (a) $A|_F$ is closed in $C(F)$; (b) F is an intersection of peak sets for A; (c) $\mu_F \in A^\perp$ for every $\mu \in A^\perp$.*

Proof. It will suffice to prove that (a) implies (c).

Suppose that $A|_F$ is closed. Then by Theorem 38, $\exists c \ge 1$ such that $\|v + A_F^\perp\| \le c \|v + A^\perp\|$ for every $v \in M(F)$. We have to prove that if $\mu \in A^\perp$ then $\mu_F \in A^\perp$; we may assume that $\|\mu\| = 1$. Since A is an algebra, $f\mu \in A^\perp$ for every $f \in A$, and $\|f\mu_F + A_F^\perp\| \le c \|f\mu_F + A^\perp\| \le c \|f(\mu_F - \mu)\| = c \|f\mu_{X \backslash F}\|$.

Let $F' = X \backslash F$. Given $0 < \varepsilon < 1$, there is a compact set $K \subset F'$ with $|\mu|(F' \backslash K) < \varepsilon$. But $\exists f \in A^{-1}$ with $\|f\| \le 1$, $|f| < \varepsilon$ on K, and $|f| > 1 - \varepsilon$ on F. (Use Urysohn's lemma to find $u \in C_R(X)$ with $u = \varepsilon/2$ on K, $u = 1 - \dfrac{\varepsilon}{2}$ on F, $\dfrac{\varepsilon}{2} \le u \le 1 - \dfrac{\varepsilon}{2}$ on X. Then $\log u$ is continuous, so $\log |f_n| \to \log u$ uniformly, for some sequence $\{f_n\}$ in A^{-1}; hence $|f_n| \to u$ uniformly. We conclude that $\exists f \in A^{-1}$ with $-\varepsilon/2 < |f| - u < \varepsilon/2$. So $|f| < 1$ on X, $|f| < \varepsilon$ on K, $|f| > 1 - \varepsilon$ on F.) For any $v \in A_F^\perp$, $\dfrac{1}{f} v \in A_F^\perp$ also (since $1/f \in A$), so

$$\|\mu_F + A_F^\perp\| \le \left\| \mu_F - \frac{1}{f} v \right\| = \left\| \frac{1}{f}(f\mu_F - v) \right\| \le \frac{1}{1 - \varepsilon} \|f\mu_F - v\|. \text{ Choose } v \text{ so}$$

that $\|f\mu_F - v\| < \varepsilon + \|f\mu_F + A_F^\perp\|$. Then $\|\mu_F + A_F^\perp\| < \dfrac{1}{1 - \varepsilon}(\varepsilon + c \|f\mu_{F'}\|) \le$

$\dfrac{1}{1 - \varepsilon}(\varepsilon + 2c\varepsilon)$ (since $\|f\mu_{F' \backslash K}\| \le \varepsilon \|f\| < \varepsilon$ and $\|f\mu_K\| \le \varepsilon \|\mu\| = \varepsilon$). Letting $\varepsilon \to 0$, we conclude that $\mu_F \in A_F^\perp$, so $\mu_F \perp A$.

EXERCISE SET 7.6

1. Suppose that $F_1, \ldots, F_n$ are intersections of peak sets for a function algebra A. Prove that $F_1 \cup \cdots \cup F_n$ is an intersection of peak sets. Prove that if $\{F_n\}$ is a sequence of sets each of which is an intersection of peak sets for A and if $F = \bigcup_n F_n$ is closed, then F is an intersection of peak sets.

7.7 THE LOCAL MAXIMUM MODULUS PRINCIPLE

In this section we discuss several versions of the local maximum modulus theorem for function algebras, due to H. Rossi. (For a proof of the theorem see [147] or [C]. Geometrical formulations and applications of the theorem can be found in [182].) The theorem has found application to many problems in function algebras, but so far no proof of it has been found which does not use profound results from the theory of several complex variables (as well as the Arens-Calderôn lemma and Šilov's theorem). We will state one form of the theorem and derive several others from it.

First some definitions: Let A be a commutative Banach algebra with identity. Let $\mathscr{M}(A)$ be the space of complex homomorphisms of A, and let $\hat{A}$ be the representing algebra for A on the compact space $\mathscr{M}(A)$. Let $\Gamma(A)$ be the Šilov boundary for $\hat{A}$ in $\mathscr{M}(A)$. (We have noted that if A is itself a function algebra, then $\Gamma(A)$ is the Šilov boundary of A.) An element $p \in \mathscr{M}(A)$ is a peak point for $\hat{A}$ iff there exists $f \in A$ with $\hat{f}(p) = 1$, $|\hat{f}| < 1$ on $\mathscr{M}(A) \backslash \{p\}$. A point $p \in \mathscr{M}(A)$ is a *local peak point* iff p has an open *nbhd* U in $\mathscr{M}(A)$ such that $\hat{f}(p) = 1$, $|\hat{f}| < 1$ on $U \backslash \{p\}$ for some $f \in A$. Similarly, a set $K \subset \mathscr{M}(A)$ is a *local peak set* for $\hat{A}$ iff K is nonvoid and compact and there is an open set U in $\mathscr{M}(A)$ containing K and an element $f \in A$ such that $\hat{f} \mid K = 1$, $|\hat{f}| < 1$ on $U \backslash K$; K is a peak set iff we can take $U = \mathscr{M}(A)$ in the condition above.

The version of the local maximum principle which we shall assume is the local peak point theorem.

Theorem 42. *If p is a local peak point for $\hat{A}$, then p is a peak point for $\hat{A}$.*

Theorem 43. *Every local peak set for $\hat{A}$ is a peak set for $\hat{A}$.*

Proof. Let K be a local peak set for $\hat{A}$. Choose an open set U about K and an element $f \in A$ such that $\hat{f} = 1$ on K, $|\hat{f}| < 1$ on $U \backslash K$. Let $H = \{a \in \mathscr{M}(A) : \hat{f}(a) = 1\}$. By hypothesis, $K = H \cap U = H \cap \bar{U}$, so K is open and closed in H. Note that if $a \notin H$, then $\exists g \in A$ with $\hat{g}(a) \neq 0$ but $\hat{g} = 0$ on H, namely $g = 1 - f$. So H is the set of common zeros in $\mathscr{M}(A)$ of its kernel $I = \{g \in A : \hat{g} = 0 \text{ on } H\}$. Hence H is the maximal ideal space of the Banach algebra $B = A/I$, and the Gelfand map identifies $\hat{B}$ with $\hat{A}|_H$.

Now K is an open-closed subset of $H = \mathscr{M}(B)$, so by Šilov's theorem on idempotents, $\exists x \in B$ with transform equal to 0 on K and 1 on $H \backslash K$. Thus K

is the hull (zero-set) of its kernel $J = \{h \in A : \hat{h} = 0 \text{ on } K\}$. (For consider any $a \in \mathcal{M}(A) \backslash K$. If $a \notin H$, then $\exists g \in A$ with $\hat{g}(a) \neq 0$, $\hat{g} = 0$ on $H \supset K$. If $a \in H$, then $a \in H \backslash K$, so $\hat{x}(a) = 1$, $\hat{x} = 0$ on K. In either case $a \notin$ zero-set (J).)

Set $A_K = \{g \in A : \hat{g} \text{ is constant on } K\} = J + \mathbf{C}1 = \{g + \lambda 1 : g \in J\}$. Then J is a closed ideal of A, A_K is a closed subalgebra of A, and A_K is just J with an identity adjoined. So $\mathcal{M}(A_K)$ is the one-point compactification of $\mathcal{M}(J)$. Since J is a closed ideal of A and $K = $ hull J, $\mathcal{M}(J) = \mathcal{M}(A) \backslash K$. Hence $\mathcal{M}(A_K)$ is $\mathcal{M}(A)$ with K identified to a point. (If $\psi \in \mathcal{M}(A_K)$ and $\psi(J) = \{0\}$, then $\psi(g + \lambda 1) = \lambda$, so there is only one such homomorphism. If $\psi(J) \neq \{0\}$, extend ψ uniquely to a complex homomorphism φ of A by setting $\varphi(h) = \psi(gh)/\psi(g)$ for any $g \in J$ such that $\psi(g) \neq 0$. Thus we have $\mathcal{M}(A_K) = \mathcal{M}(J)_\infty$.) Since $\hat{f} = 1$ on K, $f \in A_K$. If p is the point $\{K\}$ in $\mathcal{M}(A_K)$, then $\hat{f}(p) = 1$. Also, if $\psi \in \mathcal{M}(A_K) \cap U$ and $|\hat{f}(\psi)| = 1$, then $\hat{f}(\psi) = 1$, so $\psi \in H \cap U = K$; hence $\psi = p$. Thus on $\mathcal{M}(A_K)$, $\hat{f}$ peaks within U exactly at p; i.e., p is a local peak point for $\hat{A}_K$. Therefore p is a peak point for $\hat{A}_K$.

Thus $\exists h \in A$ with $\hat{h} = 1$ on K, $|\hat{h}| < 1$ on $\mathcal{M}(A) \backslash K$. So K is a peak set for $\hat{A}$.

Theorem 44 (Local Maximum Principle, Version I).   *Let U be an open set in $\mathcal{M}(A)$. Suppose that for some $f \in A$, (1) $|\hat{f}| \leq 1$ on U, (2) $|\hat{f}| < 1$ on bd(U), (3) $\hat{f}(a_0) = 1$ for some $a_0 \in U$. Then there is an element $g \in A$ such that*
   (a) $|\hat{g}| \leq 1$ on $\mathcal{M}(A)$;
   (b) $\{a \in \mathcal{M}(A) : |\hat{g}(a)| = 1\} = \{a : \hat{g}(a) = 1\} = \{a : \hat{f}(a) = 1\} \cap U$.

Proof.   Replace f by $\frac{1}{2}(1 + f)$. Then if $a \in U$, $|\hat{f}(a)| = 1$ iff $\hat{f}(a) = 1$. Let $K = \{a \in U : \hat{f}(a) = 1\}$. By hypothesis (3) K is not empty, and by (2) $K = \{a \in \overline{U} : \hat{f}(a) = 1\}$, so K is compact. Since $\hat{f} = 1$ on K and $|\hat{f}| < 1$ on $U \backslash K$, K is a local peak set for $\hat{A}$. Hence K is a global peak set for $\hat{A}$, so there is some $g \in A$ such that $\hat{g} = 1$ on K, $|\hat{g}| < 1$ on $\mathcal{M}(A) \backslash K$. Since $\hat{g} = 1$ precisely on K, (a) and (b) hold.

Theorem 45 (Local Maximum Principle, Version II).   *Let U be a nonvoid open set in $\mathcal{M}(A)$ disjoint from the Šilov boundary of A. Then*
   (a) bd(U) *is not empty;*
   (b) $\sup_U |\hat{f}| = \sup_{\text{bd}(U)} |\hat{f}|$ *for every $f \in A$.*
Let A_U be the closure of $\hat{A}|_U$ in $C(\overline{U})$. Then $\Gamma(A_U) \subset$ bd(U).

Proof. U is open and nonvoid in $\mathcal{M}(A)$, and $U \cap \Gamma(A) = \varnothing$. Note that U is not closed in $\mathcal{M}(A)$. For if U were open-closed, then Šilov's theorem would imply that $\exists f \in A$ with $\hat{f} = 1$ on U, $\hat{f} = 0$ on $\mathcal{M}(A) \backslash U \supset \Gamma(A)$, which is absurd. Hence bd(U) is not empty.

Assume that $\sup_U |\hat{f}| \neq \sup_{\text{bd}(U)} |\hat{f}| = \max_{\text{bd}(U)} |\hat{f}|$ for some $f \in A$. If $\max_{\text{bd}(U)} |\hat{f}| > \rho = \sup_U |\hat{f}|$, then $|\hat{f}(a)| > \rho$ for some $a \in$ bd(U). By continuity, $|\hat{f}| > \rho$ on a *nbhd* of a; this *nbhd* contains a point of U, so we have a contradiction. If the maximum is less than $\rho = \sup_U |\hat{f}|$, we can multiply by a scalar to get $|\hat{f}| < 1 = \sup_U |\hat{f}|$ on bd(U). Since $\hat{f}$ is continuous and U has compact closure, we have $\sup_U |\hat{f}| = |\hat{f}(a_0)| = 1$ for some $a_0 \in \overline{U}$. Replace

f by $e^{-i\theta}f$ where $\hat{f}(a_0) = e^{i\theta}$. Then f satisfies the hypothesis of version I, so $\exists g \in A$ with $|\hat{g}| \leq 1$ on $\mathscr{M}(A)$ and $\{a : |\hat{g}(a)| = 1\} \subset U$. Since U is disjoint from $\Gamma(A)$ and $\hat{g}$ attains its maximum modulus only within U, we have a contradiction once more. So $\sup_U |\hat{f}| = \sup_{\mathrm{bd}(U)} |\hat{f}|$.

Corollary. *Let A be a function algebra with maximal ideal space $I = [0, 1]$. Then $\Gamma(A) = I$.*

Proof. If $\Gamma(A)$ is proper in $\mathscr{M}(A)$, then there is an open interval $(x - \varepsilon, x + \varepsilon)$ disjoint from $\Gamma(A)$. By the maximum principle, $|\hat{f}(x)| \leq \max(|\hat{f}(x - \varepsilon)|, |\hat{f}(x + \varepsilon)|)$ for all $f \in A$. But A separates points, so $\hat{f}_1(x) = 1$, $\hat{f}_1(x - \varepsilon) = 0$ and $\hat{f}_2(x) = 1, \hat{f}_2(x + \varepsilon) = 0$ for some f_1, f_2 in A. Hence $\hat{f}(x) = 1$, $\hat{f}(x + \varepsilon) = \hat{f}(x - \varepsilon) = 0$ if $f = f_1 f_2$. This is a contradiction, so $\Gamma(A) = \mathscr{M}(A)$.

EXERCISE SET 7.7

1. Let $f \in A$ and $t > 0$. Then every component of the set $L = \{a \in \mathscr{M}(A) : |\hat{f}(a)| \geq t\}$ intersects the Šilov boundary of A, unless L is empty.

2. Let A be a function algebra, and let S be the topological boundary of $\Gamma(A)$ in $\mathscr{M}(A)$. Prove that S is a support set for every $a \in \mathscr{M}(A) \backslash \Gamma(A)$; hence each complex homomorphism not belonging to the Šilov boundary has a representing measure supported in S.

3. Let K be a compact set in $\mathscr{M}(A)$. Let $f \in A$ and $a \in K$. Show that $|\hat{f}(a)| \leq \max_{\mathrm{bd}(K) \cup (K \cap \Gamma(A))} |\hat{f}|$.

4. Let A be a function algebra on X, and let E be the essential set for A on X. Suppose that $X = M(A)$ and that X is metrizable. Prove that $E = X \backslash P$, where P is the set defined in Theorem 36, §7.5.

Chapter Eight

Constructions

8.1   FUNCTION ALGEBRAS ON THE INTERVAL

Let $I = [0, 1]$. We are concerned here with the construction of function algebras on I and with the properties of such algebras. One obvious function algebra on I is the entire algebra $C(I)$, but direct construction of proper closed separating subalgebras of $C(I)$ seems to be difficult. One technique which has been successful is to embed I in a suitable compact space X as a closed boundary for a function algebra A on X, and then pull A back to I via the embedding. Another approach has been to obtain I as the identification space determined by a nonseparating sup norm algebra on a suitable space, e.g., the circle.

Let us look first at the embedding idea. Let $S^2 = \mathbf{C} \cup \{\infty\}$ be the Riemann sphere (extended plane). A function f defined on S^2 is said to be analytic at ∞ iff the function $z \to f(1/z)$ is analytic at the origin, or equivalently, iff f is analytic and bounded on some deleted *nbhd* $\{z \in \mathbf{C} : |z| > 1/\varepsilon\}$ of ∞.

Given a compact set E in the plane, we define $\mathscr{B}_E \subset C(S^2)$ and $\mathscr{A}_E \subset C(E)$ as follows: $f \in \mathscr{B}_E$ iff $f \in C(S^2)$ and f is analytic on $S^2\backslash E$; $g \in \mathscr{A}_E$ iff g extends to an element of $\mathscr{B}_E$. It is clear that $\mathscr{B}_E$ and $\mathscr{A}_E$ are sup norm algebras, and for certain sets E it is clear that these algebras contain only the constants. Note that the restriction map from $\mathscr{B}_E$ to $\mathscr{A}_E$ is an isometry:

$$\|f\| = \max_{z \in S^2} |f(z)| = \|f\|_E \qquad (f \in \mathscr{B}_E).$$

Lemma 1. *Suppose that $\mathscr{B}_E$ contains a function which is not constant on $S^2\backslash E$. Then there exist f_0, f_1, f_2 in $\mathscr{B}_E$ which together separate points on S^2. (Hence $\mathscr{B}_E$ and $\mathscr{A}_E$ are function algebras.)*

Proof. By hypothesis, there exist $f_0 \in \mathscr{B}_E$ and a, b in $\mathbf{C}\backslash E$ such that

$f_0(a) \neq f_0(b)$. Define functions f_1, f_2 on S^2 as follows: $f_1(z) = \dfrac{f_0(z) - f_0(a)}{z - a}$

$(z \neq a, z \neq \infty)$, $f_1(a) = f_0'(a)$, $f_1(\infty) = 0$; $f_2(z) = \dfrac{f_0(z) - f_0(b)}{z - b}$ $(z \neq b,$

$z \neq \infty)$, $f_2(b) = f_0'(b)$, $f_2(\infty) = 0$. Since f_0 is finite at ∞, f_1, f_2 are in $C(S^2)$ and both are analytic on $S^2 \backslash E$.

Since $f_0(a) \neq f_0(b)$, f_0, f_1, f_2 separate a and b. If $z_0 \neq \infty$ and $f_0(z_0) = f_0(\infty)$, $f_1(z_0) = f_1(\infty) = 0$, then either $z_0 = a$ and so $f_2(z_0) \neq 0 = f_2(\infty)$; or $f_0(z_0) = f_0(a) \neq f_0(b)$, so again $f_2(z_0) \neq f_2(\infty)$. Hence f_0, f_1, f_2 separate z_0 from ∞. Finally, suppose $z_1, z_2 \in \mathbf{C}\backslash\{a, b\}$ and $f_k(z_1) = f_k(z_2)$ for $k = 0, 1, 2$. Since $f_0(a) \neq f_0(b)$, either $f_0(z_1) \neq f_0(a)$ or $f_0(z_1) \neq f_0(b)$. In the first case, $\dfrac{f_0(z_1) - f_0(a)}{z_1 - a} = \dfrac{f_0(z_1) - f_0(a)}{z_2 - a} \neq 0$, while in the second case, $\dfrac{f_0(z_1) - f_0(b)}{z_1 - b} = \dfrac{f_0(z_1) - f_0(b)}{z_2 - b} \neq 0$; so $z_1 = z_2$. Thus f_0, f_1, f_2 separate distinct z_1, z_2 in $\mathbf{C}$.

Next we show that if E has positive planar measure, then $\mathcal{B}_E$ separates points on S^2. However, there are sets E of measure zero such that $\mathcal{B}_E$ is nontrivial. An exposition of the basic theory of the sets E for which $\mathcal{B}_E$ does not reduce to the constants appears in [216].

Theorem 1. *If E is a compact planar set with positive Lebesgue measure, then $\mathcal{B}_E$ separates points on S^2.*

Proof. By the lemma, it suffices to find a function in $\mathcal{B}_E$ which is not constant on $S^2 \backslash E$. Our candidate is the function given by $f(\xi) = \displaystyle\int_E \frac{1}{\xi - z}\, dm(z)$ $(\xi \in \mathbf{C})$, $f(\infty) = 0$, where m is planar Lebesgue measure.

Observe that if $g \in L^1(m)$ and $\varphi \in L^\infty(m)$, then the convolution of g with φ, defined by

$$(g * \varphi)(\xi) = \int_\mathbf{C} g(\xi - \alpha)\varphi(\alpha)\, dm(\alpha)$$

exists everywhere in the plane and is continuous, since translation is continuous in the L^1 norm. (See Exercise 1.) So if $g \in L^1(m)$ and $G(\xi) = \displaystyle\int_E g(\xi - \alpha)\, dm(\alpha)$ $(\xi \in \mathbf{C})$, then G is a continuous function on the entire plane.

Now we use the fact (established in Chapter V) that $1/z$ is locally integrable in the plane. Specifically, take a bounded open *nbhd* N of E, and let D be an open disk about the origin containing $\{\xi - z : \xi \in N, z \in E\}$. Set $g(z) = \chi_D(z)/z$; then, changing to polar coordinates, we see that $g \in L^1(m)$. The corresponding continuous function G satisfies the formula $G(\xi) = \displaystyle\int_E \frac{1}{\xi - \alpha}\, dm(\alpha)$, $\xi \in N$.

Now define f as above. Since f and G agree on N, f is continuous on N. Since there are no singularities of the integrand if $\xi \notin E$, f is analytic on $\mathbf{C} \setminus E$. (In more detail, let $\delta(\xi) = \text{dist}\,(\xi, E)$. Suppose that $\xi \in \mathbf{C} \setminus E$ and $\xi_n \to \xi$. Choose n_0 so that for $n \geq n_0$, $|\xi_n - \xi| \leq \delta(\xi)/2$. Then $\dfrac{f(\xi_n) - f(\xi)}{\xi_n - \xi} = \displaystyle\int_E \dfrac{-1}{(\xi_n - \alpha)(\xi - \alpha)}\, dm(\alpha)$. The integrands are bounded by $\dfrac{2}{\delta(\xi)^2}$, so by the dominated convergence theorem, $f'(\xi)$ exists.) Since E is bounded, $|f(\xi)| \leq \dfrac{m(E)}{\delta(\xi)} \to 0$ as $\xi \to \infty$, so f is continuous at ∞. Hence $f \in \mathscr{B}_E$.

Finally, f is not constant on $S^2 \setminus E$. Indeed, $\xi f(\xi) = \displaystyle\int_E \dfrac{\xi}{\xi - z}\, dm(z) \to m(E)$ as $\xi \to \infty$, since the integrand approaches 1 uniformly. Since $m(E) > 0$ by hypothesis, f is not identically zero on $S^2 \setminus E$.

Theorem 2.   *There exists a proper function algebra on I which has three generators.*

Proof.   To apply the construction above, we need to know that there exist Jordan arcs of positive planar measure. (A Jordan arc is a homeomorphic image of I.) This was established by W. F. Osgood in 1903 (see *Transactions of the American Mathematical Society*, vol. 4). The details are complicated and we will not give the proof.†

Let $\tau : [0, 1] \to \mathbf{C}$ be a one-one continuous map such that $m(J) > 0$, where $J = \tau(I)$. By Theorem 1, $\mathscr{A}_J$ is a function algebra on J, so $A_J = \{f \circ \tau : f \in \mathscr{A}_J\}$ is a function algebra on I which is isomorphic to $\mathscr{A}_J$. The restrictions of f_0, f_1, f_2 to J separate points on J, so A_J has a closed subalgebra B which contains the constants, has three generators $f_k \circ \tau$ ($k = 0, 1, 2$), and separates points on I. It remains to show that B is a proper subalgebra of $C(I)$. This follows from Lemma 4 below; in fact, every nonconstant function $g \in B$ maps I onto a set with a nonvoid interior in the plane. Hence (for example) no nonconstant continuous real-valued function on I belongs to B (i.e., B is antisymmetric).

In order to prove a fundamental fact about the algebras $\mathscr{B}_E$, we must discuss the concept of the variation of the logarithm of a continuous function along a closed curve. Given a continuous nowhere vanishing function ψ on a closed interval $[a, b]$, a *continuous logarithm* of ψ is a continuous function v on $[a, b]$ such that $\psi = e^v$. Because of the uniform continuity of ψ and the fact that the exponential function has local continuous inverses, one can prove that every continuous $\psi : [a, b] \to \mathbf{C} \setminus \{0\}$ has a continuous logarithm.

---

† A modified version of Osgood's construction can be found in B. Gelbaum and J. Olmsted, *Counterexamples in Analysis*, Holden-Day, San Francisco, 1964.

(Just modify the proof given below.) If γ is a continuous function on $[a, b]$, and if f is continuous and nowhere zero on the curve $C = \gamma([a, b])$, then the *variation of the logarithm of f along C* is defined to be $v(b) - v(a)$, where v is any continuous logarithm of $f \circ \gamma$. (Any two continuous logarithms of $f \circ \gamma$ differ by a constant, so var log (f, C) is well defined.)

Lemma 2. *Let $\varphi : \mathbf{C} \to \mathbf{C}\backslash\{0\}$ be continuous. For each $r > 0$, let $V(r)$ be the variation of the logarithm of φ along the circle $C_r = \{z : |z| = r\}$. Then $V(r) = 0$ for every r.*

Proof. Of course, C_r is parametrized by $\gamma_r(t) = re^{it}$ $(0 \le t \le 2\pi)$. Fix $r_0 > 0$ and choose $\varepsilon > 0$ so that $r_0 - \varepsilon > 0$. Let $E = \{(r, t) : r_0 - \varepsilon \le r \le r_0 + \varepsilon, 0 \le t \le 2\pi\}$, and define $g : E \to \mathbf{C}\backslash\{0\}$ by $g(r, t) = \varphi(re^{it})$. E is compact and g is continuous, so g is uniformly continuous and assumes a positive minimum modulus: $\exists \lambda > 0$ with $|g(r, t)| \ge \lambda$ on E. Also $\exists \delta > 0$ so that if $(r_j, t_j) \in E$ and $|r_1 - r_2| < \delta$ and $|t_1 - t_2| < \delta$, then $|g(r_1, t_1) - g(r_2, t_2)| < \lambda$. Hence if $r_0 - \varepsilon \le r \le r_0 + \varepsilon, 0 \le t_1, t_2 \le 2\pi$, and $|t_1 - t_2| < \delta$, then

$$|g(r, t_1) - g(r, t_2)| < \lambda,$$

while $\lambda \le |g(r, t_2)|$. Hence $\left| \dfrac{g(r, t_1)}{g(r, t_2)} - 1 \right| < 1$. Let $D = \{z : |z - 1| < 1\}$, and let Log be the principal logarithm. Then D is contained in the domain of analyticity of Log.

Choose a positive integer N such that $2\pi/N < \delta$; and for $k = 1, \ldots, N$, define g_k on E by $g_k(r, t) = g\left(r, \dfrac{k}{N}t\right) \Big/ g\left(r, \dfrac{k-1}{N}t\right)$. Then $g_k(E) \subset D$ for each k. Also, g_k is continuous on E.

Let ψ be the restriction of φ to the real interval $[r_0 - \varepsilon, r_0 + \varepsilon]$. Then ψ has a continuous logarithm v on $[r_0 - \varepsilon, r_0 + \varepsilon]$. Now set $h(r, t) = v(r) + \sum_{k=1}^{N} \text{Log } g_k(r, t)$ $((r, t) \in E)$. Then h is continuous, and $e^{h(r,t)} = g(r, 0) \prod_{k=1}^{N} g_k(r, t) = g(r, t)$, so h is a continuous logarithm of g.

Now $e^{h(r,t)} = \varphi(re^{it})$, so for each fixed r in $[r_0 - \varepsilon, r_0 + \varepsilon]$, h_r is a continuous logarithm of φ on C_r, where $h_r(t) = h(r, t)$. By definition, $V(r) = h(r, 2\pi) - h(r, 0)$. So V is continuous at r_0.

Since $\varphi(r) = \varphi(re^{2\pi i})$, $e^{h(r, 0)} = e^{h(r, 2\pi)}$, so $\dfrac{1}{2\pi i} V(r)$ is an integer; i.e., V takes on discrete values. Since $r_0 > 0$ is arbitrary, V is continuous on $(0, +\infty)$, so V is constant. But $\varphi(0) \ne 0$, so by continuity, there exists $\delta_1 > 0$ such that $|\varphi(z) - \varphi(0)| < |\varphi(0)|$ if $|z| < \delta_1$. But there is a continuous branch L of the logarithm on the disk $D_1 = \{w : |w - \varphi(0)| < |\varphi(0)|\}$. So if $0 < r < \delta_1$, then $e^{L(\varphi(re^{it}))} = \varphi(re^{it})$, and by definition of $V(r)$, it follows that $V(r) = L(\varphi(re^{2\pi i})) - L(\varphi(r)) = 0$. Hence V is identically zero.

Lemma 3.   *Let E be a compact set in the plane. Then for each $f \in \mathcal{B}_E$, $f(E) = f(S^2)$.*

Proof.   Let $f \in \mathcal{B}_E$, $w \in f(S^2)$. Assume that $w \notin f(E)$. $f - w$ is analytic on $S^2 \backslash E$, continuous on S^2, but has no zeros on E. So $f - w$ has a nonempty finite set of zeros $z_0, z_1, \ldots, z_n$ (repeated according to their multiplicities). (Suppose $f - w$ has infinitely many zeros. Then since S^2 is compact, the zeros have a limit point z^*. $z^* \notin E$ since $f - w$ has no zero on E. Since $f - w$ is analytic and has a nonisolated zero, $f - w$ is constant on the component U of $S^2 \backslash E$ containing z^*. So $f - w$ is constant on $\bar{U}$, which meets E. Hence $f(z) = w$ for some $z \in E$, contrary to assumption.) Set

$$g(z) = (z - z_0)^{-1}(z - z_1)^{-1} \cdots (z - z_n)^{-1}(f(z) - w).$$

Then $g \in \mathcal{B}_E$, $g(\infty) = 0$, but g has no zero in $\mathbf{C}$. By Lemma 2, the variation of $\log g$ along each C_r is 0. But $g(\infty) = 0$ and g is analytic at ∞, so $V(r) \neq 0$ for all sufficiently large r. (In fact, $\dfrac{1}{2\pi i} V(r)$ is the order of the zero of g at ∞.) So we have a contradiction.

Lemma 4.   *Let J be a Jordan arc in the plane. Then for every nonconstant function $g \in \mathcal{A}_J$, the interior of $g(J)$ is not empty.*

Proof.   Since J is a Jordan arc in the plane, J does not separate the plane and the interior of J is empty. (These are two basic facts about the topology of $\mathbf{R}^2$.) By definition, g has an extension $f \in \mathcal{B}_J$. Since f is analytic and not constant on the open connected set $\mathbf{C} \backslash J$, f is an open mapping, so $U = f(\mathbf{C} \backslash J)$ is a nonvoid open subset of the plane. Hence $g(J) = f(S^2)$ contains a disk.

So in the function algebra A_J of Theorem 2, every nonconstant function parametrizes a Peano curve in the plane (i.e., its image has a nonvoid interior).

There is a proper function algebra B on I which has three generators g_1, g_2, g_3. The map $t \to (g_1(t), g_2(t), g_3(t))$ is a homeomorphism of I onto a Jordan arc Γ in $\mathbf{C}^3$. Observe that $P(\Gamma) \neq C(\Gamma)$. For if $\varphi \in P(\Gamma)$, then $\varphi(g_1, g_2, g_3)$ is a uniform limit of polynomials in g_1, g_2, g_3 and hence belongs to $B \neq C(I)$. So there is an arc in $\mathbf{C}^3$ on which the polynomials are not dense in the continuous functions. Note that this cannot be the case for an arc in the plane. For if J is an arc in $\mathbf{C}^1$, then J has a connected complement and empty interior, so $P(J) = C(J)$ by Lavrentiev's theorem. Equivalently, any one-one continuous function on I generates $C(I)$.

In general, given n functions $f_1, \ldots, f_n$ in $C(I)$ which together separate points, they determine a homeomorphism γ of I onto a compact set in $\mathbf{C}^n$ given by $\gamma(t) = (f_1(t), \ldots, f_n(t))$. If B is the function algebra generated by $f_1, \ldots, f_n$, and if Γ is the arc $\gamma(I)$, then $B = P(\Gamma) \circ \gamma = \{\varphi \circ \gamma : \varphi \in P(\Gamma)\}$, $P(\Gamma) = B \circ \gamma^{-1}$. Thus questions about finitely generated function algebras on I are equivalent to questions about polynomial approximation on arcs in $\mathbf{C}^n$.

There exists an arc in $\mathbf{C}^2$ on which the polynomials are not dense—that is, there is a doubly generated proper function algebra on I. The construction is a rather involved variation of the technique already used.

Let E be a totally disconnected compact perfect set in the plane which has positive planar measure. (For example, let $E = K \times K$ where K is a Cantor set of positive one-dimensional measure, $K \subset I$. To form K, take $\alpha \in (0, 1)$ and delete from I the middle open subinterval of length $\alpha/2$, then the two middle open subintervals of length $\alpha/2^3$, the four middle intervals of length $\alpha/2^5$, etc., and let K be the complement of the union of the deleted segments.) Set $f_0(\infty) = 0$, $f_0(\xi) = \int_E (\xi - z)^{-1} \, dm(z)$ $(\xi \in \mathbf{C})$, and let $g_0(\xi) = \xi f_0(\xi)$. Then f_0, g_0 lie in $\mathscr{B}_E$ and the map $\sigma = (f_0, g_0)$ carries E continuously onto a compact set E^* in $\mathbf{C}^2$. Note that σ is one-one on $E_0 = \{\xi \in E : f_0(\xi) \neq 0\}$. It follows that E^* is totally disconnected. Note that $P(E^*)$ is isomorphic to the closed subalgebra of $\mathscr{B}_E$ generated by (1 and) f_0 and g_0. In particular, $P(E^*) \neq C(E^*)$.

To get an algebra on the interval, we need to know that through any compact totally disconnected set in $\mathbf{R}^n$ there passes a Jordan arc. (This was established by Louis Antoine in 1921; see *Journal de Mathématiques Pures et Appliquées*, vol. 4, pp. 302–304.) So there is an arc L in $\mathbf{C}^2$ with $E^* \subset L$. Since $P(E^*) \neq C(E^*)$, $P(L)$ is a proper subalgebra of $C(L)$; in fact, every non-constant element of $P(L)$ is a Peano curve. Since L is an arc in $\mathbf{C}^2$, there is a proper function algebra on I which has two generators.

The scarcity of examples of function algebras on I and the fact that in the known examples, functions with pathological properties predominate, have led to the conjecture that a proper function algebra on I cannot be generated by smooth functions. Due to the work of Wermer, Bishop, and Stolzenberg it is now known that if A is a function algebra on I generated by C^1 functions, then $A = C(I)$. (See [183].) Furthermore, work of Pelczynski [140] shows that any function algebra on I must contain many unsmooth functions. Rudin [155] shows that the polynomials are dense in the continuous functions on any arc lying in $\mathbf{C} \times \mathbf{R}^n$; i.e., if $f, g_1, \ldots, g_n$ separate points on I and $g_1, \ldots, g_n$ are real-valued, then $f, g_1, \ldots, g_n$ generate $C(I)$.

As far as I know, there is no example of a function algebra $A \neq C(I)$ with maximal ideal space I. For the algebras A_J defined above, it is clear that $\mathscr{M}(A_J) \supset S^2$ (in fact, in view of a theorem of Arens [5], $\mathscr{M}(A_J) = S^2$), so $\mathscr{M}(A_J) \neq I$. We can also show that if $\mathscr{M}(A) = I$, and if A is generated by functions f such that the plane curves $f(I)$ all have measure zero, then $A = C(I)$. This is a special case of the following theorem.

Theorem 3. *Let A be a function algebra on a compact space X with $X = \mathscr{M}(A)$. Suppose that there is a subset $\mathscr{F} \subset A$ such that* (i) *$\mathscr{F}$ separates points, and* (ii) *for each $f \in \mathscr{F}$, $f(X)$ has planar measure 0. Then $A = C(X)$.*

Proof. Let $B = \{f \in A : \bar{f} \in A\}$. B is a self-adjoint sup norm algebra on X. We shall show that $\mathscr{F} \subset B$. Let $f \in \mathscr{F}$. If q is any polynomial on $\mathbf{C}$ which vanishes nowhere on $K = f(X)$, then $q(f) \in A$ and has no zeros. Since $X = \mathcal{M}(A)$, $q(f)$ is invertible in A for each such q. Hence $r(f) \in A$ for every rational function r which is finite on K. But $m(K) = 0$ by (ii), so $C(K) = R(K)$ by the Hartogs-Rosenthal theorem. (See §5.3.) So $\bar{z}$ is a uniform limit of rational functions on K, and $\bar{f}$ is therefore a uniform limit of rational functions $r_n(f)$. So $\bar{f} \in A$ for every $f \in \mathcal{F}$. Hence $\mathcal{F} \subset B$, and since $\mathcal{F}$ separates points on X, $B = C(X)$ by the Stone-Weierstrass theorem.

EXERCISE SET 8.1

In these problems, m is planar Lebesgue measure.

1. Let $g \in L^1(m)$. For ξ, α in $\mathbf{C}$ define $g_\xi(\alpha) = g(\alpha - \xi)$. Show that the map $\xi \to g_\xi$ is continuous from $\mathbf{C}$ into L^1 (indeed it is uniformly continuous).

2. Suppose that E is a compact set in the plane and φ is a bounded Borel measurable function on E. Set $\tilde{\varphi}(z) = \int_E \varphi(\alpha)(z - \alpha)^{-1} \, dm(\alpha)$. Show that $\tilde{\varphi} \in \mathcal{B}_E$ and that if $\int_E \varphi \, dm \neq 0$, then $\tilde{\varphi}$ is not constant.

3. Suppose that E is compact and $m(E) > 0$. Show that if $g \in \mathcal{A}_E$ and g has no zeros on E, then $1/g \in \mathcal{A}_E$, yet E is not the maximal ideal space of $\mathcal{A}_E$.

4. A point $z_0 \in E$ is a *density point* iff $m(E_r) > 0$ for all $r > 0$, where $E_r = \{z \in E : |z - z_0| < r\}$. If $m(E) > 0$, then E has density points. Show that if z_0 is a density point of a compact set $E \subset \mathbf{C}$, and if $\delta > 0$, then $z \to (z - z_0)^{-1}$ is uniformly approximable on $\{z \in \mathbf{C} : |z - z_0| \geq \delta\}$ by members of $\mathcal{B}_E$.

5. We know that a function algebra on I can have a one-dimensional maximal ideal space: $C(I)$ is an example. If J is a planar arc of positive measure, then A_J is a function algebra on I whose maximal ideal space contains S^2, and hence is two-dimensional. Show that there is a function algebra A on I such that $\mathcal{M}(A)$ contains $S^2 \times S^2$, hence has dimension at least 4; A can be chosen to have six generators. (Take f_0, f_1, f_2 in $\mathcal{A}_E$ which together separate points on S^2, where E is a compact totally disconnected set of positive planar measure. Use f_0, f_1, f_2 to define a homeomorphism F of $S^2 \times S^2$ into $\mathbf{C}^6$, and find an arc L through $E^* = F(E \times E)$ such that $F(S^2 \times S^2) \subset \mathrm{hull}(L)$.)

8.2   DIRICHLET SUBALGEBRAS

In this section we construct a proper Dirichlet subalgebra of $C[0, 1]$. Our example will be a subalgebra A' of the restriction of the disk algebra to the unit circle, and the interval I will be obtained by identifying points on the circle which are not separated by A'. Along the way we discuss some general techniques for constructing Dirichlet subalgebras of given Dirichlet algebras.

Lemma 5. *Let U, V be w^*-closed linear subspaces of E^*, where E is a Banach space. If there is some $k > 0$ such that $\|u\| + \|v\| \leq k\|u + v\|$ for all $u \in U$, $v \in V$, then $U + V$ is w^*-closed.*

Proof. Since $U + V$ is a linear subspace of E^*, it suffices (by the Banach-Dieudonné theorem) to show that $(U + V) \cap \Sigma$ is w^*-compact, where Σ is the unit ball in E^*. Let $Q = \{u + v : u \in U, \ v \in V, \ \|u\| \leq k, \ \|v\| \leq k\} = (U \cap k\Sigma) + (V \cap k\Sigma)$. Since U is w^*-closed and Σ is w^*-compact, $U \cap k\Sigma$ is w^*-compact. So Q is the vector sum of two w^*-compact sets and is therefore w^*-compact.

Since $Q \subset U + V$, it is clear that $Q \cap \Sigma \subset (U + V) \cap \Sigma$. But if $\|u + v\| \leq 1$ then $\|u\| + \|v\| \leq k$, and so $\|u\| \leq k$, $\|v\| \leq k$; hence $(U + V) \cap \Sigma \subset Q \cap \Sigma$. So $(U + V) \cap \Sigma = Q \cap \Sigma$ and is therefore w^*-compact.

Theorem 4. *Let A, B be Dirichlet algebras on a compact space X. Suppose that every $\mu \in A^\perp$ is singular with respect to every $\nu \in B^\perp$. Then $A \cap B$ is a Dirichlet algebra on X.*

Proof. $A \cap B$ is certainly a sup norm algebra on X, so we need only show that no nonzero real measure lies in $(A \cap B)^\perp$.

Note that $A^\perp + B^\perp \subset (A \cap B)^\perp$ and indeed $A^\perp + B^\perp$ is w^*-dense in $(A \cap B)^\perp$. For if a w^*-continuous linear functional $\sigma \to \int f \, d\sigma$ (where $f \in C(X)$) annihilates $A^\perp$ and $B^\perp$, then we have $f \in A$ and $f \in B$ by the Hahn-Banach theorem, and hence $\int f \, d\sigma = 0$ for all $\sigma \in (A \cap B)^\perp$. On the other hand, given $\mu \in A^\perp$ and $\nu \in B^\perp$, $\|\mu + \nu\| = \|\mu\| + \|\nu\|$ since μ, ν are mutually singular by hypothesis. So $A^\perp + B^\perp$ is w^*-closed in $M(X)$, by Lemma 5. Therefore $(A \cap B)^\perp = A^\perp + B^\perp$.

Any real measure $\sigma \in (A \cap B)^\perp$ has the form $\sigma = \mu + \nu$, where $\mu \in A^\perp$ and $\nu \in B^\perp$. Since μ, ν are concentrated on disjoint sets, μ and ν are also real-valued. Since A and B are assumed to be Dirichlet algebras, $\mu = \nu = 0$; so $\sigma = 0$. Therefore $A \cap B$ is a Dirichlet algebra.

Now suppose that X is a compact space and that ψ is a homeomorphism of X onto itself. For each measure μ in $M(X)$, we define a measure $\mu \circ \psi$ on X by setting $(\mu \circ \psi)(E) = \mu(\psi(E))$ for each Borel set $E \subset X$. As a linear functional, $\mu \circ \psi$ is given by $\int f \, d(\mu \circ \psi) = \int f \circ \psi^{-1} \, d\mu$ ($\forall f \in C(X)$). Note that $\|\mu\| = \|\mu \circ \psi\|$. ψ also defines an algebra automorphism ψ_* of $C(X)$ given by $\psi_*(f) = f \circ \psi$. Observe that if $A \subset C(X)$ and $B = \psi_*^{-1}(A) = \{f \in C(X) : f \circ \psi \in A\}$, then $\nu \in B^\perp$ iff $\nu \circ \psi \in A^\perp$; i.e., $A^\perp = B^\perp \circ \psi$. If A is a function algebra, then B is a function algebra (isometrically) isomorphic to A. Set $A(\psi) = A \cap B = \{f \in A : f \circ \psi \in A\}$.

Theorem 5.   *Let A be a Dirichlet algebra on X, and ψ a self-homeomorphism of X. Suppose that there is a Borel set $F \subset X$ such that for each $\mu \in A^\perp$, μ is concentrated on $F \cap \psi^{-1}(X \backslash F)$. Then $A(\psi) = \{f \in A : f \circ \psi \in A\}$ is a Dirichlet algebra on X, and unless $A = C(X)$, $A(\psi)$ is a proper subalgebra of A.*

Proof.   Let $B = \{f \in C(X) : f \circ \psi \in A\}$. Then $A(\psi) = A \cap B$, and B is a Dirichlet algebra on X. Let F be as in the hypothesis. Given $\mu \in A^\perp$, we have $|\mu|(X \backslash F) = 0$ by hypothesis, so μ is concentrated on F. If $\nu \in B^\perp$; then $\nu = \sigma \circ \psi^{-1}$ for some $\sigma \in A^\perp$. Hence $|\nu|(F) = |\sigma|(\psi^{-1}(F)) = 0$ by hypothesis, so ν is concentrated on $X \backslash F$. Hence by Theorem 4, $A(\psi)$ is a Dirichlet algebra on X.

Suppose that $A(\psi) = A$: Then $A \subset B$, so $B^\perp \subset A^\perp$. But $A^\perp$, $B^\perp$ are concentrated on disjoint sets, so $B^\perp = \{0\}$ and hence $B = C(X)$. Hence $A = \psi_*(B) = C(X)$.

Corollary.   *Let A^1 be the boundary value algebra on the unit circle T. Then there exist proper subalgebras of A^1 which are Dirichlet algebras on T.*

Proof.   Let m be normalized Lebesgue one-dimensional measure on T. There exist a Borel set $F \subset T$ and a self-homeomorphism ψ of T such that $m(F) = 1$, $m(\psi^{-1}(F)) = 0$. (See the remarks below.) By the theorem of F. and M. Riesz, every $\mu \perp A^1$ is absolutely continuous with respect to m, so $|\mu|(T \backslash F) = 0 = |\mu|(\psi^{-1}(F))$. The hypothesis of the theorem is satisfied, so $A^1(\psi) = \{f \in A^1 : f \circ \psi \in A^1\}$ is a proper Dirichlet subalgebra of A^1.

Remarks.   Let I be the unit interval $[0, 1]$, and let m be Lebesgue measure on the Borel sets of I. Each continuous nondecreasing real-valued function φ on I determines a finite positive Borel measure $\mu = \mu_\varphi$ on I, where $\mu(E) = m(\varphi(E))$ for all Borel sets $E \subset I$. (If E is an interval, then $\varphi(E)$ is an interval. So $\varphi(E)$ is a Borel set if E is a relatively open subset of I. But $\{E : \varphi(E)$ is a Borel set$\}$ is a σ-ring, so $\varphi(E)$ is a Borel set for every Borel set $E \subset I$.) In particular, $\mu([a, b]) = \varphi(b) - \varphi(a)$ for any $[a, b] \subset I$. It is a fundamental fact about measures on the line that μ and m are mutually singular iff $\varphi' = 0$ except on a Lebesgue measurable set of m-measure zero. (This is essentially proved in [K], Chapter 8.)

Lemma 6.   *There is a strictly increasing continuous function φ from I onto I such that $\varphi' = 0$ a.e. For any such function, there exists a Borel set $E \subset I$ such that $m(E) = 0$ but $m(\varphi(E)) = 1$.*

Proof.   If φ is a strictly increasing continuous map of I onto itself such that $\varphi' = 0$ outside a set of measure zero, then the induced measure $\mu = m \circ \varphi$ is singular; thus there is a Borel set E with $m(E) = 0$ but $m(\varphi(E)) = \mu(E) = \mu(I) = m(\varphi(I)) = m(I) = 1$.

Let φ_0 be the classical Cantor function on I extended to $\mathbf{R}^1$ by constancy. ($\varphi_0 = 0$ on $(-\infty, 0]$, $\varphi_0 = 1$ on $[1, +\infty)$). $\varphi_0 = 1/2$ on $[1/3, 2/3]$, $1/4$ on

[1/9, 2/9], 3/4 on [7/9, 8/9], etc.; φ_0 is extended to all of [0, 1] by continuity.) Consider the sequence of intervals $I_n = [a_n, b_n]$, where $I_1 = [0, 1]$, $I_2 = [0, \frac{1}{2}]$, $I_3 = [\frac{1}{2}, 1]$, $I_4 = [0, 1/4]$, $I_5 = [1/4, 2/4]$, $I_6 = [2/4, 3/4]$, $I_7 = [3/4, 1]$, ..., and let $\varphi_n(t) = \varphi_0\left(\dfrac{t - a_n}{b_n - a_n}\right)$. ($\varphi_n$ is the Cantor function rescaled relative to the interval I_n.) Finally, set $\varphi = \sum\limits_{n=1}^{\infty} \dfrac{\varphi_n}{2^n}$. The series converges uniformly, so φ is continuous and nondecreasing on $\mathbf{R}^1$. Since $\varphi(0) = 0$ and $\varphi(1) = 1$, $\varphi(I) = I$. A little reflection shows that φ is strictly increasing on I, and $\varphi' = \sum\limits_{n=1}^{\infty} \varphi'_n/2^n = 0$ a.e. by Fubini's theorem on differentiation of series of monotone functions.

Consider a singular homeomorphism φ of I onto I as in Lemma 6. Define ψ on the circle by setting $\psi(e^{2\pi it}) = e^{2\pi i\varphi(t)}$. ψ is a homeomorphism of T onto T. If E is a Borel set on I such that E has measure 0 while $\varphi(E)$ has measure 1, and if we let $F = \{e^{2\pi it} : t \in \varphi(E)\}$, then F has measure 1 on the circle while $\psi^{-1}(F)$ has measure zero. This establishes the existence of ψ and F which was asserted in the proof of the corollary to Theorem 5.

Observe that for the algebras A, B in Theorem 5, not only are the measures in $A^\perp$ mutually singular with the measures in $B^\perp$, but there is a fixed set F such that $A^\perp$ is concentrated on F and $B^\perp$ is concentrated on the complement of F. In this case one can determine the maximal ideal space of $A \cap B$.

Theorem 6. *Let A, B be Dirichlet algebras on X. Suppose that there is a Borel set F such that every $\mu \in A^\perp$ is concentrated on F while every $\nu \in B^\perp$ is concentrated on $X \backslash F$. Then $\mathscr{M}(A \cap B)$ is homeomorphic to $\mathscr{M}(A) \# \mathscr{M}(B)$, the space obtained by attaching $\mathscr{M}(A)$ to $\mathscr{M}(B)$ via the embeddings of X in each.*

Proof. Let $x \to \varphi_x$ be the embedding of X in $\mathscr{M}(A)$ and $x \to \tilde{\varphi}_x$ the embedding of X in $\mathscr{M}(B)$. To form $\mathscr{M}(A) \# \mathscr{M}(B)$, we take the disjoint union of $\mathscr{M}(A)$ with $\mathscr{M}(B)$ (say $(\mathscr{M}(A) \times \{1\}) \cup (\mathscr{M}(B) \times \{2\})$) with the obvious topology and identify each φ_x with the corresponding $\tilde{\varphi}_x$. The content of the theorem is that the map $h \to h' = h | A \cap B$ is a homeomorphism of $\mathscr{M}(A) \# \mathscr{M}(B)$ onto $\mathscr{M}(A \cap B)$. Since $\varphi_x | A \cap B = \tilde{\varphi}_x | A \cap B$, $h \to h'$ is a well-defined mapping. Clearly $h' \in \mathscr{M}(A \cap B)$ and, by definition of the Gelfand topologies, $h \to h'$ is continuous. It remains to be shown that it is one-one and onto.

Note that $A \cap B$ is a Dirichlet algebra. If $h \in \mathscr{M}(A) \cup \mathscr{M}(B)$, then h and h' have the same representing measures. For example, if $h \in \mathscr{M}(A)$ and σ_h is the representing measure for h on X, then $\int f d\sigma_h = h(f) = h'(f)$ for all $f \in A \cap B$; so by uniqueness, σ_h is the representing measure for h'. It is therefore clear that if $h'_1 = h'_2$ and if h_1, h_2 are both in $\mathscr{M}(A)$ or both in $\mathscr{M}(B)$, then $h_1 = h_2$ since they have identical representing measures.

Let us now show that if $h \in \mathcal{M}(A)\backslash X$, $k \in \mathcal{M}(B)\backslash X$, then $h' \neq k'$. Let σ_h, σ_k be the representing measures for h, k. It will be enough to show that σ_h is concentrated on F and σ_k on $X\backslash F$.

Take $f \in A$ such that $h(f) = 0$. Then $f\sigma_h \in A^\perp$, so (1) $f\sigma_h$ is concentrated on F: $\int_{X\backslash F} |f| \, d\sigma_h = 0$ if $h(f) = 0$. For each $x \in X$, choose $f_x \in A$ with $h(f_x) = 0$, $f_x(x) = 1$. ($\hat{A}$ separates points.) By compactness, there is a function g of form $\sum_{i=1}^{n} |f_{x_i}|$ such that $g > 0$ on X. But $\int_{X\backslash F} g \, d\sigma_h = \sum_{i=1}^{n} \int_{X\backslash F} |f_{x_i}| \, d\sigma_h = 0$, by (1). Since $g \geq \delta > 0$ on X, $\sigma_h(X\backslash F) = 0$. So indeed σ_h is concentrated on F. By symmetry, σ_k is concentrated on $X\backslash F$. So $h' \neq k'$. Thus the map is one-one.

Let $q \in \mathcal{M}(A \cap B)$ be arbitrary, and let σ_q be its representing measure. Then $\sigma_q = \alpha + \beta$ where α is the restriction of σ_q to F, $\beta = \sigma_q | X\backslash F$. Since $\int 1 \, d\sigma_q = 1$, either $\alpha \neq 0$ or $\beta \neq 0$. We may assume that $\alpha \neq 0$. If $f \in A \cap B$ and $q(f) = 0$, then $f\sigma_q = f\alpha + f\beta$ is an annihilator of $A \cap B$. But $(A \cap B)^\perp = A^\perp + B^\perp$, as we showed in the proof of Theorem 4, so $f\sigma_q = \mu + \nu$ where $\mu \in A^\perp$, $\nu \in B^\perp$. Since μ, ν are concentrated on F, $X\backslash F$ respectively, we have $f\alpha = \mu$, $f\beta = \nu$. So $f\alpha \in A^\perp$ if $q(f) = 0$. Let $M_0 = \ker(q)$; then α annihilates the ideal AM_0 of A spanned by M_0. Since α does not annihilate 1, $1 \notin AM_0$. There are two conclusions: AM_0 is proper in A, and hence is contained in some maximal ideal $M = \ker(h)$ of A, $h \in \mathcal{M}(A)$; and $AM_0 \cap (A \cap B)$ is a proper ideal of $A \cap B$ containing M_0, so $AM_0 \cap (A \cap B) = M_0$. So $M_0 = M \cap (A \cap B)$ and $q = h'$. Thus the map is onto $\mathcal{M}(A \cap B)$.

Corollary. *Suppose that A and ψ satisfy the hypotheses of Theorem 5. Then $\mathcal{M}(A(\psi)) = \mathcal{M}(A) \#_\psi \mathcal{M}(A)$, the space obtained by attaching $\mathcal{M}(A)$ to $\mathcal{M}(A)$ along X via the homeomorphism ψ.*

Proof. Let $B = \{f \in C(X) : f \circ \psi \in A\}$. Then $\mathcal{M}(A(\psi)) = \mathcal{M}(A) \# \mathcal{M}(B)$. There is a homeomorphism $h \to \dot{h}$ from $\mathcal{M}(A)$ onto $\mathcal{M}(B)$ given by $\dot{h}(f) = h(f \circ \psi)$. If $h = \varphi_x$ for some $x \in X$, then $\dot{h}(f) = f(\psi(x))$, so $\tilde{\varphi}_x = \varphi_{\psi(x)}$. (Here $x \to \varphi_x$, $x \to \tilde{\varphi}_x$ are the embeddings of X into $\mathcal{M}(A)$, $\mathcal{M}(B)$.) So $\mathcal{M}(A) \# \mathcal{M}(B)$ is obtained from the disjoint union of $\mathcal{M}(A)$ with itself by identifying x with $\psi(x)$ for each $x \in X$.

For example, if ψ is a homeomorphism of the circle onto itself which carries some set of measure zero onto a set of full measure, then $\mathcal{M}(A^1(\psi))$ is obtained by attaching the closed disk $\Delta = \mathcal{M}(A^1)$ to itself along the circle, with each point $e^{i\theta}$ attached to its image $\psi(e^{i\theta})$, and is homeomorphic to S^2.

Now suppose that A is a function algebra on X and that ψ is a homeomorphism of X onto X such that (a) $f \circ \psi \in A$ for each $f \in A$ and (b) $\psi \circ \psi$ is the identity mapping on X. Let $X' = X/\psi$ be the orbit space determined by ψ. The points of X' are the pairs $\{x, \psi(x)\}$ with $x \in X$, and X' is given the quotient topology defined by the quotient map $Q : x \to x' = \{x, \psi(x)\}$. Observe that $C(X')$ separates points on X', so X' is a Hausdorff space. For suppose that x', y' are distinct points of X'. There are distinct points x, y in X with $x' = Q(x)$, $y' = Q(y)$, and $y \neq \psi(x)$. There is a continuous function f on X such that $f(y) = 0$ but $f(x) \neq 0$, $f(\psi(x)) \neq 0$. Set $F = (f \circ \psi) \cdot f$. Then $F \in C(X)$, $F = F \circ \psi$, and $F(x) \neq 0$, $F(y) = 0$. If F' is defined on X' so that $F' \circ Q = F$, then $F' \in C(X')$ and F' separates x' and y'. Note too that $A' = \{f \in A : f = f \circ \psi\}$ can be identified with a function algebra on the compact space X', since we could have chosen f above to lie in A.

Theorem 7. *Let A be a Dirichlet algebra on X. Suppose that $\psi : X \to X$ is a continuous map such that* (a) $f \circ \psi \in A$ *for each* $f \in A$, (b) $\psi \circ \psi$ *is the identity mapping on X. Then* $A' = \{f \in A : f \circ \psi = f\}$ *is a Dirichlet algebra on X/ψ.*

Proof. Let $g \in C_R(X/\psi)$. Then there is some $u \in C_R(X)$ such that $u = u \circ \psi$ and $g(x') = u(x)$, $x \in X$. Let $\varepsilon > 0$. Since A is a Dirichlet algebra, $\|u - \mathrm{Re}\,(f)\| < \varepsilon$ for some $f \in A$. But $\psi \circ \psi$ is the identity, so $f + f \circ \psi$ belongs to A'. Since $u = u \circ \psi$, $\|u - \mathrm{Re}\,(\frac{1}{2}(f + f \circ \psi))\| < \varepsilon$. So A' is a Dirichlet algebra on X/ψ.

We can now find our long awaited proper Dirichlet algebra on the interval. Let A^1 be the boundary value algebra. Suppose that ψ is a homeomorphism of the circle T onto itself which has the following properties: (a) ψ is singular (i.e., ψ carries some Borel set E of measure 0 onto a set of measure 1), (b) $\psi \circ \psi$ is the identity mapping. Let $A_\psi = \{f \in A^1 : f \circ \psi = f\}$; A_ψ should be a small subalgebra of A^1. But recall that $A^1(\psi) = \{f \in A^1 : f \circ \psi \in A^1\}$ is a Dirichlet algebra on T, and clearly $A_\psi = \{f \in A^1(\psi) : f \circ \psi = f\}$. Hence by Theorem 7, A_ψ is a Dirichlet algebra on the identification space T/ψ.

If ψ also satisfies the condition: (c) ψ reverses orientation on T, then T/ψ is homeomorphic to the interval I, and A_ψ is a proper Dirichlet algebra on I. (Let φ satisfy the conditions of Lemma 6. Set $h = -\varphi$. Then h is a strictly decreasing continuous mapping of $[0, 1]$ onto $[-1, 0]$, and $h' = 0$ a.e. Set $\psi(e^{i\pi t}) = e^{i\pi h(t)}$ if $0 \leq t \leq 1$ and $\psi(e^{i\pi t}) = e^{i\pi h^{-1}(t)}$ if $-1 \leq t \leq 0$. Then ψ satisfies conditions (a), (b), (c).)

One can go a step further and construct a new Dirichlet algebra on the circle.

Lemma 7. *Let ψ be a homeomorphism of the circle T onto itself such that* (a) ψ *is singular,* (b) $\psi \circ \psi = $ *identity. Let* $A_\psi = \{f \in A^1 : f = f \circ \psi\}$. *Then* $A_\psi{}^\perp = (A^1)^\perp + \Theta$, *where Θ is the set of all odd measures ν on T. By definition, $\nu \in \Theta$ iff $\nu = -\nu \circ \psi$.*

Proof. Note that $C(T/\psi)$ can be identified with the set of all $f \in C(T)$ such that $f = f \circ \psi$, and that $\nu \in \Theta$ iff ν annihilates all such functions. Since $A_\psi = A^1 \cap C(T/\psi)$, the lemma asserts precisely that $(A^1 \cap C(T/\psi))^\perp$ is the sum of the annihilators $(A^1)^\perp$ and $C(T/\psi)^\perp$. As in Theorem 4, we need only verify that $(A^1)^\perp + \Theta$ is w^*-closed.

But if $\mu \in (A^1)^\perp$, then μ and $\mu \circ \psi$ are mutually singular, so $\|\mu + \mu \circ \psi\| = \|\mu\| + \|\mu \circ \psi\| = 2\|\mu\|$. Hence if $v \in \Theta$,

$$\|\mu\| = \tfrac{1}{2}\|\mu + \mu \circ \psi\| = \tfrac{1}{2}\|\mu + v + \mu \circ \psi + v \circ \psi\|$$
$$= \tfrac{1}{2}\|\mu + v + (\mu + v) \circ \psi\| \le \tfrac{1}{2}(\|\mu + v\| + \|(\mu + v) \circ \psi\|)$$
$$= \|\mu + v\|.$$

From this it is easy to see that the unit ball of $(A^1)^\perp + \Theta$ is w^*-closed, and hence $(A^1)^\perp + \Theta$ is also w^*-closed, by Banach-Dieudonné. (Suppose that $\{\mu_\alpha + v_\alpha\}$ is a convergent net in the unit ball of $(A^1)^\perp + \Theta$. Then $\|\mu_\alpha\| \le 1$ also, so some subnet $\{\mu_\beta\}$ of $\{\mu_\alpha\}$ is w^*-convergent with limit $\mu \in (A^1)^\perp$. Thus v_β also converges w^* to some $v \in \Theta$, and $\lambda = \lim_\alpha (\mu_\alpha + v_\alpha)$ must lie in the unit ball of $(A^1)^\perp + \Theta$.) So the lemma is proved.

Theorem 8. *Let ψ be an orientation-reversing homeomorphism of T onto T satisfying conditions (a), (b). Suppose that $\psi(1) = 1$, $\psi(-1) = -1$. Set $B = \{f \in A_\psi : f(1) = f(-1)\}$. Then B is a Dirichlet algebra on the space obtained from T/ψ by identifying 1 and -1; hence B is a Dirichlet algebra on the circle.*

Proof. To see that B is an algebra on the circle, it is perhaps best to consider A_ψ as a function algebra on the upper semicircle of T and to note that B identifies its endpoints but no other points.

Since A_ψ separates points on the upper semicircle, we choose $g \in A_\psi$ such that $g(1) = 0$, $g(-1) = 1$, and fix g. For any $f \in A_\psi$, $f + (f(1) - f(-1))g$ is in B. Let λ be a real measure on T which annihilates B. We must show that λ is orthogonal to all continuous functions on T/ψ which identify 1 and -1.

Set $c = \int g \, d\lambda$ and let $\sigma = \delta_1 - \delta_{-1}$, a difference of point masses. We calculate that $\int f \, d(\lambda + c\sigma) = \int f \, d\lambda + (\int f \, d\sigma)(\int g \, d\lambda) = 0$ for all f in A_ψ. Hence by Lemma 7, $\lambda + c\sigma = \mu + v$ where μ is in $(A^1)^\perp$ and v is odd relative to ψ. By an F. and M. Riesz theorem, $\mu = km$ where m is normalized Lebesgue measure on the circle and k is an H^1 function. We shall show that k is real-valued and hence $\mu = 0$. (For suppose $k \in H^1$ is real-valued. Then $\int kz^n \, dm = 0$ for $n = 0, 1, 2, \dots$ and so $\int kz^n \, dm = 0$ for $n = -1, -2, \dots$ (take complex conjugates). So the Fourier coefficients of k vanish, and $k = 0$ a.e. $[m]$. Hence $\mu = km = 0$.)

Now $\lambda + c\sigma = \mu + v$, and λ is real; so $\lambda + a\sigma = k_1 m + v_1$, $b\sigma = k_2 m + v_2$ where $c = a + ib$, $k = k_1 + ik_2$, $v = v_1 + iv_2$. Note that v_1, v_2 are also odd. We have $v_2 - b\sigma = k_2 m$, so $v_2 - b\sigma$ is absolutely continuous with respect to m. Since ψ is singular, there is a Borel set $E \subset T$ with $m(E) = 0$, $m(\psi(E)) = 1$. Let $E_0 = E \cup \{1, -1\}$; then $m(E_0) = 0$ and $m(\psi(E_0)) = 1$. Given any Borel set F on T, set $G = F \setminus E_0$. Then since $v_2 - b\sigma \ll m$, we have

$$(v_2 - b\sigma)(E_0) = 0$$

and $(v_2 - b\sigma)(\psi(G)) = 0$ (since $m(\psi(G)) = 0$). But $\sigma(E_0) = 0$ and $\sigma(\psi(G)) = 0$ (since $\psi(1) = 1$ and $\psi(-1) = -1$ do not lie in $\psi(G)$), so $v_2(E_0) = 0$, $0 = v_2(\psi(G)) = -v_2(G)$. Thus $v_2(F) = 0$, and since F is arbitrary, $v_2 = 0$.

Hence $b\sigma = k_2 m$, so k_2 and b must both be zero, since σ is supported on $\{1, -1\}$. Hence $k = k_1 + ik_2$ is real-valued a.e. and in H^1, so $k = 0$, $\mu = 0$. We conclude that $\lambda + a\sigma = v_1$. In particular, $\lambda + a\sigma$ is odd, so it is clear that λ annihilates any $f \in C(T)$ such that $f = f \circ \psi$ and $f(1) - f(-1) = 0$. So B is a Dirichlet algebra on the circle.

One can show that B is isomorphic to no subalgebra of the boundary value algebra. The idea of the argument is that the homomorphisms of A_ψ determined by 1 and -1 are identified in $\mathcal{M}(B)$ and thus $\mathcal{M}(B)$ is a two-sphere with a pair of antipodal points identified, whereas the circle is contractible to a point in the maximal ideal space of any Dirichlet subalgebra B^1 of A^1 since B^1 must separate the points of $\Delta = \mathcal{M}(A^1)$.

EXERCISE SET 8.2

1. Let A be a function algebra on X. Suppose that G is a finite set of homeomorphisms of X onto itself which forms a group under composition and that $f \circ \varphi$ belongs to A for every $f \in A$ and $\varphi \in G$. Let $X' = X/G$ be the space whose points are the orbits $x' = \{\varphi(x) : \varphi \in G\}$ as x ranges over X. Then X' is compact (Hausdorff) in the quotient topology.
    (a) $A' = \{f \in A : f = f \circ \varphi$ for all $\varphi \in G\}$ is a function algebra on X/G.
    (b) Each $\varphi \in G$ determines a homeomorphism $\hat{\varphi}$ of $\mathcal{M}(A)$ given by
       $\hat{\varphi}(h)(f) = h(f \circ \varphi)$.
    (c) $\mathcal{M}(A') = \mathcal{M}(A)/\hat{G}$.
    (d) If A is a Dirichlet algebra on X, then A' is a Dirichlet algebra on X/G.

2. Determine the maximal ideal space of $A_\psi = \{f \in A^1 : f \circ \psi = f\}$, where $\psi : T \to T$ satisfies (a), (b), (c).

3. Let B be a Dirichlet algebra which is a subalgebra of a function algebra A. Show that distinct complex homomorphisms of A have distinct restrictions to B.

8.3 LIMITS

Recall that a directed set is a partially ordered set D such that for all α, β in D, $\exists \gamma \in D$ with $\alpha \leq \gamma$ and $\beta \leq \gamma$. Let D be a directed set. Suppose that $\{S_\alpha\}_{\alpha \in D}$ is a family of sets indexed by D, and that for each pair $(\alpha, \beta) \in D \times D$ with $\alpha \leq \beta$, σ_α^β is a mapping from S_β to S_α. The pair $(\{S_\alpha\}, \{\sigma_\alpha^\beta\})$ is an *inverse system* iff (i) σ_α^α is the identity map on S_α ($\forall \alpha \in D$) and (ii) $\sigma_\alpha^\beta \circ \sigma_\beta^\gamma = \sigma_\alpha^\gamma$ whenever $\alpha \leq \beta \leq \gamma$ in D. Given an inverse system of sets S_α and maps σ_α^β, let S be the Cartesian product $\prod_{\alpha \in D} S_\alpha$ and let $p_\alpha : S \to S_\alpha$ ($\alpha \in D$) be the coordinate projections. Let S_∞ be the set of all $x \in S$ such that $\sigma_\alpha^\beta(p_\beta(x)) = p_\alpha(x)$ for all

$\alpha \le \beta$ in D, and let $\pi_\alpha : S_\infty \to S_\alpha$ be the restriction of p_α to S_∞ ($\alpha \in D$). Observe that for all pairs $(\alpha, \beta) \in D \times D$ with $\alpha \le \beta$, the diagram

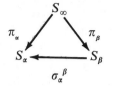

is commutative. The pair $(S_\infty, \{\pi_\alpha\})$ is called the *inverse limit* of the system $(\{S_\alpha\}, \{\sigma_\alpha^\beta\})$.

If all the S_α are topological spaces and the σ_α^β are continuous mappings, and if we give S_∞ the topology induced by the product topology on S, then the π_α are continuous. If the S_α are groups (or modules, algebras, etc.) and the σ_α^β are homomorphisms, then S_∞ is a subgroup (submodule, etc.) of $\prod_\alpha S_\alpha$ and the π_α are homomorphisms.

Lemma 8. *Let $(\{S_\alpha\}_{\alpha \in D}, \{\sigma_\alpha^\beta\})$ be an inverse system of compact spaces and continuous maps. Then the inverse limit of the system is also compact.*

Proof. The set on which two continuous maps into a Hausdorff space coincide is closed, so $S_\infty = \bigcap_{\alpha \le \beta} \{x \in S : \sigma_\alpha^\beta(p_\beta(x)) = p_\alpha(x)\}$ is a closed subset of the compact space $S = \prod_{\alpha \in D} S_\alpha$. It remains to be shown that S_∞ is nonvoid. To do this we will make use of compactness of S and the directedness of D in choosing preimages of points.

Given $\beta \in D$, set $F_\beta = \{x \in S : \sigma_\alpha^\beta(p_\beta(x)) = p_\alpha(x) \text{ for all } \alpha \le \beta\}$. Each F_β is closed in S, and the intersection of the F_β ($\beta \in D$) is S_∞. So it suffices to prove that any finite intersection $F_{\beta_1} \cap \cdots \cap F_{\beta_n}$ is nonvoid. But D is directed, so $\exists \gamma \in D$ with $\beta_1 \le \gamma, \ldots, \beta_n \le \gamma$, and hence $F_\gamma \subset \bigcap_{i=1}^{n} F_{\beta_i}$. So we are reduced to showing that each F_β is nonvoid. But this is clear. Just choose any element $x_\beta \in S_\beta$, and for each $\alpha \in D$ with $\alpha \le \beta$, let $x_\alpha = \sigma_\alpha^\beta(x_\beta)$. By the axiom of choice, $\{x_\alpha\}_{\alpha \le \beta} \times \prod \{S_\gamma : \gamma \in D, \gamma \not\le \beta\}$ is nonvoid; so $F_\beta \ne \emptyset$.

Lemma 9. *Let $(\{S_\alpha\}_{\alpha \in D}, \{\sigma_\alpha^\beta\})$ be an inverse system of compact spaces and continuous maps. Then for each $\alpha \in D$, $\pi_\alpha(S_\infty) = \bigcap \{\sigma_\alpha^\beta(S_\beta) : \beta \in D, \alpha \le \beta\}$. In particular, if $\sigma_\alpha^\beta(S_\beta) = S_\alpha$ for all α, β with $\alpha \le \beta$, then $\pi_\alpha(S_\infty) = S_\alpha$ for all $\alpha \in D$.*

Proof. Given $x_\alpha \in S_\alpha$, we form an inverse system (Y, ρ) as follows. If $\alpha \le \beta \in D$, set $Y_\beta = \{x_\beta \in S_\beta : \sigma_\alpha^\beta(x_\beta) = x_\alpha\}$, while if $\alpha \not\le \beta \in D$, set $Y_\beta = S_\beta$. Note that if $\beta \le \gamma$ and $x_\gamma \in Y_\gamma$, then $\sigma_\beta^\gamma(x_\gamma) \in Y_\beta$; so there is a mapping $\rho_\beta^\gamma : Y_\gamma \to Y_\beta$ given by $\rho_\beta^\gamma(x_\gamma) = \sigma_\beta^\gamma(x_\gamma)$. Let $(Y_\infty, \{\rho_\alpha\})$ be the inverse limit of the inverse system $(\{Y_\beta\}, \{\rho_\beta^\gamma\})$. If $y \in Y_\infty$, then $\pi_\alpha(y) = p_\alpha(y) = \rho_\alpha(y)$ belongs to $Y_\alpha = \{x_\alpha\}$ and to $\pi_\alpha(S_\infty)$; i.e., if $Y_\infty \ne \emptyset$, then $x_\alpha \in \pi_\alpha(S_\infty)$.

Hence if $x_\alpha \in S_\alpha \backslash \pi_\alpha(S_\infty)$, the inverse limit $\varprojlim Y_\beta$ is empty. So for some $\beta \geq \alpha$, the space Y_β is empty; i.e., $\bigcap_{\alpha \leq \beta} \sigma_\alpha{}^\beta(S_\beta) \subset \pi_\alpha(S_\infty)$. Conversely, given $\beta \geq \alpha$ and $x \in S_\infty$, $\pi_\alpha(x) = \sigma_\alpha{}^\beta(\pi_\beta(x))$ belongs to $\sigma_\alpha{}^\beta(S_\beta)$, so the reverse inclusion is also true.

Remark. Any space S is the inverse limit of the trivial system $(\{S\}, \{i_S\})$, where i_S is the identity map on S.

If the directed set D is the set of integers or the set of nonnegative integers, then a system of maps $\{\sigma_n{}^m : n, m \in D, n \leq m\}$ satisfying the consistency conditions (i), (ii) is completely determined by the specification of all the maps $\{\sigma_n{}^{n+1} : n \in D\}$, and conversely, every family $\{\sigma_n{}^{n+1} : S_{n+1} \to S_n\}$ determines a unique consistent system $\{\sigma_n{}^m\}$ by composition. In this case we speak of inverse *sequences* $\cdots \leftarrow S_n \xleftarrow{\sigma_n{}^{n+1}} S_{n+1} \leftarrow \cdots$.

Now we turn to direct systems.

Let D be a directed set. Suppose that R is a commutative ring with identity and that $\{A^\alpha\}_{\alpha \in D}$ is a family of R-modules indexed by D. Suppose also that for each pair $(\alpha, \beta) \in D \times D$ with $\alpha \leq \beta$, $\varphi_\alpha{}^\beta : A^\alpha \to A^\beta$ is an R-linear map. The pair $(\{A^\alpha\}, \{\varphi_\alpha{}^\beta\})$ is a *direct system* iff (i) $\varphi_\alpha{}^\alpha$ is the identity on A^α for each α in D, and (ii) $\varphi_\beta{}^\gamma \circ \varphi_\alpha{}^\beta = \varphi_\alpha{}^\gamma$ if $\alpha \leq \beta \leq \gamma$ in D. Let $A = \sum_{\alpha \in D} A^\alpha$ be the direct sum of the A^α; A consists of all $f \in \prod_{\alpha \in D} A^\alpha$ such that only a finite number of coordinates of f are not zero. For each $\alpha \in D$ there is an embedding $i_\alpha : A^\alpha \to A$; given f^α in A^α, $i_\alpha(f^\alpha)$ is the element of A with αth coordinate f^α and all others 0. Let S be the submodule of A generated by the ranges

$$(i_\beta \circ \varphi_\alpha{}^\beta - i_\alpha)(A^\alpha)$$

for all pairs $(\alpha, \beta) \in D \times D$ with $\alpha \leq \beta$. Set $A^\infty = A/S$, let $\kappa : A \to A^\infty$ be the canonical map, and set $j_\alpha = \kappa \circ i_\alpha$ for each $\alpha \in D$. Then $j_\alpha : A^\alpha \to A^\infty$ is R-linear, and if $\alpha \leq \beta$ in D, the diagram

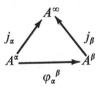

is commutative. The R-module A^∞ is called the *direct limit* of the given system.

One basic property of A^∞ is this: $A^\infty = \bigcup_{\alpha \in D} j_\alpha(A^\alpha)$. For take any element $\kappa(f) \in A^\infty$, $f \in A$. By definition of the direct sum, $f = \sum_{k=1}^N i_k(f^k)$ where $f^k \in A^{\alpha_k}$ and $i_k = i_{\alpha_k}$. Since D is directed, there is some $\alpha \in D$ with $\alpha_k \leq \alpha$ for $1 \leq k \leq N$. Set $g = \sum i_\alpha(\varphi_{\alpha_k}{}^\alpha(f^k))$. Then $g - f$ is in S, so $\kappa(f) = \kappa(g) = j_\alpha\left(\sum_k \varphi_{\alpha_k}{}^\alpha(f^k)\right)$.

We shall need a lemma about direct limits which we shall not prove. For a proof, see page 221 of Eilenberg and Steenrod, *Foundations of Algebraic Topology*.

Lemma 10. *Given a direct system $(\{A^\alpha\}, \{\varphi_\alpha{}^\beta\})$ with direct limit $(A^\infty, \{j_\alpha\})$, suppose that $g^\gamma \in A^\gamma$ and $j_\gamma(g^\gamma) = 0$. Then $\varphi_\gamma{}^\delta(g^\gamma) = 0$ for some $\delta \geq \gamma$.*

Lemma 11. *Suppose that $f^\alpha \in A^\alpha$, $f^\beta \in A^\beta$. Then $j_\alpha(f^\alpha) = j_\beta(f^\beta)$ iff $\varphi_\alpha{}^\gamma(f^\alpha) = \varphi_\beta{}^\gamma(f^\beta)$ for some γ such that $\alpha \leq \gamma$ and $\beta \leq \gamma$.*

Proof. Suppose that $\varphi_\alpha{}^\gamma(f^\alpha) = \varphi_\beta{}^\gamma(f^\alpha)$ for some $\gamma \geq \alpha, \beta$. Then $g_\alpha = (i_\gamma \circ \varphi_\alpha{}^\gamma - i_\alpha)(f^\alpha)$ and $g_\beta = (i_\gamma \circ \varphi_\beta{}^\gamma - i_\beta)(f^\beta)$ belong to S, and $g_\alpha - g_\beta = i_\beta(f^\beta) - i_\alpha(f^\alpha)$. So $0 = \kappa(g_\alpha - g_\beta) = j_\beta(f^\beta) - j_\alpha(f^\alpha)$.

Conversely, suppose that $j_\alpha(f^\alpha) = j_\beta(f^\beta)$. Choose $\gamma \in D$ with $\alpha \leq \gamma$, $\beta \leq \gamma$, and set $g_\gamma = \varphi_\alpha{}^\gamma(f^\alpha) - \varphi_\beta{}^\gamma(f^\beta)$. Then $j_\gamma(g_\gamma) = 0$, by commutativity in the fundamental diagram, so $\varphi_\gamma{}^\delta(g_\gamma) = 0$ for some $\delta \geq \gamma$ in D. Hence $\varphi_\alpha{}^\delta(f^\alpha) = \varphi_\gamma{}^\delta(\varphi_\alpha{}^\gamma(f^\alpha)) = \varphi_\gamma{}^\delta(\varphi_\beta{}^\gamma(f^\beta)) = \varphi_\beta{}^\delta(f^\beta)$. (Thus f^α, f^β determine the same element of A^∞ iff their images under the φ's agree from some step on.)

If the A^α are R-algebras and the R-linear maps $\varphi_\alpha{}^\beta : A^\alpha \to A^\beta$ ($\alpha \leq \beta$) are algebra homomorphisms, then we can turn A^∞ into an R-algebra in such a way that the maps $j_\alpha : A^\alpha \to A^\infty$ are algebra homomorphisms. We would like to take $f^\alpha \in A^\alpha$, $f^\beta \in A^\beta$ and define the product of $j_\alpha(f^\alpha)$ and $j_\beta(f^\beta)$ in A^∞ in a natural way. As a first step, note that if $\gamma_1 \geq \alpha, \beta$ and $\gamma_2 \geq \alpha, \beta$ in D, then $j_{\gamma_1}(\varphi_\alpha{}^{\gamma_1}(f^\alpha)\varphi_\beta{}^{\gamma_1}(f^\beta)) = j_{\gamma_2}(\varphi_\alpha{}^{\gamma_2}(f^\alpha)\varphi_\beta{}^{\gamma_2}(f^\beta))$. (To check this, consider any $\gamma \geq \gamma_1, \gamma_2$ and note that both sides equal $j_\gamma(\varphi_\alpha{}^\gamma(f^\alpha)\varphi_\beta{}^\gamma(f^\beta))$.) Note too that if $j_\alpha(f^\alpha) = j_\alpha(g^\alpha)$ and $j_\beta(f^\beta) = j_\beta(g^\beta)$, then $j_\gamma(\varphi_\alpha{}^\gamma(f^\alpha)\varphi_\beta{}^\gamma(f^\beta)) = j_\gamma(\varphi_\alpha{}^\gamma(g^\alpha)\varphi_\beta{}^\gamma(g^\beta))$ for some $\gamma \geq \alpha, \beta$ (and hence, by the first step, for all $\gamma \geq \alpha, \beta$); indeed, by Lemma 11, $\exists \gamma \in D$ with $\varphi_\alpha{}^\gamma(f^\alpha) = \varphi_\alpha{}^\gamma(g^\alpha)$, $\varphi_\beta{}^\gamma(f^\beta) = \varphi_\beta{}^\gamma(g^\beta)$. Thus we can unambiguously define $j_\alpha(f^\alpha)j_\beta(f^\beta)$ to be $j_\gamma(\varphi_\alpha{}^\gamma(f^\alpha)\varphi_\beta{}^\gamma(f^\beta))$ for any $\gamma \geq \alpha, \beta$. Since $A^\infty = \bigcup_\alpha j_\alpha(A^\alpha)$, the multiplication is defined on all of A^∞, and it is clear that A^∞ is an algebra and that $j_\alpha : A^\alpha \to A^\infty$ is an algebra homomorphism.

Suppose now that $\{A^\alpha\}_{\alpha \in D}$ is a family of commutative complex Banach algebras with identity and that $(\{A^\alpha\}, \{\varphi_\alpha{}^\beta\})$ is a direct system, where the homomorphisms $\varphi_\alpha{}^\beta : A^\alpha \to A^\beta$ ($\alpha \leq \beta$) send 1 to 1. Let A^∞ be the direct limit of this system; A^∞ is then a commutative complex algebra with identity. Let $\mathcal{M}_\alpha$ be the maximal ideal space of A^α. By definition of the Gelfand topology, the dual of $\varphi_\alpha{}^\beta$, defined by $\sigma_\alpha{}^\beta(h_\beta) = h_\beta \circ \varphi_\alpha{}^\beta$ ($h_\beta \in \mathcal{M}_\beta$), is a continuous mapping from $\mathcal{M}_\beta$ to $\mathcal{M}_\alpha$. Also, $\sigma_\alpha{}^\beta \circ \sigma_\beta{}^\gamma = \sigma_\alpha{}^\gamma$ if $\alpha \leq \beta \leq \gamma$, as we check directly. So $(\{\mathcal{M}_\alpha\}, \{\sigma_\alpha{}^\beta\})$ is an inverse system of compact spaces. Let $(\mathcal{M}_\infty, \{\pi_\alpha\})$ be the inverse limit of this system; $\mathcal{M}_\infty$ is a compact space.

Corresponding to each $f \in A^\infty$ we shall define a function $\hat{f}$ on $\mathcal{M}_\infty$. Since the ranges of the $j_\alpha : A^\alpha \to A^\infty$ fill A^∞, $f = j_\alpha(f^\alpha)$ for some $\alpha \in D$, $f^\alpha \in A^\alpha$. If $f = j_\beta(f^\beta)$ also, then by Lemma 11 there is some $\gamma \in D$ with $\alpha \leq \gamma$,

$\beta \leq \gamma$, and $\varphi_\alpha^{\ \gamma}(f^\alpha) = \varphi_\beta^{\ \gamma}(f^\beta)$. So $\widehat{f^\alpha}(\pi_\alpha(h)) = \pi_\alpha(h)(f^\alpha) = \sigma_\alpha^{\ \gamma} \circ \pi_\gamma(h)(f^\alpha) = (\pi_\gamma(h) \circ \varphi_\alpha^{\ \gamma})(f^\alpha) = \pi_\gamma(h)(\varphi_\alpha^{\ \gamma}(f^\alpha)) = \pi_\gamma(h)(\varphi_\beta^{\ \gamma}(f^\beta)) = \widehat{f^\beta}(\pi_\beta(h))$, $h \in \mathcal{M}_\infty$. We now define $\hat{f} : \mathcal{M}_\infty \to \mathbf{C}$ by setting $\hat{f}(h) = \widehat{f^\alpha}(\pi_\alpha(h))$ for any α such that $f = j_\alpha(f^\alpha)$. Since $\widehat{f^\alpha}$ and π_α are continuous, $\hat{f} \in C(\mathcal{M}_\infty)$.

Given f, g in A^∞, we can check that $\hat{f} + \hat{g} = (f + g)^\wedge$ and $\hat{f}\hat{g} = (fg)^\wedge$. For choose α, β in D with $f = j_\alpha(f^\alpha)$, $g = j_\beta(g^\beta)$ where $f^\alpha \in A^\alpha$, $g^\beta \in A^\beta$, and choose $\gamma \in D$ with $\alpha \leq \gamma$, $\beta \leq \gamma$. Set $f^\gamma = \varphi_\alpha^{\ \gamma}(f^\alpha)$, $g^\gamma = \varphi_\beta^{\ \gamma}(g^\beta)$. Then f^γ, g^γ are in A^γ and $f = j_\gamma(f^\gamma)$, $g = j_\gamma(g^\gamma)$. So $f + g = j_\gamma(f^\gamma + g^\gamma)$ and $fg = j_\gamma(f^\gamma g^\gamma)$. Hence $(f + g)^\wedge(h) = \pi_\gamma(h)(f^\gamma + g^\gamma) = \hat{f}(h) + \hat{g}(h)$ and $(fg)^\wedge(h) = \hat{f}(h)\hat{g}(h)$. So $f \to \hat{f}(h)$ is a complex homomorphism of A^∞ for each $h \in \mathcal{M}_\infty$, and $f \to \hat{f}$ is an algebra homomorphism of A^∞ into $C(\mathcal{M}_\infty)$.

On the other hand, every complex homomorphism q of A^∞ comes from evaluation at some $h \in \mathcal{M}_\infty$. For define $h_\alpha(f^\alpha) = q(j_\alpha(f^\alpha))$ $(\alpha \in D, f^\alpha \in A^\alpha)$; then $h_\alpha \in \mathcal{M}_\alpha$ since it is a composite of homomorphisms sending 1 to 1. If $\alpha \leq \beta$ in D, then $\sigma_\alpha^{\ \beta}(h_\beta)(f^\alpha) = h_\beta(\varphi_\alpha^{\ \beta}(f^\alpha)) = q(j_\beta \circ \varphi_\alpha^{\ \beta}(f^\alpha)) = q(j_\alpha(f^\alpha)) = h_\alpha(f^\alpha)$ for all $f^\alpha \in A^\alpha$. Hence $\{h_\alpha\}_{\alpha \in D}$ are the coordinates of some $h \in \mathcal{M}_\infty$. Obviously $q(f) = \hat{f}(h)$ for every $f \in A^\infty$.

Let $\hat{A}^\infty = \{\hat{f} : f \in A^\infty\}$. $\hat{A}^\infty$ is a subalgebra of $C(\mathcal{M}_\infty)$ which contains the constants, and the homomorphisms of $\hat{A}^\infty$ onto $\mathbf{C}$ are the point evaluations. Furthermore, $\hat{A}^\infty$ separates points on $\mathcal{M}_\infty$. (Given $h \neq h'$ in $\mathcal{M}_\infty$, there is some $\alpha \in D$ with $\pi_\alpha(h) \neq \pi_\alpha(h')$. $\hat{A}^\alpha$ separates points, so $\widehat{f^\alpha}(\pi_\alpha(h)) \neq \widehat{f^\alpha}(\pi_\alpha(h'))$ for some $f^\alpha \in A^\alpha$. Set $f = j_\alpha(f^\alpha)$. Then $\hat{f}(h) \neq \hat{f}(h')$.) The uniform closure of $\hat{A}^\infty$ is therefore a function algebra $\mathscr{A}^\infty$ on $\mathcal{M}_\infty$ which has maximal ideal space $\mathcal{M}_\infty$.

It is not always the case that the mapping $f \to \hat{f}$ from A^∞ into $\mathscr{A}^\infty$ is one-one, but it will be one-one if we add suitable hypotheses.

Now suppose that for each α in a directed set D, X_α is a compact space and A^α is a function algebra on X_α. Suppose homomorphisms $\varphi_\alpha^{\ \beta} : A^\alpha \to A^\beta$ $(\alpha \leq \beta$ in $D)$ are given and conditions (i), (ii) for a direct system are satisfied. Suppose too that $\varphi_\alpha^{\ \beta}(1) = 1$, and that the dual maps $\sigma_\alpha^{\ \beta} : \mathcal{M}_\beta \to \mathcal{M}_\alpha$ have the property that $\sigma_\alpha^{\ \beta}(X_\beta) = X_\alpha$ whenever $\alpha \leq \beta$ in D. Let $p_\alpha^{\ \beta} : X_\beta \to X_\alpha$ be the restriction of $\sigma_\alpha^{\ \beta}$. Then $(\{X_\alpha\}, \{p_\alpha^{\ \beta}\})$ is an inverse system. The inverse limit space $(X_\infty, \{p_\alpha\})$ is a closed nonvoid subset of $\mathcal{M}_\infty$. Since each $p_\alpha^{\ \beta}$ is onto $(\alpha \leq \beta)$, $p_\alpha(X_\infty) = \pi_\alpha(X_\infty) = X_\alpha$ for all $\alpha \in D$, by Lemma 9.

Take $f \in A^\infty$ such that $\hat{f} = 0$. Then $f = j_\alpha(f^\alpha)$ for some $\alpha \in D$, $f^\alpha \in A^\alpha$, and $\hat{f}(h) = \widehat{f^\alpha}(\pi_\alpha(h)) = 0$ for all $h \in \mathcal{M}_\infty$. Therefore $\widehat{f^\alpha}$ vanishes on $\pi_\alpha(\mathcal{M}_\infty) \supset \pi_\alpha(X_\infty) = X_\alpha$, so $f^\alpha = 0$. Hence $f = 0$. So the map $f \to \hat{f}$ from A^∞ onto $\hat{A}^\infty \subset \mathscr{A}^\infty$ is one-one. We can therefore regard $A^\infty = \varinjlim A^\alpha$ as an algebra of continuous functions on $\mathcal{M}_\infty$, and its completion $\overline{A^\infty}$ as a function algebra on $\mathcal{M}_\infty$ with maximal ideal space $\mathcal{M}_\infty$. In the following we identify $\overline{A^\infty}$ with $\mathscr{A}^\infty$.

Theorem 9. *Let* $(\{A^\alpha\}, \{\varphi_\alpha^{\ \beta}\})$ *be a direct system of function algebras, with* $\varphi_\alpha^{\ \beta}(1) = 1$. *Assume that the dual maps* $\sigma_\alpha^{\ \beta}$ *take* X_β *onto* X_α $(\alpha \leq \beta)$. *Let* X_∞

be the inverse limit of $(\{X_\alpha\}, \{p_\alpha{}^\beta\})$ *where* $p_\alpha{}^\beta : X_\beta \to X_\alpha$ *is the restriction of* $\sigma_\alpha{}^\beta$. *Then the map* $f \to f|\,X_\infty$ *from* $\overline{A}^\infty$ *to* $\overline{A}^\infty|_{X_\infty}$ *is an isometry. We may thus regard* $\overline{A}^\infty$ *as a function algebra on* X_∞.

Proof. It suffices to show that if $f \in A^\infty$, then $\hat{f}$ assumes its maximum modulus over $\mathcal{M}_\infty$ at some point of X_∞. But if $f = j_\alpha(f^\alpha)$, where $f^\alpha \in A^\alpha$, and if $h \in \mathcal{M}_\infty$, then $|\hat{f}(h)| = |\widehat{f^\alpha}(\pi_\alpha(h))| \leq \|\widehat{f^\alpha}\| = \|f^\alpha\|$, so $\|\hat{f}\| \leq \|f^\alpha\|$. But $\|f^\alpha\| = |f^\alpha(x_\alpha)|$ for some $x_\alpha \in X_\alpha$. Since $p_\gamma{}^\beta(X_\beta) = X_\gamma$ for all $\gamma \leq \beta$ in D, $\pi_\alpha(X_\infty) = X_\alpha$, so $x_\alpha = \pi_\alpha(x)$ for some $x \in X_\infty$. Hence $\|f^\alpha\| = |f^\alpha(x_\alpha)| = |f^\alpha(\pi_\alpha(x))| = |\widehat{f^\alpha}(\pi_\alpha(x))| = |\hat{f}(x)|$. So $\|\hat{f}\| = \|f^\alpha\|$ and $\hat{f}$ assumes its maximum modulus on X_∞.

Theorem 10. *Suppose that the hypotheses of Theorem 9 are satisfied and that A^α is a Dirichlet algebra on X_α for every $\alpha \in D$. Then $\overline{A}^\infty$ is a Dirichlet algebra on X_∞.*

Proof. The continuous maps $p_\alpha{}^\beta : X_\beta \to X_\alpha$ induce homomorphisms $k_\alpha{}^\beta : C_R(X_\alpha) \to C_R(X_\beta)$ given by $k_\alpha{}^\beta(u_\alpha) = u_\alpha \circ p_\alpha{}^\beta$. Let $(D^\infty, \{q_\alpha\})$ be the direct limit of the direct system $(\{C_R(X_\alpha)\}, \{k_\alpha{}^\beta\})$ of real function algebras. As we did for A^∞, we can make D^∞ into an algebra of continuous real-valued functions on X_∞ by setting $u(x) = u_\alpha(x_\alpha)$ if $x \in X_\infty$, $u = q_\alpha(u_\alpha)$, and $x_\alpha = \pi_\alpha(x)$. Now D^∞ is a subalgebra of $C_R(X_\infty)$ which contains the constants and separates points, so D^∞ is dense in $C_R(X_\infty)$.

Take $u \in D^\infty$ and $\varepsilon > 0$. Choose $\alpha \in D$ with $u = q_\alpha(u_\alpha)$, $u_\alpha \in C_R(X_\alpha)$. Since A^α is a Dirichlet algebra on X_α, $\exists f^\alpha \in A^\alpha$ with $|u_\alpha - \text{Re}\,(f^\alpha)| < \varepsilon$ on X_α. Define $f = j_\alpha(f^\alpha) \in A^\infty$. Then for all $x \in X_\infty$, $|u(x) - \text{Re}\,(f(x))| = |u_\alpha(x_\alpha) - \text{Re}\,(f^\alpha(x_\alpha))| < \varepsilon$ (where $x_\alpha = \pi_\alpha(x)$). So $\text{Re}\,(A^\infty)$ is dense in D^∞. Hence $\overline{A}^\infty$ is a Dirichlet algebra on X_∞.

Theorem 11. *Let $(\{A^\alpha\}, \{\varphi_\alpha{}^\beta\})$ be a direct system of function algebras, with $\varphi_\alpha{}^\beta(1) = 1$. Suppose that the dual maps $\sigma_\alpha{}^\beta : \mathcal{M}_\beta \to \mathcal{M}_\alpha$ carry Γ_β onto Γ_α, where Γ_α is the Šilov boundary of A^α. Then $\Gamma_\infty = \varprojlim (\{\Gamma_\alpha\}, \{\sigma_\alpha{}^\beta : \Gamma_\beta \to \Gamma_\alpha\})$ is the Šilov boundary of the limit algebra $\overline{A}^\infty$.*

Proof. Γ_∞ is compact, being an inverse limit of compact spaces. By Theorem 8, the map $f \to f|\,\Gamma_\infty$ is an isometry, so Γ_∞ contains the Šilov boundary of $\overline{A}^\infty$.

Conversely, suppose that $x \in \Gamma_\infty$, and let U be open about x in $\mathcal{M}_\infty$. U contains a *nbhd* of x of the form $\pi_\alpha{}^{-1}(U_\alpha)$ for some $\alpha \in D$ and some open *nbhd* U_α of $x_\alpha = \pi_\alpha(x)$ in $\mathcal{M}_\alpha$. (By Exercise 1, U contains a finite intersection $\bigcap_{j=1}^{n} \pi_{\alpha_j}{}^{-1}(U_{\alpha_j})$. Since D is directed, $\exists \alpha \in D$ with $\alpha \geq$ all α_j. Set $U_\alpha = \bigcap_{j=1}^{n} (\sigma_{\alpha_j}{}^\alpha)^{-1}(U_{\alpha_j})$. Then $x \in \pi_\alpha{}^{-1}(U_\alpha) \subset U$.) Since the Choquet boundary of A^α is dense in Γ_α and $x_\alpha \in \Gamma_\alpha$, $\exists y_\alpha \in c(A^\alpha) \cap U_\alpha$. Hence there is some $f^\alpha \in A^\alpha$ such that $f^\alpha(y_\alpha) = 1 = \|f^\alpha\|$, $|f^\alpha| < 1$ outside U_α.

Set $f = j_\alpha(f^\alpha) \in A^\infty$, and choose $y \in \Gamma_\infty$ with $y_\alpha = \pi_\alpha(y)$. (This is possible since $\pi_\alpha(\Gamma_\infty) = \Gamma_\alpha$.) Then $\hat{f}(y) = 1 = \|f\| = \|f^\alpha\|$ and $y \in \pi_\alpha^{-1}(U_\alpha) \subset U$. But if z is outside U, then $\pi_\alpha(z) \notin U_\alpha$, so $|\hat{f}(z)| = |\widehat{f^\alpha}(\pi_\alpha(z))| < 1$. Thus $\exists f \in A^\infty$ such that $\hat{f}$ assumes its maximum modulus in U but nowhere in $\mathcal{M}_\infty \backslash U$. Therefore $x \in \Gamma(\overline{A^\infty})$. So both inclusions have been established.

Suppose that G is an additive abelian group and Γ is the character group of G. Γ is a compact abelian group in the topology of pointwise convergence on G. For $x \in G$ and $\gamma \in \Gamma$, let $\gamma(x) = \langle x, \gamma \rangle = \hat{x}(\gamma)$ (so that $\hat{x}$ is what was called φ_x in Exercise 6, §6.7). A *trigonometric polynomial* on Γ is a finite linear combination $\sum c_i \hat{x}_i$ with c_i scalars, $x_i \in G$. By the Stone-Weierstrass theorem, the trigonometric polynomials are dense in $C(\Gamma)$.

If G^+ is a subsemigroup of G which contains 0, then G^+ defines a partial ordering in G if we say that $x \geq y$ iff $x - y \in G^+$. Then we have $x \geq x$; $x \geq y$ iff $x - y \geq 0$; $x \geq y$ and $y \geq z$ imply that $x \geq z$; and if $x \geq y$ then $x + z \geq y + z$ for all $z \in G$. Let $P(G)$ be the set of all trigonometric polynomials $\sum c_i \hat{x}_i$ with $x_i \in G^+$, and let $\mathbf{A}(G)$ be the uniform closure of $P(G)$ in $C(\Gamma)$. Then $\mathbf{A}(G)$ is a sup norm algebra on Γ. The members of $\mathbf{A}(G)$ are called the *generalized analytic functions* on Γ (corresponding to the ordering defined by G^+); we denoted $\mathbf{A}(G)$ by Λ_{G^+} in Exercise 6, §6.1. Clearly $\mathbf{A}(G)$ separates points on Γ iff $P(G)$ does, and this happens iff $\{\hat{x} : x \in G^+\}$ separates points on Γ. That is, $\mathbf{A}(G)$ is a function algebra iff $\gamma_1 \neq \gamma_2$ in Γ implies that $\langle x, \gamma_1 \rangle \neq \langle x, \gamma_2 \rangle$ for some $x \in G^+$. Note that if G^+ generates G this condition is satisfied, whereas if G^+ generates a proper subgroup G_1 of G there exists a character $\gamma \in \Gamma$ with $\gamma = 1$ on G_1 but $\gamma \not\equiv 1$ (since G/G_1 is a nontrivial abelian group and hence has a nontrivial character in its dual). So $\mathbf{A}(G)$ is a function algebra iff G^+ generates G.

Suppose that G and H are additive abelian groups ordered as above by semigroups containing 0. Suppose that $\varphi : G \to H$ is an order-preserving homomorphism: $\varphi(x + y) = \varphi(x) + \varphi(y)$ if $x, y \in G$, and $\varphi(x) \geq 0$ in H if $x \geq 0$ in G. Let $\varphi^t : \Gamma_H \to \Gamma_G$ be the dual map to φ, given by $\varphi^t(\gamma) = \gamma \circ \varphi$; then φ^t induces an algebra homomorphism $\tau : C(\Gamma_G) \to C(\Gamma_H)$ defined by $\tau(f) = f \circ \varphi^t$. Since φ is order-preserving, it is easy to see that τ maps $P(G)$ into $P(H)$. For if $f = \sum c_i \hat{x}_i$ where the $x_i \geq 0$, then $\tau(f) = \sum c_i \widehat{\varphi(x_i)}$ and all $\varphi(x_i)$ are nonnegative. But an algebra homomorphism of sup norm algebras is continuous, so τ maps $\mathbf{A}(G)$ into $\mathbf{A}(H)$. So we see that an order-preserving homomorphism $\varphi : G \to H$ of abelian ordered groups induces a homomorphism $h : \mathbf{A}(G) \to \mathbf{A}(H)$ of their algebras of generalized analytic functions, given by $(h(f))(\gamma) = f(\gamma \circ \varphi)$.

Suppose now that $(\{G^\alpha\}, \{\varphi_\alpha{}^\beta\})$ is a direct system of ordered additive abelian groups and order-preserving homomorphisms, and that $G^\alpha{}_+$ generates G^α for each α. The direct limit $(G^\infty, \{\varphi^\alpha\})$ is also an ordered group in a natural way (see Exercise 2), and $G^\infty{}_+$ generates G^∞. So the generalized analytic functions on G^∞ form a function algebra $\mathbf{A}(G^\infty)$. On the other hand, the original direct system determines a direct system of function algebras $(\mathbf{A}(G^\alpha), \{h_\alpha{}^\beta\})$ which has a limit function algebra $\overline{A^\infty}$, with maps $h_\alpha : \mathbf{A}(G^\alpha) \to A^\infty$. It turns out that the processes of forming generalized analytic functions and taking direct limits commute.

For each α, let Γ_α be the dual group of G^α, and for $\alpha \le \beta$, let $\sigma_\alpha{}^\beta : \Gamma_\beta \to \Gamma_\alpha$ be the dual map to $\varphi_\alpha{}^\beta : G^\alpha \to G^\beta$; so $\sigma_\alpha{}^\beta(\chi_\beta) = \chi_\beta \circ \varphi_\alpha{}^\beta$ for $\chi_\beta \in \Gamma_\beta$. Now $(\{\Gamma_\alpha\}, \{\sigma_\alpha{}^\beta\})$ is an inverse system of compact abelian groups, so its limit $(\Gamma_\infty, \{\sigma_\alpha\})$ is also a compact abelian group. (Note that there are dual maps $\tau_\alpha{}^\beta : \mathcal{M}(\mathbf{A}(G^\beta)) \to \mathcal{M}(\mathbf{A}(G^\alpha))$ to the $h_\alpha{}^\beta$. If ψ_β is given by evaluation at some χ_β in Γ_β, then $\tau_\alpha{}^\beta(\psi_\beta)$ is given by evaluation at $\sigma_\alpha{}^\beta(\chi_\beta)$. Hence $\tau_\alpha{}^\beta$ takes Γ_β into Γ_α and its restriction to Γ_β is just $\sigma_\alpha{}^\beta$.) Each element χ of the limit space Γ_∞ defines a character of G^∞, as follows. Given $x \in G^\infty$, choose α so that $x = \varphi^\alpha(x^\alpha)$ for some $x^\alpha \in G^\alpha$, and set $\langle x, \chi \rangle = \langle x^\alpha, \chi_\alpha \rangle$ where $\chi_\alpha = \sigma_\alpha(\chi)$. The map $x \to \langle x, \chi \rangle$ is well defined and is a character of G^∞, and furthermore every character of G^∞ is given by some $\chi \in \Gamma_\infty$. Note that in a sense $\sigma_\alpha : \Gamma_\infty \to \Gamma_\alpha$ is dual to $\varphi^\alpha : G^\alpha \to G^\infty$, since by definition $\langle \varphi^\alpha(x^\alpha), \chi \rangle = \langle x^\alpha, \sigma_\alpha(\chi) \rangle$.

Theorem 12. *Given a direct system $(\{G^\alpha\}, \{\varphi_\alpha{}^\beta\})$ of ordered abelian groups and order-preserving homomorphisms, we have* (a) $P(G^\infty) \subset A^\infty = \varinjlim \mathbf{A}(G^\alpha) \subset \mathbf{A}(G^\infty)$ *where* $G^\infty = \varinjlim G^\alpha$, *and* (b) $\mathbf{A}(G^\infty) = \overline{A^\infty}$. *So the generalized analytic functions defined by G^∞ coincide with (the completion of) the direct limit of the system of algebras of generalized analytic functions defined by the G^α.*

Proof. The maps $h^\alpha : \mathbf{A}(G^\alpha) \to A^\infty$ are given as follows: $h^\alpha(f^\alpha)(\chi) = f^\alpha(\sigma_\alpha(\chi))$. (We are considering A^∞ as an algebra of functions on Γ_∞.) In particular, if $x^\alpha \in G^\alpha{}_+$, then $h^\alpha(\widehat{x^\alpha})(\chi) = \langle x^\alpha, \sigma_\alpha(\chi) \rangle = \langle \varphi^\alpha(x^\alpha), \chi \rangle$, so $h^\alpha(\widehat{x^\alpha}) = \widehat{\varphi^\alpha(x^\alpha)}$. So since φ^α is order-preserving, h^α carries $P(G^\alpha)$ into $P(G^\infty) \subset C(\Gamma_\infty)$. Conversely, if $x \ge 0$ in G^∞, then, by definition, $x = \varphi^\alpha(x^\alpha)$ for some $x^\alpha \ge 0$ in G^α. Thus $\hat{x} = h^\alpha(\widehat{x^\alpha})$. So $P(G^\infty) = \bigcup_\alpha h^\alpha(P(G^\alpha))$.

Hence we have $P(G^\infty) \subset \bigcup_\alpha h^\alpha(\mathbf{A}(G^\alpha)) = A^\infty$. Each h^α is continuous, and $h^\alpha(P(G^\alpha)) \subset \mathbf{A}(G^\infty)$ for each α, so $h^\alpha(\mathbf{A}(G^\alpha)) \subset \mathbf{A}(G^\infty)$ also. So $A^\infty \subset \mathbf{A}(G^\infty)$. Hence (a) is proved, and (b) follows immediately.

In the course of the arguments above, a number of identifications have been made but have not been made explicit. To make the details technically correct, it appears that we should require that the G^α be simply ordered and that the maps $\varphi_\alpha{}^\beta$ be strictly increasing. (G is simply ordered by G_+ iff $G = G_+ \cup (-G_+)$ and $G_+ \cap (-G_+) = \{0\}$.)

Let us look briefly at a class of examples in which the "generalized analytic functions" are the ordinary analytic functions on the disk, restricted to the boundary. Let $\mathbf{Z}$ be the additive group of integers, T the unit circle (which is a compact abelian group under multiplication), and let $\langle m, \lambda \rangle = \lambda^m$

for $m \in \mathbf{Z}$, $\lambda \in T$. Under this duality, T is the character group of $\mathbf{Z}$. The usual ordering in $\mathbf{Z}$, given by the semigroup $\{m : m \geq 0\}$, determines the boundary value algebra $A^1 = \mathbf{A}(\mathbf{Z})$ on T.

Fix a prime number p. For each $n \geq 0$, let $G^{(n)} = \mathbf{Z}$, and let $\varphi_n{}^{n+1} : G^{(n)} \rightarrow G^{(n+1)}$ be given by $m \rightarrow pm$. The direct limit of the sequence $\mathbf{Z} \overset{\varphi}{\rightarrow} \mathbf{Z} \overset{\varphi}{\rightarrow} \mathbf{Z} \rightarrow \cdots$ can be identified with the additive subgroup $G_p = \{m/p^n : m \in \mathbf{Z}, n \in \mathbf{Z}, n \geq 0\}$ of $\mathbf{R}$, with the maps $\varphi^n : G^{(n)} \rightarrow G_p$ given by $\varphi^n(m) = m/p^n$.

The dual inverse system is $T \overset{\sigma}{\leftarrow} T \overset{\sigma}{\leftarrow} T \leftarrow \cdots$, where $\sigma_n{}^{n+1}(\lambda) = \lambda^p$, since $\langle pm, \lambda \rangle = \lambda^{pm} = \langle m, \lambda^p \rangle$. The inverse limit Σ_p of this inverse sequence is called the *p-adic solenoid*. Observe that Σ_p is a compact connected metric space (an inverse limit of compact connected spaces is connected). Observe too that $a \in \Sigma_p$ iff $a = (a_0, a_1, a_2, \ldots)$ where $|a_0| = 1$ and $a_n = (a_{n+1})^p$ for $n = 0, 1, 2, \ldots$; the metric is given explicitly by $\rho(a, b) = \sum_{n=0}^{\infty} |a_n - b_n|/2^n$.

Passing again to dual maps, we have a direct sequence $A^1 \overset{\tau}{\rightarrow} A^1 \overset{\tau}{\rightarrow} A^1 \rightarrow \cdots$ where $\tau_n{}^{n+1}(f)(\lambda) = f(\lambda^p)$. The completed direct limit $\overline{A_p{}^\infty}$ of this system of algebras of analytic functions is precisely the algebra $\mathbf{A}(G_p)$ of generalized analytic functions on Σ_p. (Note that $\sigma_n{}^{n+1}(T) = \{\lambda^p : \lambda \in T\} = T$ for all n, so no identifications are being made. The ordering in G_p is the same as that which it has as a subgroup of $\mathbf{R}$.)

EXERCISE SET 8.3

1. Let $(S_\infty, \{\pi_\alpha\})$ be the inverse limit of an inverse system $(\{S_\alpha\}, \{\sigma_\alpha{}^\beta\})$ of topological spaces (and continuous maps). Show that the topology of S_∞ is the weak topology defined by the maps $\pi_\alpha : S_\infty \rightarrow S_\alpha$.

2. Suppose that $(\{G^\alpha\}, \{\varphi_\alpha{}^\beta\})$ is a direct system of ordered abelian groups and order-preserving homomorphisms. Let $(G^\infty, \{\varphi^\alpha\})$ be the direct limit of this system. Show that $G^\infty{}_+ = \bigcup_\alpha \varphi^\alpha(G^\alpha{}_+)$ is a subsemigroup of G^∞ containing 0 and hence orders G^∞. Show that if each G^α is fully ordered (i.e., $G^\alpha{}_+$ generates G^α), so is G^∞.

3. A homeomorphism ψ of a metric space X onto itself is said to be *unstable* iff $\exists \delta > 0$ such that if x_1, x_2 are distinct points of X, $\exists n \in \mathbf{Z}$ such that $\rho(\psi^n x_1, \psi^n x_2) > \delta$. (Here if $n > 0$, ψ^n is the n-fold composition of ψ with itself and $\psi^{-n} = (\psi^{-1})^n$; ψ^0 is the identity map.)
   (a) Consider $\psi : \Sigma_2 \rightarrow \Sigma_2$ given by $\psi(a_0, a_1, a_2, \ldots) = (a_0{}^2, a_1{}^2, a_2{}^2, \ldots)$. Show that ψ is a homeomorphism of Σ_2 onto itself, with inverse given by $\psi^{-1}(a_0, a_1, a_2, \ldots) = (a_1, a_2, \ldots)$. Prove that ψ is unstable.
   (b) Show that $\mathbf{A}(G_2)$ is invariant under ψ, in the following sense: if $F \in \mathbf{A}(G_2)$, then $F \circ \psi \in \mathbf{A}(G_2)$.

8.4 TENSOR PRODUCTS OF FUNCTION ALGEBRAS

Tensor products provide a convenient means for embedding two or more function algebras, defined on possibly different compact spaces, in a single function algebra. We shall also see that forming tensor products is a powerful tool for constructing function algebras with pathological Gleason parts.

Let A, B be function algebras on compact spaces X, Y. Let $A \otimes B$ be the subspace of $C(X \times Y)$ spanned by the functions of the form $f \otimes g$ ($f \in A$, $g \in B$), where $(f \otimes g)(x, y) = f(x)g(y)$. Since A and B are algebras, $A \otimes B$ is an algebra, and the identity element of $A \otimes B$ is $1 = 1 \otimes 1$. It is clear that $A \otimes B$ separates points on $X \times Y$, so its uniform closure $A \hat{\otimes} B$ is a function algebra on $X \times Y$.

Proposition 1. *The Šilov boundary of $A \otimes B$ is $\Gamma(A) \times \Gamma(B)$.*

Proof. The Šilov boundary of $A \hat{\otimes} B$ is the same as that for $A \otimes B$; indeed, a closed boundary for a dense subset is always a boundary for the entire algebra.

If $x_0 \in \Gamma(A)$, $y_0 \in \Gamma(B)$, then $(x_0, y_0) \in \Gamma(A \otimes B)$. For let N be any *nbhd* of (x_0, y_0) in $X \times Y$, and choose open *nbhds* U, V of x_0, y_0 such that $U \times V \subset N$. Since $x_0 \in \Gamma(A)$, there is some $f \in A$ with $\|f\| = 1$, $|f| < 1$ on $X \backslash U$; similarly, $\|g\| = 1$, $|g| < 1$ on $Y \backslash V$ for some $g \in B$. But $f \otimes g \in A \otimes B$, $\|f \otimes g\| = 1$, and $|f \otimes g| < 1$ outside N. So $(x_0, y_0) \in \Gamma(A \otimes B)$. Therefore $\Gamma(A) \times \Gamma(B) \subset \Gamma(A \otimes B)$.

On the other hand, $\Gamma(A) \times \Gamma(B)$ is a boundary for $A \otimes B$, so $\Gamma(A \otimes B) \subset \Gamma(A) \times \Gamma(B)$. A typical element of $A \otimes B$ is a function of the form $\sum_{i=1}^{N} f_i \otimes g_i$ with the f_i in A, g_i in B. Take any point $(x^*, y^*) \in X \times Y$ at which $\sum f_i \otimes g_i$ assumes its maximum modulus. Then $\sum f_i(x^*)g_i$ belongs to B, so

$$\left| \sum f_i(x^*)g_i(y^*) \right| = \left| \sum f_i(x^*)g_i(y_0) \right|$$

for some $y_0 \in \Gamma(B)$. Similarly, $\sum g_i(y_0)f_i \in A$ assumes its maximum modulus at some $x_0 \in \Gamma(A)$, so $\left| \sum f_i(x^*)g_i(y^*) \right| = \left| \sum f_i(x_0)g_i(y_0) \right|$; i.e., $\sum f_i \otimes g_i$ assumes its maximum modulus at $(x_0, y_0) \in \Gamma(A) \times \Gamma(B)$. So $\Gamma(A) \times \Gamma(B)$ is a boundary for $A \otimes B$.

Lemma 12. *Let $f_i \in A$, $g_i \in B$ ($1 \leq i \leq n$). Then*

$$\left\| \sum f_i \otimes g_i \right\| = \sup \left\{ \left| \sum \varphi(f_i)\psi(g_i) \right| : \varphi \in A^*, \ \psi \in B^*, \ \|\varphi\| \leq 1, \ \|\psi\| \leq 1 \right\}.$$

Proof. If $x \in X$, $y \in Y$, then $\varphi_x \in b(A^*)$, $\psi_y \in b(B^*)$, where φ_x is the evaluation functional determined by x and $b(A^*)$ is the unit ball in A^*. So if $\left\| \sum f_i \otimes g_i \right\|_\lambda$ is the supremum above,

$$\left\| \sum f_i \otimes g_i \right\|_\lambda \geq \sup_{(x, y) \in X \times Y} \left| \sum f_i(x)g_i(y) \right| = \left\| \sum f_i \otimes g_i \right\|.$$

For the reverse inequality it must be shown that if $\varphi \in b(A^*)$, $\psi \in b(B^*)$, then

$(\star)$ $$\left| \sum \varphi(f_i)\psi(g_i) \right| \le \left\| \sum f_i \otimes g_i \right\|.$$

Now $\left| \sum \varphi(f_i)\psi(g_i) \right| = \left| \psi(\sum \varphi(f_i)g_i) \right| \le \left\| \sum \varphi(f_i)g_i \right\|$, since $\|\psi\| \le 1$. Choose y_0 such that $\left\| \sum \varphi(f_i)g_i \right\| = \left| (\sum \varphi(f_i)g_i)(y_0) \right| = \left| \sum \varphi(f_i)g_i(y_0) \right|$. ($y_0$ depends on φ.) Then $\left| \sum \varphi(f_i)\psi(g_i) \right| \le \left| \varphi(\sum g_i(y_0)f_i) \right| \le \left\| \sum g_i(y_0)f_i \right\| = \left| \sum g_i(y_0)f_i(x_0) \right|$ for a suitable $x_0 \in X$. So $\left| \sum \varphi(f_i)\psi(g_i) \right| \le \left| \sum (f_i \otimes g_i)(x_0, y_0) \right| \le \left\| \sum f_i \otimes g_i \right\|$, proving $(\star)$.

Proposition 2. *There is a one-one mapping from $\mathcal{M}(A \hat{\otimes} B)$ onto $\mathcal{M}(A) \times \mathcal{M}(B)$ given by $h \to (\xi, \zeta)$, where $\xi(f) = h(f \otimes 1)$ $(f \in A)$, $\zeta(g) = h(1 \otimes g)$ $(g \in B)$.*

Proof. If $h \in \mathcal{M}(A \hat{\otimes} B)$ and ξ, ζ are defined as above, then $\xi \in \mathcal{M}(A)$, $\zeta \in \mathcal{M}(B)$. Furthermore, ξ, ζ determine h on the dense subalgebra $A \otimes B$, since $h(\sum f_i \otimes g_i) = h(\sum (f_i \otimes 1)(1 \otimes g_i)) = \sum \xi(f_i)\zeta(g_i)$. So the map is one-one.

Given (ξ, ζ) in $\mathcal{M}(A) \times \mathcal{M}(B)$, we want to define a complex homomorphism h_0 of $A \otimes B$ by setting $h_0(\sum f_i \otimes g_i) = \sum \xi(f_i)\zeta(g_i)$, and then extend h_0 to a complex homomorphism of $A \hat{\otimes} B$. If $\sum f_i \otimes g_i = \sum f_i' \otimes g_i'$, then $\left\| \sum f_i \otimes g_i + \sum (-f_i') \otimes g_i' \right\| = 0$, so by Lemma 12,

$$\sum \varphi(f_i)\psi(g_i) - \sum \varphi(f_i')\psi(g_i') = 0$$

for all (φ, ψ) in $b(A^*) \times b(B^*)$. Since complex homomorphisms have norm 1, $\sum \xi(f_i)\zeta(g_i) = \sum \xi(f_i')\zeta(g_i')$. So h_0 is well defined as a function from $A \otimes B$ to $\mathbf{C}$. Since $(f' \otimes g')(f' \otimes g') = ff' \otimes gg'$, h_0 is a complex homomorphism of $A \otimes B$. Again by Lemma 12, $\left| h_0(\sum f_i \otimes g_i) \right| = \left| \sum \xi(f_i)\zeta(g_i) \right| \le \left\| \sum f_i \otimes g_i \right\|$, so h_0 is continuous. Hence h_0 extends to some $h \in \mathcal{M}(A \hat{\otimes} B)$, and it is clear that (ξ, ζ) is the image of h under our mapping.

Theorem 13. *The mapping $h \to (\xi, \zeta)$ given in Proposition 2 is a homeomorphism.*

Proof. Let $\mathcal{A} = A \hat{\otimes} B$, and $\mathcal{F} = \hat{\mathcal{A}}$ be the family of Gelfand transforms of members of $\mathcal{A}$. The topology of $\mathcal{M}(\mathcal{A})$ is the weak topology defined by $\mathcal{F}$. We shall show that it coincides with the product topology of $\mathcal{M}(A) \times \mathcal{M}(B)$ (carried over to $\mathcal{M}(\mathcal{A})$ via the correspondence $h \leftrightarrow (\xi, \zeta)$). Since the finite sums $\sum f_i \otimes g_i$ are norm dense in $\mathcal{A}$, the topology of $\mathcal{M}(\mathcal{A})$ is the same as the weak topology defined by $\mathcal{F}_0 = \{ \widehat{\sum f_i \otimes g_i} \}$.

Observe that $\mathcal{F}_0$ separates points on $\mathcal{M}(A) \times \mathcal{M}(B)$. (For if $\xi \ne \xi'$, then $\exists f \in A$ with $\xi(f) \ne \xi'(f)$; so

$$\widehat{f \otimes 1}(\xi, \zeta) = \xi(f)\zeta(1) = \xi(f) \ne \xi'(f) = \widehat{f \otimes 1}(\xi', \zeta')$$

for any ζ, ζ' in $\mathcal{M}(B)$. Similarly, if $\zeta \neq \zeta'$, then $\mathcal{F}_0$ separates (ξ, ζ) from (ξ', ζ') for any ξ, ξ' in $\mathcal{M}(A)$.) Furthermore, if $F \in \mathcal{F}_0$, then the map $(\xi, \zeta) \to F(\xi, \zeta)$ is continuous relative to the product topology. (For $F(\xi, \zeta) = \sum_{i=1}^{n} \xi(f_i)\zeta(g_i)$ where $f_i \in A$, $g_i \in B$. By definition of the Gelfand topologies, $\xi \to \xi(f)$ is continuous on $\mathcal{M}(A)$ for each fixed $f \in A$, and $\zeta \to \zeta(g)$ is continuous on $\mathcal{M}(B)$ for each fixed $g \in B$. Since multiplication is continuous from $\mathbf{C} \times \mathbf{C}$ to $\mathbf{C}$ and addition is continuous from $\mathbf{C}^n$ to $\mathbf{C}$, the map $(\xi, \zeta) \to F(\xi, \zeta)$ is continuous.) So $\mathcal{F}_0$ is a separating family of continuous functions on the compact space $\mathcal{M}(A) \times \mathcal{M}(B)$. Hence the topology of $\mathcal{M}(A) \times \mathcal{M}(B)$ is the weak topology defined by $\mathcal{F}_0$; i.e., $\mathcal{M}(\mathcal{A})$ is homeomorphic to $\mathcal{M}(A) \times \mathcal{M}(B)$.

Lemma 13. *Let* $F \in \mathcal{A} = A \hat{\otimes} B$ *and* $y_0 \in Y$. *Set* $F_{y_0}(x) = F(x, y_0)$ *for* $x \in X$. *Then* $F_{y_0} \in A$. *Similarly,* $y \to F(x_0, y)$ *is in* B *for fixed* $x_0 \in X$.

Proof. If (f_i, g_i) are finitely many elements of $A \times B$, then $\|\sum g_i(y_0)f_i\| = \max_{x \in X} |\sum g_i(y_0)f_i(x)| = \max_{x \in X} |\sum \varphi_x(f_i)\psi_{y_0}(g_i)| \le \|\sum f_i \otimes g_i\|$, by Lemma 12. So there is a continuous linear mapping $T : A \hat{\otimes} B \to A$ such that $T(\sum f_i \otimes g_i) = \sum g_i(y_0)f_i$ on $A \otimes B$, i.e., $T(F) = F_{y_0}$ for F in $A \otimes B$. Since T is continuous, $T(F) = F_{y_0}$ for every F in $\mathcal{A}$, so $F_{y_0} \in A$.

Theorem 14. *Let* $c(A)$, $c(B)$ *be the Choquet boundaries of* A, B. *Then* $c(A \hat{\otimes} B) = c(A) \times c(B)$.

Proof. Recall that $x \in c(A)$ iff $\{x\}$ is an intersection of peak sets for A.

If $x \in c(A)$ and $y \in c(B)$, and if $(x, y) \in U \times V \subset N$, then there exist $f \in A$, $g \in B$ with $|f(x)| = \|f\|$, $|f| < \|f\|$ on $X \backslash U$, $|g(y)| = \|g\|$, $|g| < \|g\|$ on $Y \backslash V$. So $F = f \otimes g$ belongs to $A \hat{\otimes} B$, and F assumes its maximum modulus at (x, y) but nowhere on $(X \times Y) \backslash N$. Hence $(x, y) \in c(A \hat{\otimes} B)$.

Conversely, suppose that $(x_0, y_0) \in c(A \hat{\otimes} B)$. Let U be open about x_0 in X. Then $\exists F$ in $A \hat{\otimes} B$ with $|F(x_0, y_0)| = \|F\|$, $|F| < \|F\|$ on $(X \times Y) \backslash (U \times Y)$. Set $f = F_{y_0}$. Then $f \in A$ by Lemma 13, and $|f(x_0)| = |F(x_0, y_0)| = \|F\| = \max_{(x, y) \in X \times Y} |F(x, y)| \ge \|f\|$. So $|f(x_0)| = \|f\| = \|F\|$, while $|f(x)| = |F(x, y_0)| < \|f\|$ if $x \notin U$. Thus $x_0 \in c(A)$. Similarly $y_0 \in c(B)$.

One would expect from the preceding results that the objects one associates with function algebras are determined for a tensor product as Cartesian products of those of the component algebras. This turns out to be true for Gleason parts and maximal sets of antisymmetry.

Theorem 15. *Let* (ξ, ζ), (ξ', ζ') *belong to* $\mathcal{M}(A) \times \mathcal{M}(B)$, *and let* h, h' *be the corresponding elements of* $\mathcal{M}(A \hat{\otimes} B)$. *Then* h *and* h' *are Gleason equivalent iff* $\xi \sim \xi'$ *and* $\zeta \sim \zeta'$. *Hence the Gleason parts in* $\mathcal{M}(A \hat{\otimes} B)$ *are the Cartesian products* $P \times P'$ *where* P *is a part in* $\mathcal{M}(A)$, P' *a part in* $\mathcal{M}(B)$.

Proof. If $\xi \sim \xi'$, there are f_n in the unit ball of A with $|\hat{f}_n(\xi) - \hat{f}_n(\xi')| \to 2$. Set $F_n = f_n \otimes 1$. Then $F_n \in \mathscr{A}$, $\|F_n\| \le 1$, $|h(F_n) - h'(F_n)| \to 2$. So $h \sim h'$. Similarly, if $\zeta \sim \zeta'$, then $h \sim h'$.

Conversely, suppose that $\xi \sim \xi'$ and $\zeta \sim \zeta'$. Then $(\xi, \zeta) \sim (\xi' \zeta)$ and $(\xi', \zeta) \sim (\xi', \zeta')$, so by transitivity, $(\xi, \zeta) = h \sim (\xi', \zeta') = h'$.

To show this, suppose $(\xi, \zeta) \sim (\xi', \zeta)$. By density of $A \otimes B$ in $\mathscr{A}$, there are $F_n \in A \otimes B$ with $\|F_n\| \le 1$ such that $|\hat{F}_n(\xi, \zeta) - \hat{F}_n(\xi', \zeta)| \to 2$. The functions f_n given by $f_n(\xi'') = \hat{F}_n(\xi'', \zeta)$ lie in $\hat{A}$ by Lemma 13, and $\|f_n\| \le 1$, $|f_n(\xi) - f_n(\xi')| \to 2$. So $\xi \sim \xi'$.

Theorem 16. *Let $\mathscr{K}$, $\mathscr{K}'$ be the families of maximal antisymmetric sets for A, B on X, Y. Then the maximal antisymmetric sets for $A \hat{\otimes} B$ are the sets $K \times K'$ with $K \in \mathscr{K}$, $K' \in \mathscr{K}'$.*

Proof Since $\{K \times K'\}$ is a disjoint closed cover of $X \times Y$, it suffices to prove that each $K \times K'$ is a maximal set of antisymmetry for $A \hat{\otimes} B$.

First of all, it is a set of antisymmetry. For suppose $F \in A \hat{\otimes} B$ is real-valued on $K \times K'$, and let (x, y), (x_0, y_0) belong to $K \times K'$. Then $F_y \in A$ and F_y is real on K, so F_y is constant on K. Similarly, F_{x_0} is constant on K'. So $F(x, y) = F_y(x) = F_y(x_0) = F_{x_0}(y) = F_{x_0}(y_0) = F(x_0, y_0)$; i.e., F is constant on $K \times K'$.

$K \times K'$ is therefore contained in a maximal set of antisymmetry for $A \hat{\otimes} B$, say L. Let $\pi_1(L)$, $\pi_2(L)$ be the projections of $L \subset X \times Y$ into X, Y respectively. Then $K \subset \pi_1(L)$, $K' \subset \pi_2(L)$ and $K \times K' \subset L \subset \pi_1(L) \times \pi_2(L)$. But if $f \in A$ is real-valued on $\pi_1(L)$, then $f \otimes 1$ is real-valued on L; hence $f \otimes 1$ is constant on L, so f is constant on $\pi_1(L)$. That is, the projections are sets of antisymmetry for A, B respectively. By maximality, we have $K = \pi_1(L)$, $K' = \pi_2(L)$, so $L = K \times K'$. Thus $K \times K'$ is a maximal set of antisymmetry for $A \hat{\otimes} B$.

We are going to form the tensor product of a function algebra A with an algebra of generalized analytic functions. Before doing this, we need to establish some properties of those algebras.

Let G be an additive subgroup of $\mathbf{R}$ and let Γ be the character group of the discrete group G; assume that $G \ne \{0\}$. Recall the definition of the algebra $\mathbf{A}(G)$ of generalized analytic functions determined by G: $\mathbf{A}(G)$ is the function algebra on Γ generated by the functions φ_x with $x \ge 0$ in G, where $\varphi_x(\alpha) = \langle x, \alpha \rangle = \alpha(x)$ if $x \in G$, $\alpha \in \Gamma$. Equivalently, if σ is the normalized Haar measure of Γ, then $\mathbf{A}(G)$ consists of all $f \in C(\Gamma)$ such that $\int f(\alpha) \overline{\langle x, \alpha \rangle} \, d\sigma(\alpha) = 0$ for all $x < 0$ in G. The map m^0 defined by $m^0(f) = \int f(\alpha) \, d\sigma(\alpha)$ $(f \in \mathbf{A}(G))$ is a complex homomorphism of $\mathbf{A}(G)$, corresponding to the "origin" ρ_0 in $\Delta_G = \mathscr{M}(\mathbf{A}(G))$, and unless G is isomorphic to $\mathbf{Z}$, $\{m^0\}$ is a one-point part in $\mathscr{M}(\mathbf{A}(G))$, $m^0 \notin \Gamma$. (See §6.4.)

We have observed that $\mathbf{A}(G)$ is a Dirichlet algebra on Γ. Indeed, if $\mu \in M(\Gamma)$ is a real measure which annihilates $\mathbf{A}(G)$, then $\int \langle x, \alpha \rangle \, d\mu(\alpha) = 0$ for all $x \geq 0$ in G, and so $\int \langle \overline{x, \alpha} \rangle \, d\mu(\alpha) = \int \langle -x, \alpha \rangle \, d\mu(\alpha) = 0$ also. Hence μ is orthogonal to $C(\Gamma)$, so $\mu = 0$.

Theorem 17. *Let G be a nontrivial additive subgroup of $\mathbf{R}$. Then*
   (a) $\mathbf{A}(G)$ *is a maximal closed subalgebra of* $C(\Gamma)$;
   (b) *for each proper compact subset F of Γ, $\mathbf{A}(G)|_F$ is dense in $C(F)$.*

Proof. Let $\mathbf{A}(G) \subset B$ where B is a closed subalgebra of $C(\Gamma)$. Since $\mathbf{A}(G)$ is a Dirichlet algebra, we know that the restriction map from $\mathscr{M}(B)$ to $\mathscr{M}(\mathbf{A}(G))$ is one-one and that its range is precisely the set of complex homomorphisms of $\mathbf{A}(G)$ whose representing measures (relative to $\mathbf{A}(G)$) are multiplicative on B. (See Theorem 6, §6.1.)

Let us prove that (i) if m^0 extends to a complex homomorphism of B, then $B = \mathbf{A}(G)$; (ii) if m^0 does not extend multiplicatively to B, then $B = C(\Gamma)$.

If m^0 extends to a complex homomorphism of B, then σ is multiplicative on B. If $f \in B$ and $x < 0$ in G, then $\varphi_{-x} \in \mathbf{A}(G) \subset B$, so $\int f(\alpha) \langle x, \alpha \rangle \, d\sigma(\alpha) = \int f\varphi_{-x} \, d\sigma = \left(\int f \, d\sigma \right)\left(\int \varphi_{-x} \, d\sigma \right) = 0$. Hence $B \subset \mathbf{A}(G)$, so $B = \mathbf{A}(G)$.

Suppose that m^0 does not extend to a complex homomorphism of B. If $x \in G$ and $x \geq 0$, then $\varphi_x \in \mathbf{A}(G)$, so $\varphi_x \in B$. But we can also show that φ_x is an invertible element of B. For take any $h \in \mathscr{M}(B)$. Then there is some $\zeta \in \Delta_G$ such that $h(f) = \hat{f}(\zeta)$ for all $f \in \mathbf{A}(G)$, and $\zeta = \rho\alpha$, where $\alpha \in \Gamma$ and ρ is a nonnegative element of Δ_G. Since $\rho_0 \alpha = \rho_0$ and m^0 does not extend to h, $\rho \neq \rho_0$. But then $h(\varphi_x) = \hat{\varphi}_x(\zeta) = \zeta(x) \neq 0$. (See (9) in §6.4: if $\zeta \in \Delta_G \backslash \{\rho_0\}$, then ζ has no zeros.) So φ_x is invertible in B; i.e., φ_{-x} is in B. Thus B contains φ_x for every $x \in G$, so $B = C(\Gamma)$.

Hence $\mathbf{A}(G)$ is a maximal algebra on Γ.

Now if $f \in \mathbf{A}(G)$ is real-valued, f is constant. Indeed, $\int f(\alpha) \langle \overline{x, \alpha} \rangle \, d\sigma(\alpha) = 0$ for all $x < 0$ in G. Taking complex conjugates, $\int f(\alpha) \langle x, \alpha \rangle \, d\sigma(\alpha) = 0$ for all $x > 0$ in G. So f and the constant $\int f \, d\sigma$ have the same Fourier coefficients, and hence f is constant. So $\mathbf{A}(G)$ is an antisymmetric maximal subalgebra of $C(\Gamma)$, and thus $\mathbf{A}(G)$ is pervasive on Γ (see Theorem 25, §7.4). This is precisely what (b) asserts.

If α is a positive irrational number and $G_\alpha = \{n + m\alpha : n, m \in \mathbf{Z}\}$, then G_α is an additive subgroup of $\mathbf{R}$ which is isomorphic to the direct sum $\mathbf{Z} \oplus \mathbf{Z}$. Hence the character group of G_α is $T^2 = T^1 \times T^1$, with the pairing given by $\langle (n, m), (z_1, z_2) \rangle = z_1{}^n z_2{}^m$. The algebra $A_\alpha = \mathbf{A}(G_\alpha)$ is the subalgebra of $C(T^2)$ generated by the functions $z \to z_1{}^n z_2{}^m$ with $n + m\alpha \geq 0$. The Haar measure σ of $T^2 \left(d\sigma = \left(\dfrac{1}{2\pi} \right)^2 d\theta \, dt \right)$ represents the complex homomorphism m^0 of A_α. Since $\{m^0\}$ is a one-point part of $\mathscr{M}(A_\alpha)$ off the Šilov boundary T^2, one can use A_α and tensor products to construct function algebras with interesting Gleason parts having no analytic structure.

Recall that if A is a function algebra (or more generally, any commutative

Banach algebra), a set H in $\mathcal{M}(A)$ is called a *hull* iff H is the set of common zeros of the ideal $\{g \in A : \hat{g} = 0 \text{ on } H\}$. The hulls form the closed sets in a topology on $\mathcal{M}(A)$ called the hull-kernel topology. Every finite set in $\mathcal{M}(A)$ is a hull, and every hull is closed (in the Gelfand topology of $\mathcal{M}(A)$).

Theorem 18. *Let A be a function algebra and H a hull in $\mathcal{M}(A)$. Let P be a part in $\mathcal{M}(A)$ such that $P \cap H$ is nonvoid. Then there is a function algebra B such that $\mathcal{M}(B)$ contains a part Q homeomorphic to $P \cap H$.*

Proof. Let X_0 be the underlying space for A. Let α be a positive irrational, and set $B_0 = A_\alpha \otimes A$. Then B_0 is the function algebra on $T^2 \times X_0$ generated by the functions $(z, x) \to f(z)g(x)$ with $f \in A_\alpha$, $g \in A$. Since $\mathcal{M}(B_0)$ is $\mathcal{M}(A_\alpha) \times \mathcal{M}(A)$, we may regard B_0 as a function algebra on $\mathcal{M}(A_\alpha) \times \mathcal{M}(A)$.

Choose a compact set F on T^2 such that $F \neq T^2$ but $\sigma(F) > 0$, where σ is the Haar measure of T^2. Set $X = (F \times \mathcal{M}(A)) \cup (\mathcal{M}(A_\alpha) \times H)$, and let B be the uniform closure of $B_0|_X$.

If $(\zeta_0, x_0) \notin X$, then $\zeta_0 \notin F$ and $x_0 \notin H$. Since H is a hull, there is some $g \in A$ with $g(x_0) = 1$ and $g \mid H = 0$. Since F is a proper compact subset of T^2, $A_\alpha|_F$ is dense in $C(F)$, so F is A_α-convex. Since $\zeta_0 \notin F$, $\exists f \in A_\alpha$ with $f(\zeta_0) = 1$, $|f| \leq \delta < 1$ on F. Choose n so that $\delta^n \|g\| < 1$, and set $h = f^n \otimes g$, i.e., $h(\zeta, x) = f(\zeta)^n g(x)$. Then $h(\zeta_0, x_0) = 1$, h vanishes on $\mathcal{M}(A_\alpha) \times H$, and $|h| < 1$ on $F \times \mathcal{M}(A)$, so $\|h\|_X < 1$. Since (ζ_0, x_0) is an arbitrary point of the complement of X, it follows that X is B_0-convex. So $X = \mathcal{M}(B)$.

Let $Q = \{m^0\} \times (P \cap H)$, where $\int f \, d\sigma = m^0(f), f \in A_\alpha$. Of course, $Q \subset X$ and Q is homeomorphic to $P \cap H$. We claim that Q is a part in $\mathcal{M}(B)$.

First of all, any two points (m^0, s), (m^0, t) in Q are Gleason equivalent. Indeed, $s \sim t$, so $\exists c < 2$ such that $|g(s) - g(t)| \leq c\|g\|$ for all $g \in A$. Let $h \in B$, $\|h\| \leq 1$. Since $F \times \mathcal{M}(A) \subset X$, $|h(z, x)| \leq 1$ for all $z \in F$, $x \in \mathcal{M}(A)$, and we have $x \to h(z, x)$ in A for each $z \in F$ (by Lemma 13). Similarly, $z \to h(z, x)$ belongs to A_α for each $x \in \mathcal{M}(A)$. Since σ represents m^0 on A_α,

$$|h(m^0, s) - h(m^0, t)| = \left| \int_{T^2} (h(z, s) - h(z, t)) \, d\sigma(z) \right|$$

$$\leq \int_F |h(z, s) - h(z, t)| \, d\sigma(z)$$

$$+ \int_{T^2 \setminus F} (|h(z, s)| + |h(z, t)|) \, d\sigma(z)$$

$$\leq c\sigma(F) + 2\sigma(T^2 \setminus F) < 2.$$

So $(m^0, s) \sim (m^0, t)$.

On the other hand, if $(\zeta_0, x_0) \in X \setminus Q$ and $s \in P \cap H$, then (ζ_0, x_0) and (m^0, s) are inequivalent. For if $\zeta_0 \neq m^0$, then $\zeta_0 \nsim m^0$, so there are f_n in A_α with $\|f_n\| \leq 1$ and $|f_n(\zeta_0) - f_n(m^0)| \to 2$. And if $\zeta_0 = m^0$, then $x_0 \notin P$, so $x_0 \nsim s$ and there are g_n in A with $\|g_n\| \leq 1$ and $|g_n(x_0) - g_n(s)| \to 2$. In the first case set $h_n = f_n \otimes 1$; in the second case set $h_n = 1 \otimes g_n$ (restricted to X). Then $h_n \in B$, $\|h_n\| \leq 1$, and $|h_n(\zeta_0, x_0) - h_n(m^0, s)| \to 2$, which shows that $(\zeta_0, x_0) \sim (m^0, s)$.

So Q is a part in $\mathcal{M}(B)$.

Remark. We now have our first examples of disconnected Gleason parts. For example, take A to be the disk algebra, P the open disk, $H = \{0, \frac{1}{2}\}$. We conclude that there is a function algebra with a two-element part.

Theorem 19. *Suppose that Y is a σ-compact locally compact Hausdorff space. Then there is a function algebra B such that $\mathcal{M}(B)$ contains a part Q homeomorphic to Y and $\hat{B}|_Q$ is isometrically isomorphic to $C(Y_\infty)|_Y = \{f \in C(Y) : f \text{ is finite at } \infty\}$.*

Proof. Let Y_∞ be the one-point compactification of Y. Then Y_∞ is a compact Hausdorff space and $\{\infty\}$ is a G_δ in Y_∞, say $\{\infty\} = \bigcap_{n=1}^{\infty} U_n$, where the U_n are open sets in Y_∞. So $\{\infty\}$ is a zero-set for $C(Y_\infty)$: there exists a continuous function k on Y_∞ such that $k(Y_\infty) \subset [0, 1]$ and $k^{-1}(0) = \{\infty\}$. (Take $k_n \in C(Y_\infty)$ such that $k_n(\infty) = 0$, $k_n = 1$ on $Y_\infty \backslash U_n$, $0 \leq k_n \leq 1$. Set $k = \sum_{n=1}^{\infty} k_n/2^n$.) Set $h = 1 - \dfrac{k}{2}$. Then $h \in C(Y_\infty)$, $h(Y_\infty) \subset [\frac{1}{2}, 1]$, and $h^{-1}(1) = \{\infty\}$. Let $H = \{(y, h(y)) : y \in Y_\infty\}$.

Let Δ be the closed unit disk, A^0 the disk algebra, $Z = Y_\infty \times \Delta$. Let A be the subalgebra of $C(Z)$ consisting of all $f \in C(Z)$ such that for each $y \in Y_\infty$, $z \to f(y, z)$ belongs to A^0 and $f|Y_\infty \times \{0\}$ is constant. It is not difficult to show that A is a sup norm algebra on Z with maximal ideal space obtained from Z by identifying $Y_\infty \times \{0\}$ to a point. (We shall prove this below. See Theorem 23, §8.5.) The points of each disk $\{y\} \times \text{int } \Delta$ are Gleason equivalent for A (since they are in the same part in $\mathcal{M}(A^0)$), and the centers $(y, 0)$ are identical in $\mathcal{M}(A)$, so $P = \{(y, z) \in \mathcal{M}(A) : |z| < 1\}$ is a part in $\mathcal{M}(A)$. (The argument just given shows that P is contained in a single part for A. But it is easy to see that $(y, 0)$ and (y, z_0) are not equivalent if $|z_0| = 1$. Just take functions f_n of norm at most 1 in A^0 which push 0 and z_0 nearly two units apart, and extend the f_n to Z by translating the disk.)

Note that $P \cap H = \{(y, h(y)) : y \in Y\}$ (with no identifications), so $P \cap H$ is homeomorphic to Y. Let us show that H is a hull for the algebra A. We have $h(\infty) = 1$, $\frac{1}{2} \leq h(y) < 1$ if $y \in Y$, and $h \in C(Y_\infty)$. Let $f_0(y, z) = \dfrac{h(y) - z}{3h(y) - z}$ $(y \in Y_\infty, z \in \Delta)$. Then $f_0 \in A$ and $H = f_0^{-1}(0)$, so H is a hull.

So by Theorem 17 there is a function algebra B such that some part $Q = \{m^0\} \times (P \cap H)$ in $\mathcal{M}(B)$ is homeomorphic to $P \cap H$, and hence to Y. Suppose now that $g \in C(Y_\infty)$ is a continuous function on Y which is finite at

∞. Set $f(y, z) = \dfrac{g(y)}{h(y)} z$. Then $f \in A$ and for $y \in Y$, $f(y, h(y)) = g(y)$; i.e., f restricts to g on $P \cap H$. Hence $A|_{P \cap H}$ is isometrically isomorphic to $C(Y_\infty)|_Y$.

But $Q = \{m^0\} \times (P \cap H)$ and $B = \overline{B_0}|_X$ where $B_0 = A_\alpha \hat{\otimes} A$ and $X = (F \times \mathcal{M}(A)) \cup (\mathcal{M}(A_\alpha) \times H)$. Given $\varphi \in B$, there are φ_n in $A_\alpha \hat{\otimes} A$ with $\varphi_n \to \varphi$ uniformly on $X \supset \mathcal{M}(A_\alpha) \times H \supset \{m^0\} \times H$. So $\varphi_n(m^0, x) \to \varphi(m^0, x)$ uniformly for $x \in H$. Each $\varphi_n(m^0, \cdot)$ lies in A, so $\varphi(m^0, \cdot)$ belongs to the uniform closure of A on H. In particular, $\varphi \mid Q$ determines a function f on $P \cap H$, given by $f(x) = \varphi(m^0, x)$, which is uniformly approximable by A on $P \cap H$. But $A|_{P \cap H}$ is uniformly closed, so $\varphi \to f$ is an isometric isomorphism of $B|_Q$ onto $A|_{P \cap H}$. This completes the proof.

Let J be a nonvoid index set. Let Δ be the closed unit disk and set $\Delta^J = \prod_{i \in J} \Delta_i$ where $\Delta_i = \Delta$ for each $i \in J$. Δ^J is a generalized polydisk lying in $\mathbf{C}^J$. Similarly, there is a generalized polydisk algebra. For $p \in \Delta^J$ and $i \in J$, let $z_i(p) = p_i$, the ith coordinate of p. Let A^J be the closed subalgebra of $C(\Delta^J)$ generated by 1 and the coordinate functions $\{z_i : i \in J\}$. A^J is a function algebra with maximal ideal space Δ^J. (If $\varphi \in \mathcal{M}(A^J)$, then $\|\varphi\| = 1$, so $|\varphi(z_i)| \leq \|z_i\| = 1$ for each $i \in J$. So $\varphi(f) = f(\lambda)$ for all $f \in A^J$, where λ is the element of Δ^J with coordinates $\lambda_i = \varphi(z_i)$, $i \in J$.)

Lemma 14. *Let θ be the element in Δ^J such that $z_i(\theta) = 0$ for all $i \in J$. Let P_0 be the Gleason part of $\mathcal{M}(A^J)$ containing θ. Then $p \in P_0$ iff $\exists \delta < 1$ such that $|z_i(p)| \leq \delta$, $\forall i \in J$.*

Proof. Suppose $p \in P_0$. Then $\exists \delta < 1$ such that $|f(p)| \leq \delta \|f\|$ for all $f \in A^J$ such that $f(\theta) = 0$. In particular, $|z_i(p)| \leq \delta$ for all $i \in J$.

On the other hand suppose that there exists such a δ, $0 < \delta < 1$. Define $\tau : \Delta \to \Delta^J$ by $\tau(\xi)_i = \dfrac{\xi}{\delta} p_i$ $(i \in J)$, where $p_i = z_i(p)$. Then τ is a continuous mapping. We have $f \circ \tau \in A^0$ when f is one of the generators z_i, so $f \circ \tau \in A^0$ for every $f \in A^J$. If $g \in A^0$ and $g(0) = 0$, then $|g(\delta)| \leq \delta \|g\|$ by the Schwarz lemma, so $|f(p)| = |(f \circ \tau)(\delta)| \leq \delta \|f \circ \tau\| \leq \delta \|f\|$ for all $f \in A^J$ which vanish at θ. This proves that $p \sim \theta$.

We can now prove a strengthened form of the last two theorems. The proof involves a modification of the argument in Theorem 19. The modification is required because infinitely many "points at infinity" may have been adjoined in forming the compactification.

Theorem 20. *Let Y be a σ-compact completely regular space. Then there is a function algebra B such that $\mathcal{M}(B)$ contains a part Q such that Q is homeomorphic to Y and $B|_Q$ is isometrically isomorphic to the algebra of bounded continuous functions on Y.*

Proof. If Y is compact, the assertion is contained in Theorem 19. So assume that Y is not compact.

Let βY be the Stone-Čech compactification of Y; $\beta Y = \mathcal{M}(BC(Y))$, and each $\psi \in BC(Y)$ has a unique extension $\hat{\psi} \in C(\beta Y)$. Y is embedded by evaluation as a proper dense subset of βY.

Set $J = \beta Y \setminus Y$. Let A be the subalgebra of the cylinder algebra $\{f \in C(\beta Y \times \Delta^J) : \lambda \to f(y, \lambda)$ is in A^J for each fixed $y \in \beta Y\}$ consisting of all those f which are constant on $\beta Y \times \{0\}$. Again one sees that $\mathcal{M}(A)$ is $\beta Y \times \Delta^J$ with the centers identified to a point and that $P = \{(y, \lambda) \in \mathcal{M}(A) : \lambda \in P_0\}$ is a part in $\mathcal{M}(A)$.

By hypothesis, $Y = \bigcup\limits_{n=1}^{\infty} K_n$ where $K_n \subset K_{n+1} \subsetneq Y$ and each K_n is compact.

For each $t \in J$, choose $h_t \in C(\beta Y)$ such that $h_t(\beta Y) \subset [\frac{1}{2}, 1]$, $h_t \leq 1 - \dfrac{1}{2^n}$ on K_n, and $h_t(t) = 1$. Let $H = \bigcap\limits_{t \in J} g_t^{-1}(0)$ where $g_t(y, \lambda) = \dfrac{h_t(y) - z_t(\lambda)}{3h_t(y) - z_t(\lambda)}$ on $\beta Y \times \Delta^J$. Each g_t belongs to A, so H is a hull in $\mathcal{M}(A)$. Note that $P \cap H = \{(y, p) : y \in \beta Y, \ p \in P_0 \text{ and } h_t(y) = p_t = z_t(p) \text{ for all } t \in J\}$. By Lemma 14, $p \in P_0$ iff $|p_t| \leq \delta < 1$ for all $t \in J$, for some fixed δ. So $P \cap H = \bigcup\limits_{n=1}^{\infty} \{(y, p) : y \in Y, \ p_t = h_t(y) \text{ for all } t \in J, \text{ and } |p_t| \leq 1 - \dfrac{1}{2^n}\}$.

Define $\tau : \beta Y \to \Delta^J$ by $\tau(y)_t = h_t(y)$, $t \in J$. τ is continuous, so the mapping T given by $T(y) = (y, \tau(y))$ is a homeomorphism of βY onto H. The last formula for $P \cap H$ shows that $P \cap H = T(Y)$, so $P \cap H$ is homeomorphic to Y.

So by Theorem 18 there is a function algebra B such that some part Q of $\mathcal{M}(B)$ has form $Q = \{m^0\} \times (P \cap H)$. Given $\psi \in BC(Y)$, we let $\hat{\psi} \in C(\beta Y)$ be its unique extension and set $f(y, \lambda) = \dfrac{\hat{\psi}(y)}{h_t(y)} z_t(\lambda)$ for any $t \in J$. Then $f \in A$ and $\hat{\psi} = f \circ T$, so $A|_{P \cap H} = C(\beta Y) = BC(Y)$. Since $A|_{P \cap H}$ is uniformly closed, $B|_Q$ is again isomorphic to $A|_{P \cap H}$.

Observe that the part Q in $\mathcal{M}(B)$ admits no analytic structure; indeed no subset of Q admits a structure relative to which all the functions in B are analytic. Since a part is always σ-compact and completely regular, none of the hypotheses in Theorem 20 can be deleted.

Now one can extend Theorem 15 to tensor products of arbitrary families of function algebras, provided that all but a finite number of the parts in the component algebras are points. (See Exercise 5.) Thus we may improve Theorem 19 as follows.

Theorem 21. *Let $\{Y_i\}_{i \in J}$ be a family of σ-compact locally compact spaces. Then there is a function algebra B such that there are parts $\{P_i\}_{i \in J}$ in $\mathcal{M}(B)$ with P_i homeomorphic to Y_i for each $i \in J$.*

Proof. There are function algebras $B_i(i \in J)$, with parts $Q_i \subset \mathcal{M}(B_i)$ such that for each i, Q_i is homeomorphic to Y_i. Let $B = \bigotimes_{i \in J} B_i$ be the completed tensor product of the B_i.

For each i, choose a_i in the Choquet boundary $c(B_i)$; then $\{a_i\}$ is a Gleason part in $\mathcal{M}(B_i)$. For fixed j in J, set $F_i = \{a_i\}$ for $i \in J\backslash\{j\}$ and $F_j = Q_j$. Then $P_j = \prod_{i \in J} F_i$ is a Gleason part in $\mathcal{M}(B)$ which is homeomorphic to Y_j.

EXERCISE SET 8.4

1. Show that $C(X) \hat{\otimes} C(Y) = C(X \times Y)$.

2. Prove that if A is a Dirichlet algebra on X, then $A \hat{\otimes} C(Y)$ is a Dirichlet algebra on $X \times Y$. Show by example that $A \hat{\otimes} B$ need not be a Dirichlet algebra even though A and B are Dirichlet algebras. Note however that it is still true that the non-one-point parts P in $\mathcal{M}(A \hat{\otimes} B)$ have an analytic structure (if A, B are Dirichlet): there is a one-one continuous map τ from D onto P such that $\hat{F} \circ \tau$ is analytic on D for each $F \in A \hat{\otimes} B$; here D is either the open disk U or the bicylinder $U \times U$.

3. Show that $A \hat{\otimes} B$ is antisymmetric iff A and B are antisymmetric.

4. Show that $A \hat{\otimes} B$ is an essential algebra on $X \times Y$ iff either A is essential on X or B is essential on Y.

5. One can define tensor products of arbitrary families of function algebras. Let J be a nonvoid set, $\{X_i\}_{i \in J}$ a family of compact spaces indexed by J, and A_i a function algebra on X_i for each $i \in J$. Let $X = \prod X_i$. Then $\otimes_i A_i$ is the linear subspace of $C(X)$ spanned by the functions of form $\otimes_i f_i$ defined as follows: for each $i \in J$, $f_i \in A_i$; for all but a finite number of values of i, $f_i = 1$; $\otimes_i f_i(x) = \prod_i f_i(x_i)$ for $x = \{x_i\}$ in X. The function algebra $\hat{\otimes} A_i$ is the uniform closure of $\otimes A_i$. Show that $\mathcal{M}(\hat{\otimes} A_i) = \prod \mathcal{M}(A_i)$, $\Gamma(\hat{\otimes} A_i) = \prod \Gamma(A_i)$. Suppose that P_i is a Gleason part in A_i for each $i \in J$ and that P_i is a point for all but a finite number of values of i. Prove that $\prod P_i$ is a part for $\hat{\otimes} A_i$.

6. Prove the following: Suppose that $\{a\}$ is a one-point part in $\mathcal{M}(A)$, where A is a function algebra, and that F is a closed set in $\mathcal{M}(A)$ containing a. Then (evaluation at) a is a one-point part in $\mathcal{M}(B)$, where B is the uniform closure of $\hat{A}|_F$.

7. Let Y_∞ be the one-point compactification of a σ-compact locally compact space Y, let $Z = Y_\infty \times \Delta$, and let A be the subalgebra of $C(Z)$ which was considered in the proof of Theorem 19.
   (a) Show that $\{(\infty, 1)\}$ is a part in $\mathcal{M}(A)$.
   (b) Let $B_0 = A_\alpha \hat{\otimes} A$. Prove that $a = (m^0, (\infty, 1))$ is a one-point part in $\mathcal{M}(B_0)\backslash\Gamma(B_0)$.

(c) Let B be the uniform closure of $B_0|_X$. Show that $\{a\}$ is a one-point part in $\mathcal{M}(B)$.

Thus, given Y, there exists a function algebra which has a Gleason part homeomorphic to Y and a one-point part off its Šilov boundary.

8.5   NEW ANTISYMMETRIC ALGEBRAS

The basic examples of antisymmetric function algebras are algebras of analytic functions of one or more complex variables. We know by now that every function algebra A determines a decomposition of its maximal ideal space into maximal sets of antisymmetry; if $\tilde{K}$ is any such set, $\tilde{K}$ is the maximal ideal space of the restriction algebra $\hat{A}|_{\tilde{K}}$. So it may seem that we have many examples of (compact connected) spaces which are maximal ideal spaces of antisymmetric algebras. But this result is abstract and does not give substantial specific information about a basic question: which spaces are obtainable as the maximal ideal spaces of antisymmetric algebras? Such a space must be compact and connected; is every compact connected space homeomorphic to $\mathcal{M}(A)$ for some antisymmetric A? Since no example of any proper subalgebra of $C(I)$ is known which has maximal ideal space I, the demonstration of an affirmative answer would require some new tools.

In this section we touch briefly on a technique for constructing new antisymmetric function algebras from given ones. We apply the construction to produce antisymmetric algebras whose maximal ideal spaces have odd (real) dimension and which are therefore quite different from algebras of holomorphic functions. (An interesting antisymmetric function algebra (on the unit ball of $\mathbf{C}^2$) which we shall not discuss here is described in [104].) Modifying the idea of welding together maximal ideal spaces, which we used in §8.2 to construct new Dirichlet algebras, we produce a nonanalytic function algebra which is analytic on its Šilov boundary (and hence is an integral domain).

Theorem 22.   *Let X be a compact Hausdorff space and let A be a function algebra with maximal ideal space $Y = \mathcal{M}(A)$. Let B be the algebra of all continuous functions h on $X \times Y$ such that for each fixed x in X, the function h_x given by $h_x(y) = h(x, y)$ belongs to A. Then $\mathcal{M}(B) = X \times \mathcal{M}(A)$ and $\Gamma(B) = X \times \Gamma(A)$.*

Proof.   Note that B separates points and is thus a function algebra on $X \times Y$. B contains a subalgebra A_1 isomorphic to A; A_1 consists of all $f \in B$ such that $f(x_1, y) = f(x_2, y)$ for all x_1, x_2 in X and y in Y. Similarly B contains a subalgebra C isomorphic to $C(X)$; C consists of all $g \in B$ such that $g(x, y_1) = g(x, y_2)$ for all y_1, y_2 in Y and x in X.

Let $\varphi \in \mathcal{M}(B)$. Restricting φ to A_1 and C, we have $x_0 \in X$, $y_0 \in Y$ such that $\varphi(f) = f(x, y_0)$ for all $f \in A_1$, $\varphi(g) = g(x_0, y)$ for all $g \in C$. We shall show that $\varphi(h) = h(x_0, y_0)$ for every $h \in B$.

Given $h \in B$, define f by $f(x, y) = h(x_0, y)$; then $f \in A_1$ and $h - f$ vanishes on $\{x_0\} \times Y$. Let $\varepsilon > 0$ be given. By continuity, there is an open *nbhd* U of x_0 in X such that $|h - f| < \varepsilon$ on $U \times Y$. Take a Urysohn function $g \in C(X)$ such that $g(x_0) = 0$, $g = 1$ outside U, and $0 \leq g \leq 1$. Extend g to an element of C. We have $g(x_0, y_0) = 0$, $\|(1 - g)(h - f)\| < \varepsilon$. So $|\varphi(h) - h(x_0, y_0)| = |(1 - g(x_0, y_0))(\varphi(h) - f(x_0, y_0))| = |\varphi((1 - g)(h - f))| < \varepsilon$. Since ε is arbitrary, $\varphi(h) = h(x_0, y_0)$, so that φ is given by evaluation at (x_0, y_0).

This proves that $\mathcal{M}(B) = X \times \mathcal{M}(A)$.

Given $h \in B$, take (x_0, y_0) in $X \times Y$ at which h assumes its maximum modulus. Then $f \in A$, where $f(y) = h(x_0, y)$ ($y \in Y$). So there is some y_1 in $\Gamma(A)$ such that $\|f\| = |f(y_1)|$. Hence $\|h\| = |h(x_0, y_0)| = |f(y_0)| \leq |f(y_1)| = |h(x_0, y_1)|$, so h assumes its maximum modulus on $X \times \Gamma(A)$. Thus $X \times \Gamma(A)$ is a closed boundary for B, hence contains $\Gamma(B)$.

Conversely, given $(x_0, y_0) \in X \times \Gamma(A)$ and any open *nbhd* W of (x_0, y_0) in $X \times Y$, we can find $h \in B$ such that h attains the value 1 in W and $|h| < 1$ outside of W. (See the proof of Proposition 1, §8.4.) So $X \times \Gamma(A)$ is contained in $\Gamma(B)$.

Theorem 23.   *Let A, B, X be as in Theorem 22. Let H be a hull in $\mathcal{M}(B)$. Set $\tilde{A} = \tilde{A}(A, X, H) = \{h \in B : h \,|\, H \text{ is constant}\}$. Then $\mathcal{M}(\tilde{A}) = \mathcal{M}(B)$ with H identified to a point and $\Gamma(\tilde{A}) = \Gamma(B)$ with $\Gamma(B) \cap H$ identified to a point.*

Proof.   Let $J = kH$ be the ideal of functions in B which vanish on H; then $\tilde{A} = J + \mathbf{C}$. So $\mathcal{M}(\tilde{A})$ is the one-point compactification of $\mathcal{M}(J)$. But J is a closed ideal in B with hull equal to H, so $\mathcal{M}(J) = \mathcal{M}(B) \backslash H$. Hence the first assertion is proved.

It is clear that $\Gamma(B)$ is a boundary for $\tilde{A}$, so in $\mathcal{M}(\tilde{A})$, $\Gamma(\tilde{A}) \subset \Gamma(B)$ with H identified to a point. On the other hand, consider any point ξ in $\Gamma(B) \backslash H$ and let W be an arbitrary open *nbhd* of ξ which is disjoint from H. Since $\xi \in \Gamma(B)$, there is some $h_0 \in B$ with $|h_0| \leq \delta < 1$ on $\mathcal{M}(B) \backslash W$ while $h_0(\xi_0) = 1$ for some $\xi_0 \in W$. Since $\xi_0 \notin H$, there is some $h_1 \in J$ with $h_1(\xi_0) = 1$. Choose n so that $\delta^n |h_1| < 1$ on $\mathcal{M}(B) \backslash W$. Then $h = h_0{}^n h_1$ is in $\tilde{A}$, $h(\xi_0) = 1$, but $|h| < 1$ outside W. W is arbitrary, so we conclude that $\xi \in \Gamma(\tilde{A})$. Hence $\Gamma(B) \backslash H \subset \Gamma(\tilde{A}) \subset \Gamma(B)$, with H identified to a point.

If every open set W in $\mathcal{M}(B)$ containing H meets $\Gamma(B) \backslash H$, then the point $\{H\}$ in $\mathcal{M}(\tilde{A})$ belongs to the closure of $\Gamma(B) \backslash H$. Taking closures above, we have $\Gamma(\tilde{A}) = \Gamma(B)$, where $\Gamma(B) \cap H$ is identified to a point. Otherwise some open *nbhd* W of H in $\mathcal{M}(B)$ is disjoint from $\Gamma(B)$. In this case, $\Gamma(B) \cap H$ is empty, so that when H is identified to a point in $\mathcal{M}(\tilde{A})$, $\Gamma(B)$ and $\Gamma(B) \backslash H$ become identical: again $\Gamma(\tilde{A}) = \Gamma(B)$, but now the identified "point" is not present.

Lemma 15.   *Define $\pi : X \times Y \to X$ by $\pi(x, y) = x$. If A is antisymmetric, then $\tilde{A}(A, X, H)$ is antisymmetric iff $\pi(H) = X$.*

Proof.   Note that $\{f \in \tilde{A} : \bar{f} \in \tilde{A}\} = C \cap \tilde{A}$, since $B \cap \bar{B} = C$. For if $h \in B$ and $\bar{h} \in B$, then for each $x \in X$, h_x and $\bar{h}_x$ lie in the antisymmetric algebra A, so h_x is constant; i.e., h is constant on every $\{x\} \times \mathcal{M}(A)$, which means that $h \in C$. Now $\pi(H)$ is a compact subset of X, assuming H is non-void. Clearly $\pi(H)$ is a proper closed subset of X iff $C_R(X)$ contains non-constant functions which are constant on $\pi(H)$. So the assertion is clear.

Note that if F is any nonvoid hull in $\mathcal{M}(A)$, $X \times F$ is a hull in $\mathcal{M}(B)$. Since $\pi(X \times F) = X$ we conclude that if A is antisymmetric and F is a non-void hull in $\mathcal{M}(A)$, then $\tilde{A}(A, X, X \times F)$ is also antisymmetric, with maximal ideal space and Šilov boundary given by Theorem 23.

We can now construct an antisymmetric algebra whose maximal ideal space is a (real) three-dimensional solid. (Actually, we have already seen an example of such an algebra. Let α be a positive irrational number and A_α the function algebra on T^2 generated by the functions $z \to z_1{}^n z_2{}^m$ where $n + m\alpha \geq 0$. Then $\mathcal{M}(A_\alpha)$ is homeomorphic to $[0, 1] \times T^2$ with the centers $\{0\} \times T^2$ identified to a point. Thus A_α is an antisymmetric algebra with maximal ideal space a solid torus.) We take $I = [0, 1]$, A the disk algebra A^0, F the singleton set $\{1\}$ in $\Delta = \mathcal{M}(A)$. The algebra B consists of all continuous functions f on $I \times \Delta$ such that for each fixed $t \in I$, $z \to f(t, z)$ is analytic on the open unit disk. The subalgebra $\tilde{A} = \tilde{A}(A^0, I, I \times \{1\})$ consists of all $f \in B$ which are constant on the segment $\{(t, 1) : 0 \leq t \leq 1\}$. $\tilde{A}$ is antisymmetric, and $\mathcal{M}(\tilde{A})$ is the cylinder $I \times \Delta$ with $I \times \{1\}$ identified to a point. So $\mathcal{M}(\tilde{A})$ is homeomorphic to a solid ball in $\mathbf{R}^3$.

Note that if we let X be a two-point discrete space $\{a, b\}$ and take $F = \{0\}$, $A = A^0$, then the algebra $\tilde{A}$ is the double-disk algebra (on its maximal ideal space; see §7.4). Here the maximal ideal space of the antisymmetric algebra $\tilde{A}$ is the union of two closed disks joined at their centers, so $\mathcal{M}(\tilde{A})$ is two-dimensional but not embeddable as a closed subset of the plane.

At this point we are going to discuss an example of a function algebra A such that A is analytic on its Šilov boundary but is not analytic on its maximal ideal space. (Recall that A is analytic on a closed boundary X iff $f \in A$, U nonvoid and open in X, and $f|U = 0$ imply that $f = 0$.) The construction is as follows.

Let E be a totally disconnected compact perfect set in the plane, each point of which is a density point; i.e., if an open set V meets E, then $V \cap E$ has positive Lebesgue measure. Let F be a Cantor set of measure zero on the unit circle T^1. There is a homeomorphism τ of E onto F. Let $\mathcal{B}_E$ be the algebra, defined in §8.1, consisting of all continuous functions h on the Riemann sphere which are analytic on the complement of E, and let $S = \mathcal{M}(\mathcal{B}_E)$. (Actually, S is the sphere S^2, but we shall not need this fact and will not prove it. For our purposes it will suffice to know that $S^2 \subset S$.) Let A^1 be the boundary value algebra on T^1, A^0 the disk algebra on the closed unit disk Δ.

Let X be the compact space obtained from the disjoint union of S and Δ by attaching E to F via the homeomorphism τ. The algebra A is defined to be the set of all $f \in C(X)$ such that $f|S$ is in $\hat{\mathcal{B}}_E$ and $f|\Delta$ is in A^0. We shall prove: (i) A is a function algebra on X; (ii) $\mathcal{M}(A) = X$ and $\Gamma(A) = T^1$; (iii) A is analytic on $\Gamma(A)$; (iv) A is not analytic on $\mathcal{M}(A)$; (v) A is an integral domain.

Observe first that the Šilov boundary of $\mathcal{B}_E$ is E. This is true whether or not E is totally disconnected.

Theorem 24. *Let E be a compact set in the plane each point of which is a density point. Let $\mathcal{B}_E$ be the algebra of Theorem 1, §8.1. Then E is the Šilov boundary of $\mathcal{B}_E$.*

Proof. Every $f \in \mathcal{B}_E$ assumes its maximum modulus on E, so $\Gamma(\mathcal{B}_E) \subset E$. On the other hand, let $z_0 \in E$. We shall show that for every open *nbhd* U of z_0 in S^2, there is a function in $\mathcal{B}_E$ which assumes its maximum modulus only in U. We may assume that U is an open disk $D(z_0; \rho)$ with center z_0 and radius ρ. Let $0 < r < \rho$ and set $E_r = E \cap D(z_0; r)$.

Define f by $f(\xi) = \displaystyle\int_{E_r} \frac{1}{\xi - z}\, dm(z)$ where m is planar Lebesgue measure. Our hypothesis guarantees that $m(E_r) > 0$. By the argument in Theorem 1, f is continuous on S^2, analytic outside $\bar{E}_r$, vanishes at infinity, but is not constant on any *nbhd* of ∞. If f assumed its maximum modulus at a point of the connected set $S^2 \backslash \bar{D}(z_0; r)$, then f would be constant on that set (by the identity principle for analytic functions), contrary to what has been shown. So if $z \notin D(z_0; \rho)$, $|f(z)| < \|f\|$. So f is the required function.

Once again assume that E is a two-dimensional Cantor set of positive density at each point, and let F be a Cantor set of linear measure zero on T^1. Form the space X and the algebra A as above. Let us denote the assertion that E and F are identified in X by $E \equiv F$.

Some of the statements (i)—(v) are easy to prove.

(iii) Let $f \in A$ vanish on a nonvoid relatively open subset of T^1. Since $f | T^1$ is in A^1, which is pervasive and hence analytic, $f | T^1 = 0$. So $A|_{\Gamma(A)}$ is analytic.

(v) We know from (iii) that $A|_{\Gamma(A)}$ is analytic. Hence $A|_{\Gamma(A)}$ is an integral domain. But A and $A|_{\Gamma(A)}$ are isomorphic algebras, so A is an integral domain.

(iv) Now we need the machinery of Chapter Seven. Since F is a closed set of measure zero on T^1, it follows from the F. and M. Riesz theorem that $\mu_F = 0$ for every annihilator $\mu \in (A^1)^{\perp}$. So $A^1|_F = C(F)$ (Rudin-Carleson) and since T^1 is metrizable, F is a peak-interpolation set and hence a zero set for A^0: there is a function $g_0 \in A^0$ with $g_0 = 1$ on F but $|g_0| < 1$ on $\Delta \backslash F$, so there is a function $g \in A^0$ with $g = 0$ on F, $|g| > 0$ on $\Delta \backslash F$. (Moreover, every element of $C(F)$ extends to a member of A^0 without increase of norm.) Actually, some of these facts are part of the content of classical theorems of P. Fatou and have more direct proofs than we have given.

Take g in A^0 with $g = 0$ on F, $|g| > 0$ on $\Delta \backslash F$. Let f^* be the function which is 0 on S and coincides with g on Δ. Since S and Δ meet only in $E \equiv F$, f^* belongs to A. So A is not analytic on X.

(i) Note that the argument just given shows that $J = \{f \in A : f \,|\, S = 0\}$ separates points on $\Delta \backslash F$. For let $z' \neq z''$ in $\Delta \backslash F$. If $g(z') \neq g(z'')$, then $f^* \in J$ and f^* separates z' and z''. If $g(z') = g(z'')$, choose g_1 in A^0 such that $g_1(z') \neq g_1(z'')$ and let $f_1 = 0$ on S and $f_1 = gg_1$ on Δ. Then $f_1 \in J$ and f_1 separates z' and z''.

On the other hand, $\mathscr{B}_E$ separates points on S. So given distinct x_1, x_2 in S, $\exists h \in \mathscr{B}_E$ with $\hat{h}(x_1) \neq \hat{h}(x_2)$. By the Rudin-Carleson theorem, $\hat{h}$ extends to a function in A. So A separates points on S. Since X is the union of S and $\Delta \backslash F$, A is a function algebra on X.

The problem is now to prove (ii). This is a little tricky. We have $X \subset \mathscr{M}(A)$, as was just shown. Conversely, let $\varphi \in \mathscr{M}(A)$. There are two possibilities: either φ annihilates the ideal J or it does not. If $\varphi \,|\, J = 0$ then φ determines a nonzero complex homomorphism $f + J \to \varphi(f)$ of the Banach algebra A/J, which is algebraically isomorphic to $A|_S$ (via $f + J \to f \,|\, S$), which is $\hat{\mathscr{B}}_E$; so if $\varphi \,|\, J = 0$ there is a point $x \in S$ with $\varphi(f) = f(x)$, $\forall f \in A$. Otherwise $\varphi \,|\, J$ is a nonzero complex homomorphism of J. Now the map $f \to f \,|\, T^1$ takes J isomorphically and isometrically onto the ideal $kF = \{g \in A^1 : g \,|\, F = 0\}$. (If $f \in J$, then $f \,|\, T^1$ is in kF since $F \equiv E \subset S$, and $\|f\| = \max_{S \cup \Delta} |f| = \max_{\Delta} |f| = \max_{T^1} |f|$ since $f \,|\, \Delta \in A^0$. On the other hand, we have seen that every $g \in kF$ extends to an element of J.) A nonzero homomorphism of an ideal into the scalars extends uniquely to a complex homomorphism of the underlying algebra, so $\varphi \,|\, J$ is given by evaluation at some point of $\mathscr{M}(A^1) = \Delta$. The same is therefore true for φ. So again φ is a point evaluation. Thus $\mathscr{M}(A) = X$.

If $f \in A$, $\|f\|_\Delta \leq \|f\|_{T^1}$ since $f \,|\, \Delta$ is in A^0 and $\|f\|_S = \|f\|_E = \|f\|_F \leq \|f\|_{T^1}$ since $f \,|\, S$ is in $\hat{\mathscr{B}}_E$, $E = \Gamma(\mathscr{B}_E)$ and $E \equiv F \subset T^1$. So T^1 is a boundary for A.

Conversely, let $x \in T^1$. We prove that $x \in \Gamma(A)$. Now there is some $g_0 \in A^0$ with $g_0 = 1$ on F, $|g_0| < 1$ on $\Delta \backslash F$. Extend g_0 to a function $f_0 \in A$ which is identically 1 on S. Let U be open about x in X. Then $U \cap E$ is a *nbhd* of x in the Šilov boundary E of $\mathscr{B}_E$, so there is some h_0 in $\mathscr{B}_E$ such that $|h_0| < 1$ on $S \backslash (U \cap E)$ but $|h_0|$ assumes the value 1 somewhere in $U \cap E$. Extend h_0 to a function $f \in A$ (again using the fact that $A^0|_F = C(F)$). Note that $\|f_0^n f\| = 1$ for all $n \geq 1$.

Now $|h_0| < \delta_0 < 1$ on $E \backslash U \equiv F \backslash U$. Hence by continuity, $|f| < \delta_0$ on some open set V containing $F \backslash U$. But $f_0 = 1$ on $F \subset V \cup U$, $|f_0| < 1$ on $\Delta \backslash F$; so $|f_0| \leq \delta < 1$ on $\Delta \backslash (V \cup U)$ and in particular, $|f_0| \leq \delta$ on $T^1 \backslash (V \cup U)$. Hence for n sufficiently large, $|f_0^n f| \leq \delta_0$ on $T^1 \backslash (V \cup U)$. But on V, $|f_0^n f| \leq |f| \leq \delta_0$, so $|f_0^n f| \leq \delta_0$ on $T^1 \backslash U$. We have found a function in A which does not assume its maximum modulus on $T^1 \backslash U$. So $x \in \Gamma(A)$, and the proof is complete.

It should be clear that a mild modification of the proof will apply to the following situation. A_1, A_2 are function algebras with $\mathscr{M}(A_2)$ metrizable. F is a compact set in $\Gamma(A_2)$ such that F is homeomorphic to $\Gamma(A_1)$ and $\mu_F = 0$ for every annihilator μ of $A_2|_{\Gamma(A_2)}$. X is the compact space obtained by attaching $\mathscr{M}(A_1)$ to $\mathscr{M}(A_2)$ with $\Gamma(A_1)$ attached to F, and $A = \{f \in C(X) : \mathscr{M}(A_1) \in \hat{A}_1, f \,|\, \mathscr{M}(A_2) \in \hat{A}_2\}$.

EXERCISE SET 8.5

1. Prove that if A is a function algebra with maximal ideal space $K = \mathcal{M}(A)$, there is a function algebra B such that $\mathcal{M}(B)$ contains a part Q homeomorphic to K and $\hat{B}|_Q = \hat{A}$.

2. Let I^n be the Cartesian product of n copies of $I = [0, 1]$. There is an antisymmetric function algebra A with maximal ideal space obtained from $I^n \times \Delta$ by identifying $I^n \times \{1\}$ to a point; give a simpler topological description of $\mathcal{M}(A)$. If K is the Cantor set and $K' = \{e^{2\pi it} : t \in K\}$, then there is an antisymmetric algebra with maximal ideal space homeomorphic to $I^n \times \Delta$ with $I^n \times K'$ identified to a point.

3. Let n be a positive integer. Show that there is an antisymmetric function algebra with maximal ideal space obtained from $I \times T^n$ by identifying $\{0\} \times T^n$ to a point. We can choose this algebra to be a maximal Dirichlet algebra on its Šilov boundary.

Bibliography

[A]   F. T. Birtel (editor), *Function Algebras*, Scott, Foresman, Chicago, 1966.

[B]   I. M. Gelfand, D. Raikov, G. E. Shilov, *Commutative Normed Rings*, Chelsea Publishing Company, New York, 1964.

[C]   R. Gunning and H. Rossi, *Analytic Functions of Several Complex Variables*, Prentice-Hall, Englewood Cliffs, N.J., 1965.

[D]   H. Helson, *Lectures on Invariant Subspaces*, Academic Press, New York, 1964.

[E]   K. M. Hoffman, *Banach Spaces of Analytic Functions*, Prentice-Hall, Englewood Cliffs, N.J., 1962.

[F]   L. Loomis, *Abstract Harmonic Analysis*, D. Van Nostrand, Princeton, N.J., 1953.

[G]   M. A. Naimark, *Normed Rings*, P. Noordhoff, Groningen, Netherlands, 1959.

[H]   R. R. Phelps, *Lectures on Choquet's Theorem*, Van Nostrand Mathematical Studies #7, D. Van Nostrand, Princeton, N.J., 1966.

[I]   C. Rickart, *General Theory of Banach Algebras*, D. Van Nostrand, Princeton, N.J., 1960.

[J]   W. Rudin, *Fourier Analysis on Groups*, Interscience-John Wiley, New York, 1962.

[K]   —, *Real and Complex Analysis*, McGraw-Hill, New York, 1966.

[L]   J. Wermer, *Banach Algebras and Analytic Functions*, Advances in Mathematics, Volume 1, pp. 51–102, Academic Press, New York, 1961.

[M]   —, *Seminar uber Funktionen Algebren*, Lecture Notes in Mathematics, No. 1, Springer-Verlag, Berlin, 1964.

[N]   L. Zalcman, *Analytic Capacity and Rational Approximation*, Lecture Notes in Mathematics, No. 50, Springer-Verlag, Berlin, 1968.

Abbreviations of Journal Titles

Acta Math.   *Acta Mathematica*
Acta Sci. Math. (Szeged).   *Acta Universitatis Szedediensis. Acta Scientiarum Mathematicarum*
Amer. J. Math.   *American Journal of Mathematics*
Amer. Math. Monthly.   *The American Mathematical Monthly*
Amer. Math. Soc. Transl.   *American Mathematical Society Translations*
Ann. Inst. Fourier (*Grenoble*).   *Université de Grenoble. Annales de l'Institut Fourier*
Ann. of Math.   *Annals of Mathematics, series 2*
Ark. Mat.   *Arkiv för Matematik*
Bull. Amer. Math. Soc.   *Bulletin of the American Mathematical Society*
Bull. Soc. Math. France.   *Bulletin de la Société Mathématique de France*
C. R. Acad. Sci. Paris Sér. A-B.   *Comptes Rendus Hebdomadaires des Séances de l'Académie des Sciences. Séries A et B*
Canad. J. Math.   *Canadian Journal of Mathematics*
Canad. Math. Bull.   *Canadian Mathematical Bulletin*
Dokl. Akad. Nauk.   *Doklady Akademii Nauk*
Duke Math. J.   *Duke Mathematical Journal*
Func. Anal. Applic.   *Functional Analysis and Its Applications*
Illinois J. Math.   *Illinois Journal of Mathematics*
J. Functional Analysis.   *Journal of Functional Analysis*
J. Math. Mech.   *Journal of Mathematics and Mechanics*
Kōdai Math. Sem. Rep.   *Kōdai Mathematical Seminar Reports*
Mat. Sb.   *Matematičeskiĭ Sbornik. Novaja Serija*
Math. Ann.   *Mathematische Annalen*
Math. Student.   *The Mathematics Student*
Math. Scand.   *Mathematica Scandinavica*
Math. Z.   *Mathematische Zeitschrift*
Mathematika   *Mathematika. A Journal of Pure and Applied Mathematics*
Mem. Amer. Math. Soc.   *Memoirs of the American Mathematical Society*
Osaka J. Math.   *Osaka Journal of Mathematics*
Pacific J. Math.   *Pacific Journal of Mathematics*
Proc. Amer. Math. Soc.   *Proceedings of the American Mathematical Society*
Proc. Japan Acad.   *Proceedings of the Japan Academy*
Proc. Nat. Acad. Sci. U.S.A.   *Proceedings of the National Academy of Sciences of the United States of America*
Rend. Circ. Mat. Palermo.   *Rendiconti del Circolo Matematico di Palermo*
Rev. Roumaine Math. Pures Appl.   *Académie de la République Populaire Roumaine. Revue Roumaine de Mathématiques Pures et Appliquées*
Rev. Un. Mat. Argentina.   *Revista de la Unión Matemática Argentina*
Soviet Math. Dokl.   *Soviet Mathematics. Doklady*
Studia Math.   *Polska Akademia Nauk. Studia Mathematica*
Tôhoku Math. J.   *The Tôhoku Mathematical Journal*
Trans. Amer. Math. Soc.   *Transactions of the American Mathematical Society*
Uspehi Mat. Nauk.   *Akademija Nauk SSSR i Moskovskoe Matematičeskeo Obščestvo. Uspehi Matematičeskih Nauk.*
Vestnik Leningrad. Univ.   *Vestnik Leningradskogo Universiteta*

References

[1] P. R. Ahern, On the generalized F. and M. Riesz theorem, *Pacific J. Math.*, 15 (1965).

[2] P. R. Ahern and Donald Sarason, The H^p spaces of a class of function algebras, *Acta Math.*, 117 (1967).

[3] —, On some hypo-Dirichlet algebras of analytic functions, *Amer. J. Math.*, 89 (1967).

[4] Richard Arens, A Banach algebra generalization of conformal mappings of the disk, *Trans. Amer. Math. Soc.*, 81 (1956).

[5] —, The boundary integral of log $|\Phi|$ for generalized analytic functions, *Trans. Amer. Math. Soc.*, 86 (1957).

[6] —, The maximal ideals of certain function algebras, *Pacific J. Math.*, 8 (1958).

[7] —, The group of invertible elements of a commutative Banach algebra, *Studia Math., Seria Spec.*, (1963).

[8] R. Arens and A. P. Calderôn, Analytic functions of several Banach algebra elements, *Ann. of Math.*, 62 (1955).

[9] Richard Arens and I. M. Singer, Function values as boundary integrals, *Proc. Amer. Math. Soc.*, 5 (1954).

[10] —, Generalized analytic functions, *Trans. Amer. Math. Soc.*, 81 (1956).

[11] E. L. Arenson, Certain properties of algebras of continuous functions, *Soviet Math. Dokl.*, 7 (1966).

[12] W. Badé and P. Curtis, The Wedderburn decomposition of commutative Banach algebras, *Amer. J. Math.*, 82 (1960).

[13] —, Embedding theorems for commutative Banach algebras, *Pacific J. Math.*, 18 (1966).

[14] Heinz Bauer, Silovscher Rand und Dirichletsches Problem, *Ann. Inst. Fourier (Grenoble)*, 11 (1961).

[15] H. S. Bear, A strong maximum modulus theorem for maximal function algebras, *Trans. Amer. Math. Soc.*, 92 (1959).

[16] —, Complex function algebras, *Trans. Amer. Math. Soc.*, 90 (1959).

[17] —, Some boundary properties of function algebras, *Proc. Amer. Math. Soc.*, 11 (1960).

[18] —, The Šilov boundary for a linear space of continuous functions, *Amer. Math. Monthly*, 68 (1961).

[19] —, A strict maximum theorem for one-part function spaces and algebras, *Bull. Amer. Math. Soc.*, 70 (1964).

[20] —, A geometric characterization of Gleason parts, *Proc. Amer. Math. Soc.*, 16 (1965).

[21] —, The integral representation of functions on parts, *Illinois J. Math.*, 10 (1966).

[22] H. S. Bear and M. L. Weiss, An intrinsic metric for parts, *Proc. Amer. Math. Soc.*, 18 (1967).

[23] Alain Bernard, Ensembles d'algèbres fondamentales, *C. R. Acad. Sci. Paris Sér. A-B.*, 260 (1965).

[24] —, Sur-algèbres d'une algèbre fondamentale, *J. Functional Analysis*, 2 (1968).

[25] Arne Beurling. On two problems concerning linear transformations in Hilbert space, *Acta Math.*, 81 (1949).

[26] Errett Bishop, Subalgebras of functions on a Riemann surface, *Pacific J. Math.*, 8 (1958).

[27] —, The structure of certain measures, *Duke Math. J.*, 25 (1958).

[28] —, A minimal boundary for function algebras, *Pacific J. Math.*, 9 (1959).

[29] —, Some theorems concerning function algebras, *Bull. Amer. Math. Soc.*, 85 (1959).

[30] —, Boundary measures of analytic differentials, *Duke Math. J.*, 27 (1960).

[31] —, A generalization of the Stone-Weierstrass theorem, *Pacific J. Math.*, 11 (1961).

[32] —, A general Rudin-Carleson theorem, *Proc. Amer. Math. Soc.*, 13 (1962).

[33] —, Analyticity in certain Banach algebras, *Trans. Amer. Math. Soc.*, 102 (1962).

[34] —, Holomorphic completion, analytic continuation, and the interpolation of seminorms, *Ann. of Math.*, 78 (1963).

[35] —, Representing measures for points in a uniform algebra, *Bull. Amer. Math. Soc.*, 70 (1964).

[36] —, Uniform algebras, *Proceedings of the Conference on Complex Analysis*, Minneapolis, 1964 (Springer-Verlag, 1965).

[37] Errett Bishop and Karel de Leeuw, The representation of linear functionals by measures on sets of extreme points, *Ann. Inst. Fourier (Grenoble)*, 9 (1959).

[38] Louis de Branges, The Stone-Weierstrass theorem, *Proc. Amer. Math. Soc.*, 10 (1959).

[39] James E. Brennan, Point evaluations and invariant subspaces, Doctoral thesis, Brown University (1968).

[40] Andrew Browder, Cohomology of maximal ideal spaces, *Bull. Amer. Math. Soc.*, 67 (1961).

[41] —, Point derivations on function algebras, *J. Functional Analysis*, 1 (1967).

[42] Andrew Browder and John Wermer, Some algebras of functions on an arc, *J. Math. Mech.*, 12 (1963).

[43] —, A method for constructing Dirichlet algebras, *Proc. Amer. Math. Soc.*, 15 (1964).

[44] Lennart Carleson, On bounded analytic functions and closure problems, *Ark. Mat.*, 2 (1952).

[45] —, Representations of continuous functions, *Math. Z.*, 66 (1957).

[46] —, Interpolation by bounded analytic functions and the corona problem, *Ann. of Math.*, 76 (1962).

[47] —, Mergelyan's theorem on uniform polynomial approximation, *Math. Scand.*, 15 (1964).

[48] Gustave Choquet, Existence des représentations intégrales au moyen des points extrémaux dans les cônes convexes, *C. R. Acad. Sci. Paris Ser. A-B*, 243 (1956).

[49] —, Séminaire Bourbaki, December 1956, pp. 139–01 to 139–15.

[50] E. M. Čirka, Approximation of continuous functions by functions holomorphic on Jordan arcs in C^n, *Soviet Math. Dokl.*, 7 (1966).

[51] P. Civin, A maximum modulus property of maximal subalgebras, *Proc. Amer. Math. Soc.*, 10 (1959).

[52] Lewis Coburn, The spectra of generalized Toeplitz operators, *Amer. J. Math.*, 88 (1966).

[53] Paul J. Cohen, A note on constructive methods in Banach algebras, *Proc. Amer. Math. Soc.*, 12 (1961).

[54] Brian J. Cole, One-point parts and the peak point conjecture, Doctoral thesis, Yale University (1968).

[55] Don Deckard and Carl Pearcy, On algebraic closure in function algebras, *Proc. Amer. Math. Soc.*, 15 (1964).

[56] Jacqueline Détraz, Algèbres uniformes, ensembles pics, *C. R. Acad. Sci. Paris Ser. A-B*, 264 (1967).

[57] Allen Devinatz, Toeplitz operators on H^2 spaces, *Trans. Amer. Math. Soc.*, 112 (1964).

[58] —, Conjugate function theorems for Dirichlet algebras, *Rev. U. Mat. Argentina*, 23 (1966/67).

[59] —, The strong Szegö limit theorem, *Illinois J. Math.*, 11 (1967).

[60] R. E. Edwards, Note on two theorems about function algebras, *Mathematika*, 4 (1957).

[61] C. Foias and I. Suciu, Szegö-measures and spectral theory in Hilbert spaces, *Rev. Roumaine Math. Pures. Appl.*, 11 (1966).

[62] Frank Forelli, Analytic measures, *Pacific J. Math.*, 13 (1963).

[63] —, Invariant subspaces in L^1, *Proc. Amer. Math. Soc.*, 14 (1963).

[64] —, The isometries of H^p, *Canad. J. Math.*, 16 (1964).

[65] A. S. Fox, On the boundary and tensor product of function algebras, *Canad. Math. Bull.*, 9 (1966).

[66] T. W. Gamelin, Restrictions of subspaces of $C(X)$, *Trans. Amer. Math. Soc.*, 112 (1964).

[67] —, H^p spaces and extremal functions in H^1, *Trans. Amer. Math. Soc.*, 124 (1966).

[68] —, Embedding Riemann surfaces in maximal ideal spaces, *J. Functional Analysis*, 2 (1968).

[69] John Garnett, Disconnected Gleason parts, *Bull. Amer. Math. Soc.*, 72 (1966).

[70] —, A topological characterization of Gleason parts, *Pacific J. Math.*, 20 (1967).

[71] —, On a theorem of Mergelyan, (to appear).

[72] John Garnett and Irving Glicksberg, Algebras with the same multiplicative measures, *J. Functional Analysis*, 1 (1967).

[73] Andrew Gleason, Function algebras, *Seminars on Analytic Functions*, Vol. 2, Princeton (1957).

[74] —, Finitely generated ideals in Banach algebras, *J. Math. Mech.* 13 (1964).

[75] Andrew Gleason and Hassler Whitney, The extension of linear functionals defined on H^∞, *Pacific J. Math.*, 12 (1962).

[76] Irving Glicksberg, The representation of functionals by integrals, *Duke Math. J.*, 19 (1952).

[77] —, Measures orthogonal to algebras and sets of antisymmetry, *Trans. Amer. Math. Soc.*, 105 (1962).

[78] —, A remark on analyticity of function algebras, *Pacific J. Math.*, 13 (1963).

[79] —, Function algebras with closed restrictions, *Proc. Amer. Math. Soc.*, 14 (1963).

[80] —, Maximal algebras and a theorem of Rado, *Pacific J. Math.*, 14 (1964) (correction, *idem*. 19 (1966), p. 587).

[81] —, Some uncomplemented function algebras, *Trans. Amer. Math. Soc.*, 111 (1964).

[82] —, The abstract F. and M. Riesz theorem, *J. Functional Analysis*, 1 (1967).

[83] —, Dominant representing measures and rational approximation, *Trans. Amer. Math. Soc.*, 130 (1968).

[84] I. Glicksberg and John Wermer, Measures orthogonal to a Dirichlet algebra, *Duke Math. J.*, 30 (1963) (addendum, *idem*. 31 (1964), p. 717).

[85] M. Hasumi, Invariant subspace theorems for finite Riemann surfaces, *Canad. J. Math.*, 18 (1966).

[86] —, Interpolation sets for logmodular Banach algebras, *Osaka J. Math.*, 3 (1966).

[87] Morisuke Hasumi and T. P. Srinivasan, Invariant subspaces of continuous functions, *Canad. J. Math.*, 17 (1965).

[88] S. Ya. Havinson, On the Rudin-Carleson theorem, *Soviet Math. Dokl.*, 6 (1965).

[89] Elizabeth A. Heard, A sequential F. and M. Riesz theorem, *Proc. Amer. Math. Soc.*, 18 (1967).

[90] Henry Helson and David Lowdenslager, Prediction theory and Fourier series in several variables, *Acta Math.*, 99 (1958).

[91] H. Helson and Frank Quigley, Maximal algebras of continuous functions, *Proc. Amer. Math. Soc.*, 8 (1957).

[92] —, Existence of maximal ideals in algebras of continuous functions, *Proc. Amer. Math. Soc.*, 8 (1957).

[93] Kenneth Hoffman, Fatou's theorem for generalized analytic functions, *Seminars on Analytic Functions*, Vol. 2, Princeton (1957).

[94] —, Boundary behavior of generalized analytic functions, *Trans. Amer. Math. Soc.*, 87 (1958).

[95] —, Minimal boundaries for analytic polyhedra, *Rend. Circ. Mat. Palermo*, 9 (1960).

[96] —, A note on the paper of I. J. Schark, *J. Math. Mech.*, 10 (1961).

[97] —, Analytic functions and logmodular Banach algebras, *Acta Math.*, 108 (1962).

[98] —, Bounded analytic functions and Gleason parts, *Ann. of Math.*, 86 (1967).

[99]   K. Hoffman and Arlan Ramsay, Algebras of bounded sequences, *Pacific J. Math.*, 15 (1965).

[100]   K. Hoffman and H. Rossi, The minimum boundary for an analytic poly-hedron, *Pacific J. Math.*, 12 (1962).

[101]   —, Function theory and multiplicative linear functionals, *Trans. Amer. Math. Soc.* 116 (1965).

[102]   —, Extensions of positive weak*-continuous linear functionals, *Duke Math. J.*, 34 (1967).

[103]   Kenneth Hoffman and I. M. Singer, Maximal subalgebras of $C(\Gamma)$, *Amer. J. Math.*, 79 (1957).

[104]   —, On some problems of Gelfand, *Amer. Math. Soc. Transl.*, 27 (1963).

[105]   —, Maximal algebras of continuous functions, *Acta Math.*, 103 (1960).

[106]   Kenneth Hoffman and John Wermer, A characterization of $C(X)$, *Pacific J. Math.*, 12 (1962).

[107]   Eva Kallin, A non-local function algebra, *Proc. Nat. Acad. Sci. U.S.A.*, 49 (1963).

[108]   —, Polynomial convexity: the spheres problem, *Proceedings of the Conference on Complex Analysis*, Minneapolis, 1964 (Springer-Verlag, 1965).

[109]   Y. Katznelson, A characterization of all continuous functions on a compact Hausdorff space, *Bull. Amer. Math. Soc.*, 66 (1960).

[110]   A. Kerr-Lawson, A filter description of the homomorphisms of H^∞, *Canad. J. Math.*, 17 (1965).

[111]   Heinz König, Zur Abstrakten Theorie der Analytischen Funktionen, *Math. Z.*, 88 (1965).

[112]   —, Zur Abstrakten Theorie der Analytischen Funktionen II, *Math. Ann.*, 163 (1966).

[113]   K. de Leeuw and H. Mirkil, Translation-invariant function algebras on abelian groups, *Bull. Soc. Math. France*, 88 (1960).

[114]   —, Rotation-invariant algebras on the *n*-sphere, *Duke Math. J.*, 30 (1963).

[115]   J. Lewittes, A note on parts and hyperbolic geometry, *Proc. Amer. Math. Soc.*, 17 (1966).

[116]   Gunter Lumer, Analytic functions and Dirichlet problem, *Bull. Amer. Math. Soc.*, 70 (1964).

[117]   —, Herglotz transformation and H^p theory, *Bull. Amer. Math. Soc.*, 71 (1965).

[118]   —, Intégrabilité uniforme dans les algèbres de fonctions, classes H^Φ, et classe de Hardy universelle, *C. R. Acad. Sci. Paris Sér. A-B*, 262 (1966).

[119]   —, Classes H^Φ et théorème de Phragmen-Lindelöf, pour le disque unité et les surfaces de Riemann hyperboliques, *C. R. Acad. Sci. Paris Sér. A-B*, 262 (1966).

[120]   Robert McKissick, A nontrivial normal sup norm algebra, *Bull. Amer. Math. Soc.*, 69 (1963).

[121]   M. S. Melnikov, Structure of the Gleason parts of the algebra $R(E)$, *Func. Anal. Applic.*, 1 (1967).

[122]   S. N. Mergelyan, On the representation of functions by series of polynomials on closed sets, *Dokl. Akad. Nauk.*, 78 (1951), *Amer. Math. Soc. Transl.*, No. 85 (1953).

[123]   —, Uniform approximation to functions of a complex variable, *Uspehi Mat. Nauk.*, 7 (48) (1952), *Amer. Math. Soc. Transl.*, No. 101 (1954).

[124]   Samuel Merrill, Analytic embedding and mean square approximation, *Proc. Amer. Math. Soc.*, 18 (1967).

[125]   Nozomu Mochizuki, A characterization of the algebra of generalized analytic functions, *Tôhoku Math. J.*, 16 (1964).

[126]   —, The tensor product of function algebras, *Tôhoku Math. J.*, 17 (1965).

[127]   —, Isometry between $H^p(dm)$ and the Hardy class H^p, *Tôhoku Math. J.*, 18 (1966) (correction, *idem.* 19 (1967), p. 379).

[128]   —, A note on the Choquet boundary of a restricted function algebra, *Tôhoku Math. J.*, 18 (1966).

[129]   Robert E. Mullins, The essential set of function algebras, *Proc. Amer. Math Soc.*, 18 (1967).

[130]   M. Nagasawa, Isomorphisms between commutative Banach algebras with an application to rings of analytic functions, *Kodai Math. Sem. Rep.*, 11 (1959).

[131]   Stelios Negrepontis, On a theorem by Hoffman and Ramsay, *Pacific J. Math.*, 20 (1967).

[132]   Donald J. Newman, Some remarks on the maximal ideal structure of H^∞, *Ann. Math.*, 70 (1959).

[133]   Yoshiki Ohno, Remarks on Helson-Szegö problems, *Tôhoku Math. J.*, 18 (1966).

[134]   —, Simply invariant subspaces, *Tôhoku Math. J.*, 19 (1967).

[135]   Bernard V. O'Neill, Parts and one-dimensional analytic spaces, *Amer. J. Math.*, 90 (1968).

[136]   A. Pelczynski, The universality of certain Banach spaces, *VestnikLeningrad. Univ.*, 13 (1962).

[137]   —, On simultaneous extension of continuous functions, *Studia Math.*, 24 (1964).

[138]   —, Supplement to my paper "On simultaneous extension of continuous functions," *Studia Math.*, 25 (1964).

[139]   —, Uncomplemented function algebras with separable annihilators, *Duke Math., J.*, 33 (1966).

[140]   —, Some linear topological properties of separable function algebras, *Proc. Amer. Math. Soc.*, 18 (1967).

[141]   Robert R. Phelps, Extreme positive operators and homomorphisms, *Trans. Amer. Math. Soc.*, 108 (1963).

[142]   —, Extreme points in function algebras, *Duke Math. J.*, 32 (1965).

[143]   C. E. Rickart, Analytic phenomena in general function algebras, *Pacific J. Math.*, 18 (1966).

[144]   —, The maximal ideal space of functions locally approximable in a function algebra, *Proc. Amer. Math. Soc.*, 17 (1966).

[145]   —, Holomorphic convexity for general function algebras, *Canad. J. Math.*, 20 (1968).

[146]   Daniel Rider, Translation-invariant Dirichlet algebras on compact groups, *Proc. Amer. Math. Soc.*, 17 (1966).

[147]   Hugo Rossi, The local maximum modulus principle, *Ann. of Math.*, 72 (1960).

[148] —, Algebras of holomorphic functions on one-dimensional varieties, *Trans. Amer. Math. Soc.*, 100 (1961).

[149] —, Holomorphically convex sets in several complex variables, *Ann. of Math.*, 74 (1961).

[150] H. L. Royden, On the multiplicative groups of function algebras, *Stanford University Technical Report*, No. 18 (1960).

[151] —, Function algebras, *Bull. Amer. Math. Soc.*, 69 (1963).

[152] L. A. Rubel and A. L. Shields, Bounded approximation by polynomials, *Acta Math.*, 112 (1964).

[153] Walter Rudin, Analyticity and the maximum modulus principle, *Duke Math. J.*, 20 (1953).

[154] —, Some theorems on bounded analytic functions, *Trans. Amer. Math. Soc.*, 78 (1955).

[155] —, Subalgebras of spaces of continuous functions, *Proc. Amer. Math. Soc.*, 7 (1956).

[156] —, Boundary values of continuous analytic functions, *Proc. Amer. Math. Soc.*, 7 (1956).

[157] —, Continuous functions on compact spaces without perfect subsets, *Proc. Amer. Math. Soc.*, 8 (1957).

[158] —, On the closed ideals in an algebra of continuous functions, *Canad. J. Math.*, 9 (1957).

[159] —, On the structure of maximum modulus algebras, *Proc. Amer. Math. Soc.*, 9 (1958).

[160] Walter Rudin and E. L. Stout, Boundary properties of functions of several complex variables, *J. Math. Mech.*, 14 (1965).

[161] Donald Sarason, Doubly invariant subspaces of annulus operators, *Bull. Amer. Math. Soc.*, 69 (1963).

[162] —, The H^p spaces of an annulus, *Mem. Amer. Math. Soc.*, No. 56 (1965).

[163] —, On spectral sets having connected complement, *Acta Sci. Math. (Szeged)*, 26 (1965).

[164] —, Generalized interpolation in H^∞, *Trans. Amer. Math. Soc.*, 127 (1967).

[165] I. J. Schark (pseud.), Maximal ideals in an algebra of bounded analytic functions, *J. Math. Mech.*, 10 (1961).

[166] S. J. Sidney, Properties of the sequence of closed powers of a maximal ideal in a sup-norm algebra, *Trans. Amer. Math. Soc.*, 131 (1968).

[167] —, Point derivations in certain sup-norm algebras, *Trans. Amer. Math. Soc.*, 131 (1968).

[168] S. J. Sidney and E. L. Stout, A note on interpolation, *Proc. Amer. Math. Soc.*, 19 (1968).

[169] G. E. Šilov, On decomposition of a commutative normed ring into a direct sum of ideals, *Mat. Sb.*, 32 (1954), *Amer. Math. Soc. Transl.*, Ser. 2, Vol. 1 (1955).

[170] T. P. Srinivasan, Simply-invariant subspaces, *Bull. Amer. Math. Soc.*, 69 (1963).

[171] —, Doubly invariant subspaces, *Pacific J. Math.*, 14 (1964).

[172] —, The disk algebra and its generalizations, *Math. Student*, 33 (1965).

[173] —, Simply invariant subspaces and generalized analytic functions, *Proc. Amer. Math. Soc.*, 16 (1965).

[174] T. P. Srinivasan and M. Hasumi, Doubly invariant subspaces, II, *Pacific J. Math.*, 14 (1964).

[175] T. P. Srinivasan and Ju-Kwei Wang, On the maximality theorem of Wermer, *Proc. Amer. Math. Soc.*, 14 (1963).

[176] —, On closed ideals of analytic functions, *Proc. Amer. Math. Soc.*, 16 (1965).

[177] Lynn A. Steen, On uniform approximation by rational functions, *Proc. Amer. Math. Soc.*, 17 (1966).

[178] Gabriel Stolzenberg, Polynomially convex sets, *Bull. Amer. Math. Soc.*, 68 (1962).

[179] —, An example concerning rational convexity, *Math. Ann.*, 147 (1962).

[180] —, A hull with no analytic structure, *J. Math. Mech.*, 12 (1963).

[181] —, The maximal ideal space of the functions locally in a function algebra, *Proc. Amer. Math. Soc.*, 14 (1963).

[182] —, Polynomially and rationally convex sets, *Acta Math.*, 109 (1963).

[183] —, Uniform approximation on smooth curves, *Acta Math.*, 115 (1966).

[184] I. Suciu, On the algebras generated by the inner functions, *Rev. Roumaine Math. Pures Appl.*, 10 (1965).

[185] Jun Tomiyama, Some remarks on antisymmetric decompositions of function algebras, *Tôhoku Math. J.*, 16 (1964).

[186] R. E. Valskii, Gleason parts for algebras of analytic functions and measures orthogonal to these algebras, *Soviet Math. Dokl.*, 8 (1967).

[187] A. G. Vitushkin, Approximation of a function by rational functions, *Soviet Math. Dokl.*, 7 (1966).

[188] —, Necessary and sufficient conditions on a set in order that any continuous function analytic at the interior points of the set may admit of uniform approximation by rational functions, *Soviet Math. Dokl.*, 7 (1966).

[189] Michael Voichick, Ideals and invariant subspaces of analytic functions, *Trans. Amer. Math. Soc.*, 111 (1964).

[190] —, Invariant subspaces on Riemann surfaces, *Canad. J. Math.*, 18 (1966).

[191] Junzo Wada, On Šilov boundaries of function algebras, *Proc. Japan Acad.*, 39 (1963).

[192] —, On the interpolation of some function algebras, *Osaka J. Math.*, 1 (1964).

[193] James H. Wells, Multipliers of ideals in function algebras, *Duke Math., J.*, 31 (1964).

[194] James H. Wells and C. N. Kellogg, Invariant subspaces, *Illinois J. Math.*, 10 (1966).

[195] John Wermer, On algebras of continuous functions, *Proc. Amer. Math. Soc.*, 4 (1953).

[196] —, Polynomial approximation on an arc in C^3, *Ann. of Math.*, 62 (1955).

[197] —, Subalgebras of the algebra of all complex-valued continuous functions on the circle, *Amer. J. Math.*, 78 (1956).

[198] —, Rings of analytic functions, *Seminars on Analytic Functions*, Vol. 2, Princeton, (1957).

[199] —, Function rings on the circle, *Proc. Nat. Acad. Sci. U.S.A.*, 43 (1957).

[200] —, Function rings and Riemann surfaces, *Ann. of Math.*, 67 (1958).

[201] —, Rings of analytic functions, *Ann. of Math.*, 67 (1958).

[202] —, The hull of a curve in C^n, *Ann. of Math.*, 68 (1958).

[203] —, An example concerning polynomial convexity, *Math. Ann.*, 139 (1959).

[204] —, Dirichlet algebras, *Duke Math. J.*, 27 (1960).

[205] —, Subalgebras of $C(X)$, *Symposium on Linear Spaces*, Jerusalem (1960).

[206] —, Uniform approximation and maximal ideal spaces, *Bull. Amer. Math. Soc.*, 68 (1962).

[207] —, Maximal ideal spaces, *Proceedings of the International Congress of Mathematicians*, Stockholm (1962).

[208] —, The space of real parts of a function algebra, *Pacific J. Math.*, 13 (1963).

[209] —, Approximation on a disk, *Math. Ann.*, 115 (1964).

[210] —, Analytic disks in maximal ideal spaces, *Amer. J. Math.*, 86 (1964).

[211] —, Polynomially convex disks, *Math. Ann.*, 158 (1965).

[212] —, Bounded point derivations on certain Banach algebras, *J. Functional Analysis*, 1 (1967).

[213] John Wermer and Bernard V. O'Neill, Parts as n-sheeted coverings of the disk, *Amer. J. Math.*, 90 (1968).

[214] Donald R. Wilken, Maximal ideal spaces and A-convexity, *Proc. Amer. Math. Soc.*, 17 (1966).

[215] —, Lebesgue measure of parts for $R(X)$, *Proc. Amer. Math. Soc.*, 18 (1967).

[216] Lawrence Zalcman, Null sets for a class of analytic functions, *Amer. Math. Monthly*, 75 (1968).

Index of Notations

Index

15 14 13 12 11 10 9 8 7 6 5 4 3 2 1   74 73 72 71 70 69